CHARLES
FOURIER

Portrait of Fourier by Jean Gigoux, 1836.

CHARLES
FOURIER

The Visionary and His World

JONATHAN BEECHER

University of California Press
BERKELEY   LOS ANGELES   LONDON

University of California Press
Berkeley and Los Angeles, California
University of California Press, Ltd.
London, England
© 1986 by
The Regents of the University of California
Printed in the United States of America
1 2 3 4 5 6 7 8 9

Portions of chapter 15 originally appeared in
"Parody and Liberation in the *New Amorous World*
of Charles Fourier," *History Workshop: A Journal
of Socialist and Feminist Historians,* 20
(Autumn 1985), 125–133. Reprinted by
permission of *History Workshop.*

Library of Congress Cataloging-in-Publication Data

Beecher, Jonathan.
  Charles Fourier: the visionary and his world.

  Bibliography: p.
  Includes index.
  1. Fourier, Charles, 1772-1837. 2. Socialists—
France—Biography. 3. Utopian socialism—History.
I. Title.
HX704.F9B34 1987   335.2′3′0924 [B]   85-28931
ISBN 0-520-05600-0 (alk. paper)

To
Guy and Brigitte Vourc'h
Michel and Colette Cotté
AND
Merike Lepasaar Beecher

In a little while I'll be able to teach a course on socialism; at least I know all about its spirit and its meaning. I have just been swallowing Lamennais, Saint-Simon, and Fourier, and I am rereading Proudhon from beginning to end. . . . There is one fundamental thing they all have in common: the hatred of liberty, the hatred of the French Revolution and of philosophy. All those fellows belong to the Middle Ages; their minds are stuck in the past. And what pedants! What schoolmasters! Seminarians on a spree, bookkeepers in delirium!

Flaubert to Madame Roger des Genettes, summer 1864. Gustave Flaubert, *Correspondance 1859–1871* (Paris: Club de l'Honnête Homme, 1975), 211.

Fourier was certainly correct in considering the passions as impulsions that guide man and societies. . . . The passions are indeed the movements of the soul; thus they are not bad in themselves. In taking this position Fourier has, like all the great innovators, like Jesus, broken with all the world's past. According to him, it is only the social milieu in which the passions move that renders them subversive. He has conceived the colossal task of adapting the milieu to the passions, of destroying the obstacles, of preventing the conflicts. But to regularize the play of the passions, to harness them to the wagon of society, is not to give rein to the brutal appetites. Is it not to promote intelligence rather than sensuality?

Balzac, *Revue parisienne,* August 25, 1840, in Honoré de Balzac, *Oeuvres diverses* (Paris: Louis Conard, 1938), III, 314.

CONTENTS

[Contents]

ILLUSTRATIONS

Frontispiece. Portrait of Fourier by Jean Gigoux, 1836. (Photo from Cabinet des Estampes, Bibliothèque Nationale.)

(Plate section follows page 258)

1. Fourier's birthplace. Lithograph published by the Librairie Phalanstérienne. (Photo by University of California at Santa Cruz Photographic Services.)

2. Galleries of the Palais Royal around 1800. Engraving by Coqueret from a watercolor by Garbizza. (Photo from Cabinet des Estampes, Bibliothèque Nationale.)

3. Lazare Carnot writes "Citizen Fourrier." AN 10AS 25 (10). (Photo by Service photographique des Archives Nationales.)

4. Fourier's Lyon. "Lyon vu de la Croix-Rousse." Lithograph by Viard. (Photo from Cabinet des Estampes, Bibliothèque Nationale.)

5. Diligences. Louis-Léopold Boilly, "L'Arrivée d'une diligence dans la cour des messageries," 1803. (Photo from Cabinet des Estampes, Bibliothèque Nationale.)

6. Prostitution in 1802. "Le Sérail parisien, ou le Bon Ton de 1802." Engraving by Blanchard. (Photo from Cabinet des Estampes, Bibliothèque Nationale.)

7. Prostitution in 1815. "Sortie de la Maison de Jeu du numéro 113," after a watercolor by Opiz. (Photo from Cabinet des Estampes, Bibliothèque Nationale.)

8. The Fatalistic or Resigned Cuckold. "Coiffe-moi bien ma petite femme! . . ." Engraving by Naudet, 1820. (Photo from Cabinet des Estampes, Bibliothèque Nationale.)

9. The Manageable or Benign Cuckold. Anonymous engraving from *Le Colin Maillard,* 1816. (Photo from Cabinet des Estampes, Bibliothèque Nationale.)

10. Fourier at thirty-six. Lithograph by Brandt after an anonymous portrait. (Photo from Cabinet des Estampes, Bibliothèque Nationale.)

11. Lithograph of Fourier by Cisneros, 1847, after the portrait by Gigoux. (Photo from Cabinet des Estampes, Bibliothèque Nationale.)

12. Engraving of Fourier by Flameng, published by Jean Journet. (Photo from Cabinet des Estampes, Bibliothèque Nationale.)

13. Pen and ink drawing of Fourier by Dr. A.-F. Baudet-Dulary, 1833. (Photo from Cabinet des Estampes, Bibliothèque Nationale.)

14. Lithograph of Fourier by Vayron after a drawing by Lise V. . . , c. 1837. (Photo from Cabinet des Estampes, Bibliothèque Nationale.)

15. Anonymous oil portrait of Fourier, 1835. (Photo by Yves Hervochon.)

16. Fourier's Paris. Detail from *Nouveau Plan Itinéraire de la Ville de Paris,* gravé par Perrier et Gallet, 1824. (Photo from Département des Cartes et Plans, Bibliothèque Nationale.)

17. Manuscript from the 1830s. "Autres inépties de la morale." AN 10AS 24 (1). (Photo by Service photographique des Archives Nationales.)

18. Victor Considerant's design for a Phalanstery. *La Phalange,* Vol. I, 1836. Kress Library, Harvard University. (Photo by Harvard University Library Reproduction Services.)

19. General view of a Phalanstery. "Vue générale d'un Phalanstère ou Village organisé d'après la théorie de Fourier." Drawn by Jules Arnoult after plans by A. Maurize and published by the Librairie Phalanstérienne. (Photo by Service photographique des Archives Nationales.)

20. Plan for the ideal city of Chaux, by Claude-Nicolas Ledoux. "Vue perspective de la Ville de Chaux," from *L'Architecture considerée sous le rapport de l'art, des moeurs, et de la législation,* 1804. (Photo from Cabinet des Estampes, Bibliothèque Nationale.)

21. Plan for a water inspector's house, by Ledoux. "Maison des Directeurs de la Loue. Vue perspective," from *L'Architecture*. (Photo from Cabinet des Estampes, Bibliothèque Nationale.)

22. House of Madame de Thélusson, by Ledoux. "Vue perspective de l'entrée de la maison de Madame de Thélusson," from *L'Architecture*. (Photo from Cabinet des Estampes, Bibliothèque Nationale.)

23. Victor Considerant. Engraving by Lafosse, 1848. (Photo from Cabinet des Estampes, Bibliothèque Nationale.)

24. Prosper Enfantin. Lithograph by Didion from a drawing by Leclerc, 1832. (Photo from Cabinet des Estampes, Bibliothèque Nationale.)

25. Fourier replies to the Saint-Simonians. "Horoscope des Saint-Simoniens en réplique à leur article du 28 juillet." AN 10AS 20 (11). (Photo by Service photographique des Archives Nationales.)

26. History of human societies. "Tableau du cours du mouvement social" from *Théorie des quatre mouvements* (1808 ed.), p. 56. Kress Library, Harvard University. (Photo by Harvard University Library Reproduction Services.)

27. The *archibras* in action. "M. Victor Considerant ayant la chance de se voir tout à coup gratifié d'une organisation phalanstérienne avant les temps prédits par Fourier!" Cartoon by Cham (Amédée Noé), *Folies du jour. Caricatures politiques et sociales* (1849), p. 8. Houghton Library, Harvard University. (Photo by Harvard University Library Reproduction Services.)

28. The *archibras* in action. "Les Phalanstériens trouvant moyen d'utiliser leur queue en Californie pour l'extraction des blocs d'or." Cartoon by Cham (Amédée Noé), *Coups de crayon* (1849), p. 5.

29. The Fourierists' heaven. Frontispiece for the *Almanach Phalanstérien pour 1845* by Dominique Papety. (Photo by University of California at Santa Cruz Photographic Services.)

30. Fourier's grave in the Montmartre Cemetery. (Photo by Merike Lepasaar Beecher.)

PREFACE

When I first read Fourier in the early 1960s I found him attractive in part because of his sheer strangeness and in part because, of all the thinkers in the socialist tradition, he seemed to offer the widest, most generous vision of human possibility. Since there was then no scholarly biography of Fourier I decided—without quite realizing what I was getting into—that I would write one. It took me the better part of two decades to finish the book. In the process the world has changed and so have I. But I still find Fourier a source of delight, and I believe that we need his capacity for indignation, his compassion, and above all his utopian imagination even more now than we did in the 1960s.

This said, I should add that what I am offering here is not a Fourier for our times. What I have tried to do is to see Fourier in relation to his world and to situate his ideas in relation to the worlds of discourse that he challenged. The approach I adopt here is not the approach with which I began, and I would just as soon forget some of my own earliest efforts to make historical sense of Fourier's thought. But I do not wish to forget the help I received along the way from many friends, colleagues, and teachers.

I began work on the doctoral dissertation that was the first modest incarnation of this book in 1962, during the first of two years as a foreign student at the Ecole Normale Supérieure. I finished the book in the spring of 1984 while a visiting scholar at the Center for European Studies of Harvard University. I have spent most of the intervening years as a member of Adlai Stevenson College at the University of California, Santa Cruz. I would like to express my thanks for the support I have received from each of these institutions. I would particularly like to thank Louis Bergeron, then *caïman d'histoire* at the Ecole Normale Supérieure, Stanley Hoffman, chairman of the Center for European Studies, and Dean

McHenry, whose vision and persistence made UCSC and Stevenson College possible. If UCSC never was the Fourierist Phalanstery it has sometimes been taken for, it has been for me a wonderful place to teach and write, a fertile garden in which my book could ripen and grow at its own slow pace and to its own considerable proportions—rather like the pumpkins just north of here around Half Moon Bay.

In working on this book I have benefited from financial assistance offered by the French government, the Tower Fund of Harvard University, and the Faculty Research Committee of UCSC. I am particularly indebted to the American Council of Learned Societies, whose fellowship made it possible for me to spend the academic year 1976–1977 in Paris at a time when it was vitally important for me to be there. I have also benefited from many kindnesses on the part of librarians and archivists at the following institutions: the Archives Nationales, the Bibliothèque Nationale, the Bibliothèque de l'Arsenal, the library of the Ecole Normale Supérieure, the Institut Français d'Histoire Sociale, the International Institute of Social History (Amsterdam), the municipal libraries of Besançon and Lyon, the municipal archives of Belley (Ain), the departmental archives of the Doubs and the Rhone, the Widener, Kress, and Houghton libraries of Harvard University, the Baker Library of Dartmouth College, and the McHenry Library at UCSC. I particularly want to thank the staff of the Archives Nationales, where I was almost a permanent resident for two years, and René Lacour, formerly director of the Archives du Département du Rhone, who gave me the keys to his castle, making it possible for me to commune at all hours with the shades of the Lyon counterrevolution.

My personal debts are many. At the outset I received valuable help and encouragement both from my actual teachers, Crane Brinton, H. Stuart Hughes, Jr., and Judith Shklar, and from friends and adopted teachers including Leon Bramson, Robert Darnton, Harvey Goldberg, Temma Kaplan, Edward Morris, David Thomas, and Renée Watkins. Friends at the Ecole Normale—and notably Pierre-Yves Pétillon, Eric Walter, and Christian Baudelot—helped me more than they perhaps realized to find my way in the several directions I wished to travel. At an early stage in my work I also benefited from talks about Fourier with Vincent Bounoure, Simone Debout, Emile Lehouck, and Nicholas Riasanovsky, and from an extended correspondence about Fourier with the late I. I. Zil'berfarb. More recently I have been greatly helped by the comments and criticism of a number of friends and colleagues who have taken the trouble to read my manuscript or portions of it. I would like particularly to thank George Baer, Edward Berenson, Richard Bienvenu, Victoria Bonnell, Joseph Butwin, Peter Kenez, Emile Lehouck, Karen Offen, Mark Poster, Nicholas Riasanovsky, Buchanan Sharp, Gareth Stedman Jones, Mark Traugott, and Laurence Veysey. I also wish to thank the members of the Berkeley French History Seminar, and especially Lynn Hunt and Susanna Barrows, for their shrewd and thoughtful comments. The encouragement and criticism I have received from all these friends and colleagues has enabled me to appreciate what it means to belong to a community of scholars.

There are a few special debts I would like to acknowledge. I was nearing the end when I got to know Gareth Stedman Jones. But his interpretation of the history of utopian socialism helped me to clarify my own thoughts and to see Fourier in a perspective far more satisfying than that with which I began. I owe much to his work, and to his encouragement. I would also like to record my indebtedness to Frank Manuel and to Norman O. Brown: I am sure that neither is aware of how much his work has stimulated me. My greatest debt is to Richard Bienvenu. Over the years he and I have carried on a running dialogue on Fourier, the utopian socialists, and problems of work and socialism that has always heartened and at times inspired me. This book owes much to his influence, and in several chapters I have drawn extensively on the introductory essay we wrote together for an anthology of Fourier's writings first published in 1971.

At the time this book was completed I was living with my family in a beautiful old farmhouse in Barnard, Vermont. As I finished my climb up "Mt. Fourier," it gave me pleasure to contemplate Mt. Ascutney—as I could from my study window. For the use of that farmhouse, and for many other kindnesses, I wish to thank Holly and Dan Field.

Finally, I would like to thank Alain Hénon and Barbara Ras of the University of California Press for their encouragement, their confidence in me and my huge manuscript, and for all the pains they have taken to turn that manuscript into the handsome book that I hoped it would be. I am dedicating this book to five people. To Guy and Brigitte Vourc'h and to Michel and Colette Cotté, dear friends who have nurtured and educated my love of France and have made me feel that their country is mine also. And to Merike Lepasaar Beecher, my wife and partner, to whom I owe much more than I could or should say here. I would like to have offered each of them a separate book. If Fourier is right in promising each of us 810 lives, I may yet be able to do so.

INTRODUCTION

Charles Fourier was the nineteenth century's complete utopian. A social critic who advocated "absolute deviation" from established philosophies and institutions, he surpassed Rousseau in the intransigence of his rejection of the society in which he lived. A psychologist who celebrated the passions as agents of human happiness, he carried to its ultimate conclusion the rejection of the doctrine of Original Sin that had been the hallmark of utopian thinking ever since the Renaissance. A social prophet whose blueprints included everything from color schemes for work uniforms to designs for nursery furniture, he was more concerned than any of his radical contemporaries to give precise definition to his conception of the good society. A visionary who foresaw an age in which oranges would grow in Warsaw and sea water could be turned into lemonade, he had a faith in the power of human beings to shape their own world that was remarkable even in the age of Napoleon.

Because Fourier's intellectual ambitions were so grandiose and because he persisted in linking his social and economic theories to a strange cosmology and an even stranger "theory of universal analogy," it has proved impossible for almost anyone to swallow his doctrine whole. The disciples who gathered around him during his last years quickly learned to practice what one of them described as a "useful weeding-out" of his ideas. In their restatements and popularizations of his doctrine they emphasized his economic critique and his plan for the organization of work while neglecting his call for sexual liberation and denying the importance of his cosmology.

Scholars have had almost as hard a time with Fourier as have his disciples. Many historians of ideas who have been attracted by some aspects of his thought have nevertheless found it difficult to write about Fourier without questioning his sanity. Most commonly, he has been seen as an interesting but somewhat daft precursor of saner and more profound thinkers. Making distinctions between his "shrewd insights" and his "wild speculations," historians have considered his ideas, not in their own right, but in relation to subsequent intellectual systems—whether Marxism or surrealism or psychoanalysis. It is true that shortly after Fourier's death, during the decade of the 1840s, "Fourierism" emerged as one of the most significant of the early socialist sects in France. In North America, where Fourier's ideas were popularized by the astute journalist Albert Brisbane, some two dozen Fourierist experimental communities were in existence by 1846. But the failure of the communities in America and the debacle of the European left in 1848 brought an end to the history of Fourierism as a significant social movement. Since that time Fourier has commonly been seen, along with Saint-Simon and Owen, as one of the utopian precursors of a socialism that only acquired scientific status with the work of Marx and Engels.

It was Engels who provided the classic assessment of Fourier as one of the triumvirate of utopian and hence prescientific socialists. In a section of *Anti-Dühring* (1878), later published separately as *Socialism: Utopian and Scientific,* Engels offered an appreciative and shrewd but also highly selective analysis of utopian socialism. Engels's aim was not to write the history of early socialism, but rather to respond to Eugen Dühring's ill-informed criticisms of the utopians by emphasizing those aspects of their thought that anticipated the critique of capitalism he and Marx had worked out. The rest he dismissed as "fantasy" unavoidable "at a time when capitalist production was still so little developed."[1]

Although Engels made no claim to comprehensiveness, his essay in fact defined the parameters within which several generations of historians were to discuss Fourier. The very substantial body of Soviet writing on Fourier remains to this day wedded to ideas and phrases from Engels's essay and from the section on the utopian socialists in the *Communist Manifesto.*[2] Similarly much of the work of West European Marxists treats Fourier's thought and the question of its relation to that of Marx and Engels as problems fully intelligible within the framework established by Engels.[3] But also among non-Marxist writers Fourier's thought was for several generations considered largely from the standpoint of its contribution to the development of a socialist ideology that was understood to have reached maturity long after Fourier's death. Thus the first major academic study of Fourier's thought, the Sorbonne thesis by Hubert Bourgin, presented itself as a "contribution to the study of socialism." Similarly in numerous books and articles by Charles Gide, who was the first writer to gain a wide audience for Fourier in France, Fourier was presented as a "prophet" or "pioneer" of cooperatist socialism.[4]

In recent years, and especially since the Second World War, Fourier has been considered from other perspectives. There has been a new appreciation of Fourier's psychological writings and notably his analysis of love and repression. He has been seen as a precursor not of Marx but of Freud—or at least of the radical Freud recovered in the 1950s and 1960s by Herbert Marcuse and Norman O. Brown.[5] A new look has also been taken at aspects of Fourier's doctrine, such as his cosmological speculations, which were formerly regarded as evidence of his "madness." Much of the impetus for this reorientation was provided by André Breton, whose *Ode à Fourier* (first published in 1947) was only the first of Breton's many efforts to rescue Fourier from the political economists. For Breton what was central to Fourier's thought was, not the critique of capitalism and the scheme for the organization of labor, but rather Fourier's celebration of desire and his affirmation, in the face of the prejudices and constraints of specific cultures, of the world's hidden unity. Breton's aim was not only to place Fourier in the tradition of the great visionaries but also to claim him as an ancestor of the surrealist movement.[6]

Although Fourier has never been widely read, his name meant enough by the late 1960s that it occasionally appeared in graffiti on the walls of the Sorbonne; and during the turmoil of May 1968 his statue was ceremoniously returned to its pedestal near the Place Clichy. To some student radicals of the time Fourier appeared as an embodiment of the challenge to all authority—the *contestation globale*—that was at the heart of the "events of May."[7] But to other admirers of Fourier, writing in the early 1970s, what was interesting in Fourier was not so much the content of his work as its form—the verbal inventiveness revealed in his linguistic experiments, or the playfulness and exuberance of his writings on analogy. Michel Butor's long poem, *La Rose des vents,* which appeared in 1970, was at once a celebration and a poetic extension of Fourier's cosmological vision. And the following year, in an influential essay, Roland Barthes argued that a concern for language was actually at the center of Fourier's project. According to Barthes, Fourier was a "logothete," an inventor of language for whom writing was an end in itself.[8]

None of these perspectives is without merit. Barthes' view of Fourier as a writer like Flaubert whose great dream was to write a book about nothing might seem to be simply an ingenious provocation. Yet one clearly positive result of the interest in Fourier generated by Barthes, along with Breton and Butor, has been a heightened appreciation of Fourier's imaginative gifts, an increased consciousness of his literary strategies, and a greater willingness to reckon with subtleties and ambiguities in his mode of presentation.[9] Similarly the interest in Fourier as a precursor of Freud has been valuable because it emphasizes that Fourier was not simply a humanitarian critic of early capitalism insisting that men did not get enough to eat: a vision of instinctual and emotional liberation was central to his thought. But still, one of the striking features of much of the recent writing on Fourier is its a-contextual and even teleological character. If Fourier is now less often seen as a forerunner of Marx, he is still seen as a forerunner—of Freud, or surrealism, or the linguistic preoccupations of the Parisian intelligentsia of the early 1970s. The problem with these perspectives is not so much that they are limited—what perspective isn't?—but that they are anachronistic. It is not hard to establish that many of Fourier's ideas "anticipated" those of Marx or Freud. But this does little to deepen our understanding of Fourier himself and of what he sought to achieve. To insist on the modernity of some of Fourier's ideas makes it all the more difficult to understand why he held others that we would now find silly or archaic. What easily gets lost in all such efforts at retrospective evaluation is a sense of the inner logic of an individual's thought.

One of the things I have tried to accomplish in this book is to present an account of Fourier's thought that conveys some sense of its "inner logic." I have tried, in other words, to describe how Fourier arrived at his ideas and how they fit together in what he regarded as a coherent system. There are obviously limits to one's ability to enter the mind of a thinker as unconventional and idiosyncratic as Fourier. Yet he was, after his own fashion, a systematic thinker. The vision of the good society that he elaborated in such obsessive detail was based on an almost equally detailed theory of human motivation (which he called the theory of passionate attraction), and the whole was subsumed within a larger "theory of the destinies," which purported to explain everything from the creation of the universe and the immortality of the soul to the significance for human sexuality of the cauliflower and the artichoke. Fourier apparently worked out the main elements of the system at an early point in his career as a thinker. At the age of thirty-one, in his first attempt to draw attention to his ideas, he could already present himself as the "inventor" of the "calculus" of the destinies. During much of the rest of his life he devoted himself to filling in the details and working out the implications of what he subsequently referred to as his discovery.

My principal aim has been to present as plausible an account as possible of the theory itself, of the process by which it took shape in Fourier's mind, and of his unremitting attempts to find a patron able to finance the establishment of a community or Phalanx based on his plans. From the beginning I conceived of the book as a biographical study in which Fourier's ideas would be seen in relation to his experience and set against the background of the various worlds he traversed. My hope was that by grasping the interplay between the dreams and aspirations of this extraordinary man and the circumstances in which he lived, I could present a fuller and richer account of his theory than those offered by commentators whose chief concern was with Fourier's "modernity," or the relevance of his ideas to our world. I was motivated in part by the belief—or prejudice—that there is no genuine understanding of the life of the mind outside specific historical and biographical circumstances. But I was also reacting against the conventional view of Fourier as a kind of inspired lunatic who lived in a completely self-contained mental universe. For generations scholars interested in Fourier had been treating him as a picturesque crank—a maniacal *vieux garçon*—who lived a life without events and whose biography could be reduced to a few choice anecdotes. The implication of this view was that, growing out of no lived experience, Fourier's utopia was a work of pure imagination and could be mined for interesting details and "modern" insights, but as a whole had little bearing on any larger world.

During the past generation a new picture of Fourier has begun to emerge. One of the results of the revival of interest in Fourier after World War II was to stimulate research on his biography as well as on various aspects of his thought. Articles by Emile Poulat, Jean-Jacques Hémardinquer, and Pierre Riberette have shed light on Fourier's early and middle years, and there has been a good brief biography by Emile Lehouck. At the same time, Simone Debout, one of the most thoughtful of contemporary Fourier scholars, has appealed for studies showing the roots in reality of Fourier and his utopia.

> It is important not to judge Fourier in isolation, but to link him to the world which he confronts, to the hypocritical conventions and to the culture of his time, in order to understand precisely what was exceptional about him and what his disciples themselves ignored or barely grasped.[10]

This intellectual biography is the fruit of my own effort to discover the experience behind the texts—to establish bridges between Fourier's mind and the world around him, and to treat him not as a curious species of exotic fauna but as part of a larger world.

When I began work on this book there was no scholarly biography of Fourier in any language. I soon discovered why. The main problem was that although the sources were rich for some parts of Fourier's life, they were barren for others. After 1816, when Fourier entered into regular correspondence with his disciple Just Muiron, his life is relatively well known. But for the whole decade of the French Revolution, which was his crucial formative period, there is only a handful of sources. The mere task of putting together a coherent narrative turned out to be much harder than I had anticipated. And it was made no easier by the fact that Fourier spent much of his early life working in subordinate positions for provincial cloth merchants. He belonged, in other words, to a world far removed from that frequented by most of the intellectuals of his time—a world not easy to recapture. The result is that in writing a biography of the sort I wished to write I found that I had to give considerable time not only to establishing the narrative but also to reconstructing the various settings in which Fourier lived and moved: the worlds of the soldier in the Revolutionary Year III; of the traveling salesman, the unlicensed broker, and the provincial journalist during the Napoleonic period; and of publishing and advertising in Restoration Paris. I have tried to treat these various social and cultural settings as at least partly discrete worlds, and then to situate Fourier within them, just as in the chapters on Fourier's theory I have attempted wherever possible to situate his ideas within a larger world of intellectual discourse.

The main sources on which I have drawn are of three sorts. First, there is the great mass of Fourier's papers now preserved at the Archives Nationales. Among these papers are the drafts of many of Fourier's published works and the manuscript notebooks constituting the enormous *Grand Traité,* the almost-completed full exposition of the theory on which Fourier labored between 1816 and 1820.[11] There is also a substantial collection of letters received by Fourier, and a large mass of loose papers—including drafts of letters, notes, doodles, and jottings—some of them in a private code devised by Fourier to foil snoopers.[12] During the 1840s and 1850s, when "Fourierism" had become a relatively prominent social movement, many of the more substantial manuscripts were published by Fourier's disciples. Unfortunately the published versions must be used with care, since they were often published in fragmentary or even censored form. The disciples frequently omitted and occasionally simply "revised" passages they thought likely to provoke scandal or invite ridicule. And they published almost nothing at all from the five manuscript notebooks describing Fourier's sexual utopia and constituting his treatise entitled the *Nouveau monde amoureux,* which finally appeared only in 1967.[13]

Although Fourier's manuscripts are of unequal value, I found them as a whole to be an essential source. The notes, drafts, and correspondence provided a wealth of detail that gave the account of Fourier's later years a much richer texture than it would otherwise have had. In one instance (chapter 6) the hastily scrawled drafts of a few letters by Fourier served as the basis for a whole chapter, one that could not have been written without them. The notebooks constituting Fourier's *Grand Traité* were fascinating for the sense they gave of the sheer scope of Fourier's theory and for the answers they provided to a number of specific questions. But I found them to be of limited use for Fourier's biography. In his manuscripts, as in his published works, Fourier referred only rarely to himself or to his own experience; and much of what he did say was either cryptic or trivial. There is, to be sure, a series of autobiographical fragments in which Fourier speaks as the "inventor" of the theory of passionate attraction.[14] In these fragments he describes the process by which he arrived at his "invention," chronicles the trials of the inventor in a hostile world, and stipulates the "duties of critics toward unlettered inventors." What is particularly striking about all these writings, however, is the conventional and stereotypical character of the persona created by Fourier. His picture of himself as "the maligned inventor" is in a sense both poignant and true, but it gives us little insight into his inner life and his searchings.

The second group of sources for this intellectual biography consists of works published by Fourier. These include three major expositions of the doctrine, various polemical writings and "announcements" designed to stir up interest in the major works, a large number of newspaper articles, and finally Fourier's last and strangest work, a "mosaic" of articles and polemics that got out of hand and ran, uncontrolled, to over eight hundred pages. One of the striking features of all these works is that none of them is complete. They all refer to a body of doctrine that is anticipated, introduced, summarized, or alluded to, but never presented in its entirety. As Roland Barthes has written, "Fourier spends his time putting off the decisive formulation of the doctrine. He never gives the reader anything more than examples, enticements, 'appetizers.' The message of his book is the announcement of a message to come: 'Wait just a little more. I will tell you the essential part very soon.' "[15]

One reason for Fourier's failure to publish a definitive treatise is that the doctrine, as he initially envisaged it, was simply too vast and too multisided for Fourier himself ever to elaborate it fully. It was a universal system, and many of its branches required specialized knowledge that he did not possess. Thus as early as 1803 he was already announcing that he would leave to others the honor of working out the lesser branches. But modesty was not one of Fourier's more pronounced intellectual traits, and he had other motives for reticence besides a sense of his own limitations. These included the fear of plagiarism, the fear of ridicule, and the desire to play the fool so as to anticipate and confound the criticism he knew his ideas would provoke. As we shall see, there appears to have been an element of willful obscurity in much of Fourier's published work; some of his silences and certain aspects of his presentation are difficult to understand on any other terms.

The reticence or coyness that marks all of Fourier's published writing poses problems not merely for his biographer but for anyone who seeks to read him sympathetically. But these problems are minor compared to those presented by the bizarre form of his works. Not only was Fourier a careless, digressive, and at times simply ungrammatical writer; he also had a penchant for outlandish neologisms that has always bewildered his readers. His books came furnished with incomprehensible tables of contents and varying schemes of pagination and typography; and his ideas were presented in a strange private language in which "pivots" and "cislogomenas" mingled with "mixed scales" and "bicompound accords."

Since Fourier described himself as an "unlettered shop sergeant" and as a "stranger to the art of writing," one is tempted to conclude that he was simply *not able* to present his ideas in an intelligible form. This was in fact the view of his disciples, who took upon themselves the task of restating and "clarifying" Fourier's ideas in order to render them intelligible to a wider audience than he was ever able to reach. But if the disciples understood their public, it is not at all clear that they understood Fourier. The problem is that, when he chose to use them, this self-proclaimed "stranger to the art of writing" had remarkable gifts as a prose writer, one of which was a rare ability to vary his tone. He had a didactic and professorial voice, which he unfortunately appears to have regarded as his most effective form of expression. But he could also write in terms of inspiration, playful wit, clinical detachment, and dry and searing irony. Parody was one of his great talents; and much of his most effective social and cultural criticism was delivered in the form of tongue-in-cheek evocations of the "perfectibilities" of philosophy, the "beauties" of commerce, and the "joys" of married life.

The general problem all of this raises is how self-conscious a writer Fourier actually was. Was he the naive "shop sergeant" he made himself out to be? Or was he a shrewd and calculating writer quite capable of distancing himself from his own work? Or was there something of both in him? Was there actually a method in the apparent disorder of Fourier's principal works? If so, what sort of method? And how are we to reconcile the elements of humor, buffoonery, and parody in Fourier's writing with his oft-repeated description of himself as the successor of Newton, the "inventor" of the "new science" of passionate attraction?

I have tried to confront these questions. They are in fact central to the chapters on Fourier's cosmology and on "the riddle of the *Quatre mouvements*." But they are broader in their application: they hang over all of Fourier's work and apply to each of its separate parts. And they point to a larger and seemingly paradoxical question, which was raised at the outset of an excellent recent study of Fourier's thought: Did

Fourier actually *want* to be read?[16] Did he really believe (as he often claimed) that his eccentricities of presentation—the strange neologisms, the misleading clarifications, and the seemingly arbitrary analogical tables—were heuristic devices that would aid his readers in grasping the theory? Or was Fourier playing a more complex game? Were his books actually obstacle courses set up in the way of his readers? The question may seem strange, but I do not find the answer obvious.

If there is something deeply problematic about Fourier's own writings, there is no hint of this in the work that is, all by itself, the third main source for Fourier's modern biographer. This is the "official" biography of Fourier, first published shortly after his death by his disciple, Charles Pellarin.[17] This book, which went through five editions between 1839 and 1871, became one of the Holy Scriptures of the Fourierist movement. Along with Victor Considerant's *Destinée sociale* and Hippolyte Renaud's *Solidarité,* it was more widely read during the nineteenth century than the works of the Master himself; and it was virtually the sole source both for a number of popular biographies prepared by his disciples in the 1840s and for the biographical comments in studies subsequently devoted to Fourier by scholars and journalists outside the movement.

For an official biography, Pellarin's *Vie de Fourier* was in some respects a remarkable piece of work. Pellarin was a diligent researcher; and his book is based not only on Fourier's extensive correspondence with his disciple Just Muiron but also on interviews with a sister of Fourier's and with several childhood friends. While Pellarin's aim was to inspire love for "the qualities of [Fourier's] heart" as well as respect for his "incomparable genius," he had the broad-mindedness to suppose that a liberal use of the correspondence with Muiron—which gives unique insight into Fourier's foibles and eccentricities—might serve this purpose. "Our Fourier is a man who loses nothing by being seen *en déshabillé,*" wrote Pellarin in a letter of 1842.[18] Indeed, the warmth and disarming naiveté of his presentation of Fourier "undressed" constitutes the chief merit of the book.

Not surprisingly, Pellarin's biography has many of the characteristics of a work of piety. The portrait of Fourier has a doggedly antiseptic quality; one is constantly reminded that he was after all a *lovable* eccentric. Pellarin also downplayed aspects of Fourier's thought that he and the other disciples feared would shock or offend mid-nineteenth-century readers. Fourier's sexual radicalism is never mentioned; and in the final edition, published in 1871, Pellarin went to inordinate lengths to defend Fourier against the accusation that his ideas might have had anything to do with the "atrocities" and the "carnage" of the Paris Commune.[19] All this is perhaps to be expected. More disappointing, however, is the spottiness of Pellarin's documentation concerning the three most important decades of Fourier's intellectual life, the period running from the beginning of the French Revolution to Fourier's first personal encounter with Muiron in 1818. Fourier's early life is presented as a series of uplifting or pathetic vignettes or *images d'épinal,* some of which have been shown to bear little relation to the facts that can be established.[20] The treatment of purely biographical matters also suffers from the fact that, as is now known, Fourier's chief disciple, Victor Considerant, withheld from Pellarin at least one document of major biographical interest.[21] Nevertheless, given the limitations of the genre, Pellarin's official life of Fourier remains an engaging and in many ways uncommonly valuable work. It is also a work that has the character of a primary source. For Fourier's correspondence with Muiron, which is extensively reproduced in Pellarin's book, disappeared after Muiron's death. The excerpts published by Pellarin are thus all that we have left of this precious source concerning Fourier's later life.

In this biography I have attempted to move beyond both the pieties of Pellarin's book and the rather trite image of "the maligned inventor" presented by Fourier in his autobiographical fragments. My efforts have naturally been aided by the work of those contemporary scholars who have helped establish a fuller and more accurate picture of Fourier's life and thought than that offered by Pellarin or by Hubert Bourgin in his massive and richly documented but no longer definitive Sorbonne thesis. At the same time I have taken a long look at Fourier's manuscripts and papers. I have found the less formal writings—the notes, drafts, and loose papers—particularly valuable, and in the end I managed to squeeze more out of them than I had initially thought possible. I have tried to date these writings whenever I could, and to work them into a narrative framework. I have also attempted to track Fourier's movements and activities (especially during the early years) through research in public archives in Besançon, Lyon, Belley, and Paris. Above all, however, I have been concerned to put Fourier in a context—to see his life and thought in relation to his time and to the various milieus that he traversed. If I had to characterize my method as a biographer in one word, I would call it a kaleidoscopic method. I have tried to organize the sources into a series of relatively discrete patterns, thus locating Fourier's ideas and activities in a wide variety of settings. I hope that in so doing I have still been able to convey a sense of the larger shape of Fourier's life and of the coherence, the originality, and the beauty of his utopian vision.

There is one final question that I feel I should touch on, if only because it has loomed large in much previous writing on Fourier. This is the question of his sanity. Having lived (in a fashion) with Fourier for the better part of two decades, I think I know him better than I know a number of my closest friends. I would not care to argue that the man was entirely sane. On the other hand, I fail to see what might be gained if we could establish, beyond a doubt, that Fourier was mad. It is not given to all of us to imagine a world populated by antilions and anti-crocodiles. Nor is it given to all of us to see as clearly as Fourier saw into the contradictions, the wasted opportunities, and the hidden possibilities of our own lives. Fourier's speculations in cosmology and cosmogony have often been dismissed as insane (or at least nonsensical) by readers who simultaneously express the utmost admiration for his insights as a social and cultural critic. I would simply reply that there is a close connection between the "madness" of his cosmogony and the insight of his social criticism. Both are radical affirmations of man's power to shape himself and his world. Both are rooted in the belief that the only limit to our possibilities is our desire. Fourier's "madness," like that of his contemporary William Blake, is of a piece with his radical utopian optimism.

I

Provincial Autodidact

I ALONE shall have confounded twenty centuries of political imbecility, and it is to me alone that present and future generations will be indebted for their boundless happiness.

OC I, 191.

My reservoir of ideas is like the source of the Nile: it is not known but it yields in abundance.

"Détérioration matérielle de la planète,"
La Phalange, VI (1847), 504.

1

Early Years

WHEN THE mature Charles Fourier wanted to evoke an image of intellectual sluggishness and narrow-minded piety, he sometimes simply referred to the province and the city in which he was born. The province was Franche-Comté, a mountainous, heavily forested region on France's eastern frontier. One of the last parts of present-day France to be integrated within "la grande nation," Franche-Comté was in fact something of a cultural backwater during the eighteenth century. It had scarcely been touched by the Enlightenment, and it remained throughout the eighteenth century a bastion of the Counter-Reformation, which, in the words of one historian, "had an influence in Franche-Comté that was later, more profound, and more lasting than elsewhere."[1]

Fourier's birthplace was the city of Besançon, the capital of Franche-Comté and an attractive if somewhat drowsy town of gray stone houses located within a loop in the Doubs River and dominated by the impressive citadel that Vauban had constructed following the French conquest of 1674. With a population of about thirty-five thousand, Besançon had a few small industries and was the marketplace for a region rich in iron and salt mines as well as dairy farms and vineyards. But at the end of the Old Regime Besançon was notable much less for its economic activity than for its role as an administrative and military center and as the seat of an archiepiscopal diocese. The single greatest property owner—and employer—in the city was the Catholic church. In addition to its cathedral chapter and its seven parish churches, the Church in Besançon could boast four abbeys, six hospitals, eight monasteries, ten convents, a large *collège* run by secular priests, a "vast" seminary, and a house of detention appropriately named the Good Shepherd. Because of the proximity of the frontier, the army was also a significant presence in the life of the city. There was an artillery school at Besançon and a large permanent garrison at the citadel. But Besançon was best known as an administrative center—as the seat of a *parlement,* a provincial government, an intendancy, and numerous courts.[2]

Much of this was to disappear with the French Revolution, which reduced the size of Besançon's diocese and turned the proud provincial capital into the seat of a mere prefecture. Although he had left Besançon by then, Charles Fourier could occasionally become quite exercised by the treatment of his native city as "a pariah, a proscript . . . the Cinderella of the capitals."[3] But he was not one to spend much time looking back regretfully, as did the city fathers, to the days when "Besançon could pass for rich with its provincial government, intendancy, archbishopric [and] *parlement*" and when the life of the city revolved around its nobles, "whose needs, customs, wealth, and luxurious habits caused money to circulate and trade to prosper."[4]

I

Although the world in which Fourier grew up was that of the affluent commercial bourgeoisie, there were aristocratic pretensions on both sides of his family. One of his mother's brothers had purchased letters of nobility, and in his father's family tradition had it that the Fouriers descended from a tradesman named Dominique Fourier who had been ennobled by the duke of Lorraine in 1591. One of Dominique's sons was Pierre Fourier, a priest who had been beatified and later canonized for his work in founding religious orders and in reforming the Catholic church in Lorraine. The other descendants of Dominique Fourier were supposed to have left Lorraine to settle in Burgundy and Franche-Comté, where Charles's father was born. Although they were never able to prove their relationship to Dominique and Pierre Fourier, all the members of Charles's family took it for granted. One of his nieces eventually entered a religious order founded by the saint, and as an old man Fourier himself could refer to the Catholic reformer with no discernible trace of irony as "mon saint oncle."[5]

Fourier's ancestors seem to have been small tradesmen and artisans for the most part and to have resided at Dampierre-sur-Salon, a village not far from Gray, for several generations prior to Charles's birth. Charles's father—he spelled his name with an extra *r*: Fourrier—was born in 1732. He worked for a time in the family cloth business at Dampierre, and then early in the 1760s he established himself as a cloth merchant at Besançon. He was not a cultured individual, but he had a good head for business and he did well at Besançon. He also managed to marry into one of the city's most prominent commercial families, the Muguets. Aided by the dowry of Marie Muguet, he succeeded in acquiring a fortune of some two hundred thousand livres and a fine three-story stone house on the Grande rue. We know little more about him except that he was sufficiently respected by his fellow merchants to be elected to the post of premier juge consulaire in 1776, a position that required a good reputation and some knowledge of commercial law.[6]

Fourier's mother's family, the Muguets, were natives of Villefranche in the Beaujolais wine country. Her oldest brother, François Muguet (1732–1795), is described by Charles Pellarin as "the first in Besançon to set the example of large-scale commercial transactions."[7] A wholesaler who engaged in banking activities on the side, François Muguet was in fact a notable—and at times notorious—figure in the commercial life of the city. Having managed to purchase letters of nobility and a seigniory at Nanthou in 1780, he married twice, had fourteen children, and left a fortune of two million livres. Pellarin, who refers to the Muguets as "the first family of Besançon commerce," says nothing about the means by which François Muguet acquired his wealth. But there are documents that make him sound like a speculator and a profiteer in the grand Balzacian manner. He was, according to his enemies, a "fervent man who had made it his business to get rich" and who "speculated on events of every sort."[8] He was said to have made his fortune smuggling gold across the Swiss frontier. Then, "having ruined the majority of his allies in smuggling," he was widely accused during the 1780s of helping to precipitate a local financial crisis through his complicity in the circulation of worthless bills of exchange and in the fraudulent bankruptcies of numerous Besançon ironmasters. The charges against Muguet were never proved in court, but they appear to have been well founded and they were in any case sufficient to sustain a war of pamphlets and factums that lasted from 1786 until the outbreak of the French Revolution.⁹

François Muguet had three sons by his first marriage. The youngest, Hyacinthe Muguet de Nanthou (1760–1808), was to go down in history as the "unknown" Lamethist deputy who delivered the Constituent Assembly's report on the inviolability of Louis XVI following his flight to Varennes.¹⁰ The other two sons, Fourier's cousins, were Felix (1757–1835) and Denis-Louis (1758–1829) Muguet. Both were to play an important role in the commercial life of Besançon and to "enjoy in the area a sort of celebrity for the breadth and range of their knowledge, for their integrity, and for their strength of character, which did not, however, rule out a number of eccentricities."¹¹ Marie Muguet's other brother, Claude-François Muguet, dit de Roure (1748–1826), stood as Fourier's godfather. Having made a comfortable fortune in partnership with François Muguet, he devoted much of his later life to religious and charitable activities. His relations with Fourier were often strained. An intractable and tightfisted old bachelor, Claude-François Muguet frequently crossed swords over money matters with his nephew and godson.¹²

Although she came from a prosperous commercial family, Fourier's mother had received little education. Like many a well-to-do eighteenth-century bourgeoise, she was barely literate. "Very pious, very parsimonious, and above all extremely hostile to fancy dress"—such is Pellarin's description of Madame Fourrier.¹³ She and Charles Fourrier had six children. The first four were girls: Mariette (born in 1765), Antoinette (1767), Lubine (1768), and Sophie (1771).¹⁴ It was only on April 7, 1772, that the long-awaited son arrived. He was a frail little baby, born with his left arm so abnormally weak that it seemed to be paralyzed. Fearing that he might not survive, his parents had him baptized on the day of his birth. He was christened François-Marie-Charles Fourrier.¹⁵

II

In discoursing upon any one of the thirty-six "crimes of commerce," the mature Charles Fourier rarely neglected to point out that he knew whereof he spoke: he had been "raised from the cradle" in the mercantile brotherhood.[16] This was no exaggeration. Not only did he come from merchant stock; the very room in which he was born was located directly above his father's store. The Fourriers' house was a solid stone structure with a gabled roof and a spacious courtyard. The ground floor was entirely occupied by his father's office and storerooms, and the family lived in the two upper stories. Built in the sixteenth century, the house was situated in the center of Besançon on the corner of the Grande rue (number 83) and the old ruelle Baron (now rue Moncey). It was almost entirely demolished in 1841, but on the site there is a plaque honoring "Charles Fourier, le Phalanstérien," which sometimes catches the eye of tourists strolling down the Grande rue to visit the cathedral or the house at number 140, where, just thirty years after Fourier, Victor Hugo was born.[17]

Most of what we know about Fourier's childhood comes from several pages of reminiscences dictated a few years after his death to three of his disciples by his favorite sister, Lubine.[18] The elder Fourier emerges from these sources as a rather distant figure, fond of his only son but too much absorbed in his business affairs to spend much time on his children. He died when Charles was nine. Thus, with four older sisters and no brothers, the boy grew up in a strongly feminine atmosphere and in a household dominated by his mother. Madame Fourrier, whom the judicious Pellarin describes as "meticulous and unenlightened in her piety," seems in fact to have been a despotically prudish and narrow-minded woman, a nagging parent, suspicious of her children's extravagances, and forever warning them of the dangers of impiety and self-indulgence. When her daughters took to wearing fancy dresses and ribbons in their hair, she was quick to remind them that this was not the way to catch a husband who would unite virtue with good looks and riches.[19] And when Charles spent his pocket money on the purchase of maps and atlases, she made such a fuss that as an old man he could still recall how his father had "conspired" with him "against his mother for the purchase of maps that he desperately wanted and [she] considered to be hardly worth a mite."[20] Charles quickly learned to keep his intellectual interests to himself. In later life he never spoke to his mother of his writings; and when friends told her of his first book, the pious old lady apparently "fell into a great sadness," fearing that her Charles might become "another Luther, another Voltaire."[21]

According to his sister, Fourier was a precocious child. "Charles was very young when he flew with his own wings," Lubine recalled.

"His facility in learning everything was extreme." He had a "wonderful aptitude" for arithmetic, she boasted, and even before he went to school, he was capable of performing complicated calculations in his head. He was always fascinated by geography, and he also loved music. Although he had never had lessons, Lubine reported, he could play several instruments and read music at sight. An amateur of "musical theory," he often reproached his sisters for having learned music by traditional methods, because "he had found a method by which he was certain of teaching anybody in less than six months what ordinary masters took years to teach." He had never had a writing or a drawing teacher, but he learned to draw and to write in a "wonderful" round calligraphic hand by sitting in on the lessons intended for his older sisters. They marveled at his virtuosity. "While our teacher was there, instead of doing his own work, he listened to what was said and afterward came and gave us advice. He told us what ought to be shaded, in what manner flowers should be represented. He drew some himself and showed them to the professor, who would not believe Charles had never been taught drawing. He liked especially to make drawings of emblems, of dogs lying at the feet of their masters. Everything was well colored, and his flowers especially were as brilliant as possible."[22]

After his father's death, Lubine remembered, young Charles was given a room of his own. He had the only key and he allowed no one to enter without his permission. The room became a private sanctuary within which he could pore over his maps and atlases or practice the violin without fear of interruption. But of all his solitary interests the most intense was his love of flowers. He filled his room with pots of flowers and arranged them carefully by species and color. His passion for order extended even to the pots, which were similarly crowded together according to color, size, and quality. This solitary, secretive boy guarded his kingdom jealously. But Lubine recalled that one day a friend got in and accidentally broke one of the pots, disturbing the perfect symmetry of the floral arrangement. Charles's reaction was violent. "At the sight of the damage [he] became enraged and leapt for the clumsy fellow's throat."[23]

Charles kept his room until he had finished school and was sent off to work. By that time, his sister recalled, he had managed to bring enough dirt into the room to dispense with the pots. Except for a narrow pathway running from the door to the window, the whole room was covered with a thick, rich coating of soil, and the flowers were literally growing out of the floor. "On each side the floor was adorned with the prettiest flowers, tuberoses, tulips, and others. Of course when he left us and the soil was removed from on top of the floorboards, they had all rotted and it was necessary to do the whole room all over again."[24]

Although physically frail, Fourier was remembered by his schoolmates as a stubborn and combative little boy. He also seems to have been capable of an often quixotic sympathy for the underdog, joining the side of the weaker whenever a dispute broke out. Sometimes this left him battered and bruised. His sister remembered him coming home "completely exhausted and in great disorder. 'But where have you been?' Mamma would ask him. 'What a state you're in!'" And Charles would reply, "'It is because, Mamma, I have been defending little Guillemet, or Wey, or someone else.'" "He was a faithful and affectionate comrade," one of his childhood friends recalled, but "when he thought he was right, his obstinateness was invincible."[25]

III

Most of the anecdotes in Charles Pellarin's biography seem intended to illustrate some edifying moral trait of the young Fourier: his "sympathy for the downtrodden," his "irresistible tendency to right wrongs," his "hatred of injustice and oppression." He is shown defending the weak, sharing his lunch with a crippled beggar, or writing an ode on the death of a pastry seller. There is no reason to doubt the truth of these stories. Fourier must have been an uncommonly sensitive and impressionable boy with a remarkable capacity for pity. Still, there is a disappointingly antiseptic quality to the characterization of the young Fourier offered by Pellarin. The hero is depicted as a precocious youth, somewhat eccentric to be sure, but generous, considerate, and steadfast.

Much of this stands in conspicuous contrast to the general observations on the tendencies and penchants of "civilized youth" to be found in Fourier's own writings. There children appear as a "demonic breed" of destructive animals, averse to useful labor but indefatigable when it comes to making mischief, deceiving parents, tormenting teachers, and breaking things. They have their moments of great generosity, but on the whole they are dirty, gluttonous, thieving, apish, mutinous creatures. In a typical passage Fourier described, not without relish, the misdeeds of children who, in the heat of common excitement, undertake the most difficult and dangerous tasks for the perverse pleasure of wreaking destruction, above all when it is a question of making trouble for teachers and guardians. During childhood everyone has participated in those glorious expeditions in which the actors, without fear of cold or heat or mud or dust, spend two or three hours in a row demolishing and breaking things. Going at it with unbelievable ardor and enthusiasm, they get more done at the age of eight or ten than would strong workers who were paid to spend the same amount of time on a similar task without being strongly motivated. What is the children's motive? It is the pleasure of doing damage, hatred, vengeance.[26]

Tormented by authority, the children of civilization were in Fourier's view at once envious of their oppressors and ready to rise and wreak vengeance upon them.

Along with his general observations on civilized youth, Fourier's writings also contain a few explicitly autobiographical passages concerning his own childhood. These passages are rare. But such as they are, they offer a more vivid—and certainly less angelic—picture of the young Fourier than that provided by the official biography. They also suggest that Fourier's picture of the destructive and mutinous tendencies of the young was in great part autobiographical. When, for instance, Fourier wished to describe the unconscious destructiveness of the three or four year old child, he cited one of his own earliest memories: the destruction of an entire fruit orchard.

At the age of three I was left alone one day in the garden of a canon who was away at vespers. It was the moment when fruit is just beginning to form. The apples, pears, and peaches were still no bigger than hazelnuts, and the garden was full of beautiful espaliers. I busied myself for half an hour picking all this young fruit. I destroyed at least two hundred dozen; the ground was covered with precious fruit. I put several hundred in my smock and brought them back to the two servants, my own and the canon's. In seeing that harvest, they swore profusely, calling me a "little devil," a "hellion of a child," etc.

It was the two servants' fault. They were having a good time drinking a bottle in the canon's cellar, and they left me alone in the garden. They went out and woefully gathered up all the traces of destruction and threw them out of sight.

There you have civilized children, a demonic breed whose instincts always impel them to make trouble even when they are acting innocently, for I did this damage without malice, purely for the fun of it.[27]

Similarly, when the elderly Fourier was talking with his disciples and wished to illustrate a point about the conspiratorial and thieving penchants of children, he could do no better than to tell them how as a little boy he had conspired with friends to steal a massive collation of cherry tarts prepared for all the participants in a religious procession in which he was supposed to be a censer bearer.[28]

Some of Fourier's other recollections add vivid color to the picture of his pious upbringing. Particularly interesting is a story meant to demonstrate the absurdity of Catholic religious education in which mere infants were lectured on the dire punishments awaiting adulterers, fornicators, and sodomites.

I was at the age of seven quite terrified by the fear of boiling cauldrons. I was taken from sermon to sermon, from novena to novena. Finally, terror-stricken by the threats of the preachers and the dreams of boiling cauldrons that besieged me every night, I resolved to confess to a multitude of sins of which I had no understanding and which I was afraid of having committed without realizing it. I thought it would be better to confess to a few too many than to leave out a single one. Thereupon I composed a litany of all the sins that I couldn't understand, such as fornication, and I went to recite them all to Abbé Cornier, the vicar of the Eglise des Annonciades. First of all I recited the minor, everyday sins like having forgotten to say my prayers. Then I started on the list of sins that were mysterious to me, and I accused myself of lust. (I was seven years old.) "You don't know what you are saying," the vicar answers. I stop somewhat abashed. "Come on, let's hear the rest." I continue and accuse myself of having committed simony. "Ah! Simony! Come now, you're talking nonsense." Very much confused, I try to place the blame on someone else, and I answer, "They told me at home to confess to that." Whereupon a new rebuke from the pious vicar: "You're a little liar. They did not tell you that!" At this point I terminated my learned confession.[29]

Fourier soon outgrew his fear of boiling cauldrons. But he never ceased to resent the mystification of the young, and the exploitation of their fears, by the Church.

The tyrannical abuse of children by figures of authority—by parents, priests, and teachers—was one of the dominant themes of the critique of civilization contained in Fourier's mature writings. Frequently in treating this subject he made it clear that he spoke from personal experience, and that this experience had been particularly bitter at the dinner table. "How many canings did I not receive for refusing to eat turnips and cabbage, barley, vermicelli, and other moral medicine that caused me to vomit, not to mention my feelings of disgust."[30] One incident in particular stuck in Fourier's mind. The villain was his schoolmaster, "the Pedant."

> One day while dining at the Pedant's I got rid of a fat quarter turnip that he had served on my plate because he hated me and wanted to force me to eat turnips. I cleverly hid this turnip under my clothing, and when everybody got up from the tables I was one of the last to rise. I let the crowd go out and then chose the right moment to throw the turnip out the window, which was open during the summer. But through fright and haste I aimed poorly and the turnip landed on a wooden stairway where someone who was passing by cried out. The Pedant arrived. I was caught red-handed and forced to go fetch the turnip, which was covered with dust, and eat it for the honor of offended morality.[31]

Judging from Fourier's own testimony, such torments were typical of his childhood. He claimed that in his childhood he was "whipped every day with a leather strap" and that his fingers were continually rapped with a rod, "a punishment that frequently caused me inflammation and made all my nails fall out with frightful pain."[32]

These stories are not as implausible as they might seem, given what we now know about discipline and child-rearing practices in the Old Regime. Still there is room to doubt that Fourier was quite the childhood martyr he made himself out to be. As the youngest child and only son, he almost certainly enjoyed a privileged status in the Fourrier household. Pellarin suggests that many of his eccentricities were tolerated by the family; and according to Lubine, the elder Fourrier had a special fondness for his only son. Her reminiscences also include one dinner table scene in which the father's will was not a match for the son's digestion. "My brother was very delicate about his food," she remembered. "In his childhood Papa, who wished to accustom him to cleaning his plate because, as he said, no one knows the situation in which he may find himself placed in life, one day compelled him to eat leeks. Poor Charles was so sick, so sick, he vomited so violently that my father, who loved him as one loves an only son, was very anxious and promised himself that he would never again force the tastes of his son, and would let him do as he chose in the matter of food."[33] The recollections of his schoolmates suggest that Charles was often a stubborn, willful boy; and it may be that his memories of familial or pedagogical coercion were vivid precisely because such incidents were rare. But what matters is that Fourier *thought* of himself as a martyr, tyrannized by parents and teachers. Later, in devising his utopia, he made it clear that disciplinary functions could best be left to a child's peers and the proper role of parents would be to indulge their children and to cater to their whims.

IV

However things may actually have been at the Fourrier family dinner table, there was one matter on which the parental dictate was unyielding. It was assumed by everyone in the family that Charles, as the only son of a successful merchant, would naturally succeed his father at the head of the family business. Many of the boy's tastes and interests—his love of music, drawing, horticulture—hardly befitted a future cloth merchant. But his parents were encouraged by his good head for figures. Dotingly they would ply him with little problems in business arithmetic, and he "would answer at once in livres, sous, and deniers without ever making a mistake."[34] In order to accustom his son to the business, the elder Fourrier began, when Charles was only six, to give him small chores to do around the store. This apprenticeship had not lasted long before, as Fourier dryly put it many years later, he discovered "the contrast that reigns between commerce and truth." Taught at catechism and at school that one must never lie, he was shocked to observe that his father's customers were often sold defective or falsely labeled fabric. He began to alert them when he saw that they were about to be taken in. But one day an angry client betrayed him. His parents rewarded him with a sound spanking and a bitter reproof:

"This child will never amount to anything in commerce." It was from this point that Fourier subsequently dated his "secret aversion" to commerce: "At the age of seven I swore an oath like that which Hannibal swore against Rome at the age of nine: I swore myself to an eternal hatred of commerce."[35]

Of all the traditions surrounding Fourier's childhood, none was more piously preserved by his disciples than this story of his spanking and his "Hannibalic oath" against commerce. Fourier himself often retold it in his writings and in conversation with the disciples, and it figured prominently in the funeral oration delivered by Victor Considerant in 1837.

> This oath, to which he was so faithful, was the origin of his discovery. For it was in seeking the means to introduce *truth* and *honesty* into the commercial mechanism that he eventually arrived at the discovery of [his theory of] agricultural association.[36]

Stories such as this, of youthful revelations and "Hannibalic oaths," rarely deserve to be taken literally; and Fourier's realization of "the contrast that reigns between commerce and truth" may well have taken place more gradually than he later claimed. It is certain that whatever sharp practices his father may have engaged in were modest compared to the vast operations perpetrated by his uncle, François Muguet, during the 1780s. In his lengthy dissections of "the crimes of commerce" the mature Fourier never mentioned the activities of François Muguet.* But he must have been well aware of them, and it is hard to believe that they too did not play an important role in nurturing his "secret aversion" to commerce. In any case, and even if hindsight made Fourier exaggerate the significance of his spanking and oath, there is an important sense in which they can be seen as "the origin of his discovery." Thereafter he was always to regard the "crimes" of commerce with the outraged innocence of a child. And insofar as it is possible to retrace the steps that led him to the working-out of his own utopian theory, it would seem that he began with a long period of rumination on the possibility of establishing a "truthful system of commerce."[37]

---

*There is, however, among Fourier's papers a letter from his godfather, Claude-François Muguet (the younger brother and former business partner of François Muguet), responding angrily to an allegation by Fourier concerning "the profit you say I made on my bankruptcy." Muguet to Fourier, April 15, 1806, AN 10AS 25 (4).

If Fourier's father had not died at the age of forty-nine, or if his younger brother had survived, it is possible that he might not have been forced into a career that he detested. In fact the pressure on him to become a merchant was intensified as a result of his father's early death. The elder Fourrier left a very large fortune—the inventory drawn up immediately after his death set its value at slightly over 200,000 livres. According to the terms of his will, his wife was to inherit a sum equivalent to the value of her dowry and personal property, and the balance—almost 110,000 livres—was to be divided among the children with Madame Fourrier retaining control over it until the daughters married and Charles came of age. As the only son, Charles was to inherit about 43,000 livres, or twice the amount left to each of his sisters.* But the will also specified that Charles was to receive his full patrimony only if he had embarked on a career in commerce by the age of twenty. If he decided on another career he would receive nothing until the age of thirty, and then only half of his full inheritance.†

Although Charles Fourrier *père* could thus attempt to dictate his son's future from beyond the grave, he could not help his widow manage the family business. Since she felt incapable of doing so by herself, she decided, shortly after her husband's death, to form a partnership with her brother-in-law, Antoine Pion, the proprietor of a small retail cloth business. This partnership, which lasted just three years, was not a profitable one for the Fourrier family. Taking advantage of Madame Fourrier's lack of business experience and modest education, Pion managed to make what the family later described as "a scandalous profit" on the appraisal of the goods that each brought to

---

*It is notoriously difficult to give modern equivalents for the currency of the Old Regime. But to convey some idea of what these figures meant, one might say that during the latter part of the eighteenth century an income of two or three thousand livres a year was generally adequate to meet the needs of an artisan's family, and that the *portion congrue* (or minimum annual fixed income) of an unbeneficed priest was just five hundred livres a year prior to 1786 and seven hundred livres thereafter. Of course disparities of income were enormous during the Old Regime and there were nobles who found it impossible to live properly in Paris on an income of twenty thousand livres. The fact remains that for a provincial merchant, Charles Fourrier was a very rich man indeed, and his son's inheritance was more than many landless farm laborers could expect to earn in a lifetime of hard work.

†According to the terms of the will Fourier's inheritance was to be paid in installments: one-third at the age of twenty, provided he had entered a career in commerce; one-third at twenty-five, provided he had married and was still in commerce; and the final third at the age of thirty. In fact he received his entire inheritance at the age of twenty-one. For the text of the will see Pellarin, *Fourier,* 170–171.

the partnership. Within three months after the papers were signed, he had already paid off a personal business debt of 30,000 livres. When, after three years, Madame Fourrier had had enough of Pion's partner-ship, she was unable to recover more than 84,000 of the 204,000 livres she had entrusted to the care of her brother-in-law. Only in 1793 did the balance finally get back to her—in depreciated *assignats*. When Fourier claimed his inheritance in 1793, it was in that form that he was paid.[38]★

V

In 1781, shortly after his father's death, Fourier entered the Collège de Besançon. The dark stone buildings in which he spent his six years as a *collégien* are still standing, and today they form the central section of Besançon's Lycée Victor Hugo. Already in Fourier's time the Collège de Besançon was a venerable institution.[39] Founded by the Jesuits at the end of the sixteenth century, it had been directed by secular priests since the Jesuits' expulsion from Franche-Comté in 1765. All the professors were priests, and daily attendance at mass was compulsory for all stu-dents at the college. Throughout much of the eighteenth century the student body had been drawn only from the most privileged ranks of Besançon society. But there was no charge for tuition; and by the time Fourier entered the school, it had begun to serve as a melting pot in which members of the Parlementary nobility found themselves placed side by side with the sons of functionaries, shopkeepers, and artisans. As its most recent historian writes of the college in the 1780s:

> At the beginning and end of the school day a young and noisy crowd enlivened . . . the austere rue Saint-Antoine. You could recognize by their fine clothing the children of the Comtoise

---

★The machinations by which Pion managed to turn the partnership into a windfall for himself are chronicled in detail in a printed broadside entitled "Tableau des bénéfices qu' Antoine Pion a eu l'art de se créer dans la succession de Charles Fourrier, en s'associant avec sa veuve," AN 10AS 20 (10). Although neither signed nor dated, this broadside may well have been drawn up by Fourier himself. It concludes on a note of pathetic exaggera-tion: "Is there any cause for astonishment that Antoine Pion, who before forming his partnership with the widow Fourrier only had a small retail business, suddenly had a brilliant success in business when one sees that his affluence is founded on the ruin of a family whose whole fortune has passed into his hands and which retains of its former prosperity only the rags that could be drawn from the dust of its warehouses."

aristocracy, the Terrier de Santans, the Mareschal de Longue-villes, the Damey de Saint-Bressons, the Varin d'Ainvelles. But they were lost in the growing mass of sons of functionaries, merchants, and even peasants, the Martins, the Tourailles, the Moutrilles, the Pions, etc.[40]

A number of these sons of the bourgeoisie were subsequently to play important roles in the life of the region. Fourier's best friend at the college, Jean-Jacques Ordinaire, was to become a leading French disciple of Pestalozzi and rector of the University of Besançon; another classmate, Pierre-Claude Pajol, was to serve as a general in the Napoleonic army; and two years ahead of Fourier was Pierre-Joseph Briot, a man whose path was to cross Fourier's several times in later life and who was soon to gain notoriety in Franche-Comté as a Jacobin journalist and deputy.[41]

Although the education that Fourier received at the Collège de Besançon was not a bad one by the standards of the time, it did little to engage his energies or to satisfy his curiosity. It was a severe classical education stressing logic, rhetoric, and theology as well as Latin and Greek. Among the marks it left on Fourier, one was the ability to coat the most fanciful speculations with all the trappings of apparent logical rigor. It also left him with an intimate knowledge of the catechism and a command of Latin that was manifest in the occasional Latinate outbursts scattered throughout his writings and in the neologisms he was fond of forming from Latin and Greek roots. The Collège de Besançon offered Fourier little, however, by way of science, mathematics, and French literature. Physics and mathematics, both of great interest to Fourier, were poorly and archaically taught; and even in the final year of rhetoric, the study of French literature largely consisted of readings in Bossuet, Bourdaloue, Massillon, and other theologians. Fables by La Fontaine were given to first-year students, but Corneille, Racine, Molière, and Boileau were not taught. As Fourier later complained: "I studied for six years in a school in which professors were forbidden to teach French versification."[42] History—both ancient and modern—was taught at the college; and judging from Fourier's manuscript writings on education, he seems at least to have enjoyed ancient history. But whereas Madame Roland and Camille Desmoulins wept at not having been born in classical times, Fourier shed no tears over his books. His own enthusiasm was of a less sentimental variety.

Children are seditious. They love the cabalistic system of Greece and Rome in which the common people, always at odds with the aristocracy, offer them an image of the atmosphere of schools with their intrigues and conspiracies against the masters.[43]

As for French history, he found the "insipid series" of its kings—"Charles the Simple, Charles the Bold, etc."—distinctly less inspiring. "I have read the history of all these poor kings and, like all Frenchmen, I haven't remembered any of them except for Charlemagne. [In reading about the kings] you learn of lots of assassinations and poisonings committed by their wives, their priests, their courtiers, but you never find anything grandiose."[44]

Despite his distaste for much of the curriculum and, no doubt, for many of his teachers, Fourier did extremely well at the Collège de Besançon. Among the early editions of the *Almanach historique de Besançon et de la Franche-Comté* now gathering dust at Besançon's municipal library, there are several dating from Fourier's school days, which list the prizes awarded annually by the college. For the academic year 1781–1782, Fourier's first at the school, there is no mention of his name. But the following year "Charles-François Fourrier" emerged as winner or cowinner of *all* the prizes—translation, composition, history, and catechism—except the "prix de diligence." In 1783–1784 "M. Fourier" was awarded first prizes in composition and memory. Again in 1784–1785 he won the prizes for composition and Latin poetry.[45]

Such a record was enough to impress even the widow Fourrier; and in the fall of 1785 she wrote to a friend in Paris, one Monsieur Martinon, requesting his advice on the possibility of sending Charles to Paris to finish his studies. Martinon did his best to discourage her. "I know that your son has done very well in his studies and that he has won prizes every year." But so, observed Martinon, had Felix Muguet when he was a student at Besançon. Nevertheless, when he arrived at Paris, he had to repeat a grade, and so would Charles. Martinon also noted that even though the environment in Paris might be stimulating, it would expose a young man to dangerous influences. This argument may well have proved decisive; in any case Charles was not sent to Paris.

The letter from Martinon also sheds some light on the continuing family controversy over Charles's future. Madame Fourrier had reported that Charles had displayed "a desire to study logic and physics." "This is not necessary for a merchant," commented Martinon, adding: "You believe he has a taste for commerce; I fear the contrary." He continued:

> I advise you not to constrain your son. Let him choose the profession he wishes. Having made the choice himself, he will have nothing to blame you for. If you force him to take up a profession he does not like, he will abandon it and he will blame you for having tried to force it on him. . . . In your place I would let my son study his humanities at Besançon. Afterward, if he spoke to me about philosophy, I would try to find a man who could come to my home and teach him the essentials of logic, physics, and mathematics during the course of a year. One year would be enough, since your son likes these subjects; it would take three years at the college to do these courses.[46]

Whether or not Charles got his private tutor, he seems in any case to have completed his studies at the Collège de Besançon in the spring of 1787.

Little is known about Fourier's activities during the years immediately following his graduation from the Collège de Besançon. It is possible that he spent 1787–1788 doing a supplementary year of rhetoric at Dijon.[47] Later he apparently made a brief effort to study law at the University of Besançon, only to discover, as he told one of his disciples, that he had "a pronounced repugnance and also a notable incapacity" for the study of the law.[48] Far more interesting to Fourier than the law would have been the opportunity to study engineering at the exclusive Ecole de Génie Militaire at Mézières. But admission to this school, which was one of the great centers of scientific education in eighteenth-century France, was limited to those of noble birth. For a time Fourier hoped that his family would be able to obtain documentary proof of their descent from the ennobled Dominique Fourier of Lorraine. Shortly before his death, his father had in fact contemplated undertaking the necessary research at the Abbaye de Theuley between Gray and Langres. "That would have given us at least four hundred years of nobility," wrote Fourier many years later, "but he was already sick and he didn't act on the idea, which my mother opposed because it would have cost at least twenty-five louis in expenses."[49]

VI

The years immediately following Fourier's graduation from the Collège de Besançon were those that came to be known as the pre-Revolution. It was during this time that the longstanding conflict between the monarchy and the *parlements* reached the breaking point. In order to raise money to meet the interest payments on the enormous state debt, Louis XVI was obliged to call a meeting of the Estates General, the first that had been held in France since 1614. Several of Fourier's relatives were to figure in these events and in the revolutionary ferment that followed. His cousin, Hyacinthe Muguet de Nanthou, participated in the Estates General as a member of the Third Estate, elected by the *baillage* of Aumont (Haute Saône). Antide de Rubat, the husband of his oldest sister, Mariette, was elected to the Legislative Assembly in 1791.[50] Whereas these men were moderates in their politics, there was also at least one militant Jacobin among Fourier's close relatives. The husband of his sister Lubine Clerc was to emerge during the course of the Revolution as one of the most influential members of Besançon's Revolutionary Committee.

In later life Fourier was to express nothing but contempt for the "vandalism" and the "illusions" of the French Revolution; and in his first published work he referred specifically to "the catastrophe of 1793" as the event that first inspired him "to suspect the existence of a still unknown social science."[51] Given the depth of his hatred of the Revolution and its importance in the development of his thought, one would like to know as much as possible about his attitude toward the Revolution during its initial stages. Unfortunately there is not much to be gleaned from his writings and surviving papers. We do know that in Dijon in 1787 Fourier was still quite indifferent to discussions on the conflict between the *parlements* and the king and the respective prerogatives of Dijon's *parlement* and its provincial estates. "I took little interest in all that," he recalled long afterward. "I was in Rhetoric, fifteen years old, and busied more with amusing myself than with political discussions."[52] Among Fourier's manuscripts, however, there is a brief personal comment to be found in one of his discussions of the "illusions" of liberty, equality, and fraternity. "I myself shared these illusions in 1789," writes Fourier. "How much more likely they are to reign among the fanatical or the blind."[53]

Whatever Fourier may have felt about the great events of 1789, his mother believed that, two years after his graduation from the Collège de Besançon, it was time for him to follow in his father's footsteps and to enter the world of business. A position was therefore found for him at Lyon in a banking house directed by the Swiss financier Schérer. Fourier allowed himself to be talked into making the trip to Lyon, and his description of the outcome of the trip is graphic.

> Lured to Lyon by the prospect of a trip and having arrived at the door of the banker Schérer, where I was being taken, I deserted in the middle of the street, announcing that I would never be a merchant. It was like backing out of a marriage on the altar steps.[54]

Fourier could walk out on a job, but he could not so easily walk out on the vocation for which his family had destined him. By the end of the year he was once again obliged to yield to his family's insistence that he enter commerce. This time the destination chosen for him was Rouen. To make the prospect more attractive he was granted permission to spend a few days en route in Paris, where he could stay with his brother-in-law, Antide de Rubat, and Rubat's close friend, Anthelme Brillat-Savarin.★

It is hard to imagine that any young provincial could have visited Paris for the first time at the end of 1789 without being awed and overwhelmed by the city. This was certainly true of Fourier. He does not seem to have been particularly interested in the political agitation of the French capital. But he was delighted by the boulevards and the buildings and above all by the Palais Royal, which, with its newly completed interior galleries and its cafés and shops and performers and its women of easy virtue, had become a mecca for visitors to Paris in the years immediately prior to the French Revolution. Fourier described his first impressions in a letter to his mother.

> You ask me if I found Paris to my liking. Of course. It is magnificent, and I who am not easily astonished was amazed at the sight of the Palais Royal. The first time you see it, you think you have entered a fairy palace. There is everything there that one could desire: plays and performances, magnificent edi-

---

★This was the famous Brillat-Savarin, the future author of *La Physiologie du goût* (1755–1826). When Fourier met him, he was serving in the Constituent Assembly as a representative of the Third Estate from Bugey and Valromey, and he was still better known as a lawyer and political liberal than as a writer and gourmet.

fices, promenades, the latest fashions, just everything one could desire. When you see all that, you will scarcely think about the Palais des Etats [at Dijon]. Then there are the boulevards where you see stone grottoes and little houses, each of which is prettier than the others. Add to that all the superb buildings, the Tuileries, the Louvre, the quays, the churches. One can say that this is the most pleasing place in the world, but if you don't have a carriage here it's very tiring and you get covered with mud. I'm a good walker, though, and I don't need one.[55]

So entranced was Fourier by Paris that years afterward he could speak of this visit as the inspiration for his first speculations on utopian architecture. "It was thirty-three years ago," he wrote in 1822, "as I walked for the first time along the boulevards of Paris that their appearance inspired in me the idea of unitary architecture, for which I soon determined the rules."[56] Although Fourier's stay in Paris was only supposed to last a few days, he prolonged it to more than a week and went on to Rouen regretfully.

When the English traveler Arthur Young visited Rouen in 1788, he described it as a "great, ugly, stinking, close and ill-built town which is full of nothing but dirt and industry."[57] Fourier's reaction was similar. He wrote his mother that to go from the "beautiful city" of Paris to the "affreux pays" of Rouen was to "fall from a palace to a prison."

> You ask me if Rouen is beautiful. I will tell you that there cannot be another city on earth equally abominable. It is full of wooden houses of an inconceivable ugliness. They are dark and each floor hangs out over the street by a foot more than the one below it. The sod huts in Bresse are a thousand times less ugly. . . . Saint-Rambert is magnificent by comparison.[58]

As for Rouen's commerce, Fourier reported that it was considerable, especially in the linen trade. But his first impression was that it would be very difficult to get established at Rouen and that, in any case, the work of a linen merchant would be "extremely monotonous" with few opportunities for travel.

Fourier seems to have remained at Rouen through the winter and spring of 1790, working as an apprentice to a cloth merchant named Cardon. Among his papers there is a faded manuscript fragment that enables us to catch a glimpse of him at this time. It describes a trip taken by Fourier in March of 1790 across the Pays de Caux in Normandy.

I was traveling through the countryside in the month of March at daybreak. A very cold north wind was blowing. As I went on my way, I met two little girls in wooden shoes. The older of the two, who might have been six or seven years old, was crying bitterly. "My child," I asked her, "why are you crying, and where are you going so unhappily?" "Sir," she answered, "my mother is sick. There is no soup in our parish. We are going toward the steeple you see over there to ask another curé for soup. I am crying because my little sister cannot walk any more." She wiped her eyes with a piece of rag that served her as an apron. While she was lifting those tatters to her face, I saw that she did not even have a blouse. Economists, remember that Normandy is the richest of our provinces. That is how the common people lived under the glorious monarchy of fourteen hundred years.[59]

This was certainly not Fourier's first contact with extreme poverty, but it seems to have left a deep impression on the seventeen-year-old boy.

Sometime during the course of 1790 Fourier quit his job at Rouen and returned to Besançon. A few months had been enough to convince him that he would rather learn the silk trade at Lyon than remain stuck in "the fog, the mud, and the rain" of the "dismal" city of Rouen. In due course his mother, or one of her advisers, managed to find yet another position for him, this time as an apprentice merchant with the firm of Bousquet and Viala, cloth merchants at Lyon. In the early months of 1791 Fourier traveled to Lyon to take up this new job. There, in the "second city of France" and in a time of revolution, Fourier began his life as an adult.

2

Revolutionary Decade

THE DECISIVE period in Fourier's intellectual life was the decade of the French Revolution, for this was the time when his utopian vision took shape. In later years he generally assigned a precise date to his "discovery": he claimed that it was in April of 1799 that he hit upon "the germ, the fundamental operation," of his theory of association. Fourier's accounts make it clear, however, that this discovery was preceded by a long gestation period, which began almost ten years earlier, at the end of 1789, when "walking for the first time along the boulevards of Paris" he first began to ponder the idea of a new type of "unitary architecture."[1]

It is unlikely that we will ever know with certainty much about Fourier's inner life during these crucial, formative years. Almost nothing he wrote during this period has survived, and his own later accounts of "the indices and methods that led to the discovery" are disappointingly vague and incomplete.[2] What we can do, however, is trace Fourier's external biography during the revolutionary years, and thus provide a context for our attempt in the next chapter to reconstruct the stages in the intellectual itinerary that led up to Fourier's discovery.

The city of Lyon, where Fourier went to work in 1791, lies at the confluence of two great rivers and at the foot of two hills. The winding, unhurried Saône has long been known to Lyonnais as their "meditative" river and the swift and powerful Rhone as their "industrious" river. The two hills have been similarly contrasted. For centuries Catholic pilgrims have flocked to the "mystical" hill of Fourvière, at whose summit has stood a succession of churches dedicated to the Virgin Mary. Lyon's other hill, the Croix-Rousse, takes its name from a cross of reddish stone erected at its summit in the sixteenth century. But in Fourier's time it became known as Lyon's "industrious" hill because of the ateliers of the *canuts* or silk weavers that began to line its slopes at the end of the eighteenth century. According to local tradition, the two rivers and the two hills represent two contrasting aspects in the character of the city and its inhabitants.

Lyon was the second-largest city in France.[3] Its population of roughly 125,000 made it almost four times as big as Besançon and the only French city outside of Paris to exceed 100,000. With its huge silk-weaving industry, Lyon was also the largest manufacturing center in southern France. This silk industry, which had long been the principal source of Lyon's prosperity, had been established by Italian immigrants in the sixteenth century.[4] It had always been a luxury industry and the period of its greatest prosperity was probably the reign of Louis XV, when the European market for the elaborate hand-woven fabrics that were Lyon's specialty was at its height. Production declined during the 1780s. But still it has been estimated that on the eve of the Revolution over 40 percent of Lyon's population was supported by work in some way connected with the production of silk. The city's ten thousand active looms were capable of occupying some twenty-eight thousand weavers, journeymen, apprentices, and helpers; and thousands more workers of both sexes were employed in related trades. As a specialized luxury industry, however, the *Fabrique,* as it was known, was chronically unstable even during the periods of its greatest prosperity. Catering to the courts of Europe and above all to that of Versailles, it remained dependent on the vagaries of fashion and trade legislation. Even a small event, like the declaration of a period of court mourning, could be a disaster for the industry, throwing thousands of people out of work.

In the last years of the Old Regime the situation of the Lyon silk weavers was particularly difficult. Following the lead of Marie Antoinette's court, the French aristocracy began to demand light English cottons and muslins and printed white linens rather than the ornately woven silk materials in which Lyon excelled. Lyon's weavers were unable to adapt to the new "anglomania," and the signing of the Treaty of Eden in 1786, which opened France to imports of cheap English fabrics, only worsened the situation. Yet the collapse of the market was just one of the problems confronting the Lyon silk weavers. Equally serious was that during the course of the eighteenth century the traditional structure of the silk industry had broken down at Lyon, and the master weavers, who numbered about six thousand, had become dependent on the four hundred master merchants who controlled both the supplies of raw material and the outlets for finished goods. Deprived of their traditional right to sell their work to individual consumers, the weavers were reduced to the status of wage laborers working for a piece wage or *tarif de façon,* which was set by the merchants. Deep hostility grew up between the two groups, and the last years of the Old Regime were marked by constant and sometimes violent conflict over wage rates. The reduced demand for Lyon silks, together with the rising cost of living, created a situation in which the wages offered by the merchants were often simply insufficient to enable the master weavers to feed their families and pay for the upkeep of their looms and ateliers. Similarly, the women who worked in the industry—the thousands of *brodeuses* and *fileuses* and *devideuses*—were so poorly paid that prostitution in one form or another became almost a necessity for those who were not married.[5] As the apprentice to a wholesale cloth merchant, Fourier was in a position to appreciate the hardships of the Lyon *canuts.* And as the Revolution reduced the silk industry to a state of complete stagnation, he also saw unemployment and hunger and mass poverty of a sort he could not have imagined in his sheltered life at Besançon.

In addition to being a great economic center, Lyon was also a city with a strong tradition of mystical speculation and utopian social thought.[6] It had long been a center of esoteric Freemasonry and illuminism; and on the eve of the French Revolution, Rosicrucianism, Swedenborgianism, Mesmerism, and a variety of other mystical cults were all flourishing at Lyon. Influential hermetic thinkers like the "unknown philosopher" Saint-Martin were attracted to the city at this time, as were adventurers and charlatans like Cagliostro. The rich merchants who dominated Lyon's silk industry provided a ready audience for such figures; and they, together with the office-holding nobility and the professional bourgeoisie, constituted most of the membership in the city's numerous Masonic lodges.

During the course of the French Revolution, as the difficulties of the silk industry increased and the problems of unemployment became acute, Lyon was also the scene of intense discussion of plans for radical economic and social reform.[7] Particularly interesting to the student of Fourier are the various utopian projects and the proposals for fixing the price of bread advanced between 1790 and 1793 by the quasi-socialist justice of the peace François-Joseph L'Ange. The central idea of L'Ange, who was a victim of the Terror in 1793, was that to avoid speculation in basic foodstuffs a national share-holding company should be formed through which each year the totality of French consumers would pay a fixed and predetermined price for the nation's entire harvest. Grain and other basic commodities would then be distributed through a network of associations or *centuries,* each consisting of a hundred families and each with its own warehouse, school, and assembly. Although there is no mention of L'Ange in Fourier's writings, it is possible that some of his initial utopian reflections were inspired by the schemes and projects of L'Ange.[8] But what seems certain is that the city of Lyon itself—with its poverty and social unrest, and with its ferment of mystical and utopian thought—was a revelation to Fourier. After his pious upbringing in a bastion of Catholic traditionalism, Lyon opened up new worlds for him.

II

During his first months in Lyon Fourier worked as a subordinate clerk for the firm of Bousquet and Viala, Marchands Drapiers. He probably spent much of his time in their business house on the Place de L'Herborie, tending the counter, cutting and measuring cloth, helping with inventories, and learning how to keep accounts. He was paid no wages, and his food and lodging were provided by his employers in return for a substantial subsidy from his mother.[9] All of this was part of the traditional commercial apprenticeship accorded by prosperous merchants to young men of similar background. The senior partner,

François-Antoine Bousquet, may well have known Charles's father. At any rate his relationship with the young man was paternal. It was not long before Bousquet began to take him along as a *commis* on business trips through the south of France. In July of 1791, while Charles was on a brief vacation in Bugey visiting his married sisters, Bousquet wrote approvingly to Madame Fourrier: "I assure you, Madame, that nothing can equal the good character of Monsieur your son; he is gentle, honest, and well educated; he has been a great pleasure to me on our trips."[10]

Fourier, whose curiosity for new places and sights was great, seems to have found the life of a commercial traveler far more appealing than working behind a counter. Soon he was traveling by himself on behalf of his employers. And then in 1792, at his own request, he was sent to Marseille, possibly to handle the transshipment of levantine silk and cotton and other goods needed by Bousquet and Viala at Lyon. For a young man eager to know the world Marseille was an exciting city.[11] Upon its quays mingled all the peoples of the Mediterranean world, and in its warehouses were piled masses of carpets, printed cotton and calico, rice, grain, hides, Italian olives, and Cyprus wines. A rough and ebullient port of trade, Marseille at this time was, in the words of Jean Jaurès, "still traversed by as many corsairs as merchants, and more than once its commerce resembled a pitched battle." It contributed richly to Fourier's commercial education. Years afterward he recalled having been a spectator in 1792 while Marseille brokers reaped profits as high as three thousand francs on the sale of a single ship cargo. "These profits of three thousand francs are called a 'broker's luncheon,'" Fourier wrote. "He has less trouble in striking fine bargains than a merchant has in selling a couple of cloth coats." In a manuscript critique of commercial speculation Fourier also recalled having "heard tales at Marseille in 1792 [about] the late Magon, Escalon, and others who made a hundred thousand francs most years on bartering in wheat and soap." Fourier's manuscripts include a reference to a trip to Toulon in 1792, and it is possible that he also attended the great trade fair at Beaucaire in July of that year.[12]

While Fourier worked in commerce at Marseille, the Revolution was running its course in Paris and the provinces. Already in June of 1791 the prospects of the constitutional monarchy had been gravely compromised by the king's abortive attempt to flee France. Then in the spring of 1792 the French declared war on Austria and Prussia. The subsequent military reverses, food shortages, and rumors of treason stimulated the growth of a radical "popular movement" in Paris and of revolutionary clubs and *sociétés populaires* throughout the rest of France. In July of 1792, when the famous battalion of volunteers from Marseille departed for Paris to rescue the capital from its enemies both foreign and domestic, the municipal governments of both Lyon and Marseille were in the hands of radicals affiliated with the Jacobins of Paris.

Exactly how Fourier reacted to these events is unknown.[13] It is possible that until the end of 1792 he retained some of his initial sympathy for the Revolution and its ideals. But it is clear that the year 1793 was to leave Fourier with a fierce and lifelong hatred of revolutionaries in general and of the Jacobin "clubbists" in particular.

III

In the spring of 1793, not long after his twenty-first birthday, Fourier traveled to Besançon to collect his inheritance. The sum he received after "a stay of one or two months" in Besançon came to almost forty-three thousand livres.★ Even though this sum was paid to Fourier in depreciated paper currency, it was still a sizable amount of money—more than most Frenchmen could expect to earn in a lifetime. Having collected his inheritance on May 23, 1793, Fourier returned immediately to Lyon.[14] Apparently planning to set himself up as a merchant dealing in colonial goods, he ordered shipments of rice, sugar, coffee, and cotton to be sent from Marseille.

There could hardly have been a worse time or place for the sort of commercial venture Fourier had in mind. For just as he attempted to establish himself in business, the city of Lyon was falling into political turmoil. During the month of May a violent reaction developed in Lyon against the policies of the revolutionary government in Paris and against the revolutionary dictatorship established at Lyon by the Jacobin leader Chalier. At the end of May an insurrection broke out at Lyon. The result of it was the establishment of a new "federalist" government, which promptly arrested Chalier and the other leading Jacobins

---

★According to the terms of his father's will Fourier should only have received one-third of his inheritance at the age of twenty. In fact, the sum that he received—42,932 livres, 16 sous—represented full payment. The notarial act, reproduced in Pellarin, *Fourier*, 180–181, specifies that the payment was made in *assignats*, the paper currency of the Revolution, which were then worth about 40 percent of their face value.

and broke off relations with Paris. Although the inspiration for the insurrection of May 29 and 30 came largely from moderate Girondins, they soon lost control of the federalist movement. By the middle of July Chalier had been executed and Lyon had become a rallying point for royalists and counterrevolutionaries from all over the south of France. At the same time an army was formed at Lyon under the leadership of the royalist general Précy, and at Paris orders were given to place the rebellious city under siege.[15]

For sixty days the city of Lyon withstood the siege organized by the revolutionary government. During that time Fourier saw his bales of cotton requisitioned and turned into barricades. His rice, sugar, and coffee were also requisitioned without compensation and used to feed the soldiers and the wounded in the hospitals. By the end of August virtually all the able-bodied men in Lyon had been placed under arms, and Fourier himself was conscripted into Précy's ragtag army. Apparently he participated actively in the fighting and took part in a sortie that came close to costing him his life.[16]*

The insurrection of Lyon began as part of a more general counterrevolutionary movement that threatened to sweep across the south and west of France. By early September it was clear that the movement had failed. But the city of Lyon held out for another month against the troops of the Convention. During the last days the supply of bread gave out, and the city's population was reduced to living off rotten potatoes and the flesh of domestic animals. Finally on October 9 Lyon capitulated and was occupied by troops under the direction of Georges Couthon of the Committee of Public Safety. Three days later the Convention voted to make an example of the rebellious city.

> The city of Lyon shall be destroyed. Every building formerly inhabited by the rich shall be demolished. . . . The name of Lyon shall be effaced from the list of cities of the Republic. . . . On the ruins of Lyon a column shall be raised that will be a

---

*In his writings Fourier never spoke about his own role in the defense of Lyon, but he did occasionally comment on what he had witnessed. See for example OC X, PM (1851), 118: "It takes so little to transform children into fanatics. During the siege of Lyon companies of young cavalrymen were formed, some of whose members were barely twelve years old. They joined up out of a desire to have an epaulet, and they were the boldest under fire. I heard more than one of them say before enlisting: 'Will I have an epaulet?' 'Yes.' 'Well, let's go.' . . . All that is needed is a paltry ornament, a tuft of wool, to lead a child to his death."

witness to posterity of the crimes and the punishment of the royalists of this city. On it shall be the inscription: LYON MADE WAR ON LIBERTY. LYON IS NO MORE.[17]

By the time this decree reached Lyon, the repression was already under way. Committees of surveillance were organized to seek out and arrest suspected counterrevolutionaries, and special tribunals were created to judge the rebels as quickly as possible.

One of the victims of the repression at Lyon was Fourier's old employer, François-Antoine Bousquet, whose royalist sympathies were too well known for him to escape the attentions of the Commission de Justice Populaire. One of his sons had been killed in the fighting, and the other had served as an adjutant to General Précy. Now his store and apartments on the Place de l'Herborie were placed under lock and key and his merchandise confiscated. His country home in the commune of Oulins was similarly sequestered, and he was placed under surveillance.[18] As for Fourier himself, the record is less clear. I have been able to find no trace of his name in the records of the revolutionary tribunals.[19] But according to his own account—and that of Pellarin—Fourier was taken into custody on several occasions and narrowly missed being included in one of the mass executions organized by Joseph Fouché in early December. In Pellarin's words:

> Having once gotten out of the hands of those who had arrested him, Fourier was, during the following days, rearrested and then released on a number of occasions. For several weeks he remained in the same situation, subject to a continual threat of death. He was subjected to as many as four domiciliary visits a day, and each time he had to sacrifice to the agents [of the Convention] one of the objects that still remained in his possession. Thus he was even forced to turn over to them his watch and, in the final instance, an excellent collection of maps of which he was extremely proud.[20]

According to his own account, it was only by a lie that Fourier managed to escape execution: "Three times in one day I lied to the revolutionary committee and its agents during their domiciliary visits. On this one day alone I escaped the guillotine three times by telling good lies."[21]

At last Fourier managed to escape Lyon and, like many another suspect, he took refuge in the woods overlooking the city. For several weeks he lived off potatoes and bread that he managed to beg, borrow, or steal from peasants. Finally, hungry and exhausted, he made his way back to Besançon. Reunited with his family, he found that most of them had had an easier time than he in making their peace with the Revolution. His rich uncle, François Muguet, was prudently making large financial contributions to the local authorities.[22] And one of his brothers-in-law, the husband of his sister Lubine Clerc, had become a member of the all-powerful Revolutionary Committee of Besançon.*

On Fourier's return to Besançon, his family and friends urged him to remain in hiding. But apparently he was sick of traveling incognito. Believing himself safe in Besançon, he came and went freely about the town. Since he had neither papers nor a passport to his name, it was not long before he found himself back in jail. Fourier could probably have sought help from his brother-in-law. He did not do so, his official biographer maintains, because he feared compromising his family. He may also have found life in jail agreeably restful. In any case, he does not seem to have felt himself in danger. Much later his sister Lubine recalled that during his stay behind bars Fourier passed his time "without much worry, playing the violin and picking at the guitar." Within a few days word of his plight had reached Madame Fourrier via the wife of the prison concierge. A speedy intervention on the part of Léger Clerc then won his release.[23]

Fourier's independence was short-lived. No sooner had he been released and given a fresh set of papers than he became subject to the *levée en masse,* the decree of August 23, 1793, that placed all French citizens on permanent requisition in the service of the Republic. For single men between the ages of eighteen and twenty-five, this decree had stipulated: "They will be the first to march. They are ordered to travel without delay to the principal town of their district. There they

---

*Léger Clerc, who was born in 1760 and died early in the Restoration, had married Fourier's sister in 1789 or 1790. The Revolution made him both rich and powerful. During the sales of *biens nationaux* in 1793 he was able to purchase the splendid Hôtel des Gouverneurs for sixty-five thousand francs in paper currency. After Thermidor he was arrested along with other members of Besançon's Revolutionary Committee. According to the act of arrest, he was one of the most "ferocious" and "incendiary" of Besançon's revolutionaries. He was also accused of having smuggled silver ingots across the Swiss frontier. Whatever truth there may be in this charge, he remained until his death the fiery Jacobin of the Year II. On Léger Clerc see ADD L 69, AMB I²8 #566 and I²15 #9950; Gaston Coindre, *Mon Vieux Besançon. Histoire pittoresque et intime d'une ville* (Besançon, 1960), 136; Jules Sauzay, *Histoire de la persécution révolutionnaire dans le département du Doubs de 1789 à 1801,* 10 vols. (Besançon, 1867–1873), V, 337; VII, 24, 32.

shall occupy themselves with daily practice in the handling of arms while they await the hour of departure."[24]

Fourier did not respond to the *levée en masse* with undue haste. He was probably released from jail sometime in February or March, but it was only on June 10, 1794—the day of the voting of the "law of extermination" that inaugurated the Great Terror—that Fourier was enrolled in the eighth regiment of light cavalry attached to the Army of the Rhine. In entering an elite cavalry unit—rather than the infantry, like most conscripts of 1794—Fourier apparently managed once again to profit from the intervention of a relative. In this case his benefactor was a Colonel Brincour, the husband of one of his Pion cousins.[25]

It was difficult for those who knew Fourier in later life to imagine the figure he must have cut on horseback in the army in the Year II. It was democratically organized, an army without substitutes, a school of patriotism in which men were taught to hate the counterrevolutionary, the refractory priest, and the émigré as much as the English, the Austrians, or the Prussians. During the days of its greatest glory—and these were also the days of the Terror—this mixture of professional soldiers from the old royal army, volunteers of 1791 and 1792, and conscripts of 1793 fused to beat back the enemy all along the French frontier. But during the period of the great victories—notably that of Fleurus on June 26, 1794—Fourier was doubtless still in training at the Besançon depot of the eighth regiment. When he did get into action there was surely little about it to appeal to his love for the heroic and ceremonial aspects of military life. For during his eighteen months as a soldier, the Army of the Rhine was engaged in a series of holding actions and fruitless blockades in the Palatinate on the left bank of the Rhine, which prompted Carnot to observe that while all other armies had adopted the offensive, the Army of the Rhine seemed to have sworn to remain always on the defensive.[26]

Nowhere along the Rhine was the fighting less heroic than outside of Mayenne, where the eighth regiment of light cavalry participated in a prolonged and ultimately futile blockade of a large Austrian garrison. When the blockade began, some four months after Fourier had joined his regiment, the surrounding countryside had already been plundered of all its available resources. Food for the men and fodder for their horses had to be brought in from outside. But the roads were full of potholes that ruined such carts and wagons as could be requisitioned to haul supplies. The army's artillery wagons soon met a similar fate, throwing the whole supply system into chaos. By winter of the Year II (1794–1795) many of the troops were without shoes or adequate clothing. They were reduced to eating roots dug out of the ground with their bayonets and a substitute for bread composed mainly of oat and pea flour that was "repugnant to sight and smell." In the spring special armed detachments were unable to prevent them from ravaging the countryside and stripping the fields of unripe grain. The number of deserters multiplied, and by spring the actual size of the army had been cut almost in half. "I have often had the occasion," a Napoleonic marshal later wrote of this winter's campaign, "to see our troops suffer great privations. But if other times were just as hard, they never lasted so long. I do not except the Russian Campaign of 1812."[27]

Hostilities were suspended in March of 1795 with the signing of the Treaty of Basel. But in September the fighting was resumed, and the French forces at last went on the offensive. The Army of the Rhine, now united with the Army of the Moselle and commanded by Pichegru, took Mannheim on September 20 without firing a shot, and the road to the east lay open. But Pichegru, who was subsequently to defect to the Austrians, was unwilling or unable to exploit his advantage. Then at the end of October 1795 the Austrians counterattacked and drove the French in frantic retreat from Mayenne and Mannheim. In the course of the retreat more than fifteen thousand soldiers deserted, pillaging the stores and warehouses of their own army on their way back to France. But to some contemporary observers the thefts committed by desperate soldiers seemed modest compared to those that could be attributed to the purchasing agents and suppliers and other officials employed by the *administrations militaires*. In summarizing the "disasters and atrocities" that accompanied the retreat of the Army of the Rhine and Moselle, the Representative of the People Becker observed: "While [our soldiers] are suffering a thousand hardships, they must watch while the employees of all the administrations mock their destitution through a display of wealth and a prodigality that betray [the employees'] dishonesty."[28] A week later the same representative, charged with the "god-awful commission" of reorganizing the cavalry, wrote a vivid description of its condition as it went into winter quarters.

> I cannot tell you what bad shape the cavalry of the Army of the Rhine is in. No money: the coffers are empty. No horses: only

ones that are exhausted and sick. Soldiers without clothing, and there's absolutely nothing to be done about it. No stirrups for the horses. In fact, everything is missing here. What's worse, no discipline. Just a bad lot of thieves, and a good-for-nothing bunch of drunken officers who are the cause of our ruin.[29]

Such was the condition of the cavalry of the Army of the Rhine in early December 1795. Barely six weeks later, on January 23, 1796, Charles Fourier received his discharge for reasons of ill health.[30]

It is not certain that Fourier had to share all of the hardships of the Army of the Rhine during the campaigns of 1794 and 1795. Throughout this period the actual number of men under arms never totaled much more than half of the paper enrollment. Even without relatives as strategically placed as Fourier's cousin, Colonel Brincour, many a soldier still managed to sit out much of the war in depot or on sick leave.* But whatever Fourier's particular vantage point may have been, these years of army service left him with bitter memories. In later years he spoke angrily and apparently from personal experience of the forced marches and miserable rations and rain-soaked bivouacs that were the lot of the soldier. "At the end of a campaign," he could write, "whoever has not been exterminated by enemy fire is laid flat by fever in a hospital bed or crippled by rheumatism and the other habitual privileges of the bivouac."[31] Like many other contemporary observers, Fourier believed that most of these hardships had a quite specific cause: the profiteering of corrupt suppliers and army officials. As he wrote a few years later in a manuscript entitled "Petitesse de la Politique," some of the worst "horrors" of the war were perpetrated by "merchants in league with the military authorities." "These merchants are the suppliers who, by starving and denuding men and by plundering hospitals, destroy more soldiers than the cannons of the enemy. They know that they will never be punished when they commit their crimes with the complicity of mercenary generals."[32]

Fourier was not wrong in laying much of the blame for the hard-

---

*The "Tableau general des forces de l'armée de Rhin-et-Moselle for 25 brumaire an IV" (November 16, 1795), for instance, records that no less than 62,119 soldiers, or two-fifths of the total enrollment of 168,770, were in hospitals outside the battle zone (Bourdeau, *Les Armées du Rhin,* 151). Fourier's specific references to military hospitals in both of the following quotes—and, of course, his own discharge on grounds of ill health—would suggest that he spent at least a part of his time as a soldier on sick leave.

ships of the soldiers in 1795 on the profiteering of army suppliers. A number of these individuals—both private *fournisseurs* and agents of the official *administrations militaires*—were making fortunes at this time by means of a variety of devices ranging from speculation in paper money to the fraudulent sale of requisitioned goods.★ But all this was only one aspect of the more general economic crisis that was engulfing France during the bitterly cold winter of the Year III. The roots of this crisis lay partly in government policy and partly in the extreme scarcity of food and other basic commodities that resulted from the combined effects of war and the bad harvest of 1794.

The overthrow of Robespierre in August 1794 had heralded the end not only of the Terror but also of the brief Jacobin experiment in a controlled economy. It meant the end, in particular, of the government's attempt to enforce the *maximum* on commodity prices and wages, which had been in force since September of 1793. Although it could never be vigorously enforced, the *maximum* had served as a fairly effective means of war rationing. It had enabled the government to buy food and supplies for its armies in a market under relatively firm control. Supplemented by policies of requisition and nationalization, and by some restraint in the printing of paper money, it had enabled the revolutionary government to survive at a time of great economic, political, and military distress. But in the wake of Thermidor came the relaxation of economic restraints. In December 1794 the *maximum* was abolished. Between then and the end of 1795 the value of the *assignat,* which had remained relatively constant during the period of Jacobin dictatorship, plummeted from about 20 percent to less than 1 percent of its nominal face value. At the same time speculation became the order of the day—speculation in national lands and grains, in wigs and rabbit skins, in anything that could be bought and sold with the constantly depreciating paper. Finally the government itself was forced to refuse to accept its own paper in the payment of taxes.

★The Directors were well aware of the problem and repeatedly advised the War Ministry about abuses committed by "public vampires" in its own administration. But such warnings made little difference. Earlier the Thermidoreans had made an attempt to reform the system of military supplies. But its main consequence had been merely to make private *fournisseurs,* rather than government functionaries, the principal beneficiaries of graft. On this whole subject see Jacques Godechot, *Les Commissaires aux armées sous le Directoire,* 2 vols. (Paris, 1937); Bourdeau, *Les Armées du Rhin,* esp. 203–245 and 299–380; and Georges Lefebvre, *La France sous le Directoire (1795–1799)* (Paris, 1977), 506–511.

IV

It was at the height of the economic crisis—in late January 1796—that Fourier was released from the army. Upon receiving his discharge papers he returned to Besançon, where he remained for the next six months. One of his immediate concerns was to straighten out his financial affairs and to salvage what remained of his inheritance. Just how much Fourier had left after his losses during the Lyon insurrection is not entirely clear, but it seems to have been a considerable amount. Apparently Fourier invested this money at Livorno. Among his papers there is a letter to the banker Luc Preisverch at Basel, acknowledging receipt of 33,026 francs, "which forms the remainder of my account at Livorno."[33] A few years later almost all the money was lost. Just how it was lost is again unclear: Pellarin describes Fourier's fortune as having been "swallowed up" in a shipwreck off the Italian coast near Livorno.[34] But in any case by the end of the Directory almost all the money that Fourier had inherited in 1793 was gone. He and his mother and sisters still hoped to force their cousin, Antoine Pion, to reimburse the money that he had "stolen" from them during his partnership with Madame Fourrier in the 1780s. The family eventually brought suit against Pion. But the only result of several years of litigation in three different courts was the loss of another forty thousand francs in lawyers' fees.[35]

During the period immediately following his discharge Fourier also seems to have been preoccupied by the need to make sense of his experiences as a soldier and to work out his own ideas concerning military organization and strategy. Thus during the spring and summer of 1796 he set down in writing his reflections on a variety of military matters. Some of these reflections took the form of letters sent by Fourier to various members of the government. On June 21, 1796, he wrote a letter to the Directorate, urging that the boundary between France and Switzerland be redrawn so as to give the French army a rapid passage from the Rhine to the Alps.[36] At about the same time Fourier also apparently sent a proposal to the Ministry of War advocating the creation of a corps of portable gunners (*arquebusiers*).[37] It seems likely, however, that in the spring of 1796 Fourier's concern with military matters went far beyond a simple interest in troop movements or in particular corps. According to one of his old friends, Fourier was preoccupied at this time with more comprehensive schemes and projects that dealt with the whole question of the supply system and the overall organization of the army.[38]

In the late summer or fall of 1796 Fourier returned to Lyon—which had now become in Richard Cobb's words "the capital of counter-revolution in France"[39]—and went back to work for his original employer, François-Antoine Bousquet. It was not without difficulty that the Maison Bousquet had weathered the Revolution. Denounced, imprisoned, then placed under surveillance during the Terror, the elder Bousquet had had to wait until after Thermidor to receive the "certificate of nonrebellion" that enabled him to regain legal ownership of his business and property.[40] But two years later, when Fourier arrived, Bousquet's business was back on its feet and Fourier was apparently able to resume his duties as a *commis*. In December of 1796 he traveled from Lyon to Paris on a passport that identified him as a "commis fabricant de Lyon."[41] But soon after that time he moved to Marseille. Judging from the tiny handful of documents relative to this period among his papers, Marseille seems to have remained Fourier's base of operations from the beginning of 1797 until early in 1799.

The Marseille to which Fourier returned in 1797 was a very different city from the one he had known five years earlier.[42] The whole economic life of the city had traditionally centered around its port. But now the war and the British naval blockade had reduced the activity of the port to only a fraction of what it had been in 1792. The harbor of Marseille was still full of small cargo ships, which plied the coast between Spain and Italy. But the Levantine and North African trade had collapsed, and in the Year V on the revolutionary calendar (September 22, 1796, to September 21, 1797) the number of ships arriving at Marseille via the straits of Gibraltar had fallen to just twenty-seven, from a high of over three hundred in 1792.[43] At the same time the city was in a state of almost constant political unrest. Just like Lyon, Marseille had been the scene of Jacobin Terror, counterrevolution, and finally occupation by the armies of the Convention. Like Lyon also, Marseille had been "debaptized" by the government, and for a few months it was referred to in the correspondence of the revolutionary authorities as "Ville sans nom." Then after Thermidor came the reprisals. At Marseille they took the form of a White Terror in which notorious Jacobins were shot in the streets and massacred in the prisons by armed bands who called themselves the "Compagnons du Soleil" and the "Compagnons de Jéhu." Under the Directory repeated efforts were made to put an end to the violence. The city was declared in a state of siege, and dictatorial powers were given to a series of military governors and commissioners. These authorities managed to establish a semblance of order in the city. But throughout the late 1790s most of the rough mountainous country that lay behind the port of Marseille was actually controlled, not by the government, but by bands of army deserters, counterterrorists, and criminals who plundered food convoys, attacked diligences, and robbed travelers almost at will.[44]

There is no period of Fourier's life about which a biographer would like to know more than the two years or so that he spent in Marseille. Whatever he may have brought with him to Marseille, his experiences in this "workshop of revolutions and arsenal of anarchy" must have exercised a vital, shaping influence on his thought.[45] Unfortunately the record of Fourier's activities—and thoughts—at this time is scant. We know that in May of 1797 "Citizen Fourrier" was living in a furnished room at the Hotel des Turcs on the Place de la Liberté at Marseille.[46] And just a year later, when the French fleet commanded by the twenty-nine-year-old General Napoleon Bonaparte set sail for Egypt from Marseille and Toulon, we know that Fourier was on hand to witness the preparations for the voyage. Long afterward he was still able to comment sarcastically on the "sterile" admiration bestowed by the citizens of Marseille upon the scientists who participated in the Egyptian expedition.

> I saw at Marseille all of these savants of the Egyptian expedition regarded as if they were a menagerie of wild animals. Usually they walked about the city in groups, and the populace ran after them shouting without meaning harm, "Des savannes! Des savannes!" just as one would shout, "Bears! Bears!" I saw them all go into the Café Casati on the Place Necker. The public was crowding around them on stools in order to watch them drink their coffee; and when they left everyone shouted, "I saw the savannes!" People were stupefied by the fact that they drank their coffee like other human beings.[47]

During these years at Marseille Fourier apparently remained in contact with the Maison Bousquet at Lyon. He also had business dealings with one Fréderic Fournier of Lyon, who seems to have replaced Viala as Bousquet's partner.[48] Fourier's writings tell us next to nothing about these contacts and activities. But there is one anecdote that turns up several times in his published work, which he apparently often related to his disciples. He recalled that while working as a merchant's clerk at Marseille, he had often had occasion to see people throwing into the sea supplies of grain that a merchant had allowed to rot while waiting for a rise in prices. "I have myself presided as a clerk over these foul operations," he wrote, "and one day I jettisoned twenty thousand quintals of rice that could have been sold for a fair profit before it rotted had the owner been less greedy for gain."[49] This incident was later described by Fourier's disciples as having had a "decisive influence" on his intellectual development. It is more likely that it was just one of many events at Marseille that served to dramatize to Fourier that "some reversal of the natural order had taken place within industry."[50]

V

As difficult as it is to trace Fourier's movements or to catch more than a fleeting glimpse of the man himself during the later years of the revolutionary decade, it is clear that it was at this time that his theory took shape. His experiences during the period of Jacobin dictatorship had already left Fourier with a lasting horror of political revolution and social turmoil. Now it was the financial chaos and the food shortages and the widespread poverty of the Directory that made him a bitter enemy of what he was subsequently to describe as "the anarchic and perverse mode of exchange . . . known as 'free competition.' "[51] At Lyon and Marseille Fourier was well placed to observe the devastating effects of inflation on small wage earners and pensioners and others with fixed incomes. He was also able to witness the dislocations caused by the collapse of the Lyon silk industry and by the stagnation of the port of Marseille. And alongside this, at Marseille in particular, he could see great fortunes being made through speculation in paper money, the creation of artificial shortages, and profiteering in supplies for the Army of Italy.

According to his later accounts, it was during the early years of the Directory that Fourier first began "to suspect the existence of a still unknown social science" that would provide a remedy for the "calamities afflicting social industry."[52]★ These calamities—"poverty, unemployment, the success of dishonesty, maritime piracies, commercial monopoly, the taking of slaves"—convinced Fourier that there was something wrong with the whole economic system based on free or (as he called it) "anarchic" competition. He accordingly began to formulate a general critique of commercial capitalism that emphasized the parasitism of the merchant and the middleman as the chief cause of economic ills. He also began to consider various schemes for the control or elimination of the middleman and the establishment of direct contact between producers and consumers. At the same time that Babeuf was launching the "conspiracy of equals" and Henri Saint-Simon was developing his first schemes of social reorganization and Robert Owen was making his first practical experiments in industrial reform, Fourier thus began to ponder the idea that a cure for many of the ills produced by the system of free competition might be obtained through the establishment—within the capitalist system—of small, self-sustaining communities or associations of producers and consumers.

Fourier's proposals for economic reform only represent one facet of his intellectual activities during the Directory. During this period his mind seems to have been churning with a variety of other projects related to his experiences as a tradesman and a soldier. Not long after his discharge from the army, he began to bombard public authorities with a host of proposals and petitions. These include the letters concerning troop movements and military affairs that have already been mentioned. There was also a proposal to the minister of the interior for the transfer of the fair at Beaucaire to the city of Arles.[53] (This proposal was forwarded to the Commission on Fairs and Markets of the Council of Five Hundred, where it was characterized as "one of those dreams that the mind of a *négociant* should have been the last to conceive.") There were letters to the foreign ministers Delacroix and Talleyrand concerning peace treaties and the adjustment of national boundaries.[54] And there was an important epistle to the city fathers of Bordeaux concerning plans for the renovation of certain quarters of that city.[55] In 1796 or 1797 Fourier made one or more trips to Paris to get a hearing for his ideas. Apparently he also tried to enlist the support of Pierre-Joseph Briot, an important figure in

★It has traditionally been assumed that Fourier's formative years were spent almost entirely at Lyon. A number of the "calamities" to which he refers, however, could only have been observed at a seaport such as Marseille. See Hémardinquer, "Notes critiques," esp. 51–54.

Besançon politics during the revolutionary period, who was to be elected to the Council of Five Hundred in April of 1798.★ Nothing came of these efforts; and in any case it seems clear that in 1797 Fourier had not yet made his crucial discoveries. But still in his letter of December 1796 to the municipality of Bordeaux he was already able to claim that in his travels around France he had been so struck by "the monotony and ugliness of our modern cities" that he had conceived "the model of a new type of city" designed in such a way as to "prevent the spread of fires and banish the stenches that, in cities of all sizes, literally wage war against the human race."[56]

Proposals like these were not uncommon at the time: unknown provincial philosophers had been submitting them to government officials and learned societies throughout the eighteenth century. But Fourier was no common provincial philosopher; and in 1797 and 1798 his private speculations took a bolder turn.[57] He began to see the problems of urban squalor and cutthroat economic competition as symptoms of a deeper social sickness. The frustrations of his own life and the wretchedness and chaos of postrevolutionary society sufficed in his mind to demonstrate the futility of the Revolution and to discredit the philosophical ideas that had inspired its leaders. As he saw it, the French Revolution was simply a spectacular proof of the vanity of the whole tradition of rationalist and enlightened philosophy. The philosophers had always attempted to impose rational norms on human behavior, to repress and stifle the passions. The cause of their failure was quite simply that they had refused to accept man as he was. Institutions could be changed, but man could not. The passions were God-given and they were meant to be expressed.

Fourier's first efforts to bring together all his earlier speculations into a comprehensive view of man and society date from 1799. It was at this point that he began to conceive of his model community not merely as an experiment in city planning or economic reform but rather as part of a larger theory of social organization designed to provide a

---

★Passport records at the Archives Nationales show that in December of 1796 "Citizen Fourrier" was granted a passport for travel from Lyon to Paris, AN F^7 6239^A. Pellarin, whose source is apparently the recollections of Désiré Ordinaire, speaks of Fourier as having traveled to Paris in 1797 to consult about his ideas with the deputy Briot, who was "too absorbed by his legislative responsibilities . . . to make a careful study of Fourier's proposals." Pellarin, *Fourier* (5th ed.), 51. Since Briot was only elected to the Council of Five Hundred in April 1798, that trip must have taken place the following year, if at all.

useful outlet for every human passion. The task he set himself was to work out a scheme of "natural association" that would make the gratification of individual desires and passions serve the general good. In his sole surviving account of "the indices and methods that led to the discovery" Fourier passed blithely over "the stages of my research on the problem of natural association." He merely observed that he eventually hit upon a scheme for the organization of a community into small "passional" groups whose members would be inspired to work at socially useful tasks by "rivalry, self-esteem, and other stimuli compatible with self-interest."[58] This scheme was based on an elaborate theory of human motivation, which Fourier described as "the geometrical calculus of passionate attraction" and which, he claimed, was in "complete accord" with the Newtonian principle of gravitational attraction.

Fourier's crucial breakthrough came in April 1799. He was then employed as a clerk for a business house at Marseille. Quitting work, he traveled to Paris in order to undertake the scientific studies he believed necessary to "complete" and "confirm" his theory. Apparently he spent a good part of his time in Paris at the Bibliothèque Nationale: one of his favorite images—the imminent "downfall" of "the four hundred thousand volumes" of philosophy owned by the library—seems to date from this period.[59] It is possible that he also attended public lectures (which were popular during the Directory) at the Musée de Paris, or the Lycée Republicaine, or at the Collège de France, where the faculty included Cuvier and Lalande.[60] At any rate, in his reading during this period Fourier evidently concentrated on mathematics and natural sciences—on books like Montucla's *Histoire des mathématiques* and Castel's *Histoire naturelle des poissons,* both of which titles are scrawled on the back of a promissory note endorsed by Fourier at Paris in September of 1799.[61]

As his studies advanced, Fourier soon managed to persuade himself that he had hit upon the key to "the riddle of the destinies." Not only had he discovered the means to gratify and harmonize all the human passions. He had also discovered the principles on which it would be possible to explain "the plans adopted by God" in assigning "passions, properties, forms, colors, and tastes" to everything that existed in the animal, vegetable, and mineral kingdoms.[62] This vision of a "total science," which would explain everything in the universe, was to haunt Fourier for the rest of his life.

After less than a year in Paris, however, a number of "misfortunes" compelled Fourier to give up his studies and to go to work once again for the Maison Bousquet in Lyon. Fourier never specified the exact nature of these misfortunes. But almost certainly they included the loss of that part of Fourier's fortune which remained after the siege of Lyon.[63] Thus in June of 1800, shortly after the *coup d'état* that brought Napoleon to power, Fourier returned to Lyon to reenter what he described as "the jail house of commerce."

3

From Architectural Reform
to Universal System

THROUGHOUT his life Fourier's thought continued to bear the marks of the period in which his ideas first crystallized, the period of the Thermidorean reaction and the Directory. Thirty years later he was still inveighing against hoarders and speculators, the principal economic villains of the Directory, and still illustrating his indictment of commerce with examples drawn from the 1790s. Under Napoleon and the Bourbons he also continued to rail against the political ideals and models of the revolutionary period. For Fourier Robespierre was always "the executioner from Arras," Marat was a "drinker of blood," and Sparta, the model of a democratic nation in arms, was actually "a league of ambitious and tyrannical monks, living in laziness at the expense of the Hellots, whom they massacre as a reward for their services."[1]

If the speculation and shortages of the Directory figured prominently in what Fourier was to call the "bad dream" of civilization, it was the ideal of republican asceticism that became his permanent political nightmare. Thus he rarely missed an opportunity to expose the hypocrisy of a Robespierre, or to denounce Cato, the prototype of the virtuous republican, as in fact "the most shameless of egotists."[2] Even

[57]

under the restored Bourbon monarchy he persisted in ridiculing the efforts of the authorities during the Directory to inculcate an ethic of self-denial and civic virtue. "There are no collective social virtues without wealth," Fourier insisted.[3] And when he sought an example of the absurdity of appeals to republican virtue, he repeatedly cited the maxims—such as "Pay your taxes with joy"—from Saint-Lambert's *Catéchisme universel* that François de Neufchâteau, the interior minister of the Directory, had ordered posted in every primary school in the Republic in 1799. When it was pointed out to him in 1821 that Saint-Lambert was no longer cited as an authority on moral questions, Fourier shrugged. Since moral and philosophical systems came in and out of fashion as quickly as clothing, Saint-Lambert's "outmoded moral frippery" was "just as good as the moral frippery of 1821."[4]

There is little doubt that by 1800 Fourier had identified most of those aspects of contemporary life that were subsequently to figure prominently in his critique of civilization. In his thinking about human nature and human motivation, and in the elaboration of his cosmology and of his utopian vision, he was less advanced. He could write later that it was only in 1806 that he managed to complete the basic "calculus of the mechanism of the passions." His first full description of life in his ideal community dates from the years 1805–1808.[5] According to his own testimony his cosmology was not finally established until after 1814. And it was not until as late as 1817 that he gave final form to his vision of a sexually liberated society. Taking all these later developments into account, however, it is still clear that the essential and formative period in Fourier's intellectual life was the decade of the French Revolution, the period running from Fourier's first visit to Paris in the winter of 1789–1790 to his great discovery of 1799. One of the main problems confronting anyone who sets out to write Fourier's intellectual biography is to account for the transformation that took place within him during these years—Fourier's transformation from the callow youth of 1789 to the self-described "inventor" of the calculus of passionate attraction.

Having traced Fourier's external biography in the preceding chapter, we must still attempt to reconstruct the inner logic of his intellectual development during the 1790s. Then we will consider the problem of Fourier's literary and philosophical sources and the question of what impelled him to work out a universal system.

I

As a young man Fourier was what Jonathan Swift would have called a "projector." He claimed that by the age of twenty he had already drawn up a proposal for the creation of a steam-powered locomotive to run on iron rails.[6] Although nothing is left of this proposal (which was not taken seriously by the engineers to whom he showed it), we do have some record of the numerous projects and proposals that the young Fourier submitted a few years later to the authorities of the Directory. As we have seen, these projects dealt with a wide range of topics including army organization and supply, the reform of commerce, and geopolitics. But there were two topics that Fourier found particularly absorbing during the chaotic years of the Thermidorean reaction and the Directory. First of all, he was fascinated by questions of architecture and city planning. Second, he was interested in working out a program of commercial reform that would serve to moralize economic relations and thus remedy the ills produced by the system of free or "anarchic" competition.

Fourier's interest in architecture and urban planning went back to his first visit to Paris at the age of seventeen. In later years Fourier referred more than once to the way in which, as a young man taking his first steps in the world, his imagination had been stirred by his first glimpse of Paris with its broad boulevards, its elegant town houses, and above all its "fairy palace," the Palais Royal. He recalled in 1822 that it was while walking on the boulevards of Paris and admiring two small town houses located on the Boulevard des Invalides, "between the rue Acacias and the rue N. Plumet," that he first conceived of "the idea of unitary architecture, for which I soon determined the rules."[7] Elsewhere Fourier explained that it was the contrast between the elegance and spaciousness of Paris and the darkness and dirt of such cities as Rouen and Troyes that had first set him to pondering the problem of how to create a more rational and attractive form of urban organization. At the time when he first began to formulate his economic critique, he wrote, he had already "been occupied for four years by a [study] of the blunders in the physical arrangement of civilized edifices."

> I had been so struck by the ugliness of the cities of Rouen and Troyes that I conceived a plan for a kind of city very different

from ours. (I will explain the arrangement in the section on Guarantism.) This plan, which I have since recognized as a highly precious invention, involved innovations in the domestic order and led by degrees to the invention of the calculus of passionate series.[8]

One version of this plan, which marked the beginning of Fourier's career as a utopian, is contained in his letter of December 1796 to the city government of Bordeaux.[9]

In this letter Fourier argued that the large number of foreigners who visited Bordeaux made it an ideal location for the establishment of a model city that might inspire city planners to improve on the "shabby" and "insipid" design of most of the new cities established in Europe and America during the eighteenth century.

> I observe that since the city of Bordeaux is a major point of arrival for foreigners, it would be a particularly suitable place to offer the whole world the model of a new kind of city constructed in a very different manner than Petersburg, Philadelphia, Nancy, Mannheim, Karlsruhe, and other such shabby efforts. In this location such a model would be seen by a large number of Americans and might correct the ideas of that nation, which is building a large number of cities, each more insipid than the others.

Fourier went on to discuss some of the advantages of the plan.

> The rules that I have established would render a city much more healthy than the majority of villages because it will be impossible for the [common] people to crowd into filthy sinkholes such as the tumbledown hovels of the poor quarters, and because the population would not be permitted to concentrate in any quarter.

Fourier then proceeded to enumerate a set of regulations that reflected (despite his insistence on the originality of his ideas) the widely shared preoccupation of contemporaries with the need for correct proportion, open space, and the free circulation of air in urban design.

> There will be created a Commission of Architecture responsible for overseeing the construction of edifices both public and private. No house may be built until the commission accepts its plan as consistent with the rules adopted. . . . The commission

should require of all buildings if not luxury at least an elegant simplicity. . . . Every house must be surrounded by an amount of open space at least equivalent to its surface area. This open space should form a court or garden. . . . The least separation between two buildings must be six *toises*. . . . This space will increase in proportion to the size of the buildings. . . . The separation must be at least equal to half the height of the façade before which it is placed. On the side facing the street buildings may rise only to a height equal to the width of the street.[10]

In all of this Fourier's main concern seems to have been with aesthetic matters. But in describing his plan to the city fathers of Bordeaux he insisted that even though it would indeed make cities pleasing to the eye, it would also yield "more precious" social benefits such as a reduction in crowding and fire damage and in the incidence of contagious diseases.

This proposal to the city of Bordeaux was only a fragment of a larger scheme of urban reform that Fourier had already worked out by the end of 1796.* We know from Fourier's later writings that in the larger scheme he had much more to say about the exterior decoration of buildings in the model city and about the need for precise and carefully graduated distinctions between streets, buildings, and ornamentation in the central city, the suburbs, and adjoining rural areas.[11] We also know that these initial reflections on the reform of urban architecture eventually inspired Fourier to consider the idea of a city, or community, within which the storage, preparation, and consumption of food would be carried on collectively. For one of the consequences of Fourier's regulations—with the premium they placed on open space and on elegance and proportion in architecture—was that they would require the construction of relatively large dwelling units. In the ideal city envisaged by the young Fourier none but the very rich could afford to own an entire building with the required amount of land around it. The

*Fourier was explicit about this in the introduction of his memoir to the municipality of Bordeaux: "Struck by the monotony of our modern cities, I have imagined a plan absolutely different from the plans that have been in vogue the past few years. I will not send it to you in its entirety since I have much to say in the plan about the ornamentation of the surrounding area, and it is only a matter here [at Bordeaux] of a quarter the surroundings of which have already been built." AN 10AS 15 (18), p. 1. The larger plan was eventually to find a place in Fourier's mature system as one of a number of reformist proposals that might facilitate a gradual transition from civilization to Harmony. See OC X, PM (1851), 17.

rest—the members of the bourgeoisie and the lower classes—would necessarily be housed in private apartments within large dwelling units. But if large numbers of people were lodged in a single building, Fourier observed, the building could easily be designed with communal kitchen, dining room, and cleaning room. As he wrote later, the "principal advantage" of the large dwelling units he had in mind was that they would "lend themselves to the partial association of households at least in the preparation of meals, which is the greatest expense of the common people." Without imposing association, such houses would make it "easy to provoke."[12]

Thus it was that Fourier's earliest speculations on the reform of urban architecture inspired him to consider the advantages of certain forms of domestic association. His first critical reflections on commerce pointed in the same direction.

If Fourier's concern with urban planning and design can be traced back to 1789, his interest in the reform of commerce had an even earlier genesis. By Fourier's own account, the initial stimulus was provided by the "reprobation" he earned as a young man for his inability to conform to the dishonest commercial practices that his family and his first employers accepted as a matter of course.

> Disposed since childhood to incline to honesty and trust, I was declared by everyone to be incompetent at commerce. . . . The reprobation with which I was universally honored provoked my disdain at an early age and inspired me, out of a spirit of rivalry, to make calculations concerning a means of success that will surprise all the merchants, the means of truth!!![13]

On the basis of his own experience and observation, it seemed evident to Fourier that honesty was *not* the best policy for someone who wished to succeed in commerce. The merchant who misrepresented his goods and cheated his customers was far more likely to prosper than one who attempted to conduct his affairs honestly. But was it possible, Fourier asked, to imagine a situation in which a merchant could conduct his affairs with the utmost probity and still be assured of prospering? It was with this question that Fourier began an inquiry that he subsequently described as the "hypothetical calculus of truth." "I followed the algebraic method," Fourier wrote, "I took for granted the existence of problematical unknowns, of truth, justice, liberty, and association . . . as if there were no obstacle to their employment."[14]

These reflections on the relationship between commerce and individual morality seem to have preoccupied Fourier from the very beginning of his career in commerce. He later described himself as having spent "several years" in "vain research" without discovering any means by which the individual could avoid ruining himself through the practice of absolute probity. But at some point not long after the beginning of the Directory—probably in 1796—Fourier's reflections took a bolder turn. He began to consider the possibility of collective or institutional solutions to a problem that he had initially perceived only in terms of the behavior and moral standards of individuals. Honesty would only become good economic policy, Fourier surmised, in a society where the honest individual could count on others to observe the same standards as himself. The problem therefore was to devise new institutions that would either offer all merchants an incentive for the practice of truth, or oblige them to deal honestly with each other and with the general public, whether they liked it or not.

What Fourier was looking for was, as he put it, a "method of collective guarantees" that would compel every merchant to act as if honesty and the love of virtue were his most fundamental impulses. Fourier apparently spent many months devising a series of institutional schemes that would accomplish this task. Among these schemes was a proposal for the organization of the whole corps of merchants in a group of insurance companies that would be "collectively responsible for the goods society confides to them for exchange and distribution."[15] There were also various licensing schemes designed to reduce the number of merchants and to control their activities through the establishment of trade associations whose members would be obliged to pay an increasingly high licensing fee or *patente* each year—or devote themselves "to farming, industry, and productive enterprise."[16] There was even a scheme for the creation of a network of cooperative warehouses, which Fourier called the *entrepôt concurrente,* within which goods would circulate and undergo evaluation without ever becoming the property of merchants and other middlemen.[17] It was this last plan, which implied the elimination of the whole corps of merchants, that seems to have convinced Fourier that the remedy for what he was soon to call the "crimes of commerce" lay in the proper application of the principle of association.

During the last half of the eighteenth century the idea of association retained some resonance in France.[18] While Turgot and the Physiocrats were arguing that the key to economic prosperity lay in the destruction of the guilds and other archaic forms of community that served to inhibit the circulation of wealth and the movement of goods and people, the opposition to economic individualism persisted. It was sometimes argued that the misfortunes of the small peasant farmer in particular might be remedied through the establishment of self-sustaining communities or associations of producers and consumers in which property would be held and work performed in common. Even the *Encyclopédie,* which was in many respects favorable to economic individualism, published an article recommending "associations de bons citoyens" and "associations de gens laborieux" as "the only way of assuring the happiness of men . . . and of sparing them an infinity of cares and worries that it is impossible to avoid in the state of desolation in which men have lived up to now." There is also evidence for the growth among householders at Lyon and other large cities of rudimentary consumers' associations to purchase food and fuel in common. And in Fourier's own Franche-Comté there was already by the end of the eighteenth century a significant development of peasant producers' associations—called *Fruitières*—for the manufacture of Gruyère cheese.[19]

Fourier had some familiarity with the *Fruitières;* and although it is not clear how closely he followed the development of other types of association, we do know that by the early years of the Directory he had become fascinated by the whole idea of association. His interest in urban reform had led him to conceive of a "new kind of city" in which the purchase, preparation, and consumption of food would be carried on in common by lower and middle class householders. His interest in the reform of commerce had prompted him to devise various associations to regulate the exchange and distribution of goods. It was only a small step for him to move in his reflections on association from the spheres of consumption and distribution to that of production. As he wrote later, the problem that particularly intrigued him at this time was that of agricultural association.

> More than once people have supposed that incalculable savings and ameliorations would result if one could bring together the inhabitants of a village in an industrial society, if one could associate two or three hundred families of unequal wealth according to their capital and their work. . . . Three hundred

families of associated villagers could have just a single well-kept granary instead of three hundred rundown granaries, a single wine vat instead of three hundred poorly maintained vats. In many cases and especially in summer, these villagers could have just three or four large ovens instead of three hundred. They could send a single dairymaid to town with a wagon bearing a cask of milk and thus save a hundred other dairymaids the time and trouble it takes to carry their pitchers into town. These are just a few of the savings that diverse observers have recognized; and yet they have not indicated one-twentieth of the advantages that will result from agricultural association.[20]

The main problem, as Fourier saw it, was reconciling the conflicting desires, interests, and passions that the members of such a community would be sure to have. The "incalculable savings" that an agricultural association might yield could only be obtained if a way were found of harmonizing the passions and the interests of all.

It was at this point—in beginning to reflect upon ways of integrating the passions of individuals within a harmonious community—that Fourier first entered the new intellectual world he was to inhabit for the rest of his life. His task was to work out what he called a theory of "NATURAL or ATTRACTIVE association." By this he meant the construction of a model of a new form of social organization within which the gratification of individual desires would serve the general good and individuals would want to work at socially useful tasks. Having formulated the problem to his own satisfaction in April of 1799, he made his first crucial intellectual breakthrough shortly thereafter.[21] This was the discovery that work could become attractive and conflict could be harmonized if people who shared particular penchants were divided into groups and series of groups within which differences in age, wealth, character, and education were carefully nuanced and contrasted. The name Fourier gave to the fundamental unit that was to harmonize the passions and structure life within his natural association was the "passionate series."

This initial flash of inspiration was what prompted Fourier to quit his job at Marseille and to travel to Paris to embark on the program of scientific studies described in the previous chapter. During his eight or nine months in Paris Fourier seems to have had two main intellectual preoccupations. First of all, he attempted to give substance to his new theory of natural association. Second, he began to generalize his ideas and to seek "proofs" in the realm of science and mathematics. He was soon able to assert that far from being arbitrary and unscientific like the concepts of other social theorists, his passionate series were "on every point analogous to geometrical series, all of whose properties they share."[22] He could also argue that his resolution of the problem of natural association had provided him with the "key" to "several new sciences." Chief among them was the science (or "theory" or "calculus") of passionate attraction.

> The first science that I discovered was the theory of passionate attraction. When I had recognized that the progressive series assure full development to the passions of both men and women, and to people of diverse ages and diverse classes; when I had recognized that in this new order the more passions one has, the stronger and wealthier one will become, I surmised that if God had given so much influence to passionate attraction and so little to reason, its enemy, his purpose was to guide us to the system of progressive series, which is completely consistent with attraction. Then I supposed that attraction, which is so much maligned by the philosophers, must be the interpreter of the designs of God concerning the social order. By this means I arrived at the ANALYTIC AND SYNTHETIC CALCULUS OF PASSIONATE ATTRACTIONS AND REPULSIONS.[23]

This calculus was also "an exact science and wholly applicable to geometrical theorems." Thus Fourier could boast that in working out the theory of passionate attraction, he was completing the work of Isaac Newton—but extending it from the realm of pure curiosity (the equilibrium of the stars) to that of the most urgent utility (the equilibrium of the passions).

A second new science discovered by Fourier was what he described as the science of universal analogy. Convinced that the laws of passionate attraction were "entirely consistent" with the laws of material attraction, he concluded that the material world and the inner or passionate world constituted a unified system. Any development in one sphere was necessarily accompanied by an analogous development in the other. And Fourier went on:

> I suspected that this analogy could extend from general laws to particular laws, that the attractions and properties of animals, vegetables, and minerals were perhaps coordinated to the same

plan as those of man and the stars. I convinced myself of this after the necessary research.[24]

Thus Fourier found himself embarked on the exploration of "a new scientific world." Armed with his theories of passionate attraction and universal analogy, he began to "read in the mysterious book of nature," to decipher its strange language, to lift its "supposedly impenetrable veil." In due course he began to see himself not only as the successor of Newton but also as the founder of a universal system that would explain "the plans adopted by God" for everything from the destiny of man and the future of the solar system to "the most minute alterations of matter in the animal, vegetable, and mineral kingdoms."

There is much that remains obscure about these initial discoveries. It is clear, for example, that Fourier felt greatly indebted to Newton, and that he was deeply serious when he spoke of himself as having "continued" or "completed" Newton's work.* But it is difficult to say what he actually owed to Newton. Certainly he shared with many European thinkers of the eighteenth and early nineteenth centuries a sense of awe at the underlying harmony and simplicity of the principles Newton had shown to be at work in the physical universe. Clearly he believed, as did many of these other thinkers, that the key to the right ordering of human affairs must lie in the discovery of some social or moral analogue to the principle of gravitational attraction. But what, apart from the name and the assumption of a preestablished harmony, was so "Newtonian" about Fourier's psychological theory? He never explained.[25]

II

There are many other questions to raise concerning the extraordinary intellectual journey taken by Fourier during the last five years of the revolutionary decade. It is still difficult to be specific about the precise

---

*The study of Fourier's earliest manuscripts shows that at the outset of his career he was trying in a very literal way to make use of concepts borrowed from physics and astronomy in the development of his psychological and social theories. Thus his ideal community, which he eventually named the Phalanx, was originally sometimes called *le tourbillon;* and the names he originally gave to the three distributive passions (later named the Cabalist, Butterfly, and Composite) explicitly identified them as varieties of movement: Composition, Oscillation, and Progression. See Fourier's notes to the "Ode sur la découverte des lois divines" (1803), AN 10AS 23 (16).

chronology of Fourier's intellectual development, and the connection between Fourier's ideas is at times so obscure as to defy interpretation. Furthermore, if Fourier's debt to Newton was indeed as superficial as it appears, then one would like to know what thinkers, if any, *were* his intellectual guides. Not much light is shed on this question by Hubert Bourgin's classic study of Fourier's sources.[26] The only writings that Bourgin saw as "definite and certain sources" for Fourier were a few articles in the journal *La Décade philosophique* on the ideas of Count Rumford and Cadet de Vaux.[27] But this, argued Bourgin, was only to be expected in the case of an uncultured autodidact like Fourier. For Bourgin Fourier was the "unlettered shop sergeant" he proclaimed himself to be. He owed little if anything to books, and his main sources were observation and introspection. "From the day he left the college of his town," wrote Bourgin, "provided with the mediocre and super-ficial education that was offered at that time, Fourier ceased studying. His occupations scarcely permitted it; he had neither the leisure nor the means to continue his studies. His doctrine took almost complete shape in his mind during a time when, as a clerk and traveling salesman, he had no other resource than himself; and when his doctrine was fully elaborated in a manner that he found satisfying, there was nothing more for him to seek in books."[28]

In some respects it is hard to quarrel with Bourgin's conclusion. There is no doubt that Fourier's principal source was reflection on his own experience or that once the main outlines of the theory had taken shape, he looked to other people's writings principally for the confirmation of his own ideas. Where Bourgin's account is deeply mislead-ing, however, is in its claim that Fourier's studies—and presumably his serious readings—came to an end with his graduation from the Collège de Besançon. In fact, there is ample evidence to suggest that as a young man Fourier was a voracious reader and that if there was a point at which he ceased to study, it was not in 1787 but rather in 1808 after the failure of his first book. After that date Fourier does indeed seem to have retreated into a private world. Henceforth he could describe him-self as "bored" by long books and treatises on metaphysics. And he became increasingly selective in his readings, concentrating on newspa-pers like the *Journal des débats* and the *Gazette de France* and journals such as the *Revue des deux mondes* and the *Revue encyclopédique,* which he combed in search of detail and anecdote to support his theory.

Fourier was never, to be sure, a systematic reader. Rather he was an intellectual *bricoleur,* eager to instruct himself in the wide range of questions that interested him, which he needed to consider in the elaboration of his theory. He seems to have done a large amount of reading simply for information: encyclopedias, learned treatises, travelers' tales, and a wide variety of atlases are all cited in his writings. In discussing the passions, for instance, he drew on the articles on the passions in both Diderot's *Encyclopédie* and Panckoucke's popular *Encyclopédie méthodique.* Even in sexual matters he supplemented what he had learned from personal experience and from conversation with references to treatises such as Tissot's *Onanisme* and the *De Matrimonio* by the sixteenth-century Spanish Jesuit Tomas Sanchez.[29]

Fourier was particularly interested in deepening his knowledge of what he described as the "fixed" sciences such as chemistry, physics, biology, and astronomy. His approach to these sciences was naturally idiosyncratic. He always denied, for example, having any special expertise in astronomy: his own specialty was "astrosophy"—"the theory that brings astronomical science in line with [the science] of the human passions." Nevertheless, evidence of his desire to draw on the natural sciences in the elaboration of his own theory may be found in a cahier of reading notes entitled "Cosmology, Physics, etc." that dates from the years 1806 to 1809. This notebook includes excerpts and summaries of articles by and about Buffon, Guyton de Morveau, Fourcroy, and the abbé Rozier. There are also long excerpts from various articles on the work of Hyacinthe Azaïs and his "seductive" promise to "explain by a single fact . . . the universality of physical and chemical phenomena." And there are reading lists including works on chemistry by Fourcroy and Lavoisier as well as an article (listed with its *côte* at the Bibliothèque Nationale) from the *Journal de physique* of September 1781 on "the physical cause of the color of the different inhabitants of the earth."[30] All of this suggests that Fourier continued well into the Empire to read in the field of science and apparently also to use the Bibliothèque Nationale during his business trips to Paris.

What philosophical and literary works were particularly important to Fourier? Among the major figures of the eighteenth century the one whom Fourier appears to have known best is, not surprisingly, Rousseau. His abundant, varied, and detailed references to Rousseau's works—and especially to *Emile,* the *Confessions,* and the *Nouvelle Héloïse* more than to the political writings—suggest that at the very least Fourier found in Rousseau an important interlocutor in his own attempts to define a social order consistent with man's true needs.[31] Fourier had some (probably secondhand) knowledge of the work of the Physiocrats; he was intrigued by Bernardin de Saint-Pierre's *Etudes de la nature;* and he made frequent use of the abbé Raynal's *Histoire des deux Indes* in his discussion of patriarchal and barbarian societies. In general, however, Fourier was not steeped in the literature of the radical Enlightenment. There are no significant references to Helvétius and Holbach in his work, and his allusions to Voltaire and Diderot are for the most part perfunctory. Nor was Fourier greatly interested in the main writings of the utopian tradition. There is no mention in his writings of Morelly's *Code de la nature,* Mercier's *L'An 2440,* or any of the utopian writings of Restif de la Bretonne. He was indeed familiar with Fénelon's *Télémaque* and Mably's *Entretiens de Phocion.* But his references to Mably consist largely of derogatory comments concerning the cabbage, gruel, and turnips served by Phocion's frugal wife; and the "dogmatic nonsense" of Fénelon he proposed as a model for the "social cacographies" to be published in his ideal society for amateurs of "burlesque social archaeology."[32]

If as a young man Fourier did not read deeply in any of the major writers of the Enlightenment except for Rousseau, he was able to draw throughout his life on a relatively solid foundation in the classical writers and their seventeenth-century French followers. Curiously perhaps for a thinker who is in some respects rightly identified with the romantic movement, Fourier's strongest intellectual roots lay in the neoclassical seventeenth century. The poets whom he most often and most freely cited were Horace and Boileau; he was a great lover of Molière and La Fontaine, whose texts and protagonists he often used to illustrate his own observations about the passions; and in his own aesthetic tastes he was firmly on the side of the classics. While many of his contemporaries could exult in the sublimity of craggy mountains, wild cataracts, and raging seas, Fourier's preference went to the calm, the orderly, and the harmonious. His architectural dream was to replace the "crowded huts" and the "foul swamps" of rural France with "symmetrical constructions," and he professed nothing but scorn for "the savants" who wished to accustom contemporaries to such "hideous sights" as "the bare mountains of Provence" and the "horrible Fountain of Vaucluse."[33] His own ideal, epitomized in his descriptions of the Phalanx, was of a landscape dotted with belvederes and planted with flowers, a landscape in which nature was clipped and ordered and the eye was led, along paths and under arbors, to columned rotundas and brightly colored tents. It was a vision in the tradition of a Poussin or a Claude Lorrain.

III

The preceding comments on Fourier's literary preferences and aesthetic sensibilities tell us something about the form that his utopian vision was to take, but very little about its content and inception and nothing at all about the intriguing question of what prompted Fourier to present his theory of association within the larger framework of a "theory of the destinies." What drove Fourier beyond his "modest calculus" on association and into an intellectual realm he had previously associated with "astrologers and magicians"? Why did he originally feel it necessary to work out a universal system? It seems to me that these are fundamental questions and that one way of approaching them fruitfully is to attempt to situate Fourier in the intellectual history of the postrevolutionary period.

Fourier needs to be seen, I believe, as one of a group of thinkers for whom the French Revolution was the decisive experience and whose main intellectual concern was to find their bearings in a world torn apart by the Revolution. Of these thinkers some, like the Catholic counterrevolutionaries Louis de Bonald and Joseph de Maistre, and like Fourier's fellow utopian socialist Henri Saint-Simon, were Old Regime aristocrats who had reached maturity prior to the outbreak of the Revolution. Others like Fourier himself, like the romantic philosopher Pierre-Simon Ballanche, and like a host of minor monist visionaries, were members of what Léon Cellier has described as a "sacrificed generation" of French writers and intellectuals.[34] Too young to figure actively in the French Revolution, hampered in their ability to reach an audience by the restrictions of the Napoleonic period, the members of this generation were nonetheless deeply marked by the Revolution and obliged to spend much of their adult lives coping with its consequences.

The group that Fourier belonged to was thus a diverse group including reactionary theocrats, mystics, and utopian socialists. What they all had in common was, first of all, an acute awareness of the inadequacy of the world outlook of the Enlightenment in the face of the problems confronting Europe in the aftermath of the Revolution. For most of them, the result of the Revolution was not only to wipe out the aristocratic and feudal social order but also to reveal the bank-ruptcy of the Enlightenment confidence in human reason, progress, and equality. The Revolution in Fourier's view was the *coup d'essai* of the philosophes—an experiment that demonstrated by its failure that their "torrents of political and moral enlightenment" were "nothing more than torrents of illusions." Saint-Simon could also write: "It is chiefly to the vicious direction followed by the Encyclopedists in their works that one should attribute the insurrection that broke out in 1789, as well as the bloody character the Revolution assumed from its beginning." Again, Ballanche could describe the Revolution as a "monstrous" event, a "calamity" that was "the fruit of the cruel war" waged by the philosophes "against all illusions." All three were echo-ing the language and the judgments of counterrevolutionary theorists like de Bonald, who described "the oppression caused by false doc-trines and by impious and seditious writings" as "the veritable and unique cause of the Revolution and of all the crimes by which it has terrified the world."[35]

Hostile to the philosophes, Fourier and his contemporaries were Napoleonic in their own intellectual ambitions. Moving away from the empirical and critical traditions of the Enlightenment, they attempted to construct vast systems and to formulate general theories that would fill the intellectual and spiritual vacuum of the postrevolutionary period. "The philosophy of the eighteenth century has been critical and revolu-tionary," wrote Saint-Simon, "that of the nineteenth century will be inventive and organizational."[36] What this meant for the reactionaries de Bonald and de Maistre (who similarly separated themselves from the "critical" eighteenth century) was the construction in de Bonald's *Théorie du pouvoir* (1796) and de Maistre's *Du Pape* (1819) of great new Catholic systems embracing questions of politics, history, theology, and language. For Ballanche invention and construction meant the search for an epic form and for symbols appropriate to his conviction that a new birth would come out of the destruction of the revolutionary period. Saint-Simon's initial goal was, as he later explained, the devel-opment of a universal system, a unitary or total science based on a single law that would be equally valid for the physical and social worlds.

> I wished, like everyone else, to systematize the philosophy of
> God. I wished to descend successively from the level of the

universe to that of the solar system; from there to terrestrial phenomena and finally to the study of the human species considered as an element of the sublunary world; and to deduce from this study the laws of social organization, the original and essential object of my research.[37]

Fourier's initial aim as a thinker was no less grandiose. Convinced that there must be one law governing both the material and moral worlds, he set out to establish his own universal system. And like Saint-Simon, he believed that Newton's law of gravitational attraction could, if properly understood, serve as the basis for that system.

In the systems devised by all of these thinkers there was one common and underlying conviction: the belief in the need to reach an understanding of man and society deeper and richer than that of the Enlightenment. Rejecting the philosophes' view of all men as essentially similar in nature and equal in rights, both the reactionaries and the utopian socialists stressed human uniqueness and diversity. For them the human mind was not a blank slate: all human beings were born with innate dispositions and propensities. They also agreed that the Enlightenment philosophes had been much too sanguine about the rationality of man and about the feasibility of establishing by legislative fiat a just, free, and egalitarian social order. Both the reactionaries and the utopian socialists agreed on the primacy of the nonrational ties that bound people together in society, on the crucial influence of the passions on human behavior, and on the importance of status and hierarchy as guarantors of social order.

Finally, in their attempts to make sense of the French Revolution and to devise systems that would fill the intellectual vacuum of the postrevolutionary period, each of these thinkers claimed to have discovered some sort of providential plan at work in the world. For de Maistre and de Bonald the French Revolution represented something radically evil—something "satanic" or "diabolical." But both saw a providential force working behind the events. "Never," wrote de Maistre, "has the divinity shown itself so clearly in any human event. If it employs the vilest instruments, that is because it punishes in order to regenerate."[38] The idea that the French Revolution was a "punishment" that would enable France to expiate its sins and thus prepare the way for a great movement of regeneration was central to the thinking of de Maistre, de Bonald, and (with a somewhat different emphasis) Ballanche. Saint-Simon and Fourier did not invoke Satan and they did not use the language of sin and damnation, but they too found a providential power at work in the world and believed themselves privy to its designs. Saint-Simon's first and last works included passages that, he claimed, had been dictated to him by God. And Fourier consistently, throughout his career, could speak of himself as having discovered "God's plan" for the universe.

When Fourier first acquired a significant following, the French Revolution had been over for more than a generation, and the whole intellectual world out of which Fourier's thought had come had vanished. Fourier's providentialism, his hostility to the French Revolution and its ideals, and his dream of establishing a universal system were all, in varying degrees, alien to the thinking of the young men and women who turned Fourierism into a democratic and humanitarian social movement in the 1830s and 1840s. It is hardly surprising, therefore, that Fourier's ideas were misunderstood or distorted in fundamental respects by almost all his disciples. Nor is it surprising that several generations of historians should have interpreted Fourier's thought in light of their own republican and socialist ideals. What needs to be kept in mind, however, as we follow the unfolding of Fourier's doctrine, is that it arose as a reaction to the French Revolution and that from the beginning it reflected the desire to create order in a world shaken to its foundations. Fourier was never to cease presenting his ideas as antithetical to the theory and practice of the Revolution. And he was never entirely to renounce his initial dream of elaborating a universal system that would fill the intellectual void created by the Revolution. In these respects, as in others, his thought was always to bear the mark of the period between Thermidor and the coming of Napoleon.

4

Provincial Shop Sergeant

TODAY THERE are parts of old Lyon that remain very much as they have been for centuries. On the right bank of the Saône in the quarters of Saint Jean and Saint Paul the narrow streets and Renaissance town houses nestled at the base of the Colline de Fourvière have been jealously preserved. The massive stone spiral stairways have not disappeared, and one must still stoop to enter the dark courtyards of these houses through long, low entryways. The spacious Place de Bellecour with its monumental Louis XVI façades is no less imposing now than when its linden trees provided shade for the bourgeois aristocracy of Imperial Lyon. Across from the "praying" hill of Fourvière stands the "laborious" hill, the Croix-Rousse; and on its slopes there is still the labyrinth of the *traboules* to remind one that this was once the redoubt of the *canuts*. At the foot of the Croix-Rousse lies the Place des Terreaux, a bustling square lined with cafés and shops, and dominated now as in 1800 by the Hotel de Ville and the Palais de Saint Pierre. But the quartier des Terreaux, the area between the two rivers and running south from the Place des Terreaux toward Bellecour, has changed beyond recognition since Fourier's time. Then a maze of winding streets, of shops and ateliers, it was subsequently rebuilt and aired out with the construction of broad avenues like the rue de la République and the rue du Président Herriot. It still remains the commercial center of the city. But there is little left to evoke the surrounding in which Fourier lived except a few street names—rues Mercière, de la Poulaillerie, Mulet, Bat d'argent, de l'Arbre sec—streets described by a journalist of the time as "rues sales, obscures, rues éternelles, marchandes, indignes de négociants."[1] The quartier des Terreaux was the small tradesman's Lyon, the quarter of the *marchand* but not the *négociant,* that of the *boutique* but not the *magasin;* and it was here that Fourier took up residence on his return from Paris in 1800. It remained as much of a home as he had throughout the Consulate and Empire.

Louis Reybaud, a Marseillais who knew his Lyon, has left a description that will do as well as any to evoke the atmosphere in which Fourier lived and worked during these years.

> What strikes one most sharply in traversing the city of Lyon is the care with which its inhabitants have husbanded and made use of all available space. Here and there one barely perceives a few large open spaces like the Places des Terreaux and de Bellecour. Everywhere else there is only a confused pile of houses so tall that they practically intercept the daylight. Except for the line of the quays one would seek in vain for a regular perspective, one of those wide and open streets where the light and the air play freely. The heart of the city . . . is furrowed with alleys that cut across each other irregularly and form a labyrinth that is almost always obscured by a veil of fog and a thick cloud of smoke. . . . The two great waterways leave only a narrow tongue of land . . . a most restricted area, locked in by the heights of the Croix-Rousse on one side, and on the other by the slopes of Saint-Just and Fourvière. Whence the necessity of compressing the dwelling places and raising them high, while the space given over to traffic and the public way is reduced beyond all measure. Thus a sort of luxury that all provincial towns possess . . . that of courtyards and gardens, is absolutely unknown in Lyon. Vegetation is so to speak suppressed, and the interior empty spaces permitted in buildings are scarcely sufficient to light and ventilate them enough to render them habitable. Nowhere do houses more closely resemble hives, and the ceaseless buzzing that rises from this bustling enclosure makes this resemblance the more striking and the more exact.[2]

To evoke in more specific terms the physiognomy of Fourier's Lyon one turns in vain to the guidebooks and almanacs—and even the engravings—of the period. There one is confronted by a wealth of details concerning Lyon's monuments, its churches, the dimensions of its Hotel de Ville. There are paeans to the shade provided by the thick lindens of the Place de Bellecour, to the sumptuous town houses of Perrache and Saint-Clair, the new citadels of the city's fast-growing mercantile aristocracy. But of the quartier des Terreaux, the commercial heart of a commercial city, there is scarcely a word. The tourist is hurried through. If he pauses, it is perhaps only to observe, in the words of an aristocratic visitor, that unlike the quartier de Bellecour, the quartier des Terreaux is "poorly constructed: its streets are narrow and dirty, the houses are high, and the multitude of passages are so many sewers. These as well as the butchers' shops, the dye works, and the hospitals make you breathe the foulest, the most contaminated, and the most dangerous air."[3]

I

It was on the Place des Terreaux—and just in front of the Bourse, the "palace of falsehood" as Fourier liked to call it—that the diligence from Paris deposited Fourier on June 4, 1800. The program of studies on which he had embarked in Paris following his "discovery" had lasted no more than eight or nine months. He estimated that to work out his theory in all its details three or four more years of sustained effort would have been necessary.[4] But now he found himself obliged to return to Lyon and take up work once again as a clerk for his old employer, François-Antoine Bousquet. A few days after his arrival Fourier was accompanied by Bousquet's son and one of his partners, Fréderic Fournier, to the City Hall, where he signed his temporary residence permit. This document identified him as "Citizen Charles Fourrier of Besançon," a *commis marchand* by profession and a man of small stature with a large oval face, gray eyes, and a high forehead. He was temporarily lodged "with the Citizen Chevalier" at 165, rue Lafond, next door to the residence of his employer.[5] After a brief stay at this address he found a widowed *marchande,* Pauline Guyonnet, with a room to rent at 74, rue Saint-Côme, a narrow, busy street that ran crookedly from the Place de l'Herborie up toward the Place des Terreaux. In the spring of 1808, Fourier found another furnished apartment nearby on the rue Clermont. This was a wine merchants' street running just behind the Bourse. Fourier remained there, in rooms overlooking the umbrella merchants' stalls on the Place du Plâtre, until the end of 1815.

The events of 1799–1800 had brought two decisive changes in Fourier's life. In the first place, he now had a mission. For the next eight years he was to devote himself to the elaboration and perfection of the "Newtonian calculus" that was the core of his system. At the same time writing became a regular part of Fourier's daily routine. Every day after work he would spend at least a few hours working out his ideas in an ever-growing set of notebooks, which he jealously guarded and carried about with him on his peregrinations. By his own account Fourier continued to make intellectual discoveries. But so far as one can judge from his rather obscure references to his own intellectual development, these discoveries all took place within a common framework and they served primarily to refine and develop aspects of the initial revelation.[6]

In terms of Fourier's external biography the turn of the century also marked an important break. For with the loss around 1800 of the last remains of his inheritance, he was definitively "declassed." Condemned to a career in the lower reaches of commerce, Fourier was too precise in his habits ever to fall into dire poverty. He always managed to earn enough to permit himself a few indulgences, and during good years in Lyon his earnings reached a quite comfortable four or five thousand francs annually. But for the next fifteen years, while he mapped out the contours of his ideal city and chronicled the glorious adventures and amorous intrigues of its inhabitants, he was to lead a life of dull work and trivial distractions. Not again until 1816 would he be free to devote all his time and energy to the thinking and writing that was all that really mattered to him.

Embarked on the exploration of a "new social world," Fourier compared himself to Newton and Columbus. He was convinced that the full working-out and acceptance of his theory would bring an end to the old, mercantile, "civilized" world. But for the time being at least that world had a claim on him.

> It is worth recalling [he wrote in 1820] that since the year 1799, when I found the germ of the calculus of attraction, I have been constantly absorbed by my mercantile occupations and scarcely able to devote a few moments to passional problems, a single

one of which often requires sustained research for several years. After having spent my days participating in the deceitful activities of the merchants and brutalizing myself in the performance of degrading tasks, I could not spend my nights acquiring a knowledge of the true sciences, which would enable me to draw upon them in the elaboration of my theory.[7]

Throughout the Napoleonic period Fourier remained at Lyon and frequented its banks, its business houses, and its Bourse. Punctual at work, frugal in his habits, scrupulously neat in his dress, he dined in the cheap *tables d'hôte* of the quarter and took his glass of white wine each morning at a small café on the rue Sainte-Marie-des-Terreaux. His distractions were those of a hundred other modest employees of the Terreaux: an occasional evening in the upper reaches of Lyon's Grand Théâtre, a solitary stroll at dusk along the quays of the Rhone, a weekly visit to the flower market on the quai de Villeroi. He had friends with whom he shared some of his ideas and dreams. But at work he hid behind the mask of a conscientious employee. For he knew that in a business house a reputation as an intellectual was worth that "of a vandal at the Academy, or of a Huguenot in the Catholic church."[8]

Of course Fourier did have a number of quirks and eccentricities. He became notorious in the Terreaux for his love of cats and flowers and marching bands. Acquaintances recalled the detached and preoccupied air that would often come over him. Sometimes he became so lost in thought as to have no awareness of the season or the weather. He was also occasionally to be seen standing before the great map of Germany at the Prefecture of Lyon, scrutinizing its details in rapt silence for hours on end. But the trait for which Fourier was best remembered was his constant gravity. As a friend recalled later, Fourier was never known to laugh. "Under no circumstance and for no reason did Fourier ever abandon himself to mirth. In the middle of the jokes and the merry talk of his friends, he maintained a perpetual impassivity and an imperturbable composure. He had a particular dislike of wits, pranksters, and makers of puns. . . . Generally it was only by some sally, by some original sortie against the civilized, that he would involve himself in the conversation. Then everyone might laugh; he alone would maintain his habitual gravity and calm."[9]

Most of Fourier's friends during these years were clerks and small-time brokers like himself, modest employees with whom he dined *table d'hôte,* shared a game of dominoes or billiards after work, and occasionally picnicked and poeticized on the banks of the Bedaine River near Arbresle. A number of them seem to have belonged to a fraternal group called "Les Amis du Vieux Coin," which met frequently for dinners and informal poetic tournaments. The "Vieux Coin," which Fourier celebrated in a poem published in the *Bulletin de Lyon* in 1805, was apparently the name of a restaurant or *table d'hôte* where he and his friends liked to gather.[10] Few of these friends left any mark on history. Like Henri Brun, a tradesman and poetic *amateur* who was Fourier's boon companion for a few years, most of them are known to us only through a letter or two preserved among Fourier's papers.[11] Those whom we know better—those like Jean-Baptiste Gaucel and Louis Desarbres whose names turn up occasionally in the archives at Lyon—are only the more successful, clerks who eventually managed to go into business for themselves.

Jean-Baptiste Gaucel, a much-traveled *commis marchand* from the Aveyron, lived during the Consulate at 81, rue Saint-Côme, just across the street from Fourier's room at number 74. Gaucel was a bachelor of about Fourier's age, a former infantry captain, a liberal in politics, a Freemason, and, like Fourier himself, a friend and admirer of Lyon's republican surgeon, L.-V.-F. Amard. By 1807 Gaucel had gone into business for himself as a linen merchant, and he seems to have provided Fourier with a number of commissions during the latter's stints as a self-employed commercial broker. Although Fourier frequently complained about the philistinism of his commercial associates, Gaucel was clearly an exception. In 1808 he helped Fourier publicize the *Théorie des quatre mouvements;* and in later years, after moving his business to Lille, he was to remain in touch with Fourier, to read his major works, and to subscribe to the first Fourierist journal, *Le Phalanstère.*[12]

Another business associate with whom Fourier was to keep in touch was Louis Desarbres. A clerk and traveling salesman like Fourier during the Consulate, Desarbres was to become by the end of the Empire a prosperous banker with offices on the elegant rue Saint-Clair. The precise nature of his relationship with Fourier is not clear. Although he is known to have served as Fourier's banker from time to time, he may also have employed him during the Empire. At this time Desarbres apparently had little interest in Fourier's theory. But by the beginning of the July Monarchy, when Desarbres had accumulated a fortune of "two or three million," several of Fourier's disciples had begun to think of him as a potential benefactor, and Desarbres himself was boasting of his friendship with Fourier. "Desarbres does not lack self-esteem," wrote Clarisse Vigoureux to Fourier in 1834. "When he hears your name discussed in public, he never neglects to say that you are his best friend and that he would very much like to see you and that he is most interested in you."[13]

A closer friend of Fourier's during these years was the civil servant Jean-Baptiste Dumas. A division chief at the Prefecture of Lyon, Dumas had literary pretensions. He had been elected to the Academy of Lyon at the age of twenty-four and was soon embarked on a long and prolific career as an author of poems and odes for ceremonial occasions and as the academy's specialist in funeral orations. Dumas was also active in local journalism and was in fact one of the few members of the intellectual establishment of Imperial Lyon with whom Fourier was on close terms. The two probably became acquainted during the Consulate when Fourier collaborated on several newspapers edited by Dumas. During the Restoration, when Dumas served as judge on the Tribunal of Commerce and as a member of Lyon's Conseil d'Arrondissement, they remained in touch; and judging from the affectionate tone of Dumas' letters, their friendship survived Fourier's departure from Lyon.[14]

II

Were there women in Fourier's life at this time? The solitude of his later years was so profound that it is sometimes assumed that by the age of thirty he had already become the lonely, embittered, and somewhat maniacal recluse whom the disciples knew after 1830. Yet the image that can be pieced together from his private papers and from the recollections of Jean-Baptiste Dumas suggests that the young *commis marchand* of Imperial Lyon was anything but a recluse. Among Fourier's papers there are, for example, drafts of a number of poems addressed (around 1803 or 1804) to young women encountered by Fourier at the theater. One of the most elaborate of these is an epistle to a Mademoiselle Justine, whose "lively charms, graces, and playful humor" had inspired in Fourier "secret desires." The epistle concludes with a portrait of the author.

En habit gris, en habit noir, / Romaine ou ronde chevelure,
Chevalier de sombre figure, / Au théâtre il va chaque soir.
Il vous ferait son nom savoir, / Mais il craint que
  d'indifférence
Vous ne payiez la confidence / Du plaisir qu'il trouve à vous
  voir.

If Fourier was a modest suitor, he also appears to have been a persistent one; for a similar self-portrait with only slight changes was also addressed by him to a Mademoiselle Sandroc and preceded by the statement "I have made a hundred rhymes like this and for many a young lady."[15]

Fourier was far from handsome; and as a young man he was quite self-conscious about his small stature, his large head, and his plain, rather nervous features. "Even at the age of twenty-five," he wrote later, "I had nothing to attract the attention of any woman."[16] He was also so stiff, awkward, and shy that when he attempted to take dancing lessons, not long after his return to Lyon, the result was simply to provide his friends with an entertaining spectacle.

Busy during the day, he was obliged to take his lessons at six o'clock in the morning in the middle of the winter. These dancing lessons, which went on for at least three months, were vividly remembered by everyone who knew Fourier at that time. They went around waking each other well before sunrise just for the pleasure of watching their comrade. . . . This malign curiosity will be easily understood when one realizes that Fourier danced in short breeches, slippers, and without socks, and with a funereal seriousness and gravity.[17]

Despite his awkwardness and his lack of the conventional social graces, it is clear that in Lyon as in his later life, many of Fourier's closest friends were women, and in his relations with them he displayed a courtliness and a kindness that many remembered long afterward. Almost all of the letters from women preserved among Fourier's papers contain expressions of thanks for his "many kindnesses," his "proofs of a veritable friendship," and his attentiveness in "making ladies happy." Some of these letters—for instance, one from a young actress studying with Talma in Paris—show Fourier in an apparently paternal role. Others, such as those written in 1808 by his former landlady, Pauline Guyonnet, are more ambiguous.[18]

What remains particularly cloudy is the role physical intimacy played in Fourier's relations with women. Fourier seems to have had numerous affairs. Many of them were apparently no more than passing infatuations or purely sexual encounters—"amours faciles" as Jean-Baptiste Dumas put it. But Fourier also seems to have made his own the role of the philanthropic lover, which he attributed in his *Nouveau monde amoureux* to the "amorous nobility" who provided consolation to the lovelorn and to rejected suitors. In 1818 in a letter to his nephew he could boast with what appears to be an affected cynicism that he still had a "pretty clientele" in Lyon. His "relations with rich and worldly friends" had provided him "by ricochet" with more women than he needed, and "from the leavings of the feast" he had "been able to make up for [himself] a pretty assortment."[19] Did Fourier have physical relations with the rejected lovers who came his way "by ricochet"? We don't know, though this certainly is Fourier's implication. What we do know is that some of Fourier's most intense relations with women were perfectly chaste. Among the warmest letters preserved by him are those from a Madame Laporte, who addresses him as "my dear iron-legs" and thanks him for the "illusions" that his "sweet words" have inspired in an aging woman. "In you," she writes, "the sentiment of friendship has all the fire of that of love." She continues: "There are so few men disposed to be the friends of women with whom they do not make love (to speak like the Italians) that I have formed a high idea of you, and of myself—since a woman needs to find some way of maintaining her little vanity." But in another letter Madame Laporte seems less pleased with Fourier's self-control: she chides him for conforming to the ascetic ideal of the philosophers, "who are so self-possessed that the only thing they know about love is the name, and who retain their detachment to the point of experiencing nothing."[20]

In his own writings Fourier made a sharp distinction between physical love and platonic or sentimental love (*l'amour céladonique*), and he seems to have been a person who in his own affairs found it difficult to combine physical relations with emotional or intellectual intimacy.* It is possibly for this reason that he found himself particularly attracted

---

*For one specific instance see Fourier's letter to his nephew, Georges de Rubat, August 1818, 10AS 20 (2), p. 12. Fourier writes that he owed an important discovery to a woman for whom he had formed a "sentimental attachment" (*une céladonie*). "I had set a rendezvous to go to bed with her. But as soon as she provided me with the discovery I had been seeking . . . for six years, I couldn't stand the idea of possessing her and I backed out."

to lesbians. "I was thirty-five years old," he wrote in the *Nouveau monde amoureux,* "when by chance a scene in which I was an actor made me realize that I had the taste or mania of Sapphianism, the love of lesbians and the eagerness to aid them in every way possible."[21] What forms did Fourier's "aid" of lesbians take? It does not seem far-fetched to suggest that they included participation, as an observer, in lesbian lovemaking. There was clearly something of the voyeur in him. He was endowed with both an intense curiosity about the world and a powerful capacity for vicarious experience. Both of these impulses, which found one expression in his persistent questioning of friends and acquaintances concerning sexual matters, may have found another in the "Sapphianism" he claimed to have discovered in himself at the age of thirty-five.

Although Fourier was an intensely private person, his papers do provide some remarkably intimate glimpses into his own erotic life. But what they all add up to is not entirely clear. Emile Lehouck is no doubt correct in criticizing the kind of psychological reductionism that would derive almost everything in Fourier's thought from frustrated sexual drives.[22] As a young man at least Fourier was not the isolated, embittered figure he was later to become; and if his most intense relations with women were platonic, there is no reason to suppose that (as Manuel and others have suggested) he was impotent. Beyond this, however, what more positive conclusions can we draw concerning Fourier's sexuality? Possibly the most revealing evidence is provided by the passages from the *Nouveau monde amoureux* dealing with the amorous propensities of the omnigyne, an individual endowed (like Fourier himself) with twelve dominant passions. These passages are particularly interesting to Fourier's biographer because Fourier described himself as the only omnigyne whom he had ever met.

> Omnigynes must be very inconstant in love [wrote Fourier]. The average duration of the illusion is limited for them to one-eighth of a year, or six weeks following the first intercourse. On the other hand, they are constant forever in friendship, and the women whom they have been in love with for only a month or two will find them as faithful in friendship after ten years as on the first day.[23]

An inconstant lover, Fourier himself seems to have been the most faithful of friends.

III

The social and intellectual life of Lyon during the Empire has been zealously chronicled by generations of local *érudits* anxious to refute conventional judgments concerning the city's "exclusively mercantile" character and to show the antecedents of the regional revival that took place in the 1830s and 1840s. But in reading these secondary works one is struck that Fourier's name virtually never appears.[24] Nor is it to be found in the membership lists of Lyon's numerous learned societies and fraternal associations, which appeared annually in the *Almanach de Lyon*. Fourier never held a chair at the Academy of Lyon, or at the city's Société de l'agriculture, its Société des amis du commerce et des arts, its Société littéraire, or in any of its Masonic lodges, or even—so far as is known—in any of its more ephemeral gastronomic and literary groups like the Société épicurienne, the Petite Table, and the Société des Diners. He had a number of friends who belonged to these organizations. Among them were Jean-Baptiste Dumas; the Masonic leader and man of letters, Dr. Aimé Martin *ainé;* and the republican surgeon, L.-V.-F. Amard.* Fourier was also acquainted with Pierre-Simon Bal-

---

*L.-V.-F. Amard (1777–1847), who was chief of surgery at the Hôpital de la Charité, was an important figure in the political and literary life of Lyon under Napoleon and the restored Bourbon monarchy. A leader of the liberal opposition to the Bourbons, he was also the author of works on both medical and philosophical subjects including a *Traité analytique de la folie* (1807) and *Association intellectuelle, méthode progressive et d'association, ou de l'art d'étudier et d'opérer dans toutes les sciences* (1821). This latter work contained ideas on the organization of scientific research and on the human impulse to form associations (to which Amard gave the name "collectisme") that were of interest not only to Fourier but also to the disciples of Saint-Simon and some of the early Carbonari. See articles by Buchez in *Le Producteur* III (1826), 177, and IV (1826), 168ff., and François de Corcelle, *Documens pour servir à l'histoire des conspirations, des partis et des sectes* (Paris, 1831), 59–60, 77.

In addition to publishing treatises on association at almost exactly the same time, Amard and Fourier were united in their hostility to the Parisian literary and philosophical establishment, which Amard described in a letter to Fourier, December 7, 1821, AN 10AS 25 (2), as "a narrow and petty group . . . puffed up with a sterile and false science, rotten with prejudices and vanity." On Fourier's personal relations with Amard see J. Loysel to Victor Considerant, Wissenbourg, February 1838, AN 10AS 39 (11): "One of our friends here is a tax collector who knew a Monsieur Amar [sic], a distinguished doctor at Lyon. This Amar knew very well and had profound esteem for the views and the character of Charles Fourier, whom he often invited to dinner and to whom he demonstrated his affection in all sorts of friendly ways. It seems that he had ideas about association analogous [to Fourier's] and developed them in a *special work*." Amard was also a close friend of Fourier's comrade Jean-Baptiste Gaucel, who spoke of him in a letter to Fourier of February 12–13, 1824, AN 10AS 25 (2), as "the good and gallant Doctor Amar [sic] to whom I beg you to say a thousand affectionate things for me."

lanche, who was to become one of the leading philosophers of French romanticism and the guiding spirit of the "Ecole mystique" of Lyon. But except for Amard, none of these individuals seems to have taken Fourier's intellectual aspirations very seriously. When Dumas wrote to Fourier, it was generally to express less concern for "the success of the famous system" than for "the prosperity of its author."[25] As for Ballanche and the members of his circle, to them Fourier was simply "a modest person . . . who enjoyed among us, the young men of that time, a fine reputation for his knowledge of geography."[26]

Throughout his years at Lyon—except for two brief moments of notoriety occasioned by the publication of a few newspaper articles in 1803 and of the *Quatre mouvements* in 1808—Fourier remained completely outside the public and institutional manifestations of the city's intellectual life. Pained as he was by his lack of recognition, Fourier tried to make a virtue of it, to boast of his obscurity and to flaunt his lack of academic credentials in the face of the intellectual establishment. Thus in his first major exposition of the theory he chided his contemporaries for having left the discovery of passionate attraction to a "near illiterate," a "scientific pariah." "It is a *shop sergeant*," he wrote, "who is going to confound all the weighty tomes of political and moral wisdom. . . . Eh! This is not the first time that God has made use of a humble agent to bring low the mighty."[27] Until the end of his life Fourier continued to harp on his lack of intellectual sophistication, to lament it but also to boast of it. What, he asked, was there to learn from Locke, Condillac, and the whole "philosophical cabal"? Their torrents of enlightenment and their elegant prose had done nothing to increase human happiness. Had he tried to understand their controversies, he would have betrayed his natural gifts and deprived the world of his discovery.

> The world should be grateful for my ignorance [he wrote] and it should thank the fate that, in tearing me from my studies to exile me and imprison me in banks and countinghouses, forced me to cultivate my own intelligence, to neglect other people's controversies, and to concern myself only with my own ideas and to utilize the inventive genius with which nature has endowed me.[28]

Fourier did not lack self-understanding. He knew that his gifts were unique and quite alien to the conventional wisdom and traditional philosophy of his time. He did not, in fact, have anything to learn from Locke and Condillac. There is nonetheless a hollow note not only in the labored exaggeration of his boasts about his own ignorance and illiteracy but also in his tirades against "the philosophers." He was eager to win their recognition and quite unable to understand his failure to do so. And if he could vaunt his lack of learning, he could also deplore that having embarked on the exploration of a new scientific world, he was "pursued by poverty" and obliged to spend his days in the exercise of "mercantile occupations," which were "trivial and incompatible with study."[29]

IV

The "mercantile occupations" that absorbed most of Fourier's time and energy throughout the Consulate and Empire would seem, at first glance, to have been diverse in nature. When he arrived from Paris in 1800 his papers identified him as a *commis marchand.* In most of the surviving passport records he is similarly described as a *commis* or *commis marchand en draps.* But we know that he did not spend all his time at Lyon in the employ of one—or several—of the city's *marchands de draps.* Pellarin informs us that during at least a part of the Napoleonic period Fourier was self-employed. "In order to have more freedom and more time for his own work he became a *courtier marron,* that is to say, a commercial broker without a license or official authorization."[30] On at least two occasions apparently, Fourier was also employed by the government. In 1811 the prefect of the Rhone, Count Taillepied de Bondy, appointed him to the post of expert cloth inspector at the military warehouses of Sainte-Marie-des-Chaines at Lyon. Although this particular job lasted no more than a few months, it was enough to arouse his ire against the Ministry of War. As late as 1824 he was still vainly dunning the ministry with requests for vacation pay due him from 1811.[31] In 1815 during the Hundred Days Fourier also served briefly in the Bureau of Records of the city of Lyon.[32]

In viewing Fourier's professional career as a whole, Hubert Bourgin has written: "He often changed employers and often changed occupations too." In Auguste Ducoin's words, he was "by turns a cashier, bookkeeper, shipping clerk, correspondence clerk, commercial broker."[33] The impression one gets is that in his professional life, as in his emotional life, Fourier's own dominant passion was the one he called the Butterfly. But insofar as the years at Lyon are concerned, this impression is misleading. Most of the jobs listed by Ducoin were held by Fourier only later, during the Restoration. And as for his two stints as a petty functionary, they were but brief interludes in a commercial career that centered mainly around two poles: the Lyon Stock Exchange, where Fourier spent most of his time as an unlicensed and self-employed commercial broker, and the Maison Bousquet, for which he worked throughout much of the Napoleonic period as a clerk and traveling salesman.

In considering Fourier's career as an unlicensed broker, a word should be said about the functions and the legal status of the *courtier* and of his disreputable twin, the *marron*.[34] The nearest English equivalents for the term *courtier* are "broker" or "middleman." In its original—and broadest—sense the term referred to all those whose function it was to facilitate the sale or exchange of merchandise or money in return for a small commission. During the seventeenth century a distinction developed between *courtiers de commerce,* who dealt in merchandise, and *agents de change,* who exercised banking functions. Both groups were organized in closed corporations, each with its governing syndicate; and the lucrative titles of *courtier de commerce* and *agent de change* were sold by the crown as offices with life tenure. Legally the right to perform brokerage functions was limited to the titulary members of the corporations. In fact, however, the legal privileges of the titulary brokers were never respected by those unable to buy their way into the corporations. Throughout the Old Regime the *titulaires* continually complained that their functions were being usurped through the practice of clandestine brokerage. Their unwelcome rivals eventually became known as *coulissiers,* referring to the fact that they did not have access to the floor of the Bourse and had to hang about the outside corridors. But in the eighteenth century they acquired a more picturesque name, which derived from the accounts of old Creole life made popular by Bernardin de Saint-Pierre. Like the fugitive slaves of Saint Domingue and the Ile de France, these clandestine and unauthorized brokers were called *marrons.*[35]

The coming of the French Revolution temporarily erased the distinction between titulary and clandestine brokers. In 1791 the corporations of *courtiers* and *agents de change* were abolished along with all other professional guilds and associations. The profession of brokerage was thrown open to anyone upon payment of a small licensing fee. The result was a rapid increase in the number of individuals acting as brokers. With the advent of Napoleon, however, French commercial institutions once again became subject to strict regulation; and in 1801 the monopoly of the titulary brokers was restored.

With the reestablishment of the legal monopoly, many a small broker found himself once again outside the law. But few of them ceased their activity. During the Consulate and Empire the legal restriction on clandestine brokerage—*marronage*—was even more widely ignored than during the Old Regime. For the *marrons* actually served a useful commercial function in acting as intermediaries in small transactions on which the licensed brokers were reluctant to waste their time. Since the *marrons* had not posted any security and since they enjoyed no recognized, legal status at the Bourse, however, it was sometimes a risky business to deal with them. In the eyes of the *titulaires* they were a disreputable breed of lower animal whose very existence was a menace to business.

Although the *marrons* resented the privileged status accorded to the titulary brokers, they were reluctant to challenge the principle of monopoly. For most of them hoped eventually to become *titulaires* themselves. In Fourier's words they were "pretenders" who "cherish the hope of acquiring a share in the monopoly."[36] Fourier himself was no exception to this rule. Several times during his years in Lyon he addressed petitions to the local authorities calling for a widening of the monopoly. In 1808, for instance, he learned of a proposal for the creation of a new category of licensed brokers specializing in transportation. Immediately he wrote a long memorandum to the prefect, supporting the proposal and asking to be considered as a candidate. The reply was polite but negative.[37] Behind the prefect's refusal, however, Fourier saw the malevolent hand of the corps of licensed brokers ("les exclusifs") and the Lyon Chamber of Commerce. "The monopolists got wind of my request," Fourier wrote later, "and they put pressure on the Chamber of Commerce to refuse it."[38]

In 1812 Fourier once again found himself at odds with "les exclusifs" and the Chamber of Commerce over the brokerage monopoly. On February 5, 1812, a number of Lyon merchants had addressed a petition to the Ministry of Commerce, requesting an increase in the number of licensed brokers. Their petition also contained a strong denunciation of "the abusive and scandalous uses" to which the *titulaires* had put their monopolistic privilege. They complained that the licensed brokers were simply unwilling to handle the affairs of small merchants, and that they derived illicit profits of up to thirty thousand francs on the sale of their offices. This petition was forwarded by the ministry to the prefect of the Rhone, who in turn requested an opinion from the Lyon Chamber of Commerce. Its negative verdict was enough to end the matter.[39]

In the meantime, however, Fourier had gotten into the act. On behalf of the petitioners he drafted a long memorandum urging the prefect to ignore the advice of the Chamber of Commerce. Reiterating the arguments of the original petition, Fourier went on to denounce the collusion between the *titulaires* and the Chamber of Commerce. "The Chamber of Commerce has no interest in putting a stop to the abuses perpetrated by the licensed brokers. The members of the chamber are in fact their accomplices in these abuses." Even the less prosperous members of the chamber had been accorded easy credit and special treatment by the licensed brokers, whose "secret policy" was to "flatter and pay court to the Chamber of Commerce." Indeed, from the moment of its creation, the Lyon Chamber of Commerce had been "manipulated most adroitly by the licensed brokers and coaxed into undertakings that too obviously served their interests." Fourier professed no surprise at the alacrity with which the Lyon chamber defended the interests of the licensed brokers. But, he continued menacingly, these "compagnies affiliées" would do well to change their tune.

> Despite the silence maintained by the Chamber of Commerce of Lyon, it has good cause to wish that a reform be made without delay. Otherwise the merchants might renew their grievances and new supporting documents might be forwarded to the minister. . . . Other memoranda might call attention to the secret operations of these affiliated companies and to the system of vexations that they practice on merchants who do not belong to their association and who lack other means of self-defense. The revelation of these intrigues would be unfortunate for the titulary brokers and for their protectors. The petitioners will wait until the last moment before taking this extreme step. But despite the efforts of some individuals who have an interest in the suppression of their demand, they will renew it nonetheless; and if they have to they will deliver to the minister a document demonstrating that the treasury has been

deprived of *THIRTY MILLION FRANCS* and more as a result of false information given to the government.[40]

Fourier's threats and promises were to no avail. The prefect ignored
his appeal and the French treasury lost its "thirty millions and more."
As for the "other memoranda" in which Fourier threatened to reveal
the intrigues and the "secret machinations" of the licensed brokers and
their protectors, there is no trace of them in the archives. Nevertheless
it is clear that Fourier did prepare at least one such memorandum at the
request of his fellow *marrons,* and that they themselves prevented him
from submitting it to the prefect on the ground that its criticism of
existing practices was so outspoken as to jeopardize their own position.
As Fourier wrote later:

> One day at their request [that of his fellow *marrons*], I drafted a
> memorandum in which I disclosed the principal grievances
> against the monopoly of the licensed brokers including their
> theft of 50 percent from the public treasury. When I read it to
> them, they turned pale and exclaimed: "All is lost if the minis-
> try finds out about this. We will lose what business we have." I
> advised them that they would be lost so long as they limited
> themselves to half-measures. Useless remonstrances! They
> were so afraid that they might lose some of their own profits
> that they would not hear of raising further objections. They
> wouldn't let me finish reading the memorandum.[41]

Unable to limit himself to "half-measures," Fourier had simply scan-
dalized the *courtiers marrons,* whose interests he aimed to serve.

Two drafts of this second 1812 memorandum are to be found
among Fourier's papers at the Archives Nationales. The earliest, entitled "On the Monopoly Exercised by the *Agents de Change* or
Brokers," appears to have been the one Fourier read to his colleagues;
the more succinct, revised version seems to have been written later
with an eye to publication in a journal.[42] In both versions Fourier's
critique of the brokerage monopoly was elaborated in some detail. He
cited the numerous fraudulent bankruptcies recently perpetrated in
Paris and Lyon by titulary *agents de change* and *courtiers* as dramatic
evidence of the inadequacy of the legal statutes governing these corps.
He also noted that the twelve-thousand-franc *cautionnement* required by
the government of licensed banking brokers was "ridiculously low."
The actual selling price of such offices was eighty thousand francs, he

observed, of which not one sou found its way into the public treasury. In ceding the monopoly privilege at a mere fraction of its market value, Fourier asserted, the government had acted like Esau, who
gave up his birthright for a plate of lentils. Fourier then went on to
claim that the clandestine brokers had in fact rendered a great service
to France by serving as a check against the "clubbist intrigues" of the
licensed brokers. Were the government actually to enforce its laws and
to crack down on the *marrons,* that would leave the licensed brokers
free

> to become by means of their secret intrigues the masters of the
> marketplace, capable of turning every rise and fall in price to
> their own advantage. Once rid of their rivals, these corpora-
> tions will form coalitions throughout the whole Empire, and
> they will organize by their intrigues perpetual fluctuations in
> prices and runs on goods and on public and private funds.
> From then on all the profits of commerce will fall into the
> hands of the licensed brokers, as has already happened in times
> of active speculation.[43]

If the licensed brokers had not already succeeded in their "disastrous
machinations," Fourier concluded, it was only because—in spite of the
law—they were still faced with the competition of the clandestine
brokers.

During the Restoration, long after he had left the ranks of Lyon's
courtiers marrons, Fourier returned often in his writings to the question
of the broker and his misdeeds. In these later writings Fourier managed
to take a somewhat more detached view than in 1812, or managed at
least to consider the activity of the licensed brokers in a broader context, as one of many branches of commercial fraud and speculation.[44]
He was also able to find in his experiences as an unlicensed broker
excellent material for satire. In fact some of the best and sharpest satirical writing he ever did is to be found in his "Analyse du mécanisme
d'agiotage" with its humorous taxonomies of various types of bourse,
its parodies of commercial jargon, and its mock-heroic accounts of "the
marching order of the brokers in the great maneuvers at the Bourse."

Although Fourier's initial critiques of the brokerage monopoly are
scarcely of earthshaking importance, they are interesting from a biographical standpoint because they give us insight into the experience
that lay behind the broader critique of commercial institutions and prac-

tices that he subsequently formulated in such mature writings as the "Analyse du mécanisme d'agiotage." And Fourier's various letters and petitions against the brokerage monopoly are interesting on another count as well. They represent one of the very few times in his career when he wrote, not as an independent social theorist or critic, but rather as the representative of a specific interest group. Just how difficult it was for Fourier to play this role is suggested by the consternation of the *courtiers marrons* when they heard what Fourier had written on their behalf. He could never do anything by halves.

V

Two decades after Fourier left the profession, the traveling salesman or *commis voyageur* attained literary immortality with Balzac's creation of the Illustrious Gaudissart, the ebullient and smooth-talking hat salesman who learned about the inside of men's heads by providing for the outside, and who incidentally slipped Saint-Simonian brochures into the lining of his wares. Although Gaudissart was, in Balzac's words, the "paragon of his species," he had many literary rivals, and almost all of them were endowed with the same expansiveness and *joie de vivre,* the same eloquence and good humor. Among them was Louis Reybaud's Potard, "the famous Potard, otherwise known as the Old Troubadour, the dean of Lyon's traveling salesmen in dry goods and drugs." Known to all the diligence drivers from Lille to Bayonne, Potard was "the Don Juan of the cafés, the Balthazar of the *tables d'hôte.*" Yet Reybaud's novel, written in 1841, just nine years after *The Illustrious Gaudissart,* was entitled *Le Dernier des Commis Voyageurs.* Its message, insofar as it had one, was a lament for the decline of the profession. "Like aerial navigation, hot water bottles, Phalansteries [!], and other inventions intended to heal the ills of humanity," wrote Reybaud, "the commercial traveler belongs to the nineteenth century." But with the rise of the railroad, the postal service, and newspaper advertising, Reybaud believed in 1841 that the traveling salesman's days were numbered. The heroic period was over.[45]

It is probable that few who exercised the profession during its heroic days conformed less than Fourier to the literary model of the *commis voyageur* created by writers like Balzac and Louis Reybaud. But one fact that emerges from their fictional accounts, and is confirmed by the historical evidence, is that the heyday of the traveling salesman was relatively brief.[46] Until the last years of the Old Regime roads were too slow and travel by diligence too expensive for businessmen to make much use of this type of traveling representative. Merchant drapers of the late eighteenth century, like Fourier's father and like his employer François-Antoine Bousquet, had already begun to establish wide commercial contacts and to adopt new techniques for the marketing of their goods. But for the most part they transacted their business personally or through the good offices of numerous "correspondents," fellow tradesmen in other cities whom they occasionally met at the big commercial fairs.[47]

Down through the revolutionary period the *marchand colporteur* was a more familiar sight on the byroads of France—and responsible for a greater proportion of commercial transactions—than the *commis voyageur*. The *colporteur* generally traveled by foot or horseback. Packing his merchandise with him, he catered to a limited market. He was usually self-employed and his goods were often of dubious origin. He was distrusted by the more prosperous members of the trade guild, and the *cahiers de doléances* of 1789 are full of recriminations against *colportage*—"this passport for fraud and vagrancy"[48]—and its practitioners. The *commis voyageur,* on the other hand, enjoyed a more elevated social status. He traveled by diligence, dressed respectably, and slept in hotels. He almost always served as the representative of a *maison de commerce* whose samples he carried and whose business he transacted.

Although many of these transactions took place in the stores of the established merchants and wholesalers whom he visited, the *commis voyageur* also did a considerable amount of business at the fairs that were held regularly along the major trade routes of Europe. By 1800 these trade fairs had become something of an anachronism in western Europe.[49] They continued to attract vast numbers of mountebanks, performers, confidence men, prostitutes, and curiosity seekers. But with some exceptions like the famous Beaucaire Fair, the volume of business was falling. In eastern Europe, however, and notably in Germany and Russia, the trade fair was flourishing as never before. And with the Continental System in force, it was to central Germany and Russia that Lyon's silk manufacturers began to look increasingly for markets for their material and manufactured goods, a large part of which was sold each year at the biennial fairs at Leipzig and Frankfurt.[50]

During the Napoleonic period the job of *commis voyageur* could not have been entirely distasteful to a lover of geography and travel. For in an era of great restrictions on the right to travel, the *commis voyageur* enjoyed a privileged status. Hardly anyone else but a soldier could say, as Fourier could, at the end of the Empire: "I have traveled all over Europe."[51] It would probably be impossible to reconstruct a detailed record of Fourier's travels during this period. But there is no doubt that they took him not only all across France and Germany but also to the chief commercial centers of Italy, Spain, and the Low Countries. It is also probable that every year between 1800 and 1814 he bought and sold cloth on commission at at least one of the great trade fairs of Beaucaire, Frankfurt, and Leipzig. Passport records for the Consulate and Empire are fragmentary; but those that have survived at Lyon and Paris indicate that for the period from June 1801 to August 1802 alone, Fourier took no less than four business trips—to the fair at Beaucaire, to Huningue, Toulouse, and to Germany.[52]

It was through these trips by diligence and canal barge that Fourier came to know the "grassy banks of the Saône" and the "ravaged rocks" of the "arid hinterlands of Provence," the "clean and well-constructed villages of Flanders and Brisgau" and the "disgusting" peasant villages of Picardy, Bresse, and Champagne with their "miserable earthen huts" and their "dirty wooden shacks."[53] Long afterward in his manuscripts he could occasionally evoke these trips, reflecting with particular bitterness on the contrast between the poets' and philosophers' visions of "la belle France" and the sights, the sounds, and above all the odors of the France he knew.

> The workers of the great manufacturing towns of France like Lyon and Rouen spend their lives most apathetically in stinking hovels where they are packed in by the score and where there is a perpetually putrid stench, which spreads outside, infecting the stairways, the courts, and the narrow streets.

The philosophers could talk all they wanted about "the perfectibility of sensations of perception." They had never walked through

> these loathsome streets where the French common people live, and where the noise of looms, hammers, quarrels, and beggars, the sight of ragged clothes, dirty dwellings, and the thankless labors of the poor, the suffocating odor of the filthy holes in which they are crammed affect so disagreeably the senses of sight, hearing, and smell, and contradict so forcefully the brag-

ging about the perfection of sensations of perception that our ideologists find in their fair France!

Fourier's wish for these "preachers of progress" was that they might be condemned to live out their days in some small town in the south of France where the only discernible indication of progress would be the slow thickening of the "ancient crust of fecal matter" that had been accumulating on the streets and in the gutters since the beginning of time.[54]

As a traveler Fourier was constantly counting, collecting, and classifying. He carried a meter stick with him on his trips to measure the dimensions of any building or monument that attracted his attention. His disciples claimed that even as an old man he was able to quote these dimensions from memory, along with detailed information about the population and topography and climate of most of the cities he had visited during his years as a traveling salesman.[55] In his writings, however, he made few specific comments about the places he visited and the sights he saw. He almost never merely reported his experiences and observations as a traveler. Instead once his conception of utopia had begun to take shape, he digested what he saw and assimilated it into the system. An attractive building by the architect Ledoux became a model for imitation in Harmony.[56] So did the elegant meals that Fourier was served for just thirty sous at an inn in Basel in 1808 or 1809, and the "collective service" performed by the *Kellner,* "the waiters in German inns . . . who have a standing higher than that of ordinary domestics."[57] Similarly when Fourier wished to explain what he meant by the term *monogyne,* a person dominated by a single passion, he could do no better than to describe a man whom he had encountered on one of his trips: "He was a drinker, a monogyne dominated by the passion of taste with drink as his tonic passion. I encountered him in a public carriage. He was not a simple drunkard, but a man endowed with a marvelous ability to relate all of life's happenings to wine."[58]

If the diligence was, as Louis Reybaud put it, "a confessional," Fourier surely had the key to many of its secrets. Reluctant to share his most intimate feelings with those who knew him well, he seems to have been more at ease with total strangers. He thrived on chance encounters, on the short-lived but intense intimacy that springs up between traveling companions thrown together for the duration of a trip. It was with strangers—and especially foreigners encountered on his trips—that he found it easiest to talk about his own theories.[59] And in return for his own confidences, he was richly rewarded with theirs. Time and time again in his writings, and above all in his unpublished manuscripts, one encounters phrases like "a traveler told me" and "I once heard someone say." On sexual matters in particular Fourier seems to have owed much of his rich documentation to confessions made by chance acquaintances.[60] It was to these, and also to his persistent curiosity about people in all walks of life, that he himself attributed a great part of his knowledge of human nature. As he wrote near the end of his life:

> If I have succeeded in the study of attraction, I owe it in part to the care with which I have studied the common people and chosen places where I could hear their conversation. . . . On a canal barge, when I am given the choice between two cabins, I avoid the one reserved for fancy people. There one doesn't learn anything new; one only hears hypocritical conversations. But in the section assigned to ordinary people I hear a great many astonishing and naive remarks that lay bare the real attitudes of the people and give the lie to all the theories of the philosophers on the progress of morality and liberalism.[61]

If, as Fourier so often lamented, his jobs and travels were scarcely conducive to study and writing, they did give him an insight into the real life of his society that was denied to more cloistered observers. He had seen at first hand the condition of the silk workers, the cheats of commerce, and the frustrations of the poor. Pension dinner tables and travel by diligence had brought him into contact with a wide variety of men and gave him an understanding of their needs and desires that he would never have acquired from books. This experience, together with introspection into his own desires and needs, was the raw material out of which he fashioned his utopia.

5

Lyon Journalism

LIKE FIGARO, a journalist of the Napoleonic period was free to write what he pleased, provided of course he said nothing about the duc d'Enghien or Poland or the Bourbons, the Jesuits, the high price of sugar, the movements of troops and ships, the defeats in Spain, or anything at all to do with politics or religion or morals—unless it had already appeared in the *Moniteur officiel.* The tone for the times had been set, barely two months after the *coup d'état,* by the First Consul's decree of January 17, 1800. This "monument to the servitude of the press" brought the immediate suppression of all but thirteen of Paris's seventy-three political journals. By 1811 only four remained, and they were kept in line by Imperial subsidies, strict censorship, and the surveillance of Fouché's police. The bulk of the "news" consisted of texts of Imperial decrees, accounts of Imperial festivities, and odes to the emperor. Only the *Journal des débats* (renamed the *Journal de l'Empire* in 1805), which was the redoubt of the ferocious (and corruptible) feuilletonist Julien-Louis Geoffroy, managed to provoke the slightest tremor of popular interest. But its owners, the Bertins, were constantly harrassed by the government, and it was finally confiscated in 1811.[1]

In the provinces, as in Paris, the Napoleonic period was no great age in the history of French journalism. The Imperial policy was, in general, to assure the existence of "one journal per department," and in many areas this represented a numerical advance on prerevolutionary journalism. But these departmental journals were drab affairs. Each was a sort of regional *Moniteur* in which bulletins and acts of law emanating from Paris vied for attention with local *faits divers*. As early as 1801 a ministerial circular forbade publication in the departments of any news detrimental to commerce or likely to disturb public opinion. In fact censorship was erratic in the provinces. But provincial editors were timid, and they were not exactly in the intellectual vanguard. When in 1806 readers of the *Bulletin de Lyon* were informed of "the recent death by apoplexy" of Immanuel Kant, the Königsberg philosopher had already been two years in his grave.

It was in the same *Bulletin de Lyon* that on December 3, 1803, Charles Fourier first revealed the existence of his "mathematical theory of the destinies of all the globes and their inhabitants." The revelation came almost incidentally, since for some time previously the unknown "shop sergeant" had been trying to make a name for himself through the publication in the local press of poems and articles that seemed to have little to do with the theory of the destinies.[2]

I

Fourier's first journalistic venture came barely two months after his return to Lyon. Together with a young playwright named Alphonse Martainville, he composed a prospectus for a newspaper to be named the *Journal de Lyon et du département du Rhône*. On August 11, 1800, the two would-be editors wrote the newly appointed prefect Raymond Verninac to request official authorization. "For a long time no journal has been printed at Lyon," they wrote, adding judiciously, "the existence of a periodical newspaper in all the large communes of the Republic proves the utility of this kind of undertaking when it is inspired by the love of order and respect for the government."[3] The proposal was supported by the Lyon police commissioner, François Noël. But the prefect took a different view. After calling in Fourier and Martainville, he informed Fouché, the minister of police, that "one of the editors, Citizen Martainville, has been pointed out to me in the past by the police as a dangerous man and one who must be watched. The other individual, Citizen Fourrier, similarly offers little grounds for the confidence of a republican administration." As for the printing house of Tournachon-Molin, which was supposed to publish the journal, its owners had in the prefect's view "prostituted themselves to calumny and counterrevolution."[4] This was enough to doom the proposal.[5]

Although nothing came of the journal, Fourier's association with Martainville is worthy of note. Five years younger than Fourier, Martainville was already a veteran of the literary wars of the Directory.[6] After Thermidor he had joined Fréron's *jeunesse dorée;* and in February of 1795, at the age of seventeen, he helped organize the demolition of busts of Marat at the Salle Feydeau. During the period of the White Terror he displayed his considerable polemical gifts in such ferociously anti-Jacobin pamphlets as *Donnez-nous leurs têtes ou prenez les notres.* His huge belly and his capacity for alcohol won him a reputation for gourmandise that equaled his notoriety as a baiter of Jacobins. In the last years of the Directory he began to write vaudevilles, dramas, and *féeries;* and it was to get some of these plays produced that he had come to Lyon in 1800.

In later life this debonaire bon vivant became a champion of austere morals and *ultra* Catholicism and, as editor of the *Drapeau blanc,* one of the most influential publicists of the Restoration. But according to a contemporary portrait there was nothing austere about the Martainville of the Consulate.

> Concealing a lively and original wit under a rude exterior; seeking his pleasures where he found them, and success without regard for dignity; ready and waiting for anything; loose in his conduct, easy in his morals, beset by debts, but leading joyously a life of expedients and adventures; a good fellow besides, not at all malicious and endowed with an inexhaustible good humor. . . . He did everything to make a living, being at once a journalist, a dramatist, a *chansonnier,* a writer of little books, smelling of the quarters he frequented, even talking from time to time about morality and virtue; he was Figaro in the guise of Sancho Panza.[7]

A man of huge appetites, a habitué of cafés and theater lobbies, master at dominoes, womanizer, "garçon de bonne humeur": such was Martainville when Fourier knew him. It would be hard to imagine a personality more unlike that of the meticulous and taciturn *commis voyageur* of the Maison Bousquet.

Martainville returned to Paris at the beginning of 1801. He remained a prolific dramatist, satirizing many of the contemporary follies—fraudulent bankruptcies and complicated cuckoldry—that were to provide Fourier with the targets for his own more trenchant brand of satire. In 1806 Martainville and Louis Ribié became the toasts of Paris with their *Pied du mouton*, a "mélodrame-féerie comique à grand spectacle." Although Fourier's relationship with Martainville was brief and perhaps of small significance, his love of the theater was intense and lasting. It is at least conceivable that when he set about describing the wonders of the ideal world that he called Harmony, Fourier may have found some inspiration in the baroque fantasies and special effects contrived by the playwright.

Fourier's initial rebuff at the hands of the prefect only served to postpone his journalistic debut. Another occasion soon arose. At the beginning of 1802 Lyon enjoyed a brief moment of glory as the scene of the *Consulta* of cisalpine delegates organized by Napoleon to mark the founding of the Italian Republic. To publicize the sessions of the *Consulta* and to describe the fetes accompanying Napoleon's election as president of the new Republic, the government authorized Antoine-François Delandine and Jean-Baptiste Dumas to found a newspaper, the *Journal de Lyon et du Midi*. Dumas, a young functionary at the Rhone Prefecture, was soon to become a good friend of Fourier's. The older Delandine was a local savant and bibliophile who is known to posterity probably less for his treatises on magnetism and ancient myths of hell than for a line in Benjamin Constant's journals concerning his "excessive ignorance."[8]*

The extent of Fourier's collaboration on the *Journal de Lyon et du Midi* is difficult to estimate. Most of the articles were unsigned. Among those that may have been written by Fourier are a number of brief character sketches bearing such titles as "Theory of Egotism," "On Gaiety," and "Counsels for a Young Man, by a Woman." There are also hints of Fourierist rhetoric in "Observations on Bankruptcies."[9] The one article that can definitely be attributed to Fourier is a letter to the editor signed "Four . . ." questioning the prestige attached by Lyonnais to the banking profession. The only men who play an essential

*Delandine (1756–1820) had, nonetheless, sat in the Estates General, taught legislation at the Ecole Centrale, and was soon to be appointed director of the Bibliothèque Municipale de Lyon.

role in commerce, writes Fourier, are manufacturers and shipowners. "All the other classes of traffickers, commissioners, bankers, wholesalers, or retailers are only their accessories and agents." The manufacturer makes his fortune slowly, and the shipowner "shares the perils of the state" by risking his ships and capital on its behalf. But the banker is a speculator more interested in his own pocketbook than in the national welfare.

> When a coalition of bankers, like that which recently caused a sudden rise in the price of Spanish woolens, [is] provided with immense sums of capital and able to invest them in great and noble ventures in productive industry [but instead] speculates only on monopolies, is it not comparable to a swarm of birds of prey that ravages one by one the diverse regions where it comes to rest?[10]

This letter is significant first of all as an attack on the parasitism of bankers, middlemen, and all *manieurs d'argent*—a theme that was to remain central to Fourier's whole critique of contemporary economic life. Also significant is the foretaste it offers of Fourier's polemical style, and of his ability—a real asset in Napoleonic times—to leave his readers in doubt as to the real import of his radical social criticism. For no sooner had he described the banker as a "bird of prey" than—disclaiming all intent to "break the golden calf"—he began to chide his fellow Lyonnais for not being bankers enough, for their reluctance to accept bills of exchange in commercial transactions. He concluded by inviting the bankers of Lyon to adopt a more adventurous policy so that "the enormous profits of banking" might flow back "into one of their natural channels, into Lyon, the crossroad of the commercial relations of Europe."

II

With the conclusion of the cisalpine *Consulta,* the *Journal de Lyon et du Midi* lost its *raison d'être;* and after March 20, 1802, it ceased publication. By the standards of the Consulate, however, the journal had been successful. It was not long before the publishers, Ballanche *père et fils,* obtained authorization for a new biweekly journal, the *Bulletin de Lyon,* to be edited by Jean-Baptiste Dumas and the younger Ballanche. The latter was Fourier's junior by four years. But the publication in 1801 of his *Du Sentiment considéré dans ses rapports avec la littérature et les arts* had already won him a reputation. A close friend of Ampère, Madame de Récamier, and Chateaubriand, Pierre-Simon Ballanche was embarked on a career as one of the principal philosophers of the romantic religious revival in France, and he was later to become the guiding spirit of Lyon's "École mystique."*

No more than its predecessor could the *Bulletin de Lyon* properly be described as a bold journalistic enterprise. During the first year of publication an occasional local crime, a controversy over the use of fireworks, or a review of a new book on phrenology provided the only spice to the familiar diet of official dispatches, exchange quotations, and lengthy extracts from Paris journals. Then in November of 1803 Fourier made his debut—in poetry.[11] The occasion was a riddle contest sponsored by a literary amateur named Antoine-Gabriel Jars.† Interest in the contest seems to have been particularly keen among the women of Lyon; and in October and November of 1803 a number of their entries appeared in the pages of the *Bulletin*. One of the entrants, a "Femme A.F . . .", described herself in verse as "not accustomed to sharing," and she advised Jars to combine the two prizes he offered so that she might win them both. Her poem aroused Fourier's curiosity. He suspected that it had been composed by Jars himself in an effort to stir up interest in the contest; and he wrote a poem of his own lampooning the inaptitude for poetry of the ladies of Lyon.[12]

Fourier's poem was a conventional piece of badinage intended "to be read in male company" but too "salacious," he thought, for publication. Jars thought otherwise, and the poem was published. This touched off an exchange of couplets, epigrams, and articles. "We prefer fat financiers to skinny poets," proclaimed one Sophie D., and a Clothilde D. wrote the

---

*Although Ballanche was to publish more than a dozen articles by Fourier and although he was later to give Fourier an entree into Charles Nodier's salon at the Arsenal, the two had little in common. It was the geographer and not the visionary that Ballanche admired in Fourier; for his part Fourier regarded Ballanche as "most estimable in himself" but the unfortunate victim of a "religious mania." See OC X, PM (1852), 32.

†Antoine-Gabriel Jars, whose father, Gabriel Jars, had been a pioneer in the development of French metallurgy, was a military engineer and a native of Ecully. A number of his plays and operas were performed at Lyon during the Consulate and Empire. He was to serve as mayor of Lyon during the Hundred Days and as deputy from the Rhone during the late Restoration and most of the July Monarchy. He died in 1857. See J. Vaesen and Joseph Vingtrinier, *Une Commune du lyonnais: Ecully* (Lyon, 1909), 312. On Fourier's later efforts to interest Jars in his theories see Pellarin, *Fourier*, 235.

Bulletin to denounce Fourier as a "shameless author" of "erotic" verse. Insisting that his style was "*grivois,* which is different from the erotic," Fourier replied with a "Mercurial in Rose Water." Then "Femme A.F . . ." reentered the lists: "If it were possible that this letter was not the work of a woman, it is you, Fourrier, whom I would accuse; I would imagine that you needed a pretext to launch your satire against us." But she went on to take up his defense in verse:

> Je vous aime, Fourrier, malgré tous vos travers.
> Vous êtes fou; mais vous êtes aimable. . . .

And she added a note in which she reproached Fourier for his excessive discretion with regard to his theory of universal harmony:

> Harmony! On this point I will reproach you for your negligence. I will ask for an account of your studies concerning the social harmony that is going to follow civilization. You promise us great benefits in that new state. Will they be worth those that I now enjoy? Love is my god, friendship my guardian angel, and you are my folly. Adieu. If you guess who I am, don't betray me.[13]

Although nothing is known about the author of these lines, her specific references to "social harmony" and "civilization" show that she belonged to the small circle of friends with whom Fourier had already begun to discuss his ideas. Her pressing invitation was all the encouragement he needed to let badinage give way to inspiration.

On December 3, 1803, the *Bulletin de Lyon* included an article by Fourier entitled "Universal Harmony." This article, which was his first public revelation of his ideas, deserves to be cited in full:

> The calculus of harmony, for which Madame A.F. seeks publicity, is a discovery that the human race was far from expecting. It is a mathematical theory concerning the destinies of all the globes and of their inhabitants, a theory of the sixteen social orders that can be established on the diverse globes throughout eternity.
>
> Of the sixteen possible societies, only three are to be seen on our globe: Savagery, Barbarism, and Civilization. Soon they will come to an end, and all the nations of the earth will enter the fifteenth society, which is simple harmony.
>
> Great men of all the centuries! Newton and Leibniz, Voltaire

and Rousseau, do you know in what you are great? In blindness. You will soon seem like no more than great madmen for having thought that Civilization was the social destiny of the human race. How could you have failed to understand that these three societies, the savage, the barbarian, and the civilized, are steps to be climbed, that they are reason's age of childhood and imbecility, and that God would be improvident if he had conceived of nothing better adapted to human happiness. These three societies are the most disastrous among the sixteen. Of the sixteen there are seven that will see the establishment of perpetual peace, universal unity, the liberty of women.

I owe this astonishing discovery to the analytic and synthetic calculus of passionate attraction, which our savants have judged unworthy of attention during their twenty-five hundred years of study. They have discovered the laws of material movement; that's all very well, but it doesn't get rid of poverty. It was necessary to discover the laws of social movement. Their invention is going to lead the human race to opulence, to sensual pleasures, to the unity of the globe. I repeat, this theory will be geometrical and applied to the physical sciences. It is not an arbitrary doctrine like the political and moral sciences, which are going to meet a sad fate. There is going to be a great disaster at the libraries.

If ever war was deplorable, it is at this moment. Soon the victors will be on the same level as the vanquished. What point is there in conquests when the entire globe will comprise but a single nation, will be run by a single administration? In spite of this unity, there will be no equality in Harmony.

To the chief of France can be reserved the honor of extracting the human race from social chaos, of being the founder of harmony and the liberator of the globe. The rewards this honor entails will not be modest, and they will be transmitted in perpetuity to the descendants of the founder.

Some readers will cry out, "Dream," "Visionary." Patience! In a short time we shall wake them from their own frightful dream, the dream of civilization. Blind savants, just look at your cities paved with beggars, your citizens struggling against hunger, your battlefields and all your social infamies. Do you still believe that civilization is the destiny of the human race, or rather that J.-J. Rousseau was right in saying of the civilized: "These are not men, there is a disorder in things, the cause of which we have not yet fathomed."[14]

Fourier's article was written hastily and in what can best be described as his exalted mode of discourse. But it carried conviction and it provoked considerable discussion. A few days after its appearance a broadside entitled "Conversation on the Man of the Day" began to circulate through Lyon.[15] In it Fourier was celebrated as the "commis faiseur d'Harmonie"—a "deep thinker" and a "universal genius" who was also a witty destroyer of prejudice. Not all the readers of the *Bulletin* were quite so impressed by Fourier's article; and some commentators have marveled that the publication of "Universal Harmony" produced no official reaction from the local police authorities, who exercised immediate responsibility in matters of censorship.[16] The Lyon police commissioner, Dubois, may have regarded Fourier's ideas and even the attack on civilization as a "frightful dream," as too extravagant to be dangerous. But in referring briefly to the menace of war, Fourier had violated one of the canons of Napoleonic journalism. Two weeks later, when he published an article with more specific references to war and politics, the reaction was swift.

"Continental Triumvirate and Perpetual Peace within Thirty Years" appeared in the *Bulletin* on December 17, 1803.[17] At the outset Fourier described the French Revolution as a mere "bagatelle" compared with the impending crisis. "Europe," he wrote, "is approaching a catastrophe that will cause a disastrous war and terminate with perpetual peace." There were four powers to be reckoned with in continental Europe: France, Russia, Austria, and Prussia. According to customary practice, the weakest of the four—Prussia—was sure to be dismembered by the others. This would leave three powers competing for European dominance. "The upshot of any triumvirate is well known: one dunce and two rivals who tear each other apart." Fourier was sure that "the role of Lepidus" would be played by Austria. France and Russia would divide Austria and then fight over its cadaver for global empire. England could be discounted. The winner on the continent would seize control of India and close the ports of Asia and Europe to English trade. If need be, she would burn to the ground any port receiving English goods. England, a purely mercantile power, would collapse without a blow. The sovereign of Europe would exact tribute from the entire globe, and a reign of temporary peace would ensue. By what means could this peace be perpetuated? Who would emerge victorious from the struggle between France and

Russia? Fourier left these questions unanswered. He merely warned his readers not to count too heavily on France's recent triumphs. He offered to demonstrate "in other articles" that the present conjuncture was unfavorable to France.[18]

This article was to inspire a whole series of legends. In later years Fourier's disciples claimed that it came to the attention of Napoleon himself, and that it won Fourier the offer of a job in the Ministry of Foreign Affairs.[19] An eager disciple could write Fourier in 1834 about "talk in the *école*" of an article in which Fourier had allegedly anticipated the battle plan adopted by Napoleon at Austerlitz.[20] Reality was more prosaic. But Fourier's article did make trouble for the editors of the *Bulletin de Lyon*. Having reported on it to his superiors, the police commissioner, Dubois, was ordered to conduct an investigation. Ballanche was summoned to the commissariat, and he informed Dubois that "Fourrier" was not a pseudonym but the name of a young *commis marchand de draps* employed by the Maison Bousquet. Ballanche described Fourier as "a modest man, foreign to any sort of intrigue and ambition."[21] Dubois then called in Fourier, who agreed to exercise more prudence in the future. After issuing warnings to author and editor, Dubois let the matter drop.

The public reaction to "Continental Triumvirate" was mixed. Several readers apparently denounced the article in letters to the authorities in Paris. In another letter published in the *Journal de Lyon* Fourier was advised that he would find at the Charenton madhouse all the acclaim and admiration he deserved.[22] Fourier replied that if all madmen were sent to Charenton, its population would soon exceed that of Paris. And he reminded his critics that the accusation of madness had also been leveled against Columbus and Galileo.[23]

A few days later Fourier returned to the attack with an article entitled "Invitation to Echoes" in which he contrasted his own "varied follies" with the banal accusations of his critics. "Should I have expected such a burst of indignation?" he asked.

> Many a time I have addressed political observations to the government. In reply I have received flattering letters signed by Carnot, Talleyrand, and others who, I hope, know something about politics. When one has their approbation, he can console himself for not being in favor among the diplomats of the Grand-Côte.

Fourier called for an end to the "deluge of taunts" he had provoked, and challenged his critics "to say something new and to fly with their own wings without waiting for me to stimulate them."[24]

III

During the month that had elapsed since the publication of his initial satire Fourier had gained considerable notoriety. In scrimmaging with his critics he had shown himself to be a hardy controversialist. He had also begun to draw attention to his discovery. But he was eager to reach a wider audience. Thus on December 25, 1803, he sent a long letter to the High Judge (attorney general) of France, asking for official protection and access to the Paris journals.[25]

Fourier's "Letter to the High Judge" is a document of great importance. For in support of his appeal for governmental protection, he provided both a far more detailed formulation of his theory than that contained in "Universal Harmony" and also his fullest known statement concerning his early development and initial ambitions as a thinker. This statement makes it clear that at the outset of his career Fourier conceived of passionate attraction as much more than the rationale for his utopian plan. Instead it was the central element in a comprehensive vision of the universe; it was a "universal law" whose discovery would enable him not only to lay plans for the harmonious organization of society but also to uncover the secrets of the natural world—to explain everything from the origins of the heavenly bodies to "the most minute alterations of matter in the animal, vegetable, and mineral kingdoms."

Dismissing his article on the "Continental Triumvirate" as a "trifle," Fourier began his letter by introducing himself as the successor of Isaac Newton. Newton had discovered the laws of material attraction, and Fourier those of passionate attraction. Passionate attraction, which had eluded the philosophers for two thousand years, was the "key" to the theory of the destinies; it was "the archetype according to which God has regulated all the modifications of matter, the order of universal movement, and of the social movement of human societies in all the worlds." The theory of the destinies could be divided into three principal branches.

1st. The theory of creations, that is to say, the determination of the plans adopted by God concerning the modifications of matter, including everything from the cosmogony of the universes [*sic*] and the invisible stars to the most minute alterations of matter in the animal, vegetable, and mineral kingdoms; the plans followed by God in the distribution of the passions, properties, forms, colors, tastes, etc., of the diverse substances.

2d. The social movement, that is to say, the future and past destinies of human societies on the diverse globes, their ordering, their changes, their characters, etc.

3d. Immortality or the future and past destiny of God and of souls in the diverse worlds they have traversed and will traverse throughout eternity.[26]

The elaboration of so vast a theory was, Fourier informed the High Judge, too difficult a task for a single individual. Thus he had confined himself largely to the single most urgent problem, that of the "social movement" or historical development of human societies. He had worked out a theory of history that specified the sixteen periods or "social orders" through which all inhabited globes were destined to pass. At the apex of his schema was the era of Full Harmony, a social order totally consistent with the "plans of God," in which men and women would freely obey the dictates of their passions. The "mechanism" of this new social order was too complex for Fourier to describe in detail; he simply advised the High Judge that he had worked out everything to do with Harmony—"from the methods of its central administration to the most minute aspects of its domestic relations, which are diametrically opposed to our own."[27]

As to the other branches of his theory, Fourier explained that he had limited himself to establishing the general principles for each one and to seeking verifications "in each of the fixed sciences and even in the fixed arts like music." But he had not found the leisure at Lyon to pursue his studies. Unknown and destitute, he had resolved to share a part of his future glory with "the physicists and the naturalists." He would concede to them the honor of confirming his theory by the findings of their own sciences. He would claim for himself only the honor due the inventor of the essential element, the theory of passionate attraction.

Fourier had just two requests to make of the High Judge. First, he asked permission to publish "detached articles" concerning his discovery in the Paris journals. Naturally he would consent to any changes proposed by the censors; and of course he would not reveal the *fond* of his theory in his published articles. He would communicate the essential "in private" to the First Consul. Fourier's second request was that his letter be brought to the attention of Napoleon. "Extremes touch," concluded Fourier. "If I am unknown and destitute, I expect to inspire the confidence of the first of men by the very excess of my obscurity."

The "Letter to the High Judge" did not reach its destination. It was intercepted by the Lyon police and forwarded to the Police Ministry at Paris along with several of Fourier's other articles and a note, apparently in the hand of the Lyon police commissioner, Dubois.

> Almost every day the journals contain some new piece of madness signed "Fourrier." Today he mocks those who had the stupidity to complain about his article on the "Triumvirate," which was denounced by the commissioners of the government. Would it not be advisable to forbid the journals to insert any political article by this individual?[28]

In the margin of this note a functionary in the Bureau des Journaux of the Paris Police Ministry added: "We have advised the commissioner to see to it that nothing improper is inserted in this journal. Accompanying is another *brevet de folie* this Fourrier had addressed to the High Judge."

This directive from the Paris police did not bring an immediate end to Fourier's active collaboration on the *Bulletin de Lyon*. He published two more articles in the first weeks of 1804. But neither of them dealt with politics, and they were in fact his last signed contributions to the journal.[29]

Although Fourier's career as an active journalist lasted scarcely two months, he was to remain in daily contact with the editor of the *Bulletin*, Jean-Baptiste Dumas, for the next few years.[30] During this time he apparently submitted for publication a number of articles on subjects ranging from the embellishment of Lyon to the question of the civil rights of Jews.[31] These articles were not published. But Fourier did manage to get back in print between 1805 and 1807 with a poem and a few anonymous articles on the theater.[32] Of the three articles I have been able to identify two were relatively insignificant pieces in which he took to task "H.T.", one of the *Bulletin's* regular critics, for his harsh treatment of the young tragedian Joanny.[33] More interesting was the first, a long article lamenting the "eclipse" of the classic theater in the provinces and calling upon the government to organize schools of drama and opera in the major provincial cities as a means of refining popular taste.[34] The ideas expressed in this article on the social function of the theater and on the dangers of the cultural monopoly exercised by Paris were to be elaborated in identical terms in his first book.[35] In the meantime, however, Fourier had begun to cast about for some new means of waking his contemporaries from the "frightful dream" of civilization.

IV

For a few weeks at the end of 1803 Fourier had been the talk of the town—the "commis faiseur d'Harmonie" celebrated in the pages of the *Bulletin de Lyon* as "a deep thinker, a universal genius," and ridiculed in the *Journal* as a candidate for Charenton. No doubt he enjoyed notoriety for its own sake. He may also have briefly regarded the *Bulletin de Lyon* as a sort of springboard that would bring his theory to the attention of the public. But the storm created by the publication of "Continental Triumvirate" and by the "Letter to the High Judge" dispelled any such hopes. The police put an end to the publication of his *brevets de folie,* and he bade farewell to the skeptics of Lyon with a curt invitation to "reflect upon my defiance."

After his brief moment of celebrity, however, Fourier continued to discuss his doctrine in public. Some of his listeners were strangers, chance acquaintances encountered in cafés, diligences, or at pension dinner tables; others were his cronies from the "Vieux Coin," functionaries like Dumas and literary-minded tradesmen like Henri Brun and Jean-Baptiste Gaucel. To such "curieux" as these Fourier provided "diverse explanations" of his theory during his early years in Lyon.[36] But many of his warmest admirers in Lyon seem to have been women; and they may well have been chief among those whom he later described as having "shuddered with impatience" at his oral descriptions of the delights of Harmony and of the "voluptuous refinements that this new order will introduce even in the most insipid occupations."[37]

Shortly after the appearance of his newspaper articles Fourier composed a number of brief works—poems, "bagatelles," and short essays—for circulation among this small group of friends and admirers. One of these is a little collection of poems, a "galimatias of society verse," composed for "adepts who have conversed with me."[38] The

[111]

fifteen-page manuscript bears the title "Notice to Serve as an Announcement of the Discovery of the Geometrical Calculus of the Universal Destinies and of the Social Harmony of the Human Globe." Including verses of all sorts—sonnets, odes, rondos, and ballads—it opens with an "Epistle of Discharge to the Authors of the Uncertain Sciences." This is followed by a "Sonnet or Sonnette of Warning to the Curious"; a few stanzas to the "indolent cohort" of riddle lovers (complete with riddles and "hieroglyphical applications" drawn from his theory); and a "Catalinaire" in which Fourier mocks in turn the pretensions of each of the "uncertain sciences": philosophy, politics, political economy, and morality. There are also odes to "the just" and to "the unfortunate nations," and even a "Nuptial Song to Young Women on the Imminent Fall of Civilization, Barbarism, the Harems of Marriage, etc." In a concluding prose statement Fourier made his intentions clear.

> Readers will be surprised that I have permitted myself a jest like this galimatias of society verse in [treating] a subject that seems so grave, in an announcement of the divine laws that are going to overthrow the civilized, barbarian, and savage order. But they would be mistaken if they supposed that the calculus that is going to occupy us is as serious, as arid as human legislation. The only solemn thing about my subject will be the analysis of the misfortunes caused by the pretensions of the uncertain sciences. Since these misfortunes are about to end, we ought to focus our attention on the felicities of the future and on the absurdities of our sciences, subjects that provoke gaiety rather than gravity. Moreover this bagatelle is not something to be spread abroad; it is for adepts who have conversed with me. Their accounts have brought me many requests for "at least a brief summary." In providing it I don't want to wear sack-cloth. I explain myself in a familiar way.[39]

By means of such "familiar" explanations as these, Fourier managed to keep alive the interest in his ideas that his newspaper articles had provoked. But apparently a few poems were not sufficient to satisfy the demands of his "adepts." He later reported receiving numerous requests for a more detailed summary of his doctrine and even for "instructions" concerning "appropriate behavior during the remainder of civilization."[40] All this was to lead eventually to the publication of a "prospectus" entitled *Théorie des quatre mouvements*. But an examination of Fourier's early manuscripts shows that several years prior to the writing of the *Quatre mouvements* (most of which was done in 1807), he had already begun to prepare a different sort of introduction or "prospectus" to his theory. The project that had begun to take shape in his mind was to "prepare the way" for a full exposition by issuing a purely critical "manifesto" that would demonstrate the bankruptcy of the philosophy and political science of civilization.[41]

During the period 1803–1806 Fourier devoted much of his creative energy to the composition of this manifesto. Among his early manuscripts there are two relatively complete drafts, both entitled *L'Egarement de la Raison démontré par les ridicules des sciences incertaines* and both completed in 1806.[42] His papers also include a number of manuscripts dating from the three previous years. Some are mere fragments; others are long treatises. With a few obvious exceptions, most of these seem to be earlier, less complete drafts of the same manifesto.[43] This is notably the case of a long essay entitled "Petitesse de la Politique" (written in 1803), which corresponds to the second section of the *Egarement*.[44]

Unlike Fourier's later works, the *Egarement de la Raison* was clear and straightforward in its broad outlines. It was divided into three parts, each of which constituted an indictment of one of civilization's three "uncertain sciences": metaphysics, politics (including political economy), and moral philosophy. The charge he leveled against them all was that they had failed to make any real contribution to human happiness. After pointing out the means by which each might have done so and thus hastened the advent of Harmony, Fourier then analyzed the "vice" that had caused it to fail: the "timidity" of metaphysics, the "narrowness" of politics, and the "absurdity" of moral philosophy. Although the structure of Fourier's manifesto was relatively straightforward, his prose was polemical, hortatory, often bristling with irony. Turn by turn he chided his readers, reasoned with them, lectured, scolded, and menaced them for the neglect of his discovery. Throughout he carried on a running dialogue with the three uncertain sciences. Addressing each corps collectively as "vous," he pointed out their past errors, anticipated their objections to his arguments, and advised them on their future conduct. He interrupted this dialogue repeatedly to engage in long digressions, and dropped numerous hints concerning his own discoveries and the "immense delights reserved for Harmony." Sometimes he developed these allusions in systematic fashion. But more often they remained vague and fragmentary, worked out only so far as was necessary to establish the waywardness of the philosophers.

Although the preparation of the *Egarement de la Raison* absorbed much of Fourier's time and energy during the period 1803–1806, he never published it; it stands as a private declaration of war against "civilized philosophy." In 1808 Fourier finally did publish an introductory work that was far more ambitious—and more enigmatic—than the *Egarement*. He titled it *Théorie des quatre mouvements et des destinées générales*. Although it included some passages from the *Egarement,* the bulk of the *Quatre mouvements* was written in 1807.* Fourier spoke later of having composed the work hastily under the menace of a strict censorship law, such as was actually promulgated in 1810.

> In 1807 my discovery was only in its eighth year: I still had an infinite number of problems to resolve in order to work up a complete body of doctrine. I would not have been so hasty about making my debut but for the entreaties of a few *curieux* who were asking me for at least a sketch of the doctrine. They got me to do it by talking of a censorship law that was in the offing and that muzzled France the following year [*sic*]. I composed this work precipitously in order to elude it.[45]

It was easy enough for Fourier to compose a prospectus to his theory, but it was another thing to ensure it a wide audience. Unversed as he was in literary matters, he decided to seek the advice of professionals about the problem of publication.

Thus sometime in 1807, with his manuscript nearing completion, Fourier conferred with several of his literary acquaintances, members of the Academy of Lyon. The advice he got was to find a protector—preferably the all-powerful literary critic, Julien-Louis Geoffroy—and to publish his work in Paris. Some years later in a manuscript diatribe against "the monopoly of genius exercised by the city of Paris," Fourier wrote a summary of his conversations with the Lyon academicians:

---

*In 1807, shortly before the appearance of the *Quatre mouvements,* Fourier also published a short brochure entitled *Sur les charlataneries commerciales.* In this brochure he attacked the business practices of Parisian merchants at Lyon who destroyed the confidence of the public by selling shoddy goods at huge discounts. He concluded by urging the *négociants* of Lyon to get tough with "the fly-by-night merchants and the tailors of the Palais Royal who come to Lyon to set up commercial establishments." For Fourier their activities were just one example of the baneful influence of Paris on the life of provincial France. This brochure was reprinted by Fourier's disciples in *La Phalange,* 3d series, II (April 11, 1841), cols. 732–736.

Savants. If you don't get your work published in Paris, it
   cannot succeed. *Gniak Paris.* ["Il n'y a que Paris": "Paris is
   the only place that counts."]

Author. Alas! I can't afford to set myself up in Paris. I live at
   Lyon, and if I left I'd lose my job.

Savants. Ah! Too bad. Paris wants the debut. Paris wants to
   be the sole judge of new works. *Gniak Paris. Gniak Paris.*

Author. But if my discovery is correct, it would be as useful
   to the Parisians as to anyone else and it would bring them
   the wealth for which they are so avid. Couldn't they accept
   the favor even if it came from an outsider, a provincial?

Savants. Bah! Bah! That's just talk. Paris doesn't want the
   provinces to play a role in the learned world. *Gniak Paris.*
   Gniak Paris.

Author. All right, I know that Paris exercises a monopoly of
   genius in France. But what measures should you take when
   you have the misfortune to be a helot, a pariah, in short, a
   provincial? Must you bury your discovery because you
   haven't the honor to be born in Paris, or the means to live
   there in style?

Savants. Ah! If you don't have Geoffroy with you, you can't
   do anything. You won't get far in Paris. . . . You
   absolutely must find yourself protectors in Paris. *Gniak
   Paris.*[46]

Fourier did not find himself "protectors in Paris." When the *Quatre
mouvements* did appear in April of 1808, it was published by a Lyon
printer named Mathieu Rusand whose specialty was books of theology.

6

"*The Parody before the Play*"

WHEN FOURIER delivered the manuscript of the *Théorie des quatre mouvements et des destinées générales* to his printer, the good Monsieur Rusand expressed stupefaction. "This title seems strange to you," said Fourier. "It has to be. Some day you will know why."[1] Upon encountering a similar reaction from his bookseller in Paris, Fourier replied only that the book's title, like its contents, was a "riddle" that he would explain later.[2] A riddle: so the book must surely have seemed to its few contemporary readers. It is still the most obscure and enigmatic of Fourier's works. The Fourierists of the 1840s approached it cautiously: for them it was a difficult work, which could only be properly appreciated by "grown men and mature minds." But the modern reader may well be attracted by the very qualities that disturbed Fourier's disciples: the relatively free treatment of sexual matters, the boldness of Fourier's cosmological speculations, the spontaneity, the apparent lack of system, and above all the imaginative exuberance of the work.

I

The enigma of the *Théorie des quatre mouvements* began with its title page. The author's name was not given; the place of publication was identified as Leipzig; and the book was described in its subtitle as the "prospectus and announcement" of an unidentified "discovery." At the outset Fourier stated that this was the first of two introductory volumes and that it would offer only a few "glimpses" of the theory. Fourier announced that his second prospectus would be "an extension of the first" but he would be guided in his choice of subjects by the comments of his readers. Observing that he was "a man foreign to the art of writing," he also requested help on questions of style and nomenclature.

> You will find in the course of the work . . . a number of tableaux in which the nomenclature may seem improper and poorly chosen, for I have very little mastery of the French language. Thus you must pay more attention to the ideas than to the words, on the choice of which I confess my insufficiency. I will adopt more correct nomenclature when it is communicated to me.[3]

Identifying himself only at the end of the book as "CHARLES, at Lyon," he announced that he would begin to publish a full six-volume theoretical treatise only after the first two preliminary volumes had brought him one thousand subscribers.

Fourier divided the book into three parts, each supposedly designed to appeal to a different type of reader. Thus the first and "most difficult" part was aimed at "studious men who will not be afraid of surmounting a few obstacles in order to penetrate profound mysteries." But even though this first part bore the promising title "Exposition," it shed little light on the basic elements of Fourier's doctrine—the theory of passionate attraction and the ideas on work, small group behavior, and community organization, which by 1808 he had already worked out in some detail.★ Nor did the "Exposition" do much to clarify just what was meant by the "four movements" themselves. As he blithely noted in a postscript: "I have avoided discussing anything with regard

---

★Fourier's discussion of passionate attraction and of the twelve radical passions was confined to two brief—and very general—chapters (OC I, 72–76, 82–86). In the note on passionate groups and series that he placed at the end of the book (OC I, 292–306), he dealt only with the material organization, deferring all discussion of the "mechanism" itself and of its operation until a third volume. Throughout the whole book virtually nothing was said about Fourier's ideal community, the Phalanx. An examination of Fourier's early manuscripts, however, makes it clear that he had already resolved most of the essential problems and his reticence about them in the *Quatre mouvements* was quite willful. See OC X, PM (1851), 80–174: "Formation d'une Phalange d'attraction dans laquelle s'organisent les sectes groupées."

to the animal and organic movements."[4] In a page of definitions and a "most insufficient" footnote on the "hierarchy of the four movements," Fourier simply apprised his readers of two facts: (1) Human, animal, and organic life was endowed with passions and properties that had their own laws ("movements") of attraction and repulsion similar to those discovered by Newton in the material universe. (2) The social movement, which dealt with the interaction of the human passions throughout history, was the first and noblest of the four. It dictated to the others in such a way that all of nature could be read as a vast hieroglyph, a *tableau vivant* of the harmony or discord of the human passions at any given historical period.[5] Having safely buried most of his commentary on the "four movements" in an abstruse footnote, Fourier then proceeded to embark upon a breathless account of the various stages of social, zoological, and climatic evolution on "the third planet named earth." He announced with pedantic gusto that the whole process was to encompass four phases, eighteen creations, and thirty-two periods. Its "approximate duration" would be eighty thousand years, of which about one-sixteenth, or five thousand years, had already transpired.

Whereas the first part of the *Quatre mouvements* was directed at "the studious," Fourier advertised the second part as a series of "descriptions" designed to provide his "voluptuous" or "sybaritic" readers—and especially women—with a foretaste of the delights of Harmony.[6] To them he offered a set of contrasting tableaux of the "vices of the conjugal system" in contemporary civilization and the amorous, artistic, and gastronomic pleasures the future held in store. Here Fourier focused primarily on the condition of women. He began with an extensive critique of marriage and the family system. Arguing that "the extension of the privileges of women is the fundamental cause of all social progress," he went on to consider a variety of proposals for the gradual emancipation of women.[7] Each of these proposals was characterized by Fourier as appropriate to one of the several stages in social evolution that lay between civilization and the establishment of Full Harmony. But he refused to discuss the sexual relations that would prevail during the final stage of full female emancipation. It was only at the end of part II—in turning to the less touchy topics of gastronomy and the arts—that Fourier offered a hint of the splendors of Full Harmony.

Although the first two parts of the *Quatre mouvements* contained a few "glimpses" of what life would be like in Fourier's utopia, the third part, the "Confirmation," was critical. It consisted of three "demon-strations" of the errors of the civilized philosophers or, as Fourier put it, their "methodical mindlessness"—their inability to understand the reasons for their own failures or even to define correctly the problem with which they were confronted. Here his tone changed once again. Having precipitously plunged his "studious readers" into an account of the entire course of the earth's "social movement," he had gone on to tease the "voluptuous" with his contrasting tableaux of the pleasures of Harmony and the pains of civilization. But now he adopted a more clinical tone and focused on problems of immediate concern. Drawing heavily upon his drafts of the *Egarement de la Raison,* he devoted his first two demonstrations to the failure of the politicians to establish Euro-pean unity and the failure of the moralists in their "pitiful" attempts to create artificial religious cults during the Revolution and Directory. In his third demonstration he took on the political economists and ana-lyzed at length the "known vices and unknown dangers" inherent in the system of free competition. The theme that ran throughout this portion of the *Quatre mouvements,* as well as Fourier's epilogue on "the social chaos of the globe," was that civilization was an anarchic order. The incoherent organization of its industry and agriculture, the frag-mentation of its political and administrative structures, the diversity and contradiction of its philosophies, the "amorous confusion" created by its repressive moral codes—all of these were longstanding manifesta-tions of the same sickness, the same lack of "unity."

An outline such as the above can convey some sense of what the *Théorie des quatre mouvements* is "about," but it cannot convey the im-pression produced on the reader by Fourier's text or even by a glance at his index. For between each of his major sections is inserted a bewilder-ing variety of preambles and epilogues on such subjects as "the destitu-tion of moral philosophy," "the proximity of the social metamorpho-sis," and "methodical mindlessness." The book as a whole has no discernible logical continuity; references are repeatedly made to future volumes and to aspects of the doctrine that Fourier does not choose to discuss; and within each section one encounters long and apparently gratuitous notes and digressions on everything from the breakup of the Milky Way and the melting of the polar icecaps to the decadence of the French provincial theater and the *maîtrise proportionnelle.* Finally, the whole is preceded by an "Introduction," a "Preliminary Discourse," an "Argument" and an "Outline," and followed by "Omitted Chapters," a "Note," a "Nota," a "Notice to the Civilized," several epilogues, and a huge fold-out "Tableau of the Course of Social Movement" beginning with the first infection of the seas by stellar fluid and culminating with the cessation of the earth's rotation on its axis.

What is one to make of this extraordinary book? Was there any method whatsoever in its obscurity? In a number of later manuscripts Fourier provided an answer to "the riddle of the *Quatre mouvements*" in which he described the book as an intentional travesty, a work of "studied bizarreness."[8] In an "Explanatory Preamble to the First Announcement" written several years later and entitled "The Sphinx without Oedipus" he wrote: "This work in which I announced the theory of universal unity was a sort of parody published before the play."[9] Unable to publish a full exposition of his theory in 1808, he had begun with a "trial balloon," which was designed to interest his readers but also to mystify them. Though there was "not a syllable" to disavow, the book was a parody in its bizarre organization, its stylistic affectations, and its fragmentary and "tempestuous" presentation of the doctrine.

His purpose had been twofold. In the first place, he wished to *sonder l'opinion,* to fathom the depths of prejudice that a full revelation of his theory would encounter. With this in mind he had donned the garb of Harlequin. He had intentionally assumed the masks of inspiration, salaciousness, and pedantry. He began with a few details drawn from his cosmogony, which he knew would seem shocking and unbelievable, since he had intentionally neglected to provide the key to his theory. Having "launched the scoffers," he went on to more serious business: to his revolutionary attacks on the marriage system and on commerce. He knew that the philosophers were particularly sensitive on the question of free love—"even more intolerant than the priests"— and so he had treated it in a facetious tone, merely hinting that it was "the most important branch of the theory of attraction."[10] Commerce, on the other hand, was "secretly despised" by the whole continent, which was now feeling the full weight of the English blockade. Thus in his third part, in his critique of "commercial license," he had adopted a more sober tone and had proved that when it pleased him he could be "no more bizarre than anyone else." Meanwhile, like a scout venturing behind enemy lines, his purpose was to observe his public, to test their reactions, to note the points on which, while scoffing, they gave ground and conceded that all was not nonsense in his book. The second purpose of his parody was to confound potential plagiarists. By presenting his theory in a bizarre and visionary manner—by playing the fool—he had set out "a snare for the snarling critics." In holding his book up to public ridicule, they would neglect to look for "the pearl in the mud." Nevertheless, it was there. He did not wish to give away his secret, but he had to reveal enough to lay claim to his discovery.

Fourier's explanation of "the riddle of the *Quatre mouvements*" raises almost as many questions as it answers.* The writings in which it is advanced date for the most part from several years after the book's publication. By that time he had become convinced that its failure was the result of a conspiracy launched by the "philosophical cabal" in Paris, and he thirsted for revenge. It is clear that he did not anticipate the ridicule that greeted its publication, and there is much in his talk about the "trap" laid for the critics that sounds like later rationalization. It is also true that in his later works, when he seems to have been making every effort to express himself as clearly and as unambiguously as possible, Fourier produced books that were only slightly less bizarre than this one. Yet there was in fact a riddle: in his correspondence with the bookseller Brunot-Labbe, Fourier was already describing his book as such before the disastrous reviews appeared.† The text itself, which was indeed a "patchwork" of articles and essays in various tomes, is quite consistent with his explanation. There also seems to have been an element of willful obscurity not only in what Fourier failed to say but also in some of the things that he did say. He later noted that when some of his friends read the proofs of the book's "Preliminary Discourse" and found it "soberly written," he immediately added an intro-

---

*The only scholar who has given serious attention to Fourier's writings on "the riddle of the *Quatre mouvements*" is Frank Manuel, to whose brilliant chapter on Fourier in *The Prophets of Paris* (Cambridge, Mass., 1962) I am greatly indebted here and in many other places. But I would dissent from some of Manuel's conclusions. "If Fourier's explanation of the secret of the *Quatre mouvements* were accepted," Manuel writes (p. 245), "many of his extravagances would have to be interpreted in a different spirit. Actually much of this is a later rationalization constructed to steel himself against ridicule." The evidence cited here has convinced me that Fourier's rationalization was prepared in advance and that it does not represent a disclaimer of extravagant elements in his doctrine but of his manner of presentation.

†See Brunot-Labbe to Fourier, January 14, 1809, AN 10AS 25 (2): "At first glance the title seems to be that of a mathematics book rather than of a book presenting a system of extraordinary imagination. Many people have come to buy it who have changed their minds once they saw it. Since you say that it is a riddle that you will explain later, it would be advisable for you to provide the explanation right now in order to promote sales." This is a reply to a letter written by Fourier on November 18, 1808—before the book met disaster at the hands of the Paris critics.

duction written in his most "visionary" tone.[11] Whether the riddle was contrived with all the cunning premeditation that Fourier later attributed to it is another question. As he said himself: "My mind is naturally bizarre and impatient with methods. Thus it suited me to speculate on the use of my natural propensities."[12]

II

Whatever one chooses to make of the riddle of the *Quatre mouvements,* there can be no doubt about Fourier's eagerness for the book to command a wide audience. When it came off the press at the beginning of April 1808, he immediately set about assuring it a wide distribution and organizing a fanfare of publicity to greet its appearance. He had twelve cartons containing a total of six hundred copies dispatched to agents in Frankfurt, Leipzig, Milan, Hamburg, Amsterdam, Geneva, Basel, and Brussels.[13] He sent copies to celebrities like Madame de Staël, to aristocrats like Louis de Bauffremont,[14] and to such influential friends as his former schoolmate, Jean-Jacques Ordinaire, who was now a celebrated educator.* Obliged to remain at Lyon himself, he prevailed upon friends and business associates in Paris and abroad to help publicize the book.

In early May answers to his letters began to arrive. Amsterdam was the first to reply. His agents there informed him that the bookseller Dufour was willing to handle the *Quatre mouvements,* but not at his own risk; Fourier would have to pay all expenses in advance. From Basel a friend wrote that he would see to the book's distribution.[15] But the response from Geneva was less encouraging. According to his instructions, Manget and Cherbuliez had forwarded a copy to the editor of the *Bibliothèque brittanique,* Maurice, "who thanks you for the gift but refuses to review the book." Sales would be "nonexistent," they advised, "so long as the journals don't advertise the book." As for Madame de Staël, they informed him that she was not at Coppet.[16] Sometime later

---

*As a professor at the Ecole Centrale du Doubs, Jean-Jacques Ordinaire had already begun to acquire a reputation as one of Pestalozzi's most gifted French disciples. In 1810 he was named rector of the Académie de Besançon. Although he had been Fourier's closest friend at the Collège de Besançon, they had seen little of each other since, and Pellarin writes that on a visit to Besançon "one or two years later" Fourier found his old friend "more inclined to laugh at a few details than to take the *Quatre mouvements* seriously as a whole." Pellarin, *Fourier,* 18.

Fourier did receive an acknowledgment from Madame de Staël of "the letter in which you requested me to give your work publicity." But it was only to inform him that "I did not find the book here on my return, and I am really very sorry not to have had the chance to be useful or agreeable to you."[17]

Fourier always regarded "northerners" as particularly well disposed to new ideas, and he doubtless placed great hopes on the large carton of books sent to Schramm, Therstens and Company at Hamburg. But when they wrote in midsummer, it was to say that communications with Sweden and Denmark were broken, that the neighboring countries were so devastated that there was no market for books of any sort, and that sales in Hamburg itself "surely won't exceed five copies." The situation in Leipzig was no better; not a single copy was sold, and Fourier's carton remained for years, unopened, in a Leipzig warehouse. Nor was Belgium interested. On August 25 Fourier's agents there wrote that they "could not very well understand" his letter, but in any case they could find no one in Brussels to take charge of his book.[18] All over Europe the response was virtually the same. The trunks containing the treatise meant to topple civilization shuttled about Europe for the course of the summer. Then, one by one, each came to a final resting place in a bookseller's basement.

Had the *Quatre mouvements* received even modest critical acclaim in Paris, that would have more than compensated for its failure abroad. Fourier had been advised that the key to success was to secure the backing of an influential Paris journal. There was one obvious choice. With a circulation of more than twenty thousand, the *Journal de l'Empire* was the most widely read newspaper in France. It was also the redoubt of the brilliant feuilletonist, Geoffroy. A word from him—even an unfavorable review—would suffice to bring the theory before the public eye. Fortunately, Fourier had an old friend at Paris, Henri Brun, who was acquainted with Lenormant, the publisher of the *Journal de l'Empire*.

The matter was too important to be entrusted to the mails. So at the end of April 1808 Fourier entrusted another Paris-bound friend, Jean-Baptiste Gaucel, with a letter to Brun and several copies of the *Quatre mouvements*. Taking no chance, he also wrote an "impartial" review of the book that the editors could publish anonymously if Geoffroy was unwilling to sign it himself.[19] Brun replied immediately that Lenormant was willing to have the book reviewed in the *Journal de l'Empire* and would also take charge of a carton of forty copies to be sold or distributed gratis to the editors of Paris's other leading journals. "As for me," wrote Brun, "I think it will be enough to have it announced by the *Journal de l'Empire,* since there is not a single hamlet in France that does not receive that journal." Although he had only time to leaf through the book hastily, Brun wrote that he was impressed by the wit and vigor of Fourier's style. "There is no doubt that you will obtain a sufficient number of subscribers to publish [the work] that you are announcing. Anyway you should be assured of complete success, even if it is only because of the curiosity that dominates almost the entirety of the *civilized."* In a postscript Brun observed "with pleasure that the women are encouraged by your work. I hear that the ladies of Lyon are mad about it. It ought to do as well among *cuckolds* of every sort, and there are quite a few of them at Lyon."[20]

If the women of Lyon were enthusiastic about the *Quatre mouvements,* most of their husbands seem to have ignored the very existence of the book. It was neither reviewed in the local journals, nor mentioned in the annals of any of Lyon's numerous learned societies, nor even included among the acquisitions of the public library.[21] In Paris the situation was scarcely more encouraging. Toward the end of May a four-line *annonce* of the *Quatre mouvements* appeared in the *Journal de l'Empire,* and a few days later Lenormant wrote Fourier that a review was soon to come.[22] But in the weeks that followed he waited vainly for its appearance. As the summer wore on he began to make inquiries. Finally in September Brun wrote that Lenormant, "who combines an unheard-of negligence with indifference to everything that doesn't strike him as lucrative," had simply forgotten about the *Théorie des quatre mouvements.* Out of forty copies he had sold six, kept two, and distributed none to the other Paris journals. There was nothing more to hope for from "the *cajots* of the *Journal de l'Empire."*[23]★

Five months had been wasted. But Fourier still had some cause for optimism. For Brun had managed to retrieve the volumes from Lenormant, and they were now in the hands of a more trustworthy book-

---

★Fourier always felt that the real *cajot* was not Lenormant but Geoffroy himself. It seemed to him that the announcement of his book was Geoffroy's way of saying that he expected a favorable review to be paid for in advance. As he wrote later: "The famous Geoffroy lived up to his reputation. He began by announcing the title and promising a review as if to tell me, 'If water doesn't come to the mill, the mill won't grind.'" AN 10AS 14 (49), p. 9.

seller, Claude Brunot-Labbe. This "honest fellow," wrote Brun, "felt that the book might profit from a less austere title." But he had agreed "to have the journals publish the review of the book just as you wrote it."[24] At last Fourier had found an ally on whom he could count. Once again he sprang into action, dispatching a shipment of 105 additional copies to Brunot-Labbe. On his side the bookseller did what he could, distributing copies to the editors of ten Paris journals.[25] Now Fourier had only to await the verdict.

If, as Fourier later claimed, his purpose in beginning the *Quatre mouvements* with the "incredible perspectives" of part I was to "launch the scoffers," one can only say that the results surpassed his expectations. For the prophecies contained in this section—the talk of eighteen creations and seas of lemonade—constituted a stockpile of "extravagances" on which Fourier's critics were to draw freely for the next four decades. In the 1830s Balzac was to spell out the commonly accepted formula with his account—in the *Monographie de la presse parisienne*—of how "the *blagueur,* the second variety of small Parisian journalist," managed to earn his ten francs a day by regaling his readers for weeks on end with absurdities drawn from the *Quatre mouvements.*[26] The first historical incarnation of the *blagueur* was in fact Fourier's very first reviewer. On November 30, 1808, the literary feuilleton of the *Journal du commerce* opened with a long parody of Fourier's book.

> I have furtively slipped into the boudoir of the universal destinies [began the reviewer] and I have seen the ladies without their veils, like Venus rising from the bosom of the sea. I have come upon the analytic and synthetic calculus of passionate attractions and repulsions. I have discovered the theory of the four movements. A new Micromegas, I have voyaged around Sirius, sailed in the sign of the Virgin, surveyed Jupiter, stolen Saturn's ring, traversed the galaxies, and grabbed the moon by its horns.

All this, commented the anonymous reviewer, was obviously the work of a sick man.

> If we lived in the time of the enchanters, we would beg Astolph, that courtly paladin, to help the patient as he helped the celebrated Roland. But if there are no more necromancers or paladins or winged horses, fortunately we still have doctors, pharmacologists, who know how to prescribe and administer

the remedies suitable for the restoration of the organs of the brain. We believe we have detected grave disturbances in the cerebral organs of M. Charles.

The patient's malady was diagnosed as irritation of the nerves and "firing of the blood"—attributable no doubt to his vain efforts to solve the problem of human happiness. The reviewer noted that Fourier's "paroxysms" were occasionally interrupted by "such well put, such coherent observations that we believed for a moment that he had recovered the use of his reason." But since "six more outbursts" were apparently in store, he urged the Faculty of Medicine to come to the rescue at once.[27]

The following day, December 1, the first of four lengthy feuilletons devoted to the *Quatre mouvements* appeared in the Catholic *Gazette de France*.[28] It is doubtful that the author had actually bothered to read the book from cover to cover. But after characterizing it in promising but ambiguous terms as "a book such as has never been seen, a book as extraordinary in its conception as in its execution," he managed to entertain his readers for two weeks with a series of paraphrases of the more bizarre portions of the text, interspersed with ironic commentary. "Doubtless many people are going to believe that this book was written at Charenton," he concluded. Not at all. "You write directly to M. Charles in Lyon. He gives neither the name of the street, nor the number of the house he lives in; but they used to write to Voltaire in Europe, and one can perfectly well write to M. Charles in Lyon."[29]

In mid-January of 1809 Brunot-Labbe, the Paris bookseller, wrote Fourier to bring him up to date on the book's sale. He regretted that the publication of reviews had not served to stimulate sales. After giving away sixteen free copies to journalists, he had sold exactly nine. Perhaps the fault lay in the title. *Théorie des quatre mouvements* seemed "at first glance to be the title of a book of mathematics" rather than the introduction to a "system of extraordinary imagination."

> I would like to do more with it, but as long as the trumpets refuse to sound it will be difficult to make it known. It is only with time, and in writing other volumes, that you will succeed, because one volume, a prospectus that must be purchased, cannot have a wide sale. You were surely expecting it.[30]

The kindly bookseller's words could not soften the blow. The prospectus was a failure, and Fourier had not expected it. He had naturally taken his precautions with regard to the plagiarists, and donned the garb of Harlequin to fathom the depths of prejudice that subsequent volumes would encounter. But he had supposed that this "studied bizarreness" would only serve to heighten the curiosity of his readers. "It was wholly unimportant that my prospectus lacked method," he wrote later, "since one could find in it sure signs of a great discovery. This prospectus recommended itself by its very bizarreness."[31]

III

During the years that followed, Fourier was to be haunted by the rejection of his prospectus by "the Parisians."[32] "Absorbed by mercantile functions that left no margin for studies," he had neither the time nor the inclination to come to grips with the problems he had promised to treat in subsequent memoirs. Until the end of 1814 he virtually stopped writing. From time to time he set to work on a "second prospectus," but it never appeared. All that remains of his efforts is a series of manuscript prologues and introductions in which he catalogued the "litany of jeers" to which he had been subjected in 1808, unraveled "the riddle of the *Quatre mouvements*," inveighed against the spirit of sarcasm and raillery dominant in France, and called for the creation of a *police d'invention* that would protect the rights of "unlettered inventors" like himself.

Fourier began to see the rejection of his work as the result of a conspiracy mounted by the philosophers of Paris. They exercised a "literary monopoly" whose dominion extended throughout the Empire. Whenever they felt their position threatened by a writer with something new to say—an "inventor"—they quickly had him silenced. Such had been their tactic in 1803 when the word came down from Paris that he was to write no more in the journals of Lyon. When a simple signal proved insufficient to silence a writer, they called on their acolytes, the journalists, to drown him in torrents of detraction and abuse. This was the way they had dealt with the *Quatre mouvements*: "The philosophical cabal, all of whose systems I was menacing with destruction, was obliged to order its trumpeters to launch cries of 'Madman' or 'Maniac!' Thus the philosophical journals talked of sending me doctors, apothecaries to bring me to reason."[33]

The Parisians were afraid to challenge his arguments against civilization; and hackneyed accusations of madness constituted the chief weapons in their critical arsenal. Yet even in their raillery Fourier detected a note of confusion. After calling him a madman, one of them had gone on to describe his observations as "so well put, so coherent." This single line of praise, accorded by an anonymous reviewer in the *Journal du commerce,* is repeatedly cited in Fourier's manuscript writings; he saw it as an "avowal" that he had wrung from the philosophers. "Aren't they afraid of indicting themselves by this contradiction," he asked, "and of betraying their secret, their league to crush anyone who refuses to pay the tribute of incense to the scientific minotaur, to the philosophical libraries?" And he went on to chide them for their timidity.

> Far from capitulating to this army of five hundred thousand volumes, I announce its utter ruin, the imminent collapse of all the galleries of books. Such audacity disconcerts the cabal; it hesitates about its means of defense; it deliberates about whether I should be declared half a fool or a complete fool. These half-measures betray the secret. They should have realized that I am nothing by halves. Whoever reads me can judge that my role, whatever it may be, in wit or in idiocy, will be played to the hilt. [34]

Fourier took delight in egging on his accusers. He announced his readiness to concede, on their authority, that he was weak-headed, an imbecile, that his brain was diseased. He would accept the verdict rendered by the high court of the Paris feuilletons; in view of the court's past performance, the judgment would shortly be regarded as a title of glory.

In his explanations of "the riddle of the *Quatre mouvements*" Fourier gloated over the charges of madness the book had brought down upon him. He had planned it that way to put the plagiarists off the track. His ruse was a success and the philosophers were its victims. He dramatized the trick he had played on them in a dialogue entitled "The Conversation." [35] He assigned himself the role of a humble Athenian who had stumbled upon the invention of the compass. Taking care not to give away his secret, the inventor boasted of the wonderful results it would yield. At last the Athenian philosophers learned of it. But when they came to visit, he expressed no interest in their metaphysical babble. They decided after an instant's conversation that he was mad. To quiet him on the way to the insane asylum, they laughingly conceded him all rights of priority on his "useless invention." This was just what Fourier had hoped to attain through the publication of the *Quatre mouvements*—a public admission that, whatever its value, the discovery of the "social compass" was his alone. One day his book would be known as "the act of accusation against the nineteenth century"; like Columbus, he would one day find his own Isabella.[36] Then the philosophers would regret their ridicule. But until that time his priority was established and he had nothing to fear from the plagiarists.

Fourier's dreams of ultimate recognition were accompanied by elaborate fantasies of revenge in which he visited terrible reprisals on all those who had scorned his work—on his countrymen, the philosophers, civilization, and the city of Paris itself. In manuscripts bearing such titles as "On the Alternative of Blood Baths, or an Examination of the Discovery,"[37] he described the French losses in the Napoleonic wars as a tribute he had exacted for the neglect of his discovery. He boasted that the insults of his critics had been "washed in rivers of French blood."[38] He had punished civilization by allowing it "to plunge into an abyss of misery where I saw it heading and from which I could have suddenly withdrawn it."[39] Was it fortuitous, asked Fourier in 1815, that the outbreak of the war in Spain, the first of the great French defeats, had taken place in the same year as the rejection of the *Quatre mouvements?*

> Opprobrium, ruin, public servitude, in fact all the calamities that have assailed, devoured [France], date from the time when she reviled the discovery of the calculus of passionate attraction. The capital where this discovery was reviled has twice been invaded, sullied by the outrages of its enemies; she thought that she would rule the world, and she has become its plaything. . . . If I had any power over destiny, could I have asked of it a more signal vengeance?[40]

Fourier's vow of silence had proved costly to his countrymen; and in his manuscript writings he warned them that if they continued to disdain his discovery, they would have even greater cause for sorrow. What if he died prematurely? The advent of Harmony might be delayed for generations. Or else, to punish his century, he might reveal his theory only in bits and snatches, in fragments like the first prospectus. If the stupidity of his contemporaries drove him to it, he would simply wait until they had been "subdued by torture."[41]

Most of these fantasies of revenge and ultimate triumph were set down by Fourier in manuscript introductions to a "second prospectus" that never appeared. Only once during the last six years of the Empire did he air in public his grievances against his generation and his reflections on the failure of the *Quatre mouvements.* The occasion was provided by a letter published in the *Journal de Lyon* on October 19, 1811, under the pseudonym "Philoharmonicos." Its real author was Aimé Martin *aîné,* the prominent Lyon surgeon, literary figure, and Freemason, whom Fourier had probably known ever since the days when they both collaborated on the *Bulletin de Lyon.*★ Taking note of the discussions provoked by the great comet of 1811, Martin added:

> I am truly surprised, and I am not alone, that the author of the *Théorie des quatre mouvements* has not seized upon this occasion to remind us of the daring conceptions and views with which his prospectus abounds. Perhaps his situation is that of "bonus aliquando dormitat Homerus." May this lesson stir him from his lethargy.[42]

In his response, which appeared in the *Journal* two weeks later, Fourier observed that he was indeed uniquely qualified to provide his contemporaries with "new" and "reassuring" information concerning the comet—and a great many other astronomical mysteries. "But why should I unveil these mysteries?" he asked. He was an "innovator" and his theories would contradict those of the all-powerful philosophical cabal. The public was hardly likely to be interested. They would do better to address themselves to one of Paris's "transcendent geniuses" such as Monsieur Azaïs, who, only two years earlier in a lecture at the Athénée, had undertaken to unveil the whole universe.†

★A leading member of the Academy of Lyon, Aimé Martin presided during the Empire over Lyon's Masonic lodge, La Parfaite Harmonie, and he was also active in the city's informal literary cenacles like the Petite Table and the Société des Diners. He was described in a "list of influential electors" drawn up by the government in 1811 as "one of the distinguished doctors of Lyon" and a man of "good morality, loyal to the government, a highly fluent speaker, very well educated, and entirely upright." AN F⁷ 4352A, cited in Lehouck, *Vie de Fourier,* 134. Although Fourier was acquainted with many of Lyon's Freemasons, the section in the *Quatre mouvements* (OC I, 195–202) on the "still unknown properties of Freemasonry" may have been inspired by his conversations with Martin in particular.

†Fourier refers here to the *Discours prononcé à l'Athénée le 15 mars, 1809 sur la vérité universelle* (Paris, 1809) by Hyacinthe Azaïs. Azaïs (1766–1845) was one of the most prolific and (in his time) fashionable of the minor monist visionaries of the early nineteenth century. Around 1800 he worked out a relatively simple-minded "Newtonian" theory of "universal explanation," which he stated and restated during the next forty

Fourier concluded his "Reply to Philoharmonicos" by promising to resume publication in 1812 with a "volume that . . . will contain the treatise on the passionate mechanism" as well as "some piquant details on the intrigues and the past and future revolutions of the planets and comets."[43] This volume did not appear. In 1813, however, Fourier made one more effort to rouse his contemporaries. Sometime that year he learned that the University of Aberdeen in Scotland was offering a prize for the best essay demonstrating the existence of a just and good God. He wrote the mayors and principals of the colleges of Aberdeen, announcing his intention "to enter the lists as Newton's successor." His demonstration would be founded, he said, "upon a determination of the entire system of God's laws of movement, of which Newton had discovered only the fourth class." Confident that the prize was his, he assured the judges that they would have nothing to fear in bestowing it upon a Frenchman. His theory would prove "as useful to the English as to other nations," and the prize money would go toward the publication of a deluxe treatise "with diagrams and plates."[44]

The University of Aberdeen failed to acknowledge Fourier's letter; and although he had prepared an entry, a "Discourse on the Attributes

---

years in more than two dozen separate treatises. Fourier seems to have first become interested in Azaïs in 1806 or 1807 while he was working up the elaborate cosmogony included in part I of the *Théorie des quatre mouvements.* A manuscript cahier labeled "Cosmologie, Physique, etc." (AN 10AS 24 (2), #100) includes long excerpts from several of Azaïs' early pamphlets and from reviews of his *Essai sur le monde* (1806): passages dealing with Azaïs' theory of "stellar emanations" and with his "seductive" (Fourier's word) "promise to explain by a single, simple fact the universality of physical and chemical phenomena."

After 1808, however, Fourier came to regard Azaïs as a "marauder on my domaine," and the latter's speech at the Athénée is repeatedly cited in Fourier's manuscripts as a typical example of the philosophers' toadyism and "incense bearing"—as well as of the vanity of their promises to "unveil the universe." See OC X, PM (1851), 38–45; *La Phalange,* IV (1846), 309; *La Phalange,* VIII (1848), 349; AN 10AS 13 (32); 10AS 10 (8), pp. 6–8; 10AS 16 (42): letter of December 1, 1824, to the *Journal des débats,* protesting their favorable review of Azaïs' *Système de l'explication universelle.*

Fourier's comments concerning Azaïs' unction were well founded. The man had a honeyed tongue, and in fact during the 1830s he was to make several efforts to proselytize among Fourier's disciples. One of them, Brémond, even tried to arrange a "confrontation" between the two. Fortunately for both parties, it did not take place. See Azaïs to Jules Lechevalier, May 4, 1833, Bibliothèque de l'Arsenal, MS. 13462, #7; and Brémond to Reydor, January 13, 1836, AN 10AS 36 (9).

On Azaïs see Michel Baude, *P. H. Azaïs, Témoin de son temps. D'Après son journal inédit (1811–1844),* 2 vols. (Lille-Paris, 1980), and J. Guadet, "Notice sur Azaïs" in the latter's *Des Compensations dans les destinées humaines,* 5th ed. (Paris, 1846), i–xlviii.

of God," he never sent it.[45] There were plagiarists in Scotland as well as
in France; and apparently he feared that without a formal request from
the Scottish judges, his discovery might be stolen. Thus once again he
abandoned civilization to its own devices—but with reluctance. For two
years later he was still grumbling about the "base jealousy" and "sordid
avarice" of a nation that begrudged twelve hundred pounds to a for-
eigner while robbing millions in India.[46]

IV

Fourier's psychological "case history" does not begin with the rejection
of the *Quatre mouvements*. He seems to have been beset by the fear of
plagiarists from the very outset of his career, and in his earliest writings
one can find wild and occasionally sadistic fantasies of ultimate triumph
and revenge. But it may be said that the years that followed the publication of the *Quatre mouvements* marked a crucial and apparently culminating stage in his psychological development. For the fantasies and
rationalizations he had initially constructed to steel himself against his
personal misfortunes and the taunts of his Lyon critics now assumed
their final form; they were to serve him for the rest of his life in his
dealings with a world that simply had no use for his discovery.

If the period between 1809 and 1815 marked a significant stage in
Fourier's psychological development, it was less important for his intellectual growth. These years marked a hiatus in the development of his
theory. So far as one can judge from his surviving manuscripts, most of
Fourier's writing during these years had to do with commerce. Some of
it, such as his critiques of the brokerage monopoly, bore directly upon
his own experience. But he also worked at a number of more ambitious
schemes concerning the reform of commerce. In a long 1810 manuscript on the *entrepôt fédérale,* for example, he called for a government-
sponsored association of producers that would provide easy credit for
capital investment as well as liberating agriculture and industry from
"the speculative extortions of commerce." In a similar vein were various schemes of "reductive competition" designed to reduce the number
of commercial middlemen and inhibit the growth of speculation.[47]
These plans—many of which were reformulations of proposals for the
reform of commerce first developed by Fourier in the 1790s—were to
be more fully elaborated in Fourier's later writings. They were the

ancestors of a host of proposals designed to promote a gradual transition from civilization into Harmony. But to Harmony itself, and to the broad speculative problems he had left unresolved in 1808, Fourier gave little thought during these years. For the time being he was "absorbed in mercantile functions that left no margin for studies."[48]

Fourier's mother died at the beginning of May 1812. His relations with her had long since ceased to be close; and his sister later recalled that he never once mentioned his book to her. Meticulously pious to the last, she instructed her children in her will "to celebrate for my soul's rest the quantity of two hundred masses."[49] By the time of her death the family fortune had dwindled considerably. Almost twenty years of efforts to recover the gains made by Antoine Pion in his brief partnership with the widow had cost the family forty thousand francs in legal fees;[50] and the total value of Mme. Fourrier's estate—including the house on the Grande rue in Besançon—amounted to less than fifty thousand francs. According to the terms of her will, this sum was to be divided equally among her four children. But she made an additional stipulation in her son's favor: he was also to receive a life annuity of nine hundred francs "to provide for food and clothing." She instructed her three daughters—"particularly and in the first place" the most prosperous of the three, Sophie Parrat-Brillat—to guarantee its payment out of their own inheritances if need be.[51] This stipulation was later to cause much ill feeling among the children. But for the time being at least Fourier's financial position was relatively comfortable. For the first time since his arrival in Lyon in 1800 he could begin to think of quitting the "jail house" of commerce for good and retiring to the countryside to devote all his efforts to working on his theory.

The logical setting for the rural retreat Fourier had begun to meditate was the region of Bugey in the Jura foothills to the east of Lyon, where he had standing offers of hospitality from Sophie Parrat-Brillat and the children of his oldest sister, Mariette de Rubat. He visited them at the beginning of 1813 to participate in a family council. But his stay was brief and not entirely harmonious. It was only several years later, at the end of 1815, that Fourier finally accepted their invitations. Apart from a few business trips, he remained in Lyon throughout the intervening period.

Lyon was the vantage point from which Fourier witnessed the collapse of Napoleon's Empire. At the end of 1813 thirty thousand troops from Suchet's army in Spain began to concentrate around Lyon to meet the allied invasion. But on March 21, 1814, after heavy fighting around Villefranche and Limonest and the hasty withdrawal of Augereau, some forty thousand Austrian troops under the prince of Hesse-Homborg entered Lyon in triumph. The following day a proclamation was issued ordering the mayor of Lyon to provide food and lodging for the army of occupation.[52] In later years Fourier was to criticize the attitude of Lyon's municipal authorities during the occupation as a striking example of "the persecution of the poor." Modest householders were required to billet as many as eight soldiers at once, he recalled, while the municipal authorities never sent the rich more than a single officer, "who ate at their table, and caused them neither embarrassment, nor expense, nor vermin." Were his own friends, his landlady, among those victimized? In any event he insisted on the point.

> All complaints were in vain. The municipality and the local commissioners overburdened [the poor] on the pretext that the petty bourgeoisie was numerous and that, there being few nobles, the privilege, the immunity they were accorded, made little difference. Such is the spirit of all municipal bodies; cajoled by the great property owners, they do everything for the rich at the expense of the poor.[53]

The Austrian occupation ended on June 9, 1814. A month later Fourier was traveling again as a *commis voyageur*. He sold straw hats and silk stockings on commission for Bousquet's partner, Frederic Fournier, at the Beaucaire Fair in July.[54] Trade was slow as a result of the war, but in September another business trip took him as far as Naples.[55] This was, apparently, the last of his long voyages.

Although Fourier's life during the great events of 1814 and 1815 was outwardly calm, he did have one brush with the authorities similar to that which had occurred in 1803 following the interception of his "Letter to the High Judge." Once again the occasion was an attempt on Fourier's part to make contact with Napoleon. On June 14, 1814, shortly after the restoration of the Bourbon monarchy in France and the exile of Napoleon to Elba, Fourier addressed a letter to General Bertrand, Napoleon's companion in exile, indicating his desire to communicate to the fallen emperor "a discovery . . . that will be worth more to him than all he has lost."[56] This letter was intercepted and forwarded to Count Beugnot, the director general of the police, who ordered the arrest of Fourier and the seizure of his papers. Fourier was brought before the prefect of the Rhone for questioning. But the prefect quickly decided that Fourier posed no threat to the restored Bourbon monarchy. As Beugnot put it in a report to Louis XVIII:

> The prefect of the Rhone . . . became convinced that this Fourier was a visionary, a quite innocent madman from whom there is nothing to fear, moreover a peaceable and decent man who sincerely believes that "God has revealed to him the true social state," and who would like to appeal to Bonaparte to put his theory into practice on the island of Elba. The text of his interrogation, of which I have the honor to enclose a copy, is of a sufficiently curious species of extravagance that the king may deign perhaps to take a look at it.[57]

Like Napoleon's police in 1803, the police of the First Restoration treated Fourier as a harmless crank. He was promptly released, but remained under surveillance for the rest of the First Restoration.

Fourier may well have been in the large throng that gathered at the outskirts of Lyon on March 11, 1815, to hail Napoleon on his return from Elba. At any rate, his difficulties with the authorities of the Restoration had won him a local reputation as a Bonapartist sympathizer.[58] It was probably because of this reputation that his name was included on a list of "responsible, firm, and modest" citizens sent anonymously to the new minister of the interior, Lazare Carnot, in April, not long after Napoleon's return to power. In proposing the appointment of Fourier as one of several deputies to the mayor of Lyon, Carnot's anonymous correspondent described him in these terms:

> M. Fourrier, Place du Plâtre, bachelor, but entirely devoted to his system of regeneration. He must be employed to show his abilities. He is a man full of erudition, speaking knowledgeably about everything, not at all pedantic, above all a profound geographer. Somewhat bizarre, but a very reliable and very trustworthy man. Utterly disinterested, work is easy for him.[59]

Fourier was not named a deputy mayor during the Hundred Days. Nor was he appointed (as his disciples later asserted) by his namesake, the eminent mathematician Jean-Baptiste Fourier, to a position at the Prefecture of the Rhone.[60] But Fourier does appear to have held a minor position in the mayor's office during the Hundred Days—as an employee in the Bureau of Records.[61] He probably owed this job to personal connections. For Jean-Baptiste Gaucel, his old friend and now a prosperous linen merchant, had been appointed deputy mayor. And the mayor himself during the Hundred Days was Antoine-Gabriel Jars, the sponsor of the riddle contest that, twelve years earlier, had occasioned Fourier's stormy entry into the pages of the *Bulletin de Lyon*.[62]

V

Fourier's reaction to the events of 1814–1815 was less spectacular than that of his utopian contemporaries, Robert Owen and Henri Saint-Simon. He penned no appeals to the sovereigns assembled at the Congress of Vienna, and he made no effort to redefine his mission in light of the new European order. The comments he set down in his manuscripts on the events of this period were ironic and detached. He referred to the political opportunism of the Paris philosophers as the confirmation of what he already knew. In shamelessly paying court to a succession of new masters, they had merely revealed their true colors. They were a servile band of intriguers whom Napoleon had quite properly despised.[63]

More interesting are the reflections that, sometime during the First Restoration, Fourier set down on the "political outcast" whom he had celebrated in the *Quatre mouvements* as a "new Hercules." His aim was to show what the French "could have derived" from Napoleon "had they not been enslaved by the sophisms of the Parisian philosophers."[64] Napoleon was a "unityist"; and like all representatives of that rare passional type, he was as incapable of half-measures in evil as in good. All "unityists" were filled with magnanimous inclinations. Their profound scorn for the human race disposed them to distinguish themselves by "social virtues" that it lacked. But when their character was denied fulfillment, it underwent "inverse" or "subversive" development. They became "the most wicked of men without ceasing on that account to include all humanity in their plan for happiness." This was what had happened to Napoleon. Early in his career he had manifested a salutary contempt for his fellow man; and long before ascending to the throne he had worked out his brilliant "plan of unity": "the conquest and rational organization of the globe." Frustrated in his efforts, his character had undergone inverse development; and his plan had served only to "render humanity excessively wretched." But had he succeeded in imposing his will on all mankind, the "fine seeds of magnanimity" in his character would have burst forth.

> Having once attained Unity (which he missed by very little), Napoleon would have suddenly changed his administrative methods and, to uphold Unity, he would have assured the peoples of the world as much peace as he had caused them torture.[65]

Universal conquest would have set the stage for Harmony.

This was not new. As early as 1803 Fourier had argued that a universal monarchy—under either Napoleon or Alexander I—would serve to create a climate of peace and "unity" propitious for the establishment of Harmony. He had appealed directly to Napoleon in the "Letter to the High Judge" and in the *Théorie des quatre mouvements*. To the end of his days he continued to refer to "coercion" as one of the possible "ways out" of civilization. And more than once under the feebler rulers of the Restoration and July Monarchy he was to look back with nostalgia at the time when a "unityist" controlled the destinies of France.[66]

These reflections on Napoleon were an exercise or diversion of a sort in which Fourier frequently engaged. But they were relatively unimportant compared to a theoretical discovery he made at about the same time. While working in somewhat desultory fashion on "accessory problems," he hit, apparently by chance, upon the "key" to a major theoretical problem that had remained a mystery to him in 1808. He dated this discovery precisely: "On November 17, 1814, I solved the pivotal calculation, that of the general clavier of creation, which completes my theory."[67] Elsewhere he characterized his discovery in these terms.

> It was only in November 1814 that I resolved the brilliant problem . . . of the general clavier of creation or of the dispositions that God determines systematically before undertaking the creation of a universe, a galaxy, a globe, and of their products in every realm: animal, vegetable, and mineral.[68]

Like most of the major breakthroughs that punctuated Fourier's intellectual career, this one remains somewhat mysterious. What he seems to have discovered was a rationale or formula that would enable him to use mathematics rather than intuition in the working-out of a coherent pattern of analogies linking everything that occurred in the natural world to the play of the human passions. What he discovered, in other words, was a way of substantiating (at least to his own satisfaction) his claim in the *Quatre mouvements* that "everything, from the atoms to the stars, constitutes a tableau of the properties of the human passions."[69]

Fourier's fullest account of the significance of his discovery of November 1814 comes in an important manuscript where he describes it as having endowed him with the "key" to "the theory of universal analogy or the application of the passional system to the whole of created nature, of which it is the type." He continues:

> Until then my efforts at application in cosmogony and anatomy and in other areas were vague and tentative. My instinct for these calculations guided me fairly well. My errors were not grave: for instance, I speculated only on four movements, unmindful of the aromal; I confused the passional with the others of which it is the pivot. These were errors of detail; the essence was good nonetheless, and I already knew, as I know today, that a passional Tourbillon [Phalanx] is composed of 810 personality types. I defined by instinct some of its arrangements, like that of the parade order in 16 choirs and 32 half-choirs. Now I can proceed with a sure step. My progress is slow and difficult, but any solution I reach is certain.[70]

Fourier was never more specific than this concerning his discovery of 1814, nor did he specify the intellectual process that led up to the discovery. Indeed, his sparse comments concerning the general clavier of creation suggest that he hit upon it quite by accident. But he left no doubt as to the importance of this "pivotal calculation . . . which completes my theory." In later years he described it as second in significance only to the discovery of 1799. In providing him with insight into other mysteries—notably the existence of a hitherto unknown "aromal" movement—this "unhoped-for success" served to renew his interest in the elaboration of a complete doctrinal treatise. Together with the "industrial stagnation caused by the events of 1814 and 1815," it also helped precipitate his decision to quit commerce and retire to the countryside "to devote myself exclusively to my discovery."[71]

At the end of 1815 Fourier left Lyon for good and moved to Bugey to take up residence in the village of Talissieu with the children of his sister Mariette de Rubat. Among the manuscripts he took with him was the "plan" in thirty-two parts of an immense doctrinal work.[72] During the five years that he spent in Bugey, Fourier was to labor at the preparation of a *Grand Traité* far more ambitious than that which he had "announced" in 1808.

7

"The Virtuous Countryside"

THE FIVE years Fourier spent living in Bugey constituted the most productive period of his intellectual life.[1] When he moved out to Talissieu to take up residence with the Rubats his discovery was already seventeen years old. The wayfaring life of a commercial traveler had provided him with an enormous fund of experience on which to draw in the elaboration of his theory. But it had left him, as he often lamented, with little time for the act of writing, which was for his imagination a more necessary stimulus than any amount of experience.[2] In Bugey he was at last able to devote all his energies to the preparation of the full theoretical treatise heralded by the *Quatre mouvements*.

As absorbing as was his work, however, it did not cut him off completely from the life that went on around him. Fourier always had his feet planted in two worlds; and some of the strangest passages in his theoretical writings—the numerous projects concerning the reform of the brokerage monopoly, for example, or the seven-page footnote on the "distress" of French provincial theaters in the *Quatre mouvements*—can only be understood in light of his daily activity. During his stay in Bugey the mundane world continued to intrude upon and alter the contours of the universe that he had long since begun to spin out of his imagination.

This was the only period of Fourier's existence in which he got a prolonged taste of rural life. His conviction that the major ills besetting civilization were those of urban society was to survive his exposure to the countryside. The "vices" of commerce remained his central preoccupation. But henceforth his criticism of "parcelized industry" and of peasant small-holding was informed by a new appreciation of the realities of French farming and viticulture. And specific references to the local agricultural crisis of 1818 figured prominently in his subsequent indictments of civilization.[3] If this city dweller's utopia remained a rural one, he now began to view with a more skeptical eye the traditional paeans to the virtues of the pastoral life.* His later writings were filled with ironical sketches of "les vertueuses campagnes," stories of peasant incest and "secret orgies" that can also be traced directly back to the years in Bugey.[4]

These years also marked the only prolonged period in his adult life during which Fourier lived in a family, sharing the burdens and pleasures of domesticity. An unrepentant bachelor when he arrived, he would take up once again upon his departure the solitary life of a *vieux garçon* with its rented rooms and dinners *en pension*. But for a while in Bugey he was even the head of a family. Given the seriousness with which he took this responsibility, it is not surprising that he soon found himself deeply embroiled in the daily trials and tribulations of his relatives.

I

Fourier had two sets of relatives in Bugey.[5] The youngest of his three sisters, Sophie, lived in the town of Belley. Philibert Parrat-Brillat, whom she married in 1790, had weathered the storms of the Revolution (which he served in 1793 as Belley's town prosecutor) and the Empire (during which he became Imperial notary). Under the reign of Louis

---

*The abbé Delille (1753–1813) became Fourier's chief target among the "poetic charlatans" who extolled the innocence and virtue of rural life. His first blasts at Delille appear in manuscripts dating from the years at Bugey; and the *Traité de l'association domestique-agricole,* which appeared shortly after Fourier had quit the countryside for good, abounds in sarcastic allusions to Delille's vision of rural life. See *La Phalange,* IV (1846), 21, 43, 47, 217, 307; AN 10AS 2 (8), pp. 78–79; OC IV, 294–295, 499–500, and especially OC V, 561–573: a long "countergloss" on Delille's poem "L'Homme des Champs." Fourier advocated the reprinting in Harmony of texts like Delille's with appropriate commentary to be provided by "amateurs of burlesque social archaeology."

XVIII he remained town notary at Belley. The family was now large and well-to-do. Twenty years younger than her husband, Sophie possessed a strong will, a sharp tongue, and a tight purse. She was the one Fourier child who had managed to retain her paternal inheritance.

Fourier's oldest sister, Mariette, had fared even better on the marriage market. Prior to the Revolution her husband, Antide de Rubat, was already an influential lawyer, entitled to preside over the local *baillage* court. Elected mayor of Belley in 1790, he then changed places with his friend, Anthelme Brillat-Savarin, to become deputy at the Legislative Assembly. He was elected public prosecutor of the Ain during the Directory, and was appointed subprefect of Belley in 1800. Three years later, however, he died, leaving Mariette with eight children ranging in age from eighteen to one. Mariette may already have had a history of mental instability: Pellarin's biography is silent on this score and Fourier seems never to have discussed the matter with his disciples. In any case, not long after her husband's death, Mariette had to be committed to a mental institution. She was to remain there the rest of her life; and the children were left to take care of themselves at the Rubat country estate in Talissieu, a village of about forty households in Valromey, about twenty kilometers north of Belley.

As Mariette's only brother, Fourier had long felt somewhat responsible for the Rubat children. During his years in Lyon he had visited them from time to time, and he had also helped look after one of his older nieces in Lyon. He performed these paternal functions with a solicitude that his niece Clarisse remembered long afterward. "I have never forgotten and I will never forget," she wrote in 1832, "all your services to us at the time of my poor mother's sickness, and all that you also did for my dear Fanny when she was living in Lyon."[6] It was apparently in 1804, shortly after her father's death, that Fanny, then nineteen years old, had come to Lyon, where Fourier was able to find her a job with a lace mender.[7]

While still at Lyon Fourier had also been asked occasionally to join the Parrat-Brillats in family councils concerning the upbringing of the Rubat children. But sometimes his advice was unwelcome. Such was the case in 1813 when the family met to consider a marriage proposal to Fanny. Fourier's conduct in the affair is revealing. For it shows him to have been a sharp practitioner in his own blunt way of just the sort of mercantile marriage calculation that he had attacked in the *Quatre mouvements*.

Fanny was then twenty-eight, and the suitor was six years younger. Fourier knew that the Napoleonic wars had rendered eligible bachelors a scarce commodity. "In Bugey," he observed, "there is not one young man for ten girls, and in this penury a wigged monkey would be heartily welcomed." Despite his youth, the suitor was a gentleman. This had been enough to impress Fanny's Uncle Rubat and "les dames du pays." But Uncle Fourier's requirements were more exacting. When he arrived on the scene, he put his ear to the ground and soon discovered that the "gentleman's" fortune was no greater than his wit, and that his haste to enter the state of blessed matrimony betrayed another preoccupation, that of evading the draft. He told Fanny that her suitor would have to undergo a brief examination.

> Mesdames Durand and Benoit [he wrote afterwards] examined the mind and spirit and decided right away that the young man could aspire to the kingdom of heaven. As for me, without dwelling on superficial matters or on wit, which is not necessary in marriage, I went straight to the most important point, wealth; and I wrote from his dictation a page that contains so many contradictions and absurdities that I saved it to take to Belley where everyone told me, "We knew nothing about all this. He didn't tell us this." Well, what in the world were they doing then and where were they getting their information? I, who only spent ten minutes talking to him, found out enough to reduce him to his true worth.[8]

Fourier's veto was sufficient to prevent the marriage. But he felt obliged to justify his handling of the affair in a letter to his nephew, Georges de Rubat, the tone of which suggests that the other members of the family were not entirely convinced that "such a booby isn't even worth inquiring about."

II

In spite of such minor disputes the whole family was agreed, when Fourier decided to retire to the countryside in 1815, that his presence would be useful at Talissieu. For the Rubat children were in need of supervision. Their mother had long since been committed; and the burden of supporting her had fallen on the oldest son, Georges, who was trying to get a start in business in Paris.[9] The other seven children, who ranged in age from twelve to thirty, remained at Talissieu. They had been left to their own devices; and the girls in particular had received little formal education. Fanny was still unmarried. Two of her younger sisters, Hortense and Clarisse, both in their early twenties, had won a certain reputation in the region for their free and easy style of life. Indeed word of their escapades had already reached Fourier in Lyon. But priding himself on being "tolerant by principle," he had thought nothing of it.

On the contrary, what surprised him from the moment of his arrival at Talissieu in December 1815 was not his nieces' loose behavior but rather their lack of frankness about it.[10] The girls led an active social life, and the house was often full of their boisterous and rough-talking soldier-friends. There were mysterious comings and goings and odd nocturnal noises. Fourier had a pretty good idea of what all this signified, and he didn't exactly disapprove. But he wanted to make clear to the girls that he was no dupe. He thought it perfectly consistent with his parental functions to tease them about the "peculiar" behavior of their cavaliers. When he attempted to do so, however, they struck attitudes of outraged innocence. It seemed, for instance, that one of their most frequent visitors, Garin de Lamorflanc, treated them like "low-class whores" (*grisettes de bas étage*). But Fourier's pointed comments produced such a torrent of tributes to Garin's "saintly" character that he was obliged to say no more. Another visitor, an army captain named Labatie, honored the household with such long-winded sermons on Christian morality that Fourier began to wonder whether his guest was in fact a captain or a Capuchin. Such ostentatious piety seemed hypocritical to Fourier; and from the first months he began to discern in the behavior of his nieces and their friends a sort of affected prudishness—a "bégueulerie calculée"—that offended him more than straightforward licentiousness. But he held his tongue.

Absorbed in his work, going out only for an occasional meal in the village or for solitary walks in the woods, Fourier was content to let his nieces talk and act as they pleased. Often he left Talissieu on weekends to visit the Parrat-Brillats in Belley, leaving the girls with the run of the estate and never asking questions on his return. They were grateful for his discretion and, for their part, they offered him solicitude and affection, which had long been absent from his life. Thus Fourier remained on excellent terms with his nieces throughout the first six months of his stay. For Clarisse, the most attractive of the girls, he even developed a "brin d'amour"; but he was careful to suppress it, and in so doing he discovered within himself hitherto unknown reservoirs of "parentism." Far from taking advantage of Clarisse's affection, he would pass at night on tiptoe through her bedroom to avoid disturbing her sleep. He had also been attracted to a young friend of his nieces, a girl named Rosine ("whose partisan I became because everyone mistreated her"). But he did not pursue her because, as he later wrote, "I had come [to Talissieu] with the intention of disregarding women."[11] His nieces may not have been particularly impressed by his restraint; they may, as he later claimed, already have begun to make fun in private of his hermit's life and his unwillingness "to imitate the local public and to cut [his] slice of the cake." But if so he was still unaware of it.

In the month of May Hortense began to show new signs of affection toward her uncle. She began to clean up his room with unusual diligence and to sew up his manuscript cahiers; she also changed her place at the dinner table to be next to him. She stayed up sometimes in the evenings to keep him company. Fourier enjoyed her conversation and companionship. She was not as pretty as Clarisse; indeed, Fourier believed her "the dupe of the lovers whom I saw treating her so cavalierly." But she seemed to talk out of a vast experience of unrequited love. This made her particularly attractive to Fourier not only because he sympathized with downtrodden women but also because he felt he might have much to learn from her concerning the passion of love, to which he planned to devote a major portion of his *Grande Traité*. He had already begun to work on the introductory sections; and before long he allowed her to peek at his cahiers. She would read a few lines and laugh, sometimes adding such "sharp and judicious" criticisms that he declared himself "stunned." As he observed later, "I still remember two bits of advice she gave me at that time, and they serve as my guide in all texts of a similar nature."[12]

This unexpected display of sympathy and encouragement could not have come at a more opportune moment. For in that spring of 1816 Fourier had begun to lose courage in the face of the enormous intellectual task confronting him. He had come to Talissieu with a fairly clear idea of the treatise he wanted to write; the outline of its thirty-two parts had taken shape in his mind before he left Lyon.[13] But in the five months since his arrival, he had not moved beyond the initial stages. He had "invoked God and the devil" in a whole series of preliminary justifications, diatribes against civilization, and explanations of the "riddle" of the *Quatre mouvements*. He had also composed a number of occasional pieces—many of them dealing with questions of astronomy and cosmogony—for his own amusement and perhaps with an eye to publication.[14] But he could not get down to work on the body of the treatise. He was again plagued by an old "mal de nerfs," which he had suffered at Lyon. To make matters worse, the "wits" of Talissieu had found out that he was trying to write a book. They mocked him openly about it and encouraged his nieces to do the same. Under these conditions the task of "drawing from nothingness" a whole body of doctrine seemed almost hopeless. "I bent under the burden," wrote Fourier later, "I was truly in a desperate state."[15]

In these circumstances Hortense's unexpected gestures of sympathy and interest in his work had a devastating effect on Fourier. There seemed to be something almost providential about her sudden responsiveness to his needs. He grasped at her as at "a support that fate was sending me." In the weeks that followed Fourier simultaneously became infatuated with his niece and increasingly impressed by her critical gifts. He asked her advice on a multitude of problems connected with his work, and it soon became evident to him that he had at his side "a Little Geoffroy with an innate talent for criticism." He began to think of Hortense as the "talisman" of his intellectual enterprise, and to nourish the hope that her encouragement would enable him to carry his project through to its conclusion.

> It seemed to me very natural to hope for such aid from Hortense. Rightly or wrongly, I convinced myself that she would be of great assistance to me, that her criticism would aid me with the literary part and that that would give me the courage to come to grips with the dogmatic part. Authors need illusions: they are good when they help you to reach the goal.[16]

Stimulated by his new-found "illusion," Fourier set to work in May 1816 on the body of the treatise. As he wrote, his mind raced ahead of his pen. He saw that with the continued encouragement of Hortense, he could soon begin work on the most difficult portion of the treatise, the exposition of the theory of passionate attraction. "I believed that the work would go quickly, that I could do in less than a year the twelve dogmatic sections which frightened me." In a year the worst would be over; he only needed to be sure of her sustained collaboration.

But at this point doubts beset Fourier. He knew that Hortense was a flighty, capricious woman. Was it really likely that she would remain interested in the treatise for very long? What if he were suddenly deprived of his "talisman"? Tormented by this possibility, he decided to appeal to his niece's mercenary instincts. She had often told him that what she wanted from life was a husband worth at least fifty thousand francs and old enough to allow her complete amorous liberty. Why couldn't he play the role of this undemanding old husband? It was an absurd idea perhaps, but Fourier soon managed to convince himself that only by promising his niece the fifty thousand francs she wanted from a husband could he be sure of the encouragement he needed to complete his treatise. Thus barely a month after Hortense had come to his rescue, he resolved to return to commerce—for her sake and for the sake of his work.

In quitting Lyon he had not severed all his ties with the cloth industry. He still had connections, and he could easily reestablish his clientele as a broker. Furthermore, he had friends who would gladly take him into their business as a *voyageur associé*. If he worked at it full time, he could easily gain one hundred thousand francs in ten years. He would offer half of it to Hortense, provided only that she would guarantee to stay at his side and help him with his work for the year to come.

In early June 1816 Fourier notified his business associates in Lyon that he wished to return to commerce the following year. It was decided that he would go to Lyon to sign the papers at the beginning of July. Until the negotiations were settled, he would say nothing to Hortense. But upon his return he would make his proposition to her. He would make of her only two requests.

> The first is to take off your mask. Certain scenes have explained everything to me. If your sisters want to play at being prudes with me, that's all right. I only ask that you be frank. . . . In addition I will ask you to listen to portions of the treatise from time to time, and to provide me with criticism as to the general effect, the tone, and even the details. I want your advice, from which I have profited more than once. In return I will take the place of the *vieux mari* whom you are looking for and I will earn you the fifty thousand francs.[17]

In light of subsequent events—and the girls' claim that their uncle had been trying all along to "seduce" Hortense—this whole scene looks very much like a curiously sublimated amorous proposition concocted by a terribly lonely man whose longing for affection was at least as great as his need for advice on the treatise. Perhaps it was. But in any case Fourier had managed to convince himself that neither he nor his treatise could do without Hortense.

III

During the month of June a series of events ruined Fourier's relationship with Hortense and her sisters and shattered his carefully laid projects. He had long suffered in silence the "Tartuffery" of Labatie, Garin, and the rest of his nieces' entourage. But if he had any illusions about the real state of affairs, they were dispelled by a discovery he made on an afternoon's walk in the woods surrounding Talissieu. Suddenly and quite by accident (or so he later maintained), he came upon Garin and two of the girls in a singularly compromising position. As he bluntly described the scene: "Garin was reaching with his arm all the way up to the elbow under the skirts of Hortense, and he was doing it right in front of her sister Clarisse."[18] The trio failed to notice him, and he claimed that he took the incident in his stride. "Tolerant about such details, I interpreted everything favorably, saying, 'It's better to agree about sharing men than to fight over them.'" Nevertheless it was only the fear of antagonizing Hortense that prevented him from making an issue of the discovery. The real *casus belli* came shortly thereafter.

Fourier chose to regard his relationship with the girl as paternal. But this did not preclude a certain amount of physical intimacy. Sometimes as he teased with Hortense, for instance, they would pull each other's ears or she would come and sit in his lap. One day in the midst of these flirtations, she pushed him away brusquely. Then Fourier observed that her "titulary lover," Labatie, was in the next room looking on. "I thought she was going to get a scolding," he wrote later, "but he went farther than that and ordered a rupture." The next day when Fourier asked Hortense to sew up one of his cahiers, she curtly refused. Then Labatie himself insulted Fourier in front of the girls concerning satirical verses that Fourier had been circulating among his friends. But this was only the beginning.

In the meantime Hortense, who was "nothing less than laborious," had taken a job as a laundress with three respectable ladies of Talissieu. After a few days she lost patience and quit, only to find another job in the nearby village of Marlieux with none other than the sister of Captain Labatie. Before long she found so much work to do that she had to spend the night at the Labaties' instead of returning home. Soon Clarisse, too, began to spend her nights in the neighboring village of Billieux. This was too much for Fourier. He concluded that the household had become "a regular bordello where the public came in search of women to sleep with." Upon the girls' return he confronted them with evidence of their previous misbehavior, warning them that unless these overnight visits were terminated, he would be obliged to inform their brother of "all the details of this escapade as well as the preliminaries" on which he had discreetly shut his eyes. He reminded them that his own reputation was at stake as well as theirs. In the eyes of society he was responsible for them; and if they behaved like "arrant libertines," the public would have every reason to assume his complicity. "The public could compose *chansons* about them . . . and I would have had the pimp's couplet." But the girls were hardly impressed by the menace of a few *chansons*. They struck the old attitude of virtuous innocence, which Fourier now recognized as "pure hypocrisy." "They put on the same prudish airs, claiming that captains in the grenadiers were very timid in female company, and that chairs creaked all by themselves in rooms where a pair of lovers happened to be. It was this nonsense that caused the trouble."[19]

As the date of his departure for Lyon approached, Fourier began to suspect that Hortense was pregnant. Inspection proved inconclusive. But then Hortense threatened suicide, whereupon Fourier's agitation reached such a point that he felt a recurrence of the stomach cramps he had suffered for three years at Lyon. This did not prevent him, however, from writing on the eve of his departure a deliciously sarcastic letter to Laurette Labatie, the sister of Hortense's "titulary lover." Hortense's new-found enthusiasm for her work, wrote Fourier, constituted "a truly miraculous metamorphosis." But public opinion believed in appearances and not in miracles. As for himself, he shared the opinion of the public, at least insofar as it was liable to affect the family's reputation.

> It is a principle of mine [he wrote Mademoiselle Labatie] that since young women are the victims of prejudice, they are right to seek compensation in secret. . . . Thus I am the most obliging of blind men with those who look out for appearances. But I do not feel the same way about indiscretions that can hold a family up to ridicule.[20]

By no means eager "to play the role of a troublesome censor who disrupts love affairs," he was nevertheless obliged "as a good parent" to take steps to ensure that the girls behaved more prudently in the future. With this parting shot, Fourier left for Lyon. In spite of everything he was still determined to reenter commerce and to make his proposition to Hortense.

When Fourier arrived in Lyon at the beginning of July he found the political life of the city tense and agitated. Bonapartist sentiment was strong, and a plot involving a number of army officers had been uncovered six months earlier. The alleged ringleader, a Grenoble lawyer named Jean-Paul Didier, had escaped only to foment a genuine insurrection at Grenoble in May. Renewed conspiratorial activity throughout the east had served to intensify the vigilance of the Lyon police; and now a full-scale witch hunt was under way.[21] Fourier had brought a few manuscripts with him and unwittingly he contributed to the unrest by publishing an article in one of the Lyon journals in which he attributed the prevalence of sunspots and bad weather to corrupt odors emanating from the earth and Mercury.[22] His references to these planets as "Kinglet" and "Vestal" were taken as veiled allusions to the king of Rome and Marie Louise, and he narrowly escaped being arrested as the author of Bonapartist propaganda.[23] As for his business negotiations, they were quickly terminated; it was decided that he would begin work the following year. This would give him ample time, he felt, to complete the most difficult portion of the *Grand Traité* if only he could convince Hortense to cooperate with him.

On Fourier's return to Talissieu in mid-August, however, matters only got worse. Hortense refused even to speak to her uncle; when he entered a room, she would abruptly get up and walk out. After a week he realized that the situation was hopeless and decided to "abandon the battlefield." Preferring to stay away from Lyon until the atmosphere there had cooled, he paid two months' rent on a room in the nearby village of Artemare. Informed of his decision on August 25, Hortense had second thoughts. She began to fear that his departure would set tongues wagging. Late that night she appeared in his room and begged him to stay. When he refused, she subjected him to what he later described as "a torrent of insults, oaths worthy of a Messalina or a barmaid." In addition, she began to challenge his manhood. He had not, she exclaimed, "acted like a man." He claimed to be an apostle of amorous liberty, but he "had not profited from the good opportunities" he had been offered. The foulness of Hortense's tirade surpassed anything to which Fourier had thus far been subjected—and it made him change his mind about leaving. "The extreme indecency of her talk," he wrote afterward, "determined me to take a closer look at just what was going on in this house . . . to try to unravel this maze of hypocrisy." Thus the next morning he left a note informing his nieces that he was willing to stay on. He said he would answer their charge of "not acting like a man," and in fact he made them what he later described as "propositions." But these were "idle words," he asserted. His real purpose in staying on was to find an explanation for the behavior of his nieces, for the "profligacy plastered with prudery" that he was still unable to understand.[24]

That week Fourier began to make inquiries in the village about his nieces, and he quickly discovered that the multiplicity of their amours had become legendary in the region. They enjoyed a reputation for being attracted to military men, for whose distraction one of their schoolteachers, "a veritable Messalina," had organized "secret orgies." They had, it seemed, an Italian teacher, "a sly character," who made a practice of seducing his pupils. Broadening the scope of his investigation, Fourier inquired into the general sexual mores of the region. He was rewarded with stories about the deflowering of ten-year-old children, about the ravages wrought among the local peasant girls by the *demi-soldes,* the prematurely retired veterans of the Napoleonic wars. "You don't know the country you live in," he was told by an "expert" in the matter. Faithfully recorded in his notebooks, such tales were to give Fourier's vision of the "virtuous countryside" a radically new dimension. As he wrote in an 1818 draft of the *Grand Traité:*

> I witnessed in a hamlet of forty households where I had gone to work on this book, I witnessed I say, secret orgies as well organized as in a big city; young women twenty years old more experienced, more jaded than Laïs and Phryne at forty; peasant women who were used to seeing their daughters deflowered at the age of ten; fathers and mothers who knew about the whole business and played along as dispassionately as the mothers of Tahiti collaborated in the prostitution of their daughters. All of this debauchery was nicely garnished, nicely powdered with prudery, communion, and sacrilege. That's what you can see everywhere just as I saw it in a hamlet.[25]

With these discoveries in mind Fourier began—at last—to view the behavior of his nieces in a new light. He had at first been attracted to Hortense because she always seemed to be duped and victimized by her lovers. But on the contrary, he now realized, it was she who mystified them all. "She was the ringleader of the intrigues, managing love affairs with a rare deftness." But this made her even more desirable. She possessed a mine of information on amorous matters, and would have been of inestimable aid in the composition of the treatise. Even in her insults he detected an enormous satirical gift.

As the year wore on Fourier continued to regret the loss of Hortense's counsel. Without her aid he was simply unable to get down to work on the body of his *Grand Traité*. But he had to do something more than the preliminary exercises that had consumed most of his energies at Talissieu. Thus not long after his return from Lyon he embarked on the composition of a fairly modest work, a sequel to the *Quatre mouvements,* which he hoped to publish "at the end of 1817" and "elsewhere than in France." At one point he talked boldly of addressing it to rich philanthropists—the Count de Merode at Brussels, Count Marescalchi at Milan, Pourtalès at Neufchâtel—to "interested sovereigns" like Alexander I, the prince of Belgium, and the United States Congress, and to "dethroned princes who are inclined to believe that everything is not for the best in this world."[26] Although such wishful thinking sustained Fourier for a few months, nothing came of this sequel. He later described the entire year of 1816 as "wasted, half in preliminary studies and the straightening out of manuscripts, half in almost useless labor on too limited a project."[27]

There was no doubt in Fourier's mind that Hortense was the "veritable cause" of his failure "for having deprived me of an illusion that stimulated me." Nevertheless he was unable to give up his illusion. He continued to hope that by promising to return to commerce and share his earnings with her, he might be able to enlist her help and proceed with his treatise. But she refused, apparently seeing in his offers no more than some kind of curiously backhanded and not very attractive amorous proposition.

By fall Fourier's infatuation with his niece had begun to wear off, but for the sake of his work, and his peace of mind, he kept on trying to reestablish good relations with her. He told her of his own new penchant for one of her friends, hoping to elicit from her details concerning the amorous intrigues at which she was such a past master. But to no avail.

Sometimes she would appear to respond to his overtures, only to subject him later to withering abuse. The most humiliating outburst came one morning when he arrived for breakfast to find Hortense in the company of two women. Seeing that it was only her uncle, she shouted disdainfully: "Who is that? That's not a man! I need broad-shouldered men of five feet eight inches. Can somebody find me a man! Go ahead, Emilie, call Hippolyte."[28] This was more than Fourier could endure.

By the end of the year Fourier finally decided to quit Talissieu, and he made plans to retreat to the Parrat-Brillats' at Belley. On New Year's Day 1817, however, he made a last attempt at reconciliation with Hortense. Once again he attempted to enlist her help with the treatise. Again she refused—with a "shower of insults" to which, this time, Fanny added her share. At last he had had enough; and on January 15 he advised his friends in Lyon that he was no longer interested in returning to commerce. He set his departure for the end of March.

On the evening of January 26 a confrontation took place that hastened his departure. Suffering from a bad stomachache, he had been drinking *eau de vie* throughout the evening. When the girls chided him for being drunk, Fourier suddenly flew into a rage. He exploded with a "sally in which I responded to six months of insults with a quarter-hour of bitter verities. I parried the habitual sobriquet of 'old bastard' with its counterpart: 'young bitches.'" The next morning the girls walked out, announcing that they would stay with Fanny's friend, Garin de Lamorflanc, until their uncle left.

At this point Fourier took the affair outside the family circle. On February 1 he wrote a long letter to the judge of Belley. Although his purpose was to justify his own conduct and to request the judge's aid in bringing the girls back to Talissieu, he could not restrain himself from heaping invectives on them. They were "arrant libertines, profligates who swear like troopers in secret and who only judge men by their size and shoulders." He traced the quarrel from its origins, dwelling on the girls' overnight visits but omitting his own infatuation with Hortense and his proposals concerning the treatise. He explained that his attitude toward his nieces' behavior had been motivated solely by concern for their reputation—and his own.

Accustomed to towns and provinces that mercilessly lampoon people who spend their nights in suspect quarters, at a lover's domicile without the presence of a father or mother, I found it highly scandalous that Mlle. Hortense should sleep for a whole week and on frivolous pretexts at the lodging of a soldier who was her declared lover.

I was far from condemning these amusements, being by system a partisan of the liberties of the fair sex. I only took exception to the nocturnal absences that comprised the household and myself indirectly. For if the young lady had returned pregnant from these excursions, her relatives and her older brother would have rightly criticized me for having held my tongue about this mode of visiting. I would have risked having a line in the customary *chanson* as a pious spectator or as a mutually interested party paying court to one of the other nieces.[29]

This fear of being made the butt of other people's jokes was characteristic of Fourier. A born satirist, he knew the power of public ridicule. He had more than once turned his own hand to a *chanson*. And, in fact, before leaving he composed another one ostensibly to teach his nieces a lesson, to show them "the risk they had been running." He observed that he was only acquainted with the three declared lovers, but "if I could find so much material for couplets, what might be written by someone who knew all the secret intrigues!" On February 16 he left Talissieu for good.

IV

When Fourier arrived in Belley to take up residence with the Parrat-Brillats, he found that word of the quarrel had preceded him. He was accused of being a Peeping Tom, an enemy of the younger generation, a jealous old lecher, of having (unsuccessfully) attempted to seduce all the girls of Talissieu, beginning with his own nieces. Tracking these "ridiculous accusations" down to their source, he discovered that his "innocent" niece, Fanny, had written the Parrat-Brillats a letter containing (according to him) "more than thirty calumnies." Months later, after Fanny and Garin had finally married, Fourier continued to refer to his oldest niece as a "viper" and a "false Agnes," to Garin as a "Tartuffe," and to their household as a "fable factory."[30]

The following year, long after he had become absorbed once again in the preparation of his treatise, Fourier still felt called upon to dispatch an occasional missive to a relative or friend to refute his nieces' "calumnies." It took him approximately ten thousand words, for instance, to bring his nephew, Georges de Rubat, up to date on the quarrel, which he described as "a mix-up that they have passed off as an attempt at seduction." The problem, he explained, was that his nieces were "cynics" who saw everything in terms of sex. He had been misunderstood by them all, and particularly by Hortense. He assured his nephew that

> at Talissieu as today I was bent upon matters very different from amourettes . . . I considered women and men alike only with regard to the help that they might lend to my exclusive occupation. . . . If one of the Rubat girls hadn't seemed to be a useful assistant, a sort of raft in the storm, at the moment when I was drawing back like Jesus from the chalice, if I had only been excited by desire for the little thing, I wouldn't have bothered.[31]

Although echoes of the quarrel with his nieces died slowly, Fourier's stay with the Parrat-Brillats in Belley was on the whole far more harmonious than his year at Talissieu. It was not of course without its ups and downs. Fourier was far too outspoken and mischievous to avoid crossing swords occasionally on domestic matters with his sister Sophie. He let it be known that he did not approve of the domineering way in which she ran the Parrat-Brillat household, and he regaled his friends with imitations of her husband's servile admiration for her. Sophie doubtless knew nothing of Fourier's "Hierarchy of Cuckoldom" (in which her husband figured as a model for the "extolled cuckold").[32] But she was, at any rate, quick to hold Fourier responsible for a *chanson* entitled "The Bride of Three Months"—with the refrain "Just like my mother does"—which began to circulate around Belley in the summer of 1819. The same year Fourier managed to provoke the ire of the whole family by sabotaging a marriage planned for his niece, Agathe Parrat-Brillat. But these were later developments. Throughout most of his stay Fourier seems to have been a welcome addition to the Parrat-Brillat household. There were six children—five girls and a boy—and he spent many a delightful evening entertaining them with his virtuosity as a mimic and joining in games of *Dos Condos*. He had a special fondness for the youngest child, Olympe; and fifteen years later she could still write with warmth about the time when he had been a part of the family.[33]

When Fourier moved to Belley in February 1817, he originally planned to stay only six weeks. His spirits were low. Unable to get down to work on his *Grand Traité,* he still thought only of publishing a second "prospectus." But at the Parrat-Brillats' he found an atmosphere far more congenial to his work than at Talissieu. During the month of March he made a breakthrough that determined him not only to prolong his stay but also to begin work on the *Grand Traité.* The "most perplexing problem" he managed to resolve was that of the "system of passional accords." "During my first nineteen years of study," he wrote later, "I believed that societary harmony required the complete development of the twelve passions. I was the more convinced of this in that I did not understand the system of accords. It was invented only in March 1817."[34] Emboldened by this discovery, Fourier threw himself into work on the first half (or Major Octave) of his *Grand Traité.*[35] This was the most difficult portion of the treatise, the part he had always feared. By the fall of 1817, however, he had managed to complete several long and troublesome sections on the equilibrium of the passions, and he had also embarked on what was to become *Le Nouveau monde amoureux.* Within a few weeks he made another discovery concerning the uses of platonic love in his ideal community. As he wrote later:

> In 1807 my elaboration of the Theory of Harmony scarcely went beyond questions of sensual love, which, being the easiest to calculate, had to be the object of my first studies. Only since 1817 have I possessed the simple and exponential theory of sentimental or Celadonic ties in Harmony. This theory will occupy an important place in the treatise and will send back to school our sentimental champions, our troubadours and shepherds of Lignon. They will be shown to be merely disguised cynics; and so will our Pamelas and our false Agneses, those from the city as well as those from the innocent countryside, which outdoes the city in hypocrisy without conceding anything to it in cynicism.[36]

Some of the "disguised cynics" and "false Agneses" whom Fourier had the pleasure of "sending back to school" with his reflections on the value of sentimental love were, of course, his own nieces.

By the summer of 1818 Fourier could boast that he had "completed the most difficult portion of the calculus." He was convinced that its publication would bring him fame and fortune. And as he brought his nephew Georges up to date on the quarrel with his nieces, he could not resist adding that Hortense would soon find that she had made a very bad mistake in rejecting his proposition. In five years, when Fourier had published his treatise and when the broad-shouldered cavaliers had begun to turn their backs on Hortense, then she would begin to view the affair at Talissieu in another light. "She will have thirty years of old age to reflect upon a folly for which, on my side, I have every reason to be happy."

In such fantasies of triumph and revenge Fourier found the stimulus—the "illusion"—that he had vainly sought in his niece. He advanced rapidly through the concluding sections of the first half of his treatise. In February 1819 he began work on the second half. Within a matter of weeks he was to make a discovery that would alter his plans and hasten the publication of a very different sort of treatise. In the meantime he had found a new "talisman" in the person of Just Muiron. A "Geoffroy" not so gifted, perhaps, as Hortense, nor so knowledgeable in *affaires galantes*, Muiron was nevertheless to become Fourier's first genuine disciple.

8

The First Disciple

DURING HIS years at Lyon Fourier had managed to provoke some interest in his theory among a small group of friends and admirers. It was in answer to a query from one of them—the unknown Amélie F.—that he had made the first public announcement of his discovery in the *Bulletin de Lyon*. He had also composed announcements in light verse for private circulation among "adepts who have conversed with me"; and the *Quatre mouvements* itself was written in part, he said, to satisfy the demands of "a few of the curious" whom he had previously entertained with oral accounts of the wonders of Harmony.[1] Some of these early sympathizers, such as the doctors Amard and Aimé Martin, were professional men and members of Lyon's intellectual establishment. A few were cronies from the "Vieux Coin" like Henri Brun and Jean-Baptiste Gaucel. Others were the married women with whom he had exchanged verses in the *Bulletin de Lyon*.

There were few in this heterogeneous group who could properly be described as Fourier's disciples. Jean-Baptiste Dumas was probably typical in expressing greater concern for Fourier's personal prosperity than for that of the "famous system." And even at the height of her enthusiasm Amélie F. could declare to Fourier: "Vous êtes fou: mais vous êtes aimable." Whatever reservations the rest may have had, the publication of the *Quatre mouvements* does seem to have produced at least a ripple of excitement at Lyon. Henri Brun wrote Fourier in May of 1808 that the local ladies were "agog" about the book, and some of Fourier's business friends were apparently impressed by his analysis of the vices and hidden tendencies of commerce. More than three years later Dr. Aimé Martin still found it appropriate to remind the readers of the *Journal de Lyon* of "the new views and bold conceptions" contained in Fourier's "prospectus."[2]

Fourier's principal aim in publishing the *Quatre mouvements*, however, had been to bring word of his discovery to the world at large. In this respect his book seemed a total failure. The reviews were caustic; it did not sell; and such correspondence as it brought Fourier consisted mainly of "loose chatter, stale and trivial invectives, and offers of medical assistance."[3]

During the first years of the Restoration, however, a few copies of the *Quatre mouvements* did reach sympathetic readers outside Fourier's Lyon circle. Two of them, Fulcrand and Benjamin Mazel from Montpellier, who were subsequently to pay Fourier the compliment of plagiarism, had come upon the work in a Paris bookstall in 1818. Although confused by the "extravagant" chapters on the earth's origins and future destinies, they were impressed by the author's "healthy views" on commerce and association.* This reaction was to prove

*Benjamin Mazel, *Théorie du mouvement social: dediée à toutes les chambres legislatives* (Paris, 1822), 3. Benjamin Mazel practiced law at Montpellier and his brother Fulcrand had gone into business at Lodève. In 1822 they jointly published a work entitled *Recherches sur le mécanisme social de la France* (Montpellier, 1822), which contained a "critique of the usurious monopoly of the Bank of France," including several pages lifted verbatim from the epilogue to the *Quatre mouvements*. They were not in quotations but were followed by the comment (p. 44): "To speak to you I gathered these *words of peace* cast to the winds fifteen years ago by a friend of humanity, forced no doubt to withhold his name from our gratitude. May the buds from this fertile seed one day cover his tomb with the rich fruit he has merited."

The *Théorie du mouvement social* published by Benjamin the following year was little more than a confused résumé of the critique of civilization and the analysis of association contained in the *Quatre mouvements*. The author acknowledged his debt to the anonymous "M. Charles" in this fashion (p. 6): "The silence he has maintained since 1808, his death perhaps, and the domaine of thought [sic] authorized me to present more methodically a truth that belonged to everyone as soon as it was published, but which, because of the manner in which it was presented, has remained unintelligible and even extravagant to most readers." Fourier eventually heard about these books, and he let the Mazels know what he thought of their "methodical" presentation of his ideas. In *Le Phalanstère*, June 21, 1833, he was to refer to Benjamin Mazel as "an odious little plagiarist." See Benjamin's ensuing correspondence with Fourier and his disciples, AN 10AS 40 (1) and 10AS 25 (3).

typical of most of the later disciples, who were simply embarrassed by his cosmogony and metaphysics. But judging from the known sources, a majority of Fourier's first isolated admirers had no such reservations about the book.[4] Many of them were eclectic dabblers in the occult sciences; they were readers of Swedenborg, Saint-Martin, Mesmer, and Fabre d'Olivet, and Fourier's providentialism, his cosmogony, and his theory of universal analogy did not seem entirely extravagant to them. They were attracted to his work primarily because he seemed to speak their language—because his cosmic vision of the human destinies was cast in terms familiar to them.

Particularly interesting in this respect are the letters addressed to Fourier in 1818 and 1819 by an army captain from Nantes named Felix Bernard.[5] Describing himself as "imbued with a sense of the importance and truth" of Fourier's "sublime" discovery, Bernard filled his letters with long citations from the great esoteric writers and asked Fourier to consider the "striking analogies" between their work and his. He asked, for instance, whether "the existence of a subtle magnetic fluid" could not be reconciled with Fourier's discovery of "the universal laws of movement." And he pointed out that other "savants and philosophers [had] glimpsed more or less clearly the errors of civilization." Sénancour in his *Rêveries* had even "recognized that the passions tend toward harmony." But instead of "proceeding to the mathematical analysis of the human passions, he [had] strayed like the rest into the realm of conjecture."[6] Bernard praised Fourier by contrast for his "positive discovery." In concerning himself with "the ways and means" of "establishing a universal social system" he seemed to have added a new dimension to the purely abstract and "moral" conjectures of his predecessors.[7]

By 1819 Bernard was addressing Fourier as "the man of destiny," and it seems that he managed to get in contact with at least one of Fourier's other early partisans, Désiré-Adrien Gréa.[8] But his correspondence with Fourier was short-lived. His brief fling with Fourier's ideas is mentioned here as indicative of a state of mind that was widespread in illuminist circles at the time.[9] Most of Fourier's other early readers were eclectics who attached great importance to the "affinities" of his doctrine with those of the theosophists, and Bernard was not the only one who saw in it a means of "completing" their abstract and moral "conjectures." Another was Just Muiron, who became Fourier's first genuine disciple and, eventually, the "dean" of the Ecole Sociétaire.

I

On an August afternoon in 1814 Just Muiron left his desk at the Besançon Prefecture to take a stroll across the Pont de Battant to the high ground overlooking the city.[10] Habitually this studious young man took a book to read on his afternoon walks. Lacking one, he paid a call on his friend Charles Weiss, the local bibliophile. While browsing through Weiss's books, Muiron came upon a copy of the *Théorie des quatre mouvements*. "What sort of book is this with such a strange title?" he asked. Weiss replied that he had not read the book, but he had heard that its author was from Besançon and that its contents were "a great deal stranger" than its title. Muiron took another volume and proceeded on his way. Two or three weeks later, however, he encountered the "strange" book once again. This time it was in the library of Raymond de Raymond *père,* a retired postal inspector who was also Besançon's foremost partisan of esoteric or Scottish Freemasonry.★ "Is this madness?" asked Muiron. "By no means," replied Raymond gravely. The book had been loaned to him by one Simon de Troyes, a retired professor at the Collège de Besançon, and they were agreed that it contained "ideas of the highest significance." The next day Muiron revisited Weiss and procured his copy. He was later to describe his first reading of the *Quatre mouvements* as a revelation comparable to that bestowed upon Saint Paul on the road to Damascus.[11]

At the time of his discovery of the *Quatre mouvements* Just Muiron was twenty-seven years old and already a veteran of more than ten years' service in the French public administration. Following his graduation from the Ecole Centrale de Besançon in 1802, his father, Jean-François Muiron, a prosperous merchant, had found him his first job at

---

★Raymond de Raymond *père* (also spelled Raimond) was born at Nevers in 1752 and died at Besançon in 1838. After retiring as Besançon's postal inspector, he served during the Restoration as vice-president and treasurer of the Academy of Besançon. His allegiance to the esoteric brand of Freemasonry propounded by Knigge and Adam Weisshaupt was longstanding. He had attended the famous Wilhelmsbad Congress of 1782, and during the Empire, while most of Besançon's lodges rallied docilely to the officially sponsored Grand Orient, he became the leader of dissident Masonry at Besançon. As a high dignitary in the Ordre des Elus Cohens, Raymond also had international connections with the surviving disciples of Martinès de Pasqually. See Octave Chevalier, *Monographie de la famille Filiol de Raimond* (Besançon, 1965), 27–62; Gerard van Rijnberk, *Un Thaumaturge au XVIIIᵉ siècle: Martinès de Pasqually* (Paris, 1935), 96, 107, 136–137; René Le Forestier, *La Franc-maçonnerie templière et occultiste aux XVIIIᵉ et XIXᵉ siècles* (Paris-Louvain, 1970), 785, 884–894, 911, 915, 921, 932–933.

the prefecture. After appointments in the departments of Basses-Alpes, Sarthe, and Simplon, he returned to Besançon at the end of the Empire as division chief. So far as one can judge from his own writings and from the comments of his friends, Muiron was a faithful and unselfish human being, but also sententious, literal of mind, and incapable of sarcasm or irony. Conscientious in all things and fiercely dedicated to the "truth" once it had been shown to him, his plodding intellect was devoid of the qualities of creative imagination, which he admired in Fourier's work. Muiron possessed, in short, many of the gifts and limitations of a meticulous and loyal petty functionary.[12]

One quality, however, set Muiron apart from his colleagues at the Besançon Prefecture: he was totally deaf. Ever since the childhood accident that had cost him his hearing, he had been an omnivorous reader. His memory was good and he had acquired an early mastery of geography and several of the exact sciences. But his tastes ran particularly to the uplifting—to works on religion and philosophy—and during his adolescence he had found a solitary happiness in the practice of "the most austere virtues." By the end of the Empire, however, a series of severe illnesses had made the consolations of literature and philosophy seem increasingly vain. In 1814 he underwent a spiritual crisis of which he wrote an account two decades later under the pseudonym of Virtomnius (anagram for Just Muiron).

> His wide reading had sometimes satisfied his intellect but almost never his heart. In vain he had sought in books a satisfying definition of happiness, an adequate explanation of the causes of evil. . . . [In the theories of the day] Virtomnius found no more than scattered and uncoordinated fragments, which constituted, in their learned complication, a universal incoherence. He felt in 1814 that a deadly disgust and a universal skepticism were beginning to master his soul. Life was becoming a burden to him. In a few months he would have put an end to it if new studies had not led him back to *hope* and *faith*.[13]

It was a partial cure of his frequent maladies—though not of his deafness—by animal magnetism that put Muiron back on the road to moral recovery. This cure inspired him to study the theoretical writings of Mesmer, Puységur, and Lavater, in which he found his "first indications of the true laws of humanity in the present life, especially from the standpoint of physiology and psychology." Muiron then went on to the theosophists, Madame Guyon, Swedenborg, Saint-Martin, Fabre d'Olivet—"sublime writers . . . who are called illuminists by cold and narrow-minded people who do not understand them." But still he found something missing, something too abstract in their writings.

> They had nothing to say about the most efficacious means of realizing their plans, of carrying out their ideas by making them pass from the realm of possibility to that of action.[14]

It was at this point on his spiritual itinerary that Muiron encountered the *Quatre mouvements;* and for him, as for Felix Bernard, it seemed to "complete" the theories of the theosophists. The new dimension that Fourier added to their writings was precisely his preoccupation with the "realization" of his plan—with the transition from "possibility" to "action."

As he read the *Quatre mouvements* Muiron began to see order in his past readings and to detect a certainty that had hitherto eluded him.

> All that he had read, studied, learned for the past fifteen years . . . the whole philosophical chaos that encumbered his mind was bathed in a shaft of light he had not dared hope for. It all came clear as if by enchantment. Doubt fled from his mind: Virtomnius at last understood the causes of evil and error. He felt that he was going to learn the *sense* and the *purpose* of everything.[15]

Hastening to tell his friends about the work, Muiron found that his enthusiasm was not universally shared. Some, like Weiss, were unable to get beyond the title page. Others who had perused the book—and they included "men of age and experience"—were dismayed by it; a few even accused its author of "lunacy." The general reaction was hostility or bemused indifference. There were a few exceptions, however. Raymond was one; another was Muiron's friend, Désiré-Adrien Gréa, the son of a wealthy landowner in the Jura and, like Muiron, a partisan of animal magnetism and theosophy. It turned out that Gréa had already heard of the *Quatre mouvements:* his father owned a copy. Gréa read the book at Muiron's behest and was intrigued by it. Although he could never muster up anything like Muiron's zeal for the doctrine, Gréa was to become in his later years as a deputy one of the most influential allies of the Fourierist movement.★

During the two years that followed his discovery of the *Quatre mouvements* Muiron continued to talk about the book whenever he could find an audience, and he soon became known in Besançon as a "zealous partisan" of the theory of passionate attraction.[16] Muiron also attempted to get in touch with Fourier. But since he had signed himself only as "M. Charles, at Lyon," this was no easy task. It was not until the beginning of 1816—apparently with the help of Fourier's nephew, Georges de Rubat—that Muiron finally managed to determine the author's whereabouts.

In February 1816, shortly after Fourier's arrival in Bugey, Muiron wrote him an initial letter telling of the impression the *Quatre mouvements* had made on him and asking for news of the subscription it was meant to open. Although this letter went unanswered, Muiron persisted. In mid-April he had another letter delivered personally to Fourier by none other than Garin de Lamorflanc, Fanny de Rubat's future husband. This time he received a reply in which Fourier described his tribulations since 1808 and his plans for the future.

> The subscription for the founding of a canton of Harmony has not been opened [wrote Fourier]. In 1808 the journals were hostile to the announcement and made sport of the theory of attraction before it was published or known. I resolved at the time to let the French undeceive themselves by the misfortunes that lay in store for them and not to tell them of the discovery until they had paid a ransom of a million heads for the impertinent reception they gave to the announcement.
>
> The year 1813 brought full payment of the tribute. But since that time circumstances have been unfavorable for the publication of such an extraordinary discovery, and I have not thought of bringing it to light. It was only last winter that I retired here to attend to the matter. . . .
>
> Since you are interested in the publication of the treatise on

★Désiré-Adrien Gréa (1787–1863) succeeded his wife's uncle, Jean-Emmanuelle Jobez, as deputy from the Department of the Jura in 1828, and held a seat in the Chamber until 1834. He also sat—well to the right of his cousin Victor Considerant—in the Constituent Assembly of 1848. Although his enthusiasm for the theory of passionate attraction was always somewhat tepid, he did help Muiron secure loans for the publication of Fourier's works. In the election campaign of 1831 he was attacked as a "partisan of Fourierism and magnetism." *L'Impartial,* III, 20 (June 9, 1831).

attraction, I can tell you that it will not appear until 1818 and only then if it gains the approval of the censors. But they will find in the work such enormous advantages for France that they will have no hesitation about accepting it.

As to the generally negative response to the *Quatre mouvements* at Besançon, Fourier expressed no surprise. He observed that Franche-Comté had long enjoyed a deserved reputation as "the Boeotia of France."[17]

Although perfectly courteous, Fourier's letter was dry, haughty, and a bit laconic in tone. It might have dampened the enthusiasm of another man. But to Muiron it seemed "an expression of frankness, modesty, and good will," and he wrote a long reply.[18] Fourier reciprocated—somewhat more warmly this time—and within a few months a regular correspondence had been established. It was to continue until the end of Fourier's life.

II

It is one of the misfortunes of Fourier's modern biographer that almost all of the several hundred letters constituting his correspondence with Muiron have been lost. Fortunately, however, Charles Pellarin, the "official" biographer appointed by the Ecole Sociétaire, had access to the complete collection and recognized its value. Pellarin drew heavily on the correspondence in the preparation of his biography, and he published long excerpts from it as appendixes to several of the editions that the book went through. For the period 1816–1820 these excerpts are substantial, and they cast much light both on the blossoming of Fourier's relationship with Muiron and on the preparation of the *Grand Traité*.

Muiron was an assiduous correspondent, and he filled his letters with news of his efforts to proselytize for Fourier in Franche-Comté, as well as innumerable queries about theoretical problems and about the progress of Fourier's work. His meticulousness and his passion for detail were at least as pronounced as Fourier's, and he allowed none of the omissions and ambiguities of the *Quatre mouvements* to go unchallenged. In one letter, for instance, he wrote:

> What bothers me most right now about the organization of the Phalanx is the means of determining doubtful cases of paternity

once the serial order is established. What sort of research can be undertaken? How is one to resolve the difficulties created by the concurrence of several lovers at the moment of conception?[19]

Although Fourier often had to apologize for the tardiness of his replies ("When I have a problem on my mind, I have the habit of forgetting about my correspondence until it is resolved"),[20] he was obviously flattered by the disciple's interest. At the same time, however, he often had to moderate Muiron's high hopes for an immediate practical application of the theory. He also commented wryly on Muiron's inability to emancipate himself completely from his old, "civilized" habits of thought. It took some time, for instance, before Muiron managed to silence all his doubts about the origin of evil, and Fourier had to remind him repeatedly that "the question is not to know its origin but its remedy." But sometimes the master became impatient: "Your zeal is misdirected," he informed the disciple in 1818. "You stop at accessory matters and forget the most important points. You value the brushwood of subtle metaphysics, which yields nothing but skepticism."[21]

There was one symptom of Muiron's entanglement in the metaphysical "brushwood" that Fourier found particularly irritating. This was the disciple's continuing addiction to the esoteric writings that had first put him on the road to spiritual recovery. Muiron's espousal of Fourier's theory did not alter his conviction that Swedenborg, Saint-Martin, and Fabre d'Olivet had "occasionally grasped the truth"; and in his letters he frequently urged Fourier to seek "verifications" of his ideas in their works. Fourier, who now hardly read anything but the newspapers, was not interested. "I won't take the trouble to consult the books you mention to me," he replied on one occasion. "I have tried out these verifications on a few works and they were no help at all."[22]* Nevertheless, throughout the first few years of their correspondence, Muiron kept plying Fourier with citations from the great theosophists. He was particularly enthusiastic about the "science and erudition" of

---

*In a manuscript dating from the same period Fourier wrote: "I have been urged to read a number of works by such ideologists and archaeologists as Court de Gébelin (*Monde primitif*), Dupuis (*Origine des cultes*), and Saint-Martin on I don't know what, since he doesn't give any titles to his chapters; you hope to find out the subject as you read him, but after having finished you still don't know what he's talking about. All that I have found in the works of these savants is the misuse of science, a tricky erudition, a mania for filling volumes and fabricating systems." "Des Transitions," *La Phalange, VI* (1847), 210.

Fabre d'Olivet, whose commentaries on the Bible and on the *Vers dorés* of Pythagoras had buttressed his faith in Divine Providence, human perfectibility, and the essential goodness of the passions. In 1820 he even proposed the publication of a work in which Fourier's cosmogony would be "vindicated" by its conformity with Fabre d'Olivet's inter-pretation of the Book of Genesis.[23] Fourier testily rejected this proposal, claiming that the sacred books were "two-edged swords" that could only compromise the work of a true inventor. In any case, he had it on the authority of the *Journal des débats* that Fabre d'Olivet did not know Hebrew.[24]

Fourier usually replied angrily whenever Muiron urged him to seek "confirmations" of his theory in the writings of the philosophers. He had no need of "debasing" his discovery by appeals to the doubtful authority of "charlatans" and "quacks." He had made it all very clear to the disciple in a letter of 1817.

> You speak to me of the means of reconciling my theory with those of various sects, without compromising their doctrines, without supposing any retraction on their part. . . . What have those sciences produced in the last three thousand years? Indi-gence, knavery, oppression, and carnage. If I reconcile myself with those doctrines, the results will be the same. I will not do it.[25]

Throughout his life Fourier continued to insist upon the uniqueness of his own intellectual enterprise and to dismiss the universal systems of the philosophers as sterile "hoax" and "verbiage." Muiron was upset by these outbursts, but he never lost his occult predilections.*

During its first two years the correspondence between Fourier and Muiron remained formal. Fourier addressed his disciple simply as "Monsieur," and though he answered all Muiron's questions about doctrinal matters, he had little to say about his difficulties with the treatise and nothing at all about his quarrels with the Rubat girls. Fou-rier always remained reticent about his private life. But after the move to Belley in February 1817, which permitted him to get down to work on the body of his *Grand Traité,* he kept Muiron posted on the progress

---

*During the 1820s Muiron continued to organize study groups on the *Arcana Celesta* and to urge Fabre d'Olivet's *Langue hébraïque* on his fellow disciples. His *Nouvelles transac-tions* (1832) was liberally sprinkled with citations from Fabre's translation of the Bible and Saint-Martin's *Crocodile.* See Muiron to Clarisse Vigoureux, August 4, 1827, AN 10AS 4 (4), and Muiron to Fourier, June 29, 1832, AN 10AS 4 (5).

of his work. In October he wrote that "the *Traité de l'attraction* advances, though slowly. I have only reached the ninth of the thirty-two parts of the work. Various problems of which I despaired have been solved."[26] Two months later the treatise was still progressing "very slowly," but Fourier took heart in reflecting upon the distance he had traveled since the composition of the *Quatre mouvements*. After quitting Lyon he wrote:

> I lost ten months in working on a faulty outline, which got me involved in a most inadequate abridgment. Since then I have decided to adopt the fully elaborated outline, which at first frightened me by the quantity of the problems to be solved. This arduous task advances little by little, and of the thirty-two parts I am at the tenth. Each day I discover new beauties, and everything is marvellously linked to the [idea of] unity of system. I can now say that the science was but an embryo when I published the prospectus. If I manage as well as I hope in putting this theory to rights, it will necessarily cause a sensation, not by the prose of the author, but by the magnificence of the subject.[27]

Although Fourier believed that two years' work still lay ahead of him, he and Muiron now began to discuss the publication of the treatise. It was obviously going to be an enormous work; at the end of 1817 Fourier wrote that it would fill four thick volumes, and by October of the following year his estimate had risen to seven volumes of five hundred pages each. Muiron, who was eager to see Fourier in print as soon as possible, urged him to consider publishing the treatise in installments, as he had in fact proposed in the *Quatre mouvements*. But Fourier's thinking had changed. "If you send your regiments to battle one by one, they will be beaten," he wrote in February 1818. He had now decided to publish everything at once. The piecemeal method was "suitable for compilations," he observed, "but not for an original discovery, which must strike a great blow and present at the outset a whole body of doctrine and all the proofs."[28]

Until this point the relationship between Fourier and Muiron had remained purely epistolary. In the spring of 1818, however, Muiron received a letter from Joseph Bruand, an old friend from the Ecole Centrale who had been serving as subprefect at Issoire. Bruand announced that he had been transferred to the Subprefecture at Belley and asked Muiron to come and serve for a few months as his secretary. Barely a week later Muiron received a letter from Fourier also urging him to come to Belley. Although Muiron's deafness made personal contacts difficult, two years' correspondence had made him eager to meet Fourier. Thus he accepted the double invitation. In May of 1818 he took a leave of absence from his job at Besançon and set out for Belley to work for Bruand and to meet Charles Fourier.[29]

The first encounter between the two was a great success. Fourier received Muiron graciously in his small room at the Parrat-Brillats'; it was so cluttered with notes and manuscripts that there was hardly room to sit down. But Fourier made space for his disciple, and they spent long hours together—the one poring over his master's finished cahiers, and the other hard at work on the problems of love and gastronomy, which formed the final sections of the first half (or Major Octave) of the treatise. It was an overwhelming experience for Muiron, something approaching a second initiation. For the theory he found elaborated in Fourier's multicolored cahiers was vastly more complete and systematically worked out, more explicit in its details and more rigorous in its proofs, than the *Quatre mouvements* had led him to expect. Sometimes he found it difficult to follow Fourier's imagination in its flight. But the master was at hand to guide him through all complexities. Although conversation was at first a problem, the two soon hit upon the expedient of having Fourier write out answers to his deaf disciple's questions. A number of his scribbled notes to Muiron have been preserved, and they lend immediacy to our impression of this first encounter. "It is always a pleasure for me to reply to your observations," writes Fourier in one note. "Don't worry about coming to ask me questions whenever you like." In another written conversation Fourier exhorts his disciple: "You apply yourself too little to questions of attraction and especially to those concerning the mechanism of the passional series, their property of stimulating industry, economy, all that is useful. These are beautiful problems and they merit the attention of a disciple."[30]

Muiron's stay at Belley lasted throughout the summer; and this gave him ample time to make arrangements with Fourier concerning the publication of the *Grand Traité*. He had decided to do all he could to help pay for the printing costs. Although he knew that they were likely to be beyond his own means as well as Fourier's, he believed he could convince friends in Franche-Comté to help. In addition, the wife of one of his colleagues at the prefecture, Claude-François Mourgeon, was the owner of Besançon's principal printing house.★ Certain that favorable terms could be arranged, he urged Fourier to honor Franche-Comté by publishing his treatise at Besançon. Fourier was dubious at first. He knew the perils of publishing in the provinces, and it is doubtful in any case that he had the slightest desire to honor "the Boeotia of France." But his own income, the nine-hundred-franc annuity left him in his mother's will, was meager, and he had little choice about the matter. He finally accepted Muiron's offer.

Muiron left Belley in early September 1818, and he wasted no time in soliciting money from his wealthy friends. On his way back to Besançon he visited Gréa and another friend named Puvis at their country estates in the Jura. He described Fourier's treatise to them in glowing terms, and as he later put it, "his impassioned words made them share his conviction. From then on he counted on their support in facilitating his publishing venture."[31] In Besançon Muiron received further encouragement from a number of friends, among them an old acquaintance of Fourier's, the ex-Jacobin Pierre-Joseph Briot.† Mourgeon and his wife were also sympathetic. Soon all seemed in readiness at Besançon, and it only remained for Fourier to complete the treatise.

III

As Muiron was soliciting financial backing in Besançon, Fourier kept hard at work on the *Grand Traité*.[32] By the end of 1818 he had finished the first half or Major Octave, and he could boast that the most difficult stage of composition lay behind him. For the portion that remained, the

---

★Claude-François Mourgeon was a *conseilleur de préfecture* at Besançon. The printing house was run under his wife's former name, Madame *veuve* Daclin.

†Pierre-Joseph Briot (1771–1827), whom Fourier had attempted to interest in some of his first projects of social reform, sat in the Council of Five Hundred during the Directory. Under Napoleon he became a counselor of state in Italy. After Waterloo he professed to make his peace with the Bourbons, and when Muiron talked with him he was receiving a regular salary from Decazes for "secret services." At the same time, however, he seems to have played a leading role in bringing Carbonarism back to France, and until his death he remained interested in various projects for the reform of banking and commerce. In 1820 Muiron described him to Fourier as "a man who seems to dream of nothing but *association* . . . and who should be able to give you much help." Muiron to Fourier, October 4, 1820, AN 10AS 25 (2). The question of Briot's relations with Fourier bears further study. See M. Dayet, *Un Révolutionnaire franc-comtois: Pierre-Joseph Briot* (Paris, 1960).

Minor Octave, was to focus primarily on subsidiary branches of his theory: the cosmogony, the critique of civilization, and the analysis of the transitional or "mixed" stages prior to the advent of Harmony. Most of the important doctrinal problems relating to Full Harmony had been dealt with in the Major Octave. It was there that Fourier had undertaken to discuss the organization of the Phalanstery itself, and to set forth a definitive and minutely detailed exposition of the theory of passionate attraction. In five initial sections he had presented the rudiments of the theory. He had characterized each of the twelve radical passions, revealing their specific properties and the "exponential degrees of intensity" to which each was subject. He had outlined the system of education in Harmony and discussed in an elementary way the theory of attractive labor and the functioning of the industrial groups and series.

In the second book of the Major Octave Fourier had entered the realm of "superior" harmonies and "high synthesis." The seven sections that constituted this book were the most difficult of the whole treatise, and it was not until his move to Belley that Fourier had been able to make any headway with them. His first breakthrough had come in March 1817 with the discovery of the system of passionate accords.[33] During the two years that followed he had devoted himself almost exclusively to working out an analysis of the most complex and subtle varieties of passionate interaction, the "transcendent" accords and *ralliements* necessary for the maintenance of a perfectly equilibrated series. He had worked up his fragmentary discussion of gastronomy in the *Quatre mouvements* into a systematic analysis of the role good food and good mealtime companionship would play in promoting intragroup harmony in the new order. Following his discovery in 1817 of the theory of harmonious sentiments (*céladonies*), he had also been able to add new refinements to his analysis of the social uses of love.[34] All of this was now complete; and Fourier's manuscript, which filled a multitude of colored notebooks, already ran to several thousand closely written pages. It constituted a veritable *summa* of the doctrine of passionate attraction.

With the Major Octave behind him, Fourier was ready by the beginning of 1819 to begin work on the secondary problems that he had relegated to the Minor Octave of his treatise. At the outset he planned to discuss the "societary approximations," the intermediary forms of social organization that were (possibly) to precede the advent of Full Harmony.[35] The problems that now confronted him were familiar. In the *Quatre mouvements* he had left some ambiguity about the means by which the transition from civilization to Harmony would take place. He had insisted that the time was ripe for an immediate "leap" into Full Harmony. But he had also entertained the possibility that humanity *might* be destined to pass through two transitional stages. To the first of these periods he had given the name of Guarantism. It would be marked, he said, by various reforms in sexual mores and commercial relations that would serve to ease mankind "by gradual degrees" into a somewhat more advanced period, which he described simply as "Vague Series. The Dawn of Happiness." Like everything else in the *Quatre mouvements,* Fourier's discussion of these two periods was fragmentary and ambiguous; he merely suggested that it might be possible during the second transitional period to make a trial of the theory of passionate attraction on a smaller scale than that of a full-sized Phalanx. If such a "reduced trial" were successful, it would serve to verify his calculus and hence stimulate interest in the founding of a real Phalanx.[36]

Prior to 1819 Fourier had never bothered to see whether such a reduced trial was actually feasible. He had devoted all his efforts to the study of the ideal order in which the passions were perfectly harmonized: the full Phalanx, which associated twelve to sixteen hundred individuals of varying age, wealth, aptitudes, and intelligence in carefully nuanced groups and series. The study of mere "approximations" seemed a waste of time. "I was so satisfied," wrote Fourier later, "with the theory of full-scale association . . . that I didn't even dream of seeking something *less* impressive."[37] Furthermore, he believed that there was an essential, qualitative difference between the transitional stages and those of Harmony. He had long assumed that any "reduced" form of association would not allow full expression to all of the twelve radical passions; and he simply took it for granted that attraction could not come into play so long as one of them was fettered.[38]

Thus it was mainly for the sake of theoretical completeness, and perhaps also as a sort of *jeu d'esprit,* that in February 1819 Fourier began his analysis of the transitional stages with a consideration of the problem of the reduced trial.[39] But he soon became absorbed by the problem. For ten weeks he experimented with ways of harmonizing the passions on a more modest scale than he had hitherto envisaged, of devising a new system of association that would enable him to do without passions and harmonies he had hitherto regarded as essential. He tried suppressing all "transcendent" accords that required the participation of rare passional types. He also attempted to eliminate certain activities and some grandiose ceremonies that required the interaction of numerous groups and series. Then he thought of focusing his groups and series on a few branches of industry. Rejecting extensive cultivation, he concentrated on vegetable gardens, fruit orchards, and poultry. Finally, on April 3, 1819, Fourier was able to inform Muiron that he had worked out a system of "mixed association," a model of passionate equilibrium appropriate to associations of only five or six hundred members.[40] This discovery was "less brilliant" than full association, he wrote, but "much more economical." It could indeed serve as the basis for a reduced trial, as a practical and inexpensive means of verifying the calculus of passionate attraction.

Having discovered that a reduced trial was actually feasible, Fourier was reluctant to stop short at mixed association. During the month of April he began to work out an even more modest system of association that would have the added advantage of being fully compatible with civilized mores.[41] Eager to see what he could devise without the stimuli of sex and luxury, he decided to cut down on amorous and gastronomic revelry and to suppress almost all but the purely industrial groups and series. On Good Friday 1819, after several weeks of arduous calculations, he made a great breakthrough. As he jubilantly wrote Muiron on May 11:

> I must tell you about an event of great importance for my discovery. On Good Friday I hit upon the equilibrium of simple association, a theory I did not think attainable. . . . Having reached the fourteenth key, the second in the Major Octave, I conceived the bizarre and lucky idea of stripping down or castrating association in three ways.
>
> First: Instead of establishing graduated harmonies between rich and poor, I utilized only the poor and people of plebeian habits, excluding families with no more than a thousand francs of income.
>
> Second: Instead of employing modulations from the Major and Minor Octaves, I eliminated the whole Minor Octave, all the modulations in love and familism, the minor cardinal passions.
>
> Third: Instead of working out the passionate equilibrium in

direct proportion to the masses and in inverse proportion to the square of the distances, I reduced the equilibrium to the direct proportion of the masses and suppressed the inverse proportion of the square of the distances.

By means of this triple mutilation we attain an equilibrium that is perfect although extremely simple.[42]

As the rationale for a reduced trial, this new system of simple association had two distinct advantages. In the first place, it did not require the participation of the rich.

> The result [wrote Fourier] is that we can try out association with a handful of those poverty-stricken families you see emigrating every day, embarking for America from the ports of Germany and England, or indeed with a few poor peasants such as one finds in the villages of Bons [near Belley] or Bregille [near Besançon]. . . . This opens up possibilities very different from those created by composite association, which requires a whole range of inequalities, from the poor to the millionaire, from the ignoramus to the savant, etc.[43]

The second advantage of simple association was that it did not rely upon harmonies involving the passions of love and familism. For these were the passions least understood in civilization. Having managed to do without them, Fourier could describe simple association as "an *entirely moral* institution" with which even the Spanish Inquisition could find no fault.

Fourier concluded his letter to Muiron by announcing a change in plans.

> Since I am now provided with a means of trial so economical, so appropriate to the tastes and prejudices of the age, I have resolved to publish it separately, and to issue next year a *partial* treatise, which will outline the system of simple association even while it hints at the composite. The rich will demand the composite the day after they have seen the simple from which they are excluded and in which the poor will be manifestly more happy than the sybarites are now.[44]

This letter to Muiron has been cited at such length because the discovery it announced marked a great turning point—the last decisive one—in Fourier's intellectual life. Ever since his arrival in Bugey his sole concern had been to elaborate a systematic body of doctrine, and such theoretical innovations as he had made prior to 1819 only served to widen the scope and increase the complexity of that doctrine. Prompted in large part by sheer intellectual curiosity and relying when in doubt on the trusty principle of analogy, Fourier had sought in writing the *Grand Traité* to provide a key to all the branches of "the destinies." During this time he had given little thought to the actual founding of a Phalanx. When Muiron expressed impatience about the matter in 1816, he replied that "first of all a regular treatise, a body of doctrine is required."[45] He believed that his main task was to work out *everything* in advance; he was sure that the "realization" would pose no problems if only he could first elaborate the system of the passions in adequate detail.

It was precisely Fourier's desire for theoretical completeness that had induced him to devote a substantial portion of the treatise to the question of societary approximations. But his discovery, while working on this question, of the system of simple association brought about a change in his preoccupations. The problem of realization now began to dominate his thoughts. Convinced that he possessed a foolproof and economical scheme for the immediate application of his theory, Fourier was henceforth to become increasingly absorbed in the search for a backer, for the rich capitalist who would help launch the first trial Phalanx. Henceforth his main concern was not to widen the scope of his doctrine—this was the last of his "discoveries"—but to simplify it and to scale it down to "the tastes and prejudices of the age."

9

The Preparation of the Treatise

DURING HIS early years in Bugey Fourier often reflected bitterly on the failure of the *Quatre mouvements*. Even his friends in Lyon had criticized him for burying his sober reflections on commerce and industry beneath a mountain of wild speculations on love and cosmogony. They had urged him to withhold his extravagant ideas and to devote his future works to the more palatable elements of the doctrine, notably the theory of industrial association. But this was impossible. The theory was a total and indivisible truth, and to remove any one element was to damage the whole. "When they advise me to mutilate my theory," he wrote in 1816, "to accommodate it to the small-mindedness of the century, it is as if they told Praxiteles to disfigure his Venus." He knew what Praxiteles would have answered, and it was his own reply to those who urged him to cut his theory into pieces to render it more acceptable: "I'd rather break the arms of all the philosophers than those of my Venus; if they don't know how to appreciate her, I'll bury her rather than disfigure her." Philosophy could go back to the depths of hell for all he cared. "As for me, I'll bury my theory a hundred times rather than alter a single syllable."[1]

Fourier did in fact bury his theory for fourteen years. Between the ages of thirty-six and fifty his published works amounted to a grand total of two newspaper articles. In both cases he broke the silence only to heap abuse on his critics and to boast that the neglect of his discoveries had cost his contemporaries a million lives lost in the Napoleonic wars.[2] From 1808 to 1815 Fourier was content to "punish" France by his silence. After his move to the country at the end of 1815, however, he at last found the time and energy to work out on paper the vision that had been haunting him since 1799: that of elaborating a "total science," a complete and organic explanation of the universe based on the theory of passionate attraction. His silence during the early years of the Restoration was less a vengeful one than a reflection of his absorption in the task.

Although the discovery in 1819 of simple association did not induce Fourier to abandon his dream of someday publishing a comprehensive theoretical treatise, it did alter his thinking about the tactical questions of the "realization" of his theory and its presentation to the public. Since simple association was both economical and "appropriate to the tastes and prejudices of the age," he now saw his task as one of salesmanship. His most pressing concern was no longer to work out "all the proofs," but to make his ideas palatable to the public. For the rest of his life he was to try to "mutilate" and simplify his doctrine in very much the sense he had so scornfully rejected a few years earlier.

In May of 1819, while he was exulting over the discovery of simple association, Fourier wrote Muiron that his "partial treatise" would appear the following year. In fact the preparation of the work took much longer than that. There were times when he rebelled against the idea of "mutilating" his theory and went back to work on the *Grand Traité*. At other moments he believed that even a simplified presentation would fall flat unless it was heralded by a vast publicity campaign. In 1819 and 1820 he was to dissipate much of his energy in the composition of brief newspaper articles (none of which was published) designed to awaken interest in his forthcoming book. At the same time Fourier also managed to get himself involved in local affairs, which distracted his attention from his work.

I

By the summer of 1819 Fourier found himself once again embroiled in a family quarrel. This episode, a falling-out with the Parrat-Brillats, is less well documented than his misadventures with the Rubat girls at Talissieu.[3] But what seems to have brought matters to a head was his ill-advised meddling in a marriage planned for his niece, Agathe Parrat-Brillat. The circumstances were similar to those of his 1813 intervention in negotiations concerning Fanny de Rubat. Agathe was no longer young and her mother was eager to have her married. The candidate in question was a young man from Besançon named Combet. Fourier knew the Combets, and he subsequently claimed that he himself had suggested the marriage in 1816. But when negotiations became serious, he made detailed inquiries. He soon became convinced that the Combets were "not the least bit interested in the girl, whose dowry was the only thing they wanted." He advised his brother-in-law to seek another suitor. "I could not be more explicit with Parrat-Brillat," he wrote later, "for he thinks his wife is the Real Marvel of the World. . . . He trembles before her and replies to her invectives: 'Eh! What an idiot I am! Ah! Isn't my wife intelligent!'"

Despite Fourier's efforts, plans for the marriage went ahead. But then, in August of 1819, a *chanson* began to circulate around Belley. Entitled "The Bride of Three Months," it prophesied that the horns of a cuckold would sprout on the forehead of any husband of Agathe; and the refrain "Just like my mother does" cast Sophie Parrat-Brillat's husband in the same inglorious role. Sophie naturally was furious; and, not unnaturally, she pointed an accusing finger at her brother (who had in fact assigned Philibert a place in his hierarchy of cuckolds). She charged him with having "defamed" her household, and she wrote to friends in Besançon that Agathe had "fallen under his blows." Fourier maintained his innocence, and eventually Sophie's wrath subsided. But this episode did compromise Fourier's relations with his sister's family; thereafter his presence was not entirely welcome.

In addition to such domestic squabbles Fourier became involved the following year in local affairs of another sort. Toward the beginning of 1820 he received word from Joseph Bruand, the local subprefect, that an agricultural society was to be formed at Belley and that his name had been included on the membership list. Although he had acquired a certain local notoriety, Fourier was surprised by the invitation. (It may have been suggested by Bruand's friend, Just Muiron.) But he accepted it eagerly.

Like many of the *académies d'arrondissement* created during the early Restoration, the Société d'agriculture, sciences et arts de Belley enjoyed an ephemeral existence.[4] It is remembered chiefly because Fourier belonged to it, and the only evidence of his participation in its sessions is contained in two notes conserved among his papers. The first is a letter from Bruand inviting "C. Fourier, man of letters," to a meeting at the subprefecture on Sunday, February 27, 1820, "to establish our rules." The second is a printed invitation to the meeting of July 30, 1820, with a handwritten note asking when Fourier might wish to present a report to the society on his own work.[5]

Among Fourier's papers, however, there are also several manuscript drafts of a twenty-page *Note remise à l'Académie de Belley*, dated May 28, 1820, and a much longer *Mémoire à l'Académie de Belley*.[6] From a theoretical point of view these texts are interesting chiefly because they provide insight into Fourier's efforts to formulate a systematic critique of peasant small-holding analogous to the critique of commerce that he had already worked out at Lyon. They include an analysis of the "twelve principal vices" of agricultural techniques and conditions in the region of Bugey that is more precise and detailed than anything to be found in his published writings.[7] They also afford a glimpse into Fourier's methods as a publicist, an illustration of the manner in which he tried to adapt his presentation of the doctrine to the requirements of a particular audience.

In the longer *Mémoire* Fourier enumerated the diverse "obstacles" opposing any project of agricultural reform initiated in the provinces. These included the lack of capital, the prejudice and routine of provincial society, the poverty of the farmers, and the ignorance of the Parisian savants who would be passing judgment on any of their proposals. Just as the recent attempt to establish a tree nursery near Belley had failed because of local prejudice and lack of funds, these obstacles would assure the failure of any subsequent project of piecemeal agricultural reform. "Plans for local improvement will fail," Fourier wrote, "if they are not linked to a general system of operations." Another difficulty was posed by "the Parisians." They would be sure to greet the proposals of any provincial society with a torrent of scorn, abuse, and satire. The spirit of satire was an endemic French vice; and to avoid becoming its victim the Academy of Belley would have to make a striking debut in the learned world. The "affaire d'éclat" that Fourier had in mind was the opening of a competition—to be described in a brochure he offered to write himself—for the discovery of a "new industrial compass" that would serve to correct the evils of agriculture. Fourier did not wish to prejudice the deliberations of the academy. But he advised them that they could count on "at least one contestant who will not be frightened by the army of four hundred thousand philosophical volumes."

It is doubtful that Fourier's proposals were actually discussed by the academy. In any case, they came to nothing. No competition was held and no individual member of the society emerged to sponsor Fourier's plans. Indeed, the academy itself was probably a very short-lived venture. For Joseph Bruand, who appears to have been its organizer, died prematurely in 1820, and the academy most likely succumbed not long after.[8] There is a faintly nostalgic passage in Fourier's *Traité* that can stand as the epitaph to Fourier's dealings with the Academy of Belley: "The academy of which I was a member has since lost its richest associate, D. d'A., a man who enjoyed an income of sixty thousand francs and had just one son. He could easily have afforded to bequeath a year of his revenue to the society."[9]

II

By the fall of 1820 Fourier was still not very far along in his work on the treatise. But he was becoming restless and eager to "entrer en scène." He had already begun to send the Paris journals brief articles designed to call attention to his forthcoming book. In one of these *annonces,* sent to the *Bibliothèque universelle,* he promised that the book would provide proof of the existence of "five unknown planets."[10] In another article, meant for the *Censeur européen,* he announced that the book would include a scheme whereby the English could liquidate their national debt.[11] When these articles failed to appear in print, Fourier talked of making a trip to Paris to "scout out the terrain" in person. In September he wrote Muiron, requesting letters of introduction to some of the disciple's friends in the capital. Muiron, however, urged Fourier to come first to Besançon. There were final arrangements to be made for the book's publication; and now there was also a small group of disciples at Besançon who were eager to meet Fourier.

> I have prepared for you a gathering of *twelve* [wrote Muiron].
> During the time you can give to us you will be what in all your
> calculations you call the *thirteenth.* I might say maliciously that
> this is yet another analogy with the traditional dogmas on the
> Last Supper.[12]

Fourier accepted Muiron's invitation. Postponing his trip to Paris, he left Belley for Besançon in the latter part of December 1820. It was during this visit that the two made final arrangements for the publication of the treatise. Muiron agreed formally to handle all financial matters and Fourier promised to have the manuscript ready for printing by the following year.

Fourier's visit to Besançon lasted something over a month. During this time he stayed with his sister, Lubine Clerc. Now a widow with two grown daughters, Lubine was still living at the Hôtel des Gouverneurs, the sumptuous town house on the rue de l'Orme-de-Chamars that her husband had bought with *assignats* in 1793. After the death of her husband, who had remained to the last the zealous Jacobin of the Year II,★ Lubine had had difficulties with her daughters; and in 1818 she was obliged to enlist Fourier's aid in dissuading the elder of the two, Cornélie, from entering a nunnery. Fourier complied somewhat too enthusiastically for his sister's taste: his correspondence includes an angry letter from Lubine expressing shock at Fourier's "fulminations" against Cornélie's religious zeal and denying his "unfounded" allegations that his niece was in fact carrying on with one of the local priests.[13] By 1820, however, this episode was forgotten, and Fourier received a warm welcome from his Besançon sister. He brought his manuscripts with him, and Lubine recalled later that he was no less touchy about them than he had been as a child about his floral arrangements. "Sometime before publishing his book," she remembered, "he came to spend a part of the winter with me at the Hôtel des Gouverneurs where I was then living. His room was actually out of bounds. He wished no one to enter it, and he forbade anyone to touch his papers, which were scattered about on all the furniture, tables, chairs, and dressers."[14]

This visit enabled Fourier and Just Muiron to put their relationship

---

★Lubine's husband, Léger Clerc, had been a member of Besançon's Comité révolutionnaire in 1793 and 1794. During the Empire he was known as the leader of a little group of *éxagérés* whom the police had allowed to grumble harmlessly in the back room of the Café Marullier; and his name had appeared in the reports of the prefect, Jean de Bry, as one of Besançon's "*êtres tarés* . . . who miss the time when yelling took the place of reason . . . [and] who call themselves enslaved because they no longer hold their fellow citizens in chains." As the Austrians besieged Besançon in April of 1814, Léger Clerc emerged briefly from the shadows to urge de Bry to save the city by declaring the *levée en masse*. He apparently died a year or two later. See Léonce Pingaud, *Jean de Bry (1760–1835)* (Paris, 1909), 221–222, 346.

on an intimate footing. Although they were never to *tutoyer* each other, Fourier was henceforth to address Muiron in his letters as "mon cher ami." The two spent hours together conversing by means of pencil and paper—the method they had hit upon during their first encounter. Of course most of their conversations had to do with Fourier's theory and with arrangements for the publication of his book. But Fourier also wanted to be brought up to date on local politics. Despite his long absence, he had not lost interest in Bisontine affairs; and in his conversations with Muiron he expressed outrage at "the machinations of the Dijonnais" that had led to the reduction of Besançon's military garrison and to the transfer of its university to Dijon. In his letters Fourier had also frequently asked the disciple for information about new building and other architectural changes that were taking place at Besançon. Now Muiron was able to escort him around the city to view such recent developments as "the additions to our superb library on the rue Saint Maurice." With Muiron's help, Fourier set about measuring the dimensions of the city's streets, squares, buildings, and military installations. He carefully recorded all these measurements, and began work on a project concerning the modernization and embellishment of the city of Besançon, which was to serve for the next decade as one of his principal intellectual diversions.[15]

During his stay at Besançon Fourier's social life was not neglected by his attentive disciple. The Besançon social season was under way, and Muiron succeeded in getting him invited to several formal dances. Fourier's unsuccessful Lyon dancing lessons had not dampened his enthusiasm for such functions. But he enjoyed them best, he said, from the spectator's point of view. Of course he was as serious as ever about the rules of etiquette. "I have a ticket for the ball on Saturday," he wrote Muiron on January 4, 1821. "I suppose I can go in loose pants and wide stockings, the same as to a minister's. I have not brought my silk breeches. Let me know if full dress is required, for I have only blue pants here. If they are not suitable, I won't go."[16]

The lengthy conversations with Muiron and his friends and the distractions provided by the disciple took up most of Fourier's time at Besançon. But he had also come to attend to family matters. For a dispute had arisen over the payment of the nine-hundred-franc annuity, which was his principal means of support.[17] Following the death of Madame Fourrier, the children had rented out the old family house on the Grande rue. Although Fourier had sold his share in the property to his sister, Sophie Parrat-Brillat, in 1815, it was understood that the annuity to which he was still entitled should be paid to him from the income on the house. At first the income it yielded was more than sufficient. But gradually it had fallen into a state of disrepair; and no member of the family was willing to pay for renovations out of fear that the others would fail to reciprocate. After complaining in vain, the tenants stopped paying their rent. By 1819 the annual payments of Fourier's annuity had ceased to arrive, and soon he was writing dunning letters to his relatives and to the family's notary at Besançon. Finally in the fall of 1820 he informed his nephew Georges de Rubat that his patience was exhausted. The house would have to be sold to guarantee payment of his annuity.[18] When Georges failed to reply immediately, Fourier's impatience turned to suspicion and hostility. He began to believe that his relatives were in league to deprive him of his rightful inheritance.[19]

What Fourier learned upon his arrival at Besançon was that property values had declined and that the house could not be sold without a considerable loss. Nevertheless, as he wrote his brother-in-law, Philibert Parrat-Brillat, from Besançon, his mother's will had expressly stipulated that her three daughters—"and in the first place Sophie Parrat-Brillat"— were to be jointly responsible for the payment of the annuity. If the income from the house did not suffice, it would have to be sold and the loss borne by Sophie.[20] Such demands, coming after the dispute over the marriage of Sophie's daughter, further irritated the Parrat-Brillats. A venomous correspondence ensued, with threats of legal action on both sides. Before leaving Besançon, Fourier went to the Registry of Deeds to establish a lien on the house as security for a claim of 15,946 francs representing the capital and back payments due on his annuity.[21]

Several months after Fourier's return to Belley, the house was finally sold for 23,500 francs, and Fourier eventually managed to recoup most of his annuity. But the affair continued to drag on; and more than a year later, with the *Traité de l'association* just coming off the press, Fourier was still insisting on his legal right to claim damages for his sister's failure to honor the terms of his mother's will.[22]

Fourier left Besançon toward the end of January 1821. On the eve of his departure he wrote to Muiron to express "a thousand thanks for the kindnesses you have lavished on me during my stay." He had spent his last morning in "recreational promenades during which I checked all the measurements that had to be examined in accordance with our discussion with M. Lapret," the town architect. They would soon have a chance to talk further about the project for the embellishment of Besançon. But "for the time being," he wrote, that project was of "no importance." Fourier's pressing concern was to ready his manuscript for publication. "Nothing will distract me from my copying. . . . It will begin again as soon as I am back in Belley." Promising to return as soon as he had settled matters with the Parrat-Brillats concerning the sale of the house, Fourier concluded dramatically: "Let us labor together on the great enterprise."[23]

III

Fourier's final stay at Belley lasted close to three months, from the end of January until mid-April 1821. It was not a pleasant time. Upon his return he found that the Parrat-Brillats had "begun to spread any number of calumnies against me." His insistence in demanding the sale of the Besançon house and the full reimbursement of the capital and payments due on his annuity had been the last straw for his sister Sophie. Resurrecting the old quarrels concerning marriage matters and the infamous *chanson,* she had bruited it about town that her brother was a malicious gossip, an enemy of the female sex, that he had accepted the hospitality of her family only to pry into their private lives and to heap public ridicule on her and her daughters. These "gross calumnies" (Fourier *dixit*) had turned the women of Belley against Fourier. The wives of some of his associates on the Academy of Belley refused even to nod when they met on the street. Affairs reached such a pass that Fourier finally advised the mayor of Belley of "the intrigues and slanderous schemes" of his sister. Since some of his fellow academicians "might have lent an ear to these calumnies," he felt he should offer his resignation from the academy. But he promised in due course to write "a brief memorandum" that would "unravel" the whole affair and "reduce many an intriguer and play actor to his just value."[24]

Such was the atmosphere in which Fourier prepared his treatise for publication. He had explained to Muiron that the text was virtually ready; he needed only to select and transcribe material already contained in his manuscript notebooks. But now that he was back at work, he could not resist the temptation to make additions. By way of introduction he decided to expand the brief article on the English debt he had sent to the *Censeur européen* into an ample twenty-page "Dédicace aux nations endettées." On February 10 he had only just completed this introduction, and he informed Muiron that his work was going slowly. He made only an oblique reference to his problems with the Parrat-Brillats: "Other matters have distracted me a bit these days."[25]

Eager to see Fourier's book finished, Muiron assumed that he had been distracted by *amusettes* such as his plan for the embellishment of Besançon. "You are mistaken," replied Fourier on March 7, "I only give to these matters the time that must be employed *en variante*." But there were new difficulties to report. In trying to write sixteen pages in a single day, he had sprained his right hand. In any case, Fourier was not merely transcribing from his manuscript notebooks. He was rewriting and reorganizing his material. Now that the establishment of a trial Phalanx seemed a real possibility, he was trying to adopt a "new tone." He had resolved to "suppress everything that is marvellous and consign it to a few chapters of sketches."[26]

One such chapter, which Fourier wrote in March 1821, was entitled "Concerning the Northern Passage and the Triple Harvest."[27] In this long dissertation on "atmospheric refinement" he argued that once most of the earth was brought under cultivation, climatic changes would take place and temperatures at the poles would rise so much as to cause the melting of the polar ice. Fourier had already made similar predictions in the *Quatre mouvements* and in his manuscript writings. But there his main preoccupation had been with the logical working-out of the theory. Now that his principal aim was to secure financial backing, he changed his emphasis. He concentrated less on the theory than on the results, and especially on those that could be presented as a source of profit. Thus the chapter on the northern passage took the form of a "demonstration" destined for "the English" of the advantages they would derive from founding the first trial Phalanx. "This is a very valuable demonstration for England," Fourier informed his disciple. "We have the strongest reason to count upon her for the trial."[28]

Toward the middle of April 1821 Fourier was at last able to quit Belley for good. He had outstayed his welcome at the Parrat-Brillats' and there were no tears shed at his departure. Muiron, of course, was delighted to have him back in Besançon; and Fourier too was glad that they could resume the daily exchange of conversational notes begun during his first visit. "I am delighted," he wrote his "cher ami" shortly after his arrival, "to be able to converse with you again and, according to my old custom, to write notes to you while we are face to face." Since he expected to remain in Besançon for some time, Fourier decided to rent a furnished room rather than stay at his sister's. Muiron accompanied him on the search. After some fruitless haggling over twenty-franc apartments, a modest eleven-franc room was found at 73, rue des Granges. "It has the advantage of being on the second floor," Fourier observed. "That is of great importance for me, who am obliged to go back to my room twenty times a day for a forgotten handkerchief or a piece of paper. I often go back three times before I can step out on the street; and on this account a room on the fourth floor would not be very convenient for me."[29] The next order of business was the discovery of a pension, one with a clientele agreeable to Fourier's tastes: "not an assemblage of youths, nor one composed entirely of soldiers." He found what he was looking for, although he regretted—yet another indication of the vassalage of the provinces—that the unfortunate Parisian custom of dining in midafternoon now prevailed in Besançon.

Absorbed as he was by the preparation of his treatise, Fourier still suffered from the lack of distractions at Besançon and even, finally, from the want of animation at his pension. In laboring over his manuscripts he could pause to note sadly that

> today in the town where I am living . . . it takes no more than a miserable game of billiards to distract the convives from an excellent meal and to drag them away from the table after half an hour when they might well spend an hour at least over dinner. Why are they in such a rush to leave the table? To unravel a series of petty intrigues on the outcome of a game of billiards or on the skill of such and such a player. This is a pitiful sort of activity, which nonetheless serves as an effective diversion to the pleasures of the table. Can one doubt that in Harmony these pleasures will be balanced by the brilliant intrigues of the industrial series, the least of which will be a hundred times more interesting and more gratifying to one's vanity than a puny game of billiards could possibly be?[30]

In July of 1821 the treatise was still far from completion. But Fourier could finally begin to hand over installments of manuscript to the widow Daclin's printers. Publication was to last more than a year. It was not until the fall of 1822 that the final sections came off the press and were ready for binding into two thick volumes of more than six hundred pages each. Fourier continued writing up to the last minute; indeed, during most of this period he had to work feverishly simply to keep up with the printers. There was no longer time for cutting or rewriting; and any error that escaped his eye on the proofs had to be corrected or explained in a subsequent section of the text. Thus the latter portions of the book included a running commentary on the preceding sections. Most of Fourier's corrections merely concerned matters of detail. But sometimes Fourier admitted broader theoretical errors. He criticized his own analysis of amorous relations, for example, as "quite incomplete . . . SIMPLISTIC, focusing only on the vices inherent in deception," explaining, "these mistakes are easy to make when a manuscript is finished only just before being handed to the worker." Elsewhere, after warning against the danger of amassing proofs, Fourier went ahead and did so, explaining that he had been "carried away by the subject." In addition, the excessive length of some articles obliged Fourier to suppress or condense others. Thus a detailed outline of the organization of the *comptoir communal* had to be eliminated because "it would require at least twenty pages," and even an *Arrière-propos* devoted to "complements and corrections" had to be drastically limited in scope, other articles having "gained ground."[31]

As usual Fourier larded his text with specific references to newspaper articles, books, poems, encyclopedias, dictionaries, and even atlases that happened to come to hand while he was writing. They were all grist for his mill. The "tardy" communication (July 8, 1821) of a "Note, signed Huard . . . in the *Mémorial universel de l'industrie française,* June, no. 54," supplied him with proof "that there exist at Paris partisans of association, desiring and seeking an effective method." The belated discovery of a map indicating a possible northwest passage provided him with a pretext for inviting the English to listen to his plan for the melting of the polar ice caps. In describing the ill-treatment of writers and intellectuals in civilization, Fourier announced: "The day I set to work on this article I was revolted three times by accounts of the poverty of savants." In the morning, while reading in the newspapers about a session of the French Academy, he had encountered some stanzas of M. Raynouard on the poet Camoens, who spent his last years begging on the streets in Lisbon. Leafing through his papers toward noon, he had found a description in an old gazette of the poverty of "M. Heyne, savant distingué d'Allemagne," who "during most of his life had no more to eat than a few potatoes." In the evening a volume of Racine brought Fourier details on the penurious old age of Dumarsais. Details such as these, discovered by chance in newspapers and odd volumes, provided Fourier with added ammunition for his assault on civilization.[32]

Fourier similarly invoked contemporary events and even the weather as confirmations of his indictment. The precocious spring of 1822 had led some to believe in an improvement of the climate. On the contrary, he observed, "it is only one more sign of disorder." After several winters that had lasted into June, the planet "finished by skipping an entire winter in 1822. This new calamity has cost us legions of rats, caterpillars, etc., premature and persistent droughts, and multiple hurricanes."[33] The disruption of the order of the seasons was only one of many symptoms of the general disorder of the material universe. In the midst of a critique of monogamous marriage, Fourier paused to note other indexes of the "subversion" of the planet.

Instead of progress it is degeneration that may be observed on all sides. We see nothing but the material subversion of the climate and the political subversion of society. As I am writing at this very moment, June 1, 1822, there are two striking effects of subversion that may be distinguished.

MATERIAL SUBVERSION: *Last week in May* 1821. Frosts that destroy half of various harvests, and prolonged wintry weather that lasts for several weeks before and after the end of May. *Last week in May* 1822. Heat of the dog days. Thermometer at 25 degrees Reaumur, with summery weather lasting several weeks although in springtime.

SPIRITUAL SUBVERSION. *May* 1822. Indifference throughout Christendom with regard to its fierce friends, the Turks, who have cut the throats at Chios of 40,000 defenseless Christians (most attempting to surrender) and of 20,000 elderly women; who have carried off into slavery 20,000 girls and 40,000 children, whom they will raise according to the Mohammedan religion. Great eulogies for Russia concerning the fact that it remains, with its 912,000 soldiers, the indifferent spectator of the massacre of a Christian nation of which it is, according to the treaties of Kainarji and Bucharest, the obligatory protector.

With regard to so many horrors mercantile Europe does not show the least sign of emotion. Is not this reversal of customs, of seasons, and of dispositions an irrefutable sign of political and moral subversion?[34]

What relationship had the weather and the massacres of Chios with each other, or with a critique of civilized marriage? "A very intimate relationship," insisted Fourier. For they provided complementary demonstrations of the "retrograde march" of civilization and the need of an instant remedy.

IV

While Fourier was putting the finishing touches on his treatise, his disciple Muiron was soliciting loans to cover the costs of publication. Several of those whom Muiron had previously contacted now proved reluctant to help. But his circle of friends was wide, and he was nothing if not a diligent fund-raiser. The "angels" eventually located by Muiron were prosperous individuals who do not seem to have had any great knowledge of Fourier's ideas; they were probably motivated more by affection for Muiron than by enthusiasm for Fourier's doctrine. The first and most generous contributor was Auguste Bouchot, an ironmaster and future deputy from the Doubs.★ Between August 1821 and May 1822 he provided Muiron with three loans totaling close to 2,000 francs. In April of 1822 Muiron obtained a loan of 1,200 francs from Mlle. Appoline Bruand of Meximieux (Ain). The sister of Muiron's deceased friend and former colleague at the prefecture, Joseph Bruand, she was later to provide most of the funds necessary for the publication of the *Nouveau monde industriel*. The third backer was Hippolyte Maistre, an associate of Muiron's at the Besançon Prefecture. His loan of 300 francs, together with 400 francs advanced by Fourier himself, left Muiron with close to 4,000 francs, a sum sufficient to pay most of the initial printing costs. He himself made up the difference (which eventually amounted to well over 1,000 francs) and took responsibility for paying interest on the loans. Thus Muiron kept his promise; and the treatise meant to topple civilization was to be published with funds provided by an industrialist, two government functionaries, and a wealthy spinster.[35]

By August of 1822 the financial situation was well in hand and the printing was virtually finished. But Fourier continued to write. The

---

★Joseph-Auguste Bouchot (1791–1858) was to serve as deputy from the Doubs in 1830 and 1831. He was perhaps known to Muiron through Clarisse Vigoureux, whose husband had also been an ironmaster.

entire first volume of his treatise was already consecrated to prefatory matter—introduction, extroduction, prolegomenas and cislogomenas. Still he could not resist adding an *Avant-propos* in which for the last time he offered a brief résumé of the doctrine, the critique of civilization, and the incentives offered to the potential *fondateur,* as well as an explanation of the book's organization and nomenclature, a response to his "benevolent critics," and a set of detailed instructions for various types of readers.

One problem to which Fourier gave particular attention was the selection of a title. "By rights," he wrote, "this work should have been entitled *Theory of Universal Unity.*" But his compatriots had been inundated with works purporting to explain the unity of the universe, and they could no longer distinguish a real inventor from a charlatan. A more modest title therefore seemed appropriate. After discussing the matter with friends and acquaintances at Besançon, Fourier finally decided to present his theory under the "most modest" title possible: *Traité de l'association domestique-agricole.*★

Having baptized his treatise, Fourier turned his attention to practical matters. The failure of the *Quatre mouvements* had taught him that he would have to make some concessions to "the Parisian literary cabal." In particular he would have to present his work to the world as a product emanating from Paris. He would have to find a reliable Parisian bookseller willing to place his name on the title page and to take charge of the book's sale and distribution. Once the book had appeared, he would also need to go to Paris himself to promote sales and to make himself available to potential backers.

In August 1822 Fourier began to send out letters to the booksellers of Paris. The first responses were cautious. Delaunay *libraire* informed Fourier that he would be willing to handle the book "provided, however, that it does not deal with political matters." In the same vein was a letter from Brunot-Labbe, in whose storerooms on the quai des Au-

---

★Fourier's choice of a title was not to the liking of the disciples he later acquired. As one of them wrote him in 1824: "In your place . . . I would change the title of the work. It does not announce the goal you are aiming at; it does not provide a hint of the grandeur of your design. . . . You are seeking a total change in the social system; the title must make that plain." Gabriel Gabet to Fourier, October 2, 1824, AN 10AS 25 (2). Others were misled by the title. The Russian radical, Peter Lavrov, owed his early introduction to Fourier to his father, who had purchased the book expecting it to be a treatise on agronomy! See N. S. Rusanov, *Biografiia Petra Lavrovicha Lavrova: ocherk ego zhizni i deiatel'nosti* (n.p., 1899), 11.

gustins a few trunks full of the *Quatre mouvements* still lay gathering dust: "You may place my name on the title page of the book only if it is a work of wholesome literature, attacking no party and saying nothing against our institutions and our government."[36]

It was not with Delaunay or Brunot-Labbe that Fourier decided to do business, however, but with two other booksellers: Bossange *père* of the rue Richelieu and Mongie *aîné* of the boulevard Poissonière. The former, whose clientele included the duc d'Orléans, was well known at Paris. Mongie, who ran a more modest business, was to go bankrupt in 1832. Both agreed to place their names on Fourier's title page and to sell his book on a commission basis. During the month of September a brisk exchange of letters ensued between the author and his two booksellers. Although Fourier's side of the correspondence is lost, it is clear from one of Mongie's replies that Fourier's hopes were running high: "Your work will certainly have a rapid success if it has all the advantages of which you tell me. I desire its success with all my heart. But during my thirty years as a bookseller I have seen so many hopes deceived that I always wait for the outcome before I am sure of anything."[37] Despite this cautionary note, it is clear that Fourier's optimism was contagious. For in the same letter Mongie had already begun to talk about the possibility of a second edition, after a first printing of ten thousand.

A final problem for Fourier was censorship. In 1820, following the assassination of the duc de Berry, a new strict censorship law was passed. Charges were brought against such popular poets and pamphleteers as Béranger and Paul-Louis Courier, and the trial of a little-known social critic named Henri Saint-Simon became a *cause célèbre*. Anxious to avoid such difficulties, Fourier advertised his work as a "diversion" to contemporary political quarrels. Still, the threat of censorship worried him. Toward the end of 1821 he made inquiries of an old friend from Lyon, the republican surgeon, L.-V.-F. Amard, who had recently published a treatise entitled *Association intellectuelle*. Amard was reassuring, but urged Fourier not to delay in getting the book published.[38]

In October of 1822 the work of printing and binding was done, and Just Muiron submitted five copies of the *Traité* to his colleague, Hippolyte Jordan, the general secretary of the Doubs Prefecture, for the preliminary inspection required by the new censorship law. Jordan's verdict was reassuring if not entirely flattering: "The reading of such strange paradoxes presents too many difficulties ever to become dangerous." On his side Fourier asked for a legal opinion from a former schoolmate, Guillaume, who was now a judge at the Besançon civil tribunal. Guillaume also assured Fourier that he need not fear prosecution.[39]

His fears dispelled and his hopes high, Fourier now prepared two shipments of two hundred copies of the treatise to be sent to Mongie and Bossange in Paris. He forwarded an even larger shipment to Paris to await his own arrival. Leaving the remainder in Muiron's care, he made ready for the trip to Paris, which was, he hoped, to decide everything.

II

The Theory

My theory is limited to *utilizing the passions just as nature gives them and without changing anything.* That is the whole mystery, the whole secret of the calculus of passionate attraction. The theory does not ask whether God was right or wrong to endow human beings with particular passions; the societary order utilizes them without changing anything and just as God has given them.

OC V, 157.

10

Critique of Civilization

THROUGHOUT his life Fourier was an outsider. From his beginnings as an isolated and unrecognized provincial autodidact to his last years as one of the odder habitués of the cafés and reading rooms of the Palais Royal, he was at pains to separate himself from the ruling ideas and the ruling thinkers of his time. He had made his position clear in 1808 with the proclamation of his two extraordinary rules of method, absolute doubt and absolute deviation. These required him in designing his utopia to deviate consistently from the teachings of all civilized philosophers and to stand in "constant opposition" to the established practices of civilization. Above all, he wrote, "the method of doubt must be applied to civilization; we must doubt its necessity, its excellence, and its permanence."[1]

Fourier's contempt for the respectable thinkers and ideologies of his age was so intense that he always used the terms *philosopher* and *civilization* in a pejorative sense. In his lexicon civilization was a depraved order, a synonym for perfidy and constraint, and philosophers were by definition thinkers whose theories were "not compatible with experience."[2] Fourier did not describe himself as a philosopher but as an "inventor," and he could boast that his discovery had "confounded twenty centuries of political imbecility."[3] Occasionally his works were reviewed indulgently by well-meaning journalists. But Fourier scorned their faint praise. As he commented on a review of his *Traité de l'association* by the liberal publicist Etienne de Jouy:

> He recognizes first of all "that I have good reason to complain about our imperfect civilization." IMPERFECT!!! I have proven, on the contrary, that it is most perfect in pushing perfidy, rapine, egoism, and all the vices to the supreme degree.[4]

This sort of verbal extravagance was typical of Fourier's replies to his critics, and it is hard to take it seriously in a work that also includes speculations on the sexual proclivities of the stars and chapters bearing such titles as "The English Debt Paid off in Six Months with Hens' Eggs." Yet it would be wrong to dismiss absolute doubt and the rest of Fourier's indictment of civilization as no more than a series of rhetorical outbursts. If we read Fourier's critical writings with care, it becomes clear that one of the great qualities of Fourier's work was precisely his ability to abstract himself imaginatively from the known world and to look at the most familiar institutions with a fresh and unsparing eye.

This is not to say that Fourier was totally emancipated from the assumptions and prejudices of his age. On the contrary, to cite only the most obvious example, his whole system was based on a set of unquestioned assumptions concerning God and the nature of Divine Providence. Nor was Fourier lacking in prejudice. There was plenty of prejudice—as well as pettiness and sheer nonsense—in his critical writings. His critique of civilization was punctuated by angry outbursts against the Jews, the English, the Parisians, and the "philosophical cabal," which he believed was deliberately suppressing his ideas. His personal hatred of commerce was so strong that he often described the merchant as a villain whose machinations were the unique source of poverty and hunger. At the same time Fourier was fiercely hostile to the movement for the political emancipation of the Jews, and there was a strain of anti-Semitism running throughout his economic writings, a clear reflection of the prejudice current in the milieu in which he was raised.[5]

Even at its pettiest and most myopic, however, Fourier's attack on civilization had qualities not to be found in the writing of any other social critic of his time. His lack of education, his *déclassement,* and his sense of alienation from the intellectual establishment were sources of insight as well as resentment. They heightened his contempt for conventional wisdom and sharpened his awareness of ills that other more successful and worldly men simply took for granted. For all of its intellectual naiveté and personal rancor, Fourier's social criticism was that of a man who absolutely refused to be taken in by the lofty abstractions others used to rationalize or hide the physical suffering and emotional deprivation that were the lot of most men and women in the world he knew.

I

Fourier's critique of civilization was nothing if not comprehensive. When the occasion demanded, he was able to list up to 144 "permanent vices" of civilization, running from the slavery of the wage system to the "excitation of hurricanes and all sorts of climatic excesses." Nonetheless there were a few central and recurrent themes in Fourier's critical writing. These were his analysis of the problem of poverty, his critique of the family system, and his attack on "the philosophers."

Civilization's most obvious and scandalous flaw in Fourier's view was poverty. One had only to open one's eyes, he wrote, to see that civilization was an "absurd" order in which the majority of working people were hungry and ill housed and miserably clothed. Ironically the problem of poverty seemed to be most severe in the most advanced societies. "The peoples of civilization see their wretchedness increase," wrote Fourier, "in direct proportion to the advance of industry." Thus he could characterize industry as "a perfidious gift, a mocking gesture" on the part of nature, and "even a punishment" for the human race, because it reduced to despair the very people who were its agents. The wage worker of civilization was "worse off even than the savage," who enjoyed occasional days of abundance in his state of nature and who was "not, like our plebeians, embittered by the sight of luxury goods displayed under his eyes to excite his desires and to render his privations unbearable."[6]

In attempting to specify the causes of poverty, Fourier focused first of all on the wastefulness and inefficiency of civilized methods of production and consumption. Like many contemporary agronomists, he bewailed the stubborn resistance of French peasant farmers to any change in their methods of farming. "The incompetence of the farmer is so great," he wrote, "that the peasants of the Paris region do not know how to grow or harvest potatoes, the objects of so many treatises. Out of four baskets of these vegetables that you buy in the markets of Paris, three will be inedible on account of their bitterness, acidity, and sliminess, even at the moment of harvest."[7] Fourier also criticized the inefficiency of a system in which the basic units of production and consumption were the family farm and the family kitchen. Most of France's grain and other food was grown by individual farmers on small plots with inadequate tools and fertilizers. Most of France's meals were prepared in individual kitchens with the result that in a given village a hundred women were daily occupied by tasks that half a dozen could have performed in a common kitchen for the whole village.

Fourier never tired of denouncing the *morcellement* or fragmentation of civilized economic life, or of pointing out the savings of labor and material that could be realized through the establishment of common ovens and wine vats and storage facilities. Instead of building a common granary and maintaining it well, he wrote, the villagers of civilization preferred to store their grain in three hundred private bins, where it was as likely as not to be destroyed by rats, bugs, dampness, or fire. Instead of baking bread in just a few common ovens, the same villagers preferred to strip their forests of wood to feed a hundred fires in a hundred separate kitchens. The waste inherent in such fragmented and inefficient methods of production, storage, and food consumption was, in Fourier's opinion, one of the great vices of the civilized economic system.[8]

Fourier recognized, however, that the establishment of large-scale productive units and efficient methods of storage and distribution would not alone cure the ills of the civilized economy. The fundamental problem was that civilized methods of production were not merely wasteful but also anarchic and uncontrolled. What was produced in civilization depended on what the individual producer thought would bring him profit. There was no control over the quality of goods, and it was only an accident if the goods produced happened to satisfy real human needs. Furthermore, in his later writings Fourier noted that the lack of coordination among producers was resulting in periodic crises of overproduction, which could throw thousands of people out of work and shut down whole industries.[9] Unemployment had become chronic in industrial society, Fourier maintained, and it was possible for trivial events to bring about catastrophes. "Is there anything sensible or *rational*," he asked, "about an order in which fifty thousand inhabitants of a city are reduced to idleness and beggary as a result of a change in fashion that takes place two thousand leagues away in the United States?"[10]

If mass unemployment was one consequence of the "industrial anarchy" of civilization, another was parasitism. Fourier asserted that the vast majority of workers in civilization were employed in jobs that didn't begin to utilize their potential as producers. In fact, he argued, two-thirds of the working population could be characterized as parasitical because the tasks they performed were useless if not positively harmful. He attempted to prove his point in a "Table of Unproductive Classes in Civilization," which appeared in the *Traité* of 1822. There he listed as "domestic parasites" three-fourths of all children and servants, and all those women who were "absorbed in housework, which entails the wasteful duplication of functions." Fourier's second category of "social parasites" included all soldiers and sailors as well as the vast majority of merchants, transportation agents, and government functionaries (for example, the twenty-four thousand members of the French customs service). Half of the workers involved in manufacturing could also be classified as unproductive because of the shoddy quality of the goods they produced. Fourier's third category, that of "accessory parasites," was made up of both the idle rich and the idle poor. Among the latter were not only beggars, vagrants, and the unemployed but also those employed workers who doubled the idleness legally permitted by drinking or sleeping through Holy Monday, "the most ruinous of all the holy days, since it is observed fifty-two times a year in factory towns." Other accessory parasites were the involuntary idlers (prisoners and the sick), the sophists (including those who railed against parasitism while practicing it), and the pickpockets, adventurers, and other dubious individuals against whom civilization was obliged to maintain a police force, which was just as unproductive as they were.[11]

The point of Fourier's "Table of Unproductive Classes in Civilization" was that one of the causes of the shameful poverty of his age was the failure of civilized society to tap the productive forces available to it. But in his analysis of the roots of poverty Fourier concentrated primarily, not on the realm of production, but rather on that of exchange. Both his own personal experience and the conventional wisdom of his age combined to persuade him that the activity of the merchant and the commercial middleman was the chief cause of poverty and all economic ills. This was not an implausible belief at a time when the textile industries were controlled, not by industrialists, but by merchant manufacturers, when the speculative orgy of the Directory was still a recent memory, and when far greater profits were to be made in commercial speculation than in industry or agriculture. Yet it should be noted that where a modern historian would consider a wide range of social, economic, and demographic factors, Fourier attributed poverty to one overriding cause. Like the sans-culottes of the revolutionary period, and like many ordinary people in preindustrial France, Fourier made the merchant into a villain responsible for high prices, food shortages, and almost all the other ills of the economy.

The central theme in Fourier's critique of commerce was that the merchant, whose proper place in the economy was that of a subordinate agent, had come to dominate the economic life of civilization. With the development of navigation and the rise of colonial empires, wrote Fourier, the "mercantile class" had acquired enormous wealth and power. Now philosophers and kings bowed down before them, and both the farmer and the manufacturer had become "enslaved" to commerce.[12] The result was that

> the mechanism of civilized industry is distorted . . . by the independence accorded to the intermediaries known as merchants, who become the owners of the goods they handle when they should only be subordinate agents. They excel at falsehood; they adulterate foodstuffs and raw materials; and they do harm to every branch of industry with their schemes in hoarding, speculation, bankruptcy, and usury. All of their maneuvers serve only to despoil agriculture and property and to concentrate all wealth in the hands of the great merchants.[13]

Fourier insisted that commerce was wrongly identified by its apologists as a branch of industry, for it created nothing. It was unproductive by its very nature and only served to divert capital from industry and agriculture, where it might be put to good use. The merchants masqueraded as the servants of the farmer and the manufacturer, but in fact they profited from the system of free competition to despoil productive industry and defraud the consumer. They were "a band of pirates . . . a flock of vultures who devour the agricultural and manufacturing industries and subjugate the rest of society in every way possible."[14] To the old "class" struggles of civilization—the war of rich against poor, old against young, and husband against wife—the rise of commerce had thus added a new dimension: the war of the merchant and commercial middleman against all the productive classes of society. "All the essential classes," wrote Fourier, "the property owner, the farmer, the manufacturer, even the government, have been mastered by an accessory class, by the merchant, who ought to be their inferior, their agent . . . and who nevertheless directs and impedes all the energies of circulation according to his whim."[15]

Whether his subject was love or commerce, Fourier's first impulse as a social critic was that of a Linnaeus. Thus he devoted a large part of his critique of commerce to a descriptive classification of the "vices" inherent in the "commercial mechanism." Drawing on his long experience as an unlicensed broker and clerk for the business houses of Lyon, he eventually elaborated a taxonomy of thirty-six distinct "crimes of commerce."[16] Without getting too deeply entangled in detail, we can briefly consider three of these crimes: fraudulent bankruptcy, hoarding, and speculation.

In his discussion of bankruptcy Fourier took strong exception to the "sentimental" view of bankruptcies as unforeseen catastrophes caused by fate or bad luck. According to him, a bankruptcy was more often than not a fraudulent, lucrative, and carefully premeditated operation—an "ingenious" and "impudent" form of trickery that enabled "any merchant to steal from the public a sum equivalent to his wealth or credit."[17] Like Balzac some years later in his "Histoire générale des faillites,"[18] Fourier classified bankruptcies into a number of distinct species, and he illustrated each by offering a series of case histories involving such protagonists as "Scapin the small shopkeeper," "the banker Dorante," and "the Jew Iscariot." There were first of all the so-called honest bankruptcies, those in which the merchant made good on at least 50 percent of his debts. There was also the "family-style bankruptcy" in which, before making his declaration, the merchant prudently confided the bulk of his fortune to relatives, leaving his creditors with nothing but honeyed words. Finally, there was the domino version, the "banqueroute en feu de file." This was a carefully premeditated operation in which the culprit first drove all his competitors into bankruptcy, and then simply absconded with his illicit gains. As diverse as were the methods employed in these three types of bankruptcy, their ultimate result was the same: to despoil the honest and productive members of society.[19]

[The Theory]

Another of the commercial vices described by Fourier was hoarding. This was the most odious of them all in that it always attacked industry where it was weakest.

> Whenever there is a scarcity of food or any sort of goods the hoarders are right there to make matters worse, to get hold of existing supplies, to buy up those that are expected, to take them out of circulation, to double, triple their prices by maneuvers that exaggerate the scarcity and give rise to fears, which are only later recognized as illusory. Their effect on industry is that of a band of butchers who go out on the field of battle to lacerate and open the wounds of the fallen.[20]

Fourier observed that the Jacobins had had some success in repressing this class of "vultures," but had been unable to find a remedy for the ills the hoarders exploited. Thus the only result of the Terror and the *maximum* (which Fourier described as a regression to the "brutal" methods of Barbarism) was that the hoarders could now perpetrate their misdeeds with impunity. The lesson the philosophers had drawn from 1793 and 1794 had been to "laisser faire les marchands"—to leave them free to "assassinate the people" through the hoarding of grain, and to "assassinate industry" through the hoarding of cotton and colonial goods.

The "brother" of hoarding and the third of Fourier's vices was speculation. He described its practitioners as "mitigated clubbists" and "industrial Jacobins." Like the demagogues of 1793 they had a talent for affiliation, and they had established their own secret "committee of inquisition." Just as the Jacobins had arranged simulated conspiracies in order to fleece the rich and eliminate their rivals, the speculators had mastered the art of organizing artificial crises in order to despoil industry. To illustrate the cunning of the speculators and the power they had gained since the Revolution, Fourier frequently cited the skillfully organized run on the Bank of France in 1805.

> During the last war against Austria an obscure mercantile plot kept in doubt the victories of Ulm and Austerlitz. At a time when France manifested the blindest confidence in the operations of the emperor, the speculators managed to produce the symptoms of a universal mistrust. . . . In two months the Parisian intriguers committed unprecedented ravages in French industry; it took a torrent of sudden and miraculous victories in order finally to muzzle the speculation, which threatened to

ruin all public credit. One shudders to think of the financial distress into which France would have fallen had the campaign been less successful.[21]

By such maneuvers as this, coalitions of speculators had begun to play a major role in politics and to direct industry according to their whim. Thus in his earliest manuscripts Fourier could warn that the system of free competition had a "secret goal" that the political economists had not foreseen. Unrestrained profit seeking was beginning to give rise to the formation of monopolies and vast "mercantile coalitions." Already French speculators had proved themselves adept at creating artificial shortages in order to drive up prices. Coalitions of hoarders and monopolists still ran the risk of governmental requisition and "the vengeance of the multitude." But nothing would stop them once they secured official protection. Civilization, Fourier predicted, was about to enter a new, and terminal, phase of "mercantile feudalism" the horrors of which would surpass those of the Spanish Inquisition and the Venetian Senate.[22]

Fourier's critique of commercial capitalism has rightly been criticized on the ground that he remains on the moral level and fails to penetrate to the analysis of structures in the manner of Marx or even of his contemporary, Henri Saint-Simon. Even the discussion of the monopolistic tendencies inherent in the system of free competition is confused and was never developed in a careful or systematic way.[23] It could also be argued that even though Fourier's economic criticism was based on firsthand observation, his principal points were not particularly original. The attack on wasteful methods of consumption, on excessively small units of production, and on the misdeeds of the merchant or middleman were all part of a long and vigorous tradition. Half a century before Fourier the French Physiocrats in particular had already sounded many of the themes that reappear in Fourier's economic writings, notably the critique of commerce and of small-scale farming.* And of course there was nothing original about Fourier's repeated derogatory references to Jews or his tendency to treat "the Jew" as the

---

*Fourier had some familiarity with, and appreciation of, the ideas of the Physiocrats. In an 1813 manuscript he referred to "the Quesnai sect" (*sic*) as "a reasonable sect . . . that wished to subordinate the whole industrial mechanism to the needs of agriculture. Quesnai set too little value on manufactures, which must be distinguished from commerce. . . . Quesnai neglected that distinction and, like all systematic thinkers, he adopted exaggerated opinions." OC XI, PM (1853–1856), 158.

epitome of the dishonest merchant. These are points that must be noted. Yet to stress them would be to risk overlooking or misunderstanding the nature of Fourier's real achievement as an economic critic.

What Fourier did accomplish at a time when the principle of free trade was being turned into a dogma and presented as a key to the "wealth of nations" was, first of all, to reveal with unparalleled clarity the hollowness of the claim that a nation could be wealthy at a time when its streets were lined with beggars. He cut through the rhetoric of liberal political economy and analyzed in detail the real vices of the system of free or "anarchic" competition. But there is also a sense in which Fourier went beyond moral indignation to an analysis of processes if not of structures. For in addition to identifying vices, he showed how they operated. He showed, for example, how a profitable bankruptcy was arranged, or how an artificial shortage was created, or how the intrigues of the Bourse were actually set in motion. His manuscripts on commerce even included satirical sketches and mock-heroic "tableaux" that parodied the language of the Bourse and rendered explicit what was hidden by the fine rhetoric of the political economists. It was in these writings, which satirized the commercial system and laid bare the disparity between rhetoric and reality, that Fourier's critique of commerce was most original and most penetrating.

II

The second vital component of Fourier's attack on civilized society was his critique of its sexual mores. If poverty was the prime source of the physical suffering in civilization, Fourier believed that the most intolerable emotional constraints of civilized society were those imposed by the institutions of marriage and family life. Thus he attacked these institutions on all fronts and with all the weapons at his disposal. His critique ranged from tirades against the moral "vices" inherent in the family system to satirical evocations of the "joys" of domestic life, from dry commentaries on the defects of the family as an economic unit and as an instrument of child rearing to pseudoscientific enumerations of the drawbacks of marriage for both partners and a taxonomy of types of cuckoldry. But through all of this ran a recurrent theme: civilization was an edifice built on the repression of man's instinctual drives, and its cornerstone was the institution of monogamous marriage.

Fourier's system was all of a piece, and in his attack on civilized marriage he repeatedly pointed out that its vices were closely related to those inherent in the economic life of civilization. Just as the principle of laissez faire had provided merchants with a philosophical sanction for dishonest business dealings, so marriage, he maintained, had sanctioned and institutionalized the practice of deceit in amorous relations. Marriage was a state of "domestic warfare" in which husband and wife were no less determined to deceive one another than the two parties to a business transaction. Only a minority took seriously the public celebrations of the "virtuous wife" and the "doting husband," and the faithful spouse was as sure to be cuckolded as the honest merchant to be swindled.[24] There was also an explicitly economic dimension to Fourier's critique of the family. What could be more wasteful and inefficient, he asked, than a system that obliged each housekeeper to do her own marketing, cooking, and child raising, whether or not she had any aptitude for these tasks? As well as being psychologically inexpedient, this gave rise to a costly duplication of functions. Fourier's attack on piecemeal labor was thus by no means limited to the agricultural or industrial sphere; it was most forcefully articulated in his critique of the family system.[25]

In evoking the "joys" of married life, Fourier described the reigning atmosphere in the vast majority of households as one of monotony and boredom, a boredom epitomized by the conjugal dinner. Rendered insipid by the "unseemly disparity in the ages and interests of the participants and by the tiresomeness of the preparations," the family dinner was not an occasion for relaxation but a servitude to be endured. The conjugal bed fared no better at Fourier's hands. He denounced marriage for having deprived sex of its mystery and charm. For the husband marital lovemaking was a bothersome obligation, for the wife another servitude. In condemning husband and wife to live perpetually together, to share bed and board day after day, civilized marriage had made ordeals—or at best routine satisfactions—out of life's greatest pleasures. It had driven both partners outside the home in search of illicit liaisons or such meager and costly distractions as could be provided by cafés, theaters, and public balls. In Fourier's eyes an order that thus victimized both husbands and wives could only be described as "the work of a third sex that wished to condemn the two others to boredom."[26]

Since the institution of monogamous marriage seemed to symbolize the failure of civilized man to devise institutions capable of satisfying the most basic human needs, Fourier never tired of pointing out its drawbacks. Sometimes, as in a chapter entitled "Gamut of the Misfortunes of the Conjugal State," he took the husband's point of view and enumerated the eight or the sixteen woes of the married man.[27] Of all these woes it was adultery or cuckoldry to which he gave the closest, most devoted attention. The watchful husband might exhaust himself in precautions, he wrote, but he could never be sure of escaping the fate shared by a host of illustrious horned predecessors. Fourier's initial reflections on the fate of the cuckold were contained in the *Théorie des quatre mouvements,* where he distinguished three basic varieties of cuckolds: (1) "The Common Cuckold," the honorable spouse who remained ignorant of his wife's misbehavior; (2) "The Short-Horned Cuckold," who knowingly abandoned his wife to all comers in order to take his pleasure elsewhere; and (3) "The Long-Horned Cuckold," the jealous maniac who, like Molière's Georges Dandin ("a paragon of the species"), vainly raged against an implacable destiny. Of these three types only the short-horned variety managed to avoid public ridicule. But like the others, he was helpless before the brutal law of civilization, "the bugbear of all men": the law that in doubtful cases "the father is he whom the marriage bond designates."[28]

During the Restoration Fourier elaborated an exhaustive "Hierarchy of Cuckoldom" in which no less than seventy-two distinct types were ranked according to class, species, and gender.[29] They ranged from the "Cuckold in the Bud" to the "Posthumous Cuckold" and were apparently based on models known to Fourier.[30] Of course, the cuckold had long been a stock figure in literature and on the stage and an easy mark for the satirist's ridicule. But Fourier's satire was more than an amusing exposure of human frailty. For what made cuckoldry important in his eyes was that it epitomized the "secret insurrection" of the human race against all legislation requiring perpetual amorous fidelity.[31]

Fourier insisted that whatever misfortunes marriage might bring to the husband, the principal victims of this institution were the women. He described marriage as a "mercantile calculation" in which the woman was no more than "a piece of merchandise offered to the highest bidder."[32] Once the transaction was concluded, she became in the eyes of the law her husband's exclusive property. Until that time, civilized society obliged her to remain chaste. If her dowry and her looks failed to attract a suitable purchaser, she was left to wither on the vine.

> Just what are the means of subsistence of impoverished women? [asked Fourier]. The bedpost or their charms, when they have any. Yes, prostitution, more or less prettied up, is their sole means of support, and philosophy even begrudges them that. This is the state to which they have been reduced by civilization with its conjugal slavery.[33]

Whether married or single, the repressed women of civilization had to defy existing moral standards in order to gain the slightest gratifications. The philosophers, who were the guardians of these standards, had naturally been quick to denounce the "innate" frivolity and deceitfulness of the female character. But Fourier did not regard the "servile and perfidious penchants" of women as innate. He attributed them to the constraints imposed by civilized society.

> When philosophy chatters about the vices of women, it is only criticizing itself; it is philosophy that has produced those vices through a social system that, repressing the development of their faculties from childhood and throughout the whole course of their lives, forces them to resort to deceit in order to obey their natural impulses.[34]

To judge women by the "defective character" they exhibited in civilization was like judging the beaver by the inertness he displayed in captivity. Their true nature, their "destiny," would be revealed only in Harmony. The examples of the great queens—Elizabeth, Catherine, Maria Theresa—and of Ninon de Lenclos and Madame de Sévigné were portents of things to come. Once emancipated from the oppressive system of conjugal slavery, women would surpass men "in dedication to work, in faithfulness, and in nobility of character . . . in all the functions of mind and body that are not dependent on physical strength."[35]

Fourier's defense of women is one of the aspects of his thought for which he was and is best known. He was the first of the early European socialists to put a thoughtful and rigorous analysis of the situation of women at the center of a comprehensive critique of his society. His writings on "the woman question" were greatly admired by Flora Tristan and a number of the other pioneer French feminists; and his disciples did much to give currency to the idea of the emancipation of women within the socialist movement of the 1830s and 1840s. This being the case, it is worth emphasizing one distinction. Unlike the position taken by the socialists of the 1840s, who argued for women's emancipation on humanitarian and moral grounds, the main thrust of Fourier's argument was utilitarian. He saw the servitude of women as a "blunder" that victimized society as a whole and retarded its development most conspicuously in the economic sphere.[36]

To prove this point Fourier devoted a part of his analysis to a consideration of non-Western societies that had been relatively liberal in their treatment of women. In such societies, he claimed, this liberality had been a driving force behind economic and social progress. The Japanese, noted (so Fourier believed) for their indulgence toward women and their lack of jealousy, were "the most industrious, the bravest and the most honorable" of the barbarian nations.[37] The discovery of Tahiti had revealed an "industrious" society in which the emancipation of women had served to compensate for the lack of certain raw materials. The customs of the Tahitian savages, proclaimed Fourier, were "Nature's admonition" to the civilized, a "glimmer of wisdom" that "should have suggested the idea of a social order that could unite large-scale industry with amorous liberty."[38] Each of these two nations was the "best" and "most industrious" of its kind. Conversely, he observed that the most vicious and laziest nations were those in which the servitude of women was the most pronounced. The decadence of barbarian China and civilized Spain was clearly the result of their lack of indulgence toward women. Fourier did not regard this correlation as fortuitous. On the contrary, he concluded his analysis of "the debasement of women in civilization" with the "general thesis" that

> social progress and changes of historical period take place in proportion to the advance of women toward liberty, and social decline occurs as a result of the diminution of the liberty of women. . . . The extension of the privileges of women is the fundamental cause of all social progress.[39]

These words became one of the battle cries of radical feminism in the 1840s. Cited as "masterly" by Marx and Engels, they were to serve Flora Tristan, who knew Fourier during his old age, as the epigraph for her *L'Emancipation de la femme*.[40]

III

Fourier's critique of civilization focused primarily on the institutions of commercial capitalism and monogamous marriage. But another important target of his criticism was "philosophy"—that is, the whole system of "reasonable" ideas that served to legitimize the institutions of civilization and to disguise its repressive mechanisms. Just like *civilization,* the terms *philosophy* and *philosophers* had a pejorative sense for Fourier. In his lexicon the philosophers were a "corps"—sometimes a "cabal"— of toadies and pedants who spent their time devising incomprehensible ways of expressing commonplace observations and concocting specious justifications for the pain and suffering that were the lot of most people in civilization.

Fourier conceded that from Socrates to Rousseau there had been a few thinkers who had recognized their own ignorance and "sought an enlightenment that they admitted was not to be found in their own learning."[41] He referred approvingly to these thinkers as "the expectant philosophers," and his own works are studded with appropriate, but generally innocuous, little quotations from theirs. For example:

> Before the Revolution the compiler Barthélemy said (in his *Voyage d'Anacharsis*): "These libraries, the so-called treasure houses of sublime knowledge, are no more than a humiliating repository of contradictions and errors; their abundance of ideas is in fact a penury." What would he have said a few years later if he had seen the philosophical dogmas put to the test? No doubt like Raynal he would have made a public confession of ignorance and said with Bacon: "We must revise our whole understanding of things and forget all that we have learned."[42]

For the majority of philosophers Fourier had no such sympathy. They were "obscurantists" who claimed that there was "nothing more to be discovered" even though they themselves had failed to solve the most basic problems within their own special domains. As he wrote in the *Quatre mouvements:*

> If they discuss *industrial economy,* they forget to consider *association,* which is the basis of any economy. If they discuss *politics,* they forget to make any stipulation concerning the *size of the population,* although its proper proportion is the basis of the

well-being of the people. If they discuss *administration*, they fail
to speculate on the means of bringing about the *administrative
unity of the globe*, without which there can be no stability or any
guarantee of the fate of empires. If they discuss *industry*, they
fail to seek measures for repressing the *swindling, hoarding*, and
speculation that despoil producers and consumers and constitute
a direct impediment to the exchange of goods. If they discuss
morality, they fail to recognize and demand the *rights of the
weaker sex*, whose oppression destroys the very principle of
justice. If they discuss the *rights of man*, they fail to lay down as
a principle the *right to work*, which, in truth, is not tolerable in
civilization, but without which all the other rights are useless.
If they discuss *metaphysics*, they fail to study the system of the
relations of God with man, and fail to seek the means of revelation that God can employ with regard to us.[43]

In view of the philosophers' propensity for neglecting fundamental
problems, Fourier maintained that one of their most striking collective
attributes might be described as "methodical mindlessness."

Fourier made no attempt to conceal the personal rancor that lay
behind his attack on the philosophers. Condemned to obscurity and
isolation, he hated them with all the bitterness of an outsider whose
opponents refuse even to argue with him. He may have found some
consolation in dreaming up schemes for the protection of the rights of
"unlettered inventors" like himself. But his chief consolation, no
doubt, was the direct attack on the doctrines of the philosophers, which
he first undertook in 1803 in the manuscripts comprising the *Egarement
de la Raison* and which he renewed in almost all his later works.

In his critique of the philosophers, Fourier generally dealt separately
with each of civilization's three "uncertain sciences": metaphysics, politics, and moral philosophy. Beginning with metaphysics, he dismissed
out of hand the "quibbles about sensations, abstractions, and perceptions" that had occupied philosophers for twenty-five centuries.[44] These
"trifles" were unworthy of occupying a group of thinkers whose proper
function was to determine the "intentions" and "plans" of God with
regard to the universe. Fourier addressed them collectively.

You have given way, philosophers, on the great problem of the
divine laws. Terrified by the spectacle of present and past evils,
you have despaired of Providence, and you have fallen into two
excesses that distance you in every way from the discovery of

the destinies. These two excesses, or rather these two weaknesses, are atheism and religious credulity.[45]

Fourier maintained that the first of these excesses, atheism, was a "pardonable" and sometimes a "noble" reaction. In denying the existence of God, the atheists had at least refused to hold him accountable for the ills of civilization. But this was a sterile viewpoint. A more fruitful attitude would have been "reasoned impiety"—the position that so perverse a civilization could only be the work of a power "infinitely skillful in moving and organizing matter, infinitely wicked and ingenious in torturing his creatures."[46] Atheism was a dead end, wrote Fourier, but in stressing the skill of the Creator, reasoned impiety would have led to enlightenment.

The more common reflex of the metaphysicians was that of religious credulity and superstition. Unable to find an explanation for the "evident disorders" of civilization consistent with their own assumptions concerning the nature of God and the universality of his providence, they had called a halt to the whole inquiry. They had asserted that the intentions of the deity were hidden behind a "mask of bronze," which no amount of reasoning could pierce. Of course the metaphysicians had continued to invoke the name of God. But it was only to "dishonor" him by vaunting as his ultimate achievement a civilization marked by almost universal poverty and suffering. They had reduced him to the status of a "roi fainéant," a front man for their own social theories, the best of which were but counsels of resignation in the face of evils that seemed insoluble.

Fourier admitted that in describing this world as a vale of tears and suffering, the philosophers of religious resignation had displayed a grain of sense: they had evaluated civilization at its true worth. They might have gone on to question its permanence. Adopting an attitude of "independent and reasoned piety," they might have questioned God's "motives" for allowing the temporary triumph of evil, and investigated the possibility of an alternative social order less insulting to God. "But," wrote Fourier, "this good impetus given to the religious spirit was thwarted by the interest and the charlatanism of the priests." Attributing the evils of civilized society to acts of divine punishment for the sins of individuals, the priests had offered the promise of individual salvation. This was a crafty maneuver designed to magnify their own importance as "influential go-betweens." But it was degrading to the deity. "The hypothesis of individual arrangements between God and man gave birth to all the dogmas that lend to God our faults and our weakness." No one could respect a God who would stoop to bargain with individuals and who was incapable of providing so much as a brief terrestrial foretaste of the pleasures promised in the afterlife.[47]

Passing in review various "fictions" concerning the future life, Fourier ridiculed the celestial paradise of the Christians as a shoddy recompense for the trials of civilization, a resting place so dull and monotonous that it seemed expressly designed "to keep the pious lukewarm in their desire for the future life." He conceded in the language of eighteenth-century euhemerism that the priestly caste had displayed a certain "political sagacity" in its exploitation of the egoism and credulity of civilized man. But his main concern was not so much to expose the base motives of the crafty priests who had invented heaven and hell as to show his readers that these fictions corresponded to their own condition in civilization. The God worshiped by the civilized was a "being in their own image," endowed with "their pettiness and their malice." The poverty of the Christian paradise betrayed the sterility of their hopes and aspirations. And as for the torments of hell, they were but the faithful image of the "massacres and miseries" of life in civilization.[48]

The second branch of philosophy considered by Fourier was politics—"the science that is charged with curing the ailments of the body social." Fourier compared its civilized practitioners to the quack doctors immortalized by Molière and Scarron. After long consultations on the nature and causes of the patient's disease, they could only repeat (in elegant Latin) that he was indeed quite sick; their medications were no more effective than the mumbled incantations of Doctors Tant-pis and Tant-mieux.[49]

Fourier's chief argument with the political philosophers of his time was quite simply that their doctrines and policies had no relevance to the way people actually lived. A case in point was the liberal theory of progress, the belief that human history was a record of more or less continuous advancement in human happiness and prosperity. In Fourier's view this was an "indecent boast" and one that was "cruelly refuted" both by the "disastrous consequences" of the French Revolution and by the failure of the philosophers to find any remedy for the fundamental problem of poverty. "At Athens as at Paris," Fourier addressed the philosophers, "the beggar standing at the palace gate has always served to demonstrate the nullity of your political wisdom and the reprobation of nature against your social theories."[50]

If Fourier dismissed the theory of progress, he was equally critical of the great revolutionary ideals. When concepts like liberty, equality, and fraternity were considered in the light of social reality, he maintained, it became evident that they were actually chimeras, mere words without meaning. In vaunting liberty, for example, the philosophers "forgot that in civilized societies liberty is illusory if the common people lack wealth." The notion of equality of rights was "another chimera, praiseworthy when considered in the abstract and ridiculous from the standpoint of the means employed to introduce it in civilization." Even more absurd, according to Fourier, was the supposition that the sentiment of sweet fraternity could exist between the refined sybarite and the coarse, hungry peasant who was dressed in rags and covered with vermin, and spoke an incomprehensible patois. In fact, Fourier maintained, the chief function served by the revolutionary ideals was to "mask the horrors" and to hide "the constraint, the police, and the gallows," which were for him, as for conservatives like Joseph de Maistre, the "actual mainstays" of the most liberal of contemporary societies.[51]

Fourier's critique of the liberal and radical ideologies of his time was rooted in his belief that they had simply failed to come to grips with the essential problem of the age, that of providing the poor with the means of subsistence and the right to work. "How impotent are our social compacts," wrote Fourier, "to provide the poor with a decent means of subsistence and . . . to assure them of the first of the natural rights, the RIGHT TO WORK!" Fourier insisted that this right had nothing in common with the "frivolous" abstractions of the French Revolution.

> By these words *natural rights* I do not mean the chimeras known as 'liberty' and 'equality.' The poor man does not aim so high; he does not wish to be the equal of the rich. He would be well content to eat at the table of their valets. The people are more reasonable than you imagine: they will consent to submission, to inequality, to servitudes, provided you can find a way to aid them when political vicissitudes have deprived them of their work, reduced them to famine, to opprobrium and despair.[52]

It was precisely in this case, Fourier observed, that the poor were "abandoned" by political philosophy.

What has it done to assure them in bad times not of aid but merely of the chance to do the work on which their subsistence depends? The people and even the educated class abound in wretched individuals who are vainly looking for employment while their fellow creatures get along without anxiety in idleness and abundance.[53]

Fourier accused the political philosophers of merely jesting with the poor by offering them the rights of sovereignty when they demanded nothing more than "the rights of servitude, the right to work for the pleasure of the lazy." He called upon them to equal "nature's bounty" in their treatment of the poor.

> If your social compacts are to equal the bounty of nature, you must give us at least what it gives to the savages and the wild animals, a job that pleases them and to which they have become accustomed during the course of their lives. . . . Give the civilized man the same privileges as those of the savage who possesses an inalienable right to the same sort of work as the chiefs of his horde, the right to hunt and to fish and to keep his catch for himself and not for a master.[54]

These words, which date from 1806, constitute one of the earliest socialist formulations of the right to work. They were to be restated, in the same antiegalitarian accents, in almost all of Fourier's subsequent writings.★

The analysis of civilized moral philosophy, which was the third element of Fourier's attack on "the philosophers," was as much a postmortem as a critique. "The sect of moralists is dead," Fourier wrote. The moralists had lost both their credit in the intellectual world and their power to influence the masses. Their visions ("always confounded by experience") were no longer taken seriously. Thus Fourier observed

---

★The right to work was recognized by Turgot (edict of February 1776) and in the French Constitution of 1793 (article 21). But in both cases what was actually being defended was the right of individuals who did not belong to trade guilds to *seek* employment in professions in which the right to work had formerly been limited to guild members. Although Fourier's formulation is idiosyncratic, it has rightly been described as the first socialist formulation of the right to work because its emphasis is on the right to find work and not simply the right to seek it. See Engels to Bernstein, May 23, 1884, in Karl Marx and Frederick Engels, *Selected Correspondence* (Moscow, n.d.), 447; Charles Gide and Charles Rist, *Histoire des doctrines économiques*, 6th ed. (Paris, 1944), 332; Anton Menger, *The Right to the Whole Produce of Labour* (London, 1899), 13–16.

that it was scarcely worthwhile to accumulate evidence of their failings. Nevertheless he did so—and with glee. As individuals, he claimed, the moralists were a band of charlatans; their prototype was Seneca, who vaunted the virtues of poverty while "gorging himself on a fortune of sixty million livres." As a group they were so inept as to bring down "torrents of ridicule" on any government foolish enough to employ their services. In this respect, Fourier cited with relish the "hail of sarcasm" that had greeted the publication by the Directory of maxims from Saint-Lambert's *Catéchisme universel* and above all its preposterous injunction to "pay your taxes with joy."⁵⁵

Fourier took particular pleasure in noting the contradictions of the moralists. He gloated over Varro's claim that the ancient Romans held 278 different opinions on the nature of true happiness. And he could wax sarcastic over a news item on the publication of treatises on morality.

> "This year we had only seventeen treatises on morality," wrote a journal of 1803, deploring the smallness of the harvest. It was only speaking about France. If one adds the other states that are involved in the commerce or manufacture of moral doctrines, which is carried on actively in England, Germany, and Italy, the number of treatises must reach at least forty a year, even in times of scarcity. And since all of these treatises are contradictory, each one overturning its predecessor, one must change one's behavior and manners at least forty times a year in order to follow docilely the lessons of sweet and pure morality. Moreover, you need a lot of money to buy these innumerable controversial works, a lot of time and patience to read them, and a lot of intelligence to understand them, since their authors do not understand them themselves.⁵⁶

Despite the contradictions in their doctrines, the moralists all had one thing in common: they believed that the way to virtue was to repress and correct the passions. Far from studying man, the moralists had only studied "the art of perverting man and repressing the soul's impulses or *passionate attractions* on the grounds that they are not suited to the civilized and barbarian order."⁵⁷

Although Fourier obviously enjoyed heaping ridicule on the moralists, he hardly bothered to analyze their doctrines. For although the priests and politicians continued to maintain some power over the masses, it seemed clear to Fourier that the moralists could no longer hope to command an audience. They were like "old codgers who, sitting by the fireside, still have their word to say about the present century, but are no longer heard."[58] The reason for this was that in an age of commercial capitalism, their doctrines of renunciation had ceased to have the slightest relevance to the way people actually lived.

> For a long time morality preached scorn for perfidious wealth. Today Seneca would hardly shine with this doctrine. The nineteenth century is entirely given over to speculation and the thirst for gold. . . . Such is the fortunate fruit of our progress in rationalism and positivism. They have pushed us from one extreme to the other; they have introduced the worship of the GOLDEN CALF and dethroned the morality of the divine Seneca and the divine Diogenes.[59]

What people really cared about in the nineteenth century was enriching themselves, and all talk about establishing the reign of virtue and justice and truth would be idle until a social system was established that would make them more lucrative than vice and iniquity and falsehood.[60]

IV

Of all the aspects of Fourier's theory it was his critique of civilized society that won the greatest respect from his contemporaries. His analysis of the frauds of the marketplace and the anarchic character of early capitalist production, his call for the organization of work, his attack on the family system and his plea for the emancipation of women—these and many other elements of his critique all made their way into the developing socialist tradition. Fourier's critical writing thus helped to mold the mentality of the generation that fought on the barricades of 1848. It also won the admiration of Marx and Engels, who assigned to Fourier a special place among the utopian precursors of scientific socialism. As Engels wrote in an oft-quoted passage:

> We find in Fourier a criticism of the existing conditions of society, genuinely French and witty, but not upon that account any the less thorough. Fourier takes the bourgeoisie, their inspired prophets before the Revolution, and their interested eulogists after it, at their own word. He lays bare remorselessly the material and moral misery of the bourgeois world. He confronts it with the earlier philosophers' dazzling promises of a society in

which reason alone should reign, of a civilization in which happiness should be universal, of an illimitable perfectibility, and with the rose-colored phraseology of the bourgeois ideologists of his time. He points out how everywhere the most pitiful reality corresponds with the most high-sounding phrases, and he overwhelms this hopeless fiasco of phrases with his mordant sarcasm.

Fourier is not only a critic; his imperturbably serene nature makes him a satirist, and assuredly one of the greatest satirists of all time. He depicts, with equal power and charm, the swindling speculations that blossomed upon the downfall of the Revolution, and the shopkeeping spirit prevalent in, and characteristic of, French commerce at that time. Still more masterly is his criticism of the bourgeois form of the relations between the sexes, and the position of women in bourgeois society.[61]

In these comments, which remain one of the most trenchant general appreciations of Fourier's critique of civilization, Engels put his finger on one of the most remarkable features of Fourier's critical writing. This was his ability to cut through the rhetoric of liberal political economy and to expose the contradiction between its promises and the reality of bourgeois civilization in the early nineteenth century.

Fourier was, as Engels recognized, a great satirist, a gifted writer whose command of parody, extended metaphor, and mock-heroic diction gave both mordancy and variety to his critique. Just as Balzac could write novels about the "grandeur and decadence" of perfume merchants and vermicelli manufacturers, Fourier could describe in meticulous detail the "pitched battles" and "transcendent intrigues" of the Napoleons and Talleyrands of a provincial stock exchange. Adopting a clinical tone, he could carefully describe the various ranks in the "knighthood" of bankrupts or the "hierarchy" of cuckoldom. He could also deftly use the Swiftian device of the extended metaphor, which is so fully and vividly elaborated that it finally becomes inseparable from the object represented. In Swift's "The Art of Political Lying," lies *become* flies buzzing around a horse's tail in summer; in Fourier's writings on analogy philosophers *become* parrots with bright plumage, sharp claws, and fluent but meaningless speech. But Fourier's principal aim as a satirist was to expose the hollowness of the rhetoric of the philosophers and political economists of his time, and one of his favorite devices was the ironic incantation of the ideas and slogans of these thinkers in such a way that their words were revealed as a litany of meaningless clichés. "Our sophists will cajole you," Fourier wrote, "saying that sensations arise from perceptions of intuitions for the welfare of commerce and of the Constitutional Charter."[62] Repeatedly Fourier criticized the philosophers as performers in an "obscurantist ballet" who claimed to be flying "on a sublime course leading to rapid progress toward perfectibilizing perfectibility."[63] This sort of language was not simply meaningless, Fourier explained; it was also deceiving.

> The two sciences, philosophy and theology, which provide the poor with so much happiness, deck themselves out in the masks of "balance," "counterpoise," "equilibrium," "guarantee," "perfectibility." These bits of verbiage can be compared with that of the Jacobins of 1793, who, with each word, caused "principles," "facts," "justice," and "the welfare of the country," etc., to resound. What a fine thing in civilization is the abuse of words! When Condillac tells us, "Words are the veritable *signs* of our ideas," wouldn't he have done better to tell us, "Words are the veritable *masks* of our ideas."[64]

Fourier's critique of civilization was thus informed by an understanding that one of the main functions of the political and economic rhetoric of his time was to throw a veil over social reality and to mask the hegemony of the "mercantile class," which had come to dominate French political life since the Revolution.

There is another feature of Fourier's critique of civilization that gives it a powerful and enduring resonance, but distinguishes it from radical social criticism in the Marxist tradition. This is the breadth of Fourier's social sympathies. Unlike Marx and Engels, Fourier attached as much importance to sexual and generational conflict as to the conflict of social classes. He was also sensitive to an extremely wide range of social ills, and particularly to the kinds of mental or psychic suffering that the sufferer himself could not explain or understand. Fourier was concerned not only with the exploitation of factory workers and the hardships of small peasant farmers but also with the drudgery of housewives, the boredom of office workers, the abuse of children, the loveless and insecure lives of the elderly, and the sufferings of the ugly, whatever their class or status. He had an immediate grasp of pain wherever he saw it, and he had the clarity of vision to recognize it where others could not. It is for this reason that Edmund Wilson could speak of Fourier as possessing an "almost insane capacity for pity."[65]

This capacity for pity was itself rooted in Fourier's steadfast rejection of the tragic view of life. He was simply unable to accept human suffering as a necessary part of things. And he was unable to accept doctrines that purported to explain or justify suffering as anything else but specious rationalizations. On the contrary, he argued, humans were made to be happy. A rich and full life was the "destiny" of every man and woman, and the only limits that could legitimately be placed on an individual were those inherent in his or her instinctual endowment. It was his conviction that both physical suffering and emotional deprivation were *avoidable* that gave Fourier's critique of civilization its extraordinary urgency and comprehensiveness.

11

The Anatomy of the Passions

BOTH FOURIER'S critique of civilization and his utopian plans hinged on a psychological theory, which he rightly regarded as the core of his whole system. According to this theory, which challenged the assumptions of the vast majority of contemporary radicals and reformers, man was neither a malleable nor a rational creature. On the contrary, Fourier insisted, human behavior was dictated by fundamental instinctual drives that could not be permanently altered or suppressed. Fourier called these drives the passions, and he believed that one of his own principal accomplishments as a thinker had been to identify and define them and to analyze their functions. His argument with "the philosophers" was that they had failed to recognize the power of the passions. For centuries they had been devising doctrines meant to curb or check the passions and thereby to alter human nature. But Fourier believed that these repressive doctrines were themselves one of the principal causes of the misery of civilized man. In his view the real task confronting the social theorist was to find a way to liberate and utilize the repressed passions. Only when the primacy and immutability of these drives was recognized, he believed, would it be possible to construct a society in which human beings could be free, happy, and productive.

I

In its broad outlines Fourier's concept of human nature represented a radical departure from the image of man as a "blank slate," a machine for the processing of sensations, which had been so compelling to Enlightenment thinkers in their attacks on the Christian doctrine of Original Sin. Still, one should not exaggerate the novelty of Fourier's insistence on the strength of the passions as determinants of human behavior. For a concern with the passions and their powers had in fact been central to much French moral and psychological thinking throughout the seventeenth and eighteenth centuries.[1] In their different ways the great playwrights Racine and Molière had explored in depth the influence of a "ruling passion" on individual behavior. Descartes had written a *Traité sur les passions* in which attention was given to the uses of the passions and their influence on "all the good and evil of this life." It is true that for Descartes and for many other seventeenth and eighteenth century thinkers the self was identified with consciousness and the passions were fundamentally modes of awareness. The idea of a passion as an unconscious or preconscious drive is largely absent from the thought of the period. It is also true that many seventeenth-century thinkers were interested in the passions mainly because they regarded them as base inclinations whose influence was to be feared. But in the century after Descartes a host of thinkers emerged to take issue with the traditional Christian disparagement of the passions, and by the mid-eighteenth century the rehabilitation of the passions had become almost commonplace. "Nothing," wrote a Catholic philosopher in 1758, "is more a la mode today than to declare yourself an apologist of the passions; it is the title of a wit, of a philosophe, of a bold thinker."[2]

Among eighteenth-century thinkers the apology of the passions took many different forms. The most commonplace was the idea that the good life involved some sort of equilibrium between reason and the passions: if human life could be compared to a voyage at sea, then reason was the pilot who steered the ship and the passions were the winds that made it go.[3] But many writers of the Enlightenment made greater claims. For Diderot and Vauvenargues, for example, the passions were exalted as the principal source of great art and great deeds. For Helvétius the passions were the stimulus of attention and thus the principal cause of an individual's intelligence, or lack of it. "We become stupid," wrote Helvétius, "as soon as we stop being passionate."[4] In the work of Holbach and many other thinkers of the Enlightenment the passions are portrayed as socially useful—as the "cement" binding people together in society and as invaluable stimuli to useful work and to interest in others. All of these arguments—and others—are to be found in the work of the eighteenth century's greatest apologist of the passions, the Marquis de Sade. In his *Histoire de Juliette* one of the characters delivers a fervent defense of the passions.

> They dare to declaim against the passions; they dare to chain them by laws. But let us compare them both; let us see whether it is the passions or the laws that have done men the most good. Who doubts, as Helvétius says, that in the moral realm the passions play the role of movement in the physical? It is only to the passions that we owe the inventions and marvels of the arts; they must be regarded, continues the same author, as the productive germ of the mind and the powerful spring of great actions. Individuals who are not animated by strong passions are only mediocre beings. . . . Granting this, I wonder what could be more dangerous than laws that hinder passions? Just compare the centuries of anarchy with those during which laws have been most effective, in any government that you choose, and you will easily be convinced that it is only at the moment when laws are silent that the greatest actions burst forth.

Elsewhere in the same work the passions are described as the source of all our happiness and as the "motive forces of our being . . . so inherent to us, so necessary to the laws that move us, that they are like the first needs that conserve our existence."[5]

There was a world of difference between the rational and often utilitarian defense of the passions carried on by most eighteenth-century thinkers and the exaltation of Passion by later romantic writers. On this point, and also in his view of the passions as motive forces analogous to gravitational attraction, Fourier was clearly a child of the eighteenth century. And yet it is clear that, with the notable exception of the Marquis de Sade, none of the eighteenth-century thinkers went as far as Fourier in his defense of the passions. Indeed, most of the apologists of the passions in eighteenth-century France were ultimately moderates who believed that some restraints were necessary if a good and relatively free society was to be established. Thus while Diderot could praise "les passions fortes" and Toussaint could insist that the passions are "good, useful, and necessary," both went on to argue against indulging the passions and to urge the establishment of a "just harmony" or balance among them. Similarly, d'Alembert warned that while good in themselves, the passions had a tendency to excess, and it was therefore incumbent on all men to strive to subordinate their passions to a rational ideal, the love of mankind.[6]

It is true that the image of an idyllic primitive society where men were free to obey their instinctual promptings was present in the minds of many of the Enlightenment philosophers.[7] But few believed that this idyllic state could be recaptured. The greatest of the philosophes—Montesquieu, Diderot, Rousseau—believed that social life necessarily involved constraint; and to them freedom meant the conscious acceptance of constraint, the agreement to abide by law. The essential psychological complement of freedom, as they understood it, was stoic moderation and ascetic self-discipline on the Spartan or Roman republican model.

Fourier was familiar with this venerable tradition of political theory, and he had nothing but contempt for it. In his writings he repeatedly mocked the republican virtue and Spartan simplicity vaunted by "the philosophers." What was good, he asked, about a society in which men were compelled to live on "republican cabbage," "Spartan gruel," and self-restraint? To his mind self-imposed constraints were no better than constraints imposed from without. There was nothing dignified about continence and rational self-discipline. Furthermore, they wouldn't work. The passions clamored for gratification and no matter how "rational" repression might be, its consequences would always be harmful to the individual and ultimately destructive to society. Fourier believed that the only happy and harmonious society would be one that would liberate and utilize the passions.

II

If Fourier's defense of the passions was far more thoroughgoing than that of almost all the great Enlightenment thinkers, there are some respects in which his views were archaic by comparison with theirs. This is particularly evident when one considers the metaphysical underpinnings of his theory. For at a time when most social philosophers had dispensed with appeals to Divine Providence and with the "hypothesis" of a supreme being, Fourier was elaborating a providentialist metaphysics that involved him in elaborate speculations concerning the "designs" of the deity and the "destinies" of all created things.[8] Although Fourier was capable of developing his metaphysics at great length, it was at bottom extremely simple. Like many of the eighteenth-century deists, he was fascinated by the orderly and harmonious pattern that Kepler and Galileo and Newton had shown to underlie the workings of the material universe. He also took seriously the argument from design. He believed, in other words, that the perfectly harmonious Newtonian universe was itself a proof of the existence of an infinitely wise creator.

But in his speculations on the properties and "intentions" of the Creator Fourier went beyond the wildest dreams of the deists. He maintained that a God possessing such attributes as infinite wisdom and universal providence was bound by his very nature to have made a provision for the terrestrial happiness of mankind.

> If it is absurd not to believe in God, it is not less absurd to believe in him halfway, to think that his providence is only partial, that he has neglected to provide for our most urgent needs like that of a social order that would make our happiness.[9]

To assure man's happiness, a just and reasonable God must have prepared some kind of "social code" analogous to the plan that regulated the movements of the stars and the planets. This was an argument that to Fourier had all the value of a "geometrical proof." Repeated (as it often was) three or seven or fourteen times, it became his "geometrical proofs." Attaining fourteen pages and sixteen proofs was the tour de force entitled "Concerning the numberless absurdities into which God would have fallen if he had been wanting in the composition and revelation of an attractional and unitary social code."[10] According to Fourier, a God who had failed to create such a code would be blind, unreasonable, bad intentioned, unjust, anarchistic, impractical, bellicose, atheistical, in short "the equivalent of the fictitious being we call the devil."[11] This was a possibility that Fourier apparently never seriously entertained.

Fourier admitted that the spectacle offered by the contemporary civilized world was in itself hardly likely to bolster anyone's faith in the wisdom or beneficence of the Creator. But this, he argued over and over again, was simply evidence that weak and fallible humans had failed to recognize the intentions of the deity. They had failed in particular to recognize that it was in the sphere of science—specifically Newtonian science—that the "key" to the divine plan could be found. Taking for granted the idea of a preestablished correspondence between the physical and social worlds, Fourier maintained that the divine plan for the organization of human societies had to be in some way analogous to the principles governing the perfectly harmonious Newtonian universe. Thus the task of the social theorist as he understood it was to translate Newton's discovery into the social sphere and to find a social correlate to gravitational attraction.

Although Fourier was apparently unaware of it, he was following in the steps of a long line of seventeenth and eighteenth century thinkers who had been inspired by the work of Galileo and Newton to hope that laws of motion could be discovered for human behavior just as for falling bodies and planets. The tradition went back at least as far as Thomas Hobbes and his attempt to construct a "new science of politics" on the model of Galilean physics. But it was the Newtonian theory of gravitational attraction that really launched the search for a science of human behavior. During the century that followed the appearance of Newton's *Principia* numerous European philosophers and moralists attempted to generalize the Newtonian paradigm and to discover the principle of "attraction" that governed life in society.[12] What were the elements in human experience through which one might most easily detect the exercise of attraction? Many eighteenth-century philosophers had held that mental life begins with sensations, and a large number of them—notably the associationist psychologists from Gay and Hartley to Hume and James Mill—had gone on to seek an understanding of human nature in the laws of the association of ideas derived from sensations. David Hume, for example, referred to the association of ideas as "a kind of attraction which in the mental world will be found to have as extraordinary effects as in the natural."[13] For Fourier on the other hand, mental life began not with sensations but with the passions. Its laws were not those of the association of ideas but of "passionate attraction." In the *Nouveau monde industriel* Fourier defined it in these terms: "Passionate attraction is the drive given us by nature prior to any reflection, and it persists despite the opposition of reason, duty, prejudice, etc."[14] For Fourier the passions were "the mistresses of the world," and his primary concern as a thinker was to define them and to analyze their workings.

Fourier's love of drawing up elaborate taxonomies was manifest in almost everything he wrote about psychological questions.[15] He was constantly counting and classifying manias, penchants, and personality types. But he believed that they could all be subsumed within a basic classification of twelve recurring or "radical" passions. In discussing these passions he generally employed the simile of a tree. The trunk of the tree he called "unityism." Although this was a passion in itself, it was of another order than the twelve radical passions: it was the result of their synthesis or harmony. He described it at one point as a state of "unlimited philanthropy and universal fellow feeling" in which the individual spontaneously linked his happiness with that of the rest of mankind.[16] But since it was unknown in civilization, he generally characterized it simply by opposition to egotism, the dominant emotional state of civilization.

Three sets of branches extended from the trunk of Fourier's "passional tree." The first set consisted of five branches corresponding to the five senses. "It is scarcely credible," wrote Fourier, "that after three thousand years of studies, men have not yet thought of classifying the senses. At present even our five senses are cited pell-mell; no distinction of rank is admitted among them." It particularly disturbed Fourier that civilized philosophers had never granted due respect to taste, the most imperious of the senses and "the first and last enjoyment of man . . . almost the only resource of children and the elderly in matters of pleasure."[17]

Fourier called the passions of the five senses the "luxurious" passions because their gratification was dependent not only on health but also on wealth, on the kind of material luxuries that only the rich could afford in civilization. Such was the inequity of the civilized order that individuals with "brilliant" appetites and strong stomachs lived on the brink of starvation and others with magnificent ears lacked the money to buy tickets to the opera. In Harmony, Fourier promised, a minimum of gratification would be provided for the sense of taste and the sense of touch.[18] At the same time each of the senses would undergo prodigious refinement. The human eye, for example, would acquire the power both to see in the dark and to stare at the sun; and the sense of smell of at least some human beings would become as keen as that of hunting dogs.[19]

Fourier's second category included the four affective passions: friendship, love, ambition, and parenthood (or familism). These four passions tended to bring people together in groups; they were impulsions directed toward other people, just as the five sensual passions were impulsions directed toward things. Like the other passions, the affective passions varied in intensity not only according to an individual's personal endowment but also according to his or her age. Thus children were generally dominated by friendship, young people by love, mature individuals by ambition, and old people by familism. Some of the worst aspects of civilization stemmed from the fact that the elderly had succeeded in imposing "their" passion on the rest of society. And although ambition assumed perverse forms in civilization, love and friendship were continually frustrated by the "insidious" alliance of the familial passion with the institution of monogamous marriage. In Harmony the family passion would not disappear, but with the abolition of marriage—and of the lugubrious family meal—it would assume new, unrepressive forms.

If the sensual and affective passions were frustrated or perverted in civilization, at least there was no doubt about their existence. But the three passions at the top of Fourier's tree were either unrecognized or completely misunderstood in civilization. These were the distributive or "mechanizing" passions, so named because their free expression was essential for the gratification of the other nine. Useless and even harmful in civilization, they were to become the "mainsprings of the social mechanism" in Harmony. Their combined action would keep the other nine passions in a state of perfect equilibrium and permit the formation of the "passionate series," which were to be the basic forms of association within Fourier's ideal community.

The first of these distributive passions was the Cabalist or intriguing passion, the penchant for conspiring, calculating, forming combinations. Fourier had watched it at work among the merchants and brokers at the Bourse of Lyon. But he also knew it to be the favorite passion of women, courtiers, and politicians. "It is such an imperious need," wrote Fourier, "that if it cannot satisfy itself in real intrigues, it will seek out artificial ones like games, the theater, or novels."[20] Of course the civilized philosophers found it disruptive; they ignored the creative role it would play in Harmony, where the spirit of cabalistic rivalry and intrigue would serve as a spur to work and to perfection in every form of activity.

The Butterfly or alternating passion was the second of Fourier's distributive passions. This was the penchant for variety and contrast, for periodic changes of scene, which Fourier recognized as one of his own most deeply ingrained impulses. It was the need to "flutter from pleasure to pleasure," which manifested itself, he claimed, about "every two hours." It flourished among the "Parisian sybarites" who boasted that they had mastered the art of "living so well and so fast." The people who suffered most from the repression of this changeling passion were those chained to the bonds of civilized work—and marriage.

The last of the distributive passions, and Fourier's favorite, was the Composite. This was the most passionate of passions, the "most romantic," and the most "inimical to reasoning." Whereas the Cabalist was a "reflective enthusiasm," the Composite was pure or "blind" enthusiasm without a trace of rational calculation. Almost wholly ungratified in civilization, the Composite was the desire for the sort of happiness that could only be found in the mixture of physical and spiritual pleasures. Its particular domain was love, but it could also be associated with the other passions. "The Composite is the most beautiful of the passions," wrote Fourier, "the one that enhances the value of all the others. A love is only beautiful if it is a composite love that engages both the senses and the soul. It becomes a trivial affair or a deception if it is limited to just one of these motives. An ambition is only powerful if it brings into play the two motives of glory and interest. It is then that it becomes capable of brilliant efforts."[21]

Although Fourier's psychology began with the identification and description of the twelve radical passions, it did not end there. As he sometimes put it, the passions were the alphabet of his science, but there was also a passional grammar with its own declensions, conjugations, and syntax. Much of Fourier's writing was devoted to the delineation of the various links that might be established among the different passions, and the permutations they would undergo when placed in combination with one another. Without exploring the more subtle refinements, one can say that each of Fourier's passions could be divided into a multitude of nuances, each had its own "exponential scale" of degrees of intensity, and each was endowed with particular "subversive" tendencies that would become manifest whenever the "harmonic" tendency was denied gratification. Thus when ambition was perverted or repressed, it could express itself in destructive competition, and the aural passion in a love of mere noise. Similarly hatred and jealousy were "subversive" manifestations of the passion of love.

The twelve basic passions were the materials out of which Fourier constructed an elaborate classification of personality types, which was to serve as the model for his theory of social organization.[22] He maintained that each of the passions played a role in the psychic life of every human being. But the intensity with which the different passions were felt varied greatly from one individual to another. Everyone was ruled by one or several dominant passions, and these "dominants" in turn expressed themselves in various ways depending on the "tonic" or nuance of the passion. Thus the hero of Molière's *The Miser* was dominated by ambition with avarice as its tonic; similarly an inveterate drinker was dominated by the passion of taste with drink as its tonic. Fourier claimed that most men and women were dominated by some nuance of a single passion; they were the "monogynes" or "solitones" who would be the common soldiers in the ranks of Harmony.

Much rarer but far more interesting to Fourier were the "polytones" or "polygynes," complex personalities who were dominated by more than one passion. In discussing these types Fourier generally cited familiar historical examples. Louis XIV, for instance, was a digyne dominated by the passions of ambition and love; Robespierre and Lycurgus were both trigynes dominated by the Composite, the Cabalist, and ambition; and Henri IV was "a magnificent tetragyne" with friendship, love, ambition, and the Composite as his principal passions. In running the gamut from the monogyne to the pentagyne, Fourier confidently asserted, one would find a total of 810 distinct personality types, each of which represented some combination of the twelve basic passions. These 810 types did not exhaust the potential of the human species—there were also the extremely rare hexagynes, heptagynes, and omnigynes—but they did constitute what Fourier called the general scale or keyboard of personality types. They represented the minimal level of psychic diversity necessary for the maintenance of "passional equilibrium" within Fourier's ideal community.

Fourier's analysis of the passions can be criticized on many grounds. It is arbitrary; it is incomplete; it leaves little room for some of the most basic human impulses—for example, laziness, jealousy, the love of privacy. It places under a single rubric impulses and appetites and tastes that would seem to be fundamentally different, both in kind and in origin. It curiously treats hunger and thirst as manifestations of the passion of taste. Some of its other categories—for instance, ambition and the Cabalist—overlap. One might reply that Fourier's system is no more arbitrary, and certainly a good deal less incomplete, than many of the reductionist psychological models, the notions of economic or sexual or acquisitive man, associated with social theories widely influential in Fourier's time. It is also worth pointing out that Fourier himself gave considerable thought to a number of the objections his theory inspires. Not all of his replies are equally convincing. But one can find in his writing interesting comments on the historical relativity of such allegedly immutable impulses as jealousy.[23] One can also find in Fourier a full and coherent explanation of the process whereby the aggressive and antisocial impulses, so widespread in civilization, would disappear in Harmony.

Another line of criticism of Fourier's psychology focuses on its form rather than its content. Fourier had considerable psychological insight, it is said, but the usefulness and even the comprehensibility of his theory of the passions is vitiated by his penchant for neologisms, taxonomies, and pseudomathematical calculations. This is hard to deny. There are times when the human element—that which is to be explained—threatens to disappear beneath a welter of terminological refinements and "exponential scales." What needs to be emphasized, however, is that alongside the mathematician Fourier, the would-be Newton of the passions, there also dwelt a poet, a writer who could illustrate his taxonomies with delightful and discerning vignettes about everyday life. Thus in the midst of a discussion of the characteristics of the monogyne, he could cite an example drawn from his own experience.

> Let us add a minor and comical example to our list of monogynes. Here is a character whom I found remarkable. He was a drinker, a monogyne dominated by the passion of taste with drink as his tonic passion. I encountered him in a public carriage. He was not a simple drunkard, but a man endowed with a marvelous ability to relate all of life's happenings to wine. Like the mystics who see everything in terms of God, he saw everything in terms of wine. For example, instead of telling time by hours and half-hours, he calculated by bottles consumed. If you asked him, "How far is it to such and such a place?", he would answer, "Why, just far enough to drink four bottles." Once when the horses had stopped, I asked him, "Will we be waiting long here?" He answered, "Why, long

enough to drink a quick one." I knew that, according to his arithmetic, "a quick one" meant five minutes and "a bottle" meant ten minutes. Once when another carriage, drawn by tired horses, passed us going downhill, he shouted at it, "Bah! Bah! We'll be drinking before you will!" What he meant was, "We'll get there before you." For why should anyone go anywhere if not to drink?

I pricked up my ears when he was in private conversation with one of his comrades. He talked of nothing but rows of bottles and open casks and taking the first drink, etc. In short for this man wine was the focal point of all nature. He judged food by the wines that could be drunk with it; for him a horse was not worth money but rather a certain number of casks of Mâcon wine. No matter what subject he discussed, he managed to relate it to wine with an extraordinary finesse and subtlety. Nonetheless he was no drunkard, but simply a strongly pronounced monogyne with drink as his tonic passion.[24]

Like his contemporary Balzac, Fourier had the ability to recognize finesse and subtlety in the most commonplace passions encountered under the most ordinary circumstances. This awareness informed and animated even the driest of his taxonomies.

IV

One of the most striking intellectual developments of the postrevolutionary period in Europe was the growth of interest in groups and communities, both as constituents of society and as influences on individual personality and behavior. The bias of Enlightenment philosophy and social thought had been individualistic: most eighteenth-century thinkers had tacitly accepted an atomistic conception of society as a network of specific and willed relationships entered into by free, autonomous and rational individuals. But this view was no longer tenable to the generation of thinkers who had witnessed the social upheaval caused by the destruction of parish, guild, and other primary groups during the French Revolution. The social thought of the postrevolutionary period was marked by a new interest in the sources of social cohesion and in the relationship between personality and culture. At the same time French thinkers as diverse as Bonald, Maistre, Comte, and

Saint-Simon became fascinated with the study of the nonrational and affective ties that bound individuals to the groups and communities within which they lived, worked, and worshiped.

In many respects this whole movement was alien to the thought of Charles Fourier. Certainly Fourier did not share the concern of thinkers like Bonald and Burke with common traditions as a source of social cohesion. Nor did he have the slightest interest in the cultural determinants of personality. He believed that the individual was what his passions made him, and that the affinity between two Cabalists, for example, was likely to transcend whatever cultural barriers might separate them. But Fourier was at one with his contemporaries in his rejection of the atomistic view of society held by eighteenth-century thinkers and in his belief that the fundamental social unit was not the individual but the group. To his mind one of the great failings of eighteenth-century thought was its preoccupation with the faculties and powers of the isolated individual. "The individual," he wrote, "is an essentially false being, because he cannot either by himself or in a couple bring about the development of the twelve passions."[25] To consider the powers of the human individual in isolation and apart from the groups to which he belonged was in Fourier's view like trying to judge the powers of the bee and the beaver outside the hive and the dam.

Fourier's belief that the passions were the primary constituents of individual personality was thus linked to the conviction that the individual was preeminently a group animal and that it was only within the context of group activity that most human passions could attain full expression. For this reason he devoted great attention to the study of groups, and his efforts to work out taxonomies of the passions and of individual personality types were complemented by an attempt to specify the properties and dynamics of group behavior. Fourier understood that according to the conventional wisdom, the group was still an unworthy—and comic— object for formal study. "Whenever you talk about groups," he complained, "at the start you've got to put up with a salvo of stale jokes. . . . 'Ha! Ha! Groups! What a silly subject that is! It must be very amusing to talk about groups!' That is the way our wits reason when one talks about groups." But comical or not, Fourier insisted on the importance of the group to an understanding of human behavior.

> We have numerous treatises on the study of man. But what can they tell us about the subject if they neglect the essential por-

tion, the analysis of groups? In all our relationships we persistently tend to form groups, and they have never been an object of study.[26]

Today Fourier could no longer complain that the study of small groups is not taken seriously. Nonetheless there is still much in Fourier's writings about groups that is difficult for a modern reader to appreciate, or even to comprehend. The main problem is that Fourier was not interested, as are modern sociologists, in the empirical study of group behavior. Nor was he interested in any kind of group. Everything he had to say about groups was clearly based on long and careful observation in the excellent laboratories provided by boardinghouses and pension dinner tables. But his principal concern as a theorist was not with patterns of interaction among the members of such groups as he was actually able to study; it was with the formulation of hypotheses concerning the particular sort of groups that would exist in his utopia.

> We give the name of group to any gathering at all [he wrote], even to a bunch of idlers drawn together by boredom, without passion and without goal—empty minds, people busy killing time, waiting for something to happen. In the theory of the passions the term *group* refers to a mass brought together by a common taste for a particular function.[27]

More precisely, the kinds of groups that interested Fourier were gatherings of seven to nine individuals of diverse age, wealth, and intelligence, all sharing a common passion.

Fourier called such groups harmonic groups, and he carefully distinguished them from the "subversive" groups, which were more characteristic of civilization. He defined a *harmonic group* as "an entirely free gathering" whose members were "united by sharing one or several common objects of affection." It was also a group that appeared to be what it actually was—a group, in other words, in which the "dominant" or real passion was identical to the "tonic" or ostensible passion. A subversive group, on the other hand, was one in which the real passion was different from the ostensible passion. Fourier's prime example of a subversive group was the civilized family, nominally united by ties of affection and trust, but actually held together more by material needs and social conventions.[28]

Fourier's interest in harmonic groups may be easier for us to understand if we attempt to spell out a few of the general assumptions that lay behind his writings on groups and group psychology. The first of these assumptions was that if people were left entirely free to do whatever they wished, they would naturally tend to form sets or series of groups based on common interests and affinities. "What is the first natural impulse among a mass of free people?" he asked. "It is to divide up into groups according to nuances of opinion, taste, and function."[29] Fourier's second assumption was that within these groups or series of groups a certain hierarchical structure would always tend to emerge. The members of any group or series would divide themselves, he believed, into at least three subgroups, which could be represented in the form of a center and two "wings." To use Fourier's favorite example, if a group were made up of pear lovers, the center would consist of the mass of lovers of ripe, juicy pears, while the two wings would be made up respectively of devotees of soft, mealy pears and hard cooking pears.[30] The minimum number of people necessary for the structure to emerge, said Fourier, was seven. If there were at least twenty-four people in a gathering, then it would be possible to establish a series consisting of three groups.

> A group may be formed with a minimum of seven members, but it is more complete with nine members and can add to its three subgroups a pivotal member or leader, and an ambiguous element or transitional member. For example:

Transition	1	Ambiguous
Upper Wing	2	Students
Center	3	Experts
Lower Wing	2	Beginners
Pivot	1	Leaders

> This division emerges naturally in any gathering for work or pleasure, if people give free play to their passions and instincts. Man being by instinct hostile to equality and inclined toward the hierarchical or progressive system, this graduated order will emerge in a series of nine groups, as in a group of nine individual members, if all are entirely free.[31]

Fourier's third assumption was that although the center of a harmonic group or series would be numerically larger than either of the wings, there would be a tendency for the members of the two wings to collaborate with one another in rivalry or opposition to the center.

Beginning with these assumptions on the structure of harmonic groups, Fourier devoted much of his writing on groups and group psychology to an attempt to classify different types of groups and to describe the role that each might play in promoting social harmony. Naturally Fourier's discussion of groups includes curious "mathematical" refinements; and one sometimes finds him pausing to lament, for example, that he lacks the space to work out an extended comparison of the properties of the four fundamental types of groups and the properties of the four conic sections.[32] But Fourier's essential points can be summarized briefly. There are four basic types of groups, he claimed, in each of which the cohesive element is provided by one of the four affective passions. Thus some groups are cemented by friendship, and others by love, family feeling, or shared ambitions. Fourier argued that each type of group has its own particular mores and "tone." Groups in which friendship is the binding passion are marked by "cordiality and confusion of ranks." Groups of ambition are marked by deference of inferiors to superiors; groups of love by deference of the strong to the weak; and groups in which familism prevails by deference of the old to the young. Fourier conceded that the moralists of civilization had another conception of the family passion. For them the father was the sole authority within the family, and everyone else owed him respect and obedience. But nature's dictate was different: the natural inclination of the father was to spoil the child and to gratify its every whim. And this was exactly what both parents would do in Harmony, where the responsibility for the education and socialization of children would be exercised by others.[33]

One of Fourier's main concerns as a student of groups was to specify as precisely as possible the basis of the cohesiveness of any group. Thus he refined his initial classification of the four basic types of group by introducing a distinction between the spiritual and material expression of each of the affective passions. Familism, for example, might be based entirely on the material bond of consanguinity, but it could also have a purely spiritual basis as in the case of ties between parents and adoptive children. Similarly, love could be rooted in physical desire or in "platonic" affinities. When just one of these two impulses was at work within a group, Fourier called it a simple group as opposed to a compound group in which both the material and spiritual impulses were brought into play. All of this was summarized by Fourier in the following table:

[The Theory]

ELEMENTARY IMPULSES OF THE FOUR GROUPS

Hypomajor or group of *friendship:*

S   Spiritual affinity of character traits.

M   Material affinity of industrial penchants.

Hypermajor or group of *ambition:*

S   Spiritual affinity, league for glory.

M   Material affinity, league for interest.

Hyperminor or group of *love:*

M   Material affinity by copulation.

S   Spiritual affinity by platonic love.

Hypominor or *family* group:

M   Material affinity, bond of consanguinity.

S   Spiritual affinity, bond of adoption.[34]

In a further refinement Fourier specified that each of the four types of group was dominant at a particular phase in the life of the individual. For the child the ties formed in groups based on friendship were most important; for the young man or woman ties of love predominated; ambition was the ruling passion of groups of mature people, and familism that of the elderly.[35]

If harmonic groups were the basic building blocks out of which community was formed in Fourier's ideal society, they could not exist in isolation. Groups functioned properly only when they were brought together to form series of groups, or "passionate series." According to Fourier, a passionate series was "a league of various groups, arranged in ascending and descending order, passionately joined together because they share a common liking for some task" or activity.[36] For a series to function properly, Fourier maintained that three conditions would have to be met. First of all, although the members of a series shared a common taste, they would have to be different in other respects such as wealth, age, and strength. Just as in music a chord is formed by excluding notes too close to one another, so contrast and antipathy were essential to the proper functioning of a series. Second, since neither groups nor series could exist in isolation, each series would have to be "enmeshed" with others. In even the most modest form of simple association there would have to be at least forty-five or fifty series, each composed of at least seven groups, and each enmeshed with at least two adjoining series. Finally, for this meshing to occur, the extreme elements in each series would have to be transitional. The series of peach growers and plum growers, for example, would be linked by the nectarine fanciers. Transitional groups thus had a vital role to play in Fourier's system. Just as he was fascinated by transitional or "ambiguous" species in the natural world—for example, the bat, the quince, and the frog—he regarded transitional or ambiguous groups as indispensable links in the social structure of the Phalanx.[37]

The ultimate purpose behind all Fourier's reflections on groups and series was to guide the organization of the Phalanx. Groups were for Fourier the elementary forms of social relations, and it was within the harmonic groups and series of the Phalanx that the disparate interests and the often destructive passions of the men and women of civilization would be harmonized and channeled in salutary directions. Within these groups differences of age, wealth, and status would be transformed from sources of social conflict into instruments for the realization of the common good. Just how this transformation was to take place is best considered in the following chapters. But at this point we should at least observe that almost all the institutions of Fourier's Phalanx—the Little Hordes, the opera, the hierarchy of honors, the novel systems of adoption and inheritance—were designed with the intent either of "creating sympathetic illusions between antipathetic people" or of "removing obstacles that prevent the accord" of such people. All these institutions had a place in what Fourier called his theory of *ralliements,* or "the art of creating passionate ties between members of classes that appear to be essentially antipathetic, such as the poor and the rich, masters and valets, graybeards and young women, heirs and possessors."[38]

V

Fourier's conviction that the passions were meant to be the agents of human happiness and social harmony rested on the assumption that almost all the evil they appeared to cause was the consequence of repression. Like Rousseau, Fourier maintained that even though man was naturally good, he had been corrupted by institutions and ideas of his own making; unlike Rousseau, he did not believe that the damage was permanent. The benevolent instincts of Rousseau's natural man had been crushed under the weight of the institutions and culture of civilized society. But the passions of Fourier's man were immutable; they could be temporarily repressed and perverted, but not permanently altered. If they had appeared to assume different forms at different stages of human history, this was merely an indication that man-made institutions had been more or less effective agents of repression.

Since the passions were the source of all human activity, Fourier argued, it was up to man to shape his institutions in accordance with their laws. But this had never been understood by the philosophers, moralists, and priests. Some of the philosophers, like the affluent Seneca, had preached hypocritical doctrines of moderation; others had vainly urged that men "smother their passions" and aspire to lives of ascetic virtue. The result of these repressive doctrines, however, was only to create a state of "internal war" within every individual and to set the passions "at odds with accepted wisdom and the law."[39] This was a war that could never be won, Fourier insisted, since the passions were imperious and could be denied only at the price of pain and mental sickness.

> It is easy to compress the passions by violence [he wrote]. Philosophy suppresses them with a stroke of the pen. Locks and the sword come to the aid of sweet morality. But nature appeals these judgments; she regains her rights in secret. Passion stifled at one point reappears at another like water held back by a dike; it is driven inward like the fluid of an ulcer closed too soon.[40]

Thus each stifled passion would only reappear and make its demands felt more urgently. If the passion was particularly strong, it would reappear in a vicious or "subversive" form.

To illustrate the consequences of repression Fourier told the story of Madame Strogonoff, a Russian noblewoman whose sadistic cruelty arose from the frustration of her unconscious lesbian tendencies.

> As Lady Strogonoff, a Muscovite princess, saw herself growing old, she became jealous of the beauty of one of her young slaves. She had the slave tortured; she herself pricked her with pins. What was the motive for her cruel behavior? Was it jealousy? No, it was lesbianism. Madame Strogonoff was an unconscious lesbian; she was actually inclined to love the beautiful slave whom she tortured. If someone had made Madame Strogonoff aware of her true feelings and reconciled her and her

victim, they might have become passionate lovers. But remaining unaware of her lesbian impulse, the princess was overcome by a counterpassion, a subversive tendency. She persecuted the person who should have been the object of her pleasure. Her wrath was all the greater in that the suffocation was caused by prejudice that blinded her to the true aim of her passion. It was thus unable to attain even mental gratification. Any form of forced deprivation, that is to say, suffocation by violence rather than by prejudice, would not provoke such wrath.

There are others who subject groups to the same sort of atrocities that Madame Strogonoff practiced on an individual. Nero loved collective or widespread cruelty. Odin made a religious system and de Sade a moral system out of such cruelty. This taste for atrocities is simply a consequence of the suffocation of certain passions. It was Nero's composite passion and de Sade's alternating passion that were suffocated, and for Madame Strogonoff it was a variety of love.[41]

This passage, which is taken from Fourier's notebooks on the *Nouveau monde amoureux,* shows an awareness of the workings of repression that is not to be found in the writings of any of Fourier's contemporaries. It seems far-fetched to see an anticipation of Freudian therapy in the suggestion that Madame Strogonoff might have been cured of her sadistic impulses had an outsider helped her to bring her repressed and unconscious desires to the surface.[42] Still there can be little doubt that this text shows a grasp of the power of the unconscious and an insight into the dynamics of repression rarely equaled prior to Freud.

Fourier recognized that psychic repression did not always have such spectacular consequences as in the case of Madame Strogonoff. But even if repression failed to produce so perverse a counterpassion, he argued, it could still cause pain and anxiety. Many individuals, although fortunate by the world's standards, were nevertheless tortured by the "perpetual anxiety" that resulted from "the pressure of a suffocated dominant, that is, from an imperious passion they cannot satisfy."[43] Fourier insisted that all this pain was unnecessary, that the passions were benign, and it was the repressive institutions of civilization that turned the passions into "unchained tigers, incomprehensible enigmas."[44] This would continue to happen, Fourier maintained, until the people of civilization learned how to create a more satisfactory social order, a social order so conceived that the gratification of individual desire always served to promote the common good. The key was Fourier's discovery that within the series even the most dangerous passions could be harmonized like chords on a piano. Thus Harmony would usefully employ the very passions that civilization called indestructible vices. It would in fact depend upon them, thrive upon them. So-called vices like gluttony and lust would be very much in evidence in the most productive Phalanxes. Indeed, every one of Christianity's seven deadly sins—with the exception of sloth—would have its uses.[45]

If the passions naturally tended to harmonize, then the most peaceful and productive society would be the one that allowed the greatest scope for the expression of individual desire. The goal, according to Fourier, was complete gratification: the perfect hedonist was necessarily the perfect Harmonian. Thus the task of social theory was to seek ways in which the passions could best be satisfied and refined. Instead of trying vainly to "repress, suppress, and compress" the passions, philosophers should have sought to widen their range and increase their intensity. "The individual must march toward the realm of the good," wrote Fourier, "by submitting himself blindly to his passions."[46]

12

The Ideal Community

ACCORDING TO Friedrich Engels, the most characteristic feature of the
thought of the utopian socialists was their propensity for drawing up
"fantastic blueprints" of future society. Unable to explain how their
schemes might be brought into existence, wrote Engels, the utopians
devoted themselves to elaborating in obsessively minute detail just what
life in the ideal society would be like. By this standard Fourier must be
judged the complete utopian. He produced thousands of pages of detailed blueprints, which included, among other things, architectural
specifications, typical work schedules, designs for nursery furniture,
color schemes for work uniforms, and directives for the marching order
of barnyard animals.

   In most of this writing on the organization of the ideal society
Fourier addressed himself to the *fondateur*, the benefactor who would
provide the capital necessary to set up the first trial Phalanx. He made it
clear that if the trial were to succeed, all the institutions of the Phalanx
would have to be perfectly adapted to the dictates of the passions. An
especially important issue was the size of the Phalanx. After his discoveries of 1819 Fourier was willing to entertain the idea that a "reduced
trial" might be made with as few as eighty families or four hundred
individuals. But for any experiment in full-scale association a minimum

of fifteen hundred and a maximum of two thousand participants would be required. Ideally, the number would be 1,620—in other words exactly twice the number of people necessary to constitute the complete "scale" of 810 passional types. In his instructions to the founder Fourier also went into great detail concerning the work groups to be formed and the crops to be raised in the trial Phalanx. He discussed the problems that were likely to arise at the outset, notably the "passional doldrums" of the first winter, and he laid down precise directives for everything from the initial yield to be expected from various types of fruit trees to the sort of housing to be provided for the multitudes of curiosity seekers who would come to visit the trial Phalanx.

But Fourier could rarely limit himself to a recitation of the "paltry" preparations required for a trial Phalanx. He preferred to let his imagination dwell on the delights and wonders of the more advanced stages of Harmony. Thus chapters that began with discussions of the trial Phalanx sometimes ended with evocations of life after several generations of Harmony. And Fourier's precise descriptions of this future state were delivered (usually in the present tense) with all the assurance of someone who had *seen* exactly what would happen.

> At sunrise on a spring morning [he would begin] one can see thirty groups with their distinctive banners and emblems passing out through the gates of the palace. These various squadrons take their places in the fields and the gardens.[1]
>
> If we could see . . . all of these groups in activity, well sheltered from the sun by colored tents, working in dispersed masses, moving about with their banners and tools, singing hymns in chorus as they march along, [if we could see] the countryside dotted with small castles and belvederes with colonnades and spires instead of thatched huts, we would suppose that the landscape was enchanted.[2]

The complete utopian was also a true visionary; he had already seen the future in his mind's eye.

I

Fourier always imagined the Phalanx in a rural setting. Ideally, he wrote, it would be situated on a square league of land.[3] The terrain would be relatively hilly; water would be plentiful; and the soil and climate would be suitable for the cultivation of a wide variety of crops. The Phalanx would also have to be located within a day's ride of a large city or capital. This was important to Fourier because he believed that an important part of the income of the trial Phalanx would come from fees paid by curious visitors—the "bénéfice des curieux" as he called it.

To a traveler approaching the Phalanx for the first time, the most striking thing about it would be the elegance and the sheer vastness of the central building or Phalanstery. This was to be a massive structure—colossal in its outlines but adorned with "a multitude of colonnades, domes, and peristyles"—a cross between a palace and a sumptuous resort hotel. The plan according to which the Phalanstery was laid out would be something like that of Versailles. An immense central section with an imposing twelve-hundred-meter façade would be flanked by two long wings. To the rear of the palace and between the wings would lie a parade ground, which would be the scene of daily maneuvers and festivities on the part of the whole community.

On entering the Phalanstery the visitor would be initially received in a special reception hall called the caravansary. This would be located in one of the wings of the building so as not to disturb the ongoing daily activities of the Phalanx. Here refreshments would be served to visitors, and large receptions and entertainments would be held to welcome the arrival of caravans from distant lands. The caravansary would also serve as the communications center of the Phalanx. It would include a sorting room for incoming and outgoing mail, a "news" room where dispatches were received from neighboring Phalanxes and news bulletins drafted, as well as stables for the Phalanx's post horses and kennels for the messenger dogs, which departed hourly with mail and dispatches for other Phalanxes.

The opposite wing of the Phalanstery would be given over largely to workshops, music practice rooms, and playrooms for the children. Thus all the noisy activities would be concentrated in a particular area, and the central section of the Phalanstery could be reserved for quieter activities. This section would include the dining rooms, the exchange, meeting rooms, a library, studies, and the private rooms and apartments of the members. In the upper stories of the central section one could also find the Phalanx's temple, its tower, and its ceremonial chimes, as well as an observatory and coops for carrier pigeons, which would carry messages to distant Phalanxes.

Fourier believed that a new social order would require a new architecture; and in a number of manuscript writings on architectural questions he roundly criticized the monotonous design and the overcrowding of civilized cities, the lack of grace and proportion in domestic architecture, and the whole principle of the division of houses into dwelling units for individual families.⁴ What he wanted was an architecture that would break down the walls between people and families and make possible the multiplication of bonds between the members of a community. For this reason he included in his designs for the Phalanstery a number of specific architectural innovations. One of these was the "seristery," a specially arranged set of rooms that would serve as a meeting place for the members of a particular series. Ordinarily the seristery would consist of three large rooms: the largest would serve as the meeting place for the groups constituting the center of the series, and the other two rooms would be reserved for the groups making up the two "wings" of the series. In addition there would be a number of small conference rooms where cliques within each series could gratify their cabalistic inclinations. "This system is very different from that followed in our large gatherings," boasted Fourier. "There, even in the palaces of kings, you can see a whole crowd thrown together confusedly according to the principle of holy philosophical equality, a principle that has absolutely no place in Harmony."⁵

Fourier's other vital architectural innovation was the "street gallery." This was a raised and covered passageway that would be heated in winter and ventilated in the summer. Running through the whole Phalanstery and connecting it with adjacent buildings, it would enable people "to pass through the workshops, stables, storehouses, ballrooms, banquet and assembly halls, etc., in January without knowing whether it is rainy or windy, hot or cold." In Fourier's time the roads of France turned to mud in winter; city streets still served as garbage troughs; and sidewalks and gas street-lamps had only reached the most elegant quarters. Thus he could take pride in an invention that would enable everyone to "travel about the Phalanx, sheltered from exposure to the elements, going to dances and the theater in frosty weather dressed in light clothes and colored shoes without worrying about the mud or the cold." All this, wrote Fourier, would be "a charm so novel that it alone would suffice to make our cities and castles seem detestable to anyone who spent a winter's day in a Phalanstery."⁶

Was Fourier's conception of the street gallery inspired by contemporary developments in architecture and urban design? Fourier himself occasionally referred to the Grand Galerie of the Louvre, which was opened to the public in 1793, as one of his models for the street gallery.[7] But Walter Benjamin has also suggested in a celebrated essay that in his vision of Phalansterian architecture Fourier was chiefly inspired by the great commercial arcades built in Paris early in the nineteenth century. For Benjamin the Phalanstery was "a city of arcades," and it was in the arcades that "Fourier saw the architectonic canon of the Phalanstery."[8] It should be noted that the flourishing of the arcade as a space for promenades and luxury commerce only dates from the late Restoration with the construction of the fashionable galleries and covered passages of Colbert, Vivienne, Choiseul, and Véro-Dodat. But still two of the earliest of Paris's arcades—the Passage de Caire and the Passage des Panoramas—date from 1799 and 1800, respectively, the period of Fourier's discovery and of his first prolonged stay in Paris. And the Galeries de Bois of the Palais Royal, which so charmed Fourier on his first visit to Paris in 1789, have been authoritatively described as "the first arcade ever built."[9] The least one can say then is that Paris's arcades were known to Fourier and were already becoming a significant part of the urban landscape at the time when he conceived of his street gallery.

Fourier freely acknowledged the influence of the Louvre and the Palais Royal on his architectural ideas. There are also a few precise references in his writings to memories of buildings and streets and parks that provided him with architectural models.[10] But were there other unacknowledged influences on his thinking about architecture? Was Fourier influenced, for example, by any of the work of the so-called visionary French architects of the late eighteenth century: Boullée, Ledoux, and Lequeu? It is particularly tempting to try to link Fourier with the greatest member of this group, Claude-Nicolas Ledoux, who was active both in Paris and in Fourier's own Franche-Comté during the 1770s and 1780s.[11] Ledoux, whose treatise on the relationship of architecture to law and mores appeared in 1804, was best known in his own time as a builder of elegant Parisian town houses and as the designer of the infamous tollhouses or *barrières* that were built around Paris during the last five years of the Old Regime. But now he is best remembered as the author of an extraordinary (and partially executed) series of designs for a model community to be established around the saltworks of Chaux at Arc-et-Senans on the river Loue not far from Besançon. There is no direct evidence that Fourier knew of Ledoux's plans, or of the remarkable group of buildings he actually did construct at Arc-et-Senans. On the other hand, Fourier must have known the impressive theater built by Ledoux at Besançon a decade before the Revolution. There are also several references in Fourier's writings to one of Ledoux's finest Parisian town houses, the "charming" Hotel de Thélusson.[12] Built by Ledoux in the late 1770s for a Swiss banker's widow, the Hotel de Thélusson had a dramatic entrance, and gardens and façades that Fourier described as worthy of imitation in Harmony.[13] But it was too aristocratic and fanciful for nineteenth-century taste. It was destroyed in 1824, much to Fourier's chagrin, "to make way for some bourgeois and moral façades."[14]

There are some aspects of Ledoux's work that cannot have been appealing to Fourier. Even his plans for the ideal city at Arc-et-Senans reflected a respect for authority and a moralism that were alien to the theorist of passionate attraction. On the other hand, Fourier would have been fascinated by Ledoux's phallus-shaped Oikema or Temple of Love, if he had known of it, and also by the House of Communal Life designed by Ledoux for "sixteen families living together in the peace of the woods, each with a complete apartment."[15] On a more general level, Fourier may have been attracted by Ledoux's preoccupation with the symbolic value of elementary geometrical forms. He may also have found inspiration in the sheer exuberance of Ledoux's work, in the mixture of the massive and the fanciful that was evident in the triumphal arch and entrance to the Hotel de Thélusson, and in Ledoux's attempt at Arc-et-Senans to carve rocks and flowing water into stone. And even if the direct influence was limited, there was certainly a kinship between Fourier and the architect, who could write of his design for a tavern for the suburb of Saint-Marceau: "For the first time a tavern will be as magnificent as a palace."[16]

II

One of the most important elements in the European utopian tradition was the strain of egalitarian communism. The good society, for thinkers from Thomas More to Babeuf and Etienne Cabet, was a society of equals in which property was held in common and strict limits were placed on luxury and ostentation. It should be evident by now how deeply unsympathetic Fourier was to this vision of utopia. He never tired of mocking the Spartan image of utopia to be found in the works of Rousseau and Mably, the virtuous republic sustained by cabbage and gruel. In his view luxury was essential for the gratification of the five sensual passions; and it was equality—that "political poison"—that Fourier proscribed from his utopia.

When Fourier turned from architecture and material conditions to a discussion of social relations in Harmony, he repeatedly made it clear that since disparities in wealth and status and talent were both natural and beneficial, they would be woven into the fabric of his utopia. Thus in addition to an elaborate hierarchy of sixteen "tribes" or age groups and thirty-two "choirs," there were also to be social classes in Harmony. It is true that Fourier's notion of class was extremely rudimentary: in both civilization and Harmony wealth was the only criterion of class that he recognized.* Nevertheless he made much of the fact that there would be three classes in each Phalanx: the rich, the poor, and the middle class. Not surprisingly, the situation of Harmony's poor would be "splendid" by comparison with their status in civilization. But still, Fourier insisted, the rich would enjoy considerable advantages. Every member of the Phalanx would have an apartment of his or her own, but those of the rich would be larger and quieter than those of the poor; their meals would be even more sumptuous; and, judging from Fourier's account of a typical day in the life of two Harmonians—"rich Mondor" and "poor Lucas"— the pleasures available to the wealthy would be both greater and more refined than those enjoyed by the poor.

In his approach to economic questions Fourier was also at odds with the egalitarian and communist traditions. For one thing, he retained, at least in a limited sense, the rights of private ownership and inheritance. He also made it possible for people to collect very generous interest on invested capital. In economic terms the Phalanx was a shareholding or joint-stock company whose members were free to purchase as many or as few shares as they liked. According to Fourier's scheme of remuneration, the contribution of each member in capital, labor, and talent would be quantified; and at the end of the year, the annual profits of the Phalanx would be divided up and distributed in the following

---

*Fourier used the term *class* very loosely, at times attributing two classes to civilization (the rich and the poor), and at other times five or sixteen (OC VI, 34, 324). Sometimes he used the term *class* to refer to any group with common interests. See OC V, 378: "classes that are today antipathetic such as the rich and the poor, the young and the old." But whenever he invoked a specific criterion for class it was wealth.

proportions: five-twelfths to labor, four-twelfths to capital, and three-twelfths to talent. Simple-minded as it may seem to the modern reader, this scheme was regarded by Fourier as one of his great discoveries, and as a means of conciliating the interests of rich and poor in Harmony.[17]

Since the Phalanx was a community in which natural differences in character and intelligence were reinforced by distinctions in wealth and status, one of the problems to which Fourier gave most careful thought was social integration. How could class differences be prevented from leading to class antagonism? How, specifically, could the poor be persuaded to accept social inequalities? And how could the rich be persuaded to tolerate the company of the poor? In a sense, all of Harmony's institutions were meant to play a role in the muting of class antagonism and the creation of an atmosphere of "unity" and social harmony throughout the Phalanx. But Fourier attached particular importance to the contribution to be made by two institutions: the "social minimum" and his system of "unitary" education. What the social minimum amounted to was a guaranteed annual income, a minimum in food, clothing, and subsistence, which was to be provided to every member of the Phalanx even if he or she was unable or unwilling to perform useful tasks. Fourier was convinced that it would be possible for the Phalanx to provide such a minimum and to offer even the humblest of its members amenities equal to those enjoyed by a Croesus in civilization. And if such a minimum could be provided, Fourier believed, there would be no need for any radical leveling of social distinctions. For in his view poverty, not inequality, was the principal cause of social conflict. As he wrote in 1803, "Inequality, so much maligned by the philosophers, is not displeasing to men. On the contrary, the bourgeois delights in hierarchy; he loves to see the bigwigs decked out and parading in their best finery. The poor man views them with the same enthusiasm. Only if he lacks what is necessary does he begin to detest his superiors and the customs of society."[18]

If the social minimum was a means of reconciling the poor to inequalities of wealth and status, there was still the problem of persuading the rich to tolerate the company of the poor. As has already been pointed out, Fourier did not share the idealization of the common people that was widespread among the early socialist thinkers. In his view it was absurd to suppose that there could be any real community between the refined sybarite and the coarse, hungry, disease-ridden peasant. For this reason he insisted that during the initial phases of

Harmony a Phalanx should admit only those relatively polite and well-mannered members of the lower classes whom the rich would not find unduly offensive. In the long run, if the rich and poor were to coexist harmoniously, Fourier believed it was essential that all children in a Phalanx should receive the same education, and that an important element in that education should be training in good manners and refinement. As he wrote in the *Traité de l'association:*

> Common norms of civility, speech, and behavior can only be established by means of a collective education, which will give the poor child the same good manners as the rich. The education that children receive in our society varies according to their wealth: the rich are taught by academicians, children of the middle classes have their pedagogues, and the poor are left to the village schoolmaster. If Harmony followed the same practice, it would attain the same results. Social classes would be mutually incompatible and each would have its own particular style: the poor would be coarse, the bourgeoisie would be petty, and only the rich would be refined. The result would be a state of general discord, which must be avoided in Harmony. It will be avoided thanks to a system of education that is THE SAME for a whole Phalanx and for the whole globe. This new system of education will make good breeding universal.[19]

The most important vehicle of social integration in Fourier's Phalanx was neither the social minimum nor the system of unitary education; it was the organization of all aspects of Phalansterian life into a multitude of passional groups and series of groups. By its very definition, the *série passionnelle* was a melting pot: it was a gathering of *diverse* individuals whose common passion would enable them to forget distinctions of age, wealth, character, and intelligence. Within the context of the series and their activities the rich and the poor and the old and the young would mix freely. Such distinctions as existed within the series would be based, not on wealth or status, but on aptitude for a particular task. Moreover, since every individual was a member of many series, he would be likely to find himself thrown into very different roles with very different associates in the course of a single day. Alternately a leader and a follower, he might find that a rival in one series was an ally in another. Thus though strong loyalties might develop within a particular group, antagonisms would focus largely on rival groups rather than on individuals.

Fourier had much to say about the process by which participation in group activities would serve to create bonds between the rich and the poor and other apparently antipathetic individuals. Particularly interesting is his discussion of the *ralliement de famillisme,* the adoption by rich Harmonians of young children who collaborated with them on particular tasks.

> A father in Harmony, being passionately attracted to forty or fifty different kinds of work, consequently becomes passionately devoted to his most intelligent collaborators, and above all to the poor children whom he sees excelling at his favorite occupations in which his son does not participate at all. This is the origin of adoptions based on industrial ties, adoptions of continuators. Such adoptions could not occur in civilization where the rich do not become passionately attracted to work or, when they do become devoted to it, they have to put up with the company of intriguers and scoundrels and never that of intelligent and enthusiastic children, worthy of the rank of titular continuators.[20]

Fourier calculated that during his normal life span of 144 years a rich Harmonian might adopt as many as a hundred such children as his heirs and continuators. Taking account of his other, natural children and the children of all his adopted and natural heirs, it was possible that at the time of his death, this individual would have established familial ties with a majority of the members of his Phalanx. Fourier's ultimate response to the problem of social integration was thus the conception of a community in which family ties would be extended to include everyone!

III

Along with work and love, eating was to be one of the three most satisfying activities of Fourier's Phalansterians. Gourmandise, he often pointed out, was the strongest passion of children and the elderly—"the first and last pleasure of man, the one that delights him from birth right up until his last hour."[21] Fourier therefore had much to say about the quality (and quantity) of Harmony's cuisine and about the place of food in the life of the Phalanx.[22] Fourier was writing at the beginning of a golden age in the history of French cuisine. During the Directory and Napoleonic period the chefs of the prerevolutionary aristocracy were setting up the first restaurants in the modern sense of the term and gastronomy was becoming a science. Writers like Grimod de la Reynière and Berchoux were preparing the way for the work of the great masters, the chef Antonin Carême and the epicure Brillat-Savarin.[23] Fourier had met Brillat-Savarin (who may have been related to Fourier's brother-in-law, Philibert Parrat-Brillat) and dined with him in 1789 at the time of his first trip to Paris. But he was no more impressed by Brillat-Savarin's gastronomic theories than by what he called the "gastro-âneries" of Grimod and Berchoux. "Savarin was a *simplist*," he wrote, "ignoring gastrosophy . . . the art of combining the refinements of consumption and preparation with rivalries and hygienic methods."[24]

According to Fourier "gastrosophy," or the art of refined gluttony, had three principal branches. First there was cooking, the "most revered" of all the arts in Harmony. All Harmonians would learn how to cook at an early age. They would also be taught as young children "to recognize and develop their tastes for particular dishes, flavors, and dressing"; they would be encouraged to demand that even the most inconsequential foods be prepared to their exact specifications. Civilized moralists (with their love of bland food and discipline) would surely be horrified at this encouragement of finicky eating habits. But Fourier maintained that refined, and even finicky, habits of consumption would stimulate the young to take an interest in the cooking and preparation of food. He claimed that in the advanced stages of Harmony every child would aspire to excel in the preparation of a particular dish. On the greatest of Harmony's cooks, those who were able to adapt a single dish to the tastes of each of the 810 passional types, titles of saintliness would be bestowed. But even those who did not excel would find the kitchen to be an important school of manual dexterity and practical knowledge.[25]

Harmonians would eat a great deal, five times a day to be exact. And Fourier stressed that even the poorest Harmonian would have "twelve types of soup, twelve varieties of bread and wine, and twelve dressings for meat and vegetables" to choose from.[26] But, he insisted, none of these courses and meals would be so filling as to take away a person's desire to return to the table within a few hours. This was because the hallmarks of Harmony's cuisine would be variety and lightness. Fruits and vegetables would be emphasized; fowl and light meat would often be served; and while many varieties of bread would be available, the traditional four-pound loaf would cease to be the staple of the poor man's diet. It would be replaced, Fourier promised, by a mixture of fruit and sugar, which would henceforth bear the name of Harmony bread.[27]

Fourier was fascinated by the culinary arts. But his science of gastrosophy dealt with more than the preparation and consumption of food. It was also a "science of high school politics" and even a branch of hygiene. As hygiene, it constituted a new form of "natural or attractive medicine" that would replace the nostrums of the doctor and the pharmacist with agreeable dietary remedies.[28] Fourier might therefore be claimed as a pioneering advocate of health foods. Certainly he shared the modern-day nutritionist's suspicion of conventional medicine. Where he differed was in the nature of the remedies he proposed. Nuts and grains were not for him. Rather, the medicines he recommended were "jams, fine liqueurs, and other delicacies."[29]

As a social science gastrosophy dealt with the role of food and eating in the establishment of passionate ties between individuals. What this meant was that in Fourier's utopia the pleasures of the table would be "compound" pleasures. Good food was always to be supplemented by good company, and the meal would become, as Henri Desroche has put it, an "elementary form of Harmonian sociability," providing the occasion for all manner of intrigues, celebrations, and adventures. Thus the day's first meal, the "gastronomic antenna," was described by Fourier as "a very delightful imbroglio" at which lovers' quarrels would be settled, visitors introduced, and cabals organized.[30]

The importance Fourier attached to gastrosophy as a social science stemmed from his belief that the love of food was one of the few passions linking the old and the young, the rich and the poor. Food was therefore to play a crucial role in the whole process of socialization within the Phalanx. It was, for example, by means of gastronomic cabals that children would first participate in the activities of the passionate series. Their advisers and collaborators in these cabals would often be the oldest members of a Phalanx. For if food and activities centering around food were the delight of the young, they were also, as Fourier put it, the "last consolation" of the elderly.

So important was food in the whole Phalansterian scheme of things that Fourier could look forward to a day when the wars of civilization would be replaced by what amounted to international cooking contests. Taking over and embroidering upon the idea of a "tasting jury" that had recently been popularized by Grimod de la Reynière, Fourier called for the organization of competitions that would test the merits of particular recipes and advance the art of preparing dishes to appeal to each of the 810 passional configurations. Gastrosophy was, after all, an art as well as a science; and the importance of food in stimulating the passions and enmeshing the series was so great that an Ecumenical Council would regularly meet to consider questions of gastronomic orthodoxy and to debate "heretical theses" just like those of "the Albigensians in France and the Hussites in Bohemia."[31]

IV

If Fourier foresaw a time when the aggressive impulses that lay behind the wars of civilization might be channeled into peaceful gastronomic competitions, what did he propose to do about politics and power? How were decisions to be made within the Phalanx? Who had authority, and how was it to be exercised? What, if any, were the methods of discipline and punishment? It is proper to ask these questions about any utopian theory, but Fourier himself would not have considered them worth much attention. For he believed that he had discovered the natural form of social organization. He had designed a set of institutions that was consistent with the full expression of man's nature, thereby freeing him from subjection to external authority and removing the principal cause for criminal or other antisocial behavior. Thus there would be no need for the state in Fourier's utopia. Nor, apart from "a few cases of arbitration," would there be a need for judges, courts, police, or any other coercive agent.[32]

There was, it is true, a nominal structure of authority within Fourier's Phalanx. Day-to-day administrative decisions would be made at the outset by a Regency consisting of the wealthiest and most knowledgeable members. In the early months, prior to the trial Phalanx's first harvest, the Regency would take responsibility for various administrative tasks such as the purchase of food, the issuing of uniforms, and the renting of apartments. But once the trial Phalanx had begun to function normally, the Regency would turn over most of its powers to other organizations, the most important of which was the Areopagus or Supreme Council of Industry.

This Areopagus, which exercised what Fourier described as "autorité d'opinion" within the Phalanx, was to consist primarily of the chief officers of the various industrial series of the Phalanx.[33] It was also to include the principal shareholders and a few other dignitaries including representatives from the three "tribes" that contained the elders of the Phalanx: the reverends, the venerables, and the patriarchs. Fourier emphasized that, "everything being dictated by attraction," the task of the Areopagus was not to make laws or issue statutes. Its main function would be to make certain necessary practical decisions such as the selection of times for sowing and harvesting or the drawing up of agendas for building and repairs. Within any Phalanx these decisions would be generally respected. But they would not be binding on any group. If, for example, a group of apple growers wished to put off their harvest against the advice of the Areopagus, they would be perfectly free to do so. Fourier also stressed that the Areopagus was to have no influence on the distribution of dividends within the Phalanx; this was to be done automatically according to his own formula. Nor would it be responsible for most other financial matters; these would be taken care of by specialists who belonged to a series of accountants.

If the actual responsibilities of Fourier's Areopagus seem limited, they would still be considerable compared to those exercised by most of the other dignitaries within Fourier's utopian world. For Fourier seems to have taken to heart Napoleon's dictum "It is with baubles that men are governed." Napoleon had created the *légion d'honneur* and a new class of barons; the monarchs of the Old Regime had enriched their treasuries through the creation and sale of meaningless offices. But Fourier went further and devised a hierarchy of titles and offices so elaborate that he could boast in Harmony out of an optimum population of four billion people there would be "roughly forty million couples" holding titles and sovereign offices of one kind or another.[34] These would run from the Primarch, one of eight couples who alternated as the heads of a single Phalanx, to the thirteen Omniarchs, or supreme dignitaries presiding over the whole Phalansterian universe. In addition, and to "provide more opportunities for the gratification of individual ambition," Fourier indicated that special dignities would be bestowed on individuals skilled in the exercise of particular functions. Thus each Phalanx would have its own sibyls and kinglets and pontifs of both sexes, not to mention its *archifées* and *archicoëres* and *archicoëresses*.

Fourier took this hierarchy seriously. His manuscripts abound in calculations and reflections on such topics as "the pivotal and cardinal scepters" and "the scale of sovereignties in Harmony."[35] Yet in all these discussions he made it clear that the functions of the various potentates in Harmony would be almost entirely ceremonial and their responsibilities virtually nonexistent. For the point of the whole hierarchy of honors and titles devised by Fourier was simply to gratify the "lust for honors" that Napoleon, and Louis XIV before him, had shown to be a vital component of human nature.

If Fourier had much more to say about the "lust for honors" than about the exercise of power, it is still worth attempting to pursue one of the questions posed at the beginning of this section. What, if any, were the methods of punishment and social control employed in the Phalanx? This was a question that Fourier generally preferred to dodge. He was willing, for example, to consider the possibility that a young child might have to be punished for intentionally pulling up flowers planted by older children. "There would be damage and a motive for repression." "But," he was quick to add, "this mischief, this vandalism, could only be encountered in a child fresh from civilization and never in those raised from infancy in association."[36] Still, unlikely as it was, what if a child raised within the Phalanx did engage in malicious destruction? Fourier's answer was that when discipline was necessary, it should be imposed not by distant authorities but rather by the peers of the offender. Generally, he claimed, peer group pressure would take the form of raillery and banter. But he was not oblivious to the fact that peer groups, and especially groups of children, can be the cruelest as well as the most effective of teachers.[37]

Fourier's system includes provisions for several other kinds of quasi-disciplinary institutions and practices. For example, work groups that produced an inadequate or shoddy product would be obliged by their fellow workers to carry a black banner indicating that they had been "eclipsed."[38] An individual who revoked a bequest granted to a lover or adoptive child might be isolated from the Court of Love and forced to wear a yellow armband.[39] But a more general point can be made. Like many other utopians from the ancient Greeks to the modern Hutterites, Fourier believed that the severest punishment and the most effective deterrent necessary within his ideal community would be exclusion, that is, the removal of an offender from the work group or educational corps or amorous gathering of which he was a member. When Fourier talked about exclusion it seems that what he generally had in mind was a temporary measure that applied only to particular facets of an individual's activity within the Phalanx. A person might be deprived of the opportunity to participate in the activities of a particular work or recreational group; he might be denied for a brief period the right to participate in the nightly Court of Love; he might simply be allowed to sleep through the *parcours* or round of pleasures to be held each morning between 4:00 and 5:00 A.M.[40] But could a person also be banished permanently from all the activities of a Phalanx? Fourier seems at least to have envisaged the possibility, and there is a curious passage in his manuscripts in which he evokes the condition of the solitary exile. If, Fourier writes, a person in Harmony is seen to be traveling alone and without identification papers, "one surmises that it is a criminal traveling as a result of banishment." How was such a person to be treated?

> He is given as much consideration as we have for the assassin who is being led to the scaffold and whom the law grants everything he asks for in his final moments. Unless a man is banished in Harmony he will hardly think of traveling alone. . . . If he travels alone far from his native country, he will pass for a criminal.[41]

There is an obvious poignancy to these words, coming as they do from a man who spent much of his life as a solitary traveler.

V

As Fourier described the institutions and structures of his ideal community, he was constantly attempting to convey to his readers a sense of what the life of the Phalanx would be like. Seeking to bring the theory to life, he filled his works with "glimpses" of the new order, vignettes in which leading roles were played by characters like Cléon the sybarite, the vestal Galatea, Damon the flower fancier, and Ithuriel the patriarch. There was Irus the poet, for example. In civilization he would have been starving in a garret. But in Harmony his talents would receive immediate recognition. While still a child, he would be made editor of the "Gazette of Knight-errantry," and the title of "High Kinglet of the Globe" would be bestowed upon him at the age of thirteen. In time he would become "the equal of Homer," and thanks to the protection of an author's rights in Harmony, he would never have to worry about a line of his verse being stolen or reprinted without due acknowledgment and recompense. Then there was the story of Céliante and Bastien. Céliante was a lady of great age and great wealth with a passionate attraction to the darning of old clothes. It would be a pleasure for her to mend the work clothes of Bastien. In return he would be delighted to water her sweet williams and to keep an eye on her favorite pheasants as he performed his duties in the garden and the birdhouse. Finally there was little Zoé, a great lover of sweets. Scolded in civilization, she would find herself sought after in Harmony, where her very gourmandise would win her friends and protectors and would be the instrument of her full participation in the life of the Phalanx.[42]

One point that emerges clearly from all of Fourier's evocations of life in Harmony is that, by civilized standards, the pace of that life would be extremely fast. In conformity with the Butterfly passion, no single activity would last more than two hours. Thus people would be constantly hurrying up and down the covered passageways from one part of the Phalanstery to another, and from the Phalanstery to the fields and orchards and back again. There would be little time for solitude or rest, and on the average Harmonians would sleep no more than five hours a night. Fourier was convinced that additional sleep would be unnecessary, given the advanced hygiene and varied work sessions in Harmony. In any case, there would be such an abundance of pleasures that it would be impossible to keep any Harmonian in bed past 4:30 in the morning.

If Harmonians would sleep little, they would eat copiously, and they would lead a life rich in entertainment and festivities as well as in productive work. Each Phalanx would have its own theater, and training in speech, singing, and acting would be part of the education of all Harmonians. This would give everyone the opportunity to develop useful skills and also to witness the competitions of thousands of actors, singers, dancers, and musicians, "any one of whom would suffice to provoke the enthusiasm of court and city."[43] In addition to the regular performances of the theater and the opera of a Phalanx, there would also be special fetes celebrating the arrival of visitors and the promotion of young children from one rank to another in the various work groups to which they belonged. These fetes would often be spectacular occasions with fanfares, salvos, and the beating of drums all preceding the welcoming of visitors or the distribution of honors by the patriarchs.[44]

A day in the life of a Phalanx would thus be such an extraordinarily full day that by nightfall the happy and exhausted Harmonians would be quite ready for bed. By eleven o'clock a few lights would still burn in the caravansary, but the noise of the day would have long since subsided. There would only be the soft sound of footsteps of a pair of watchmen pacing up and down the street galleries, tending the fires, and looking into the bedrooms of the children and the patriarchs.[45]

One of the most striking features of Fourier's work is the charm and vividness of his vignettes of life in the Phalanx. He may have described himself as an "illiterate shop sergeant," but in fact he possessed the inventiveness and the delicate touch of a rococo miniaturist. He had an eye for the significant detail, a wry irony about his characters, and above all a remarkably precise imagination. Fourier himself was well aware of his imaginative powers, and in a bitter moment at the end of his life he reminded his critics in the literary establishment that even as fiction his work was superior to theirs.

> Eh! Pitiful novelists that you are, will you ever write a novel that is worth a quarter of what mine is worth? Even if mine were a novel, and if I were reduced to the role of a novelist, couldn't I stand up to the whole gang of novel writers all by myself and beat them, proving that they are nothing but a collection of pygmies?[46]

Like his contemporary Balzac, Fourier had spun a world out of his imagination. But he could not rest content until his fiction became reality.

PLATES

1. Fourier's birthplace on Besançon's Grande Rue. His father's store, with its sign "Fourrier, Marchand Drapier," is on the ground floor.

2. The Galleries of the Palais Royal around 1800.

3. Lazare Carnot thanks "Citizen Fourrier of Besançon" for his letter to the Directory concerning the movement of troops across the Alps. 10 messidor an IV (June 28, 1796).

4. Fourier's Lyon. View from La Croix-Rousse.

5. Diligences like this carried Fourier all over Europe during the
Directory and Napoleonic period. This painting by Louis-Léopold Boilly
(1803) shows the arrival of a diligence in the Cour des Messageries at
Paris. Fourier spent his last years living in apartments near this spot.

6. Prostitution in 1802: "The Parisian Seraglio."

7. Prostitution in 1815: Russian soldiers and French prostitutes at the entrance of a gambling house in the Galleries of the Palais Royal.

8. The Fatalistic or Resigned Cuckold.

Cuckoldry was a topic of seemingly inexhaustible fascination for graphic artists of the early Restoration. Fourier's Hierarchy of Cuckoldom belongs to a satirical
tradition that was represented by the work of numerous obscure cartoonists and illustrators as well as by
such well-known literary works as Molière's *Georges
Dandin.*

De l'hymen aujourd'hui pourquoi bander les yeux?
Il les aurait ouverts, qu'il n'y verrait pas mieux......

A Paris chez Martinet, Libraire, rue du Coq, N.º 15.

9. The Manageable or Benign Cuckold.

NOTE ON THE PORTRAITS OF FOURIER

During the heyday of the Fourierist movement in the 1840s a number of lithographs and engravings of Fourier were commissioned and reproduced by his disciples. Many of them, including the 1847 lithograph by Cisneros reproduced here (figure 11), were based on the great portrait of Fourier by the Bisontine artist Jean Gigoux (frontispiece). This portrait, which was commissioned by Clarisse Vigoureux, was first exhibited at the Salon of 1836. The rocky outcropping that serves as background was painted by Gigoux in the Bois de Vincennes.

According to Fourier's disciples, several portraits were done of Fourier as a young man. The lithograph by Brandt (figure 10), which is apparently based on a painting done in 1808, is the only one that has survived. All the other portraits date from the end of Fourier's life. The unsigned pen and ink sketch (figure 13) was apparently done during a dinner in 1833 by Fourier's disciple and patron Dr. A.-F. Baudet-Dulary. Figure 12 was published in the 1850s by Fourier's self-proclaimed "apostle," the poet Jean Journet, as an aid to his efforts as a solitary Fourierist missionary.

The only portrait that rivals that by Gigoux is the extraordinary and haunting anonymous portrait done in 1835 (figure 15). Nothing is known of the painter or of the circumstances under which it was done. Yet it conveys even better perhaps than Gigoux's formal portrait the inward gaze of the visionary, whose blue eyes often shone "with a gentle, melancholy, and sad luster."

10. Fourier at thirty-six. Lithograph by Brandt
after an anonymous portrait.

11. Lithograph of Fourier by Cisneros, 1847,
after the portrait by Gigoux.

FOURIER

Dévoile de l'analogie
L'enchainement mystérieux,[1]
Que l'humanité soit régie
Comme sont ordonnes les cieux.
Proclame la foi méthodique.

Du domaine scientifique
Qu'enfin le doute soit banni.
Que le plan de Dieu se révèle.
Par l'harmonie universelle.
Par l'unité dans l'infini

(La Vision.)   J. Journet.

Flameng. Graveur   JOURNET, EDITEUR   Pierron. Imp

12. Engraving of Fourier by Flameng, published by Jean Journet.

13. Pen and ink
drawing of Fourier by
Dr. A.-F. Baudet-Dulary, 1833.

14. Lithograph of Fourier by
Vayron after a drawing by Lise
V. . . , c. 1837.

Ch. FOURIER.

Lithographie de Vayron, rue galande, N.º 51, à Paris.

15. Anonymous oil portrait of Fourier, 1835.

During the last fifteen years of Fourier's life his home was Paris. More exactly his home was the Sentier, the then bustling if somewhat seedy commercial quarter surrounding the Palais Royal and the Bourse. In figure 16, which is a detail from a map of Paris published in 1824, we see the location of each of Fourier's five residences during the period 1822–1837.

1. "chez M. Saussol," 41, rue de Grenelle
   Saint-Honoré, November-December 1822.
2. Hotel Saint-Roche, 39, rue Neuve Saint-Roche,
   December 1822–March 1825.
3. Hotel de Hollande, 45, rue Richelieu, December
   1825–May 1832.
4. Headquarters of *Le Phalanstère*, 5, rue Joquelet,
   May 1832–March 1834.
5. 9, rue Saint-Pierre-Montmartre, April
   1834–October 1837.

This quarter also includes many of Fourier's haunts, including the Palais Royal (6) and the Bibliothèque Nationale (7) as well as the offices of Curtis and Lamb at 29, rue du Mail (8), where Fourier worked in 1826 and 1827.

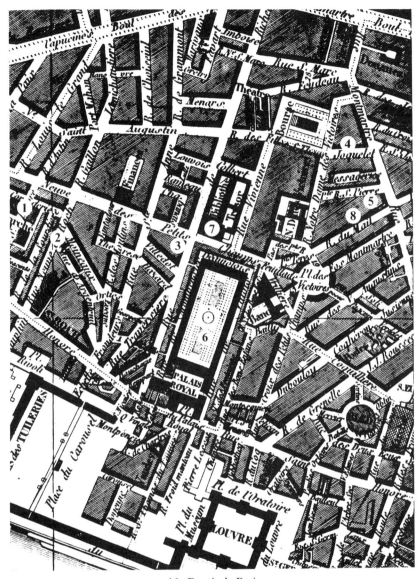

16. Fourier's Paris.

Autres inepties de la morale

Que penserions nous d'un médecin qui enterrait dans
l'autre monde tous ses malades qu'il ~~traiterait~~ quelle que fut
le m Si que pas un n'y échapperait ~~quelle que fut le genre~~
de maladie? ~~fièvre~~ chacun d'eux
~~sans~~ serait enterré sans faute, au bout de la semaine ou de
la quinzaine. On dirait de lui, cet homme là est un fléau pire
que la peste et le choléra ~~guerre~~; il faut lui interdire l'exercice de la médecine.

= Mais je suis un fort honnête homme, dirait le Carabin;
= j'ai de bonnes intentions philantropiques pour le salut de l'humanité
On lui répondrait = il ne s'agit pas ici d'intentions, c'est de la
= science qu'il faut; et il évident par vos œuvres que vous n'en
= avez point; qu'en vous donnant pour médecin vous n'êtes
= qu'un ignorant, qu'un charlatan à punir. =

Tels sont les moralistes; faux savans qui empirent
le mal par tout où ils interviennent. ~~Comme~~ quand il serait
vrai qu'ils fussent gens de probité, ce qui est plus que douteux,
leur probité ne servirait à rien contre les fléaux sociaux,
Indigence, Esclavage, fourberie ~~fausse~~ mercantile concurrence, anarchique, fiscalité
Emprunts, Agiotage, ~~des~~ prostitution, adultère, exposition,
~~les~~ Guerre, Monopole, Intempérie, révolutions, &c: pour
attaquer ces fléaux, il faut leur opposer des ressorts absorbans
et préventifs à la fois; il faut des hommes de mouvement,
connaisseurs en mécanique sociale, en progrès réel et non rêvé.

17. Manuscript from the 1830s.

JOURNAL DE L'ÉCOLE SOCIÉTAIRE

FAISANT SUITE AU JOURNAL

LE PHALANSTÈRE ou LA RÉFORME INDUSTRIELLE (1832–1854).

LA
PHALANGE

JOURNAL DE LA SCIENCE SOCIALE

DÉCOUVERTE ET CONSTITUÉE

PAR

CHARLES FOURIER.

Industrie, Politique, Sciences, Art et Littérature.

TOME I.

IDÉE D'UN PHALANSTÈRE.

Habitation d'une PHALANGE de 400 à 500 familles associées en fonctions de
Agriculture, ménage, fabriques, éducation, art, sciences, etc.;
Remplaçant, dans l'ORDRE SOCIÉTAIRE, les 400 à 500 constructions incohérentes,
maisons, masures, granges, étables, etc.,
d'une bourgade de 1800 à 2000 habitants dans l'ORDRE MORCELÉ actuel.

PARIS

AU BUREAU DE LA PHALANGE, RUE JACOB, N° 54.

1836–1837

18. Victor Considerant's design for a Phalanstery from Volume I of
La Phalange (1836).

Vue générale d'un Phalanstère ou Village organisé d'après la théorie de Fourier.
(Réduction du grand dessin lithographie par Arnoult.

19. General view of a Phalanstery, by Jules Arnoult.

Although Fourier had an intensely visual imagination, he left it to others to create pictures and architectural designs from his verbal descriptions of Phalansterian life. One of the first to do this was his disciple, Victor Considerant, who first published his own illustration of a Phalanstery in 1834. It appears here (figure 18) as part of the title page for the Fourierist journal, *La Phalange*. In the 1840s, as the Fourierist movement acquired a wide following, new illustrations were produced. In the print by Jules Arnoult reproduced here (figure 19), the main building of the Phalanstery still looks rather like Versailles, but provision has been made for factories (note the smokestacks) and even for a railroad line (note the track and trains just visible in the upper left).

Vue perspective de la Ville de Chaux

20. Plan for the ideal city of Chaux to surround the royal saltworks at Arc-et-Senans (1773–1779), by Claude-Nicolas Ledoux.

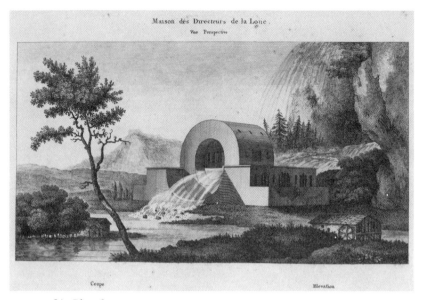

21. Plan for a water inspector's house from the Chaux project (1773–1779), by Ledoux.

22. Entrance to the house of Madame de Thélusson (1780), by Ledoux.

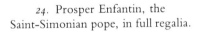

23. Victor Considerant, the leader of the Fourierist movement after Fourier's death.

24. Prosper Enfantin, the Saint-Simonian pope, in full regalia.

horoscope des St. Simoniens
en réplique à leur article du 28 Juillet.

En déclamant contre les oisifs 360 fois par an, à chaque N.º du Globe, leur Secte se dénonce elle-même, car elle est coupable de la plus honteuse oisiveté.

Elle prétend connaître l'art d'associer les travailleurs, et par conséquent l'art de quadrupler le produit de leur industrie combinément exploitée et réunissant sociétairement les trois branches productives; Cultures, fabriques, et ménage.

S'ils possèdent cet art, d'où vient qu'ils n'en font aucun essai, aucune démonstration expérimentale quoiqu'ils aient une nombreuse clientelle plus que suffisante pour former une Compagnie actionnaire et placer 3000 actions de 1000 f.r et organiser la phalange d'essai, la démonstration

Rob: Owen a pendant dix ans joué le même rôle qu'eux; il se flattait de savoir associer, mais du moins il faisait en Angleterre et en Amérique plusieurs essais; il lui eût suffi d'un seul s'il eût connu la théorie sociétaire; il n'en avait pas la moindre notion. L'expérience l'a confondu.

On voit que les St. Sim: craignant la même chute, aussi se bornent ils à pérorer sur l'association sans oser l'essayer. Leur doctrine est comme celle d'Owen toute à contresens du mécanisme sociétaire qui n'admet ni communauté, ni loi agraire (déguisée), ni phalanstère, ni main-morte, ni aucune de ces réminiscences démagogiques et féodales dont se composent les systèmes d'Owen & St. Simon.

25. Fourier replies to the Saint-Simonians. Draft of an unpublished article, August 1831.

26. The history of human societies, according to Fourier (1808).

M. Victor Considerant ayant la chance de se voir tout à coup gratifié d'une organisation phalanstérienne avant les temps prédits par Fourier!

27. The *archibras* in action. Victor Considerant sprouts a tail.
Cartoon by Cham, 1849.

During the French Second Republic a small army of journalists and political cartoonists sought to discredit the various socialist movements and factions by ridiculing the "excesses" of their founders. Fourier's *archibras* was a godsend not only to cartoonists like "Cham" (Amédée Noé) but also to conservative journalists and writers like Louis Reybaud, who included a chapter entitled "The Tails Promised to Humanity" in his *Jerome Paturot in Search of the Best of Republics*.

**Les Phalanstériens trouvant moyen d'utiliser leur queue en Ca-
lifornie pour l'extraction des blocs d'or.**

28. The *archibras* in action. Fourierist mining gold in California in 1849.
Cartoon by Cham, 1849.

If Fourier's ideas were often ridiculed in the popular press, the man himself was posthumously deified by his disciples. The full dimensions of the apotheosis he underwent become evident when one considers the caption to the frontispiece of *L'Almanach Phalanstérien pour 1845* (figure 29): "On one side Jesus offers his hand to Socrates, the pagan representative of the unity of God and Charity. Around Socrates crowd the inspired revealers, the revealers by art and science, Moses, Homer, Plato. On the other side Jesus offers his hand to the supreme inventor of modern times, to the man who has discovered the law of the kingdom of God that was promised to the earth. Jesus calls to his side the author of the *Théorie de l'Unité universelle,* Charles Fourier, our master. Next to Fourier we see the magnificent prototype of Christian love, the model of priests, Saint Vincent de Paul, the man of charity next to the man of enlightenment. Behind Fourier stands Newton; elsewhere we see all the martyrs of the faith. The oppressed, the troubled, the sick, the poor Western woman, exploited by poverty, and the enslaved woman of the Orient all offer their blessings to heaven. The hour of deliverance has sounded. In a corner of the picture Diogenes blows out his lantern: he has found his man. That man, for whom humanity has so long been waiting, is Charles Fourier, the sublime thinker, the man chosen by Christ."

29. The Fourierists' heaven. Frontispiece for the
Almanach Phalanstérien pour 1845.

30. Fourier's grave in the Montmartre Cemetery.

13

Education in Harmony

IDEAS ABOUT education and child rearing had a prominent place in all of Fourier's blueprints for the Phalanx.[1] He knew from his own experience how civilized education stifled the passions and denatured the faculties of the child, and he was convinced that his utopian vision could never be implemented unless the design for the Phalanx included a radically new system of education. The principal goals of that system would be to make possible the unrestricted development of the individual, the free expression of his or her passions, and the discovery of useful outlets for the passions in the form of productive work. Fourier laid particular stress on the role of education in the initial stages of Harmony. "It is with education that we must begin," he wrote. "It will be the branch of the mechanism that we must first organize, because children will be more susceptible to attraction than their parents, having been only slightly warped by prejudice and superstition."[2] Fourier always retained this belief. At the end of his life, when he had given up hope in virtually all else, he remained convinced that a small-scale children's Phalanx might still serve as a first step toward Harmony.

[The Theory]

I

One of the more interesting features of Fourier's discussion of education is his awareness of being part of a tradition. He did not, to be sure, admit of much respect for earlier writers on educational problems. As he wrote in the *Traité:*

> There is no problem about which people have had more foolish things to say than that of public instruction and its methods. Nature, in this branch of social politics, has perennially taken a malign pleasure in confounding all our theories and their spokesmen. The disgrace of Seneca, who was Nero's teacher, has been matched in more recent times by the failures of Condillac, who trained a political dunce, and Rousseau, who did not even dare to educate his own children.[3]

Despite such blunt pronouncements, Fourier actually seems to have been better read in education than in most other fields. He frequently referred to predecessors like Rousseau and Fénelon in ways that show a more than superficial knowledge of their work.[4] He also seems to have taken the trouble to inform himself about contemporary developments in educational theory and practice, such as the work of Pestalozzi in Switzerland and the efforts of French followers of Andrew Bell and Joseph Lancaster to introduce the monitorial system or system of "enseignement mutuel" in France.* There are at least some respects, therefore, in which Fourier's ideas about education can usefully be compared to the ideas of these schools and in general to the whole movement of liberal educational theory and practice deriving from Rousseau.

Like Rousseau and his followers, Fourier believed that the principal

---

*Fourier knew of Pestalozzi's work primarily through the reading of articles in the *Moniteur officiel* and through conversations with people who had known students from the Swiss reformer's school at Yverdon. He was quick to dismiss Pestalozzi's intuitive method but added: "I nonetheless regard his school as one of the best in Europe because it treats children gently and knows how to win their affection." OC X, PM (1851), 36. See also OC VI, 220, 240–241.

Fourier acknowledged the affinity between his conviction that children are best taught by slightly older children and the system of "enseignement mutuel," which was at the forefront of the French educational debate between 1815 and 1820. "The philosophers called 'Lancastrians,' or better 'Mutualists,' seem to have had some slight idea . . . of attractive education," he wrote in 1822 (OC IV, 155). He took pains, however, to distinguish his own method, "le mutualisme composé convergent," from "the *simple* mutualism recently introduced in civilized schools." OC V, 291–298.

[260]

aim of education was not to impart a body of knowledge or to wash children free of sin but rather to make it possible for them to discover and express their true natures. Like Rousseau and his followers, Fourier was also keenly aware of the need to avoid an overly bookish and intellectual education. He shared their aversion, and that of a number of contemporary educational reformers, to the traditional distinction between intellectual and manual education, the one reserved for the rich and the other for the poor. In Fourier's view, as in Rousseau's, the aim of education was to form both the body and the mind, and the emphasis at the outset was properly on the development of the physical rather than the mental faculties.

There are other respects, however, in which Fourier's ideas about education were antithetical to those of Rousseau and his school. First of all Fourier, who scoffed at Rousseau's celebration of the family, vigorously denied Rousseau's contention that the father is the "natural teacher" of the child.[5] Fourier also refused to follow Rousseau and the vast majority of traditional French educational theorists in their unwillingness to grant women the same educational opportunities as men. The whole notion that education should inculcate and reinforce traditional sex roles, that women should be taught to submit and men to rule, was similarly antipathetic to Fourier. Finally, whereas Rousseau and Pestalozzi, for example, had argued that manual work and intellectual activity should go together, Fourier was much more insistent than they on the importance of work to full individual self-realization. Indeed, one of the most distinctive features of Fourier's conception of education was his conviction that each child was naturally attracted to certain kinds of work.

II

To Fourier's mind one of the most pernicious vices of civilized education was its "incoherence." There was no consistency between what children were taught in school and what they actually learned from their peers and parents. Their teachers were "full of nonsensical advice" about love of country and "the merits of scorning perfidious wealth." Their fathers taught them by example, and sometimes by actual precept, about the need to sacrifice morality whenever money could be made. Their comrades taught them to scorn the advice of teachers and parents. To compound the problem, the education that was offered in schools varied according to the wealth and status of the student. The inevitable result was confusion and conflict, both in the students' minds and in society as a whole.[6]

To avoid the consequences of the incoherence of civilized education, Fourier insisted that Harmony maintain "a system of education that is ONE for the whole Phalanx and for the whole globe."[7] According to this system children would not be shut up in schools for the greater part of the day, nor would their upbringing be entrusted to their biological parents within the framework of the isolated household. Instead they would be raised and educated collectively, passing through a set number of groups or "choirs" in the course of a Harmonian upbringing. In most of Fourier's expositions there were eight of these groups, beginning with the nurslings (for infants up to about eighteen months) and culminating with the striplings (aged fifteen and a half through twenty).*

Like many other utopians from Plato down to the founders of Israel's kibbutz movement, Fourier began by proposing a system of communal child rearing. Immediately after their birth, the children of a Phalanx would be placed in a nursery where, instead of being swaddled and strapped into cradles, they would spend much of their time in specially constructed hammocks that would enable them to move freely and to see what was going on around them. They could be visited by their biological parents and breast-fed by their mothers (although Fourier criticized Rousseau for his dogmatic advocacy of breast-feeding under any circumstances).[8] But the main responsibility for their care would rest with a group of trained nurses representing the minority of women who in Fourier's view were "disposed by nature and attraction" to the task of child care.[9] Within a few days of its birth, after a child's behavior had been observed, it would be placed within one of three groups: the calm children, the unruly children, and the little devils. Each group would have its own nursery and its own special group of nurses. In this way the ceaseless cries of the little devils would not

---

*Fourier often changed the names of his choirs and the age groups they included. Here is a slightly simplified summary: *nourrissons* (up to one and a half years); *poupons* (one and a half to three); *bambins* (three to four and a half); *chérubins* (four and a half to six and a half); *séraphins* (six and a half to nine); *lycéens* (nine to twelve); *gymnasiens* (twelve to fifteen and a half); *jouvenceaux* (fifteen and a half to twenty). See OC V, 7, 13, 54–55; OC VI, 170, 205; OC X, PM (1851), 115; PM (1852), 106.

disturb the other, calmer children; and the little devils in turn could receive the care of nurses of exceptional patience and dedication.[10]

During the first two years of a child's life the main emphasis would be on the development of its senses. In order to perfect the ears of the nurslings, for example, little concerts would be given to them from the time they were six months old. Trios and quartets would be sung several times a day in the nurseries; and once a child could walk, he or she would be encouraged to march in time to the sound of instruments. An attempt would also be made to increase the acuteness of every child's hearing and "to give to children the sharpness of hearing of the rhinoceros and the cossack." The other senses would be exercised and perfected in like manner.[11]

As soon as a child could walk and move about freely, he or she would pass from the choir of nurslings to that of the *poupons* or toddlers. At about the age of three the child would again be advanced to the choir of *bambins* or urchins, where he or she would remain until the age of about four and a half. Throughout these initial stages in the child's education, no distinction would be made between boys and girls. This was important because these were the years in which the crucial "blossoming of vocations" took place, and it was essential that a child's choice of vocations not be limited by preconceived ideas concerning appropriate sex roles. Until they reached the age of four and a half Harmony's children would still be guided by adult nurses. It would be the responsibility of these nurses to introduce the children to some aspects of the adult world, and notably to the seristeries in which the adults did their work. At the same time the nurses would also take the children to visit the miniature workshops where somewhat older children would be busy playing with miniature tools.

To Fourier's mind these miniature workshops were vital arenas of self-discovery. It was in them that children could give free reign to what Fourier described as their five dominant tastes. These were:

1. FERRETING, or the penchant for handling things, exploring, running around, and constantly changing activities;
2. Industrial *din,* the taste for noisy jobs;
3. *Aping,* or the imitative mania;
4. Working on a *reduced scale,* the taste for little workshops;
5. PROGRESSIVE ENTICEMENT of the weak by the strong.[12]

Fourier believed that the opportunity to express these penchants freely and fully in the context of the miniature workshops would make it possible for children rapidly to discover their own innate vocations. These, Fourier asserted, were twenty-five or thirty in number and would remain relatively constant throughout a person's life.

When a child reached the age of four and a half, he or she was ready, according to Fourier's schema, to graduate from the choir of urchins and enter that of cherubs. At this point the child would cease to undergo surveillance by nurses. Henceforth it would receive discipline and direction from its peers, or from slightly older children. Fourier believed that this was the natural form of education, since "the child's true teacher, the only agent that could kindle in it the sacred fire of industrial emulation," was "a gathering of other children, older by six months or a year."[13] In order to merit this advancement, however, the child would be asked to pass a test. (This requirement would be repeated whenever the child advanced to a higher stage.) Fourier described the kind of standards that would have to be met by a child of four and a half.

> An urchin of four and a half seeking to enter the choir of cherubs . . . will undergo something like the following tests.
> 1. Participation in the choir and corps de ballet at the opera.
> 2. Washing of 120 plates in half an hour, without breaking any.
> 3. Peeling of a half-quintal of potatoes in a given time, without reducing their weight by more than a given amount.
> 4. Perfect sorting of a given quantity of rice or other grain in a fixed amount of time.
> 5. The art of lighting and putting out a fire carefully and quickly.[14]★

Most of the tests Fourier required of postulant cherubs had to do with the development of manual skills and physical dexterity. This was also true of the requirements for entrance into the choir of seraphs, which grouped

---

★It should be noted that this test is designed for a *bambine* or urchiness. For every stage after infancy Fourier designated both masculine and feminine choirs: for example, *séraphins* and *séraphines, jouvenceaux* and *jouvencelles.* But he made it clear that any boy or girl was free to join a choir of the opposite sex. Within the Phalanx, in other words, sex roles were chosen rather than prescribed.

children between six and a half and nine. "In the Phalanx," Fourier wrote, "no attempt will be made to create precocious little savants." One had only to observe the habitual penchants of children under nine to see that they were "very much inclined to all sorts of physical activity and very little inclined to studies." It was necessary therefore to follow "the wish of nature and attraction" by stressing physical development at the outset.[15] But Fourier emphasized that the physical development of the child was not an end in itself so much as a preparation for the subsequent development of the emotions and the intellect.

> In order to prepare the way for the education of the soul, or the noble side of man, [Harmony] begins by concentrating for a long time on the perfection of the secondary element or material shell, and on adapting it to all the habits it wishes to give to the soul, that is, to justice, truth, unity, to a horror for everything that would offend these social virtues.[16]

So the goal for Fourier was the development of the "social virtues" of justice, truth, and a sense of the unity or solidarity of the whole community. In preparing the way, in providing the young people of Harmony with the requisite physical training, Fourier utilized two resources that had no place in civilized methods of education. These were the kitchen and the opera of each Phalanx.

The importance of the kitchen in Fourier's scheme of education rested largely on the fact that gourmandise was the strongest passion of almost all children.[17] In civilization children were kept out of the kitchen for fear of their breaking dishes or being burned or cut or scalded. But this was just one of many examples of the blindness of civilized parents and moralists. If proper precautions were taken, Fourier asserted, the kitchen could become a remarkable school of manual dexterity and practical knowledge. Not only would the child's gourmandise and curiosity about the kitchen foster an interest in the preparation and cooking of food. Early training in the art of cooking would itself serve as an introduction to chemistry, biology, and agronomy. Furthermore, Fourier maintained, a child could have no better introduction to attractive work than in the kitchen, where the preparation of sugared creams, compotes, pastries, jams, and other sweets would provide "a thousand sources of industrial intrigue."[18] Thus Harmony's kitchens would provide an introduction both to the sciences and to the world of work.

The other vital institution for the education of the young in Fourier's Phalanx was the opera, which he, like many other nineteenth-century thinkers, regarded as the foreshadowing of a "total art" because of the way in which it brought together music, dance, poetry, and design in an enchanting whole.★ "An opera house is as necessary to a Phalanx," wrote Fourier, "as its plows and its herds. This is not only because it has the advantage of providing the smallest community with performances as excellent as those of Paris, London, and Naples; it also serves to educate children and to shape them in the ways of material harmony."[19] Fourier was himself a great lover of opera, but he recognized that for many of his contemporaries the opera house was "no more than an arena for amorous intrigue and an enticement to spend money." In Harmony, however, the opera would be free; it would enlist the participation and the energies of almost all the members of a Phalanx; and Fourier could describe it as "the assemblage of all material harmonies and the active emblem of the spirit of God, or the spirit of measured unity."[20] What would make it such an important vehicle of education was the fact that through participation in the opera's chorus or its corps de ballet a child would learn for the first time "to subordinate himself in every movement to unitary conventions, to general harmonies."[21] The opera was thus the "material school" of the qualities of unity, justice, and truth, which would characterize human relations in the Phalanx. It would offer an image of the harmony that actually existed in society and not, as in civilization, a momentary escape from an inharmonious world.

III

If the main aim of Harmonian education during a child's first nine years was to develop the senses and the physical faculties, the emphasis there-

★For Fourier's conception of opera as "the assemblage of all measured material harmonies" see OC V, 76–77. Fourier emphasized that Harmony's opera would include gymnastics and many related forms of popular "street art" that polite society disdained. "Little or no gymnastics is tolerated in civilized opera," wrote Fourier. "Gymnastics is supposed to be a popular genre and is relegated to the little theaters. This is an instance of corrupt taste and not of refinement. All material harmonies are noble. But since clowns, rope dancers, tumblers, etc., are pleasing to the common people, they had to be disgraced by civilized high society, which loathes the common people and their tastes. Gymnastics will be restored to favor in a state of things where the great and the common people will be ONE with respect to breeding and manners." OC V, 77.

after was on the child's moral and emotional development. Between the ages of nine and twenty, according to Fourier's schema, children would pass through three groups or choirs: the *lycéens* (for children from nine to twelve), the *gymnasiens* (twelve to fifteen and a half), and the *jouvenceaux* (fifteen and a half to about twenty). Fourier maintained that for children between nine and fifteen the passions of friendship and honor would be particularly strong. The child of nine to fifteen was not yet moved (so Fourier believed) by sexual passions, and his loyalty to his peers was much stronger than his family ties. This period was therefore one in which it was natural for children to form strong friendships; it was also a period in which the capacity for selfless devotion to the group and for great and noble actions was at its height. The task of education was to give guidance and direction to these impulses and to unite them, in a manner that would serve the common good, with selfish or antisocial impulses common among preadolescent children. With this in mind, Fourier devised two remarkable voluntary organizations for children between nine and fifteen. These were the Little Hordes and the Little Bands.[22]

The Little Hordes was a corporation that would group all those young people (of whom approximately two-thirds were boys) who were naturally rebellious, obstinate, obscene, and—above all—irresistibly attracted to filth, excrement, and danger. The Little Bands, on the other hand, would be made up of all those docile or studious children (girls for the most part) who were addicted to fancy dress and refined manners. Fourier maintained that both the attraction to dirt and danger and the love of finery could be put to socially useful purposes if they were properly combined with the penchants for friendship and honor that were particularly strong among preadolescent children. Thus the energies of the Little Hordes would be channeled into such essential tasks as the collection of garbage, the maintenance of roads, and the cleaning of butcheries and latrines. They would be encouraged to perform such work "as a pious deed, an act of charity toward the Phalanx, a service to God and unity."[23] The Little Bands in turn would be responsible for the decoration of the Phalanx, the designing of uniforms, the cultivation of flowers, and the maintenance of high standards of refinement in speech and behavior. They would be given the opportunity to satisfy their passion for finery in ways that would benefit all of society.

During the final phase of education in Harmony Fourier maintained that the primary problem would be to channel the emerging and powerful passion of love into socially desirable directions. Once again he designed two groups or corporations to serve as rallying points for the youth of Harmony. The Vestals were to group those strong-minded individuals (primarily young women) who managed to retain their virginity until the age of nineteen or twenty. The Damsels would include all those (primarily men) in whom the sexual passion burst forth early and uncontrollably. Each of these groups had an important role to play in the life of the community.[24]

Like their namesakes, the guardians of the sacred fire in the temple of Vesta at Rome, Fourier's Vestals were themselves the objects of a "semireligious cult."[25] They were revered by younger children, and especially by the Little Hordes, who served as their honor guard. The guardians of "a truly sacred fire, that of the four cardinal virtues," they played an important role at all ceremonial gatherings, serving as escorts for visiting dignitaries and carrying the banners at gatherings of the industrial armies. Unlike the Vestals of Rome, one-third of their number would be men. "To create female *vestales* without male *vestels*," Fourier explained, "would be to imitate the contradiction of our customs, which prescribe chastity for girls and tolerate fornication among boys . . . a duplicity worthy of civilization."[26]

Ordinarily, when a child reached the age of fifteen and a half, he or she would be automatically enrolled in the ranks of the Vestals. But after a few months, Fourier observed, some of the new Vestals would find the yoke of chastity too hard to bear. They would then take their place among the Damsels, one-third of whom were girls and two-thirds boys. The members of this corps were considered traitors by the younger children—the Little Hordes regarded them as "Satan's rebellious angels." But they attempted to compensate for their fall from grace by exhibiting great refinement and delicacy in love. They would be encouraged to remain faithful to their first lovers as long as possible. And in the *Traité de l'association* Fourier stressed that any Damsel who behaved dishonorably in his or her first affair of the heart would suffer the indignity of expulsion from the corps. In the unpublished *Nouveau monde amoureux*, however, he adopted a considerably more tolerant posture.

> It is customary for the female and male Damsels to remain faithful until they have reached the age of twenty. But since

everything is done by gradation in Harmony and since it would be difficult, not to say impossible, for a couple to remain faithful for four or five years, the amorous code allows for graduated exceptions to the rule of fidelity. Thus no one is expelled from the Damselate until he or she has committed three infidelities and one inconstancy, or else seven infidelities without an inconstancy.

Only half an infidelity is counted if a Damsel has an affair with one of the priests or priestesses, who, in view of their age, are given special advantages. Thus a Damsel can commit fourteen acts of infidelity with priests, and she will only be expelled after the fifteenth, whereas expulsion will occur after the eighth act of infidelity with a layman.[27]

This text, with its ironically pedantic parody of the Catholic system of indulgences, makes it clear that the fidelity imposed on the Damsels was not exactly burdensome, and that once a Harmonian became a member of that corps, he or she had already entered a "new amorous world."

The *Nouveau monde amoureux* was not known to Fourier's nineteenth-century readers. But the relatively restrained discussion of adolescent sexuality contained in Fourier's published works was quite enough to offend many of his contemporaries. Fourier was accused of advocating promiscuity and preaching complete sexual license for children. As Victor Hennequin put it in 1849: "The word that could once be read on a palace in Ferrara, *Orgia,* ought to be inscribed on the pediment of his Phalanstery."[28] In fact, when one considers the role of sexuality in Fourier's educational theory as a whole, what is striking is not Fourier's audacity but rather the cautious and conventional character of his thinking. Fourier did not believe that the child had any sexual impulses prior to the onset of puberty, and in his statutes for the organization of the Phalanx he did everything to discourage the awakening of curiosity about sexual matters in preadolescent children. Not only were all children in the Phalanx put to bed prior to the sessions of the Court of Love; their life was even organized so that they would never be exposed to the sight of dogs and cats in heat.[29] In this respect at least Harmony's children were, by the standards of twentieth-century civilization, kept in a state of extraordinary innocence.

IV

Fourier's plans for the education of children between nine and twenty focused primarily on their moral and emotional growth, on the development and channeling of the emerging passions of friendship and ambition and, later, of love. But what about the child's intellectual development during the same period? What approach did Fourier take toward the growth of the mind? Here the first point is that book learning was not to be emphasized in Fourier's new world. Fourier's works do include precise specifications for reference books and systems of typography to be employed in Harmony. There are also some delightful passages in Fourier on the contribution to be made to "burlesque social archaeology" through the publication in Harmony of critical editions of certain classics of civilized literature and philosophy.[30] In general, however, Fourier believed that books were only effective when the knowledge they contained was actively sought after by the child. In Harmony as in A. S. Neill's Summerhill, books would never be forced on children: they would be made available as a response to curiosity awakened by the experience of work and play.

Given Fourier's emphasis on the linkage between intellectual growth and practical experience, it follows that teaching in the Phalanx was not to be confined to any single, assigned space. There were to be no separate schools or classrooms. Nor was there to be a specialized class of professional teachers. Such teaching as was done would take place within the various groups and series and would be provided by individuals called sybils, who were generally the most knowledgeable members of a group. They might gather children in small groups for special instruction. But this would only be done at the request of the children. Thus Harmony would reverse the customary civilized relation between teacher and student. Students would no longer be classroom captives who detested their teachers. Able to study whatever they wished with whomever they wished, children would "regard as so many friends, as so many saviors, all those elderly men and women who are willing to give [them] instruction in work and study."[31]

Fourier did not propose to abolish tests and examinations in his scheme of Harmonian education. They would be required of children seeking to pass from one "choir" to another, and they would also be a prerequisite for a child's advancement within the various work groups of which he or she was a member. Fourier claimed that the very frequency of these examinations, and the variety of groups to which any child might belong, would reduce the fear of failure, which was endemic to the whole process of learning in civilization. Furthermore, he asserted, given the alertness and the high motivation of Harmony's children, failure would be rare. Nevertheless he did stipulate that children who repeatedly failed their examinations would eventually be relegated to "half-character" choirs composed of dull and retarded children. And such children do not seem to have benefited from the compassion Fourier so readily extended to most social deviants and outcasts. For one of the consequences of Fourier's examination system was, as he put it, to make it impossible for parents to deceive themselves about the inferiority of their children or to "extol as they now do the virtues of a little block-head."[32]

V

Fourier's name rarely appears in the standard histories of educational thought, and he does not seem to have had much direct influence on modern thinking about education. One has to go back to the nineteenth century—to Jean Macé and the movement for popular education in France and to the founders of the *école maternelle*—to find important educational movements that were in any significant way influenced by Fourier's thought.[33] Nevertheless when one considers the whole body of Fourier's writing on education, one cannot fail to be impressed by his modernity, by the many respects in which his ideas and methods anticipate those of such twentieth-century educators as Maria Montessori, A. S. Neill, and the founders of the Israeli kibbutz movement. It is true that Fourier's rejection of the concept of infantile sexuality and his whole discussion of sexual education are, to say the least, puzzlingly traditional in a thinker who can on other counts be compared with Wilhelm Reich. There seems to be no hint of irony in Fourier's proposal to remove dogs and cats in heat from the sight of Harmony's children, or in his recommendation of regular gymnastic exercises as a means of retarding the onset of puberty.[34] In his apparent fear of adolescent sexuality and of the awakening of sexual curiosity in children, the prophet of the new amorous world was in the Victorian mainstream.

There are many other points, however, on which Fourier clearly does anticipate the theory and practice of twentieth-century progressive education. He can, for example, be seen as an early advocate of the "open classroom," doing away with the school as an institution and replacing the classroom, that traditional "focal point of imposed discipline and boredom," with "the much larger and far more interesting educational arena of the Phalanx itself."[35] Fourier can also be seen as a precursor of Maria Montessori, especially in his belief that the use of miniature tools and workshops could serve as an important key to the child's discovery of vocation and development of manual dexterity. His proposals for communal child rearing are remarkably similar to the methods actually adopted in many of the kibbutzim of twentieth-century Israel.[36] And his insistence that book learning is only valuable to children when they seek it out actively themselves is in line with a long tradition of progressive education running from Rousseau to A. S. Neill.

The similarities between Fourier's educational theories and the ideas put into practice at Neill's famous school, Summerhill, are particularly striking.[37] Both Neill and Fourier stipulated that children should be left almost entirely free to choose whatever activity they wished. Both were convinced that knowledge cannot be force-fed and that when subject to a minimum of coercion, children will develop as far as they are capable as a result of their own initiative. Like Fourier, Neill also believed that many of the child's aggressive and otherwise antisocial impulses could find harmless outlets in play and even in various forms of work. Of course one very important difference between Neill's Summerhill and Fourier's Phalanx is that the one was a real school whereas the other existed only on paper, and in Fourier's mind. Neill was forced to make compromises that Fourier would have disdained. But what he shared with Fourier was the belief that children could attain their full potential only in communities marked by an absence of constraint.

It would be possible to list a number of other respects in which Fourier's ideas anticipated modern movements in education. It is perhaps in this field more than any other that his ideas have gained wide acceptance, even if he himself has had relatively little influence. But still a qualification is necessary by way of conclusion. To abstract Fourier's educational ideas from his theory as a whole and to look at him as a precursor of contemporary progressive education is to risk seriously misunderstanding him. For he was not a reformer whose ideas could be adopted piecemeal, but a visionary who dreamed of a total transformation of society. His views on education were part of a larger theory that presupposed the abolition of the family and of patriarchal authority in general. And he argued that so long as the family was maintained, and with it the assumption that the father is the "natural teacher" of the child, no amount of piecemeal educational reform could make much difference.[38]

14

Work in Harmony

THE DISTINCTIVE element in Fourier's utopian vision was not his call for a new architecture or his program of Phalansterian education or even his stipulations for Harmony's gastronomy. Rather it was his belief that work could become the gratification of man's deepest needs and the fullest expression of his powers. For Fourier, full human self-realization was only possible within the world of work.[1]

Traditionally work had been regarded as a curse. In the Christian scheme of things it was a mark of man's fallen nature, the punishment for his Original Sin; and in the Old Regime it retained the traditional Christian connotations of pain, burden, and penitence. *Travail* was defined in the dictionary of the French Academy in 1694 as the "toil, pain, fatigue taken to do something," and La Bruyère's celebrated portrait of the peasant as a subhuman beast of burden is probably representative of the attitude of the privileged classes toward physical work.[2] Rejecting all this, Fourier argued that, properly organized, work could become a means to instinctual gratification and personal fulfillment. Thus in devising the Phalanx what Fourier had in mind was not merely a planned community designed to raise living standards and increase production. His essential aim was to create an institutional framework within which work might serve as the ally rather than the enemy of the immutable human passions.

I

During Fourier's lifetime the problem of work emerged as a vital concern of European social thought. Political economists, Christian moralists, political reformers, and social utopians all sought to reevaluate work and to rescue it from centuries of classical, Christian, and aristocratic denigration. Though their perspectives and premises varied greatly, one thing they shared was the desire to establish productive work as the fundamental activity of the good society and the virtuous individual. Of course this effort to rehabilitate work did not begin with Fourier's generation. Within the Christian tradition there had long been voices arguing that disciplined work within a calling was both a barrier against temptation and a sign by which a Christian could recognize his own salvation. Similarly a long tradition of middle-class moralists had vaunted honest work as the key to happiness, respectability, and success. Again, in the writings of the Enlightenment philosophers work had been praised as a source of virtue and dignity and as a condition of human progress. Diderot, for example, in his articles in the *Encyclopédie* celebrated labor as the foundation of human happiness, and the inventions of skilled artisans as keys to the progress of human society. Finally, in the aftermath of the French Revolution, Henri Saint-Simon could proclaim the beginning of a new era in which all rights and all power would derive from the performance of productive work. Thenceforth, argued Saint-Simon, only those who worked would have the right to regard themselves as members of society.[3]

Fourier's thought can obviously be seen as part of this effort to reevaluate work. He too believed that work was a major social problem and that the reordering of work was a key to progress and to human happiness. But unlike most of his predecessors and contemporaries, Fourier did not take a moralistic position. Work for him was not a "good" to be sought after or urged on others. Thus he had no sympathy for contemporary exponents of the work ethic who regarded the world as a painful place in which work must be accepted as a destiny or duty. Nor did he share Saint-Simon's view of work as a social duty, as a means by which the individual could serve his fellows and affirm his solidarity with them. For Fourier thinkers who preached the work ethic in whatever form were simply self-interested moralists, trying to get others to do their work. His own view was that work was not a duty but a need. The desire to work was basic to man's nature, Fourier believed, and there was no full self-realization apart from work—*provided* that work was freely chosen.

The starting point of Fourier's reflections on the problem of work seems to have been his own observations on the contrast between the lethargy and loathing with which work was normally performed in civilization and the seemingly miraculous feats that workers could accomplish when they were really motivated. His favorite example was that of a group of miners in Liège who managed in 1810 to save eighty buried comrades by clearing a shaft in four days, which ordinary salaried workers could not have cleared in two weeks.[4] What Fourier sought to do was to imagine a setting in which the exceptional ardor displayed by the Liège miners would become the rule.

The problem was that the work offered by civilization simply failed to engage the energies or fire the passions of its workers. There was nothing attractive about long hours of work at boring, brutalizing, and often unhealthy jobs. On the contrary, wrote Fourier, life was a "perpetual torment" for workers obliged to work shifts of "twelve and often fifteen hours" in glassworks and chemical factories and spinning mills, which were themselves "veritable graveyards" for workers.[5] And if the factories of Lancashire and the north of France were "industrial prisons," the condition of cottage workers was even worse. The peasant of Picardy who produced muslin and kashmir cloth for manufacturers in Amiens, Cambrai, and Saint-Quentin was "living in such poverty in his earthen hut that he does not even have a bed. In wintertime he sleeps on a pile of leaves that rapidly turns into a worm-infested compost heap." The ribbon workers in the hills around Saint-Etienne lived and worked in the same conditions of poverty.[6] No wonder then, wrote Fourier, that members of savage societies had always abhorred work. No wonder, too, that the "drudges of the working class" would spend their Sundays "drowning their sorrows in wine." Most of civilization's workers were "so absorbed by worry about the subsistence of their families" that they had no other pleasure than drink, and reached "the end of the week, of the year, or of life without any other satisfaction than that of having succeeded in not dying of hunger."[7]

Although Fourier had much to say about the material suffering of the working classes, his most original and searching reflections on work in civilization focused more on the *psychological* pains that transformed the lives of civilized workers into a "permanent hell." Thus when, in the *Traité de l'association,* he came to list the "misfortunes of working people," it was fear, shame, and frustration that Fourier stressed as much as physical suffering.[8] And when he discussed the servitude of civilized workers, the boredom of office workers and the anxieties of the unemployed figured as prominently as the poverty and material needs of peasants and artisans. Fourier kept insisting that all of this was unnecessary. Work was intended to be one of life's most satisfying activities, an activity to which, in a rightly ordered society, men and women would be irresistibly drawn.

II

The great discovery that would allow work to become the gratifying experience it was always meant to be was what Fourier called his theory of attractive labor. The aim of this theory was to organize work in such a way that no socially necessary task would fail to inspire the zealous and enthusiastic commitment of at least some members of a Phalanx. Fourier maintained that this would require the fulfillment of a number of basic conditions.

1. Each worker must be an associate who is compensated by dividend and not by wages.
2. Each person—man, woman, or child—must be paid in proportion to his contribution in *capital, work,* and *talent.*
3. Work sessions must be varied about eight times a day because a man cannot remain enthusiastic about his job for more than an hour and a half or two when he is performing an agricultural or manufacturing task.
4. These tasks must be performed by groups of friends who have gathered together spontaneously and who are stimulated and intrigued by very active rivalries.
5. Workshops, field, and gardens must offer the worker the enticements of elegance and cleanliness.
6. The division of labor must be carried to the supreme degree in order to allot suitable tasks to people of each sex and of every age.
7. The distribution of tasks must assure each man, woman, or child the right to work or the right to take part at any time in any kind of work for which he or she is qualified.

X. Finally, in this new order the common people must enjoy
a guarantee of well-being, a minimum income sufficient
for present and future needs. This guarantee must free
them from all anxiety either for their own welfare or for
that of their dependents.[9]

Among these conditions are some that can be found in programs for the
organization of work devised by a number of other nineteenth-century
radicals and reformers. The proposal to abolish wage labor, for example, and to compensate workers by a system of dividends and profit
sharing was echoed by many of the spokesmen of the early producers'
cooperative movement. And while Fourier attached great importance to
his demand for clean and even "elegant" workshops, fields, and gardens, there was obviously nothing very original about it. But the other
conditions were uniquely Fourier's and they constitute the core of the
theory of attractive labor.

To make labor attractive, Fourier argued, it would be necessary to
offer workers the opportunity to choose their own tasks, to change jobs
frequently, and to work together in spontaneously formed groups and
series of groups within which the basic passions might have free play. It
would also be necessary to adopt Fourier's special scheme of remuneration in terms of labor, capital, and talent. Finally, and most importantly, it would be necessary to offer all members of a community what
amounted to a guaranteed income, even if they showed no inclination
to work. Fourier regarded this "social minimum" as indispensable. For,
he believed, it was only when men and women had been freed from the
necessity to work that they could become psychologically capable of
regarding work as attractive.

One of the key elements in Fourier's design for attractive labor
was, of course, the organization of work into passionate groups and
series. The passionate series, it will be recalled, was "a league of various
groups," arranged in hierarchical order and passionately joined together
"by a common affinity for a particular task" or function.[10] Each of the
groups into which the series was divided would specialize in one part of
a job or in the cultivation of one type of crop. The series of flower
fanciers, for example, might be divided into groups cultivating roses,
camellias, dahlias, violets, and orchids. If interest was sufficiently great,
the group of rose growers might themselves constitute a series divided
into subgroups. Fourier's best-known illustrations of the principle of

the passionate series, and one that shows just how minutely nuanced a series could be, had to do with pear growing.

THE PEAR GROWERS' SERIES
Composed of 32 groups.

Divisions	Numerical Progression	Types
1. Forward outpost	2 groups	Quinces and abnormally hard types
2. Ascending wing tip	4 groups	Hard cooking pears
3. Ascending wing	6 groups	Crisp pears
4. Center of the series	8 groups	Juicy pears
5. Descending wing	6 groups	Compact pears
6. Descending wing tip	4 groups	Mealy pears
7. Rear outpost	2 groups	Medlars and abnormally soft types[11]

Fourier emphasized that a series was not a bland gathering of people with identical tastes and personalities. On the contrary, the proper functioning of the series required the maintenance of a sort of ordered discord among its members. For this reason variety and inequality were essential; each series had to be composed of individuals who differed greatly in their "personalities, tastes, instincts, wealth, pretensions, and intelligence." Just as in music, contrast and variety were essential to the creation of harmony.

Another vital element in Fourier's theory of attractive labor was his special scheme of remuneration. According to this scheme, each Harmonian would receive an annual dividend to be based on his or her contribution in work, capital, and talent. This dividend would initially be allocated to each series, the amount being determined, not by the productivity of the series, but by the attractiveness, utility, and "necessity" of the work. Unattractive and essential work such as latrine cleaning, tripe preparation, and the supervision of noisy and hyperactive children would generally be well remunerated, whereas orchard work, which everybody loved, would not. Of course many tasks that seemed useless in civilization would be vitally important in Harmony. The painstaking care required by flower growing would be a "precious" means of introducing children to the science of agronomy. Similarly, the educational importance of the opera would place it in the "second order of necessity, immediately following repugnant tasks." Once the dividends had been distributed to each series, they would then be divided among the members according to Fourier's formula: five-twelfths for an individual's contribution in labor, four-twelfths for invested capital, and three-twelfths for talent. The special share for talent would go to the more skillful and experienced members and the share for capital to those who had made contributions or investments of benefit to the series.[12]

Fourier's theory of attractive labor was designed to reveal and utilize work instincts, which he believed were a part of the psyche of every human being. At the same time it aimed to ensure that all the passions, and above all the mechanizing passions, would be satisfied in and through the experience of work. In accordance with the dictates of the Butterfly passion work sessions would never last for more than two hours, and a worker would never become tied to a particular kind of work. The Cabalist or conspiring passion would be gratified by the intrigues and rivalries that would grow up within and between the groups and series, and these rivalries would in turn inspire each group and series to perfect its product. The great thing about the rivalries and conflicts is that they would never center on individuals. Since each Phalansterian would belong to at least thirty series (participating in the activities of seven or eight series in the course of a day), it would be commonplace for a person to find that a rival in one series would be a partner in another. Finally the Composite, the blind enthusiasm created by the simultaneous satisfaction of the spirit and the senses, would be gratified by the simultaneous fostering of a sense of *esprit de corps* among the members of each work group and of a sense of pride in the quality of the goods produced by the group.

Instead of working at the same dull task, hour after hour, day after day, Fourier's Harmonians would work in pleasant settings at jobs they themselves had chosen, which would give them the opportunity to establish amorous, conspiratorial, or simply friendly relations with many other members of the community. As varied work became the source of varied pleasures, the working day, a long ordeal in civilization, would come to seem too short in Harmony. Fourier illustrated this point by outlining the activities of two imaginary Harmonians. First there was poor Lucas, a villager participating in a trial Phalanx during the early stages of Harmony.

LUCAS'S DAY IN JUNE

Time

3:30	Rising, preparations
4:00	Session with a group assigned to the stables
5:00	Session with a group of gardeners
7:00	Breakfast
7:30	Session with the reapers' group
9:30	Session with the vegetable growers' group, under a tent
11:00	Session with the barnyard series
1:00	DINNER
2:00	Session with the forestry series
4:00	Session with a manufacturing group
6:00	Session with the irrigation series
8:00	Session at the Exchange
8:30	Supper
9:00	Entertainment
10:00	Bed[13]

By contrast Fourier described a summer's day in the life of a rich Harmonian named Mondor during the period of Full Harmony.

MONDOR'S DAY IN THE SUMMER

Time

	Sleep from 10:30 at night to 3:00 in the morning
3:30	Rising, preparations
4:00	Morning court, review of the night's adventures
4:30	Breakfast, followed by the industrial parade
5:30	Session with the group of hunters
7:00	Session with the group of fishermen
8:00	Lunch, newspapers
9:00	Session with a group of horticulturalists, under a tent
10:00	Mass
10:30	Session with the group of pheasant breeders
11:30	Session at the library
1:00	DINNER
2:30	Session with the greenhouse group
4:00	Session with the group of exotic plant growers
5:00	Session with the fish-tank group

6:00	Snack, in the fields
6:30	Session with the sheep-raising group
8:00	Session at the Exchange
9:00	Supper, fifth meal
9:30	Art exhibition, concert, dance, theater, receptions
10:30	Bed[14]

If there was little time for sleep in Mondor's schedule, Fourier explained that no more would be necessary. Improved diet, advanced hygiene, and varied work sessions would virtually eliminate the possibility of work fatigue.

Fourier's accounts of the working day in Harmony are so detailed, so minutely choreographed, that there seems to be little room for spontaneity. In his descriptions the work series are always fully staffed, there is always a qualified worker for every job that needs to be done, and Mondor is never more than a few minutes late for his afternoon sessions in the greenhouse. All this has led some commentators to raise questions concerning the degree of freedom that could actually exist within the Phalanx. Would it really be possible to coordinate the efforts of sixteen hundred people, any one of whom might belong to fifty different groups, without recourse to discipline and regimentation? Wouldn't Fourier actually have to hand over the organization of work in the Phalanx to "a giant organization and administration," which could prove even more repressive than the civil and political authorities of civilization?[15] Such questions are hard to ignore, since there does seem to be a disparity between Fourier's description of the Phalanx as a realm of total instinctual liberation and his carefully calibrated work schedules and organizational hierarchies. It should be pointed out, however, that if there is an arbitrary or coercive element in Fourier's system, it exists at the level of definitions and not in the organizational and institutional structures he devised. Fourier believed that, if given free expression, the passions of 1,620 individuals organized in Phalanxes would inevitably harmonize. But on the level of institutions there is nothing in his theory comparable, for example, to the "spiritual power" that Henri Saint-Simon called for to allocate work and provide moral guidance to the members of his new industrial society. Even more clearly there is nothing in Fourier's ideas about work comparable to the authoritarian and hierarchical industrial psychology developed by the followers of Saint-Simon toward the end of the Restoration.

How then did Fourier propose to solve the organizational problems that work in the Phalanx would inevitably entail? Specifically, how would it be possible to find the right person for every job that needed to be done? And who could design a schedule that would accommodate the immensely varied vocations and the changing desires and needs of some sixteen hundred people? Fourier's proposals for vocational education and his system of serial organization were attempts to deal with the problems of training and placement. And for the complicated task of scheduling and coordination Fourier devised a unique solution. Each evening, at the end of the day's work, all Phalansterians would attend the sessions of a Bourse or Exchange to plan their activities for the following day. These sessions, which afforded vast opportunities for the play of the cabalistic passion, were enthusiastically evoked by Fourier.

> The Exchange of a Phalanx is much more animated and richer in intrigues than those of London or Amsterdam, since every individual is obliged to use the Exchange to arrange his work and pleasure sessions for the following days. It is there that he makes plans concerning his gastronomic and amorous meetings and, especially, for his work sessions in the shops and fields. Everyone has at least twenty sessions to arrange, since he makes definite plans for the following day and tentative ones for the day after.

Fourier went on to describe the method by which each of the sixteen hundred members of a Phalanx might conclude arrangements for twenty work and play sessions in the course of a half-hour at the Exchange.

> Negotiations are carried on quietly by means of signals. Each negotiator holds up the escutcheons of the groups or Phalanxes that he represents, and by certain prearranged signs he indicates the approximate number of members whom he has recruited. Everyone else walks around the hall. In one or two circuits a given individual may take part in twenty transactions, since all he has to do is to accept or refuse. Dorimon suggests that a meeting of the beekeepers be held the next day at ten o'clock. The leaders of this group have taken the initiative according to the customary procedures. Their job is to find out whether or not a majority of the members of the beekeeping group wish to hold a session. In this case the decision is affirmative. Each of the members takes his peg from the beekeepers' board, which is placed in front of Dorimon's desk. . . .

At the other side of the hall Araminte calls for a meeting of the rose growers to be held at the same time. Since many of Araminte's rose growers are also members of the beekeeping group, they raise an objection and notify Dorimon. He conveys their message to the directorate, which tells Araminte to halt his negotiations. The rose growers are obliged to choose another hour, since beekeeping is a more necessary form of work than rose growing.[16]

There is here, as elsewhere in Fourier's accounts of Phalansterian life, a strong element of parody. Harmony's Exchange, with its elaborate procedures and benign cabals, was the civilized stock exchange, turned upside down and put to good use. As far as the organization of work is concerned, the important feature of the Exchange was that it enabled Harmonians to accomplish the work of the Phalanx and to form hundreds of work groups each day by mutual consent and without the slightest element of constraint. Harmony's Exchange was thus one of the most vital elements in Fourier's plan to reconcile work and the apparently incompatible desire for pleasure.

Some of the tasks to be performed in Fourier's utopia were naturally too vast and ambitious for the members of a single Phalanx. To accomplish these large-scale undertakings Fourier foresaw the creation of new industrial armies. Replacing the destructive armies of civilization, these harmonious and productive armies would roam the globe, digging canals, building bridges, draining swamps, irrigating deserts, and reforesting ravaged hillsides. Membership in the industrial armies would be entirely voluntary and would include women and children as well as men. Since their "campaigns" would be accompanied by splendid festivities and vast amorous and gastronomic revels, recruitment would be no problem. Harmonians would vie with one another for the opportunity to join these peaceful armies and to help turn the earth into the bountiful garden that it was meant to be. Thanks to their efforts the isthmuses of Suez and Panama would be opened to shipping, the polar icecaps would be reduced, and the greater part of the earth's surface would at last be placed under cultivation. Thus Fourier's thinking about work, which began with his reflections on the productivity of highly motivated workers, culminated with the vision of an earth transformed and wholly adapted by human labor to human purposes.

To anyone who considers Fourier's plan for the organization of labor from a skeptical, civilized perspective, a number of questions and criticisms spring to mind. First of all, even if one accepts Fourier's major premise that work *can* be made attractive, his theory of attractive labor seems to be based on a number of dubious assumptions. Isn't one of them the quite unwarranted assumption that people who have a taste for something will necessarily enjoy producing it? Is it really true, as Fourier implies, that all, or even most, fruit lovers will be attracted to orchard work? Fourier himself recognized that in the civilized world those who enjoy eating delicacies generally "scorn the agricultural work of producing them and the culinary work of preparing them." But he claimed that in Harmony, where the work of production and preparation would be rendered vastly more attractive, the love of eating certain foods would necessarily stimulate a love of producing and preparing them. Thus in the Phalanx gourmandise would "give rise to industrial attraction." Perhaps. But the point is not so much argued as asserted.[17]

Another objection, made more often but perhaps less telling, focuses on the drawbacks of Fourier's short work sessions. If Harmonians were to be changing jobs as often as Fourier's work schedules suggest, wouldn't the result be a huge waste of time? As usual, Fourier anticipated the objection, and his answer was a simple one: the ten or fifteen minutes lost in job changes would be more than offset by the increased productivity of work in Harmony. Indeed, he contended, Harmonians would be such passionate workers that their "ardor at work" would become a "harmful excess" were it not tempered by the pauses occasioned by the changing of jobs.[18]

What about the problem of maintaining work standards in the Phalanx? Given Fourier's insistence on the freedom of all Phalansterians to work at jobs of their own choosing, as often or as little as they wished, how did he propose to deal with the problem of shoddy or incompetent work? This was not a problem that Fourier found particularly troubling. In the vast majority of cases, he believed, poor work was the result of inattention, boredom, or lethargy, which simply could not exist in Harmony. Nevertheless Fourier did stipulate that the members of every group and series would be ranked according to their skill. Promotions would be determined by the vote of one's colleagues, as would the share of the profits of the Phalanx awarded to each individual for his or her work in a group. Thus poor workers, if there were any, would be poorly remunerated.

A graver problem for Fourier was that posed by a whole group that produced goods of inferior quality. What, for example, could be done about a group of melon fanciers so fanatical that they persisted in attempting to grow melons in foggy and mountainous terrain? Or artichoke addicts who insisted on growing their favorite vegetables in an area of dry weather and scorching sun? Most devotees of a fruit or vegetable totally inappropriate to a given area would be realistic enough to eat goods shipped in from outside. But in each Phalanx there would always be a stubborn few who kept trying to raise crops or produce goods utterly unsuited to their region. If a group of Dutch Phalansterians wished to grow grapes in Holland, wrote Fourier, "one would not be able to thwart them in this agricultural fantasy, since everything is free in Harmony."[19] But if the product produced by such a group was consistently rejected by the other members of the Phalanx, they would eventually be obliged to carry a black banner and join a special series of "eclipsed" groups. "I class among the *Eclipsed*," wrote Fourier, "all the groups whose work can neither do honor to the Phalanx nor serve its interests and cabalistic rivalries. These groups are considered parasites and are reduced to a quarter of the normal retribution, or to nothing at all."[20]

Finally, there is a problem that has always proved difficult, and often insurmountable, for utopians in the libertarian tradition. This is the problem of truly loathsome work, work so odious and demeaning that virtually no one would freely choose to do it. Fourier maintained that the number of jobs that fit this description would be greatly reduced in Harmony simply because no one would be wedded to a single task. Even work on a manure pile might be appealing to some people when it only had to be done two hours a week. But what about even less appealing jobs such as the cleaning of latrines, sewers, and slaughterhouses? It was here that what Fourier described as his "inspired" discovery of the Little Hordes came into play. Earlier utopians like Louis-Sébastien Mercier had sometimes argued that the truly repulsive work in any community—"the lowest, most abject, or most dangerous jobs"—might be performed by a corps of secular saints, virtuous citizens who aspired to a higher degree of perfection than their fellows and who wished to prove their virtue, not by "useless fasting" and by "saying psalms in bad Latin," but by useful acts of public service.[21]

Fourier's conception of the Little Hordes was in this tradition, but with the difference that his saints were unruly children.

What Fourier proposed was that the truly disgusting work of the Phalanx should be performed by groups of preadolescents who could conceive of no more delightful activity than wallowing in dirt and excrement. Fourier estimated that two-thirds of all boys and one-third of all girls between the ages of nine and fifteen fell into this category. Such children were passionately attracted to filth, and they were also generally foulmouthed, surly, and willing to brave any danger "simply for the pleasure of wreaking havoc." In Harmony these hitherto intolerable qualities would be put to good use. As members of the Little Hordes and entrusted with principal responsibility for such tasks as garbage collection, sewer maintenance, and the cleaning of slaughterhouses, these unruly children would be venerated by the community as "guardians of social honor" and (because they would refuse to accept pay) exemplars of "the spirit of self-abnegation recommended by Christianity."[22] They would have their own private language or slang, their own uniforms (in the "grotesque or barbarian style"), and their own leaders, called Little Khans and Little Khantes. They would be aided by acolytes called Bonzes and Druids—older people who had never outgrown the love of filth and who would accompany them on their missions. Fourier has left us an unforgettable description of their departure for work in the morning.

> The charge of the Little Hordes is sounded by a din of alarm bells, carillons, drums, trumpets, barking dogs, and mooing cows. Then the Hordes, led by their Khans and their Druids, rush forth with great cries, passing before the patriarchs, who sprinkle them with Holy Water. They gallop frenetically to labor, which is executed as a work of piety, an act of charity toward the Phalanx, the service of God and of unity.[23]

Frenzied by trumpet blasts and roars of approval, intoxicated by unending accolades, the Little Hordes would place their love of filth at the service of the Phalanx.

IV

The most striking feature of Fourier's plan for the organization of work in Harmony was his insistence on the rural character of the whole enterprise. Whenever he described a Phalanx, it was always located in a rural setting, and most of the work to be done was agricultural, with an emphasis on horticulture and stockbreeding. Fourier's favorite example of an "industrial" series was that of pear growers, and even the work projects he set for his industrial armies aimed largely at reclaiming land or increasing agricultural production. What then was to be the place of manufacturing work in Harmony? Fourier vigorously denied that he wished to banish machines and factories altogether from his ideal community. He was "far from endorsing the views of the fools who would like to tear down the factories."[24] But he did stipulate that the place of factories and machines would be limited. Manufacturing work would be a "complement" to agriculture and would serve as "a means of diversion to the passional doldrums" of winter and the rainy season.[25] There would thus be no room in the Phalanx for anything like the massive concentrations of workers, machines, and factories of the modern industrial city.

Fourier minimized the role of manufactures because he believed that although manufactured goods were necessary to man's well-being, the work of producing them could never be made very attractive. In the *Nouveau monde industriel* he distinguished between three types of attraction: direct, indirect, and divergent. Direct attraction was inspired by work that was enjoyable in itself. Divergent attraction was the detestation inspired by loathsome work. Work that inspired indirect attraction lacked intrinsic appeal but could be made to *seem* enticing under certain conditions (for instance, the presence of convivial fellow workers or the creation of intense group rivalries).[26] Early in his career Fourier came to the conclusion that most manufacturing work lacked intrinsic appeal; even in Harmony it would inspire no more than indirect attraction. This initially perplexed him because he could not understand why God would have given men a desire for the products of a kind of work they did not find appealing. But eventually he resolved the problem. If manufacturing work was not appealing in Harmony, it was because the goods produced in the Phalanx would be so well made and durable that they would rarely need replacement. Harmony's furniture and clothing would last years longer than civilization's inferior goods, and in general the need for manufactured products would be sufficiently limited that no Harmonian would be asked to spend more than one-quarter of his time producing them. The remaining three-quarters would be spent "caring for animals, raising plants and vegetables, working in the kitchens, and serving in the industrial armies."[27]

The agrarian character of Fourier's utopian blueprint has earned him in some quarters a reputation as a romantic reactionary, a primitivist, whose prescription for the ills of early industrialization was to turn backward to an idealized rural arcadia. In their influential textbook Robert R. Palmer and Joel Colton, for example, claimed that Fourier "really had little to say on the problems of society as a whole in an industrial age."[28] The economist Edward Mason was even more emphatic on this point:

> The industrial revolution passed Fourier by; he failed completely to appreciate its significance. . . . He was an economist in that older sense of the word, meaning economizer. He advertised the economies of the division of labor with the enthusiasm of Adam Smith; but division of labor meant to him the simple form well illustrated in market-gardening, not the complex form associated with machine technique. His phalanstère was based squarely on an agricultural regime and hand labor. In these respects he is exactly the opposite of his contemporary Owen, who did understand the significance of the industrial revolution, and who attempted to include the advantages of the new industrial methods in his community schemes.[29]

There is some truth to this criticism. Certainly Fourier did not share the Saint-Simonian, and Marxist, view of the ongoing process of industrialization as a positive and liberating force. He did not believe that increased production was the key to a better life for all. Nor was the exploitation of factory workers central to his critique of the civilized economy. His own analysis of economic conflict, which focused on the evils of commercial capitalism, was characteristic of a preindustrial age in which rural production and artisanal labor dominated.

Taking all of this into account, however, it is still misleading to view Fourier's utopia as an exercise in nostalgia for the preindustrial past. He was in fact caustic in his criticism of "poetic charlatans" like the abbé Delille who extolled the virtue and innocence and contentment of rural life.

> A charlatan poet, the abbé Delille, tells us that 'le sage parcourt dans leurs innombrables variétés les riches décorations des scènes

champêtres.' Eh, what are those varieties? Disgusting-looking huts, children dressed in rags, mangy and worthless livestock, gross and cheating peasants who are reduced to eating roots while the abbé Delille gorges himself in some castle. In this life the whole rustic promenade is composed of such hideous spectacles except in a few exceptional regions like Piedmont, Brisgau, Belgium. But in France the countryside is disgusting in its poverty. But, since poetry has the right to lie and since the abbé Delille makes more use of this right than most, he promenades us across rich decorations and innumerable varieties where the eye finds only poverty and monotony.[30]

This passage is from a manuscript written in Bugey during Fourier's one extended period of direct contact with the French countryside. But even earlier in the *Quatre mouvements* he could describe French peasants as more "living automatons" than men, creatures more akin to animals than to human beings and remarkable chiefly for their "extreme coarseness."[31]

If anything, Fourier's criticism of rural work was more extensive and more detailed than his criticism of the factory system. Indeed much of what he had to say about machines and factories was actually rather perfunctory and based, not on firsthand observation, but on accounts in French journals of parliamentary debates and inquiries on the effects of industrialization in England.[32] One reason for this is simply that Fourier developed his analysis of work at a time when factories, large concentrations of workers, and power machinery were still relatively marginal features of French economic life. There were, it is true, a few huge industrial enterprises in Fourier's France: the great ironworks at Le Creusot, big textile mills at Lille, Roubaix, and Mulhouse, and vast mining establishments in Alsace, Lorraine, and Le Nord. But still the French economy was predominantly agricultural, and the main units of production remained the small workshop and the cottage rather than the factory. As late as 1850 only 10 percent of the French "industrial" labor force was employed in enterprises of more than twenty workers, and in general such economic growth as did occur during Fourier's last years was not accompanied by any major change in structures but rather by an expansion of traditional forms of production.[33] Paris in particular was a city of skilled artisans and small workshops rather than big industrial enterprises. As for Lyon, the city where Fourier spent much of his formative period, its economy was dominated by the silk industry, which had long resisted centralization. During Fourier's years at Lyon, silk was still produced by hand-loom weavers, most of whom worked in their own homes or in small ateliers, weaving silk that was "put out" to them by a class of "merchant manufacturers." Given the persistently traditional character of French economic life in Fourier's time, it is hardly surprising that he consistently played down the importance of factories and manufacturing work in Harmony.

What is surprising is the degree to which Fourier's understanding of work and work-related problems has relevance for the fully industrialized societies he did not live to see. It has already been pointed out that many of the major themes in his critique of civilized work were taken up by later thinkers in the socialist tradition. His concern with the problem of boring work has lost none of its immediacy. Neither has his critique of the work ethic. Nor his analysis of the psychological costs of work in trivial and demeaning if not physically taxing occupations. Similarly his awareness of the alienation, insecurity, and frustrations of petty functionaries, workers in service occupations, and all the "little people" of the petty bourgeoisie is as relevant to our century as it was to Fourier's.

There are other respects in which Fourier's analysis of work has acquired new relevance in the twentieth century. These include his preoccupation with the problem of group dynamics in work and his skill in concocting incentives that would give a certain attractiveness to work lacking in intrinsic appeal. So attentive was Fourier to the effect of group dynamics on the morale and productivity of his work groups, and so fertile was his imagination when it came to devising work incentives, that a number of commentators have seen in him a nineteenth-century precursor of "Taylorism," of Elton Mayo, or of some of the more recent partisans of the "human relations" school of industrial psychology. The substantial return Fourier promised to investors of capital within the Phalanx lends a certain credibility to this view. But it is fundamentally misleading. For Fourier's primary concern was not with the productivity of the Phalanx but with the happiness of the Phalansterians. He did not see his task as one of adjusting the worker to his job; and his work incentives, which originated within the worker's psyche, had little in common with those of the industrial psychologists. Fourier believed that men and women were driven toward particular tasks by their own individual desires and needs. He maintained that work could become a means of self-expression and a source of pleasure only when people became free to work out of internal necessity alone. Such freedom did not exist in civilization, and its work was therefore repugnant to almost all people. But, insisted Fourier, work was not an inherently undesirable or unnatural activity. Most people *wanted* to work and would do so if given the choice between idleness and attractive work. The foundation for his theory of attractive labor, then, was his belief that people did not really need to be tricked or trapped into working, provided the work itself was pleasant. It was Fourier's belief that both happiness and self-realization were possible within the realm of work that separates him not only from the industrial psychologists and the promoters of the work ethic but also from almost all the major thinkers within the socialist tradition.

V

Toward the end of Fourier's life the awakening of working-class consciousness and the development of organized working-class movements in England and France gave a new urgency to many of the problems of work that had long preoccupied Fourier. During the early 1830s, and under the influence of the strike wave of 1833 and the two great insurrections of the Lyon *canuts* in 1831 and 1834, public discussion was initiated in the French press on the living and working conditions of the laboring classes and on the importance of labor and the laboring classes to the welfare of society as a whole. In the course of this discussion two positions emerged—sometimes in the same article or argument. On the one hand, there was a vision of the creativity of labor, of work as an expression of human power and productivity and as a source of individual dignity and collective prosperity. On the other hand, there was also a growing concern that those who lived by labor seemed to be morally and physically debilitated, threatened by complete bestiality and degradation. In fact, the awareness of the moral and physical degradation resulting from modern conditions of labor was in some cases heightened by contrast with the vision of labor as an expression of human power.[34]

Charles Fourier was a major contributor to this debate, not so much through the rather turgid articles he published at the time in *Le Phalanstère* (the journal founded by his disciples in 1832), but rather through his earlier works, which only began to acquire a significant audience after 1830. In retrospect Fourier's importance is clear. He was one of the earliest and most articulate critics of working conditions in early industrial society. His writings gave currency to the concepts of the right to work and the organization of work; and well before the socialists of the 1840s he insisted on the centrality of the problem of the organization of work in any program of radical social reform. Yet it must be stressed that Fourier's vision of what work might become was in many ways different from that of the leaders of the socialist movement that emerged in the 1830s and 1840s. In his concern with attractive work, with work as a source of passionate gratification, he had little in common with such thinkers as Proudhon and Buchez, for whom work was, among other things, an instrument of self-discipline and a rampart against vice and self-indulgence. In his insistence on including peasants, office workers, and petty bureaucrats, as well as artisans and wage laborers, in his critique of civilized work, he was almost unique among early socialists. Above all, Fourier differed from the other early socialists in his concern with the subjective experience of work. He had much to say about the material suffering and deprivation of the working classes. But his most original reflections on work in civilization focused more on fear, shame, frustration, boredom—the psychological pains of civilized work that were felt by workers at all levels of society.

Fourier's Phalanx was an attempt to imagine a society from which the material and psychological pain long associated with work might be banished, a society in which all work would be performed freely, at the urging of the passions. This vision of work as a source of passionate fulfillment and joy has rarely been taken seriously. For most thinkers within the socialist tradition Fourier's dream of an order in which work would become closely associated with erotic pleasure has in fact seemed downright silly. Thus Proudhon could write scornfully: "To turn work into intrigue, love into gymnastics, what a dream! And yet it is the dream of the Phalanstery." For Proudhon there was a "natural antagonism between work and love," and work was actually "the most powerful of antiaphrodisiacs."[35] Almost a century later Antonio Gramsci used less colorful language to make a similar point, speaking of the need "to create a new sexual ethic" suited to the rationalized methods of production characteristic of a socialist economy: "The truth is that the new type of man demanded by the rationalization of production and work cannot be developed until the sexual instinct has been suitably regulated and until it too has been rationalized."[36]

It is true that Fourier's evocations of the working day in Harmony had a certain appeal for the young Marx and Engels. There is little doubt that they were inspired by Fourier when, in a famous passage in *The German Ideology,* they looked forward to a communist society that would "make it possible for me to do one thing today and another tomorrow, to hunt in the morning, fish in the afternoon, rear cattle in the evening, criticize after dinner, just as I like, without ever becoming a hunter, fisherman, shepherd, or critic."[37] When this passage was written Marx and Engels were both familiar with Fourier's work; Engels in particular had made a careful study of Fourier, had written admiringly of his work in Robert Owen's *New Moral World,* and had even published translations of Fourier's writings on commerce.[38] It is likely that Fourier's writing on work in the Phalanx helped Marx and Engels to formulate their own initial vision of communist society as a society in which workers would hold a variety of jobs and develop their talents in a variety of areas without ever becoming tied down to or identified with a single role. In a more general sense, one can also say that there is an optimism in the early writings of Marx and Engels that links them to Fourier, an optimism about the possibility that *all* of the work undertaken within the context of a communist society could serve as a vehicle for self-realization and for the affirmation of the worker's freedom.

In their later, more mature works, however, Marx and Engels seem to have shifted their position with regard to work and its place in future society.[39] Hints of this are to be found in Marx's *Grundrisse* (1857–1858), where, while arguing against Adam Smith's "negative definition" of labor as sacrifice, Marx simultaneously criticizes Fourier for adopting a frivolous attitude toward the serious problem of work by claiming that "labor can be made merely a joke, an amusement." This, wrote Marx, was to treat a profound problem in naive "shop-girl terms."[40] In *Capital* Marx's rejection of Fourier's view of work was even more emphatic. Stressing the distinction between free labor and labor determined by need and external purposes, Marx claimed that necessary work would one day be made immensely less arduous and fatiguing. Yet, he argued, all the improvements that technology and socialization might bring would not alter the fact that much of the work to be done in a socialist society would remain painful and unrewarding. Thus he began to look forward to the day when "the development of machinery and automation would give men so much free time" that they would be able to use their leisure hours in such a way as to develop their latent and unrealized capacities.

> In fact, the realm of freedom actually begins only where labor which is determined by necessity and mundane considerations ceases; thus in the very nature of things it lies beyond the sphere of actual material production . . . [which] remains a realm of necessity. Beyond it begins that development of human energy which is an end in itself, the true realm of freedom, which, however, can blossom forth only with the realm of necessity as its basis. The shortening of the working day is its basic prerequisite.[41]

In passages such as this it is clear that the Fourierist vision of work has been left far behind.

From the point of view of the later Marx, Fourier's theory of attractive labor was not only frivolous but also fraudulent. At one and the same time Fourier guaranteed all men the right *not* to work and devised work schedules that called for each Harmonian to perform up to fifteen hours of work a day. He claimed that in Harmony everyone would be free to do exactly the work that he or she wanted, but at the same time he insisted that eager volunteers could always be found to perform the least attractive tasks. The problem for Marx was simply that Fourier refused to take seriously the repugnant character of much of the work that had to be done within any society. Whereas Marx believed certain tasks would always remain painful, Fourier would not even accept the concept of a kingdom of necessity. If Fourier had been able to reply to Marx, he would probably have argued that his whole system—the theory of the passions, the series mechanism, the system of vocational education—was an attempt to show how work and the apparently incompatible desire for pleasure could be reconciled. There was no such thing as a natural aversion to work. *All* work was meant to be a means to pleasure and an instrument of human liberation, and the social theorist's task was to define the conditions under which work could at last become what it was meant to be.

Fourier's radically optimistic assessment of work was rooted in his denial of an irreconcilable antagonism between man and nature. He did not share Marx's Promethean vision of man as constantly engaged in wresting a living out of a hostile environment. Rather, and even though in some respects Fourier's ideas were in the mainstream of nineteenth-century romanticism, his conception of man in nature was rooted in eighteenth-century classicism. Nature for Fourier was fundamentally benign; and while he expected his Harmonians to work hard, he also believed that it was in man's power to lend grace and refinement to almost all forms of productive activity. It is because of this that Fourier's utopians remind one more of the aristocrats of a Watteau than the sweating laborers depicted by a Steinlen and celebrated in many nineteenth- and twentieth-century socialist utopias. Much of the work that they performed was necessary, but, Fourier insisted, its performance would not require physical pain or instinctual self-denial. Work would become as natural, and as satisfying, to Fourier's Harmonians as dining; and just like the dinner table, the work place would become in Harmony a realm of intrigue, discovery, and pleasure.

15

The New Amorous World

DURING THE decades that followed his death, no aspect of Fourier's thought was more scrupulously avoided by his disciples than his reflections on love and sexuality. In fact, Fourier himself was partly responsible for the neglect of these ideas. After the appearance of his first book, the *Théorie des quatre mouvements,* with its tantalizing glimpses into the amorous activities of the industrial armies, he had little to say in print about the erotic dimensions of utopian life. In Bugey during the early years of the Restoration he had devoted much of his energy to the elaboration of his prescriptions for a "new amorous world." But his discovery in 1819 of the principles of "simple association" induced him thereafter to present to the public a reduced and expurgated version of his doctrine without those aspects he thought most likely to offend contemporaries.

This "censorship" of the doctrine, which was begun by Fourier himself, was continued by his disciples. During the 1830s and 1840s, in an effort to get a hearing for what they regarded as Fourier's essential ideas, they presented the theory principally as a scheme for the organization of labor. And although between 1845 and 1859 they undertook to publish a large number of Fourier's manuscript writings, they virtually ignored the five multicolored manuscript notebooks forming *Le*

Nouveau monde amoureux. It was only in 1967 that this text was finally published in an edition prepared by Simone Debout-Oleskiewicz.[1]

Le Nouveau monde amoureux is a fascinating work. A mixture of analysis, narrative, dialogue, and description, the text includes both personal revelations and lyric passages of a sort not to be found elsewhere in Fourier's work. The manuscript itself is not at all "finished": there are numerous repetitions and omissions and marginal corrections. Still it is clear that in the general body of Fourier's writing the *Nouveau monde amoureux* stands apart. Not only is it the most audacious of Fourier's works. With its long narrative passages and its extensive evocations of life in Harmony, it also comes closer to being a work of utopian fiction than anything else Fourier wrote. Critics have yet to take its full measure.[2] But it is already apparent that the publication of the *Nouveau monde amoureux*, just 150 years after its composition, has served to deepen and enrich the common understanding of Fourier's thought. It is now clear that the vision of instinctual liberation stands at the center of Fourier's thinking and that the view of Fourier as chiefly an economic thinker or as a precursor of socialism cannot account for the richness of his doctrine or the nature of his radicalism. The appearance of this text in 1967 also made it possible to situate Fourier more clearly in the utopian tradition and to relate his ideas to the reorientation of utopian attitudes toward love that took place during the eighteenth century.

I

In the great tradition of utopian thinking that runs from Thomas More through the seventeenth century there was little place for the celebration of sexual liberty or passionate love. Although most of the thinkers in this tradition rejected Christian asceticism and the mortification of the flesh, they still espoused the contemplative ideal and defined happiness in terms of moderation, balance, and self-discipline. They designed what Frank Manuel has called "utopias of calm felicity" the aim of which was to make man happy by diminishing his needs and desires.[3] In these utopias sexual questions were not avoided; indeed, there were often elaborate stipulations concerning marriage and courtship and the proper ordering of sexual relations. But sex was seen primarily in traditional terms as a potential source of discord or simply as a means of procreation. And intercourse was carefully regulated both to guard against the evils of sexual competition and to bring about the improvement of the race. Thus in More's *Utopia* there were strict laws against extramarital intercourse, and prospective mates were required to strip naked and submit to mutual inspection prior to marriage. In Tommaso Campanella's *City of the Sun* it was a capital offense for women to use cosmetics or wear high heels, homosexuals were severely punished, and married couples were to have intercourse regularly every third night "after bathing well." Selective breeding was also rigidly enforced.

> If a man becomes enamored of a woman [wrote Campanella] he may speak and jest with her, send her verses, and make emblems out of flowers and branches for her. But if his having intercourse with her is deemed undesirable by reason of the offspring that might result, it will by no means be permitted unless she is already pregnant or is sterile. As a result, only loving friendship, rather than concupiscent ardor, is recognized among them.[4]

This distrust of passionate love, which is characteristic of the tradition, was carried to its logical extreme by the French priest Gabriel de Foigny, whose utopian novel, *La Terre australe,* appeared in 1676. Foigny's utopia was populated by hermaphrodites who were capable of impregnating themselves and procreating from the thigh. Lacking both the need and the capacity for sexual intercourse, these utopians felt toward one another only a "cordial love," which they gave to all their fellow utopians equally.[5]

During the course of the eighteenth century there were many utopian writers who continued to argue, though generally in more conventional form than Foigny, that the establishment of the ideal society would require extensive restraints on erotic expression. In Mercier's *L'An 2440,* for example, monogamous marriage was the rule and women's role was to "discharge the sole task imposed on them by the creator, that of bearing children and providing consolation."[6] But alongside the relatively austere utopias of a Mercier or a Mably, there emerged a new and more tolerant vision of utopia. Inspired in part by the accounts of Cook and Bougainville of their voyages to Tahiti, by the outpouring of travelers' tales depicting new and exotic sexual mores, and by the general decline in Christian piety during the eighteenth century, a number of utopian writers began to define happiness in more explicitly sensual terms and to envisage erotic gratification as the central purpose of the ideal society. A number of works appeared idealizing the life of the Tahitians and using the gentle amours of imagined South Sea Islanders as a model against which to criticize the repressive laws and mores of civilization. In the most famous of these works, Diderot's *Supplément au voyage de Bougainville* (written in 1772 but only published in 1796) monogamous marriage was presented as a violation of the whole order of nature.

> Is there anything more senseless than a precept that forbids us to heed the changing impulses that are inherent in our being, or commands that require a degree of constancy that is not possible, that do violence to the nature and the liberty of both male and female by chaining them perpetually to one another? Is there anything more unreasonable than this perfect fidelity that would restrict us, for the enjoyment of pleasures so capricious, to a single partner than an oath of immutability taken by two individuals made of flesh and blood under a sky that is not the same for a moment, in a cavern that threatens to collapse upon them, at the foot of a cliff that is crumbling into dust, under a tree that is withering, on a bench of stone that is being worn away?[7]

For Diderot's Tahitians change was the rule in love as in all things, and polygamy and even incest were innocent pleasures. But Diderot made it clear that Tahitian customs could not be transplanted to France, where life was hard and the population already excessive. Thus his picture of Tahiti was not a model for imitation but rather a standard against which to criticize the unnatural and corrupt mores of his own society.

What was most striking about the rehabilitation of love in eighteenth-century utopian writing was its delicate pastoral tone. It was Watteau, the artist of the *fête galante* and the creator, in the *Embarkation for Cythera,* of a whole mythology of love, who established the style and the setting for the amorous utopias of the eighteenth century. Thus in Morelly's *Naufrage des îles flottantes* (1753) the initiation of the young to the rites of love was a festive, public occasion accompanied by dancing and singing on terraces decked with garlands of flowers and "under a pure and serene sky."[8] Similarly in Diderot love was an idyll performed in a pastoral setting to the accompaniment of soft flutes.

> The young Tahitian girl gave herself ecstatically to the em-
> braces of the young Tahitian boy. . . . She was proud to excite
> the desires and to attract the amorous glances of the unknown
> man, of her relatives, of her brother. In our presence, in the
> midst of a circle of innocent Tahitians, and to the sound of the
> flutes that played between the dances, she accepted without fear
> and without shame the caresses of the person to whom her
> young heart and the secret voice of her senses urged her.[9]

Here too the depiction of love had the pastel coloring and the soft tones
of a rococo painting.

In the last two decades of the eighteenth century two writers
emerged who preserved the vision of love as central to utopia while
redefining love itself. These were Restif de la Bretonne and the Marquis
de Sade. For Restif love was a terrible, overwhelming force, at once
violent and destructive and the source of man's deepest joys. The various utopias devised by Restif were systems of constraint intended to
channel and direct this force without stripping it of all its powers.[10] In
Sade's writing the cruelty and violence of love were even more dramatically represented: the erotic impulse was identified with the desire
for power and mastery, and attempts to contain or limit it were both
denounced and ridiculed as futile. For Sade love was an aggressive
passion that had to be accepted in all its forms.

It is impossible to prove that Fourier was influenced in any significant way by Restif or Sade. But (to borrow Mark Poster's expression)
the three did speak "from remarkably proximate intellectual climates."[11]
Certainly Fourier shared with Restif and Sade a sense of the power of the
sexual drive and an appreciation of the diversity of individual erotic
needs. Fourier was eminently qualified to appreciate Sade's relentless
attacks on moralists who sought the sanction of nature for certain sexual
proclivities while denying it to others. But Fourier did not celebrate
sexual abuse, and he did not see the desire for mastery or possession as
fundamental to the erotic impulse. He was convinced that most violent
and "sadistic" behavior could be understood as the result of repression.
And he was actually much closer to Diderot's optimism than to the
pessimism of Sade and Restif concerning the kind of human relations that
were likely to develop in a society free of sexual constraints. Like many
of the earlier eighteenth-century utopians, and in a pastoral tone that was
often similar, Fourier argued that sexual liberation would not lead to the
collapse of social bonds but to the reinforcement of social harmony.

Fourier's optimism on this point was rooted in a conception of love that separates him not only from Restif and Sade but also from Freud and many other twentieth-century thinkers. In *Civilization and Its Discontents* Freud argued that there was a fundamental conflict between civilization, which "endeavors . . . to bring people together into large unities," and the erotic impulse, which tends to produce fragmented self-contained pairs. "Sexual love is a relationship between two individuals in which a third can only be superfluous or disturbing," wrote Freud, "whereas civilization depends on relations between a considerable number of individuals."[12] This view of love as fundamentally exclusive and antisocial is antithetical to Fourier's. He argued that only in societies dominated by the institution of monogamous marriage did love become exclusive. "What had caused all the civilized philosophers to err concerning the destinies of love," he wrote, "is that they have always speculated on love affairs limited to a couple."[13] On the contrary, he insisted, love could be a binding element, a force for solidarity within the community as a whole. "Love is the most powerful agent of passional rapprochement," he wrote, "even between antipathetic characters."[14] What he set out to do in the *Nouveau monde amoureux* was to describe the institutional setting in which love could come to fulfill this predestined role.

II

Fourier's aim in the *Nouveau monde amoureux* was to describe the institutions and activities of what the twentieth century would call a nonrepressive society, a society capable of providing for the material needs of its members without demanding too high a price in instinctual self-denial. Fourier believed that his writings on work and on the organization of the Phalanx had demonstrated that man had long had the power to create the material foundations of a decent life for all. But the ultimate goal of the Phalanx was not merely to satisfy man's physical needs; it was to liberate man's instincts, to ensure all men and women an emotional and erotic life immeasurably freer and richer than a repressive civilization could ever provide. In such a society, Fourier argued, human relations would take on a new character, and the passion of love would necessarily undergo an extraordinary metamorphosis. No longer a diversion or a private affair, love would instead become an essential part of the collective life, a force for social harmony whose binding power would be felt even in the kitchens of the Phalanx and at its dinner tables. As Fourier wrote in a draft of the *Nouveau monde amoureux*, "love in the Phalanstery is no longer, as it is with us, a recreation that detracts from work; on the contrary it is the soul and the vehicle, the mainspring of all works and of the whole of universal attraction."[15]

To realize this vision, Fourier argued, what was necessary was a new set of laws and institutions that would promote the most diverse kinds of erotic gratification while at the same time integrating the sexual drives into the whole fabric of man's collective life. This would entail the fulfillment of three conditions. First of all, recognition would have to be given to the sheer diversity of human sexual inclinations. According to Fourier, the failure of civilized man to devise a tolerable "amorous regime" resulted in large part from the belief that all men and women were essentially the same in their sexual wants. This belief, which amounted to a kind of "erotic Jacobinism," was generally accompanied by the claim that the "natural" form of sexual grouping was the heterosexual couple. If any generalization were to be made about human sexuality, Fourier argued, it would be that most people were polygamous in their inclinations. How else could one explain the ubiquity of adultery in civilized society? But more significant to Fourier was the sheer variety and inconstancy of human sexual proclivities. Men and women had vastly different needs at different stages of their lives. And within any particular age group there was no single common denominator: some were sensualists, others sentimentalists; some were heterosexual and others homosexual. To force them all into a single mold could only result in pain and frustration.

Thus the institutions of Fourier's new amorous world would promote the gratification of many desires that civilized society condemned as perversions. It is true that in his published works Fourier occasionally spoke caustically about "modern Spartans" and members of other sexual minorities. But even a cursory reading of the *Nouveau monde amoureux* should leave no doubt that Fourier's ultimate goal was the liberation of all sexual minorities, so long as their activities did not involve the use or abuse of people against their will. Lesbians, sodomites, fetishists, and flagellants all figured prominently in his descriptions of amorous life in the higher stages of Harmony; and the highest ranks in the erotic hierarchy devised by Fourier were open only to individuals with a passionate attraction to members of both sexes. Fourier did not, to be sure, look with favor on any form of sexual activity that involved preadolescent children. But where consenting adults were concerned, he saw nothing wrong even with incest, which he could speak about with his customary detachment as "a mixture of the two minor cardinal passions, the two affective passions of love and familism."[16] Fourier believed that incest was far more common in civilization than most people were willing to admit. But he conceded that the official taboo against it was so strong that it would have to be respected during the initial stages of the transition from civilization to Harmony.

> Although it will be a rule in Harmony to authorize everything that multiplies links and gives pleasure to people without doing anyone harm, [Harmonians] will proceed only by degrees in religious and moral innovations, such as incest for example, which might be offensive.[17]

Fourier was equally accommodating on the subject of those particular erotic penchants and fixations that he referred to as amorous manias. "Manias are a diminutive form of the passions," he wrote, "they are a consequence of the human mind's need to create stimulants for itself."[18] A Freud might regard foot fetishism or a heel-scratching mania as neurotic symptoms, but for Fourier they were the expression of authentic needs, and there was a place for them in his utopia.

The second vital element in Fourier's prescription for a new amorous world was a radical alteration in the position of women. At the outset of his career, in the *Théorie des quatre mouvements*, Fourier had argued forcefully that the emancipation of women was the key to social progress in all other spheres. "The extension of the privileges of women is the fundamental cause of all social progress," he wrote.[19] He went on to argue that the main cause for the transition from barbarous to civilized societies was the breakup of the harem and the shift from the "absolute servitude of women" to the granting of some civil rights to wives under the system of monogamous marriage. Had the French revolutionaries seriously attacked the institution of marriage, further progress would have been made.

> There was very little that prevented the vandalism of 1793 from suddenly producing a second revolution as marvelous as the first was horrible. The whole human race was approaching its release; the civilized, barbarian, and savage order would have

disappeared forever if the Convention, which trampled down all prejudices, had not bowed down before the only one that had to be destroyed, the institution of marriage. . . . This is the final blow that the French Convention failed to deliver because of its timidity. How could an assembly that was so strongly hostile to half-measures have limited itself to a half-measure like divorce?[20]

Looking toward the future, Fourier suggested various proposals for the gradual emancipation of women that could open the way for the transition from civilization to Harmony. Women might simply be granted full sexual liberty at the age of eighteen; groups of eighty to a hundred people might live together in "progressive households" in which members of both sexes would benefit from flexible arrangements concerning lovemaking and the performance of domestic chores.[21] The point in any case was that since men and women were subject to the same drives and since they experienced basically the same range of emotional and sexual needs, they should enjoy the same rights and privileges. In particular women should enjoy educational opportunities equal to men, freedom from the tedium of housework, and freedom in the choice of sexual partners. Only when these rights were granted, and when the long struggle for women's emancipation was complete, could both sexes finally enter the new amorous world.

The recognition of sexual diversity and the full emancipation of women were two important conditions for the realization of Fourier's amorous utopia. The third and fundamental condition was the granting of what Fourier called the "sexual minimum." In Harmony, he wrote, every mature man and woman must be guaranteed a satisfying minimum of sexual pleasure. Whatever his or her age and no matter how bizarre his or her desires, no Harmonian could go unsatisfied. Fourier maintained that this sexual minimum would play a role in the amorous world similar to that played by the social minimum in the world of work. Labor could become an instrument of human freedom and human self-expression only when men were freed by a guaranteed income from the obligation to work. Similarly love could become the liberating and binding force that it was meant to be only when its expression had been purged of every tinge of coercion and constraint. For Fourier the important thing about the sexual minimum was that it removed the fear of sexual deprivation that corrupted and falsified amorous relations in civilization.[22]

Although Fourier's amorous imagination was nothing if not vivid, the form in which he cast his argument for the sexual minimum was curiously narrow. He seems to have taken a crudely physiological view of love, arguing that the sexual desire was an expression of the passion of touch and a hunger that could be gratified as easily and as naturally as the hunger for food. It can be argued, however, that this apparent naturalistic reductionism was a deliberate attempt to demystify the sexual act and to point the way beyond physical desire to a world of more subtle and complex relationships that would become possible only when the basic sexual needs were satisfied.[23] For the essential point, which Fourier never tired of repeating, was that as long as the basic sexual needs went unsatisfied, the true richness of the erotic impulse could not find expression.

One result of the establishment of the sexual minimum, Fourier believed, would be an awakening of sentimental or platonic love. "L'amour céladonique" he called it, invoking the name of Céladon, the chaste and faithful lover who was the hero of Honoré d'Urfé's seventeenth-century novel, *L'Astrée*. In the civilization of the nineteenth century Céladon was only conceivable as a figure of ridicule: a lover who failed to bring an amorous relation to a physical consummation was a natural butt of jokes. And those who vaunted sentimental love in civilization were "hypocrites who play the vestal virgin in public and behave like whores in private."[24] In Harmony, however, where physical gratification could be taken for granted, erotic ties would become both more complex and more broadly diffused. The "mania for exclusive possession" of a loved one would lose its force, and lovers would "seek out refined sentimental relationships to counterbalance [their] physical pleasures."[25]

III

Unlike Fourier's other utopian writings, much of the *Nouveau monde amoureux* was set not in Europe but in Asia Minor on the site of the ancient Greek city of Cnidus.[26] In choosing a classical setting for the amorous adventures of his Harmonians, Fourier was doubtless influenced by a literary tradition. Throughout the eighteenth century utopia had generally been placed far from Northern Europe; and Cnidus itself, with its famous temple to Aphrodite, had been the setting for Montesquieu's *Le Temple de Cnide*. But Fourier probably also meant to emphasize that he was describing a social order even more radically different from European ways than that described in his published works. In the *Traité de l'association* and the *Nouveau monde industriel* his account of Harmony focused on the organization of a trial Phalanx. But in the *Nouveau monde amoureux* he was discussing individuals born and raised in Harmony and completely untouched by the psychic—and physical—ills of civilization. As he explained at the outset, he was not going to write about the men and women of civilization, but rather about "an order of things in which the least of men will be rich, polished, sincere, pleasant, virtuous, and handsome (excepting the very old); an order of things in which marriage and our other customs will have been forgotten, their very absence having inspired a host of amorous innovations that we cannot yet imagine."[27]

Chief among the "amorous innovations" prescribed by Fourier for every Phalanx was the establishment of a Court of Love to be run by an elaborate hierarchy of officials: high priests, pontiffs, matrons, confessors, fairies, fakirs, and the like. This Court of Love, which was both a judiciary body and a recreational institution, would meet each evening after the children and the chaste Vestals had been put to bed. It would be run by a pontiff, who was always an elderly woman well versed in amorous intrigue. Its members were responsible for the organization of fetes, entertainments, and orgies in which all members of the Phalanx would participate. The court was also responsible for the enforcement of a minutely detailed "amorous code" that regulated the sexual activities of the members of the community.

The idea of an amorous code might seem out of place in a completely libertarian society. But the code that Fourier devised was actually no more coercive than the industrial series and groups. What it did was to stipulate the rules to be followed by members of the various amorous corporations in a Phalanx. But membership in these corporations was purely voluntary; and though the code enforced authenticity and sincerity, it did not regiment sexual life. Young men and women who belonged to the Damselate, for example, were bound by the rules of their corporation to practice fidelity. If a person transgressed the rule often enough, he or she would be "sentenced" by the Court of Love either to quit the ranks of the Damselate or to earn an "indulgence" through the performance of a virtuous act. Infidelity was not a serious crime in Harmony, but inauthenticity was. The "penances" imposed by the Court of Love were designed to discourage deception and make it impossible for anyone to claim to be what he or she was not. Fourier's system of indulgences and penances was thus both a clever parody of Catholic religious practice and a new kind of philanthropic institution. For the virtuous acts required of those who transgressed the rules of their corporations always served to provide sexual gratification for those who needed it. Indulgences and penances helped guarantee that "no one capable of love" was "frustrated in his or her desire."[28]

Variety was to be the essence of Phalansterian life, and many individuals would have amorous needs and penchants that could not be gratified within the compass of a single community. Thus there would be constant movement and travel in the new order. Bands of adventurers, troubadours, and knights-errant would traverse the globe in search of pleasures unobtainable in their own regions. People subject to extremely rare manias would regularly meet at international gatherings, which would be pilgrimages as sacred for them "as the journey to Mecca is for Muslims."[29] In this atmosphere of ceaseless movement, total strangers would be constantly encountering one another and forming new relationships. To make these encounters as rewarding as possible, the amorous hierarchy of each Phalanx had to make elaborate preparations to welcome and entertain the hordes of visitors. The tasks of these officials included everything from the mixing of punch to the organization of orgies, but their most important duty was the administration of an elaborate system of erotic personality matching.

The task of matching visitors with appropriate partners would be facilitated by the compilation of a card file—Fourier would not have eschewed more advanced techniques of data processing—identifying the passional types and amorous proclivities of each member of the Phalanx. Travelers, too, would wear insignia indicating their individual needs and penchants. Since there was a little of the Butterfly in everyone, a traveler might have momentary inclinations at variance with the basic configuration of his passions. Thus everyone would undergo periodic interviews to ascertain his or her libidinal needs of the moment. These interviews would be conducted by a group of wise and elderly psychologists—women for the most part—known as confessors. They would be assisted in their work by psychologically acute Harmonians officially designated as matrons, fairies, and fakirs. Fourier insisted that the important task of psychological analysis could not be performed by young people. Amorous experiences and, above all, female intuition were required. Thus Harmony would provide employment, prestige, and a rich sexual life for one of the classes most oppressed by civilization, the elderly. For the confessors, both male and female, would not only be held in great esteem; often they would find it necessary to intervene personally and minister directly to the sexual needs of their younger clients.[30]

Fourier's solicitude for the elderly, the poor, the "perverts," for all those to whom civilization denied sexual gratification, led him to create a variety of corps and institutions specializing in sexual philanthropy. The fakirs, for example, were assigned the task of bestowing their favors on individuals left out in the erotic matching. There were also the bacchantes, those camp followers of the industrial armies who toiled on the amorous battlefield after a night's activity by providing solace to rejected suitors of the Vestals. The members of all these groups naturally had passional inclinations for the tasks they performed. But Fourier recognized that just as there were some forms of truly loathsome work, so too there were forms of sexual philanthropy that had little intrinsic appeal. If there had to be Little Hordes to do the dirty work in the Phalanx, there also had to be an amorous nobility in each Phalanx whose main responsibility would be the providing of sexual gratification to all those whom age or physical deformity would have condemned to loneliness in civilization.

Fourier defined the amorous nobility as "the class of strong and refined individuals who know how to subordinate love to the dictates of honor, friendship, and the affections independent of pleasure."[31] The most important members of this class were the two individuals who constituted the angelic couple in each Phalanx. The partners in this angelic couple were handsome and virtuous lovers who were bound by such transcendent sentimental ties that (temporarily at least) they had no desire for physical relations. Instead, they displayed their devotion to each other, and to the community, through the performance of generous acts of erotic philanthropy.[32] Like more altruistic counterparts of Laclos' Valmont and Madame de Merteuil,[33] they served as each other's procurers, seeking out those members of the community most in need of their sexual favors. Fourier stressed that they would be amply rewarded for their service to the community. In addition to the enjoyment of public idolatry and official recognition, they would also taste "the pleasure of transcendent platonism, the highest degree of pure love, a sort of mental eroticism that raises the partners beyond their physical desires."[34]

[The Theory]

If there was a place for saints and nobles in Fourier's utopia, there was also a place for wars. But the wars of Harmony would bear no more resemblance to the bloody conflicts of civilization than did the Harmonian saints and nobles to their civilized counterparts. Wars were not to be fought with guns and cannons. Rather, they would take the form of amorous skirmishes and gastronomic competitions to be held in conjunction with the expeditions of the industrial armies. Nobody would be hurt in these wars, since, as Fourier explained, captives were taken in Harmony not as the result of combat but during the course of "a war of position, comparable to chess." Captors acquired certain amorous privileges with regard to their prisoners, but these were generally sold—or given—to the senior members of a Phalanx during the course of a ransom ceremony.

Since Fourier frequently criticized the "egotistical" sexual mores of civilization with its emphasis on the couple, it is not surprising that he had much to say in the *Nouveau monde amoureux* about various forms of collective erotic activity, and notably the orgy. "It is certain," he wrote, "that nature inclines us toward the amorous orgy, just as much as toward the gastronomic orgy, and that while both are blameworthy in the excess, they would become praiseworthy in an order in which they could be equilibrated."[35] The orgy was the expression of a universal need, maintained Fourier, arguing that the people of civilization abandoned themselves to orgies whenever they could. As evidence he cited stories drawn both from books and from the life he knew at Lyon. He had read, for example, about Muscovite noblemen who maintained underground apartments where they dallied with naked Georgian women.[36] Closer to home, he had often heard tales of Sunday outings—"parties carrées et sextines"—that culminated in promiscuous adventures in the hills above Lyon and in the scrubby woods of Les Brotteaux. Fourier even claimed that he had "witnessed" such small-scale provincial orgies and had "always been surprised at the ease with which the women quickly forget all the [dictates] of morality that they observe so carefully in public."[37] But all of this, wrote Fourier, was poverty itself. The greatest amorous exploits of civilization could be reduced to "a few foursomes or sixsomes, a few paltry high society orgies in which half a dozen Agneses or Pamelas give themselves successively to some man who has no other virtue than that of being their initiate." The sort of orgies that Harmony would offer would have nothing in common with such vulgar debauchery; they would involve "the noble expression of free love."[38] And unlike the brutal orgies of civilization, which took place in secret or in dimly lit rooms, Harmony's orgies would be carefully planned public events that would be held in broad daylight and would often involve an entire community.

Like everything else in Harmony, its orgies were classified by Fourier in a host of different categories. There were introductory orgies and farewell orgies, fortuitous orgies and bacchanalian orgies. There was an orchestrated orgy or "omnigamous quadrille" in which the movements of each participant were as carefully choreographed as those of a minuet. There was even a "museum orgy," which offered only visual gratification to its participants and was designed to encourage the development of the aesthetic faculties of the Harmonians. But Harmony's most spectacular and elaborately planned orgies were held in honor of visiting bands of adventurers and in conjunction with the work of the amorous confessors. In fact, the orgy was to become an integral part of the system of passional matching practiced by the confessors. Fourier insisted, however, that before the orgy could assume its proper place in the new amorous world, it would first be necessary to rid the globe of venereal disease. Until this was accomplished, Harmony would be "more circumspect about love than civilization now is."[39]

IV

To the modern reader Fourier's *Nouveau monde amoureux* is at once a fascinating and a perplexing work. Fourier has surprisingly little to say, given his interest in psychology, about the subjective experience of love. He tells us little about what it is like to be in love, and there is nothing in his work comparable to Stendhal's account, in the almost exactly contemporaneous *De l'amour* (1822), of the stages of love, the self-deceptions of lovers, and the process by which lovers come to recognize their own feelings. What we are offered instead is an extraordinary set of images of the erotic activities of a whole community, abundant descriptions of new "amorous institutions," and an extended discussion of what might be called the politics of love. What we are offered is, in Fourier's words, the description of a world in which love would become "an affair of state and a special sphere of social politics" possessing "its own code, its tribunals, its court, and its institutions."[40]

In Fourier's schemes for the erotic matching of strangers, and in his description of elaborately contrived orgies, there is much that appears to derive directly from his own frustrations. At the same time there is a measure of distance and control that derives in part from Fourier's penchant for ordering and classifying his material, but in part also from the mock-heroic tone he often uses in describing the amorous adventures of his Harmonians. There is no consistency of style, which is hardly surprising in an unfinished manuscript. What is surprising, however, is Fourier's inconsistency in the handling of some central issues.

The *Nouveau monde amoureux* begins with a rhapsodic celebration of love as "the divine passion" that gives mortal men "a share in the attributes of the deity," but it goes on to take what at times appears to be a narrowly physiological view of love. It argues for women's emancipation, but it frequently employs rather crude sexual stereotypes. It looks forward to the liberation of instinct, but it describes a world in which even orgies are carefully choreographed. It celebrates unfettered desire, but it offers an amorous code. Some of this makes one wonder just how far emancipated Fourier himself actually was from the prejudices he criticized. It also raises questions concerning both the form of Fourier's discourse and the nature of his vision of the sexually liberated society. How literally should the *Nouveau monde amoureux* be read? Are Fourier's new amorous institutions—the orgies, the Court of Love, the schemes of amorous matching—to be seen as the blueprint of an amorous utopia similar in kind to the economic blueprint offered in the *Nouveau monde industriel?* Or are there elements of irony, playfulness, and exaggeration in this work that distinguish it from at least some of Fourier's other writings?

In considering these questions we may make one initial observation. This is that some of the problems and apparent inconsistencies in the *Nouveau monde amoureux* may be troubling only if one insists on a literal reading of Fourier's text. To Fourier's early disciples like Just Muiron there was no doubt that all Fourier's writings should be understood as blueprints. Thus when Fourier allowed Muiron to peruse the manuscript of the *Nouveau monde amoureux,* Muiron responded with questions of a very practical sort. What "particularly troubled" the disciple was the problem of determining paternity in doubtful cases. "How," asked Muiron, "can we resolve the difficulties created by the concourse of several lovers at the moment of conception?"[41] Fourier's answer is unknown. But we might well ask whether Muiron wasn't missing the point and whether in the *Nouveau monde amoureux* Fourier wasn't offering something else besides an instruction manual for community builders. For the elaborate network of rules, regulations, codes, and complex institutional structures, which seem so out of place in a fundamentally libertarian treatise, can be seen as serving an important critical function in the larger design of Fourier's work. What Fourier may have been offering in the *Nouveau monde amoureux* is not so much the blueprint of an amorous utopia as a remarkable *parody* of the customs and institutions of civilized society, a parody in which the familiar world is turned upside down and stood on its head.

There are elements of parody almost everywhere in Fourier's writing. There are parodies of the language of the cautious moralist who always seeks the middle way, and parodies of the optimistic philosopher who claims to be flying "on a sublime course leading to rapid progress toward perfectibilizing perfectibility." There are also parodies built into the structure of Fourier's utopia. It has already been pointed out that Harmony's Bourse is a benign parody of the civilized stock exchange, and that wars in Harmony would take the form of cooking contests with the result that the renown of a nation would be founded on the success of its cooks in preparing omelettes, soufflés, and whipped cream. It might also be observed that the Little Hordes represent both a parody of monastic service and an adaptation to the needs of postcivilized society of the dirty and aggressive impulses of the barbarian hordes. But it is in the *Nouveau monde amoureux* that parody is especially concentrated, and it focuses above all on institutions, rites, and traditions associated with the Catholic church.

Fourier's Court of Love, with its female pontiff, its priests and confessors, and its fakirs and fairies, is on one level certainly a parody of the Catholic religious hierarchy. These officials had the power to issue "indulgences," to impose "penances," and to exact "amorous tithes" from the faithful. In extreme cases they could even threaten sinners with excommunication. And this would not be an idle threat, Fourier boasted, because it would entail the sinner's exclusion from the Court of Love and not merely the "trivial" menace of punishment in a distant afterlife. Of course sins in Harmony were infrequent and easily pardonable: generally they amounted to little more than lack of discernment in eating or the impolite rejection of sexual advances. And it would always be possible for a sinner to win an indulgence by providing sexual gratification to the needy.[42]

Just like the Catholic church, Harmony would also have its saints and angels and crusades. But the saints would acquire holiness through amorous and gastronomic prowess, and the one crusade most fully described by Fourier has been accurately characterized as "a massive but carefully controlled orgy, accompanied by oceans of sparkling wine and tons of meat pie."[43] As for angels, they would generally come in pairs, the highest rank being occupied by the angelic couple, those "angels of virtue" who would minister to the sexual needs of the poor, the elderly, and the unattractive. So great would be the odor of sanctity surrounding the angelic couple that their favors would become "a balm of saintliness," and all suitors would approach them "with a holy respect."[44]

Fourier naturally insisted that rigorous tests be imposed on all candidates for saintliness. Criticizing the "ridiculous idea" of rewarding "useless practices" like prayer and asceticism with the title of saintliness, he specified that the novice who wished to attain the rank of Minor Sainthood would have to undergo seven tests, beginning with the paying of an amorous tribute to all the venerables and patriarchs in a Phalanx and culminating with a "graduated omnigamy, or series of sixteen balanced orgies." In Harmony as in civilization, the road to sainthood was difficult, and Fourier emphasized that the novitiate could last as long as thirty years.[45]

Did Fourier mean all this to be taken literally? The possibility cannot be ruled out. But it seems more likely that his aim was not so much to spell out the institutions of a future society in any literal sense as to evoke the new world of possibilities that might be opened up simply by turning traditional Catholicism upside down. By peopling his new amorous world with priests and confessors and saints and sinners and by imagining amorous tithes and indulgences, Fourier was incorporating within his utopia a parody of Catholic religious practice. The point of this parody was to dramatize the implications of an ethic that attached absolutely no virtue to self-denial and isolation.

Virtue, as Fourier defined it, was "the extension of social ties," and the pathway to virtue was self-indulgence. Thus the world described by Fourier was a world in which love and gourmandise were expressions of religious piety and in which priests would "stop preaching abstinence and ready themselves to officiate at the excellent tables that will be furnished to them for their five [daily] meals."[46] It was in some respects a Rabelaisean world, a world in which Christian asceticism was mocked and close links were established between amorous and gastronomic satisfaction. But there is in Fourier little of the earthiness, the grotesque realism, and the celebration of the body and all bodily functions that one finds in Rabelais.[47] Fourier does not seem to draw, as does Rabelais, on the traditions of popular revelry and Gallic humor originally embodied in the *contes* and *fabliaux* of the Middle Ages. Insofar as his work is rooted in any tradition, it draws on—and parodies—the aristocratic traditions of chivalry and courtly love embodied in the medieval romances and troubadour songs. For Fourier's female pontiff, his priestesses, his celadonic lovers, his bands of knight-errantry, and even his elaborately worked out amorous codes are all parodies, on one level at least, of figures and conventions deriving from the tradition of courtly love.*

A second general observation may be made about the vision of sexual liberation offered by Fourier in the *Nouveau monde amoureux*. This concerns Fourier's insistence on openness and clarity in sexual relations. In the new amorous world lovemaking is generally a daytime activity. It is also usually a communal activity, and a rapidly consummated one. When people retire to their rooms at night it is almost always to sleep, and as a rule they sleep alone. Even Harmony's bands of adventurers and knights-errant would be "very sober about lovemaking at nighttime." Furthermore, Fourier insisted, outside the coteries of the monogynes all sexual activity in Harmony would be carried on in the open. There would be "nothing hidden or secret about any of the polygamous relationships."[48]

The reason Fourier gave for his insistence on openness in sexual activity was that this would put an end to the hypocrisy about sex so rampant in civilization. "Thus it will be impossible," he wrote, "for

---

*Fourier was writing at a time of revived interest in the tradition of courtly love and the troubadour songs that did much to create that tradition. In 1817 the philologist Raynouard published his *Choix de poésies originales des troubadours,* which made known Andreas Capellanus's *The Art of Courtly Love* and argued that the courts of love described by Andreas Capellanus were actual tribunals at which amorous disputes were judged. Five years later in an appendix to his *De l'amour* Stendhal could write: "There were courts of love in France between 1150 and 1200. That is a proven fact." Current scholarship sees courtly love more as a set of literary conventions than as a historical reality, and Andreas Capellanus's treatise as "a satire on, rather than a bible of, courtly love." Thus the elements of parody and satire in Fourier's work are actually consistent with the tradition as it is now understood. See Joan M. Ferrante and George D. Economu (eds.), *In Pursuit of Perfection: Courtly Love in Medieval Literature* (Port Washington, N.Y., 1975), Jacques Lafitte-Houssat, *Troubadours et cours d'amour,* 2d ed. (Paris, 1960), and Roger Boase, *The Origin and Meaning of Courtly Love: A Critical Study of European Scholarship* (Manchester, 1977).

people lacking in amorous delicacy to pass themselves off as apostles of sentimental love. Everyone will be free to behave as he wishes, but everyone will be assigned to the exact rank that his behavior merits."[49] Indeed, the particular needs and penchants of each Harmonian would be made known to all by the insignia attached to his or her clothing.

Fourier's vision of a new amorous world thus incorporates and in a sense caricatures Rousseau's dream of a society in which people might be "transparent" to each other, in which relations between individuals might be direct, spontaneous, and uncomplicated by guile and imposture. As in Rousseau, or at least the Rousseau of the *Contrat social,* this insistence on openness and transparency was accompanied in Fourier by a questioning of the worth of privacy and of the exclusive ties that might be formed between individuals. Just as Rousseau criticized private associations as an obstacle to the realization of the general will, so Fourier spoke sarcastically of the selfish egotistical love that separated a couple from the rest of society. "An empire derives no advantage," he wrote, "from the caresses of two turtledoves who spend a year cooing to each other in public meetings." Finding such behavior "indecent," Fourier did his best to proscribe it from Harmony. "This kind of love will not be protected in Harmony in any case," he wrote, "not even in the case of Vestals who have joined the ranks of the troubadours."[50]

Accompanying Fourier's celebration of the polygamous revels of his Harmonians, and of their openness and transparency, there are, it seems, darker undertones in the picture of Fourier's new amorous world. Convinced that polygamous penchants were universal, that polygamy was the "secret wish" of all mankind, Fourier still could not prevent himself from railing against the "indecent displays" and "lascivious spectacles" created by monogamous lovers who apparently never tired of each other's company. Of course Fourier relegated such lovers to the ranks of the monogynes, the lowest of the passional types. But as one reads the *Nouveau monde amoureux* one encounters a deeper strain of resentment. There are, for example, passages where Fourier revenges himself on young married couples who lie abed in the morning making love. In Harmony, he tells us, such couples will be routed out of bed at 4:00 A.M., or else "covered with ridicule for their domestic virtues."[51] There are also fantasies that combine voyeurism with punishment, such as Fourier's prediction that in Harmony a "celestial mirror" orbiting the earth will make it possible to spy on lovers who have tried to isolate themselves in woods and fields.[52]

If much of Fourier's *Nouveau monde amoureux* can be read as a parody in which Christian and courtly institutions are turned upside down, the text also invites psychological interpretation. It is certainly possible to view the new amorous institutions—the orgies, the festivities, the schemes of amorous matching—as the fruits of an effort on Fourier's part to imagine a world in which his own unappeased desires and needs would be satisfied. While parodying the Christian church and overturning its ritual, he also seems to be turning his own monastic life upside down by imaginatively banishing sexual frustration and personal detachment. By the same token there is something revealing about his emphasis on openness, his punitive and voyeuristic fantasies, and his anger at the "indecent" displays of monogamous couples. His suspicion of private relationships and genuine coupling must surely reflect his inability to achieve intimacy in his own life. And his attacks on monogamous marriage seem directed not merely against a repressive institution but also against the intense emotional ties that can unite a couple. Superficially libertine, Fourier's erotic utopia seems to betray the desire to root out precisely that kind of passion—the consuming bond to another—which eluded him all his life.

But there is obviously more than this to Fourier's emphasis on openness and transparency. If Fourier imagined a world without secrets, a world in which the insignia people wore on their clothing would proclaim their inmost desires, this was the expression of a fundamental orientation—a desire for clarity and explicitness that extended to all spheres of human behavior. Implied in this was a fierce rejection of the tragic, Pascalian view of man as an inscrutable mixture of greatness and depravity, an enigma to all but his maker. For Fourier utopia could rise only in a world from which all mystery had been banished. Thus he imagined a society in which everything had a label and a definition, in which even ambiguity presented itself as such. And thus he aspired as did James Mill, the chief disciple of that other late Enlightenment "Newton of the Mind," Jeremy Bentham, to map the human psyche in such a way that the soul of man would become as clear and as well marked as the road from Charing Cross to St. Paul's.[53]

16

History and Metempsychosis

WHEN THOMAS MORE created the first modern utopia, he placed it on an island, at an unspecified but considerable distance from sixteenth-century England. And the name he gave to it further emphasized the distance. The term *utopia* derived from a combination of Greek roots that could be read either as "the good place" or simply as "no place." More's reluctance to locate his utopia too precisely in space and time was shared by most of the great utopian writers of the next two and a half centuries. For some of them utopia was an ideal and probably unrealizable standard by which to criticize a defective reality; for others it was a measure of the moral heights to which man could rise relying only on his natural powers; for still others it was a state of perfection that would only be realized in God's good time. For almost all of the classic utopian writers, however, utopia was conceived, not as a blueprint of a specific future, but rather as a useful fiction or fantasy. As Judith Shklar has elegantly put it, utopia was nowhere "not only geographically, but historically as well." The utopian vision was a vision "not of the probable but of the 'not impossible.' It was not concerned with the historically likely at all."[1]

Toward the end of the eighteenth century a change took place in the European conception of utopia. Utopia ceased to be an island, located out of time and space. In such works as Mercier's *L'An 2440* the idea of utopia acquired at least a semblance of historical specificity; and in the writing of Turgot, Condorcet, and finally Henri Saint-Simon the vision of the good place was presented as the outcome of a long historical process. "The golden age is before us," wrote Saint-Simon; and for him and for Condorcet the task of the intellectual was to usher it in. Frank Manuel has characterized this change as a shift from the traditional static vision of utopia to the open-ended "euchronia" of the nineteenth century. Whereas before the nineteenth century utopias were generally "stable and ahistorical, ideals out of time, they now became dynamic and bound to a long prior historical series. They should henceforth be called euchronias—good place becomes good time."[2]

In terms of Manuel's distinction between the static and generally agrarian utopias of the Old Regime and the dynamic euchronias of the nineteenth century, Charles Fourier appears to be something of a transitional figure. His conception of human nature is completely ahistorical. In his view the passions were unchanging, and he never made any serious attempt to analyze the development of the human faculties or of human knowledge as a historical process. Rousseau's attempt (in the *Second Discourse*) to interpret the development of man's self-consciousness as a response to developing technologies and modes of cooperation was foreign to him. Even more so was Marx's vision of history as the creation of man by human labor. In fact, most of Fourier's descriptions of Harmony have a timeless, pastoral quality that links them to the dominant utopian mode of the Old Regime. Yet Fourier clearly wanted to give his theory a historical dimension; and in most of his presentations of the doctrine he attempted to subsume both his critique of civilization and his description of the Phalanx within the framework of a panoramic account of the whole course of human history. According to this account, which ran from "the first infection of the seas by astral fluid" to the moment when the earth would cease to spin on its axis, civilization was just the fifth—and one of the worst—of thirty-two distinct historical periods.[3]

I

In its fullest outline, which was contained in the *Théorie des quatre mouvements,* Fourier's thirty-two-stage scheme of historical development was divided into four phases. First there was a phase of "infancy" or "ascending incoherence," which was meant to last approximately five thousand years. It all began in good biblical fashion with a brief period that Fourier named "foreshadowing of happiness" or simply Edenism. This was followed by five "unfortunate periods," which Fourier collectively described as "ages of perfidy, injustice, constraint, poverty, revolutions, and bodily weakness." The first of these was a period of economic backwardness and psychic inertia to which Fourier gave the name of Savagery. Then came the even more lugubrious periods of Patriarchate, Barbarism, and Civilization. Finally, Fourier claimed, the childhood of human history would end with two transitional periods, normally called Guarantism and Sociantism or Simple Association, in which certain reforms in economic or sexual mores or both would prepare the way for the establishment of full-scale Phalanxes and the reign of Harmony.

Fourier's historical timetable thus called for an initial phase of roughly five thousand years of chaos and suffering. It was to be followed, however, by a second phase of "growth" or "ascending harmony," which would last for a full thirty-five thousand years. According to the plan, this second phase of vigor, enlightenment, and passional fulfillment would be marked by eight periods and eight new "creations" culminating with a pivotal or "amphiharmonic" period of complete happiness. Thereafter life on the planet earth would gradually retrace its steps through a third phase of gradual decline and a fourth of "caducity." Following the twenty-fifth period of its development, mankind would sink back from Harmony to Chaos, passing in reverse order through the initial seven periods. Finally, after just eighty thousand years of existence, an end would come to animal and vegetable life on the earth and the planet would cease to rotate on its axis.

Such are the broad outlines of Fourier's picture of history. It was of course an ambiguous picture in which the striving toward happiness was linked to a vision of final destruction. As Frank Manuel has written, "mankind was summoned to the worldly pleasures of the Phalanstery but was offered no promise of eternity. The earth's delights were real but necessarily transitory."[4] It should be emphasized, however, that Fourier never seriously explored the darker implications of this vision. He had much more to say about the initial stages, the movement from Edenism to Civilization and on to Harmony, than about the periods of decline. And when he asked himself how it was that a just and omnipotent God could tolerate the evils of civilization and the prior periods of injustice and perfidy, he had a quick and almost flippant answer. God had after all allotted to the harmonious periods of human history a span that was a full seven times longer than that given to the ages of constraint. That did not seem ungenerous. In any case, at a time when civilization had almost run its course and when an era of seventy thousand years of unbroken happiness was about to begin, it was hardly the moment to quibble with God or to worry about the ultimate extinction of life on earth.

II

In viewing human history as a recapitulation of the stages of individual growth from childhood to caducity, Fourier was appropriating one of the central metaphors in the great tradition of philosophical history running from Augustine to Turgot. His contemporary Henri Saint-Simon also believed in the identity of individual human development and the development of the human race. But whereas Saint-Simon saw the principal social problem of his own time, the conflict of feudal and industrial civilizations, as a "crisis of puberty," according to Fourier's timetable mankind was still coping with the teething problems of infancy.[5] And whereas Saint-Simon believed that the motor of change was scientific or industrial activity, we find Fourier in his early writings groping toward a scheme of periodization in which each historical period is defined in terms of the status of women and attempting to work out a theory of social change in which sexual rather than economic relations played the decisive role. As he wrote in the *Quatre mouvements:*

> Each historical period has an attribute that forms the PIVOT OF THE MECHANISM and whose absence or presence determines a change of period. This attribute is always drawn from love.[6]

Fourier argued that the period of Barbarism was marked by "the absolute servitude of women" and Civilization by "exclusive marriage and the civil liberties of the wife," and that the crucial feature of the ensuing period of Guarantism would be a form of "amorous corporation" within which women would enjoy considerable sexual freedom.

If the barbarians took up the practice of *exclusive marriage,* this innovation alone would soon make them civilized; if we adopted the *confinement and sale of women,* we would soon become barbarians by virtue of this single innovation; and if we adopted the system of *amorous guarantees,* which will be adopted in the sixth period, this measure alone would provide us with a means to escape civilization.[7]

Convinced that "social progress and changes of period are brought about by virtue of the progress of women toward liberty," Fourier argued in one of his earliest surviving manuscripts that if the French revolutionaries had abolished the institution of marriage, the whole edifice of civilization would have rapidly collapsed.[8]

These early writings were to win the admiration of the leaders of the emerging feminist movement in the early 1840s. But the attempt to work out a theory of social change centering on the changing status of women was not consistently pursued by Fourier. In his later presentations of the theory, he began to stress the priority of economic relations as catalysts of historical change. In doing so, he may have been motivated by the same fear that kept him from publishing the *Nouveau monde amoureux:* the fear that he could never reach an audience, or find a financial backer, if he presented himself too explicitly as a prophet of sexual liberation. Nevertheless his fullest and most interesting accounts of the historical stages leading up to civilization are to be found in the early writings and do focus on "the extension of the privileges of women" as "the fundamental cause of all social progress."

The first of Fourier's historical stages was the period of Edenism. By Fourier's account, which owed little to the Bible and much to popular commentaries on the voyages to Tahiti of Bougainville and Cook, this was a time of amorous liberty and sparse population in which strong and handsome men and women freely obeyed the dictates of their passions. It was a period of "freedom from care, of delights, of amorous festivals, of frequent and copious meals shared by people of great vigor."[9] Instinct and a concourse of favorable circumstances (such as the remoteness of wild beasts from the temperate zones originally inhabited by man) permitted the first humans to develop a form of social organization—"confused series"—that approximated that of Harmony. But this initial period of social concord was short-lived. Within a few centuries amorous liberty had disappeared and the confused series had broken up. With the emergence of the family or "incoherent household" mankind was plunged into Savagery, the first of five periods of social perfidy.[10]

Fourier noted two causes for this disastrous change. A rapid increase in population had put an end to the material abundance that was necessary for the maintenance of the series; and the migration of wild animals and reptiles into the temperate zones had stimulated the invention of "murderous weapons," which in turn served to foster "a taste for pillage" among men. Insecurity and increasing poverty thus gave rise to the family system. Soon the earlier mode of social organization was just a memory. Fables began to spread about an irretrievable terrestrial paradise. These tales had since been disfigured by cynical and conniving priests, but they still provided the only clues available to modern, civilized man concerning the first period of life on earth.[11]

In Fourier's second period of Savagery marriage replaced free love, and women fell under the authority of men. But in contrast to Civilization this period did have certain redeeming features. Savage males were free to hunt and fish and gather food when and where they wished. And they also had *insouciance,* freedom from many of the fears and anxieties that tormented civilized man. Yet Fourier was far from being an uncritical worshiper of the noble savage. For he insisted that the leisure and relative indolence savage man enjoyed was possible only because in savage society women had been reduced to the status of servants and manual laborers. Furthermore, Fourier maintained, the "inertia" of the savage was so great that as a system of production Savagery could well be described as the lowest point of human history.

The transition from Savagery to Fourier's third stage of Patriarchate was marked by the decline of a nomadic way of life and the rise of settled agricultural societies controlled by centralized and authoritarian political systems. Fourier had nothing but scorn for the whole system of patriarchy, and in describing its "odious" features he relied heavily on biblical accounts of the "crimes and brutalities" of the Hebrew patriarchs and on lurid tales from Raynal and other eighteenth-century writers concerning the practice of infanticide, commercial fraud, and "legalized piracy" in China. He also advised his readers to consider the conduct of "modern patriarchal peoples." The Circassians sold their daughters into slavery; the Corsicans were constantly feuding; and the Arabs practiced "general pederasty." "These are the virtues of patriarchal people known in our day," Fourier concluded. "They go well with the virtues of Abraham and Jacob."[12]

Fourier was never particularly clear about the distinction between Patriarchate and the period of Barbarism which followed it. The main difference seems to have been that the violence and constraint that marked patriarchal societies became even more intense with the advent of Barbarism. For Fourier Barbarism was

> an order in which every father becomes a satrap who turns his whims into virtues and exercises the most revolting tyranny over his family, following the example of Abraham and Jacob, men as vicious and unjust as have ever been seen on the throne of Algiers and Tunis.[13]

Whereas Patriarchate was a system of relatively small-scale tyranny, Barbarism in Fourier's view reached its climax with the establishment of large-scale slavery. This made it the "most unfortunate" of all the periods in Fourier's historical schema. At the same time it constituted an indispensable stage in the evolution of the human race. For large-scale slavery permitted the development of the first large-scale economic enterprises. But such enterprises, which constituted one of the vital preconditions for the establishment of Harmony, could only come into full flowering in Civilization.[14]

In his writings on Civilization Fourier often emphasized its links with the preceding stages. It was, after all, the last of the four truly disastrous periods in human history, the *lymbes obscures* that were collectively marked by the reign of poverty, deceit, and instinctual repression. In some respects it was worse than its predecessors, for "the turpitudes, the hypocrisy, and the profound perversity of Civilization" were "better masked" and therefore more insidious. It was just as repressive an order as Barbarism, Fourier could write, but "Civilization adds cunning to the violence that is enough for the Barbarians."[15] There was, however, one respect in which Civilization brought something new into the world.

> Civilization occupies an important place on the ladder of historical development. For it creates the means necessary for mankind to rise to association; it creates large-scale industry, the abstract sciences, and the fine arts. These means must be put to use if man is to rise in the hierarchy of societies.[16]

Fourier believed that man's basic instinctual drives could not be adequately gratified in an economically backward society. Refinement, luxury, and material elegance were necessary prerequisites for the establishment of his utopia, and it was the historical mission of Civilization to provide them.

Fourier often claimed that contemporary civilized society contained the seeds of its own downfall. In an effort to demonstrate the point he drew up charts in which the period of Civilization was divided into four separate phases, each with its own "germs," its pivotal institution, its counterpoise, and its "tone" or special brand of illusions.

THE SUCCESSIVE ATTRIBUTES OF CIVILIZATION

Ascending Vibration

Childhood, or First Phase

Simple Germ	Exclusive marriage or monogamy
Compound Germ	Patriarchal or nobiliary feudalism
PIVOT	*Civil rights of the wife*
Counterpoise	Alliance of great vassals
Tone	Chivalrous illusions

Adolescence, or Second Phase

Simple Germ	Communal privileges
Compound Germ	Cultivation of the sciences and arts
PIVOT	*Emancipation of those who work*
Counterpoise	Representative system
Tone	Libertarian illusions

Apogee, or Plenitude

Germs	Navigation, experimental chemistry
Attributes	Deforestation, fiscal loans

Descending Vibration

Virility, or Third Phase

Simple Germ	Mercantile and fiscal spirit
Compound Germ	Share-holding companies
PIVOT	*Maritime monopoly*
Counterpoise	Anarchic commerce
Tone	Economic illusions

Decrepitude, or Fourth Phase

Simple Germ	Urban pawnshops
Compound Germ	Fixed number of masterships
PIVOT	*Industrial feudalism*
Counterpoise	Farmers-out of feudal monopolies
Tone	Illusions about association[17]

According to Fourier, France and England had already reached the declining portion of the third phase; and now Civilization was moving rapidly toward a decrepitude evident above all in the increase in public debts and in the metamorphosis of free competition into the system of economic monopolies that Fourier described as "industrial feudalism." The philosophers of Civilization might boast about progress. But it was "progress into decadence," progress that resembled the backward crawl of the crayfish.

Fourier's theory of historical development was not an "after-thought." Nor was it (to his mind at least) an inessential part of his doctrine as a whole. He began thinking about the history of human societies at a very early point in his intellectual career; and his earliest formulations of the doctrine are full of assertions and speculations concerning the various historical phases in the earth's "social movement." In his 1803 article "Harmonie universelle," for instance, he described his principal discovery as a "theory of the sixteen social orders that can be established on the diverse globes throughout eternity." In a long manuscript dating from the same year Fourier wrote suggestively about the process of historical change.

> Every society bears within it the faculty of engendering that which will follow it. It reaches the birth crisis when it has attained the full development of its essential characteristics.

Again, in the *Théorie des quatre mouvements,* we find Fourier seeking to define historical periods and to explain historical change in terms of dominant modes of sexual relations.[18]

There are enough suggestive comments scattered throughout Fourier's writings on history to have captured the interest of commentators as diverse as Friedrich Engels and Raymond Queneau. In fact several generations of Marxist historians have followed Engels in paying tribute to Fourier's "masterly" use of historical dialectics.[19] Unfortunately, their case seems to rest on little more than a few verbal parallels between Fourier's writings and those of Marx. Fourier did describe Civilization as caught in a "vicious circle" of contradictions; he maintained that societies give rise to the forces that destroy them; and he often talked of a "class war." His concept of class, however, was at best rudimentary, and the "struggle" he discerned was simply the war between the rich and the poor, or between the merchant and his victims. The fact is that Fourier never elaborated the suggestive ideas about history that are scattered throughout his early writings. Nor did he make any serious attempt to analyze the process by which the forces at work in one period of historical development might give rise to another. Indeed, the thought that presided over the elaboration of his historical theory seems to have been less a desire to understand historical change than a penchant for symmetry. It is surely not a coincidence that in its final form Fourier's account of the thirty-two stages in the rise and fall of human societies on the planet earth was so organized as to dovetail exactly not only with his account of the various stages in the life of man but also with his conception of the "basic series" of sixteen tribes and thirty-two choirs into which the full-scale Phalanx would be divided.[20]

By and large then, Fourier's elaborate theory of history played a decorative rather than an essential role in his doctrine. He lacked both the insight and the interest of a Marx or a Saint-Simon with regard to the specifically historical dimension of human experience. Like many Enlightenment thinkers, he was more interested in uncovering nature's plan than in analyzing processes of change, and he invoked history primarily as a means of dramatizing the ills of his own age. More refined speculations on historical change were hardly necessary for a man who expected the collapse of civilization to come about through the intervention of a single wealthy capitalist.

III

If Fourier's account of the initial and "perfidious" periods of human history was largely decorative, the same might be said of his treatment of the various intermediate periods between Civilization and Harmony. Fourier's discussions of how the ideal society might come into being were set within a historical framework: he saw utopia as the outcome of a historical process. Yet in its essentials his vision of utopia was a static one, and the historical process he described had actually been completed some two thousand years earlier. By the time of the Greeks, he believed, mankind had already created the material foundations on which utopia could be built. The only reason for the delay in its establishment was simply that, until Fourier, no one had discovered the blueprint.

It follows that although Fourier wrote a great deal about the transition from Civilization to Harmony, there is a fundamental ambiguity in his reflections on how this transition might best be accomplished. In his charts on the various stages in the earth's "social movement" he always included a number of intermediate or transitional stages between Civilization and Harmony. The names that he gave to these stages varied: Guarantism, Sociantism, and Simple Harmony were three that he often used. But Fourier's essential point remained the same: it was possible for mankind to work its way slowly up from Civilization to Harmony through the establishment of model communities much smaller than an ordinary Phalanx or through the creation of small-scale producers' associations, credit institutions, collective kitchens, and the like. Fourier argued that these communities or associations would serve to accustom the men and women of Civilization to cooperation rather than competition and thereby pave the way for bolder experiments in association.[21] The same emphasis on gradualism may be found elsewhere in Fourier's writing in a manuscript entitled "Issues des lymbes obscures" and in his various classifications of the sixteen (or thirty-two) "ways out" of Civilization.[22] What is curious about all these writings, however, and about Fourier's elaborate descriptions of life under Guarantism, Sociantism, Serisophie, and the other transitional stages, is that within the larger framework of Fourier's theory they are actually quite superfluous. Since the time of the Greeks, he believed, mankind had possessed the material resources necessary to establish the full Phalanx that would mark the beginning of the period of Harmony. Thus Fourier kept reminding his readers that mankind did not need to pass laboriously through Guarantism and Sociantism on the way to Harmony. The transitional stages could simply be skipped if Fourier could only manage to find a rich capitalist or prince or chief of state who would provide the capital necessary for the immediate establishment of a full-scale Phalanx.

Given their tenuous place in Fourier's system, it would be overly fastidious to spend much time considering his proposals for rural banks and model farms and the various schemes of "reductive competition" and "truthful commerce" designed by Fourier to facilitate the transition from Civilization to Harmony. Yet these projects cannot be totally ignored. For a number of them were to serve as models for Fourier's disciples when they set about attempting to put his ideas into practice. Just Muiron in particular was tireless in his attempts to get an audience for Fourier's ideas about the "communal share-holding bank, engaging in commerce and the storage of agricultural products, serving as a warehouse and making loans of funds to its members."[23] Similarly, long after Fourier's death, his various proposals for associations of producers who would work together and market their goods in common continued to serve as an inspiration to the members of the emerging cooperative movement in France.[24]

For Fourier's biographer there is another reason to take an interest in these transitional reform proposals. At least some of these proposals seem to have been devised by Fourier at a very early point in his intellectual career. In fact, they predate his initial "discovery" of 1799. His *Traité* of 1822, for example, contains a detailed "plan of a city appropriate to the sixth period" that is in many respects identical to the proposed reforms in city planning Fourier sent to the municipality of Bordeaux in 1796.[25] Fourier's schemes of "reductive competition" and "truthful commerce" also date from the 1790s.[26] What Fourier seems to have done in all these cases was to find a way of integrating within his mature system speculations that were part of the process by which he arrived at that system. Reticent and even secretive as he was about the genesis of his theory, Fourier could not resist burying in the work of his maturity clues concerning the first steps in his own intellectual development.

IV

Fourier's reflections on human destiny did not stop with his descriptions of the enchanted world that he called Harmony. Since even in Harmony people died, he devised a theory of metempsychosis to explain what happened to their souls after death. And since life on the planet earth was destined to last a mere eighty thousand years, he incorporated in this theory an account of what would happen to the souls of all human beings after the extinction of life on the planet.[27]

According to Fourier's theory of metempsychosis, each human soul was destined to shuttle back and forth between this world and the next. During the eighty thousand years allotted to the earth, each of its souls, which were all emanations of a "great planetary soul," would enjoy 810 (or 1,620) lives, of which half would be in this world and half in the next. Of these lives 765 would be happy and 45 miserable. Thus each individual soul would be amply compensated for whatever misfortunes it had to endure during the perfidious periods of human history. There were hundreds of happy lives to be led on earth. And there was also heaven, which for Fourier's Harmonians meant hundreds of blissful extraterrestrial lives, each of which would be twice as long as its terrestrial counterpart.

Fourier emphasized that Harmony's heaven would have nothing in common with the dull and monotonous afterlife promised to Christian believers and the almost equally dull Elysian Fields of the classical tradition. In Civilization, he observed, the most religious believers could expect from the afterlife was "monotonous promenades and sterile conversations about virtue," or else an Olympus where gods and demigods ate nothing but ambrosia day after day. The civilized heaven was an "ascetic dwelling place" in which the souls of the departed had to do without their passions and also "the principal senses of taste and touch." Harmony's afterlife, on the contrary, would offer activities and entertainments to appeal to all five senses and each of the twelve passions. And the senses and passions would undergo extraordinary refinement. The human eye, for example, would acquire such sharpness that it would become possible for the souls of the dead to observe clearly everything that was happening on any of the planets in the solar system. At the same time departed souls would acquire new skills, such as the ability to plane or glide through the air, that terrestrial beings could only do in their dreams. With these powers and with their improved senses and passions, Harmony's souls would lead extraterrestrial lives more active and pleasurable than those of the living.

In the course of the eighty-thousand-year life span of the planet earth, the souls of its inhabitants would be lodged, during their extraterrestrial lives, in bodies "formed out of the element that we call Aroma, which is incombustible and homogenous with fire."[28] While away from the earth, they would be able to recall all their past lives. At the time of the earth's demise, however, the souls of all earthlings would be absorbed within the great planetary soul from which they had emanated. Individual lives would then be forgotten, and each soul would remember only the general outlines of the planet's development during its four phases. Eventually this too would be forgotten as the planetary soul attached itself to a young wandering comet, which, after a period of maturation, would itself become a new planet. A new life would then begin for the planetary soul itself.

Fourier could thus envisage the death of the planet, and his own death, without apprehension. For if he recognized death and finitude as elements of the human condition, he could also look beyond them to the merging of the human soul with that of the planet, the sun, and eventually the universe. Nor did he stop there. His vision also encompassed biniverses and triniverses. Ultimately each individual would merge with the whole. And the universe itself, as Fourier envisaged it, was pulsating with the same passions and the same sexual energies that animated the life of the individual.

17

The Cosmological Poem

IN EVERYTHING he published after 1808 Fourier's main concern was the doctrine of association. Convinced that his contemporaries had it in their power to create a social order that would liberate the passions and transform the nature of work, Fourier devoted himself in his mature works to a description of that order. Yet the *Quatre mouvements* and Fourier's manuscripts show his plan of association and his psychology and his reflections on work and sexuality to have been only parts of a larger whole, a vast intellectual system seeking to encompass, or re-place, all scientific disciplines and permitting a total and organic expla-nation of the world based on a few simple laws. Fourier described the whole project as a "theory of the destinies." By this what he seems to have meant was a comprehensive description of the created universe that would link everything to a providential plan, an overall divine scheme of purposes. Thus Fourier could talk about the "intentions" of God in creating the universe, and he could seek to explain "the plans adopted by God concerning . . . everything from the cosmogony of the universes [*sic*] and the invisible stars to the most minute alterations of matter in the animal, vegetable, and mineral kingdoms."[1]

There has always been some question about the status of Fourier's "theory of the destinies" and especially about the relationship of his cosmological speculations to the rest of his doctrine. On a number of occasions he himself indicated that he did not mean his cosmogony and his new astronomical views to be taken as the literal truth, and in his explanations of "the riddle of the *Quatre mouvements*" he boasted that in beginning with chapters on the "hierarchy of the four movements" and the "Northern Crown" and the sexual proclivities of the stars, his real intention was to "launch the scoffers." He also frequently insisted that he did not "require" his readers to accept his cosmogony or his theory of universal analogy, and that he regarded them as aspects of his doctrine that should be judged independently of his theory of association.[2]

Fourier's earthbound disciples went further. They were sufficiently interested in his theories of cosmogony and universal analogy to publish almost all his manuscripts on these topics. But in doing so they made cuts, and in their popularizations of the doctrine they often practiced what Ange Guépin described as a "useful weeding-out" of the more extravagant ideas. For they were worried about the effect that these ideas might have on their attempts to gain an audience for Fourier's economic and social theories. As Charles Pellarin put it, the writings on cosmogony and analogy were "magnificent and grandiose," but "being devoid of positive proofs," they might serve to alarm the timid and even to provoke ridicule.[3]

In purging Fourier's doctrine of its more extravagant elements, the disciples set a precedent that was long honored by scholars interested in Fourier. Thus in the monumental study of Fourier's thought published by Hubert Bourgin in 1905 Fourier's providentialist metaphysics, his cosmogony, and his theory of universal analogy were hardly mentioned. And later scholars such as Maurice Lansac and I. I. Zil'berfarb could assert that Fourier's providentialism was nothing but "a peculiar metaphysical wrapping" designed to render his social theory presentable to the bourgeois public.[4] Such claims are in fact scarcely conceivable. It was precisely the "metaphysical wrapping" that Fourier's disciples had to suppress in order to get a hearing for his doctrine. And if it were true that Fourier's cosmogony was not meant to be taken seriously, it would be difficult to understand why Fourier should have worked so hard at elaborating it not only in his published writings but also, at great length, in his unpublished manuscripts.

In fact, Fourier seems to have been quite serious about his cosmogony and about the other esoteric aspects of his doctrine. And when, in the early years of the Restoration, he made corrections in the original text of the *Théorie des quatre mouvements,* it was not, as his disciples later implied, to disavow his early stellar reveries but rather to change matters of detail.[5] It is true that the derision that greeted the publication of the *Quatre mouvements* convinced Fourier to adopt a more circumspect tone in later presentations of the doctrine. In subsequent published works he tried to pass off his theories of cosmogony and universal analogy as mere "entertainments" or "instruction for the ladies."[6] But he could never suppress them altogether. Nor could he forget his youthful ambition to elaborate a "theory of the destinies." Emile Lehouck has aptly written that the maintenance of sections on cosmogony in all of his mature works was "an act of fidelity to the dreams and ambitions of his youth."[7]

I

Just as Fourier's social theory was an effort to specify the conditions necessary for the establishment of a harmonious social order, his theory of the destinies can be understood as an attempt to discern the underlying principles of order and harmony in a universe of apparent chaos and disharmony. In seeking to discover such principles Fourier professed, like some of his contemporaries and like many moral and political philosophers of the eighteenth century, to be greatly influenced by the work of Isaac Newton. He repeatedly boasted that he was Newton's "continuator" and that whereas Newton had discovered the laws governing material attraction, he, Fourier, had gone on to grasp the laws of passionate attraction. It seems clear, however, that Fourier's debt to Newton was modest. The conception of gravitational attraction may have helped him to arrive at his own notion of a passion as a force "attracting" human beings to their predestined ends. The Newtonian image of a harmonious world order undoubtedly helped shape his social vision. But still in most important respects Fourier's scientific ideas were pre-Newtonian. Most importantly, Fourier never grasped—and apparently never tried to grasp—the modern notion of a scientific law as a descriptive proposition concerning a uniform order of sequence. The kinds of laws that Fourier invoked in his writings were not "if . . . then" propositions but rather statements concerning impulsions or tendencies inherent in things. Much more like the Scholastic philosophers than like Newton or Galileo, Fourier's real aim as a thinker was to uncover a scheme of purposes toward the realization of which everything in the world was constantly striving.★ In determining this scheme he began, as had the Scholastics, by reflecting upon the properties of God and the nature of Divine Providence.

Fourier's whole system rested on an unshakable faith in the existence of an infinitely good, infinitely wise, and infinitely powerful God. He expressed scorn for the "simplistic" and "bastard" views of the atheists. At the same time, however, his own religious views had little in common with those of orthodox Christians. He rejected the doctrine of revelation and poked fun at the Sermon on the Mount and scoffed at the Christian "inventions" of heaven and hell with the zest of a Voltairean. He also had little sympathy for the notions of divine reward and punishment and rejected the idea of a personal deity. "Begin," he addressed his contemporaries, "by shedding the political and religious prejudices by which you let yourselves be persuaded that God is a busybody who meddles in the affairs of every household, that God is a meddler who goes sticking his nose between the sheets to see if a husband is cheating on his wife."[8] For Fourier God was not such a "cuistre" but rather a "great geometer" like the God of Voltaire and of the eighteenth-century deists. He was a God who was bound by, and in fact identical with, the laws governing the universe. As Fourier wrote in the *Quatre mouvements:*

> Nature is composed of three eternal, uncreated, and indestructible principles:
> 1. *God or Spirit,* the active and moving principle;
> 2. *Matter,* the passive and moved principle;
> 3. *Justice or Mathematics,* the principle that regulates movement.

★This is not to suggest that Fourier owed nothing to Newton or that his invocation of Newton's authority was merely an attempt to clothe his own theory in the mantle of scientific respectability. On the contrary, the names that he originally gave to the distributive passions suggest that he originally conceived of himself as working out laws of psychological motion in the manner of a Newton or a Galileo. See above, p. 67n. In his Restoration writings one can still find passages in which he seems to be searching for "Newtonian" laws in the social and economic spheres. See for example *La Phalange,* V (1847), 19: "Like the stellar world, the passional world can only be harmonized by a tendency to luxury in direct proportion to the masses of capital and in inverse proportion to the square of their distances; and one can apply to the mechanism of passional harmony all the mathematical laws governing the stellar world." Nonetheless it does seem that during his years in Belley Fourier became increasingly convinced of the inadequacy of Newton as a guide to the exploration of the social world. See especially the important manuscript "Insuffisance et extension du système Newtonien en Théorie d'Attraction," AN 10AS 7 (12), pp. 23–29.

> To establish harmony between these three principles, it is necessary for God to act in accordance with mathematics in moving and modifying matter. Otherwise he would be arbitrary in his own eyes as well as in ours. . . . But if God submits to mathematical rules that he cannot change, he finds in doing so both his glory and his interest.[9]

Fourier's God was not the creator of the material world, for matter itself was as old as God. Rather, he had shaped and organized matter, he had devised "plans" for the universe, and he had done so in a manner consistent with "mathematical rules."

What were these rules that Fourier's God obeyed in devising his plans for the universe? First there was the law of universal attraction. If the movements of the stars and the planets were governed by the law of gravitational attraction, Fourier argued, there must be a similar law presiding over the movement of the passions. To assert that such a law did not exist would be to accuse God of being in contradiction with himself. Second, there was the law of serial organization. In Fourier's time the animal and vegetable worlds were still widely seen as fixed hierarchies, divided by subtle gradations into distinct species and genera. The idea that the serial order was part of God's plan for the natural universe was reinforced by the enormous prestige still enjoyed by Linnaeus and his taxonomies.[10] The claim that Fourier made was simply that if God had created finely graduated series of plant and animal species, such series must also be part of God's plan for the right ordering of the passions in human societies. The third of the laws obeyed by Fourier's God was the law of universal analogy, which held that the natural world was the mirror of the human passions. According to this law, there could be nothing arbitrary about God's creations. For the universe was a unified system, a web of hidden correspondences and hieroglyphs, each of which provided an image of the conflict or harmony of the human passions.

II

"I declare to you," wrote one of Fourier's disciples to another in 1832, "that every time I speak of Fourier I distinguish Fourier the *wise genius* from Fourier the *extravagant genius*."[11] By common agreement of the young disciples whom Fourier began to acquire in the early 1830s, the cosmogony was the work of the extravagant genius. The modern reader is tempted to agree. For Fourier's cosmogony seems at first glance to be arbitrary and fantastic.★ This self-described follower of Newton begins by announcing that the heavenly bodies are living creatures, subject like human beings to the cycle of birth, growth, and death. He then adds that many of them are androgynous organisms, endowed not only with passions but also with distinctive "aromas" that enable them to copulate with each other at a distance. Fourier goes on to discuss the sexual proclivities of the planets and the "creations" that result from their intercourse. He predicts the imminent disappearance of the moon, foretells the emergence of wondrous new animal species, and speculates about the existence of "biniverses" and "triniverses" beyond our own universe. He claims to be interested in the work of contemporary astronomers, but when he quotes one of them—Sir William Herschel—it is simply to mystify us with the reflection that the universe is not, as we thought, a "world of fire" but rather a "great and magnificent world bathing in an ocean of light."[12]

It is no wonder that Fourier's writings on cosmogony embarrassed the disciples and amused the profane. Still, one point does emerge clearly from them. This is Fourier's conviction that the earth was sick and that its sickness had infected the whole universe. The cause of the sickness was clear enough. For over two thousand years, ever since the time of Solon and Pericles, the human race had possessed the material resources necessary to leave behind the chaos and misery of civilization and to establish a harmonious social order consistent with the plans of God. But the world was still waiting. One consequence of the prolongation of civilization was that the earth was no longer able to perform its cosmic functions. It had begun to emit noxious aromas. These were partly responsible for the death of Phoebe or the moon, which now whirled through space as a pale and useless corpse. Another effect of the earth's sickness was that it could no longer provide the sun with the pure aromas it needed to continue its work of creation. As a result the sun also was languishing; and its sickness, evident in the massive sunspots of 1816, coincided with a general deterioration of the climate on earth. Hurricanes, droughts, unseasonal weather, and even the fre-

★The term *cosmogony* refers to a theory of the creation of the universe. A cosmology is a theory of the laws governing the structure or workings of the universe. Fourier used the former term to refer to both. There was a certain logic to this, since he counted twenty-six separate "creations" in the course of the earth's history.

quency of the northern lights provided proof that the planet could no longer tolerate the prolongation of civilization. "The earth is violently agitated by the need to create," wrote Fourier in the *Quatre mouvements.* "That can be seen from the frequency of the northern lights, which are a symptom of the rutting of the planet, a useless effusion of prolific fluid. It cannot form its union with the fluid of other planets as long as the human race has not accomplished the preliminary labors."[13]

Ordinarily the sickness of a single, small planet would be of little concern to the rest of the universe. But the earth and its solar system happened to be strategically situated. "Our solar system is at the center of the universe," wrote Fourier. "It is thus the foyer or pivotal system for all the starry heavens; its role in the aromal mechanism is like that of a general in the army. This means that if our solar system is backward, all the heavens fall behind in their operations."[14] To remedy the situation a rescue column of 102 planets had been organized. It had been advancing on the earth by forced marches ever since the time of Julius Caesar. But until its arrival, which Fourier believed imminent, the earth would continue to suffer.

Another symptom of the earth's sickness, in addition to the deterioration of the climate, was the proliferation of dangerous animal species. Fourier counted 130 different species of poisonous snakes, for example, and an even greater number of lizards, slugs, rats, and vermin. What possible purpose was there to the existence of such horrible creatures? What place did they have in the plans of a wise, omniscient, and benevolent God? This question, which had taxed the ingenuity of many natural philosophers in the eighteenth century, received a novel answer from Fourier.[15] Since the periods of Savagery, Barbarism, and Civilization were times of perfidy, war, and carnage, he argued, it was only natural (given the law of universal analogy) that during such periods there should be an abundance of poisonous snakes, dangerous reptiles, and other useless or harmful animals. Indeed the 130 known varieties of poisonous snakes could be described as an "exact replica" of the "130 effects of calumny and perfidy" that were the essence of these deceitful societies."[16]

Fourier insisted that with the coming of Harmony all of these harmful creatures would disappear. The earth would then undergo a series of extraordinary physical transformations culminating with a new "harmonic creation." Fourier described these transformations as a growth crisis "similar to the onset of puberty."[17] Just as pimples form on the skin of adolescents, the earth would be shaken by a series of quakes and volcanic eruptions, which would make possible the release of noxious fluids buried underground. At the same time the polar ice-caps would begin to melt, the seas would be purified, and the earth's atmosphere cleansed. The gales and hurricanes of Civilization would be calmed and replaced by a harmonic series of gentle, predictable winds that would make sea voyages "as safe as those by land."[18] The moon, sickly Phoebe, would drop out of orbit and dissolve in the Milky Way. It would be replaced in due course by five bright new satellites.[19]

Most of these extraordinary developments would become possible, Fourier explained, as a result of the formation of a ring around the North Pole. Fourier called this ring the Northern Crown, and he described its formation in a long and bizarre chapter of the *Quatre mouvements* that he described in deadpan fashion as "more curious than necessary."[20] During the course of the transition from Civilization to Harmony, Fourier explained, it would become possible for men to place previously barren areas of the globe under cultivation. One consequence of the spread of settlement and farming would be a rise in the earth's temperature. By the time farmers reached the sixtieth parallel the earth would become so much warmer that the polar ices would begin to melt. At the same time the northern lights would coagulate and form a ring around the North Pole. Sufficiently large to remain in perpetual contact with the sun's rays, this Northern Crown would stabilize climatic conditions and warm the northern latitudes with reflected light. Soon Siberians would enjoy a more temperate climate than the inhabitants of civilized Florence, Nice, or Montpellier. Grapes would grow in the suburbs of Saint Petersburg and oranges in Warsaw. With the melting of the polar icecap, the northern sea would be purified and then turned into "a sort of lemonade" by a fluid emanating from the Northern Crown.[21]

This radical improvement in climatic conditions was a necessary prerequisite to the new harmonic creation that would inaugurate the period of Full Harmony. Unlike the previous, subversive creations, which had endowed the earth with a multitude of useless and harmful creatures, this new creation would be beneficent. It would yield a plentiful assortment of useful, gracious, and hitherto unknown animals, vegetables, and minerals. Just as the reptiles, insects, and sea monsters produced by the first creations were "hieroglyphs" of the discord of the human passions during the periods of subversion, the docile and beautiful creatures produced by this new creation would reflect their new-found harmony. In due course, then, the rivers and seas of Harmony would abound in anticrocodiles providing a safe and sure means of river transportation, and antiwhales eager to tow becalmed vessels, and anti-sharks that would help fishermen secure a plentiful catch. Similar trans-formations would occur on land, where useless or dangerous species of animals would be replaced by their opposites. Instead of the handsome but dreaded lion of civilization, for example, Harmonians would bene-fit from the services of "a superb and docile quadruped" called the "antilion." This animal's huge size, long stride, elastic muscles, and extraordinary endurance would enable it to carry passengers at speeds of up to twenty-five miles an hour. Running softly, its feet hardly touching the ground, the antilion would leap over ditches, creeks, and fences at a single bound while its passengers remained as comfortable as if they were traveling in a coach with modern springs.[22]

Along with the establishment of new and docile strains of antilions and anticrocodiles, the harmonic creation would also bring remarkable physical transformations in the human species. Fourier predicted that the men and women of the new order would grow to the height of seven feet and live to the age of 144. They would acquire replaceable teeth and develop the capacity to withstand severe pain. Their senses would undergo extraordinary refinement, and they would also become sufficiently amphibious to make full use of the bottom of the sea.[23] But the most remarkable physical change in mankind, which would only take place after sixteen generations of Harmony, was the development of a new member, an *archibras,* the properties of which were described by Fourier in a manuscript censored by his disciples.

> The Harmonian arm or *archibras* is a veritable tail, a tail of immense length and with 144 vertebrae. . . . This member is as redoubtable as it is industrious. It is a natural weapon. . . . The *archibras* terminates with a very small elongated hand, a hand as strong as the claws of an eagle or a crab. . . . When a man is swimming, the *archibras* will help him move as fast as a fish. It can stretch to the bottom of the water, carrying fish nets and making them fast. With its help a man can reach a branch twelve feet high, climb up and down the tree, pick fruit at the very top of the tree, and put it in a basket tied to the *archimain.* It serves as a whip and a rein to a man who is driving a horse-drawn plow. . . . It can be used to tame a wild horse: the

rider can tie up the horse's legs with his *archibras*. It is infinitely useful, and in the playing of musical instruments it doubles a person's manual faculties since its fingers, although very small, are extremely stretchable.[24]

Why had God failed to endow human beings with such a remarkable member in the first creation? The reason was obvious. Its effectiveness as a weapon was so great that it could not be given to the human race until they had learned to settle their disputes peacefully.

III

Fourier's conviction that the advent of Harmony would be accompanied by the creation of marvelous new species of benign and useful animals derived from his belief that the natural world was a mirror of the human passions. He stated that belief clearly at the outset of the *Théorie des quatre mouvements*.

> The properties of an animal, a vegetable, a mineral, and even of a cluster of stars represent some effect of the passions in the social order, and . . . EVERYTHING, from the atoms to the stars, constitutes a tableau of the properties of the human passions.[25]

This affirmation of the correspondence between the passions and the material universe constituted the core of Fourier's theory of universal analogy. The theory rested on two premises: (1) the universe was a unified system, a web of hidden correspondences or hieroglyphs, and (2) man was at the center of the system. Like the Christian cosmographers of the latter Middle Ages and the Renaissance, Fourier believed that everything that transpired in the world of man had some echo or correspondence in the world of nature. Each of the twelve passions was represented by its own color, musical note, geometrical form, and celestial body. Similarly every animal, vegetable, and mineral species was the image of a human character trait, institution, or social relationship. "The analogy is complete in all of nature's realms," wrote Fourier. "They are, in all their details, so many mirrors of some effect of our passions. They form an immense museum of allegorical tableaux in which the crimes and virtues of humanity are depicted."[26]

Fourier's theory of analogy was a way of looking at the world so that nature lost its strangeness. "Without analogy," he wrote, "nature is no more than a vast patch of brambles; the seventy-three systems of botanical classification are only the seventy-three shafts of the thistle."[27] With analogy everything acquired a human dimension; the natural universe became not only comprehensible but also animated and even entertaining. To guide his readers through nature's tangled underbrush Fourier drew up elaborate charts in which the analogies between passions, colors, metals, animals, plants, and geometrical forms were spelled out explicitly. For example:

TABLE AND ANALOGY OF THE SEVEN PASSIONS OF THE SOUL

6	Do	Friendship	Purple	Addition	Circle	Iron
7	Mi	Love	Azure	Division	Ellipse	Tin
8	Sol	Paternity	Yellow	Subtraction	Parabola	Lead
9	Si	Ambition	Red	Multiplication	Hyperbola	Copper
10	Re	*Cabalist*	Indigo	Progression	Spiral	Silver
11	Fa	*Alternating*	Green	Proportion	Quadratrix	Platinum
12	La	*Composite*	Orange	Logarithm	Logarithmic	Gold
★	DO	UNITYISM	White	Powers	Cycloid	Mercury[28]

Fourier went on to show how different varieties of love could be represented by flowers like the iris, the tuberose, the carnation, and the hyacinth, and how one could establish a scale of degrees of stupidity, wit, and intelligence as represented by the heads of birds—their tufts, crests, plumes, collars, and other head ornaments. "Since the bird is the creature that rises above all others," wrote Fourier, "it is on its head that nature has placed the portraits of the varieties of intelligence with which human heads are provided."[29] But everything was grist for Fourier's mill, and he found as much to learn from an ear as from a head. "Why does the lion have clipped ears?" he asked. The reason was that the lion represented the king: he was prevented by his courtiers from hearing the truth just as the peasant, represented by the long-eared donkey, was forced to stand quietly listening to the worst insults.[30]

The project of a theory of analogy was not unique in Fourier's time. Indeed, the belief that nature was a realm of allegories and hidden meanings was widely held in the late eighteenth century. To cite only one example, Bernardin de Saint-Pierre's *Etudes de la nature* (1784) was a compendium of analogies purporting to demonstrate the unity, order, and harmony of nature and the wisdom of the Creator. Fourier knew this work well, but his conception of a theory of analogy differed from Bernardin de Saint-Pierre's in two respects. First of all, he scoffed at the latter's readiness to accept everything in the existing order as part of the divine plan. "Bernardin de Saint-Pierre . . . wishes to habituate us to servile admiration of the horrors of creation," he wrote, expressing particular dismay that Bernardin could find a place even for spiders in the divine plan.[31] Second, Fourier conceived of his theory of analogy as a science and claimed that its goal was to explain the causes of natural phenomena and, eventually, to provide remedies and antidotes for various diseases. "When the new science of passional analogy is pushed to perfection," he boasted, "we will learn how to determine, among other secrets, the unknown remedies that are hidden in every vegetable."[32]

Fourier insisted that there was nothing dry about his science of analogy. He was, to be sure, perfectly capable of listing in pedantic detail the precise connections that existed between the 130 distinct forms of civilized perfidy and the 130 known species of poisonous snakes. More commonly, however, he told stories or painted verbal pictures for his readers in the manner of a La Fontaine, describing exactly how the human passions were represented by specific details in the plumage of a bird or the anatomy of an animal. One of his favorite examples was the parrot.

> The parrot is the symbol of the sophists of the philosophical world: it is full of glib talk, but its words are merely verbiage without sense. Such are the brilliant systems of philosophy as represented by the contrasting variations in the colors of the parrot's plumage: one's wing is yellow on top and red at the tip. Similarly the sophists, like Epicurus and Zeno, preach contradictory dogmas. On what foundations are their lofty systems constructed? On the family system, on the division into small conjugal households; all philosophy swings on this old hinge, which is the exact opposite of the societary system. Analogy requires the pivotal parrot, which is the white one, to display a yellow stripe as the symbol of the group of paternity. This group is central to all the social systems conceived by philosophy. Thus the knight-errant of the parrots, the cockatoo, has yellow plumage on all the lower parts of his body.[33]

The elephant was another animal in whose habits and physical features Fourier could discover a world of meaning. To the discerning eye, wrote Fourier, it was evident that the elephant embodied the four affective passions in their virtuous form. The elephant was a devoted, but not servile, friend, a discreet and constant lover, a creature of large aims and ambitions, and a doting parent who was too responsible to bear children in captivity. Nature had endowed the elephant with elegant tusks and a trunk that was often ridiculed: this was its way of depicting a civilization that scorned the truly productive class and dressed unproductive soldiers in the finest of uniforms. Nature had also endowed the elephant with a puny tail and a ludicrous behind because people laughed behind the back of the virtuous man in civilization. The elephant's tiny eyes portrayed the blindness of the virtuous man who could not discern a way to make virtue triumph in civilization. His great crinkled ears depicted the suffering of those honest men who had to listen to nothing but hypocrisy or the praise of vice. Finally, if the elephant loved to roll in the mud and cover itself with dust, it was in this respect too only depicting the fate of the virtuous individual whom civilization condemned to poverty.[34]

In his readings of the book of nature Fourier took special delight in identifying and explicating analogies of love and sexuality. Here he was working within an old tradition. Ever since Linnaeus had developed his schemes of plant classification by studying the reproductive systems of plants and flowers, numerous popular writers had composed poems and treatises on the love life of the plants and flowers. Unlike most of these writers, however, Fourier did not limit himself to the "gracious" analogies provided by the more beautiful flowers. He insisted that the most humble vegetables, like the cabbage and the onion, could provide a subtle and nuanced picture of the hopes and trials of lovers. The cabbage, for example, was an emblem of clandestine love with its secret intrigues, its masks, and its hundred ruses. Like the lover, it hid its flower under the veil of a hundred nesting leaves. These puffy and undulating leaves represented the crafty efforts of lovers to conceal their relationship; and they were more blue than green because blue was the color of love. The cauliflower, on the other hand, was a hieroglyph of love without obstacle or mystery. Its ocean of white flowers depicted the delights of emancipated youth; and its leaves were neither blue nor bloated because young people who indulged themselves sexually were rarely in love and had no need to use guile like the fettered youths symbolized by the cabbage.[35]

If plants and flowers provided Fourier with most of his images of love and sexuality, he found others in the animal kingdom. One of the most memorable is his description of the male duck, the hieroglyph of many a civilized husband.

> Nature, in afflicting the male duck with a loss of voice, represents those docile husbands who do not have the right to reply when their wives have spoken. Thus when he wishes to woo his noisy partner, the duck presents himself humbly, bowing his head and bending his knees like a submissive but happy husband lulled by illusions. As a token of this the duck's head is dipped in a glistening green, the color of illusion.[36]

Silent, cowardly, and gluttonous, the duck was the very opposite of the rooster, whose proud and polygamous manners were those of the sultan in his harem.

Most of the hieroglyphs Fourier explicated so meticulously naturally referred to the vices and follies of the civilized order. But even in civilization he could detect portents of the future. Just as the wasp's nest was an image of civilization and the parrot an image of the civilized philosopher, the bee's hive and the beaver's dam were models of Harmony. In each of the plumes of the peacock's tail Fourier's eye could detect an emblem of one of the choirs of the Phalanx. And as for the transformation of the ugly caterpillar into the beautiful butterfly, what could it represent but man's future metamorphosis?

One may choose to regard all of this as a waste of time. But it has a coherence and poetry of its own. As gratuitous and arbitrary as it may seem, the theory of universal analogy was, like much else in Fourier's thought, an affirmation of underlying order and harmony in a world of apparent disorder and chaos. It was also a way of looking at the world so that everything acquired a human dimension. It was one expression, and not the least interesting, of Fourier's desire to end man's separation from nature.

IV

How did Fourier arrive at his ideas on cosmogony and analogy? Were these branches of the doctrine essentially his own creation, or was he inspired to any significant degree by other thinkers? Where, in any case, should we "locate" these ideas in an intellectual history? Fourier himself was so reticent about the genesis of his doctrine that the first of these questions may be impossible to answer in any but a superficial way. Nevertheless it has long intrigued scholars and critics, and a number of attempts have been made to connect Fourier with the great tradition of occult speculation culminating with Emanuel Swedenborg, Louis-Claude de Saint-Martin, and the other illuminati of the late eighteenth century. This was first done by Fourier's earliest disciples, many of whom were themselves dabblers in the occult sciences. More recently Simone Debout has portrayed Fourier as a crypto-Martinist, and Gérard Schaeffer has attributed to him a Pythagorean belief in the mystical properties of numbers.[37] Maurice Lansac has suggested that various chapters of the *Quatre mouvements* were first delivered as talks to the Masonic lodges of Lyon, and there has even been speculation concerning a "protective talisman" purportedly worn by Fourier.[38] In fact, Fourier explicitly disavowed number mysticism;[39] and there is no evidence to support the claims concerning Fourier's "talisman" or his alleged Masonic lectures. There are, it is true, interesting parallels between Fourier's theory and those of Swedenborg and Saint-Martin. There are even more remarkable similarities between the anthropomorphic and sexualized cosmogonies of Fourier and Restif de la Bretonne.[40] But the idealism and mysticism of the illuminati, their use of certain forms of magic, their fascination with elaborate initiation rites, and their belief in a sacred tradition were all alien to Fourier's cast of mind. He was not an illuminist like Swedenborg, describing the New Jerusalem from revelations made to him by angels. He was a self-proclaimed scientist whose aim was to map and explore a new world of hidden harmonies and meanings.[41]

Fourier did acknowledge that his general view of the universe as a tissue or web of analogies had been anticipated by a few "expectant" philosophers. There was Bernardin de Saint-Pierre, for example, whose *Etudes de la nature* was often cited by Fourier.[42] There was also the German philosopher Schelling, whom Fourier cited at second (or third) hand.

> The philosophers are all agreed in teaching that there is unity and analogy in the system of the universe. Let us hear what one of our celebrated metaphysicians has to say about matter: "The universe is constructed on the model of the human soul, and the analogy of each part of the universe with the whole is such that the same idea is constantly reflected from the whole to each part and from each part to the whole." SCHELLING[43]

Although this citation often appears in Fourier's writings, he does not seem to have actually read Schelling. His source was apparently a review of "a work by M. Ancillon of Berlin, who has commented upon and analyzed the most recent systems, those of Kant, Fichte, Schelling, and other controversialists."[44]

In general it would seem that there is little to be gained from attempts to pin down specific sources for the esoteric aspects of Fourier's doctrine. So far as we can tell, he drew on other thinkers more for the confirmation of his ideas than for inspiration. But if the hunt for influences is sterile, what we can do is "situate" Fourier's ideas within a tradition of discourse and attempt to characterize the intellectual context within which his powerfully original mind worked. The context here is the romantic reformulation of the classical and Christian tradition of analogical thinking.

The idea that the natural universe is a mirror of human concerns or of man himself is as old as civilization. When Plato wrote in the *Timaeus* (30B) that "this world is in truth a living creature endowed with a soul and with reason," he was apparently drawing on a substantial tradition of Pythagorean speculation on the macrocosm and the microcosm and the harmony of the spheres. There was also a long and influential tradition of Christian speculation about the invisible harmonies, likenesses, and proportions that bound together the universe.[45] For centuries Christian philosophers had been finding allegories of the human condition in the flowers and fields and the animals and even in the form of a nut. Renaissance architects similarly believed that the proper proportions of buildings and of the ideal city could be determined by analogy to the human body and the structure of the heavens.[46] And Kepler's *Mysterium cosmographicum* and *Harmonice mundi* constituted elaborate attempts to demonstrate that God had created the world according to models provided by music and geometry and that everything from the planetary laws to the fortunes of man could be understood in terms of these archetypes of universal order.[47] In the century of Fourier's birth there were still many who regarded the natural world not as a self-contained machine but rather as "a map and shadow of the spiritual estate of the soul of man."[48] Indeed the belief that nature was a realm of allegories and hidden meanings was central to the thought of most of the eighteenth-century illuminati. For both Swedenborg and Saint-Martin there was a correspondence between the physical and spiritual worlds, and it was by means of this correspondence that men could communicate with heaven.

What was Fourier's relation to this whole tradition of thought? Obviously he did not share the Christian preoccupation with analogy as a means of leading the mind to God. Nor was he as concerned as classical thinkers with strictly political analogies—the notion of the body politic, the analogy between the faculties of the soul and the division of functions within the state. It is true that Fourier spoke of the human body as an "epitome of the movement of the universe" and that he determined the number of the passions and the size and structure of the Phalanx on the basis of analogies relating to the number of bones, muscles, and even teeth in the human body.[49] It is also true that Fourier, who possessed a copy of Kepler's *Harmonice mundi,* was fascinated by Kepler's vision of a universe shaped and structured by music and mathematics.[50] But still there is one respect in which Fourier's thought departed radically from that of earlier thinkers who viewed the universe as a mirror of man and of human concerns. For almost all the earlier thinkers the vision of the universe as a mirror of man served to provide reasons and justifications for the existing order of things. For the eighteenth-century illuminists just as for the Christian cosmographers of the later Middle Ages, everything in the world was exactly as God had intended it to be: snakes, insects, disease, and sorrow were all expressions of God's plan, parts of a larger providential design. For Fourier, on the other hand, the natural and divinely ordained order of things was not to be identified with the existing order. It was not a given. Rather, it was an order that had to be brought into being. And analogy itself was a critical instrument that served to widen horizons and reveal possibilities.

Fourier was thus one of a number of thinkers of the romantic period who drew on the classical and Christian tradition of analogical thinking but who saw analogy as pointing beyond the known world to a new world of restored harmonies and realized visions.[51] He may have had little knowledge of Saint-Martin and Swedenborg, but he shared with some of their early nineteenth-century heirs the belief that since nature could be read emblematically, the physical world offered clues to man's future destinies. For Fourier as for Blake the physical universe was not simply a mirror of man's present condition. It was also a rich source of symbols that could be used to evoke the promise of a more perfect order.

In this sense Fourier can be connected not only with his contemporaries in the romantic movement but also with the symbolist poets of a later generation. His theory of analogy anticipated their doctrine of correspondences and their conception of the poet as a "seer" whose images and analogies reveal the world's hidden unity.[52] Like Baudelaire and Rimbaud, Fourier regarded the natural world as a "forest of symbols" that could, if rightly understood, point beyond given realities to a new mode of existence. Fourier too was a "seer," a visionary, who dreamed, as did Rimbaud, of revealing to his readers the "silent pregnancies" of language and of life.

V

Fourier's writings on cosmogony and universal analogy have been a source of both wonderment and amusement to generations of readers. His early disciples were alternately intrigued and embarrassed by them; and although his first reviewers scoffed at Fourier's "stellar reveries," later generations discovered in them what Marx and Engels referred to as a "vein of true poetry." In recent years, and thanks largely to the efforts of André Breton and his surrealist group, Fourier's creative gifts have been recognized and serious consideration has been given to the imaginative qualities of his "mathematical poem."[53] Nevertheless, there remains something deeply enigmatic about the writings on cosmogony and universal analogy, something that has struck almost all those who have studied these works with care and attention. Thus Simone Debout, the author of several of the best essays on Fourier's "mathematical poem," could speak of Fourier as the creator of a "complex, coldly calculated puzzle," and Emile Lehouck could devote a chapter of his important study of Fourier to "the riddle of the cosmogony."[54]

The first and fundamental question is that of Fourier's own attitude toward these writings. A recent critic has noted the "perplexing contrast" between Fourier's apparent seriousness in unfolding the many marvels of his cosmogony and the mock-heroic tone he often adopted in his critique of civilization and his accounts of the amorous life of the Phalanx.[55] The humorous writings were clearly meant to be taken seriously, but was Fourier's seriousness a pose? At times he was certainly capable of extraordinary detachment with regard to his own work, as, for example, when he could speak of himself as having donned the mask of inspiration in the chapters on cosmogony in the *Quatre mouvements*. In his later years, when he was desperately engaged in the search

[349]

for a backer, he often minimized the importance of the esoteric aspects of his doctrine, claiming that he did not "require" his readers to accept his cosmogony and trying to pass off his theory of universal analogy as mere "entertainment for the ladies." Fourier knew well that by the rational standards of ordinary men his antilions and his *archibras* were utterly fantastic. And yet, I have argued, Fourier himself believed in the essential truth of his own fantasies.[56] He may have warned his audience against too literal a reading of his speculations on cosmogony and analogy, but he never disowned them and when he revised the *Quatre mouvements* after 1815 it was in fact only to make corrections of detail.

Even if one assumes that Fourier took his ideas on cosmogony and universal analogy quite seriously, it is still not clear how *we* should take them. It can be argued that even though these theories are entertaining, they ultimately constitute relatively minor branches of the doctrine and can safely be relegated to a museum of inessential Fourierist curiosities. There is nothing wrong with this, if one's aim is simply to appropriate what is "living" in Fourier for one's own purposes. On the other hand, Fourier's theory was conceived as a unified whole. If one's aim is to understand how Fourier arrived at his ideas and why he held them, if one wants to understand the inner logic of Fourier's thought, it must be considered in its totality.

Another approach to the writings on cosmogony and analogy is to read them allegorically, as imaginative prophecies of subsequent developments in science and technology. This was for many years standard procedure among those historians who were primarily interested in Fourier's contribution to the development of socialist ideology. Thus, writing in 1937, Felix Armand and René Maublanc described Fourier's conception of an aromal movement as a "confused anticipation" of "electricity, radioactivity and cosmic rays."[57] Other well-meaning readers have interpreted Fourier's "unitary language" as a forerunner of Esperanto, and his antilions and anticrocodiles as "obscure predictions" of the railroad train and steamship. The problem with this approach is its sheer banality. It trivializes just those aspects of Fourier's thought in which the vein of poetry runs deepest.

It is as a poem of sorts that I think Fourier's cosmogony can best be seen, a poem that should not be taken too literally but that does give life and substance to the concept of the universe as a mirror of human concerns and translates into cosmic terms the themes and preoccupations of Fourier's social analysis. When Charles Fourier looked into the starry heavens, he did not see the "astres fainéants" to which traditional astronomy had attributed useless promenades around the empyrean. What he did see was an image of ordered spontaneity that mirrored the material and emotional life of the Phalanx. Just as each Phalanx had its officers and common soldiers, its uniforms, maneuvers, and parade groups, the stars also had their own military hierarchy, their forced marches, and their rescue columns. In Fourier's lush and varied imagery each planet was sometimes a "worker" and sometimes a "lover," and the cosmos as a whole pulsated with activity and sexual energy. In some of his descriptions the heavens had the aspect of a vast field of copulation, its space "crisscrossed like bullets on a field of battle" by the sexually charged aromas emitted by each planet. In other more prosaic accounts Fourier's imagery was domestic and agricultural: the planets had their "furnishings" of animal and vegetable species and the heavens were a "sidereal apple" or simply a "starry gourd."[58]

In all of this Fourier's constant concern seems to have been to describe the natural world in terms that stripped it of its terror and strangeness while, at the same time, affirming the centrality of human beings and human concerns in the ongoing life of the cosmos. There were, to be sure, some aspects of the natural world that Fourier found deeply disturbing. Like many seventeenth-century theists with an interest in science, he was troubled by such irregularities in the structure of the physical universe as the seemingly random distribution of the stars in space and of the planets and moons in the solar system. "What a sight is our universe," he could write, "with suns heaped up at random like piles of apples in storehouses and empty spaces without proportion or utility."[59] What sense could Fourier make of such apparent instances of disorder and chaos? Most often he attributed them to flaws in the physical design of the universe that were a necessary but transitory counterpart to a flawed social world. Just as poisonous snakes and bothersome insects would disappear with the coming of Harmony, so too the whole universe would contract to form a more compact and orderly whole.[60]

Like Pascal in one of his most famous *Pensées*, Fourier may well have been "terrified" by "the eternal silence of the infinite spaces."[61] But he could not bear to live in an incomprehensible universe ruled by a hidden God. His response to the apparent disorder and chaos of the natural world was to seek one underlying principle of order. His response to the "silence" and incomprehensibility of nature was to make

it speak a familiar language, to proceed from the assumption that everything in nature must have a human meaning.

Fourier's achievement as a cosmologist, then, was to create a myth
that placed human beings and human concerns at the center of the life
of the cosmos. The most striking feature of this myth was the stress
placed by Fourier on man's role in the whole process of cosmic change.

> Any man who has the means to found a [Phalanx] . . . can
> bring about changes in the temperament of the planet, correct
> its aromas, change its temperature and atmosphere, cleanse the
> seas, stock them with magnificent new species, make changes
> in the aromas of the sun and the various stars, move five of
> them so that they orbit around our globe, and adorn the globe
> with two rings like Saturn.[62]

It would be hard to find a more radical affirmation of the power of
human beings to shape their own universe. If Fourier issued a warning
concerning the cosmic disorders likely to result from man's continued
failure to establish a harmonic social order on earth, finally I believe, his
message was affirmative: his cosmological poem should be seen as a
celebration of human powers and human possibilities.

III

Parisian Prophet

Fourier's theory of association is making immense strides, but since Fourier was totally without elegance and since he never appeared in the
salons, it will be twenty years before he is accorded his rightful place as a sublime dreamer.

Stendhal, Mémoires d'un touriste
(Paris: Le Divan, 1929), III, 277.

18

Publicizing the Treatise

IN THE FIRST days of November 1822 Charles Fourier made final arrangements for the shipment to Paris of more than five hundred copies of the *Traité de l'association domestique-agricole.*[1] He then packed his bags, bade farewell to Just Muiron, and set off on the four-day trip by diligence from Besançon to the capital. His purpose in going to Paris was to "activate" the sale of the treatise and to seek out the *fondateur,* the rich capitalist or philanthropist who was going to subsidize the establishment of the first trial Phalanx. This move to Paris was to bring about a change both in Fourier's personal life and in the character of his work. He was now fifty years old; and he had spent all but a very small part of his life in the provinces. Henceforth, with the exception of relatively brief sojourns at Lyon and Besançon, he was a Parisian. He still had fifteen years to live. But the period of intense creative activity that had begun with his retirement to Bugey was over. For the rest of his life the search for a wealthy patron was to absorb almost all his time and energies.

In considering the earlier, provincial years, we have noted that the Fourier of Charles Pellarin's biography is at best a caricature. But at this point, beginning with Fourier's move to Paris, the caricature becomes a recognizable portrait. Whereas the young traveling salesman from Lyon seems to have been a man of diverse interests and varied ambitions, Fourier's life at Paris became completely bound up with his discovery. The story of his last fifteen years is largely a chronicle of his efforts to secure financial backing and, at the same time, to protect himself against the wiles of the plagiarists. In essence if not in literal fact, the Fourier of the 1820s and 1830s is the Fourier described in Béranger's famous anecdote: the man who was so obsessed by his vision that he made a point of returning home every day at noon because that was the hour he had set for the rendezvous with his benefactor.[2]

Just as Fourier's move to Paris had brought a change in his preoccupations and his daily activities, it also brought a change in the character of his work and in its meaning to him. During his years in Lyon and Belley writing had been for Fourier an act, or a process, of discovery. When he described himself at that time as embarked on the exploration of a "new world" he seems to have meant something quite literal. For he had succeeded in tapping, or making contact with, a deep and almost inaccessible stratum of his mind. "My reservoir of ideas is like the source of the Nile," he could write, "it is not known, but it yields in abundance."[3] This ability to enlarge upon his original insights by drawing from a hidden "reservoir of ideas" was characteristic of Fourier's work until the completion of the *Traité*. After that time he lost it. He began to repeat himself, not only out of habit but also by design. For the rest of his life his principal desire was to simplify his doctrine, to present it in a bold and striking form that would appeal to the public and win him financial backing. His later books and pamphlets were filled with lists of potential benefactors. In his zeal to win their support he began to adopt the techniques of modern advertising: pithy slogans, bold and varied typefaces, moneymaking proposals—anything that would "sell" his theory.

In his growing preoccupation, during the 1820s and 1830s, with techniques of publicity and advertising, Fourier was in step with his time. During these years, with innovations in the production of paper and the setting of type and with the flowering first of the feuilleton and then of the paid advertisement, French journalism and publishing were awakening from their long sleep during the Napoleonic period. Newspapers were growing in size and readers and influence; and the journalist was beginning to become what Balzac could describe as the "manufacturer" and "assassin" of "ideas and reputations in industry, literature, and drama."[4] The paid *réclame* had escaped the confines of the back page of the paper, and it too was burgeoning in both size and seductiveness. By the end of the 1820s an inventive publicist like Louis Véron was making a fortune vaunting the merits of the pâté Regnault on the pages of the *Quotidienne,* while lesser journalists like Balzac's Etienne Lousteau could earn thirty francs for a few hundred words of banter on some carminative water or cephalic oil. Since the commodity that Fourier had to offer—his theory—was infinitely more beneficial than all the pâtés and oils and waters ever devised, he did not expect to fare worse with the same selling techniques.

I

Upon reaching Paris Fourier found himself temporary lodgings "chez M. Saussol" at 41, rue de Grenelle Saint-Honoré. A few weeks later he took a room at the Hotel Saint-Roche at 39, rue Neuve Saint Roche. This was to remain his home until the spring of 1825. No sooner had Fourier arrived than he set about the task for which he had come: that of promoting the sale of his book and seeking out the *fondateur.* His energy was extraordinary. He dispatched copies of the treatise to members of the government, to the opposition, to influential bankers, peers, philanthropists, men of science, donors of prizes, academicians, journalists, to anyone in a position to finance, or to convince others to finance, the establishment of a trial Phalanx. Copies also went out to old friends from Besançon and Lyon like Désiré Ordinaire, Jean-Victor Couchery, and L.-V.-F. Amard; to former business associates like Jean-Baptiste Gaucel; to writers such as Charles Nodier and Amédée Pichot; and to Alexandre La Chevardière, former shareholder and director of one of Saint-Simon's more ephemeral journals, *Le Politique.*[5]

With each copy Fourier included a letter, sometimes a short treatise, showing how the immediate establishment of a trial Phalanx might serve the special interests of the recipient. In sending the treatise to Villèle, the head of the government and champion of the "émigrés' billion," he enclosed a twelve-page letter describing his theory as a sure-fire means to indemnify the émigrés. To liberals such as Benjamin Constant, Voyer d'Argenson, Girardin, and Bignon, he sent "a very forceful circular on the bad situation of the liberal party and on the means of salvation that is open to it." To Count Grégoire, an opponent of the slave trade, he promised "the freeing of all the slaves, black and white with no exceptions." And he continued: "I have heard that you are in correspondence with President Boyer [of Haiti] for whom the trial would not cost as much as a hundred thousand francs in advances on which there would be a large profit." If Grégoire could convince the Haitian president to sponsor a trial, Fourier promised to go to Santo Domingo himself to supervise activities. "In six weeks," he boasted, "our work will be concluded."[6]

Fourier seized upon the slightest pretext to gain a hearing. In notifying the minister of the interior that he had made his *dépôt légal* at the Besançon Prefecture, he added four closely written pages about the "special allure" of his theory for the king of France. Very few of these letters elicited so much as a response. And when answers did come, they were hardly encouraging. Villèle, for example, replied merely to acknowledge the receipt of "your work entitled *Projet d'organisation domestique-agricole.*"[7]

In addition to his appeals to individuals, Fourier also sent copies of his work to the major learned societies and journals of the French capital. He attempted to enter his treatise in a competition sponsored by the Paris Geographical Society, and he sought the patronage of a variety of other groups ranging from Count Chaptal's Society for the Encouragement of Industry to La Rochefoucauld-Liancourt's Society for the Promotion of Christian Morality.[8] In his appeals to the journalists Fourier stressed his reluctance to make undue demands on their time. He needed publicity. But to save them the trouble of actually reading the book, he offered to compose "reviews of any kind and in any tone."[9] Fourier's offers to serve as his own critic were not out of line with the journalistic conventions of the Restoration. They might have been accepted had be been able to pay for the opportunity. But he could not pay; and until the end of February 1823 the sole acknowledgement of the *Traité* in the Paris press was a three-line *annonce* in the *Courrier français.*[10]

At last in the middle of March a review of Fourier's book was actually published in a Paris journal. The journal, a small liberal daily called *Le Miroir,* was not particularly influential, and the review itself was ill informed and hastily written. Its initial installment consisted largely of a rehearsal of some of Fourier's more extravagant prophecies.

He promises to triple the wealth of the globe, to eliminate all debts . . . to dry up the source of the malignant passions. Finally (Oh, marvelous perspective!) he guarantees us ONE HUNDRED AND TWENTY YEARS of *active exercise* in love.

This was followed, however, by more sympathetic comment concerning the book's mixture of "satire and erudition," of "just calculation" and "frightful imagination." The reviewer concluded by describing the book in breathless if rather nebulous terms as "one of the most singular, the newest, the most bizarre, the most vast systems that the philosophical intellect has yet succeeded in constructing and in founding on bases that are sometimes imaginary and sometimes scientific and positive."[11]

In the weeks that followed two more reviews appeared. In one of them the reviewer, who admitted to having only dipped into the treatise, complained about the obscurity of Fourier's style. But he went on to observe that Fourier was "clear in his bitter satire of the social state."[12] In the other review, which Fourier believed to have been written by the well-known liberal publicist, Etienne de Jouy, recognition was given once again to Fourier's talent as a social satirist: "In those pages on which he exposes our vices he rises to a sort of satirical philosophy most worthy of notice." If this article was in fact by de Jouy, himself a satirist of some talent and great influence, this was praise that meant something. But it was hardly of a nature to satisfy Fourier, who later wrote that to be complimented for his "satirical philosophy" was an honor to which he did not aspire.[13]

In May of 1823 a fourth and final review appeared in the liberal quarterly, *La Revue encyclopédique*. The author, who signed himself "Ferry," was actually no more harsh in his judgments than any of the other reviewers. He poked fun at the "obscurity" of the book's style and organization, but conceded that "everything is not obscure in this work: we understand the author easily enough when he criticizes us; it is when he seeks to reform us that he becomes less intelligible." There was, however, a tone of ironic condescension in this review that was lacking in the others. Observing that Fourier wished to "enrich" the "science of social relations" with a new language, the reviewer remarked that the comprehension of that language was "above his strength." He then proceeded to correct Fourier on a point of Roman history, and to confess his reluctance to believe "before the proof is given, that orange trees can be made to grow . . . on the shores of the Arctic sea."[14]

II

In early June of 1823 Fourier reflected on the result of his efforts to get a hearing for his ideas in Paris.

> A discovery has cost twenty-four years of labor. The author spends six months at Paris waiting to see his book reviewed in the journals. What does he get? Cabalistic comments likely to discourage people from ever reading his work.[15]

The last review by Ferry was particularly galling to Fourier. Behind so "insidious" a "travesty" he detected the hand of his enemies, the "cabal" of Parisian philosophers. It was they who had ordered Ferry to write the review. In presenting Fourier "not as an inventor but as an ignorant *littérateur*" they were trying to make sure that his book would never be read.[16]

In an effort to justify himself, Fourier once again made the rounds of the journals. In conversation with editors, journalists, their clerks and concierges, with anyone who would lend an ear, he renewed his pleas for a fair hearing. He conceded that from a stylistic point of view the book had "none of the suppleness required in modern writings." This had given the *zoiles* the pretext they needed for discrediting it. Ridiculing the book for its bizarre form, they had failed to examine its rigorously exact *fond*. Their facetious tone had misled the public. But their real motives were clear enough: "It is for having too well defined the errors of philosophy that this work is exposed to its sinister designs."[17]

Unable to get a fair hearing, Fourier decided in the summer of 1823 to publish at his own expense a pamphlet summarizing the main points of the treatise and exposing the machinations of the philosophical cabal. This pamphlet, which he wrote in a few weeks, bore the title *Sommaires et annonce du Traité de l'association domestique-agricole*. Like the initial sections of the *Traité* itself, it was crammed full of brief doctrinal "lessons," lists of the "servitudes and duperies" of the philosophers, enticing incentives for the *fondateur,* and cross-references to the body of the treatise. There were also delightful notes on "burlesque social archaeology" and on the parrot, "the emblem of the false philosopher." But as a summary the pamphlet was confusing. For while expounding his theory, Fourier kept up a counterpoint of attacks on philosophy and comments on current events ranging from the war in Spain and earthquakes in Chile to the demolition of the Paris opera and the appearance of Dr. Amard's new book. At the same time he kept reminding potential backers of his "selling points," the *motifs d'attention:* "the tripling of income, extinction of public debts in all countries, reimbursement of ten billion in revolutionary debts, utilization of truth and virtue, accession of the savages and abundance of colonial goods, unities of every sort."[18]

Fourier's chief aim in the *Sommaires,* however, was to answer his critics and to propose a remedy for "the anarchy of criticism, the tyranny that weighs on the world of the intellect where a philosophical committee influences everything and defames or suppresses everything that gives it umbrage."[19] Thus he chronicled in detail the mistreatment that he had suffered at the hands of the Parisian journalists. He first summarized the general criticisms of his work, insisting that the charges of obscurity and lack of method were pretexts invoked to evade the issues that he had raised. Then he proceeded to analyze the reviews according to genre. The best of them, de Jouy's review, was the sole example of "decent criticism." But even there, wrote Fourier, "every line is a *social cacography,* an accumulation of errors that seem expressly designed to provide the student with instruction."[20]

Fourier insisted that there was nothing unique about the treatment he had received from the reviewers. It was the sort of welcome that France had always given to new ideas. But there was a way to be sure that inventors received a fair hearing in France. Fourier went on to propose the creation of an "examining jury" to verify discoveries made by unknown inventors, and of a *police d'invention* to punish plagiarists and settle disputes between inventors and their critics. All over Paris one could read posters proclaiming the judgment of impartial juries and expert committees on biscuits and bath waters. Fourier asked that useful inventions be accorded the same treatment: "As long as new and exact sciences are denied an examining jury of the sort that is granted to nostrums and biscuits, to PERRUQUES PHILOGENES and POMMADES PHILOCOMES, the critics will have no trouble in getting rid of inventors by treating them as academic pretenders and harrassing them on matters of form while totally ignoring the content."[21]

By September 1823 Fourier had completed the manuscript of the *Sommaires.* But while the book was in press he continued to write, grinding out more prefatory material designed to catch the eye of even the hastiest, most negligent reader. Thus when the book finally appeared, the main body of the text was preceded by an eight-page *Argument du sommaire,* a special *Avis aux journalistes,* a proposal for a Rural Shareholders' Bank, an *Avertissement aux propriétaires et capitalistes sur le triplement du revenu en association,* and finally *Instructions pour le vendeur et l'acheteur,* presenting in dialogue form the sales pitch to be used by booksellers who had not read the book. Unwilling to rely on the modest efforts of the booksellers, Fourier then began to lay plans for a new publicity campaign. He filled his notebooks with abbreviated personal directives.

> Proceed briskly and to the goal. Publicize association despite philosophers. Speak to the king. Provoke a subscription and bear in mind: no other way of full reimbursement.[22]

He carefully copied down in his notebook the names and addresses, culled from reference books like the *Almanach du Roi* and Bottin's new *Almanach du Commerce,* of highly placed individuals who might conceivably be interested in lending financial or moral support to his enterprise.

During the last three months of 1823 the distribution of the *Sommaires* was Fourier's sole preoccupation. He haunted the elegant quarters of Paris, delivering the book personally to the door of many a candidate. Generally he included with it a brief, neatly penned form letter that read:

> The intrigues of a scientific party that is all-powerful with respect to the journals have prevented the announcement of this discovery, which humiliates the sophists and undermines their systems. Thus the author is making the announcement himself by means of a summary distributed by residence. 10 francs (instead of 12) for a copy of the treatise corrected in pen if you buy it from the author, C.F., rue Neuve Saint Roche, Hotel Saint-Roche, 39. In case of absence, contact the proprietor or the porter of the hotel.[23]

At the homes of particularly promising candidates Fourier left copies of the treatise as well as the *Sommaires,* along with voluminous letters. Most of these letters were no doubt promptly relegated to the wastebasket. But one that has survived, addressed to the United States Consul at Paris, John Barnet, is probably representative of the special appeals made by Fourier to would-be *fondateurs.*

> No country [wrote Fourier] has a greater interest than yours in
> verifying the discovery that I am publishing. You need to con-
> trol your fierce neighbors, the Creeks, the Cherokees, etc.
> These savages, like all [nomadic] hordes, will only adopt agri-
> culture if it is presented to them in the natural and attractive
> order, the order of *contrasted series.* The trial that is likely to
> bring about the adhesion of all these savages will be even less
> costly in the United States than in Europe, since land and tim-
> ber are abundant in America.[24]

In addition to special appeals like this Fourier also drafted another round
of letters to the editors of the Paris journals. Attempting this time to
adopt a more circumspect tone, he informed the editor of the *Journal des
débats* that the trial Phalanx was a sober experiment in agricultural association that might involve as few as five hundred "cultivateurs."[25] And in
writing daily newspapers, he offered his services as a potential collaborator. He volunteered to write a series of "detached articles, sometimes
amusing and sometimes grave," that would focus attention on the "scientific and industrial blunders" of competing papers. All of these articles
would be linked to a body of doctrine that he would communicate to the
editors. But their readers would only be initiated gradually, painlessly,
until the journal in question could openly declare itself partisan of Fourier's theory of association.[26]

For several months this new effort to bring attention to the treatise
bore no result. Even a journal like *Le Drapeau blanc,* on which Fourier's
old Lyon acquaintance Martainville ruled supreme, refused to grant him
so much as an *annonce.* A few recipients of the *Sommaires* like Benjamin
Constant sent polite letters of acknowledgment. But from most of
them he heard nothing. Finally at the beginning of 1824 a single review
was published in a small journal called the *Bulletin universel des sciences et
de l'industrie.* The author of the review, baron de Férussac, expressed the
familiar criticism about Fourier's manner of presenting his ideas: his
work was lacking in clarity and "difficult to read in every respect." But
Férussac went on to argue that Fourier's "basic idea" of association was
"of the greatest interest." And he predicted that "if the development of
the human intellect and of the population is not halted, the force of
circumstance will lead to the application of [Fourier's] idea." Férussac
concluded by urging either Fourier himself or some other "capable and
laborious" individual to attempt to restate Fourier's ideas in a manner
more "accessible to the public."[27]

Despite the qualifications and even though he could list "seven errors" contained in this review, Fourier was delighted by it. It marked one of the few occasions in his lifetime when he was able to see his ideas taken seriously by a member of the intellectual establishment. Unfortunately it led to nothing. More typical of the response to Fourier's work was probably the comment of the American consul, John Barnet. Forwarding Fourier's book unread to a friend, Barnet described it as "appearing at a glance . . . as either a genuine curiosity or the emanation of a disturbed brain."[28]

On January 3, 1824, Fourier informed Muiron that the distribution of the *Sommaires* at Paris had stimulated sales of the treatise by a grand total of three copies. "The Parisians," he wrote, "are creatures of habit, and if they are not pushed on by the journals, nothing can stimulate them." A month later the situation had not changed. "You are astonished (and so am I) that the *Sommaire* has had no effect," he wrote to Muiron. "I did not make allowances for the fact that the so-called savant and lettered class is so despised that a man who arrives from the provinces with a discovery is regarded as someone dangerous who must be avoided. Would you believe that M. de Villebois, who at Belley asked me for a memorandum (sent in forty pages), has not even acknowledged receipt of the copy of the *Sommaire* I sent him along with a letter. After this, need we be astonished if the de Jouys, the Keratrys, and others do not wish to respond?"[29]

III

Among all of Fourier's efforts to draw attention to the theory there is one that has particular historical interest. This is his attempt to get support for his ideas from the great English communitarian socialist, Robert Owen.

Although Robert Owen was just a year older than Fourier, and although his first practical experiments in enlightened factory management dated from about the same time as Fourier's first steps as a thinker, Owen had already become a European celebrity at a time when Fourier was still buried in provincial obscurity. Owen owed his celebrity in part to the simplicity of his basic principles of social engineering: he was at bottom a thoroughgoing environmentalist with an unstinting faith in the power of good education and good working conditions to make good men. But the main reason for Owen's fame was that it seemed to many of his contemporaries that his claims about the malleability of human nature were borne out by the success of the model community he had established at the beginning of the century at New Lanark in Scotland.[30]

It was around 1818, after a triumphant tour of the Continent, that Owen's works first began to be translated into French and seriously discussed in the French press.[31] One of the major forums for such discussion was Marc-Antoine Jullien's liberal journal, *La Revue encyclopédique;* and it was probably through this journal, which Fourier read regularly, that he first heard about Owen and his community at New Lanark. At any rate, as early as 1820 Fourier was already referring in his manuscripts to New Lanark as a "forerunner" of association. In drafts of his "Note to the Academy of Belley" he criticized the large size of Owen's community but praised him for "confronting so important a problem."[32]

From the start Fourier looked on Owen as a potential convert to his own ideas. He praised Owen as an "expectant" philosopher but qualified his praise with specific criticism of Owen's plan of association. Thus in the text of the *Traité* Fourier described Owen as "the first who has made *practical* investigations and experiments in association," and he referred to New Lanark as a "precious" enterprise that appeared to yield "several of the material advantages of association."[33] But still, "relying on information provided by journalists," Fourier noted five "crucial mistakes" made in the organization of the Owenite community. First of all, at three thousand people New Lanark was too big. Second, Fourier believed that Owen's community was not sufficiently diversified. In recruiting members who were roughly equal in wealth, Owen had deprived himself of the indispensable stimulus of contrast, and he had demonstrated his incapacity to form compound series. Fourier also criticized the absence of agricultural workers in Owen's community. "In itself manufacturing work cannot suffice to establish the societary bond," he insisted. For agricultural labor was not only more attractive to most people, it was also "the principal aliment of industrial rivalries and intrigues." Fourier's fourth point had to do with the discipline at New Lanark, which he regarded as "judiciously administered but severe to the point of austerity." Owen's "monastical statutes" were "far from being an *attractive* form of association." Finally, Fourier believed that in failing to divide profits proportionally according to input in capital, labor, and talent, Owen had deprived himself of the crucial stimulus of "interest."[34]

While Fourier carefully noted all the "blunders" committed at New Lanark, he preferred in his *Traité* to emphasize the positive aspects of Owen's enterprise. Praising Owen's "speculative modesty" as well as his "visible" accomplishments, he accorded "les Owenistes" a special rank, slightly superior to Civilization, in the scheme of historical periodization included in the *Traité*. As Fourier put it in his own special terminology: "I believe that [New Lanark] merits the rank of 5¼, and that it provides a half-exit from Civilization, an ascending half-transition."[35]

Until the publication of the *Traité* all of Fourier's information concerning the Owenites seems to have come by way of the press.[36] But sometime in 1823 Fourier made the acquaintance of an Irishwoman who was able to tell him more about Owen and his work. Mrs. Anna Doyle Wheeler was a much-traveled Irish feminist of high birth and radical opinions.* In close contact with the British Owenites, the Ben-

---

*Anna Doyle Wheeler (1785–18 ?) was the daughter of an eminent Irish Protestant clergyman and a godchild of the Irish nationalist leader, Henry Grattan. Renowned for her beauty and intelligence, she was married at fifteen to Francis Massy Wheeler, the alcoholic scion of a family of "titled fools." In twelve years of dismal married life she had half a dozen children, of whom only two survived: Henrietta (1800–1826) and Rosina (1802–1882), whose divorce from Edward Bulwer-Lytton created one of the minor scandals of the Victorian era. In 1812 Anna Wheeler left her husband to begin an odyssey that took her first to Guernsey, where her uncle, Sir John Doyle, was then governor. Presiding over the cosmopolitan society of Government House, she was toasted by visiting émigrés like the duke of Brunswick and courted by the seventy-two-year-old duc de Bouillon, a cousin of the future King Charles X of France. Having driven her uncle deeply into debt, she went on in 1816 to London, Dublin, and then to Caen, where she was celebrated by a group of admirers as "the Goddess of Reason" and "the most gifted woman of the age." She returned to Ireland after her husband's death in 1820, and then moved to Paris, where Fourier met her in 1823. Their relationship soon became close; and in 1826, at the time of her daughter Henrietta's death, Fourier consoled her with his theories on metempsychosis. In the late twenties and early thirties she helped draw attention to Fourier's ideas in British cooperatist and Owenite milieus, and she also distributed copies of his later works to William Thompson, Daniel O'Connell, and Lady Byron, among others. Her friendship with Jeremy Bentham, Robert Owen, William Thompson, and their disciples dated from the early 1820s. Her relationship with Thompson was particularly close. In dedicating to her his pioneering feminist work, *Appeal of One Half of the Human Race . . .* (1825), Thompson described himself as no more than her "scribe and interpreter." See Richard K. P. Pankhurst, "Anna Wheeler: Pioneer Socialist and Feminist," *Political Quarterly,* XXV, 2 (April-June 1954), 132–143; and also Barbara Taylor, *Eve and the New Jerusalem: Socialism and Feminism in the Nineteenth Century* (New York, 1983), 59–65; Pankhurst, *William Thompson* (London, 1954), 17–18, 70–78;

thamites, and the Ricardian socialist William Thompson, she had only recently taken up residence in Paris with an entourage that included two daughters in their early twenties and a certain Lieutenant Smith. How or exactly when Fourier became acquainted with her is not known. In any case she seems to have been a gifted and outspoken woman, radical in her sympathies and eclectic in her opinions. The young Benjamin Disraeli described her as "something between Jeremy Bentham and Meg Merrilies, very clever, but awfully revolutionary."[37] Fourier's ideas appealed to her; and within a short time after their first meeting he seems to have become a regular visitor to her salon.

Apparently Anna Wheeler tried to arrange a meeting between Fourier and Owen in August of 1823. Although nothing came of it, she did bring Fourier into contact with a number of Owen's disciples, and she seems to have played a role in heightening Fourier's hopes concerning Owen. These were high by the summer of 1823 when Fourier inserted the following note into the text of the *Sommaires:*

> According to the announcement I have just read in the *Revue encyclopédique,* Monsieur Owen has decided to found a societary-agricultural community, and no doubt in a more favorable location than New Lanark. . . . If Monsieur Owen, who is going to be informed of the discovery, decides to deviate from civilized methods . . . we can regard the transition to the seventh period as certain. At present everything depends on his decision, for he has the credit necessary to get the job done. If he appreciates the plan of *compound action,* in which passionate and industrial ties are combined, then Civilization is over and done with.[38]

It was only in the spring of 1824 that Fourier managed to get in touch with Robert Owen. In a letter dated April 2, 1824, he appealed to Owen in flattering terms: "You cannot be indifferent concerning the discovery. You have made such notable trials in your experiments with association that it is important for you to know whether or not the true method has been discovered." Fourier then offered Owen his collaboration in the establishment of a Phalanx. Of course, wrote Fourier, there were many forms this collaboration might take. Owen could simply

---

Michael Sadleir, *Bulwer, A Panorama.* Part I, *Edward and Rosina* (Boston, 1931), esp. 67–77; Louisa Devey, *Life of Rosina, Lady Lytton* (London, 1887), 1–38. For Anna Wheeler's correspondence with Fourier see AN 10AS 25 (3bis) and 10AS 25 (3).

play Isabella to Fourier's Columbus. Or he could lend his name, and if possible his purse, to the organization of a competition in which Fourier's theory of association might be tested against all comers. Or he could hire Fourier as a consultant in techniques of association.

> If you are agreeable, I propose to engage myself with you, at the salary of the least of your clerks, as the individual responsible for the direction of the mechanism. I am not seeking personal profit but only the opportunity to work and to confront my detractors after two months with the denial Columbus gave to his century when it treated him as a visionary.

Accompanying this proposal were two copies of the *Traité*.[39]

On receiving Fourier's letter Robert Owen, who did not read French, passed it on to one of his disciples, Philip Orkney Skene. Skene, an ex-army officer and professor of languages who helped Owen with his foreign correspondence, replied politely and at length. He explained that "after a rapid examination of the two volumes of [the] treatise on association," he had summarized Fourier's ideas to Owen, who was interested but not in a position to use Fourier's services. Regretting Fourier's limited knowledge of Owen's doctrine, Skene proceeded to expound it in terms that he hoped would be congenial to Fourier. ("Monsieur Owen's original plans . . . are not in effect different from those of a simple domestic-agricultural association.") He then concluded in language that was both flattering and noncommittal: "I must thank you personally, sir, for the pleasure I derived from the reading of your work. Your tableaux of the vices of civilization are charming in their truth and in their strength. The idea of the passionate series seems quite original to me."[40]

Fourier was not daunted by Skene's tactful rejection of his offer of collaboration. On August 25, 1824, in informing Muiron of the letter, he was optimistic. "He praises my work a great deal and informs me that Monsieur Owen is about to found a new establishment at Motherwell in Scotland. . . . If I am employed there, as I shall request of him, I could strike the decisive blow next spring."[41] A few weeks later Fourier replied to Skene, again offering his services. The experiments at New Lanark, Hoogstraeten, and elsewhere had obviously resulted in an "avortement politique," Fourier observed, "since the neighboring populations have not been inspired to a spontaneous and sudden imitation."

But if only thirty meshed series can be formed at Motherwell and if I am employed to prevent errors from occurring, the result will be that merely by working with the poor class, we will attract the middle class, which will want to purchase shares and install itself in the place of the poor families.

The wealthy would become interested in their turn, and in no time at all, promised Fourier, London would yield a rich harvest of subscribers for the establishment of a full-scale Phalanx. Thus "Monsieur Owen could, by next summer, win over the world from Motherwell." Naturally there were mistakes to be avoided; and for this reason Fourier's own presence was necessary.

> You run a grave risk of coming to grief if you proceed without an experienced pilot. You mustn't think of me as an ordinary employee who is advancing himself out of a desire for money. My intervention will be the guarantee of a brilliant future for you and even more for Monsieur Owen, who as founder of the association will win the title of Social Messiah. . . . This is enough to let you know how important it is for all of you including Monsieur Owen to employ me at Motherwell at the wages of the lowest clerk. If I were rich I would go there at my own expense.[42]

Fourier received no reply to this second appeal. The reason may have been that by the fall of 1824 Owen and his collaborators had virtually given up on the experiment at Motherwell and had become absorbed in preparations for the community they were soon to create at New Harmony in Indiana. Fourier was not for some time aware of this. He remained optimistic about the prospects for a trial in England, and he continued to speak of the possibility of going to Motherwell to assume direction of the Owenite venture there.

Eventually Fourier was brought up to date on Owen's new ventures by Anna Wheeler and Lieutenant Smith. But this did nothing to dampen his hopes. On April 1, 1825, he could write Muiron enthusiastically about the acclaim Owen was receiving on his progress through America and about his own prospects of influencing the direction to be taken by the newly formed Owenite London Cooperative Society. He could also report that his *Traité* had captured the interest of Anna Wheeler's close friend, the Ricardian socialist William Thompson.

I know that an individual named Thompson, who is interested in association and to whom my book has been communicated, has translated a number of selections from it into English. He has also discussed it with people competent in the matter, and the result is that it should be easy to convince [the London Cooperative Society] to engage my services for the testing of the method of attraction.[43]

Fourier's hopes were as usual exaggerated. But it is a fact that William Thompson was genuinely interested in Fourier's ideas. His later works show signs of Fourier's influence, and it is likely that he was the anonymous author of a brief set of translations from Fourier published by the London Cooperative Society in 1828 under the title *Political Economy Made Easy*.

Within a year after his correspondence with Philip Skene, however, Fourier had become completely disenchanted with Robert Owen's ideas. One reason for this seems to have been simply that he learned more about them. In August of 1825 Fourier met Skene at Lyon and received from him French translations of several works by Owen.[44] He read them and was not impressed.

I was myself hopeful about his ideas [Fourier wrote later], but now that I have read his Address to the Citizens of New Lanark and his monastical statutes, I see that he is imbued with all the prejudices most contrary to the system of industrial attraction and the equilibrium of the passions. He is quite simply a moralist.[45]

Whatever doubts had been raised in Fourier's mind by a reading of Owen's works were only intensified by his encounter in April of 1826 with several members of the London Cooperative Society. "Mrs Wheeler introduced me to the members of the London Cooperative Society," he wrote Muiron. "They are not very sharp and they are bloated with dogmatism. The Owenite school is extremely weak."[46]

In a draft of the *Nouveau monde industriel* that probably dates from 1827 Fourier briefly summed up his relations with the Owenites.

I was late in learning about Owen's doctrine, and when I praised the intentions of the author in 1822, I was far from presuming that his efforts were serving *in point of fact* to render the idea of association ridiculous and to make it suspect to all governments. . . . I believed in 1822 that [the group] had some good intentions . . . but the Owenists whom I have seen since that time have convinced me by their obstination in philosophism that there is no hope of getting them to undertake an experiment in true association.[47]

What disillusioned Fourier with the Owenites, then, seems to have been a combination of factors. When viewed at close range Owen's doctrine seemed depressingly moralistic and "monastic." Most of Owen's disciples seemed like pedants beside the exuberantly eclectic Anna Wheeler. By 1827 Fourier had also begun to fear that his own theories, and the idea of association itself, would be discredited by the difficulties encountered by Owen in New Harmony, Indiana. But the main reason for Fourier's disillusionment with the Owenites was probably a very simple one: he finally realized that the Owenites were committed to the doctrines of their own leader and were not the least bit interested in converting to his, or even in giving them a trial.

19

The Provincial in Paris

FOR MORE than a year the task of publicizing the *Traité* had been Fourier's sole preoccupation. But by the beginning of 1824 it had become obvious that the book was a failure. Baron de Férussac's comments on the "repugnant" style and form of the treatise only confirmed a verdict already rendered by other less sympathetic journalists. Even at Besançon, among the friends of Just Muiron, the book received only a lukewarm reception. Some of Muiron's friends regretted Fourier's insistence on linking the "positive elements" of his theory to extravagant speculations on the melting of the polar ice and the theory of analogy.[1] Others, who were not at all disturbed by Fourier's cosmogony and his theory of universal analogy, were offended by his treatment of sex and religion. Despite their interest in esoteric ideas, Muiron's friends were for the most part pious people with conventional moral standards. Thus the old Freemason Raymond de Raymond voiced fears that the treatise would "shake his faith" and Désiré-Adrien Gréa criticized the theory of immortality as "folly."[2] François-Joseph Génisset, a professor of Latin at the University of Besançon, asked bluntly: "Who will be the God of the new association? What religion could be sufficiently flexible in its dogmas, sufficiently tolerant in its moral standards to countenance the play of all the passions and to encourage their free expression?" Could it be, asked Génisset, that "the Cross, which stands at the summit of Calvary," will be "henceforth replaced by the waving banner of the Phalanstery?"[3]

Not all the readers of the *Traité* were equally sensitive to, or repelled by, its blasphemous implications. But they all had reservations of one sort or another, and they were almost unanimous in criticizing the organization of the book and its author's penchant for neologisms. The general tenor of the criticism that Fourier received from even his most sympathetic readers is perhaps best expressed by a letter written to Fourier in 1824 by a lawyer from Dijon named Gabriel Gabet.

> The ideas that you had to present are capable of astonishing the boldest imagination. Thus you must restrain yourself as much as possible in presenting them so as not to startle your readers unduly or provoke charges of madness. It may well be that the world is running counter to its destiny as a result of a false impulse given to its movement. But I would not speak of such lofty conceptions in my published work until my plan is adopted. Then you can give free rein to all your opinions and people will listen to your reasons. Today they won't. I would even abstain from speaking about the influence that your system will have on the temperature of the globe. All of that is premature. The new social organization offers enough immediate advantages that we needn't go looking for future ones the present generation wouldn't be able to enjoy. Without going back to the causes that brought the established system into being, I would limit myself to demonstrating that it cannot make us happy. I would be sure to refrain from saying anything about the influence of the stars in all this: that is just too transcendent for nearly all of your readers. Finally, I would present my ideas in the tone of assurance that derives from conviction. But I would not address a single reproach to the philosophers who have failed to hit upon the same ideas, for their error is really the quite involuntary one of not having possessed your genius.[4]

Gabet went on to criticize Fourier's obscure language and his penchant for neologisms. "It is quite enough," he wrote, "for a Frenchman to have to familiarize himself with a system that overturns the social order and reconstitutes it on new foundations" without having to master a "new language" at the same time. "These criticisms are those of all your readers," he concluded, "and in your second edition you must silence them. You must expound your ideas in a more popular manner." Although Gabet didn't know it, the same point had been made repeatedly by Muiron's friends in Besançon. Disappointed, or in some cases simply bewildered, by the treatise, they urged Fourier to try his hand at something clearer and more modest, at what Gréa described as "a small volume limited to the theory pure and simple."[5]

I

In Fourier's later years his disciples often complained about his reluctance to listen to their advice and criticism. As Charles Pellarin put it in his biography:

> It is regrettable that the most devoted friends and partisans of Fourier never had the slightest influence on him and could do nothing to modify his own decisions on which parts of his system it was most expedient to present to the public. The habit of seeing himself misunderstood and unjustly treated . . . had thrown this extraordinary man into a state of excessive mistrust, which he never entirely relinquished in any of his relationships.[6]

The tirades against "well-meaning" but "worthless" criticism with which Fourier peppered his letters to Muiron are just one example of the intransigence of which Pellarin was later to complain. Nevertheless it seems that by the beginning of 1824 Fourier had come to share some of the reservations of his disciples with regard to his previous work. In January 1824 he wrote Muiron that he was planning to write a new book—"a small abridgment scarcely longer than the *Sommaire*"—in which he would take their advice to heart. Unlike its predecessors, this *Abrégé* would be devoid of neologisms, stylistic innovations, and unnecessary digressions. He would limit himself to a "pure and simple presentation" of the theory, a presentation that would make his doctrine accessible even to schoolchildren. He would ruthlessly strip his text of all terms that had not received the official sanction of the French Academy; he would express none of his opinions on the intrigues of the Paris philosophers. Indeed, he would offer them "a share of the spoils." In thus catering to the Parisian taste for the orthodox and the anodyne, he would produce a work that any publisher would be glad to print at his own expense. Muiron might call this "seizing the best means of advancement," but to Fourier's mind it was "dissimulation." "I say quite openly," he wrote a month later, "that I will not be frank in the *Abrégé* I am going to publish."[7]

On March 10, 1824, Fourier set to work on this new book, expecting to finish it "by the end of April." It was five years later when the work finally appeared. Fourier was slowed down in part by the fact that he was actually incapable of sustained dissimulation. Even when on his best behavior as a writer, he inadvertently launched bombs at civilization, offended its most cherished prejudices. His concessions, bribes, and ruses were part of an internal dialogue that went unnoticed by a public that found his masquerades no less shocking than the sermons he delivered in dead earnest.

There were also more mundane reasons for the long gestation period of the *Abrégé*. At the beginning of 1824 Fourier found himself in financial straits. His style of life was frugal; and the income from his pension plus some help from Muiron had hitherto been sufficient to provide for his daily needs. But during the administrative purge conducted by the *ultras* in 1823 Muiron had lost his job as division chief at the Doubs Prefecture. His back pay had been held up; and he was for the moment in no position to continue his support of Fourier's enterprise.

Thus during the winter of 1823-1824 Fourier was obliged to go back to work as an unlicensed broker, the profession he had long exercised at Lyon. He soon discovered that it was not easy for an unknown provincial to build up a clientele in Paris. He was obliged to ask his friends and former business associates at Lyon—Gaucel, Jaquet, Dr. Amard, the Bousquets—for letters of reference and commissions. As he explained to one of them:

> At Lyon you can present yourself in a business house without any need of protection or patronage. But at Paris, a place that is crawling with intriguers, any banker or businessman is fearful of getting involved with someone dangerous.[8]

Judging by their responses, Fourier had remained on good terms with most of his former colleagues and employers. They appreciated his "exactitude" in business matters, and did what they could to help him out. Particularly warm and affectionate were the letters Fourier received from Jean-Baptiste Gaucel, who was now a cloth merchant at Lille, and from François Bousquet, the son of his first employer at Lyon, who forwarded a "thick packet of letters of recommendation" to Fourier from Lyon.[9]

Fourier now began to frequent the Paris Stock Exchange, which was temporarily located on the ground floor of the Palais Royal while Brongniart's new structure was being completed. The Exchange was open officially only a few hours a day. But at all times the galleries and the garden of the Palais Royal served as a rendezvous for merchants and dealers and unlicensed brokers like Fourier himself. Thus after the official closing hour Fourier would remain at the Palais Royal, trying to drum up a little extra business at what he had described in his writings on commerce as the "post ou sous Boursasse . . . accessoire ou arrière-faix de la Grande Bourse."[10] So busy was he that he could hardly spare two hours a day to devote to his *Abrégé*. But the results were not encouraging. By the end of March he had discovered that brokerage was more time-consuming at Paris than at Lyon and yielded less. *Marrons* were abundant and the competition was greater for the small transactions that were his specialty. "People like me are crushed," he wrote, "by the licensed brokers with thick portfolios." He was not "known," he lacked a "protector," and commissions rarely came his way. His former associates were themselves provincials, and their letters of reference opened few doors at the big business houses and banks of Paris. Thus Fourier found that his services were no more useful to the "pashas" of high finance than to those of philosophy. In April, writing to Bousquet about his "vicissitudes," he was reduced to asking for a loan.[11] Shortly thereafter he began talking about returning to Lyon, where he was better known. In the summer his business began to improve slightly. A few commissions with the large houses of Périer and Chaptal (in which a young graduate of the Ecole Polytechnique named Prosper Enfantin was then employed as a *liquidateur*) began to bring him a living wage.[12] But in August he wrote Muiron: "I was expecting that the profits from brokerage would keep on increasing. But it's a line of work that only gives you half a living and no more if you don't have a carriage and a portfolio. So I am making plans to find something better by the month of September. Business got better month by month, and it was starting to yield 100 francs a month. I was hoping that the figure would rise to 200, then 300, but the obstacles I've mentioned have proved to be insurmountable!"[13]

In spite of his financial difficulties, Fourier continued to believe in the last months of 1824 that a test of his ideas was imminent. He was sure that the appearance of the *Abrégé* would suffice to set rich capitalists vying with each other for the title of *fondateur*. In the meantime his friends and disciples were doing their best to aid him in the search. At Besançon Just Muiron had just published *Sur les vices de nos procédés industriels,* and it had already elicited promises of reviews and of a formal report at the Academy of Besançon. From Gabriel Gabet at Dijon came a letter of introduction to his former colleague of the Dijon bar, the future Icarian Etienne Cabet. "I will ask [Cabet] to introduce you," wrote Gabet, "to M. Lafite [Jacques Lafitte], who is philanthropic by nature and can be of great service to you."[14] Someone else placed Fourier in contact with a rich English landowner in Touraine in whom, for a brief period, Fourier believed he had found the long-sought backer.[15] In the summer and fall of 1824 Fourier was also angling hopefully for an invitation to the Owenite community at Motherwell.

Even in Paris events seemed to be coming to a head. The success of the French intervention in Spain had brought the prospect of a long period of peace and prosperity, and investors were becoming more venturesome. During the summer a wave of speculation in land buying had engulfed Paris, and vast construction projects were being undertaken on the plain of Grenelle near the Ecole Militaire. One enterprise involved the construction of three hundred new houses and what amounted to a new community within the walls of Paris. In July 1824 Fourier wrote Muiron about this "bizarre and useless" project and about his hope that some of the funds tied up in it might soon be diverted to the construction of a Phalanstery. "Last Sunday," wrote Fourier, "the architects treated their shareholders to a fete, complete with dancing and dinner, that cost forty thousand francs. Here, when you have an architect up your sleeve, you can get hold of as many shareholders as you want because the rage for building is as common now at Paris as that of speculating on public bonds. So when I have finished my *Abrégé,* I'll be sure to send it to some architect like V. . . , who is skillful at organizing subscriptions and companies."[16] Four months later Fourier was still talking optimistically about the prospect of seeing his "system of association . . . placed in execution near Paris."[17]

Most of the schemes devised by Fourier during this period died quickly, leaving no other epitaph than a few lines in his correspondence. But concerning the strangest of Fourier's projects, the publication of an anonymous brochure entitled *Mnémonique géographique,* the record is more substantial.[18] The *Mnémonique géographique* seems to have bewildered most scholars; it has generally been ignored, or dismissed as a fantastic curiosity. Hubert Bourgin, for example, described it as containing "in reality . . . hardly anything but extravagances."[19] The work is interesting from a biographical standpoint, however, both as the byproduct of a serious effort on Fourier's part to secure a position as a teacher of geography and as the outgrowth of one of his most devious and subtle efforts to awaken interest in his theory. Ostensibly the brochure outlined a new "method for learning geography, statistics, and politics in a few lessons." It purported to enable would-be diplomats, young princes, and speculators in foreign bond issues to memorize "within two months . . . the names, territorial divisions, statistics, commercial resources, and political interests of the diverse regions of the globe."

> This new method strews flowers on the path of learning [wrote Fourier]. It consists entirely of interesting descriptions, of piquant contrasts and parallels that are easily engraved upon the memory and diversify the process of learning according to the tastes of each student.[20]

The method, which Fourier described as "picturesque mnemotechny," consisted mainly in the utilization of a variety of mental devices— mythological allegories, musical analogies, mathematical progressions— designed to prod and activate the memory. After describing a dozen such devices, the brochure concluded with a brief note: "The author of this method gives lessons in town. He will go to the homes of those persons who desire it and, if need be, he will combine other branches of instruction with the three here proposed."[21]

Fourier's intentions in publishing this curious brochure seem to have been diverse. Courses in mnemotechny were much in vogue during the 1820s; and it is clear that the publication of the *Mnémonique géographique* was in part an expedient to which Fourier was driven by financial need. Shortly after its appearance he did actually make several attempts to obtain a position as a teacher of geography. In November 1824 he sent copies of the brochure, along with additional handwritten letters, to a number of school directors, diplomats, noblemen, and businessmen. To a Monsieur Brodart, the director of a school of commerce on the rue Saint-Antoine, he described his brochure as an outline of "the program of instruction that I propose to offer."[22] But what Fourier actually wanted to teach was much more than a new system of mnemonics or a new approach to geography. He hinted at this in the brochure itself when he referred to the existence of a "new and still unknown science" the knowledge of which could (among other things) accelerate a student's progress in geography.[23] In several of his letters he was more explicit. He described his method as an introduction to the study of a host of "new sciences," and he added: "I had to mask the introduction to these new sciences under the modest title of *Mnémonique géographique,* intending to provide a more extensive account of them in my verbal instruction."[24]

If one reads the *Mnémonique géographique* in light of these comments, it becomes clear that it was in fact a "masked introduction" to Fourier's doctrine. For most of the aids to memory Fourier proposed were designed to develop the speculative capacities of the reader and to familiarize him with the serial method, the theory of universal analogy, and other key concepts. For example, in noting the utility of allegorical nomenclature as a mnemonic device, Fourier added: "Allegorical names will be systematically applicable to all of natural history when the theory of *causes in creation* has explained the tableaux emblematically presented in each animal, vegetable, or mineral." In like manner he described speculation about possibilities of land reclamation as "a fine way to provoke interest in the study of geography, above all if you inform the student of an imminent event that will soon replace destructive armies with the creation of industrial armies of several million men." Even the study of mountain chains, valleys, and other natural frontiers would serve to demonstrate the "absurdity" of conventional civilized political boundaries.[25]

The *Mnémonique géographique* was no more successful as a "masked introduction" to Fourier's doctrine than as an attempt to find work. It would have passed completely unnoticed in Paris had not a copy, signed in Fourier's hand, caught the eye of an editor of the liberal satirical journal, *La Pandore.* On November 15, 1824, readers of this journal were treated to a review ridiculing the brochure and its outlandish terminology—its allegorical nomenclature and *octaves redoublées* and *modes composées.*

Never have we seen anything so extravagant or so comical. . . . We do not know if nature was working in a simple or a compound mode when it formed M. Fourier, but we regard him as the cumulative specimen of all those who have written absurdities.[26]

When Fourier saw this article he immediately drafted an angry reply, referring to the *Mnémonique géographique* as a "private affair . . . of no concern to the journals," and sarcastically describing himself as "associated in stupidity with such fools as Newton and Kepler."[27] But the reply was not published and the matter ended there.

III

Whatever hopes Fourier nursed concerning the *Mnémonique géographique,* the brochure did nothing to improve his financial situation, which by the end of 1824 had become very shaky indeed. He still managed to pick up an occasional commission as a broker with the help of friends like Jean-Baptiste Gaucel. But his long-term prospects were dim. Finally, early in 1825, Fourier decided that the situation in Paris was hopeless; and he made plans to return to Lyon where he was known and where, with the opening of new markets in Latin America, the silk industry was prospering. He made inquiries of Bousquet, who promised to help him find steady work. Finally, gathering up his manuscripts, Fourier left the Hotel Saint-Roche, his home for the past two years, and took the diligence for Lyon, where he arrived on April 1, 1825. Three weeks later he began work at a salary of twelve hundred francs a year as a cashier for the Maison Bousquet *père et fils,* commissionaires en marchandises at 18, port Saint-Clair. As Fourier described the position to Muiron, it was "a modest but secure job that gives me no trouble and is with good people."[28]

Throughout the summer of 1825 Fourier remained behind a desk at the Maison Bousquet, keeping accounts and also handling a good deal of the firm's domestic correspondence.[29] In the evenings he kept working at his *Abrégé,* but it was still far from completion. For the brief pamphlet, "scarcely longer than the *Sommaire,*" that he had originally proposed to dash off in a few weeks had now become a treatise in thirty-six parts. On his arrival he informed Muiron that he had already "put in good order fourteen of the thirty-six parts." But by late summer he was still no more than "half" through.

News of Fourier's continued difficulties was distressing to his disciples, who were eager to see his new book completed as soon as possible. Just Muiron was still in no position to offer much more than moral support. But several of Fourier's other admirers were men of more substantial means; and they began to urge Fourier to give up his job and to finish his book in the hospitality of their own homes. From the Dijonnais Gabet came a heartfelt appeal written in a tone that Fourier had never heard before, even from Muiron.

> I bewail the obstacles that are holding you back. . . . [wrote Gabet]. Since your mercantile occupations cannot bring you wealth and rest, renounce them and come to my home to receive the friendship and the admiration that are the *minimum* required by your talents. Here in a tranquil retreat you will be able to devote your thoughts exclusively to preparing the happiness of the human race. If success crowns your enterprise, if the glory that awaits you is followed by a monetary recompense, you can return what I advance you. If your glory does not bring you wealth, it will still reflect on me and I shall be paid in full. For I will have the satisfaction of being able to say to myself: "And I too, I have served Humanity in assisting the work of the new Astrea who has come to reestablish the age of gold on earth."[30]

Désiré-Adrien Gréa was not capable of such language, or of such single-minded fervor. But he too urged Fourier to come and spend the summer months with him and his family. A wealthy man and the possessor of a magnificent country estate in the Jura foothills, Gréa could offer Fourier an ideal setting in which to complete work on his book.

Fourier was extremely reluctant to accept these offers. Jealous of his own independence, this inveterate bachelor did not relish the thought of taking "charity" or of changing his solitary ways. When Gréa renewed his invitation, Fourier again demurred. He did not wish, he said, to make trouble for the Gréa household; he also feared losing his job. When Muiron suggested that Fourier might receive special treatment from the Bousquets, Fourier replied bitterly: "You are in error if you think that in a commercial establishment the chief makes all the decisions. Furthermore you do not realize that a man loses credit, makes himself look ridiculous in a commercial establishment if he is known to be working on a book." And he continued: "I have no doubt about the pleasure that I would have at Rotalier, in addition to the advantage of having hosts who would be such agreeable company. In any case, I am the most accommodating of men, and far from needing a chateau like that at Rotalier, I could adapt myself to living in a peasant's hut. So it is useless to tell me about all the comforts that I would enjoy at Rotalier, because when I devote myself to my favorite occupation any quarters become pleasing to me."[31]

In September Fourier's scruples were finally overcome. It was decided that he would go to Rotalier and remain there as long as was necessary for the completion of his book. Gréa even agreed to help pay the costs of publication, provided he was allowed to read the manuscript before it was printed. When Fourier arrived toward the middle of September, Muiron was already there to greet him; and together he and Gréa took their friend on a tour of the estate. Rotalier was located south of Lons-le-Saunier in one of the most beautiful winegrowing regions of the Jura. The grape harvest was just under way; and as the three walked through the vineyards, Fourier spoke enthusiastically about his work and his "new chances for success."

As willing as he was to talk about his work, Fourier hesistated to let Gréa see his manuscript. Gréa's criticism of the *Traité* had been harsh, and Fourier had not appreciated it. The conversations at Rotalier seem to have convinced him that Gréa was a man of basically "civilized" tastes and aspirations, as was indeed the case. Thus while Gréa remained willing to help finance the publication of the *Abrégé*, it soon became evident that Fourier was not going to fulfill his part of the agreement. After six weeks, during which Fourier managed to complete a substantial portion of his book, Gréa had been shown no more than the chapter headings. In spite of the charm of the surroundings and the graciousness of his hosts, Fourier left Rotalier at the end of October. Fourier's departure was accompanied by no ill will on either side. Indeed, he seems to have endeared himself to the whole Gréa family by coming to the rescue of an aunt of Madame Gréa following a carriage accident that occurred during his visit. As for Fourier's secretiveness with regard to his manuscript, Gréa took it in stride; and in 1829, when the book was finally finished, he helped Muiron raise funds to pay for its publication.[32]

By the beginning of November 1825 Fourier was back at Lyon and again at work at the Maison Bousquet. But this time his stay in Lyon was brief. On December 15 he was sent to Paris on business. Although he did not anticipate remaining long in the capital, the affair dragged on; and in February he began to talk of remaining in Paris and of finding a job that would "enable me to oversee the publication of my *Abrégé*."

Not long afterward Fourier took a position as a correspondence clerk at the Paris office of an American import-export house dealing mainly in textiles. The job, which began on May 1, was with the firm of Curtis and Lamb, whose Paris offices were located at 29, rue du Mail. Fourier was to receive a salary of one thousand francs for the first year and fifteen hundred francs for the second. As he informed Muiron, the position was "not brilliant" but it was not very demanding either. Since he didn't have to appear at work until 10:00 A.M., he had several hours each morning to devote to his book; and although his manuscript notebooks were too bulky to take to the office, he had enough free time between 10:00 and 5:00 to work on his *amusette* concerning the embellishment of the city of Besançon.

This job also provided Fourier with an excellent vantage point from which to observe the effects of the economic crisis of 1826, the "plethoric crisis" to which he was to devote a few of the most suggestive and original pages of his book.[33] The success of the independence movements in Latin America had opened new markets for European exports and launched a wave of speculation and new investment that soon took on awesome proportions. Eager investors bought stock in fictitious Peruvian mines and subscribed to loans floated on behalf of nonexistent republics. Ice skates and warming pans were shipped to Rio de Janeiro; and exports of clothing and other more appropriate manufactured goods vastly exceeded the capacity of the market to absorb them. The expanding French cotton industry was particularly hard hit by the ensuing market glut; and cotton prices, which had been pushed high by speculators in 1826, plummeted the following year. Bank failures were numerous and the crisis culminated in an international depression that was to last for the next three or four years.[34]

This was a new type of crisis, quite distinct from the traditional combination of inflation and scarcity that had generally originated in bad harvests. Although its dimensions were multiple, it had many of the earmarks of the sort of international crisis of overproduction that was only to become a characteristic feature of European economic life in the latter part of the nineteenth century. There was as yet no terminology adequate to describe it; so Fourier, in typical fashion, invented his own. It was a crisis of "plethoric repression."

Repression [he wrote] is a periodic result of the blind cupidity of the merchants who, when a market is opened, immediately send out four times as many goods as can be consumed. . . . This is what was done in 1825 by our cloth merchants and those of England. They encumbered America with wares that it would take three or four years to get rid of. The result was bad sales, stagnation, depreciation of goods, and bankruptcy for the sellers. This is the inevitable result of the plethora that is always produced by the imprudence of commerce, which deludes itself about the amount of consumption possible. How could a mob of jealous sellers, blinded by greed, judge the limits to set in exportation?[35]

Perhaps it was as a result of this crisis that in the fall of 1827 the firm of Curtis and Lamb was obliged to close its Paris office. Notifying Fourier three months in advance, his employers offered him a job at Le Havre. But with work on his book advancing, he was reluctant to quit the capital; and so he turned down the offer.[36] Thus as of October 16, 1827, Fourier was once again unemployed. Toward the end of the year some of his acquaintances from Franche-Comté urged him to join them in setting up a retail outlet at Paris for wines from the Jura Mountains. This was an idea close to Fourier's heart. For in addition to being a lover of the wines of his own *pays,* he often complained about the watering-down and chemical adulteration of wines by Paris merchants. But he decided against the project in order to concentrate on his book.[37]

Although Fourier continued during the next few years to pick up an occasional commission as an unlicensed commercial broker, his days as a full-time wage earner were now over. His financial position was far from secure. But his needs were modest, and during the last ten years of his life they were provided for by his small annuity and occasional earnings as a broker, together with the help offered by an ever-growing band of disciples.

IV

The termination of his employment at Curtis and Lamb brought little change in Fourier's style of life. With the exception of one extended visit to Besançon, he lived from the end of 1825 until the spring of 1832 in a rented room at 45, rue Richelieu. Throughout this period his base of operations remained the Sentier, the heart of commercial Paris, and he rubbed shoulders daily with the clerks, employees, shopkeepers, *coulissiers,* and small functionaries of the quarter. In many of its external details his daily life was hardly distinguishable from that of any retired Parisian office clerk. He took his meals at the cheap restaurants and *tables d'hôte* of the Sentier and chatted with his table mates about the news of the day and the latest doings at the Exchange. He was in touch with cousins who lived at Saint-Mandé, and sometimes on a Sunday he would rise early and walk out to the country to spend the day with them. And in the evening he might treat himself to a visit to the Tivoli Gardens to watch the dancing, the fireworks, and the acrobats. But such entertainment, he observed, was "poverty itself," a far cry from the "composite delights" that Harmony would offer.[38] Most of his diversions were even more prosaic: a demitasse of coffee after dinner, or a game of billiards in a small café. "There is nothing new here," he wrote his cousin Laure in 1827. "Morning and night we still play at billiards, which I love as much as ever."[39]

Despite his own Butterfly passion, Fourier had always been a creature of regular habits. But in these years his daily life began to take on a more ritualized character than ever. Now there was scarcely a morning when he failed to appear in the courtyard of the Tuilerie Palace to watch the changing of the royal guards. On most days he also spent at least an hour or two at one of the *cabinets de lecture* in the Palais Royal, sometimes immersed in the daily newspapers and sometimes just staring fixedly at a page of Lebrun's great atlas.[40] But the greater part of Fourier's day was spent in writing. By this time he had begun to repeat himself so much, and to inveigh so often against his enemies, that his imagination was scarcely engaged when he wrote. But writing still had a purgative effect that made it indispensable to him.

Toward the end of Fourier's life Stendhal commented briefly on the reasons for his obscurity. "Fourier's theory of association is making immense strides," observed Stendhal, "but since Fourier was totally without elegance and since he never appeared in the salons, it will be twenty years before he is accorded his rightful place as a sublime dreamer."[41] Fourier's world was indeed a much less elegant one than that of the *notables* whom he kept trying to interest in his theory. His petty-bourgeois tastes, his meticulously plain dress, his eccentricities, his blunt conversation might have been those of an elderly resident of Balzac's Maison Vauquer, and he was no more at ease in elegant company than Père Goriot. He was often to be seen in the waiting room of a minister or in the business office of an editor, but rarely in one of their salons; and his eternal jeremiads against the literary monopoly of the Parisians reflected a sense of exclusion that he felt all his life.

There was, however, one salon at which Fourier was an occasional and always welcomed guest during the later years of the Restoration. This was Charles Nodier's at the Bibliothèque de l'Arsenal. During the late 1820s Nodier's Sunday evenings at the Arsenal became one of the principal gathering places of young men and women identified with the emerging romantic movement in France. They were also a meeting place for writers and artists from Franche-Comté, and it is probably to this that Fourier owed his welcome. At any rate, he enjoyed the warm and lively atmosphere created by the Nodiers and their daughter Marie, and he returned often enough to be remembered by several of the other guests. In the memoirs of one of them, the young painter Amaury-Duval, the Fourier of the Arsenal appears as something of a *mystifica-teur*. Fourier was leaving the Nodiers' one evening with the medical student, Alexandre Bixio. "The night was clear and the moon was full. The first thought that came into Bixio's head was to say: 'What a beautiful moon, Monsieur Fourier!' The latter answered with an air of scorn: 'Yes. Profit from its last moments because nothing can keep it from submitting to my law.'" Bixio only later learned that Fourier had prophesied the disappearance of the moon and its replacement by five new, brightly colored satellites.[42]

During the 1820s Fourier managed to make a few other acquaintances in Paris's ruling literary circles. Some of these were liberal editors, like the baron de Férussac and Marc-Antoine Jullien, who were eager to identify themselves with "advanced" ideas. Others, like Pierre-Simon Ballanche, he had first come to know in Lyon. Fourier also met a few younger journalists: Amédée Pichot of the *Revue de Paris* and the *Mercure de France,* and Ferdinand Flocon, the future member of the provisional government of 1848, who was serving at this time as an editor of the *Album National* and as stenographer to the *Messager des Chambres.* Most of these, however, were casual acquaintances at best, whose friendship proved useful to Fourier in sparing him a few indignities but not in overcoming the "conspiracy of silence" he found so frustrating. After more than five years in Paris Fourier was still very much an outsider; and insofar as he had any following at all, its center was still in Besançon.

20

"The New Industrial World"

DURING THE last years of the Restoration, while Fourier was preparing the manuscript of his "abridged treatise" and impatiently awaiting the coming of a benefactor, he began at last to acquire a small provincial following. There was still nothing like a Fourierist "movement"; that was only to develop in the more tolerant climate of the first five years of the July Monarchy. But there were by the 1820s a number of self-professed disciples who, like Just Muiron, had discovered Fourier's work more or less by accident but who, also like Muiron, had come to regard it as holy writ. Judging from their correspondence, which was carefully preserved by Fourier, none of these early disciples was any more gifted than Just Muiron. They were middle-class and in some cases middle-aged individuals—substantial *rentiers* like Gabriel Gabet of Dijon, or government functionaries like Muiron himself and like Jean-Antoine Godin, a notary and justice of the peace at Champagnole[1]— who were attracted to Fourier's ideas in part at least because of his respect for private property and his insistence on the possibility of a peaceful solution to society's ills.

One of these early disciples was the elderly proprietor from Dijon, Gabriel Gabet.[2] An ardent republican in 1792, Gabet had served as a municipal officer at Dijon during the Revolution and subsequently as a local agent of the Directory. Although he remained known at Dijon for his "advanced" ideas, this had not prevented him from rallying to Louis XVIII or from adding to his already considerable fortune under the Restoration. Gabet first became acquainted with Fourier's ideas in 1824, apparently through a reading of the *Traité de l'association*. He immediately initiated a correspondence with Fourier, which continued until the latter's death. Fourier's part of this correspondence has been lost, but most of Gabet's letters survive and they are full of questions on Fourier's theory, offers of help and encouragement, and unsolicited advice. The letters also show Gabet to have been a dedicated if not particularly effective proselytizer of Fourier's ideas.

> Apart from you [Gabet wrote Fourier in 1825] there is perhaps no one else in France who takes as much interest as I in your sublime enterprise. It is the unique object of my meditations and my conversations. I talk about it to everyone. I am becoming tiring for those who don't possess my enthusiasm, and no one can.[3]

Gabet could even boast that he was subjecting his "numerous" children to "an oral course" in Fourierism. But all that came of his good intentions was an occasional article on Fourier's theory in the *Journal politique et littéraire de la Côte d'Or*. His influence at Dijon seems to have been minimal. The same could be said of the efforts of Fourier's other scattered provincial admirers.

Until the Revolution of 1830, then, Just Muiron remained the only even modestly effective publicist of Fourier's ideas. Muiron was, as has been pointed out, a man of limited talents and extreme caution. During the 1820s his most ambitious effort to draw attention to Fourier's ideas was the publication of a small, dreary volume entitled *Sur les vices de nos procédés industriels*. The aim of this work, which appeared in 1824, was to present Fourier's theory "in a style more commonplace than that of the inventor and less overwhelming for most readers."[4] In fact, Muiron carried caution to the point of scarcely mentioning Fourier's name and of only discussing one of Fourier's most modest reformist schemes, the proposal for a rural shareholders' bank set forth in the *Sommaires et annonce* to the *Traité*. Despite these precautions, the book persuaded no one and was even less widely read than Fourier's own works. Muiron did manage to cajole a professor at the University of Besançon into delivering a formal report on his book at one of the public meetings of the Academy of Besançon.[5] But the report was vague and noncommittal, and it provoked so much laughter among the academicians at Besançon that years later Muiron was still complaining about their "sneers" and their "foolish arrogance."[6]

Muiron met with many other reverses in his efforts to arouse interest in Fourier's ideas, and more than once he was deeply wounded by the laughter and irony of his friends with regard to Fourier.* But through sheer persistence, and perhaps also through the obvious depth and sincerity of his own commitment, Muiron did manage by the end of the Restoration to create at Besançon a group of about a dozen partisans of Fourier's ideas. Two of them were to play a vital role in the later development of the Fourierist movement.

One of the first of the Besançon Fourierists was a young widow named Clarisse Vigoureux whom Muiron had introduced to Fourier's ideas around 1820. Madame Vigoureux came from a family of wealthy ironmasters. Her husband's death in 1817 had left her at the age of twenty-eight with two young children and a sizable fortune. Over the years she was to devote much of this fortune to the Fourierist movement. A reserved and dignified woman of lofty moral standards, Clarisse Vigoureux was also to become one of the "principal artisans" of the "moral purification" of Fourier's doctrine that was practiced by his disciples after his death.[7]

Another of the early Besançon converts to Fourierism was Victor Considerant, the future leader of the Fourierist movement. Considerant, who was born at Salins in the Jura in 1808, was just seventeen years old and a student at Fourier's old school, the Collège de Besançon, when he was introduced to Fourier's theory by Just Muiron and Clarisse Vigoureux. He had come to Besançon to prepare for the entrance examinations to the prestigious Ecole Polytechnique. One of his friends at the college was Clarisse Vigoureux's son, Paul; and it was through Paul and then Clarisse that he met Muiron and the rest of the small

---

*Muiron didn't take criticism of Fourier lightly. Charles Weiss, the Besançon librarian, found this out on one occasion when he poked fun at Fourier's ideas in front of Muiron. Shortly thereafter Weiss received an angry letter from Muiron warning him that the time was near when those who had scoffed at Fourier would seem more idiotic than anyone had ever seemed "since the creation of the world." Cited in Gazier, "Le Bisontin Just Muiron (1787–1881)," 12.

circle of Besançon Fourierists. Endowed with a quick mind and an outgoing personality, Considerant was soon on close terms with his elders. He devoured the books they gave him, and by the spring of 1826 he was already well versed enough in Fourier's doctrine to lecture the younger Paul on the "proofs" in the *Traité de l'association*.[8] Considerant was admitted to the Ecole Polytechnique in the fall of 1826. When he left for Paris in November, the *Quatre mouvements* and the *Traité* were in his luggage.

During his years at the Ecole Polytechnique Considerant saw much of Fourier, worked hard to master his doctrine, and was constantly discussing Fourier's ideas with his fellow students. On a trip to Paris in 1827 Just Muiron marveled at the young man's energy and quickness. "Victor is superb," he wrote Clarisse Vigoureux, "I find in him a sturdiness, a freshness, a liveliness of mind, a glow of enthusiasm with which he can very well make his way in the world even while chewing the bit as he likes to say."[9] Considerant did often bridle at the heavy workload and the "stupid regulations" imposed by the school. But he was soon on close terms with Fourier and talked of him with both admiration and filial affection. "Please give Monsieur Fourier for me all the homage that his genius merits," he wrote Madame Vigoureux at a time when Fourier was staying in Besançon, "and tell me the interesting things that you learn from him. Ah! If I were still in Franche-Comté, wouldn't he be obliged to take the stick to his disciple as the ancient Greeks did! Fortunately, he doesn't carry philosophy to that point."[10]

Victor Considerant was the one really gifted disciple to come out of the Besançon group. He was not himself an original thinker, but he was a talented organizer and a brilliant publicist. After his graduation from the Ecole Polytechnique, he was sent to Metz to finish his preparation for a career in military engineering at the Ecole d'Application there. At Metz he rapidly managed to develop a following for Fourier's ideas among his fellow officers. A few years later, at the age of twenty-six, he published the first volume of a work entitled *La Destinée sociale,* which was to become the most influential nineteenth-century popularization of Fourier's ideas.[11] But in the later Restoration, as Fourier worked on his *Abrégé,* all that was still far in the future. The immediate task confronting Fourier and his disciples was the publication of the book and the search for a backer.

I

Apart from the intermittent necessity of making a living and the ever-renewed search for a backer, most of Fourier's time between the beginning of 1825 and the end of 1828 was devoted to the composition of the *Abrégé* that he was eventually to entitle *Le Nouveau monde industriel*. The correspondence with Muiron indicates the metamorphoses the book underwent and the trouble it caused Fourier.[12] By the end of 1824 he had drafted a full outline for the work; and he was able to write Muiron from Lyon in April of 1825 that he had already completed fourteen out of a projected thirty-six chapters. But the writing progressed slowly. In mid-August he was still no more than half through. Finally in June of 1826 he could write Muiron that the work was virtually completed. All he had left to do was to finish the final section and add some new chapters on the ills of contemporary civilization. These were to take the place of a section on "societary approximations," which he had decided to suppress because it offered "too good an opportunity for plagiarists." Two weeks later, however, Fourier was beginning to talk about further additions.

> Although I have kept closely to the outline that you saw at Rotalier, I have made extensive changes in the last five chapters where I will attempt to provide an extremely detailed analysis of civilization, of the 36 traits it exhibits in each of its successive phases, [and] of its permanent traits, which I now number at 144.[13]

Ever the systematizer, Fourier decided to turn his critical chapters into "a little grammar of civilization" that would enable his readers to recognize "the elements, the motivating forces, the movement, and the goal" of their society, so that they would understand "that we need to quit civilization and not to improve it."[14]

The writing of this "little grammar of civilization" actually took Fourier almost six months. And when it was done, he still felt the need to dispatch his victim with a preface that would summarize the main points of his theory and demonstrate once and for all the confusion of the civilized philosophers and the "vicious circle of civilized industry." This preface, which Fourier began in the last months of 1826, proved to be the most difficult part of the whole book. Fourier wrote and rewrote dozens of drafts, and it was not until February 1828 that he could finally inform Muiron that he had finished. The problem lay partly in the fact that Fourier simply never found it easy to call a work done. But there was also something else. Having embarked after 1819 on the "stripping down" or "emasculation" of his theory, Fourier found that he could never emasculate it enough. He could never simplify his presentation of the theory to the point that he was fully satisfied with any single re-statement or summary of the essentials. And so for more than a year he labored on a preface that amounted, in his final version, to less than fifty pages.[15]

In July of 1827, while Fourier was still struggling over his preface, Just Muiron and Désiré-Adrien Gréa arrived in Paris. Muiron came in search of a cure for his deafness. Consultations with the renowned Dr. Koreff, with two somnambulists, and even with an *oreilliste* finally convinced him that the situation was hopeless. But the trip did give Muiron and Gréa a chance to confer with Fourier about the publication of his work. This time they were both allowed to inspect the manu-script; and they also managed to obtain his consent to their offers of financial support.

> He accepts with no less nobility than pleasure [wrote Muiron to Clarisse Vigoureux]. Definitively the *Abrégé* is reduced to about three hundred pages. He has entrusted me with the notebooks. Gréa and I have read several chapters together and he is quite happy with them. . . . Gréa's dispositions are better than ever.[16]

With financial backing assured, Fourier had only to find a publisher.

Past experience had taught Fourier the importance of the Parisian *imprimateur*. So early in 1828 he began making the rounds of the Paris publishing houses. But everywhere he tried, he was met with the same old argument: he lacked a name. "Nothing is harder," he wrote Mui-ron, "than to find a publisher here when you don't have a big name. You can tell from their replies that the subject doesn't matter at all to them. It's the author that counts. If Chateaubriand wrote that two and two make five, everyone would want to be his publisher."[17]

While Fourier vainly sought a publisher in Paris, Muiron urged him to return to Besançon and get the book published there. Fourier ac-cepted this proposal reluctantly. He still regarded Franche-Comté as the "Boeotia of France" and he doubted his disciple's assurances about the growth of interest in his thought at Besançon. "In spite of what you tell me," he wrote Muiron at the end of June, "about a change in the attitude of a few Bisontines with regard to me, I have no faith at all in their good will."[18] But since the Paris publishers were not interested in his book, he had no choice. Toward the beginning of July 1828 Fourier arrived in Besançon with his manuscript. Muiron's friend, Clarisse Vigoureux, offered Fourier a place to stay; and together with Muiron, she helped him make final arrangements for the publication of his book at the Imprimerie Gauthier.

Fourier's stay at Besançon lasted over eight months. Throughout this time he stayed with Clarisse Vigoureux and her children in their large house on the rue du Collège. Fourier's only remaining close relative in Besançon now was Lubine Clerc, the widowed sister with whom he had stayed in 1821 prior to the publication of the *Traité de l'association*. Lubine's great days at the Hôtel des Gouverneurs were finished. With the help of an infantry captain named Berthaud, she had run through most of the money left by her husband, including the portion left to her two daughters, Cornélie and Lubine. After Berthaud and his brother had established themselves as "masters" in her household, the two daughters left Besançon, both to enter religious orders. Cornélie was now at a convent in Saumur, and the younger Lubine in Paris at the convent of Notre-Dame-du-Roule, where Fourier had watched her take her final vows in March of 1828. While at Besançon Fourier attempted to recover some of the money due the girls. But his sister had none to spare, and he was left to fulminate against her "scandalous misconduct and incompetence."[19]

Much of Fourier's time at Besançon was of course spent with Just Muiron. As on Fourier's earlier visits, Muiron saw to his entertainment. Muiron also introduced Fourier to his colleagues at the prefecture and to various *notables* including the liberal philosopher, Theodore Jouffroy. Muiron, who had long known Jouffroy, apparently hoped to interest him in Fourier's ideas. But the outcome of the meeting was disappointing and Fourier could later refer scornfully to Jouffroy as "a man gangrened by the contact of philosophers."[20]★

★Although Jouffroy did not take Fourier's ideas very seriously, he did have a certain detached appreciation of Fourier's theory. See his letter to Muiron of March 14, 1832, AN 10AS 39 (3): "I am in agreement with you and the Saint-Simonians on the present situation of humanity. We differ only concerning the value of the remedy that you and they propose, namely, the social doctrine of the future. I believe in (the need for) a new dogma. . . . Has Monsieur Fourrier [*sic*] found a new dogma? Have the Saint-Simonians? I think not. That is what we have in common. Let me add that I see no comparison

Fourier's main business at Besançon was of course to see his book through publication. While it was in press, he visited the Maison Gauthier almost every day to read proof and make last-minute alterations. One of the employees of the firm left a description of Fourier as he appeared at the time.

> He had a middle-sized head, wide shoulders and chest, a wiry body. His temples were close-set, his head not very large. A certain air of enthusiasm that was spread over his face gave him the appearance of a dabbler in meditation. Nothing about him announced either a man of genius or a charlatan.[21]

The author of these lines was Pierre-Joseph Proudhon. Just twenty years old at the time, Proudhon was an autodidact like Fourier; and while working as a proofreader at the Maison Gauthier he learned what he could from the books he had to read. Until his meeting with Fourier most of his studies had focused on language and grammar and even theology. But the reading of Fourier's book opened up a new world to him. "For six whole weeks," he wrote later, "I was the captive of this bizarre genius."[22] Proudhon was not a man to remain the captive of anyone's thought for long, however; and before the book was finished he had already begun to entertain his fellow workers with jokes at Fourier's expense. In later years Proudhon was often to criticize Fourier's ideas. He had no liking for his compatriot's conception of property, his "detestable" moral views, or the veneration with which "Saint Fourier" was regarded by his disciples. But Proudhon never ceased to be fascinated as well as repelled by Fourier's thought, and it was not without some justification that he could write in his notebooks seventeen years after this unique encounter: "I am the only interpreter that Fourier has had up to now."[23]

II

The *Nouveau monde industriel,* which finally came off the press of the Maison Gauthier in March 1829, has long been regarded as the most

---

between the vast and minutely worked out conception of Fourrier and the roughly sketched edifice of the Saint-Simonians. Monsieur Fourrier is infinitely superior, but for that very reason he is more difficult to popularize."

concise and systematic exposition of Fourier's theory. It lacks the exuberance of the *Quatre mouvements* and the sheer scope of the *Traité* of 1822. But unlike either of these works, it is sufficiently straightforward in its organization that it is possible to summarize its contents in a paragraph. Essentially it is what Fourier wished to make it: a relatively clear summary of the doctrine, focusing primarily on the organization of a trial community. The preface, over which Fourier had labored so long, was largely devoted in its final, published version to a discussion of the contrast between the "enormity of the societary product" and the "vicious circle of civilized industry." Then in the initial section Fourier provided a succinct, if "elementary," review of the theory of passionate attraction. The second section dealt with preparations for a trial Phalanx. Here Fourier became as specific as possible, providing his readers with maps, diagrams, tentative budgets, and even advice on animal husbandry. In his third, fourth, and fifth sections Fourier discussed education and gastronomy, the production and distribution of goods, and the "equilibrium of the passions" that would be established within the Phalanx. The last two sections contained the critique of civilization, situated within the larger framework provided by his historical theory, and his reflections on such "transcendent" branches of the doctrine as the theory of universal analogy and the cosmogony. The book closed with a "Postface on the Intellectual Cataract" in which Fourier appealed for support and attempted to settle accounts with philosophers in general and Robert Owen in particular.

In publishing a second edition of the *Nouveau monde industriel* in 1845, Fourier's disciples described it as a "very methodical, very logical and admirably clear" summary of the doctrine. In their view the *Théorie des quatre mouvements* was a difficult and provocative work that could only be properly appreciated by "grown men and mature minds." But the presentation of the doctrine in the *Nouveau monde industriel* was sufficiently straightforward that (having omitted a few of the "cruder" passages) they believed they could make use of it in their own efforts to propagate the doctrine.[24] Fourier himself was apparently of two minds about the book. He wrote Considerant in 1831 that although it was "a good deal less substantial than the *Traité* of 1822," it was "more succinct, more specific, and most suitable for beginners."[25] Still he had reservations about the work, and he expressed them in the text itself. He repeatedly reminded his readers that he was making a great and painful effort to avoid shocking them with overly explicit discussions of the more unusual aspects of the doctrine. He was also attempting not to confuse them by treating any one subject in too much detail. Anticipating complaints, he observed that "the calculus of the passions is an extremely vast science; those who want it in abridged form must expect inadequate explanations on certain points." By hinting at some of the complexities that he could not treat in detail, he hoped his readers would "recognize how much the theory has been circumscribed and mutilated by the limits of an abridgment."[26] He promised to provide "in other volumes" all the necessary clarifications.

These reservations, apologies, and promises, which are reiterated throughout the *Nouveau monde industriel,* show that Fourier was still unreconciled to the abandonment of his initial goal as a thinker: the publication of a full-scale treatise presenting the theory of passionate attraction as the "key" to a universal system that would encompass and explain "all the mysteries of nature." But the main purpose of the book was to arouse interest in the organization of a trial community and to serve as a guide to the *fondateur* who would finance the experiment. With this end in mind Fourier attempted to be down to earth.

This concern with what he had come to refer to simply as "the realization" prompted Fourier to make a more substantial effort in the *Nouveau monde industriel* than in his earlier works to dissociate himself and his ideas from those of atheists, revolutionaries, and other compromising troublemakers. He assured his readers that his own ideas on association had nothing in common with the "diatribes against property, religion, and marriage" of a Robert Owen. He devoted twenty-four pages of his text to an elaborate exercise in scriptural exegesis intended to demonstrate the concordance of his own theory with the teachings of the New Testament rightly understood.[27] He constantly reiterated the claim that, unlike the ideas of violent revolutionaries, his own plan of association would make it possible "to satisfy all classes and all parties." All he needed was sufficient funds and just two months of time.

III

As soon as the printing of the *Nouveau monde industriel* was finished, Fourier returned to Paris and set about organizing a promotional campaign similar to that which had greeted the appearance of the *Traité* of 1822. Once again he dispatched copies of his book, along with long explanatory letters, to influential politicians and journalists and writers. To the baron de Férussac, who was responsible for the only sympathetic review that the *Traité* had received, he now sent an epistle of twenty-one pages urging the baron to lend his name (and funds) to the establishment of a Société de réforme industrielle, which would "begin by considering the true methods of extinguishing poverty, of repressing commercial fraud, and of [exposing] the false liberties that have deluded contemporaries for the past forty years."[28] A similar letter of sixteen pages went to a newly created Société de la propagation des sciences et de l'industrie, whose members included Jacques Laffitte and Casimir Périer.[29] Other letters went to Chateaubriand, Decazes, Hyde de Neuville, and the playwright Népomucène Lemercier, as well as to journalists associated with *Le Globe, Le National,* and *La Revue de Paris.* These yielded little.[30] Fourier thereupon drafted another round of letters offering to provide "verbal explanations" to all who were interested in his ideas. He solicited contributions that would cover his "publicity expenses." He pressed Muiron into service. Finally, he even tried buying space in a newspaper. On May 2, 1829, the readers of the *Journal des débats* were informed (presumably by Fourier himself) that the purchase of the *Nouveau monde industriel* would make it possible for them to familiarize themselves with a remarkable new discovery, the result of which would be to

QUADRUPLE THE EFFECTIVE YIELD OF INDUSTRY. . . . ELIMINATE ALL STATE DEBTS. . . . TRANSFORM PRODUCTIVE TASKS INTO MORE ATTRACTIVE, MORE *INTRIGUING* ACTIVITIES THAN OUR FETES, BALLS, BANQUETS, ENTERTAINMENTS. . . . FREE THE NEGROES AND SLAVES WITH COMPENSATION. . . . BRING ABOUT THE SUDDEN AND *COLOSSAL* ENRICHMENT OF ALL SAVANTS, WRITERS, ARTISTS AND TEACHERS. . . . CHIMERAS, VISIONS, YOU WILL SAY! NO, IT IS A NEW AND HIGHLY METHODICAL SCIENCE.[31]

All this (and more) Fourier managed to cram into a small paid advertisement. But for all the big words, Fourier's little *annonce* cut a modest figure next to the larger—and hardly less extravagant—advertisements for patent medicines and Turkish baths that regularly filled the back page of the *Journal des débats.*

Finally, in May and June of 1829 two fairly substantial reviews of the *Nouveau monde industriel* did appear in the Paris press. Although both were hostile, the very long review that appeared in the Catholic *Universel* at least showed signs that Fourier's book had been read. After briefly poking fun at Fourier's language and his "buffoonery," the anonymous reviewer proceeded to criticize Fourier's thought for its denial of the reality of moral choice, and for its view of society as "no more than a living machine in which the human passions are the wheels." Fourier was actually a materialist and a hedonist according to the reviewer, but "he hides his doctrine under learned and obscure sounding words." Rather perceptively the reviewer observed that Fourier "might perhaps have had an ulterior motive in sowing so many buffooneries and puerilities in the reader's path." Was this not, he asked, a means to "disorient the reader and veil a philosophical materialism" that would have proved frightening in all its nudity?[32]

The other review of the *Nouveau monde industriel* was a brief and superficial article that appeared in the *Revue française,* a semimonthly founded in 1828 by a group of liberal Orleanists including Guizot and the duc de Broglie. The reviewer began by associating Fourier with such contemporary reformers as "Robert Owen, Miss Vright [Fanny Wright], and the sect of the *Producteur* [the Saint-Simonians]." Like other partisans of association, the reviewer maintained, "Fourier . . . imagines that one can reform society in the manner of a convent; only he claims to make room within the organization that he proposes for an infinite variety of functions corresponding to the variety of man's vocations and tastes." The rest of the article was little more than a compilation of outlandish details. "It would be impossible to accumulate more bizarre assertions in a more grotesque style," concluded the reviewer.[33]

This review seems to have angered Fourier as much as any he ever received. Although it bore no signature, he managed to convince himself that it had been written by Guizot himself, and that Guizot was in fact the ringleader of the "philosophical committee" that was trying to deny him a hearing. Immediately he set to work drafting a series of "Replies to the detractor Guizot." Their general tenor can be judged from the following manuscript outline.

> Replies to the detractor Guizot: His tricks and calumnies. His ignorance in politics. Twelve absurdities in one of his pages. His role as a professional vandal.[34]

During the summer of 1829 Fourier peppered his letters to Just Muiron with bitter attacks on "Guizot and his consorts." Muiron replied
by urging Fourier to follow the example of Jesus Christ and to forgive
his persecutors.[35] But Fourier was not about to forgive anyone. What
he wanted was justice, to obtain which he spent much of the fall
composing a reply to Guizot and his other critics. It appeared in
January of 1830 under the guise of a *Livret d'annonce* to the *Nouveau
monde industriel.* In this eighty-eight page polemic Fourier made an
effort to summarize and restate the principal points of the *Nouveau
monde.* But his main concern was to reply to his critics and to unveil
the "plots" and "manoeuvres" of Guizot and the *Revue française,* the
"obscurantist plan" by which "instructions are given to certain journals by the directing coterie and, under the pretext of a sublime flight
toward perfectibility, all discoveries that offend the intellectual monopolists are crushed."[36]

The *Livret d'annonce* would have passed entirely unnoticed had it
not been for the kindness of a young journalistic acquaintance of Fourier's named Amédée Pichot. Toward the end of 1829 Pichot and Paul
Lacroix had assumed joint editorship of a small literary journal called *Le
Mercure de France au dix-neuvième siècle.* This journal had had a checkered
career since its creation in 1823. Originally a bastion of literary classicism, its editors had come by 1828 to accept the idea of a "1789 of
literature" and to identify themselves with the emerging romantic
movement. Under Pichot and Lacroix this tendency continued, and the
new editors could describe themselves as interested in "everything
youthful." On January 9, 1830, under the rubric "Economie politique,"
they published a sympathetic review of the *Nouveau monde industriel* and
of Fourier's "victorious" refutation of Guizot in the *Livret.*

> There is [in the *Nouveau monde,* they wrote] so much excellent
> criticism, so much poetry, so much eloquence, so much genius,
> let us dare say, that even at those moments when the author
> seems to be lost in imaginary spaces, we begin to doubt our
> own reason at least as much as his.[37]

This review was unsigned and actually not very substantial, since it
consisted largely of excerpts from Fourier's text. A few months later,
however, a second review appeared. This was a detailed analysis of
the *Nouveau monde industriel* signed by Victor Considerant, "élève
sous-lieutenant de génie," whom the editors generously described as

"one of the most distinguished proselytizers" of Fourier's doctrine.[38] This article by Considerant was actually the first sympathetic and well-informed account of Fourier's ideas to appear in a Paris journal. One would expect its appearance to have delighted Fourier. But judging from a letter he later wrote to the editor of the *Mercure,* his joy was less than complete: "Monsieur Considerant . . . is a highly zealous disciple," he wrote, "but one who often falls into the common error of mixing the sophisms of the philosophers with my theory. I found in his article thirty-five errors of this sort, every one of which could have required a refutation."[39]

Fourier was obviously a hard man to please. But the editors of the *Mercure* clearly believed that his ideas made good copy. For in July of 1830 they published a third article on the *Nouveau monde.* This one, which was entitled "Dénouement des utopies anciennes et modernes" and signed "Ch. Ph.", was actually written by Fourier himself.[40]

IV

Fourier's continuing struggle to get a hearing for his ideas did not absorb all his energies in the period following the publication of the *Nouveau monde industriel.* As he himself observed, his own dominant passion was the Butterfly; in moments of stress or intellectual concentration he enjoyed diverting himself with trivial amusements. One such *amusette,* which had occupied him sporadically throughout the 1820s, was his project for the renovation and embellishment of the city of Besançon. In the midst of his work on the *Abrégé* he had repeatedly written Muiron requesting the exact measurements (in paces) of buildings, walls, streets, and squares throughout the city. Fourier never lost interest in this project, and among his papers there are dozens of manuscripts and designs relating to it. But in 1829 Fourier acquired another distraction. He began to write articles for a weekly newspaper published in Besançon under the direction of Just Muiron.

Muiron's newspaper, which first appeared in March of 1829, was called the *Impartial.*[41] It was primarily a business venture of a fairly conventional sort; and the capital necessary to establish the paper was provided not by Muiron himself but by a group of Besançon businessmen. Muiron hoped that it would eventually be possible to use the newspaper as a vehicle for the publication of articles on Fourier's theory. But in asking Fourier to contribute, he made it clear that he was not free to print whatever he wished.

When Muiron first invited him to submit articles for publication, Fourier hesitated. "I have not sent you anything for the journal," he wrote Muiron in the spring of 1829, "because I am not very well informed as to the character you want the journal to have; and I am not sure if the topic that I could treat best, which is foreign relations, would be suitable for you." Fourier also warned that his habitual bluntness might prove offensive to the backers of the journal.

> It is not my way to be the echo of what everyone else is saying. . . . Nothing dull, nothing adulatory. Articles solidly backed up by facts and strong reasoning, in which I will not flatter either the liberal party or the absolutists: that's my way. If you need writing of another sort, I'm the last person to ask.[42]

Fourier's doubts were justified. For Muiron's collaborators complained about one of the very first articles that he submitted to the journal. It dealt harshly with one of Fourier's longstanding enemies, the wine merchant who adulterated his product.

> You tell me [wrote Fourier to Muiron on August 30, 1829] that the article on wines will be extensively revised because your backers are businessmen. . . . If they are wine merchants, it may be that the means I propose will offend them. But the only people who can reimburse the fifty millions that the wine sellers are stealing are the wine sellers themselves. Where else would the money come from? From the people who buy watered-down wine?[43]

At about the same time Fourier submitted an article on foreign affairs that Muiron did manage to get published. But his colleagues protested that it was less like a newspaper article than "a note to be delivered to the minister of foreign affairs."

Fourier was angered by the treatment his articles received. He believed he knew something about journalism, and he had his own ideas about what constituted good newspaper writing. "What is it that makes a journal successful?" he asked rhetorically.

> It is a vehement, audacious tone. Geoffroy attacked God and the devil (sparing only the emperor and his favorites like Fontanes), and his independent tone, his bold and colorful manner,

did wonders for the *Journal des débats,* which would never have risen to the heights if its feuilleton had been written in rose water and stuffed with mealy-mouthed academic flattery.[44]

Eventually an understanding was reached between Fourier and Muiron and the financial backers of the *Impartial.* For a time Fourier even became something like a regular contributor. Thus during the year 1830, both before and after the July Revolution, he published at least nine unsigned articles in the *Impartial.* These articles dealt with a variety of subjects: foreign affairs, population growth, teaching methods, the "inconstancy of the seasons." There was a piece in which Fourier used the decline of coach and diligence service in France as an illustration of the "vicious circle of current competition," and another in which he returned to a topic that had long been of absorbing interest to him: the "urgent need to rectify the territorial division of France."[45]

The one topic that Fourier consistently refused to treat in his articles for the *Impartial* was domestic politics. Throughout the year 1829 political conflict was brewing in France between King Charles X and an increasingly outspoken liberal opposition. By the summer of 1829 the opposition had apparently acquired a majority in the Chamber of Deputies. But in August Charles X announced the appointment of a reactionary ministry led by Prince Jules de Polignac. Thereupon the *Impartial* (along with much of the rest of the French press) joined the liberal opposition. Although Muiron knew Fourier's distaste for discussions about politics and political rights, he had become caught up in the struggle and he attempted to persuade Fourier to write an article for the *Impartial* dealing with the liberal movement for the defense of the Constitutional Charter of 1815. The reply was blunt.

> I will take good care not to write the article that you suggest on constitutional societies. I couldn't care less about all the constitutions. I never read them. I know that force and trickery are all that matter [in politics]. It looks to me as though your constitution is going to go up in smoke in a short time. Already clubs of the "Friends of Religion" are being formed, which will handle you the same way the Jacobins handled the Feuillantines in 1792. They will knock heads just as did the Companies of Jesus or Jéhu. That's their whole plan, though the means they use may be slightly less crude; and if your journal attempts to thwart them, it will be dead and buried within six months.[46]

During the first six months of 1830 the pages of the *Impartial* were full of attacks on the clergy and the Polignac ministry and what it described as "la camarilla des privilégiés." Muiron himself waxed so indignant against the clergy and the government in one article that he was condemned to a month in jail and a fine of three hundred francs. But Fourier remained quite detached.

> I see that you are so strongly preoccupied by the elections that it would be useless for me to send you articles. Unfortunately I am not as optimistic as you are about this movement of resistance. I do not believe that the liberal party will be able to maintain itself against the violence [of the *ultras*]. . . . All of this only goes to show that illusions about liberty are going to the dogs. Liberty is not made for the people of civilization. They don't know how to find the system in which liberty would coincide with the views of the government.[47]

Barely a month after Fourier wrote this letter, the government's attempt to annul the elections and suspend freedom of the press led to the outbreak of revolution at Paris. Charles X was overthrown, and a new constitutional monarchy was established under an Orleanist king, Louis Philippe. Fourier had overestimated the strength of the Bourbon monarchy and its ability to employ force against the opposition. But he doubted that the new regime would be much of an improvement over the old.

If Fourier was relatively unmoved by the July Revolution and the events that led up to it, his contributions to the *Impartial* and his correspondence with Muiron show that he was able to get very excited in 1830 over questions affecting the welfare of his native city. For all his railing against his fellow Bisontines and against Franche-Comté, Fourier was at heart very much a regional chauvinist. In his letters to Muiron throughout the 1820s he had often inveighed against the slights he believed Besançon to have suffered at the hands of the government and (especially) "the Burgundians." There was, for example, the "theft" of Besançon's university by the city of Dijon. But even more galling to Fourier—always a great amateur of military exercises and parades—was the government's "absurd" decision to transfer Besançon's school of artillery to the city of Auxonne.[48]

Fourier's long stay at Besançon during the publication of the *Nouveau monde* served to renew his interest in local affairs. Thus in one of his articles for the *Impartial* he mounted a vigorous attack on the Burgundians, "who have acquired the habit, ever since Napoleon's time, of speaking as masters whenever Besançon is concerned."[49] In another article, which was not accepted for publication, he referred to his native city pathetically as "a pariah, a proscript . . . the Cinderella of the capitals" in the eyes of the French administration.[50] At about the same time, and in the same tone, Fourier also took on the French government's corps of military engineers. In a signed letter to the *Impartial* he violently protested the engineers' destruction of a grove of trees by the Doubs that had long served as a sanctuary for birds. This was in his eyes just one of many "shameful acts of vandalism" perpetrated by the military engineers. In order to prevent further damage to the city, Fourier argued, it would be necessary to create at Besançon a "committee on beautification" that would be empowered to veto the plans of the "vandals" in the corps of engineers.[51]

In publishing these articles Just Muiron occasionally softened Fourier's language and added a few *formules de politesse*. It didn't take Fourier long to let Muiron know what he thought about such practices.

> Please tell those who are mixing their prose with mine that pettiness and baseness are not my style; that being by nature unfitted for the role of a courtesan, an obsequious phrase maker, I will not be so foolish as to play this role before the same malicious compatriots who had me defamed at the Academy [of Besançon]. . . . I know only too well that no one is a prophet in his own country. This is an added reason for me to avoid prostrating myself before the Bisontines by offering them dull and exaggerated eulogies that they themselves would not aspire to. Thus I invite those who are altering my words not to travesty me, not to give my language an adulatory tone that I despise. If they think their flattery makes sense, why don't they publish it separately? They have the whole journal at their disposal.[52]

After this letter the articles submitted by Fourier were rarely revised. But they were also rarely published.

V

Shortly after the July Revolution a young writer from Besançon named Xavier Marmier paid a call on Fourier at his small sixth-floor apartment on the rue Richelieu. Marmier's reason for seeking out Fourier seems to have been sheer curiosity. But two years later, when he had begun to make his way in Paris as a journalist, he published an article on Fourier that gives us a glimpse of the man in his surroundings.

> Monsieur Fourier lives in a small and meager sixth-floor room. You get there by climbing a narrow and winding staircase on which you constantly run the risk of stumbling and breaking your neck. You find him in front of a poor fireplace in which a few small sticks of kindling are burning their last. The room contains two or three essential pieces of furniture and a few scattered piles of manuscripts, lying here and there in a corner or spread out on a table. They constitute no doubt his greatest wealth. . . .
>
> Monsieur Fourier was wearing a white tie and a small blue frock coat. His clothing is that of a man who cares little about what is fashionable for a particular season, but who still has a laundrywoman to clean his shirts and a maid to come in and brush his clothes. Monsieur Fourier has a handsome and interesting face; his silver hair falls on his forehead and frames it without hiding it; his blue eyes possess a vivacity and an expressiveness such as I have rarely seen; the distinctive feature of his physiognomy is that of meditation. . . .
>
> I explained to Monsieur Fourier the purpose of my visit, and he promptly began to speak to me about his system as a whole and especially about the results it would yield. I must admit that these seemed to me too extraordinary . . . to take seriously.[53]

At the time of Marmier's visit it had become evident to Fourier that the *Nouveau monde industriel* was no more of a success than the *Traité* of 1822. But neither this realization nor the political upheaval of July 1830 brought much change in Fourier's private routines or in his efforts to make his theory known. He continued to spend much of his time drafting and circulating appeals for support from prominent politicians and men of affairs. Most of his letters were devoted to recitals of "the results," the prodigious benefits that his discovery would yield, and the particular motives that a given group or party might have for taking an interest in it. Thus during the first six months of 1830 he sent the ministers of Charles X a steady stream of communications bearing such titles as "Note on the necessity and the ease of making a prompt diversion to liberal and philosophical intrigues."[54] After the July Revolution the addressees changed but not the fundamental nature of Fourier's appeal. What he wanted was the opportunity to put his theory into practice, and he didn't care who gave him the opportunity. Thus in the year following the July Revolution Fourier sent long essays and statements to Jacques Laffitte and Casimir Périer and to the Committee on Agricultural Progress appointed by the Chamber of Deputies.[55] And in October of 1831 he enlisted the aid of the deputy from Lyon, J.-B. Dugas-Montbel, in circulating among his colleagues on the Chamber's Industrial Committee copies of a seventy-page "Memorandum on the vices of the system of fragmented industry."[56] A few polite letters of acknowledgment are all he received for his pains.[57]

Of all the initiatives Fourier made at this time, the most important to him was an exchange of letters with Baron Guillaume-Antoine Capelle, the minister of public works in the Polignac government. When Capelle's ministry was created in May of 1830 Fourier sent him a letter arguing that the ministry's budget was inadequate and offering to indicate a means of raising additional funds. Capelle's response was polite and not discouraging. Thereupon Fourier drafted a long essay in which his own theory was presented as a solution to all the problems confronting the Ministry of Public Works. Again Capelle replied courteously, this time advising Fourier that his ideas would be "examined with all the attention that they merit." A few days after Fourier received this letter, the Bourbon monarchy was overthrown.[58]

Baron Capelle's letters were actually no more than polite evasions. But Fourier seized on any straw of hope; and in his mind the kind, vague words soon became an "acceptance" on Capelle's part, a formal statement of the government's willingness to make a careful examination of the theory. Thus in a letter aimed at Louis Philippe Fourier could later propose that the king designate an individual to receive a complete course on the theory in ten private lessons, adding "Baron Capelle accepted such verification by his letter of July 24, 1830."[59] Just Muiron was less easily deceived. But he was unable to discourage Fourier, who wrote him a month after receiving Capelle's second letter.

> I do not share your opinion with regard to his decision. You call him evasive. You ignore the motives that I emphasized in my memorandum in order to tempt him by personal interest. And even though you have known him personally, you cannot imagine, on the basis of his dealings with the prefecture, the degree of ambition to which he was susceptible.[60]

For all the subtlety of his writings on the human passions, Fourier's practical psychology was in some respects extraordinarily crude. He was simply unable to doubt the efficacy of his own rational appeals to what he took to be other people's self-interest.

More interesting than the endless chain of illusions created by Fourier's one-sided correspondence with the ministers of Charles X and Louis Philippe were the efforts he made early in 1831 to publicize his theory by embarking on a course of lectures. Originally, it seems, Fourier's plan was to expound his theory systematically in a series of six lectures to be given in a rented hall at the Tivoli d'hiver on the rue de Grenelle Saint-Honoré. News of the lectures was spread by word of mouth and personal invitation. But Fourier also persuaded the editors of the *Mercure de France* to publish a brief announcement.

> A new social mission began last Saturday [their article ran] and will continue every Saturday at seven o'clock in the evening in one of the halls of the Winter Tivoli at 47, rue de Grenelle Saint-Honoré. Monsieur Charles Fourrier [*sic*], the inventor of the system of passionate attraction, will himself explain his doctrine of which Saint-Simonism is, in its reasonable elements, no more than a disguised plagiarism.

The editors of the *Mercure* went on to contrast the asceticism of Fourier's way of life with the "libertinism" of the disciples of Saint-Simon.

> Monsieur Fourrier has been neither a dissipater nor a libertine, like the apostle of the rue Taitbout. . . . Monsieur Fourrier is a sage in the manner of Pythagoras, of the Brahmans of India, perhaps even in the manner of the Great Newton, who died a virgin at the age of eighty. Several ladies are attending his lectures.[61]

Despite such assurances, Fourier's course of lectures did not get beyond the second session. Apparently the time and place were poorly chosen; and the second lecture, which was poorly attended, was marred according to Fourier by "trivial discussions" and "preposterous objections." In a private memorandum Fourier attributed this to the fact that the audience was insufficiently prepared. "Sessions held confusedly without a distinct core of pupils encourage trivial discussions and preposterous objections. Steps must first be taken," he wrote, "to form a corps of disciples."[62] In a letter to Muiron he added: "The organization of lectures is decidedly too difficult because the audience wants to learn everything in a single session, and they all argue on the basis of current ways of doing things. Furthermore, lectures are too expensive. It costs twenty-five francs to rent a hall of the right size in the right area. It would be better to work with a core of pupils who would consent to study the basic text."[63]

The real problem with Fourier's lectures was that he was a poor popularizer. He seems to have lacked the ability to do anything more than to present his ideas to the public as a body of doctrine, to be swallowed whole. As Just Muiron put it in a letter to his friend Gréa:

> As skillful as is Monsieur Fourier at discovering savant contri-
> vances in the sciences . . . he is very deficient when it comes to
> practical matters and to presenting his ideas in a way that will
> make them known in our civilized world. No one knows better
> than he that people have to be led from the known to the
> unknown, that they have to be led to grasp the beautiful, the
> good, and the true by means of charm and attraction. But no
> one deviates more thoroughly from that natural and wise way
> of doing things.[64]

Fourier "should play on the curiosity" of his audience, wrote Muiron. He should "develop their enthusiasm." But instead, what he was asking them to do was to "*consent* coldly to a prearranged program of study."

21

The Saint-Simonians

LEGEND HAS it that on the occasion of the Revolution of 1830 Fourier experienced a brief moment of euphoria. On the morning of July 30, having learned of the overthrow of the Bourbon King Charles X, he went to share the news with his old republican friend from Lyon, Dr. Amard. When the old doctor talked of his hope for a new republican constitution, Fourier is supposed to have replied that the time had come, not for the Republic, but for the idea of association. The new government is going to be forced, he said, "to inquire into the means of realizing association."[1] This story may be apocryphal, but in any case it is clear that Fourier's hopes with regard to the July Revolution were short-lived. Within a few months he was referring to the revolution as a merely political change without any bearing on French society. In retrospect it seemed to him that the only significant result of the revolution was to prevent what he had hoped would be a serious consideration of his ideas by Baron Capelle, the minister of public works under Charles X.

Although the ministers of the July Monarchy had no more interest in Fourier's proposals than those of the Restoration, the July Revolution turned out to be an event of considerable importance for the spread and influence of Fourier's ideas. For the establishment of constitutional monarchy under the Orleanists was accompanied by an opening up of French political life and a loosening of the restrictions on freedom of the press and freedom of association that had existed throughout the Restoration. New social and political forces that had been silenced for a generation found a voice, and hopes arose that the government might play an active role in the solution of social problems. Most of these hopes were rapidly dispelled, and by 1834 many of the old restrictions on the rights of association and free expression had been reimposed. But for an initial period of about four years the climate of French public life was freer and more open than at any time since the Directory.

These initial years of the July Monarchy were marked by a social and political awakening, which had multiple dimensions. First, there was the revival of republicanism as a significant force in French political life for the first time in a generation. This was manifest most conspicuously in the flourishing of such republican associations and clubs as the Société des Amis du Peuple and the Société des Droits de l'Homme. Second, there were important signs of a new radical consciousness among French industrial workers. Strikes, demonstrations, and above all the great insurrections of the Lyon *canuts* in November 1831 and April 1834 were evidence that the French industrial working class was beginning to acquire new habits of organization and a new sense of its own powers. A third important development of the early years of the July Monarchy was the emergence of a diffuse but significant and relatively widespread consciousness on the part of the urban bourgeoisie of the social problems caused by the spread of industrialization and the rapid growth of the cities in the preceding decade. In the wake of the July Revolution, the cholera epidemic of 1832, and the working-class insurrections at both Lyon and Paris, attention focused above all on the condition of the urban poor, and respectable middle-class journals like the *Revue des deux mondes* and the *Journal des débats* began to devote articles to what came to be known as "the social question."

It was in this context that an audience was at last found not only for Fourier's writings but also for those of a number of rival social theorists who had for some time previously been attempting to define and resolve the problems created in France and England by the rise of the new industrial society. The most important of these thinkers was Henri Saint-Simon, who had already attracted a substantial group of followers during the last years of the Restoration. Since the development of a Fourierist movement owed much to the efforts of individuals whose social consciousness had been formed by Saint-Simonism, I shall begin this chapter with a discussion of Saint-Simon and his disciples. Then I shall turn to Fourier's relations with the disciples of Saint-Simon and to the role that several of them played, after the splintering of the Saint-Simonian movement, in helping to make Fourier's ideas known to the world.

I

Ever since the appearance of Friedrich Engels's classic essay "Socialism: Utopian and Scientific," Henri Saint-Simon has had a place, along with Fourier and Robert Owen, in the great triumvirate of "utopian social-ist" precursors of Marxism.[2] Although there are other perspectives from which each of these thinkers may be viewed, this perspective remains useful. For each in his own way was a crisis philosopher, drawing plans for the reconstruction of a world torn apart by the French Revolution and Napoleonic wars. Each was a vehement critic of the waste and suffering produced by industrial capitalism in its early phases; and each believed that social control of the emerging industrial economy was the key to a richer and more abundant life for all. Saint-Simon was not, however, a utopian in the strict communitarian sense. He had no carefully articulated conception of an ideal society like Fou-rier's or Owen's. Nor did he devote his life, as they did, to the elabora-tion of a single "system." He was, as Frank Manuel has pointed out, a "man of intuitions," a seminal thinker who needed disciples, not, as Fourier did, to simplify a complex body of doctrine, but rather to build on and develop incompletely formulated insights. He was also a man whose ideas remained constantly in a state of evolution. During an initial phase of his career Saint-Simon was obsessed by the desire to create a science of society on the model of Newtonian physics. Later, after the fall of Napoleon, he became a prophet of the technocratic restructuring of society and a sort of unofficial propagandist for the liberal bourgeoisie, which had acquired wealth and power during the Empire. Convinced that the parasitism of the aristocracy was the chief bar to social progress, he began to conceive schemes of social reorga-nization to be directed by an elite of scientists and industrialists. Finally in the last years of his life, his thinking took a strongly humanitarian turn, and the partisan of industrialism became an advocate for the "poorest and most numerous class." His final work was an appeal for the establishment of a "New Christianity," the main object of which was "to improve as rapidly as possible the condition of the poorest class."[3]

When Saint-Simon died in 1825, he was still unknown to the world at large. But during his last years he had gathered around him a remarkably talented group of disciples. Many of them were graduates of the prestigious Ecole Polytechnique, where they had received superb training in mathematics and abstract science and also a fervent belief in the power of science to solve social problems.[4] They were brilliant but troubled young men who sensed acutely the political and moral anarchy of the postrevolutionary period and who saw themselves as living in a society in which traditional social bonds had collapsed. They were eager for a faith that would give their lives direction and a purpose they had failed to find elsewhere. What attracted them to Saint-Simon was not only his view of science as the key to the material and moral reorganization of society but also, and most importantly, the vision of social reconciliation suggested by the "New Christianity."[5]

A few months after Saint-Simon's death, this small group of disciples founded a journal called *Le Producteur,* which was designed to "elaborate and spread" the theories of their master. Although this journal lasted barely a year, the group stayed together. By the end of 1828 their numbers had grown, thanks to proselytizing at the Ecole Polytechnique, and they felt themselves ready to undertake the elaboration of a systematic body of doctrine. Thus throughout 1829 and 1830, in a rented hall on the rue Taranne, they collaborated on a program of public lectures, which they later published under the title *Exposition de la doctrine de Saint-Simon.*[6] The "doctrine" they elaborated was not a mere summary of the teachings of Saint-Simon; it was a "continuation" and "development" of his ideas on history, work, industry, love, and religion. By the time the lectures were finished, the disciples had radicalized their master's teaching in a number of ways; and they had also created what they themselves came to describe as a "faith," a new religion that aimed at filling what they perceived as the moral and religious vacuum of the age. In December of 1829 they constituted themselves formally as a "church" under the authority of two "supreme fathers," Prosper Enfantin and Saint-Amand Bazard.

Since the Saint-Simonian religion eventually degenerated into self-conscious posturing and a futile search throughout the Middle East for a "Female Messiah," it is easily dismissed as one of the wilder aberrations of the romantic period. But to take such a view is to risk discounting the extraordinarily deep and widespread emotional response evoked by the preaching and proselytizing of the disciples of Saint-Simon. For in the two years that followed the proclamation of the Saint-Simonian religion it acquired a large following not only in France but also in Belgium and Germany. And in retrospect it seems clear that Saint-Simonism played an important role in crystallizing the discontents and aspirations of many of the most talented members of the generation of French writers and intellectuals who reached maturity toward the end of the Restoration.

II

Like Fourier, Henri Saint-Simon finished his life as an inhabitant of the Sentier, the bustling and somewhat dingy quarter surrounding the Paris Bourse.[7] The two men may have literally rubbed shoulders on the rue Richelieu, where they both lived during the 1820s. It is almost certain, however, that Saint-Simon knew nothing of Fourier. As for Fourier, he had *heard* of Saint-Simon—there is a sarcastic reference in his manuscripts to "the economist Saint-Simon," the "learned advocate of the merchants"—but the little that Fourier knew concerning the doctrines of his fellow utopian came at second hand.[8] The real story of Fourier's relations with Saint-Simonism begins only in 1829, four years after the death of Henri Saint-Simon and just prior to the formal establishment of the Saint-Simonian church.

Fourier's first contact with the Saint-Simonians took place on May 20, 1829, when he was taken by a young acquaintance named François de Corçelle *fils* to one of their bimonthly meetings at the rue Taranne.* The *Nouveau monde industriel* had been published two months earlier, and Fourier's purpose in visiting the Saint-Simonians was, as he later put it, not only "to find out what is the doctrine of these messieurs" but also "to

---

*François de Corçelle (1802–1892) was a friend and political follower of Lafayette, whose memoirs he was to edit and one of whose daughters he married. During his student days he had been an active *carbinaro;* and though he did not consider himself a Saint-Simonian, he regarded the movement sympathetically as "a sort of religious *charbonnerie*." *Documens pour servir à l'histoire des conspirations, des partis et des sectes* (Paris, 1831), 68. This work includes a long section on Saint-Simonism but only a brief and noncommittal footnote (84–85n) on Fourier's "plan d'association domestique et agricole."

see if they could be made to take any interest in my own." When he arrived, he found a small hall crowded with about eighty spectators, who were listening intently to a lecture on "special education"—the sort of education that would enable individuals to "fulfill functions consistent both with their own aptitudes and with the needs of society." The next day Fourier noted the objections that had run through his mind while he listened.

> If I had argued I could have asked them: How with the civilized method or division by families, can you prevent a child from receiving a dozen contradictory educations, which the last, the *worldly,* will destroy? And as for special education, how will you succeed in putting a man in the place where instinct calls him? How will you develop at the age of three to five all his industrial instincts, which are often stifled for a whole lifetime? How will you make both men and women into strong and skillful workers before making savants of them? How will you teach them habits of work and cleanliness at the age of three to five when they are good for nothing and when you have to keep them out of sight to prevent them from making trouble?[9]

He kept silent, however, both during the initial lecture and the discussion afterward when he had to endure an animated debate over the merits of confession. For his part he doubted that anyone in "that crowd" would ever enter into a confessional except out of "speculation in hypocrisy."

Fourier's reaction to this first encounter with the Saint-Simonians was strongly negative. It was a wonder to him how anyone could "find credit in Paris with such weak doctrines." As he wrote Muiron:

> To give you an idea of their weakness, they claim that "the late economist Saint-Simon" was divinely inspired, and that there are three revelations: that of Moses, that of Jesus Christ, and that of the economist Saint-Simon. Isn't that making systems with an ax?[10]

He thought their "rough-hewn dogmas" were pitiful, but he added regretfully, "nonetheless they have a public and subscribers and they are talking about establishing an office." This was what Fourier found most galling: the following and the resources the Saint-Simonians had at their disposal were enormous compared to his own.

Fourier was not one to waste time where potential converts were concerned. The day after the meeting he sent the Saint-Simonians a copy of the *Nouveau monde industriel* together with a four-page letter to Prosper Enfantin in which he asked the Saint-Simonian pope to consider the idea of "changing his allegiance." Fourier conceded that "scientific vanity" might militate against such a step. But there was always the example of Augustine's conversion at the age of thirty-seven. In any case, there was little to gain from the patrimony of Saint-Simon, Fourier asserted, proceeding to criticize Saint-Simonism in terms that betrayed the superficiality of his acquaintance with it. "There is nothing at all new about this doctrine," he wrote. "It rests on all the old errors: subdivision in agriculture and housekeeping, false competition or deceitful struggle in commerce, simplistic methods of distribution, total lack of means for the development of instincts." The Saint-Simonian doctrine was "so subject to controversy," he observed (citing a point that had been raised the previous evening), "that the slightest objection involves the leaders in interminable hairsplitting." But the theory of passionate attraction had a "contrary property": it "confounds all objections by means of facts." This letter to Prosper Enfantin was accompanied by a ten-page "Note for the Saint-Simonian Society on the invention of the passionate series" in which Fourier summarized the essentials of his theory and reiterated his appeal for support from the Saint-Simonians.[11]

Prosper Enfantin may well have been amused by the naive self-confidence of Fourier's letter. But his reply was courteous. He agreed to read the *Nouveau monde industriel* with "all the attention that the questions you treat deserve, attention that has already been given to your earlier work." The proposal of a discussion seemed premature, however, since Fourier's comments suggested that he only knew the Saint-Simonian doctrine "by one or two sessions at the rue Taranne." To remedy the situation Enfantin sent Fourier "a few of the works by Saint-Simon and his school, which I now have at hand" and urged him to study them.[12]

Fourier seems to have been surprised by Enfantin's reluctance to accept his propositions. But undaunted and without wasting much time on the literature forwarded by Enfantin, Fourier drafted another long note restating his position and specifying some of his objections to the Saint-Simonian doctrine. Fourier's principal argument against the Saint-Simonians was that they were essentially moralists: they were seeking to change human nature rather than to create the material conditions that would make possible the flowering and full utilization of the existing passions. They had embarked on a "gigantic" enterprise, wrote Fourier, and one that could never succeed, whereas his own theory could be put to the test in a single community and on a modest piece of land. Fourier also objected to what he called the "plutocratic tendency" of the Saint-Simonians: their admiration for the entrepreneurial and organizational abilities of the great bankers and industrialists, whom Fourier blamed for many of the ills of modern society. Fourier went on to warn the Saint-Simonians that they were "going astray in parodying Catholicism and in attacking, peacefully or not, property, religion, and power." By contrast, Fourier boasted, his own method would work "without disturbing ministers or preachers, without taking control of the French treasury," and "without antagonizing the court and its agents."[13]

Although Fourier's knowledge of Saint-Simonism was obviously superficial, this letter to Enfantin is interesting in several respects. It does formulate with relative clarity some of the essential differences between his doctrine and theirs, and it also shows how eager Fourier was to emphasize the moderate and *un*revolutionary character of his methods when arguing with another radical. The letter was, however, neither as thoughtful nor as generous as the lengthy reply Fourier received from Enfantin a short time later. In addition to replying to Fourier's objections and formulating his own, Enfantin attempted to indicate those points on which he and Fourier stood on common ground. He criticized Fourier for his failure to indicate the historical forces tending to realize his vision of the future. He attacked Fourier's views on property and on the right of inheritance. ("No more inheritance by the right of *birth,* but by the right of *capacity.*") He criticized the idea of a small-scale test of association. But then he went on to write: "You suffer, sir. The society in which you are living seems *stinking* to you. You are disturbed by the relative position of the idle and the workers. That is enough for the followers of Saint-Simon to extend their hands to you heartily." And Enfantin continued: "The sentiment that inspires you and the dedication you display establish a real link between the followers of Saint-Simon and you." But in Enfantin's view the entente between Fourier and the Saint-Simonians was limited.

> We adhere *positively* to the sentiment that inspired you in the creation of your doctrine. We adhere *positively* to a large part of your critique of those agglomerations of incongruous and hostile beings, which people dare to describe as societies today. But we reject just as *positively* almost all your views on the future destiny

of humanity. We do not see that they are borne out by any tendency indicated by the study of human experience.[14]

Thus, finally, there was no understanding between Fourier and Enfantin; and a little later Fourier could sum up their correspondence in these terms: "The only result was an exchange of letters in which the Pope replied to me that he found his own doctrine sublime and that he [would] persist in adhering to it. As for me, I was willing to let the matter drop."[15]

If Fourier's initial reaction to the Saint-Simonians was unfavorable, his subsequent letters to Muiron show a deepening bitterness and hostility. On June 5, 1829, he was already describing them as "swindlers" from whom there was nothing more to hope. "They themselves don't believe in Saint-Simon any more than in the Koran," he wrote Muiron.[16] When Muiron suggested that the Saint-Simonians might actually be quite sincere, Fourier's response was to grumble more about their "hypocrisy," their "cossack morality," and the "evasive pathos" of their rhetoric. "I am always ready to listen to any proposition," he wrote, "but I am not ready to adopt their *tartufferie*."[17]

III

During the two years that followed Fourier's initial contacts with Enfantin, the Saint-Simonian movement was troubled by internal conflict but still continued to grow. The formal establishment of the Saint-Simonian "church" in December of 1829 occasioned the departure of a number of the earliest disciples—notably, Philippe Buchez, who went on to found a sect of his own. Nevertheless, the movement as a whole flourished. During the year 1830 members of the Saint-Simonian church at Paris began to circulate throughout the provinces, preaching and expounding their social gospel. Groups of followers grew up throughout France—at Metz, Bordeaux, Toulouse, Montpellier, Limoges, Lyon, Rouen. At Paris the meetings and lectures of the Saint-Simonians attracted such large audiences that it became necessary to rent several halls at once, and finally to move to a permanent headquarters on the rue Monsigny. Brochures were published; regular "missions" were sent out into the provinces; and in December 1830, with the purchase of *Le Globe,* the Saint-Simonians acquired their own journal.

By the end of 1830 the success of the Saint-Simonian religion was so evident that Fourier simply could not ignore or discount it. He was reminded of it by his own disciples, some of whom innocently wrote him of their own interest in Saint-Simonism or of analogies discovered between his ideas and theirs. He was also reminded of it in a more brutal way when one of his attempts to give a public lecture was interrupted by the noise emanating from a Saint-Simonian meeting in an adjacent lecture hall.[18] Incidents like this made the Saint-Simonians' success a source of intense pain to Fourier; and in his letters to Muiron the wry or ironic comments about the "niaiseries" and bad faith of the Saint-Simonians gave way to angry and rancorous tirades. He began to write about the Saint-Simonians as if he had a personal vendetta against them. And when Just Muiron professed admiration for the lofty tone and humanitarian sentiments of the Saint-Simonians, Fourier was capable of exploding.

> You want me to imitate their tone and their sentimental ser-
> mons, which you describe as "effusions of the heart." But
> that's the tone of charlatans. I could never indulge in that sort
> of trickery. I only rely on decisive arguments.[19]

Fourier's anger against the Saint-Simonians reached its height at the end of 1830 when, with some help, he managed to convince himself that in addition to being charlatans and hypocrites, the Saint-Simonians were also plagiarists. It seems that this idea was first suggested to him by his friend Amédée Pichot of the *Mercure de France*.* At any rate, Fourier

---

*See Fourier to Muiron, January 19, 1831, Pellarin, *Fourier*, 113: "They stole several of my ideas. The *Mercure* spoke of it. I was told by M. Monier *fils,* and M. Pichot told me the same thing and added that he was the one who denounced their plagiarism in the *Mercure.*" In reprinting Fourier's *Mnémonique géographique* in the *Mercure de France* Pichot had in fact included the following editorial note: "Monsieur Charles Fourier is, we dare say, one of the most distinguished thinkers of our time. He does not, however, belong to the Institute because he has as much repugnance for intrigue as he has love of true learning. We propose to prove that everything reasonable in Saint-Simonism has been plagiarized from the discovery of passionate attraction by Charles Fourier." *Le Mercure de France au dix-neuvième siècle,* XXVIII (March 1830), 453. This charge was repeated by the *Mercure* in January 1831, but no effort was made to support it.
Fourier was prone to see plagiarists everywhere—this was what Victor Considerant described as his "manie d'avare." But he may not have been entirely wrong in the case of the Saint-Simonians. Prosper Enfantin's thinking on such questions as the rehabilitation of the flesh and the emancipation of women does in fact seem to have been influenced by Fourier's work. For a full discussion of the topic see Louvancour, *De Saint-Simon à Fourier,* 146–170. See also Thibert, *Le Féminisme dans le socialisme français,* 31–39.

latched on to it, and it became one of the main articles of the indictment which Fourier launched against the Saint-Simonians in a pamphlet published in the spring of 1831 under the title *Pièges et charlatanisme des deux sectes Saint-Simon et Owen, qui promettent l'association et le progrès.*

This pamphlet, in which Fourier actually had much more to say about the "snares and charlatanism" of the Saint-Simonians than those of the Owenites, was hardly more than a litany of expletives. Its general nature is perhaps best indicated by a brief summary he wrote in a letter to Muiron.

> In a short preamble I set forth quite gaily the absurdity of their basic ideas on theocracy and mortmain and the charlatanism of their inflated manner. Then I turn to their plagiarism. . . . Before dissecting their theory and their tactics, I have devoted three articles to giving a short exposition of the two sciences they are trying to steal from me. . . . Then I examine their tricks.[20]

Fourier's criticism of the Saint-Simonian doctrine in this pamphlet is of little significance. If the pamphlet has any importance at all, it is more for its rhetorical fireworks than for its arguments. The language of invective is rich, and Fourier manages to treat the Saint-Simonians not only as "ascetic charlatans," "speculative chameleons," and "philanthropical mountebanks" but also as "inheritance hunters" and "scientific cossacks plundering and making travesties of the ideas of others."

All his life Fourier cherished illusions about his effectiveness as a polemical writer. But nowhere do these illusions seem to have been further from reality than in his assessment of the *Pièges et charlatanisme.* Fourier seems actually to have believed not only that the pamphlet was a "crushing blow" to the Saint-Simonians but also that it might help him find a protector. Thus shortly after its appearance he could write Muiron that he was planning to present the work "to those whose protection I seek, and first of all to the king and two or three of his ministers." In fact, Fourier's attacks were so violent and his rhetoric so extravagant that if it had been widely read, his pamphlet could only have proved compromising. Fortunately for Fourier, the *Pièges* passed virtually unnoticed even among the Saint-Simonians. There was a brief and derogatory allusion to it in the Saint-Simonian *Globe* and another in a lecture on Fourier delivered by the Saint-Simonian Lambert, but that was about all.[21] As for Fourier's disciples, they were embarrassed by the pamphlet. Thus Muiron could complain about Fourier's tendency "to see enemies in all men," warning that Fourier's "virulent sorties" and "lacerating invectives" could only serve to alienate potential converts. And another disciple could later observe that "more bile and gall seemed to flow from the work than honest and pure indignation."[22]

To all of this Fourier replied that he had simply told the truth. As he wrote Muiron on July 18, 1831:

> You say that they have been alienated by my "lacerating" invectives. What is so lacerating about hearing that one has been deceived for three thousand years; that it is not through administrative and sacerdotal reforms that the common good must be sought, but in industrial reform. . . . You say that we should have pity on the "poor blind who are leading the blind." But when they lead their comrades to the edge of a precipice, it would take a ferocious sort of pity to tell them: "You are headed in the right direction. Keep going." In any case, the tone I am taking with them is not one of vehement anger or even normal anger. I am using *raillery*.[23]

Two months later Fourier was still carrying on. "You accuse me of violent rage against the Saint-Simonians," he wrote Muiron. "It is not rage; it is justified scorn."

Toward the end of the summer of 1831 Fourier at last received some good news concerning his rivals. After several years of rapid growth the Saint-Simonian movement was running into financial difficulties. On August 31 the editors of the *Globe* published an urgent appeal for funds, warning that without help they would have to stop publication immediately. Fourier was delighted to learn this, and he could not resist rubbing salt into the wound. He promptly sent a long letter to the Saint-Simonians, presenting his theory as a means by which they could have increased their readership one hundred-fold while simultaneously taking credit for the reconciliation of the Poles and the Russians and the abolition of "all ancient and onerous taxes."[24]

The response to the *Globe*'s appeal for funds was sufficiently great that the editors were able to continue publication. Thus in writing Muiron two weeks later Fourier could only speak of a "distress signal" fired by the Saint-Simonians; he added with obvious disappointment that the editors of the *Globe* had not made any response to his letter, "not even a simple acknowledgment." The following month, however, and without any warning, the full text of Fourier's letter suddenly appeared in the pages of the *Globe*. It was accompanied by an introductory note that poked fun at the "infallible means" Fourier was proposing to rescue the Saint-Simonian movement and Poland at one and the same time. The editors of the *Globe* conceded that Fourier had often criticized his society "with a rare sagacity." "But," they added, "at an early point he went off on a wrong tack, and he has persisted in it, because he has always worked apart from other men."[25]

It is clear that the Saint-Simonians published Fourier's letter in the hope of discrediting his ideas.[26] Some of his disciples took consolation in the fact that he was at least getting publicity. But the more common view was expressed by Jules Lechevalier, who wrote that the letter "must appear strange and bizarre" to individuals not already versed in Fourier's theory.[27] Thus several of Fourier's disciples urged him to write another letter to the *Globe* to explain and clarify his ideas. Fourier did in fact write such a letter.[28] But he seems never to have sent it. A month later, however, he was still complaining to Muiron that he didn't have a journal of his own in which he could say whatever he liked. "If only I had a journal," he wrote, "how I would set upon those clowns."[29]

Fourier did not have a journal, or any of the other resources of the Saint-Simonians. But these were soon to come. For during the last months of 1831 a schism developed within the Saint-Simonian religion, the result of which was to make it possible for Fourier at last to acquire a significant following, and a forum for the expression of his ideas.

IV

During the two years that followed the establishment of the Saint-Simonian religion, authority within the church had been nominally shared by the two "popes," Prosper Enfantin and Saint-Amand Bazard. From the beginning, however, the dominant partner was Enfantin. Under the sway of his powerful charisma the majority of the Saint-Simonians began to espouse ideas concerning the position of women, the relations between the sexes, and the rehabilitation of the flesh that were offensive to Bazard and a number of others.★ Finally on November 11, 1831, Bazard announced his decision to quit the church. Bazard's defection opened a split within the Saint-Simonian religion. It was followed by the apostasy of other disciples, some of whom joined the Fourierists.

The emergence of Fourierism as an important social movement in Louis Philippe's France was the result in great part of the efforts of two young Saint-Simonians who were among the first to break away from the church during the schism of the winter of 1831–1832. These were Jules Lechevalier and Abel Transon. Their contributions to the spread of Fourier's ideas and the making of the Fourierist movement were so important that something needs to be said about the process by which each became a Fourierist.[30]

Jules Lechevalier was born in 1806. He was a native of Martinique who had studied law in Paris and philosophy in Berlin in the late 1820s. He joined the Saint-Simonian group in 1830 and was quick to display unusual gifts as a speaker. In the spring of 1831 Lechevalier led a Saint-Simonian "mission" to Normandy, and in the summer of the same year he preached the new gospel throughout the east of France, in Dijon, Besançon, Strasbourg, and Metz. During that summer, however, Lechevalier began to take an interest in Fourier's ideas. A discussion with Just Muiron, whose enthusiasm and obvious dedication impressed him, was as he later put it, "a first awakening for my heart and mind." Shortly afterward Lechevalier published a brief and sympathetic article on Fourier in the *Globe* (with regrets concerning the "false prejudices" and "strange judgments" of the *Pièges*); and he embarked on a thorough study of Fourier's doctrine, beginning with the *Traité de l'association*. "I was staggered," he wrote Fourier afterward, "by everything new and profound and immense that the book contains. . . . I wrote the chiefs of the doctrine that I regarded you as the *savant perfectionnant* whom we needed." But still his Saint-Simonian faith remained firm, and he saw in Fourier no more than "one of the satellites of the Saint-Simonian star."[31]

★There was little in the writings of Saint-Simon himself to justify the new direction that Enfantin gave to the Saint-Simonian doctrine in the years 1830–1831; and it is possible, ironically enough, that Enfantin was inspired in part by his reading of Fourier's *Théorie des quatre mouvements*. It seems to me, however, that the case is overstated by Louvancour, who concludes his lengthy analysis of the question of Enfantin's plagiarism of Fourier with the assertion that "when everything is taken into account, the theory of the 'rehabilitation of the flesh' and everything related to it can be considered as an importation from Fourierism into Saint-Simonism." *De Saint-Simon à Fourier,* 164.

In October of 1831 Lechevalier traveled to Metz to preach Saint-Simonism to the students at the Ecole d'Application, where Victor Considerant had been proselytizing for Fourier's theory. The two engaged in a public debate during the course of which Lechevalier made few concessions. But in private conversations with Considerant he was much less sure of himself. As Considerant informed Clarisse Vigoureux shortly after Lechevalier's departure:

> Jules Lechevalier made me some unique revelations: the Saint-Simonian religion is in a state of distress. There are money problems, the sacred college is divided. . . . We already have the Saint-Simonians and the Saint-Simonists. Soon we will have a new schism, and in fact it already exists. Jules Lechevalier has already given it a name. He talks about the Catholic *nondivorcites* and the pagan *divorcites*.[32]

In a letter to Fourier, Considerant added that if Lechevalier was not yet ready to "change colors," it was only because he was "in so deep" and because he still clung to "the idea that one can harmonize Fourier and Saint-Simon."[33]

In November of 1831, just a few days after Lechevalier's return from Metz, the crisis within the Saint-Simonian church came to a head with Bazard's announcement of his apostasy. Along with Pierre Leroux and Hippolyte Carnot, Jules Lechevalier was one of the first to imitate Bazard's gesture. At the general meeting of November 19 he declared that he could no longer remain within the church: "I confess that I have arrived at a state of DOUBT, a state of *complete* doubt with regard to the whole doctrine. I am in the very state in which I was before becoming a Saint-Simonian. . . . I am once again alone in the world."[34] Lechevalier did not long remain "alone in the world." Barely a month later, in a brochure explaining the motives for his apostasy, he announced his intention to write a work that would "render homage and justice" to Fourier and right the wrong done to his reputation by Saint-Simonian "prejudice."[35] On January 16, 1832, in a long letter to Fourier he explained that he had lost his faith in the Saint-Simonian doctrine, and that his confidence in its leaders had been "entirely destroyed." And he continued:

> At this moment I am devoting myself almost exclusively to your works, and I am urging all the Saint-Simonians whom I think capable of understanding them to study them. . . . Every day I

take new steps in your direction. The clouds are vanishing, my ideas are becoming coordinated, and already doubt has given way to the liveliest admiration. I feel that you have *given* to the world what I *promised* it in the name of Henri Saint-Simon. . . . Sir, I am very young, but my whole life is consecrated to the happiness of my fellows and to the worship of the genius who labors for humanity. Impressed by your great ideas and convinced of their power, I wish to employ all of my feeble strength to see justice rendered to you by a world that has so long misunderstood you. I want to lift the veil that priestly ambition has cast upon the eyes of men who are full of merit and devotion. I am very far from adopting all your ideas, since you yourself have not directly expounded your method, your *transcendent theory,* or the *scale of personality types.* But from what I have already learned, I am convinced that the most important social task at this time is to make your doctrine known. Thus I place at your disposition my voice and my pen.[36]

Lechevalier concluded by promising to do his utmost to "repair the wrongs of my old masters with regard to you" and by requesting permission to see Fourier to discuss some of the questions that remained in his mind with regard to the theory.

Fourier had hitherto been dubious about Lechevalier—he feared "the kiss of Judas"—but even he had to be pleased with such a letter. On January 20 he sent Lechevalier a long reply, detailing his criticism of the Saint-Simonians and renewing his charges of plagiarism.[37] Shortly thereafter he called on Lechevalier to begin discussing the questions that Lechevalier had raised. As for the disciples, they regarded the conversion of Jules Lechevalier as a "triumph." It was soon followed by that of Abel Transon.

It would be hard to imagine two individuals more different than Jules Lechevalier and Abel Transon. Unlike the ebullient, quick-witted and self-confident Lechevalier, Transon was a frail, nervous and shy individual who was constantly in need of affection and reassurance. He received it from Claire Bazard, who seems to have loved him as a mother, and from Jules Lechevalier, whom he idolized. Four months older than Lechevalier, Transon was born at Versailles on Christmas Day, 1805. After graduating at the top of his class from the Ecole Polytechnique in 1825, he worked for several years as a mining engineer. He joined the Saint-Simonians not long before the July Revolution. Frequently tormented by fits of depression and doubt, Transon several times abandoned the sect in the years 1830 and 1831. But each time Lechevalier and Enfantin brought him back to the fold. Finally in January of 1832, after several months of "pain and struggle," Transon informed Enfantin that, "having no more faith" in the Saint-Simonian religion, he had determined to follow Lechevalier into the camp of the Fourierists.[38] This time the rupture was final.

The news of the Saint-Simonian schism and of the conversions of Lechevalier and Transon spread rapidly among Fourier's disciples. To a number of them these events seemed to herald a turning point in the fortunes of the movement. From Dijon Gabriel Gabet wrote to congratulate Fourier on his "triumph" and at Metz one of Victor Considerant's comrades could boast that "everything [is] lost for the Saint-Simonians. . . . The resources of the *Globe* are going to become Fourier's booty."[39]

The activity of Transon and Lechevalier during the first months of 1832 seemed to justify these high expectations. The first writings that both of them published as Fourierists were aimed directly at the Saint-Simonians. In his *Simple Ecrit aux Saint-Simoniens,* a brochure dated February 1, 1832, Transon stressed the inadequacy of the Saint-Simonian doctrine to "realize" its visions of association.

> As long as we had nothing else to do than to *announce* a religious transformation of humanity, I entirely shared the erroneous belief that made us all suppose that Saint-Simon had bequeathed to us a universal *science,* a plan for the organization of *industry,* and a definitive RELIGION. But now that we have entered the *era of realization,* my illusion has necessarily been dissipated, in part by the awakening that Jules Lechevalier's departure gave me, in part by the reading of the works of Charles Fourier, in part by the impotence of the [Saint-Simonian] doctrine truly to *associate* men, an impotence that has become more clearly evident to me with the passing of every day.[40]

The Saint-Simonians had talked of creating craft associations in which tailors and shoemakers could work in common, sharing the profits of their labor. And yet, insisted Transon, work in these associations would necessarily have the same "repugnant and brutalizing" quality of "monastico-Christian uniformity that today characterizes all industrial labor." The Saint-Simonians had not solved the problem of rendering industrial work attractive. Nor, despite Enfantin's pronouncements, had they genuinely come to grips with the question of the role of women in modern society. Enfantin had preached equality between the sexes, but according to the latest metamorphosis of his doctrine, he was content to await the arrival of a Female Messiah before permitting even the Saint-Simonians themselves to transgress the limits of conventional morality. For his part, Transon was willing to accept the logical consequences of Enfantin's new position, the immediate emancipation of the flesh as well as of the spirit. But, he asked, had not Enfantin been anticipated by Charles Fourier? Through the rehabilitation of the passions and the doctrine of attractive labor Fourier had, according to Transon, worked out a scheme of association that was consistent with the goals of the Saint-Simonians and capable of immediate realization. Thus Transon concluded by calling upon Enfantin and his colleagues to join the Fourierist enterprise.

Transon's *Simple Ecrit* was intended less to provide a résumé of Fourier's doctrine than to show the relevance of Fourierist "means" to the "goals" of the Saint-Simonians. As such it proved to be a highly effective piece of propaganda. It did not of course inspire Enfantin to found a Phalanx. But it did provoke attention among the Saint-Simonians and, apparently, helped to bring about a number of conversions.[41] In the months that followed Transon continued his activity as a publicist for Fourier's ideas. In February and May of 1832 he published two important articles on Fourierism in Pierre Leroux and Jean Reynaud's *Revue encyclopédique*. One of these articles, his "Succinct Exposition of the Societary Theory," provoked widespread discussion and was regarded by Fourier himself as the best brief summary of the system produced by any of his disciples.[42]

Jules Lechevalier's contribution in publicizing Fourierism was even greater than Transon's. Within a week after informing Fourier of his conversion, he was already knocking on the doors of the Paris newspapers in search of publicity. On January 28, 1832, he had to tell Fourier that Jacques Coste, the editor of *Le Temps,* had burst out laughing when asked to help in recruiting "a few shareholders" for the establishment of a Phalanx. But in the same letter Lechevalier announced his intention to hold lectures on Fourier's theory for the benefit of the Saint-Simonians. "They are all very anxious to hear about it," he wrote, adding that "the Supreme Father is, I think, embarrassed by this little obstacle we are going to stick in his path, but since he doesn't lack craftiness, he pretends to be perfectly happy about the idea and has offered me the use of a hall." Reluctant to "fall into that trap," Lechevalier found a hall of his own on the rue Colombier.[43]

While preparing his lectures, Lechevalier kept in close touch with Fourier, with whom he discussed the content of each lecture.

> I will do nothing without your approval and advice [he wrote on February 3], and I am most anxious to talk with you a few moments. I would be very grateful if you would be kind enough to visit me tomorrow: I won't be going out all day. I have copied your tableau of past and future progress, which will be very useful for the lectures. I would be very much obliged to you if you would loan me the tableau that represents the diverse *ralliements*. I don't doubt, Monsieur, that a month from now we will be in a position to move ahead quickly.
>
> I believe you approve of my idea of giving only superficial treatment to your general principles and your universal synthesis. It would be advisable to save these difficult matters for another series of lectures. I confess in any case that I am not so strong on these points as on the others.[44]

Although Lechevalier had originally planned to deliver a dozen lectures, the cholera epidemic at Paris became so severe by the end of March that he was obliged to terminate his course prematurely. But the five lectures he did deliver were attended by a large and appreciative audience. Fourier himself was present at the lectures to answer questions and to add his own observations. On at least one occasion, Fourier's remarks about the Saint-Simonians were too salty for Lechevalier. "I need to tell you," he explained to his audience at the beginning of the third session on February 26, "that I am far from accepting the opinions of Monsieur Fourier concerning the Saint-Simonians or their doctrines. . . . The position of Monsieur Fourier is not the same as mine. He is and he wishes to remain *un homme sui generis*."[45] Despite such incidents, the lectures were so well received that it was decided to print each of them as a brochure for circulation among provincial disciples and potential converts. Shortly afterward, they were published together in book form under the title *Cinq leçons sur l'art d'associer, ou Réfutation du saint-simonisme au moyen de la théorie sociétaire de Charles Fourier*.[46]

The reaction of Fourier's provincial disciples to the published version of these lectures was enthusiastic. Gabet at Dijon was greatly impressed, as was Muiron's circle at Besançon. "The first installment of Jules Lechevalier's lectures arrived yesterday," Muiron wrote Clarisse Vigoureaux on March 1, 1832. "He couldn't have done better. I was enchanted. I am even happy about his reservations, about the fact that he doesn't claim to accept *everything*. He is really and truly headed in the right direction. He writes wonderfully." Ten days later Muiron added that "the lectures of Jules are working wonders here," and on March 11 the readers of the *Impartial* were informed (doubtless again by Muiron) that "amateurs of new and luminous ideas . . . and those who love an elegant, pure, engaging style, like that of our best writers, will be charmed by the *Leçons sur l'art d'associer*."[47]

In addition to the accolades they drew from longstanding Fourierists, Lechevalier's *Cinq leçons* had a significant impact on a number of his former Saint-Simonian associates. According to Charles Pellarin, who left the Saint-Simonian retreat at Menilmontant to join the Fourierists in August 1832, "his lectures contributed greatly in dissipating Saint-Simonian illusions." Eugénie Niboyet, a Saint-Simonian feminist from Lyon, was one of many whose interest in Fourier's ideas resulted largely from Lechevalier. "Fourier . . . is very fortunate to have a popularizer like you," she wrote him in July 1832. "This makes his ideas spread by giant steps. I don't doubt that you will have proselytes wherever your voice is heard, for it satisfies both the mind and the heart." Dr. Fleury Imbert of Lyon, who had been a Saint-Simonian, also had words of high praise for Lechevalier's work as a popularizer. "For ten years I regarded the *Théorie des quatre mouvements* as something to laugh and joke about. . . . Thanks to you, I now see in [Fourier's theory] one of the most astonishing products ever created by a human brain. It needed to be translated and explicated. You have undertaken that ungrateful task and fulfilled it with the talent of which you have already given so many proofs."[48]

If Lechevalier's lectures helped make Fourier's ideas accessible and appealing to many members of the Saint-Simonian group, they were also important in making Fourier intellectually respectable and in attracting the attention of the bourgeois reading public to Fourier's ideas. Lechevalier's success on this count was noted by the liberal editor Marc-Antoine Jullien, whom Fourier himself had long and vainly courted. In June of 1832 Jullien wrote to congratulate Lechevalier on his work, adding that he had "known Monsieur Fourier for a long time," and that although he "appreciated the merit" of Fourier's work, he realized that Fourier needed "to become associated with interpreters and propagators able to popularize his doctrine and to render it easily intelligible and immediately practicable."[49] No less telling are the comments of the poet Béranger, who, in a note to a poem celebrating Fourier, gave Lechevalier and Transon credit for his own "discovery" of Fourier.

> Monsieur Jules Lechevalier has explained and propagated the ideas of Monsieur Charles Fourier in a series of public lectures. Without him we might still not know what the inventor meant by Phalanstery, group, attractive functions, etc. The system of association has never been explored with more power than by this theorist who makes passionate attraction the basis of his social code. Without Monsieur Lechevalier and Transon I would have been condemned to fail to grasp the scientific character of his work.[50]

The comments of men like Béranger and Jullien, and also Fleury Imbert, deserve to be noted. Each was in his way an influential and respected figure: Béranger as an enormously popular poet, Jullien as an editor and journalist, and Imbert as a prominent Lyon surgeon. They had each known of Fourier's writings prior to 1830, but they had not been greatly impressed. In presenting the theory in a watered-down version, stripped of its more esoteric elements and of at least some of its neologisms, Lechevalier had awakened their interest. Although none of them was to become a disciple in the strict sense, each was to help make Fourier's theory better known. And in one poem, the ironically titled "Les Fous," Béranger was to celebrate Fourier's achievement before an audience that numbered in the tens of thousands.

During the twenty-three years that had elapsed since the publication of the *Théorie des quatre mouvements,* Fourier and his theory had remained virtually unknown. His books had produced more merriment than light among their few readers. His first disciple, Just Muiron, had managed to gather a small group of disciples at Besançon. But with the exception of Victor Considerant, who in the spring of 1832 was still confined to preaching Fourierism to the young engineers at the Ecole d'Application at Metz, they were a mediocre lot. Muiron's own efforts to win an audience for Fourier's ideas had been pathetically inadequate. An unread and unreadable volume on the *comptoir communal,* a superficial discussion of Fourier's ideas by the luminaries of Besançon's Académie des Sciences, Belles-Lettres et Arts, a few discreet allusions slipped into the pages of the respectable *Impartial,* and a vast number of unsuccessful appeals for publicity—this was the net result of the efforts on Fourier's behalf by Muiron and his friends at Besançon.

The Saint-Simonian schism, the conversion of Jules Lechevalier and Abel Transon, and the publication of their popularizations of Fourier's thought marked a milestone in the fortunes of Fourierism both as a body of doctrine and as a social movement. At last Fourier had, as Jullien put it, the "interpreters and propagators" he needed "to popularize his doctrine and to render it easily intelligible and immediately practicable."

22

Publishing a Journal

THE FIRST months of 1832 were a time of great hope and enthusiasm for Fourier and his disciples. The "conspiracy of silence" that had so long impeded the spread of his ideas was at last broken. The lectures and articles of Jules Lechevalier and Abel Transon had made Fourierism known to the world at large, and had also played an important role in bringing about the conversion of a number of Saint-Simonians. Fourier's older disciples were delighted by these developments. From Metz Victor Considerant wrote triumphantly about the "wonderful" news from Paris and the "beautiful" prospects for the future. At Besançon Just Muiron reveled in now being sought after by people who had formerly laughed in his face when he had tried to talk to them about Fourier's theory. At Dijon Gabriel Gabet exulted. "At last the day of your glory has come," he wrote Fourier, "the moment when your humiliated rivals recognize the superiority of your genius." Fourier himself does not seem to have been quite so overcome. But there was a note of high hope in a letter he sent to Muiron three days after Lechevalier's first lecture: "I have now reached the decisive moment," he wrote. "I am near the denouement."[1]

As winter turned into spring the news for Fourier and his disciples continued to be good. Sympathetic articles on Fourier and his thought began to appear in the Parisian press.² And encouraging letters and even a few Fourierist "professions of faith" were received from a number of former Saint-Simonians who had been introduced to Fourier's doctrines by reading Transon's *Simple Ecrit* or Lechevalier's *Cinq leçons.*³ For the first time the Fourierists began to speak of themselves collectively as a "movement" or (more often) as the École Sociétaire. And now at last it seemed possible, not only to Fourier but also to his disciples, that an experimental test of his ideas might soon be made. It also seemed possible to realize one of Fourier's longstanding dreams: the publication of a journal devoted to the exposition and spread of his ideas.

I

For several years Fourier had believed that his efforts to find a benefactor and simply to provoke interest in his ideas would be greatly facilitated if he could count on the help of a journal such as the Saint-Simonian *Globe.* In the *Nouveau monde industriel* he had called for a benefactor to subsidize the creation of such a journal, and in the midst of his polemics with the Saint-Simonians he had several times paused to lament to Just Muiron that until he had a journal of his own, he could never adequately respond to the calumnies of his rivals.⁴

In 1830 and 1831 Just Muiron's *Impartial* had given some publicity to Fourier's doctrine. But clearly this provincial *juste-milieu* biweekly newspaper could never serve as a very effective instrument for the dissemination of Fourier's ideas.* Nor could the *Mercure de France.* The editors of this Parisian monthly had published a few articles sympathetic to Fourier's theory. They had taken his side in the quarrel with the Saint-Simonians. But as their own private correspondence shows, their interest in Fourier stemmed largely from a desire to add "spice" to their journal and to strike a modern and up-to-date pose.⁵ What Fourier wanted was a journal of his own, a journal that would serve as a vehicle for the publication by installments of a simplified exposition of the

---

*Muiron does not seem to have had great confidence in Fourier's ability to write about his own theory in a manner acceptable to the owners or readers of the *Impartial.* Thus most of the articles by Fourier that appeared in the *Impartial* were *amusettes* dealing with other matters. Muiron himself, however, published occasional articles on particular aspects of Fourier's thought. See for example "Sort des classes ouvrières," *Impartial,* III, 46, 49 (September 4, 15, 1831), and "Richesses, liberté, justice pour tous," *Impartial,* III, 53, 57 (September 29, October 13, 1831).

theory. By January of 1832 he and Considerant were exchanging letters on the subject.

> Our journal should be purely scientific [wrote Considerant]. It should not have to bother about day-to-day events. It should come out once a week and be eight pages long. At least half of it should always be devoted to the publication of the elementary method on which you are working now. Whenever you wish, the whole journal should be devoted to your writing. We will utilize the space that remains to speak about the need to organize association and to provoke public discussion on the subject. Only later, and after due preparation, will we turn to [your theories on] the study of man.[6]

In his letters to Clarisse Vigoureux, Just Muiron talked about the journal in similar terms, noting that the publication in installments of Jules Lechevalier's lectures might be an excellent way to begin.[7]

By March of 1832 Fourier and his disciples had agreed to begin raising funds for the publication of a weekly journal. Clarisse Vigoureux pledged two thousand francs to the enterprise. Another large contribution was received from a wealthy banker whom Fourier had recently met.[8] With this money in hand it was possible to rent an office and to begin negotiations with a printer. By the end of April an office had been rented on the rue Joquelet, just around the corner from Brongniart's newly completed Bourse. With it came a large reception room and a small adjoining apartment. It was agreed that the apartment would be Fourier's new residence. When he moved into it in May 1832, he began the only extended period in his life when he lived in daily contact with his disciples and collaborated closely with them on a common enterprise.

The new journal, which first appeared on June 1, 1832, was called *Le Phalanstère, Journal pour la fondation d'une Phalange agricole et manufacturière associée en travaux et en ménage.*[9] It was a weekly of eight large two-column pages, which its editors described as "consecrated to making known the advantages of domestic and agricultural association and the means discovered by Monsieur Fourier to create such an association."[10] The aim of the journal was thus twofold. It was intended both to provide a forum for the elaboration of Fourier's ideas and to rally support for the establishment of a trial Phalanx. In their introductory statement Lechevalier and Considerant stressed the interconnection of Fourierist theory and practice and insisted that Fourierism was not merely a set of abstract ideas. Instead they brought "a FACT to men eager for facts and realities." They continued:

> We are writing with a particular goal in mind, a goal that is particular even within the sphere embraced by our own ideas, because we are limiting ourselves to what is most immediately and . . . most easily practicable. . . . Our journal will not even contain the theoretical development of all our principles. Except for some necessary explanations, it will be quite simply the periodical prospectus for the degree of industrial association that we wish to establish.[11]

Consistent with this initial statement, the emphasis in the first issue of the *Phalanstère* was on the realization of Fourier's ideas. Fourier himself contributed a long programmatic statement on the trial Phalanx, and a large part of the issue was given over to the publication of the official statutes of two share-holding companies the disciples proposed to create. One of them, a Society for the Foundation of an Agricultural and Industrial Phalanx, was intended to raise a capital of no less than four million francs for the trial Phalanx. The other, a Society for the Publication and Propagation of the Theory of Charles Fourier, sought to raise thirty thousand francs for the publication of the journal and of future writings by Fourier and the disciples.

Despite the professed desire of Fourier's disciples to concentrate on practical matters, there was little said in the early numbers of the *Phalanstère* concerning the actual establishment of a trial Phalanx. In fact, most of the articles that appeared in the journal during its first six months were devoted to broad and rather abstract restatements of Fourier's main ideas. The chief contributor was Fourier himself. About a third to a half of each issue was given over to contributions by him, most of which were what he liked to call "leçons particulières," essays on particular aspects of the theory ranging from architecture to cosmogony. Fourier of course had little to say about contemporary politics. But he did use the journal as a platform from which to launch renewed attacks on such "sophists" and "philanthropic comedians" as Owen, Saint-Simon, and their disciples. In this respect he was indefatigable, and almost every issue of the journal contained a new article on the "secret designs" of the Saint-Simonians, the "mindlessness of the philosophers," or the "war of the four rebellious sciences against the four faithful sciences."

Among Fourier's disciples, the chief contributors were Jules Lechevalier, Abel Transon, and Victor Considerant.★ Both Lechevalier and Considerant published long articles in serial form summarizing Fourier's economic views and his general theory of association. Transon published a number of shorter articles on particular points of theory, and he also took charge of much of the editorial work necessary to see each issue through the press. During the first six months there were also numerous occasional pieces and appreciations of Fourier's ideas by young military engineers who had been introduced to Fourier's doctrine by Victor Considerant while students at the Ecole d'Application at Metz. These articles were diverse in character and quality. But what they all had in common was the desire to make Fourier's theory accessible to a wider audience. The focus was on what one of the disciples described as Fourier's "industrial ideas" with minimal use of his private terminology and as little reference as possible to his cosmological and sexual views, or even to his theory of passionate attraction.

The efforts of the disciples to reach a wider audience were not unsuccessful. Already after just a few weeks of publication they could boast of having received a "fairly large number" of expressions of support from "individuals who had formerly studied and in part accepted Saint-Simonism."[12] They could also report that Fourier's ideas were getting attention in the provincial press. But the success of the *Phalanstère* should not be exaggerated. In fact, its press run never greatly exceeded one thousand, and its total number of paid subscribers was probably less than half that.[†] Furthermore, many of the subscribers to the *Phalanstère* had already developed at least some interest in Fourier's ideas before the appearance of the journal. Despite the expressed wishes of the disciples, much of what appeared in the journal simply could not have made much sense to someone not already familiar with Fourier's ideas.

Fourier's disciples recognized the limitations of the journal. One of

---

★When the *Phalanstère* began to appear, Victor Considerant was still at Metz undergoing advanced training in the corps of military engineers. In July of 1832, however, he was granted an indefinite leave of absence, which enabled him to devote all his time to the journal.

†"Concernant l'administration du journal le Phalanstère," AN 10AS 25 (12). By comparison *Le Globe* had thirteen hundred subscribers at the time of its purchase by the Saint-Simonians. That number soon shrank to five hundred, but throughout the period of its ownership by the Saint-Simonians the press run of *Le Globe* remained at twenty-five hundred. See Charléty, *Histoire du Saint-Simonisme (1825–1864)* (Paris, 1896), 145.

the most outspoken of them, the Polytechnicien Nicolas Lemoyne, bluntly wrote that "the journal is indigestible." It deserved to be supported by the disciples. But it would "never have any other subscribers, or even any other readers, than the most fervent disciples. . . . It satisfies neither the Butterfly, nor the Cabalist, nor the Composite. Reading it is a task that only has a small amount of attraction even for someone who is already passionately committed to the Phalanstery." Not all the disciples found the *Phalanstère* to be indigestible. Indeed, one Bertin could write in July 1832 that he was "devouring" each number of the journal with great interest; and others were equally enthusiastic. But those who attempted to use the journal as a means of arousing interest in Fourier's ideas among outsiders were generally disappointed. Thus a professor at the Collège de Nevers could write the editors in July that "up to now my efforts . . . to obtain subscribers for you have been totally futile. Nevers is a backward city like all the cities in the center of France." The story at Bordeaux was similar. "Here at Bordeaux," wrote Edouard Lanet to Lechevalier, "a few people, but a *very small number,* pay attention to your journal."[13]

Most of the disciples agreed that the trouble with the *Phalanstère* was that it was too dry and too exclusively theoretical. As Lemoyne put it in a letter to Transon:

> In all of [our] publications, not excepting your own, my friend, or Considerant's, grandiose theoretical principles predominate over practical ideas. Even in the journal you are always inflexible theorists; you don't wish to make the slightest concession to commonplace ideas.[14]

But according to many of the disciples there was another, graver problem. It concerned the role to be played on the journal by Fourier himself. Even his oldest and most loyal disciple, Just Muiron, had little confidence in Fourier's ability to make his ideas attractive, or simply accessible, to a wide audience. To the young Polytechniciens who embraced Fourierism in 1832, Fourier's limitations as a popularizer of his own ideas seemed even clearer. Within a few weeks after the establishment of the *Phalanstère* many of them had come to the conclusion that Fourier's contributions were a real liability to the journal. As one of them put it, "No one is less suited than [Fourier] to the propagation of his own ideas." Another was equally blunt: "Let him be the inspiration of the journal, but let him write less in it."[15]

Fourier's disciples had many complaints about his contributions to the *Phalanstère*. They all deplored his periodic outbursts against the Saint-Simonians. They were also disturbed by his tendency to overwhelm his readers with unexplained theoretical allusions and bizarre terminology. "In the last number of the *Phalanstère*," wrote one of them to Fourier anonymously, "you address yourself to the capitalists. You want them to bring you their money . . . and you talk to them about 'tribes' and 'choirs' and 'internal' and 'external' rivalry, about the 'three sexes,' about 'simple' and 'compound' impulsions, etc., etc. To understand all these things one has to have read your works. But you know very well that the capitalists have not read them."[16] No less offensive to some of the disciples was Fourier's "extravagance" as a polemicist and the "vulgarity" of the tone that he assumed when he was making his best effort *not* to be obscure. As Nicolas Lemoyne put it in a letter to Pellarin: "I haven't dared show the last number of the journal to anyone on account of the articles by Fourier, and still this number is one of the most remarkable. Jules surpassed himself in it. Victor and [Baudet-]Dulary write perfectly well. But the note by Fourier on the grocers will be revolting to many people's feelings, even though the only thing one can criticize it for is bad literary taste. The article on the tragedy in forty acts is a buffoonery and isn't suited to our serious journal. Finally, some passages in the article by Fourier are incomprehensible for anyone besides a disciple."[17]

Fourier was not interested in Lemoyne's notions of gravity, good writing, and good taste. He had his own ideas about journalism. In brief, he believed that a newspaper article should be piquant and entertaining and bold, and it should make a direct appeal to the interests of specific readers.[18] Thus the articles that he published in the *Phalanstère* often bore catchy and arresting titles like "The Torpedoes of Progress," "Eighty-five Model Farms and Eighty-five Follies," "The Grocers Dethroned," and "The Emancipated Woman at last Found." They included the same sort of bribes and extravagant claims that he had earlier dangled before individual "candidates." They were aggressive and rich in invective. And they went straight to the point. Here, for instance, is how Fourier began his article "The Torpedoes of Progress."

> What is your goal, braggarts who sing only of progress and association? You are insidiously seeking to suppress all attempts at real association and real progress.[19]

When the disciples complained that this was crude and in poor taste, Fourier had an answer ready for them. It was the same answer that he had given in 1830 when Just Muiron had objected to the bad taste of Fourier's contributions to the *Impartial:* "Where have you learned that there has to be so much refinement and academic dressing among journalists? . . . Refinement is not required in journalistic or literary polemics. Voltaire was certainly a refined writer, but how many insults did he not spew forth against his enemies! Without going that far, one should try to hold to a middle course and speak with firmness to vandals and calumniators."[20]

Not all of Fourier's disciples were blind to his gifts as a writer. Charles Pellarin, for example, could compare him to La Fontaine and Molière for his skill at "painting without embellishment the vices and inequities of civilization." Even a critic like Lemoyne was capable of appreciating the vein of "fantastical poetry" that ran through much of Fourier's work.[21] But almost without exception, his disciples believed that he had no aptitude for journalism. Even those who appreciated the "poetry" in his major works feared that the bluntness and extravagance of his articles in the *Phalanstère* would compromise their efforts to get a hearing for his ideas. Eventually almost all of them came to agree with the views expressed by Victor Considerant in October of 1833 as he looked back on the *Phalanstère*'s first year: "We needed a great deal of courage to keep on moving ahead with an awareness of the permanent harm [Fourier] was doing to his doctrine by his articles in the journal."[22]

Given these feelings, it is not surprising that Fourier and the disciples were frequently at odds. In fact, the tension between them seems to have existed from the beginning of their collaboration on the *Phalanstère*. In the very first issue the editors felt obliged to print a note apologizing for Fourier's insistence on accompanying his initial programmatic statement concerning the trial Phalanx with an elaborate "tableau" of the fifteen different "degrees or stages" of association. Since the nomenclature alone was enough to discourage any but the most valiant reader, the editors commented with embarrassment: "We do not claim that the totality of the tableau could be understood without extensive explanations that are a part of the general theory of Monsieur Fourier and not the special object of this publication."[23] This was just the beginning. In July 1832, after Fourier had written an exceptionally vituperative article on the Saint-Simonians, Lechevalier and Transon had to publish a categorical rejection of his position.

After having vainly tried to persuade Monsieur Fourier to adopt better ideas concerning the Saint-Simonian doctrine and its leaders, we believe it our obligation to declare on our own behalf as well as that of all the Saint-Simonians who have joined us that we do not by any means accept the terms of the preceding article. As an appreciation of the doctrine, the criticism of Monsieur Fourier seems to us to be far inferior to that which could be made with the help of all the great ideas set forth in the *Traité d'association* and the *Nouveau monde industriel.* In his judgments on men and on their intentions, we affirm that Monsieur Fourier is utterly mistaken.[24]

Fourier himself does not seem to have been greatly troubled by his disciples' disavowal. The important thing for him was to be able to speak his mind about the Saint-Simonians; and if the disciples didn't like it, they could say so.

Fourier was more disturbed about the tendency of some contributors to the *Phalanstère* to write about his theory of association as if it were no more than a plan for an experimental farm. As he wrote in the journal in August 1832:

Misled by the force of habit, our disciples frequently make mistakes, which it is important to prevent. Most of them want to attribute to the trial Phalanx the functions of a model farm that conducts experiments with livestock, tools, crop rotation, breeding, etc. They advise us to try a certain type of crop, a certain mode of planting. This is not the sort of innovation that we should be considering; we don't want too many irons in the fire. Our concern is the art of applying to productive work the passions and the instincts that small-scale subdivided industry is not able to utilize and that morality wishes to repress.[25]

In private Fourier was blunter; and his letters to Muiron in the summer of 1832 were full of complaints concerning the "avortons maladroits" who were "using our journal as a steppingstone by which to gain some education at our expense."[26]

Throughout the summer and fall of 1832 there continued to be friction between Fourier and his disciples. He was not happy with their watering-down of his theories. They in turn feared that his more outlandish ideas, his "bad taste," and his aggressiveness in polemic would alienate potential supporters. Thus Fourier continued to chastize his disciples when he discovered that "errors" or "Saint-Simonian prejudices" had crept into their work. Again, in September, after Fourier had published an article on his cosmological theories, the editors found it necessary to point out solemnly that "the art of associating in industry, agriculture, and domestic life is independent of the phenomena of the creation and of everything that may be happening on the surface of the other planets."[27]

II

Despite their recurrent disagreements, the personal relations between Fourier and his disciples remained relatively serene during the first five months of the *Phalanstère*'s publication. The mere appearance of the journal did great things for Fourier's morale, and a few days after the publication of the first issue Clarisse Vigoureux could describe Fourier as a man who seemed "rejuvenated by fifteen or twenty years."[28] Eventually the spell wore off, but for moments at least throughout the summer and fall of 1832 Fourier impressed his disciples with his hopefulness and enthusiasm and good humor. There was even a time in August when he seemed "charming" and when Jules Lechevalier could describe the reigning atmosphere in the offices on the rue Joquelet as one of "the best social harmony."[29] Again in September Lechevalier could speak of a "charming dinner" at which Fourier shined before an audience of disciples and journalists. "The director of *Le Breton* was there, as was Dubois of the Loire Inférieure. We talked a great deal about Fourier's theory; and Fourier himself, who was present at the festivities, was just deliciously witty and full of verve. The incarnate Harmonian had a score to settle with Seigneur Fénelon."[30]

The main responsibility for seeing the *Phalanstère* through the press each week rested in the hands of the disciples. But in addition to the articles he wrote, Fourier himself provided help with correspondence and bookkeeping. This was much needed. For few of the disciples had had any previous experience in business or journalism, and the first months in the life of the *Phalanstère* were difficult. Subscribers wrote from the provinces to complain that the journal was arriving irregularly; money kept mysteriously disappearing from the cash box; and an odd assortment of strangers and curiosity seekers kept flitting in and out of the new offices on the rue Joquelet. Through all of this Fourier seems to have been more successful than his disciples in maintaining his presence of mind. It was often he, rather than one of the disciples, who dealt with queries and complaints from subscribers. It was also Fourier, whose eye was more watchful than theirs in financial matters, who discovered where the money was going and confronted a thieving office boy with an itemized account of his misdeeds.[31]

Within a few months after the establishment of the journal, its offices on the rue Joquelet had become a mecca not only for Fourier's disciples but also for their friends and for strangers who had taken an interest in his doctrine. Some of these eventually became true believers. There were also foreigners like the young American Albert Brisbane, the Romanian Teodor Diamant, the German Ludwig Gall, and the Italian Giuseppe Bucellati, all of whom were subsequently to popularize and apply Fourier's ideas in their own countries. Others came simply out of curiosity. The Fourierist gatherings never became as notorious as those of the Saint-Simonians, which Balzac had advertised in 1830 as more entertaining than the vaudevilles at the Théâtre des Variétés.[32] But for a time at least in 1832 and 1833 the Fourierists were afflicted with what Victor Considerant described as a "legion of pests and parasites" whose coming and going gave the offices on the rue Joquelet a frivolous atmosphere, which was not appreciated by Fourier himself or by the older, provincial disciples.[33] Thus Just Muiron could grumble, after a visit to Paris, about "la vaine Joqueleterie," and other provincial Fourierists could complain about the "dandies" of the rue Joquelet.[34] Finally, it became necessary to set aside one evening a week for the reception of visitors who were interested in meeting Fourier or in finding out more about the doctrine.

Several of the visitors to the rue Joquelet in 1832 and 1833 left accounts of the impression that Fourier made on them. One that is well worth quoting is Albert Brisbane's portrait of the man.

> When we became acquainted with [Fourier] in 1832, he was about sixty years old. He was of middle stature, being about five feet seven or eight inches in height; his frame was rather light, but possessing that elasticity and energy which denote strength of constitution and great intellectual activity. His complexion was fair, and his hair, when young, light brown. His forehead was very high, and rather narrow—appearing perhaps more so from its great height; the region about the eyebrows, where phrenologists locate the perceptive organs, was large and full, and the upper frontal part of the forehead . . . projected

strongly and was extremely developed. . . . His eyebrows were thin; his eyes were large, and of a mingled blue and grey, the pupil extremely small, giving a look of great intensity to the face. His nose was large and high, and rather thin, projecting strongly at the upper part, and running straight to the point, which was quite sharp. His lips were extremely thin, closely compressed, and drawn down at the corners, which gave a cast of reserved and silent melancholy to his face. His features, except the mouth, were large and strongly marked, but delicately formed and moulded.

As we remember it, the expression of the countenance of Fourier was one of self-dependence, of great intensity, of determined energy, and of inflexible firmness and tenacity, but softened by thoughtfulness and profound contemplation. He was entirely unassuming in his manners; his dress was plain like that of a country gentleman, and he stooped slightly; his mien was that of a cold, unapproachable simplicity; he was thoughtful, reserved and silent, which, together with his natural firmness of character, counterbalanced his unpretending simplicity, and prevented all approach to familiarity, even on the part of his most devoted disciples. Not a shadow of vanity, pride, or haughtiness was perceptible to him; his own personality seemed sunk and lost in the vastness and universality of the great truths which he had discovered, and which he was the instrument of making known to man.[35]

Alongside this sketch of Fourier as he appeared to Albert Brisbane in 1832, another must be set. Its author, Pierre Joigneaux, was a student at the Ecole Centrale when he met Fourier. He was also a republican and something of a neo-Babouvist at the time. Much later he wrote an autobiography in which he described what could happen when a visitor happened to penetrate beyond Fourier's mien of "cold, unapproachable simplicity."

One day a week, or rather an evening, but I don't remember which one, you were sure to meet Charles Fourier in the main room at the rue Joquelet. He was the god of that place, and the faithful, who held him in profound veneration, never failed to come each week to pay him their respects. The master was seated in a large armchair; the earliest disciples—Jules Lechevalier, Victor Considerant, Doctor Pellarin, and several others—didn't leave the antechamber. The supreme honor for neophytes like me consisted in parading before the master, bowing respectfully, and saying a few pretty words in order to get better ones back. Charles Fourier didn't seem to care a bit about entering into conversation with the visitors whom curiosity brought him in greater or lesser number. He remained motionless and apparently calm. His physiognomy was not encouraging; the curve of his nose was a little bit like the beak of a bird of prey.

You can imagine that I took the trouble to work up a little speech before going to the rue Joquelet, and I expected to be heartily congratulated for it. When I entered the room where Charles Fourier was enthroned and saw that I was alone, I told myself that it was the right moment for me to bestow my compliment and make my little comments and that I had better take advantage of it. So, screwing up my courage, I drew myself up before the master and complimented him on his works. After the compliments, which didn't seem to make much difference to him, I ventured my observations about the best ways and means to bring about the realization of the Phalanstery. My view was that at that time the government was doing nothing to promote social reform . . . and that what was needed therefore was to sweep away the political obstacle and to seek in the Republic support that we were unlikely to get from the monarchy. . . .

I was going to go on, but the old man bounded up from his armchair and cut me short: "So you're another one of those frightful Jacobins whom no violence can stop. . . . All you dream of doing is turning society upside down and making blood flow. . . .

Since I wasn't thinking of anything like that, I was stunned by the brick that had just dropped on my head. I was hoping for a compliment for my good intentions; I received something less encouraging. The statue had woken up, the master had lost his temper. Madame Gatti de Gamond, who was in the adjoining room, ran up, took me by the hand, led me gently out of the throne room, and explained to me that Monsieur Charles Fourier, after twenty-four years of study and research, had such firmly decided convictions that he could tolerate neither contradiction nor advice.

"Please believe, Monsieur," added Madame Gatti de Gamond, "that Monsieur Fourier will soon regret this outburst. Great geniuses have the right to a great deal of indulgence. . . .

Whenever you have comments to make, doubts to be dissipated, or clarifications to obtain, I beg you to address yourself to the master's disciples, who will always give you a good reception and will be pleased to give you the explanations you need."

At the same time Madame Gatti de Gamond introduced me to Monsieur Victor Considerant and Monsieur Pellarin, who had no trouble in making me forget the violent attack of which I had been the object. They couldn't help laughing about it, and I laughed too.[36]

Fourier wasn't always so harsh with those who came to meet him; and according to Charles Pellarin he was capable of being positively "charming to see and to listen to" when surrounded by his disciples or others whom he trusted. But even at his best Fourier was not an easy person. He always had what one of his followers described as "a great deal of absolutism in his character."[37] And there were times when he turned on his disciples with just as much ferocity as he showed toward Joigneaux.

In November of 1832 a particularly bitter series of confrontations took place between Fourier and his disciples concerning the running of the *Phalanstère*. The documentation is sparse, and it is not wholly clear what happened or what caused it to happen. But it would seem that the root of the trouble was Fourier's growing fear of being entrapped or "enslaved" by his own disciples. For over twelve years he had been accumulating debts to Just Muiron and Clarisse Vigoureux. By 1832 they were virtually supporting him, and there were times when he could not stand the thought of it. "You are astonished that I speak of my debts," he wrote Muiron in February 1832, "I have not forgotten them. . . . Whatever you may say, I consider as a debt everything that should be envisaged as such."[38] Two months later in a fit of anger Fourier turned on Clarisse Vigoureux and accused her and Muiron of "wishing to hold him in slavery."[39] Muiron and Madame Vigoureux tried to minimize the importance of such outbursts, and the surviving documents do not tell us everything that we would want to know. But it seems clear that Fourier's feelings of dependency and enslavement were intensified by the creation of the *Phalanstère*. For it was his disciples who had provided the funds and it was they who controlled the journal. But that was not all. Fourier found it particularly galling to be told by the disciples what and how to write for the journal. Furthermore, he had begun to realize that what some of them wanted was for him to write nothing at all.

This was the background to Fourier's explosion of November 1832. His particular target was Victor Considerant, who wrote Clarisse Vigoureux a long and bitter letter about Fourier at the end of the month.

> You speak about divisions among us. Well, my God, there haven't been any [for some time]. . . . As for Monsieur Fourier, we simply let him alone. Do you know that he has twice become furious at me? On the first occasion, however, I behaved so gently that the gentle Transon, who was there, could not understand why I didn't send that bitter and unjust man packing. The cause of the second scene was simply that I told him in front of other people that it would not be worthy of him to write the kind of "amusing" articles that he said he wished to write for the journal. I have taken the utmost care to avoid having disputes with him. I speak to him very rarely and always with the greatest gentleness. If he says the opposite, he is lying and that's all there is to it.

Considerant went on to observe bitterly that he was "very glad" to report that Fourier had taken a dislike to him, for Fourier was "the very essence of injustice, jealousy, and . . . ingratitude." To be disliked by such a man was "an indication by which one knows that he has done something for the Phalansterian movement."[40]

The letters containing Fourier's side of this story have been lost. But we can gain a sense of it from a letter written to him by Clarisse Vigoureux at the beginning of December.

> Just why do you seem so sad and discontent at a time when we have such high hopes? For a year things have been going better than any of us could have hoped. [Yet] you seem dissatisfied with all your disciples, you find fault with Victor. . . . Poor Victor, I once saw you acting so unfairly toward him that I want to tell myself that the same thing is happening again today. . . . But what distresses me most is the pain and the sadness that you feel. This weighs on my heart and almost on my conscience as if we were imperiously charged with the responsibility of making you happy until the moment when the human race has accepted you as its master. . . .
>
> Monsieur, do not keep making yourself embittered, but try to believe us when we tell you that such and such a means is

appropriate with the civilized. Let me say again that you are too lofty for them to be able to understand you in all respects, and that you cannot descend to their level without losing the dignity that is necessary for success. That is why your interme- diaries have been serving you. . . . But in the name of heaven, do not become so misled as to believe that we have any thought of trying to keep you away from the journal or from anything else. Isn't your science everything? In any case I could reply to you that you have been saying that since the founding of the journal, and the result is that nobody has written in it as much as you have.[41]

Clarisse Vigoureux was speaking in good faith. But in fact Fourier's suspicions were well founded. Many of his disciples wanted very much to "keep him away from the journal." And as Madame Vigoureux was writing him from Besançon, the editors of the *Phalanstère* were con- sidering changes in the journal the result of which would be to reduce Fourier's role in it.

III

The end of the year 1832 was marked by two new developments in the life of the Fouricrist movement. One was the choice of a site for the first trial Phalanx. The other was an attempt on the part of the editors of the *Phalanstère* to make their journal less sectarian and to reach out to a wider public. The story of the trial Phalanx will be told in the follow- ing chapter. As for the changes the disciples wished to make in the journal, they seem to have been the subject of lengthy discussions in December 1832. Although the record is fragmentary, a long memoran- dum by Abel Transon gives a sense of the points at issue.[42] To Transon's mind the most important problems with the journal were its pedestrian character and the lack of coordination among its collabora- tors. Too many articles consisted simply of general restatements of Fourier's theory. "Our goal," wrote Transon, "should be to give the journal . . . the same rank in public opinion that the old *Globe* held." What this would require, he believed, was more articles on scientific and literary topics and also a more concerted effort to show the rele- vance of Fourier's theory to specific social problems. "At the point we have now reached," he wrote, "we should give as little space as possible to big generalities. . . . It is of great importance for us to prove to the public that our theories are applicable to *particular* questions of [social] organization." Significantly, throughout this whole memorandum there was just one point at which Transon referred specifically to Fourier's role on the journal. "I suppose that [in undertaking these reforms] we should previously have indicated to Monsieur Charles Fourier the maximum length of his articles, which should be considered as distinct from our editorial policies." What Transon was proposing in effect was that Fourier continue to write whatever he pleased but that its length be limited and the editorial policies of the journal be determined independently of Fourier.

Transon's proposals were adopted. Thus the final issue of the *Phalanstère* for 1832 contained the following announcement.

> Beginning on January 1, 1833, the publication of the *Réforme industrielle (ou le Phalanstère)* will no longer have as its unique object the exposition of the *societary theory*. This theory can in any case be studied in the works of Monsieur Fourier and his disciples.
> Henceforth, the articles in the journal, while continuing to have absolutely nothing to do with debates over questions of day-to-day politics, will focus primarily on those questions of general interest that fall under the rubric of industrial politics.[43]

Readers of the journal were further informed that its size was to be expanded from eight to twelve pages and that henceforth scientific, literary, and artistic topics would be treated in the journal "whenever they have a social significance." At the conclusion of the same issue there was also a brief editorial note concerning Fourier: "The article Monsieur Fourier normally contributes to each issue could not appear today, the space allotted to it in the layout having been insufficient."[44]

During the first few months of 1833 Fourier's disciples tried hard to make their journal livelier and more relevant to the concerns of the general public. They began to print book reviews and to write more articles on contemporary social problems and on current debates in medicine, education, and agriculture. At the same time they became more aggressively polemical in tone, engaging in journalistic disputes with the *Revue des deux mondes*, the *Tribune*, and the *Revue encyclopédique*. They also published large advertisements in popular Paris dailies such as the *National*, the *Temps*, the *Journal des débats*, and the *Constitutionnel*.[45]

In the midst of all this Fourier simply went his own way. He kept turning out articles for the journal. But these articles were often the source of renewed conflict between him and the disciples. Not only were they repelled by his "bad taste" and "buffoonery," they also found the articles to be too long, and they were irritated by his habit of making changes and often large additions on the proofs at the last moment. "Despite all my observations," wrote Transon to Fourier at one point, "you continue to give your articles a length that is utterly out of proportion to the size of our journal."[46] For a time the editors attempted to impose on Fourier a limit of four columns an issue. But this made no difference. His articles continued to be too long and too late. When a few lines of a late article had to be cut to fit the available space, Fourier exploded. But when he was warned ahead of time that cuts would be necessary, his immediate reaction was to withdraw the article. This was something that the disciples found hard to accept, especially when it came on the day that the paper was to go to press. "No, Monsieur," Transon protested on receiving a half-column addition to a five-column article, "you cannot wait until Thursday morning to give me that alternative. On Thursday morning the journal is done. Thursday morning *you cannot* withdraw an article the length of those you write on the pretext that it is mutilated if it can't be lengthened by half a column. Let's suppose you told me on *Monday* morning: 'I would prefer my article not to appear at all.' Then I would have time to find another. On Thursday that is impossible."[47]

If Fourier was unhappy about his disciples' editing and cutting of his own articles, he was equally unhappy about much that he read in theirs. Repeatedly during the spring and summer of 1833 he wrote articles denouncing positions taken by his own disciples in the journal. In March of 1833 Charles Pellarin had devoted two articles to a discussion of analogies between Fourier's theory of the passions and the views of the phrenologists Gall and Spurzheim. Fourier replied by filling one-third of an entire issue with an angry discussion of "the kind of service that is rendered to me by certain bumbling friends who are assassinating me while they think they are increasing my reputation." A few weeks later an article on the Saint-Simonians by Aynard de la Tour-du-Pin drew from Fourier a more succinct but equally harsh reply entitled "On a Panegyric of Theocracy and Mortmain." Then again in early July another article appeared denouncing two "adventurous disciples"— Amédée Paget and Giuseppe Bucellati—whose articles were "studded

with errors" and "completely imbued with Saint-Simonian formulas."
"The two writers should not be astonished," wrote Fourier, "that the
chief of the doctrine makes use of his right to point out heresies. This will
be an instructive gloss for less experienced disciples."[48]

The disciples' public response to all this was mild. In publishing
Fourier's attack on Pellarin, for example, they added a conciliatory
editorial note.

> Monsieur Fourier has deemed it appropriate to protest against
> the articles published in this journal on Gall's phrenological
> doctrine. It is entirely correct that he should make whatever use
> he wants of the right to distinguish his views from all others
> and to emphasize the differences that exist between him, *the
> inventor of the societary method,* and those who strive to introduce
> this great discovery into the domain of humanity.

They went on to acknowledge their sense of a "religious duty" to
publish "without change" everything written by Fourier. But they insisted on their own right to persist in fulfilling what they understood as
their duties as "intermediaries between Monsieur Fourier and the men
of their time, between the societary theory and the other ventures in
social science."[49]

In private the disciples were less delicate. For they had become fed
up by Fourier's repeated criticism. After June of 1833 Abel Transon and
Victor Considerant simply ceased to write for the *Phalanstère.* Jules
Lechevalier continued for a time, but his relations with Fourier grew
strained. In July, after the attack on Paget and Bucellati, the latter wrote
Fourier to protest the "ridicule" to which he had been subjected. "I do
not believe," he added, "that nature has given you alone the right to
investigate its laws."[50] At the same time another disciple, who chose to
remain anonymous, addressed a long letter to Fourier, complaining of
the obscurity of Fourier's articles ("You teach algebra before arithmetic") and bluntly criticizing his treatment of his own disciples.

> It may surprise you to know that one of the writers who has
> succeeded in making himself best understood by the public (I
> am here speaking of uninitiated readers and beginners) is the
> same Monsieur A. Paget whom, in the interest of the ortho-
> doxy of the journal, you felt obliged to reprimand publicly. I
> must point out that these reprimands seemed excessively severe
> and made a bad impression.[51]

A few weeks later Victor Considerant summed up the feelings of many of the disciples when he wrote that the publication of the journal should be suspended. "It is of the utmost importance that Fourier should cease to have the means to publish articles by which he is destroying both himself and his theory in the eyes of the public."[52]

By July of 1833 there was little left to the enthusiasm that Fourier and his disciples had felt a year earlier, at the time of the establishment of the *Phalanstère*. Funds were short, and the journal had never come close to paying its own way. Furthermore the attempt to establish a trial Phalanx at Condé-sur-Vesgre, which was supposedly the *raison d'être* of the journal, was running into serious difficulty. Finally, there was the widespread feeling among the disciples that the *Phalanstère* would never reach a large public so long as Fourier was free to write in it whatever he wished. For all these reasons there was considerable support for Considerant's proposal that the publication of the journal be terminated.[53] But after some discussion the disciples decided simply to reduce its size. The decision was announced by Jules Lechevalier in an article that appeared on July 19. In this article Lechevalier observed that henceforth he and several of the other disciples would be submitting most of their work to journals whose circulation was wider than that of the *Phalanstère*.[54] He went on, however, to pay tribute to "this insignificant journal that we founded by ourselves, without much help and with the most modest means." He promised that the *Phalanstère* would continue to be published and that it would "always be for us a sort of venerated birthplace, the sanctuary in which everything that has to do with the *science* and the *theory* will be carefully elaborated and proposed."[55] These fine words notwithstanding, this article was Lechevalier's next to last contribution to the *Phalanstère*. Since many of the other contributors had already drifted away, and since by July of 1833 the energies of Considerant and Transon were engaged elsewhere, the responsibility for bringing out the journal was left in the hands of just two individuals. One was Charles Pellarin and the other was Fourier himself.

Between July 19 and August 16 Fourier and Pellarin managed to get out four rather modest issues of the journal. Then its publication was shifted to a monthly basis. For another six months it continued to appear. But its circulation plummeted, and its articles—which bore such rousing titles as "The Scientific Poltroons," "Mystification of the Sirens of Progress," and "Commercial Speculation Offering a Net Profit of 300

Percent in Six Months"—were all by Fourier. Abandoned by the disciples, the *Phalanstère* had ceased to be the organ of a movement.

IV

In the last article that he wrote for the *Phalanstère* Jules Lechevalier attempted to justify the decision to reduce the journal's size and its frequency of appearance. He explained that these measures were prompted not only by a lack of funds or by the work to be done at Condé. The main reason, he said, was that "the primary effect we wanted [the *Phalanstère*] to have has been accomplished." According to Lechevalier, the journal had made it possible for "society" to "get wind of" Fourier's doctrines. The task that now confronted the disciples was "to seek to give a wider publicity to the same doctrines" through writing for more influential journals with a greater circulation. "If the *Phalanstère* had no other result than to bring us to this point, it would have already made a great contribution to the cause of ASSOCIATION."[56]

This article may well have left an unpleasant taste in the mouths of many of the collaborators on the *Phalanstère*. People who were close to Lechevalier knew that his own desire to publish his writing elsewhere was prompted largely by personal ambition and by the waning of his interest in Fourierism. Most of the disciples were acutely aware of the limitations of the journal, and few can really have believed that it had "made a great contribution to the cause of association." On the contrary, many of them seem to have come away from the experience of collaborating on the journal with the feeling that little had been accomplished except for the fulfillment of an obligation toward Fourier. As Victor Considerant wrote in October 1833, the publication of the *Phalanstère* had enabled the disciples to give Fourier "the satisfaction that thirty-four years of torment [have] made him so ardently desire, the satisfaction of being at last able to make his voice heard by the public." But in the process, Considerant maintained, the disciples had learned that Fourier was unable to make himself *understood* by the public; and they had also discovered that he was an impossible person to work with on a cooperative enterprise.[57]

Despite such comments, it would seem in retrospect that there was at least some justification for Lechevalier's positive verdict on the journal. If its circulation remained modest and if it never came close to "conquering Paris" as Fourier would have wished, the *Phalanstère* did significantly continue and extend the work of popularizing Fourier's ideas that had begun in the winter of 1831–1832. The lectures and articles of Jules Lechevalier and Abel Transon had begun the process. But their influence was felt largely in Paris and among former Saint-Simonians. What the *Phalanstère* did was to take Fourier's ideas to the provinces. Prior to the appearance of the journal there had been hardly a mention of Fourier or Fourierism in the French provincial press outside of Just Muiron's Besançon. A few months later the situation had changed radically. "We have every reason to be satisfied with the provincial press," the editors wrote in August 1832. "Spontaneously it has sought to give publicity to our opinions and to expound our ideas itself."[58] This was no exaggeration. During the first year of the *Phalanstère*'s existence articles on Fourier's ideas appeared in scores of provincial journals ranging from the *Sanglier des Ardennes* to the *Mémorial des Pyrenées,* from the *Abeille Picard* to the *Nouveau Contribuable de la Haute Vienne.* Some of these articles were original, but many were reprints taken directly from the *Phalanstère.* Thus Charles Pellarin could speak of one of his articles (on Breton agriculture) as having been so widely reprinted that "it literally made its own *tour de France.*"[59]

The editors of the *Phalanstère* attributed the relatively strong response to Fourier's ideas in the provinces to the fact that unlike Parisians, who were easily distracted by day-to-day events and political intrigues, provincial readers were able to take a longer view and to recognize that contemporary political discussion was trivial compared to the importance of the vital social question: how to provide for "the physical amelioration of the condition of the masses."[60] There may be something to this, but clearly it is only a part of the story. For in the early 1830s there were other groups, notably the Saint-Simonians and their offshoots, who were calling attention to the primacy of the social question. If Fourierism had a following among the provincial bourgeoisie, it may be due as much to the answers it gave as to the questions it posed. It is possible that many of the *Phalanstère*'s provincial readers were individuals whose social consciousness had been awakened by the Saint-Simonian movement, but who were then alienated by its religious excesses or relieved to discover (as the *Vigilant de Seine-et-Oise* put it) that Fourierism had the "profound" advantage over Saint-Simonism of showing greater deference to the rights of property and inheritance.[61]

If the *Phalanstère* carried Fourier's ideas into the French provinces, it also enabled them to reach outside the comfortable middle-class milieu to which they had hitherto been confined. It seems clear that the vast majority of the journal's readers belonged to the professional bourgeoisie; they were army officers and engineers, doctors and lawyers, small-town functionaries and *rentiers*.[62] But in at least one part of France the *Phalanstère* did manage to reach a significant number of educated working-class readers. This was the city of Lyon, where Fourier himself had spent so many years, and where the longstanding interest of the silk workers in radical and utopian ideas was stimulated by the worsening of their economic position vis-à-vis the master merchants. The master weavers or *chefs d'atelier* at Lyon had their own newspapers, one of which, the *Echo de la Fabrique,* became something like a Fourierist organ in 1832 and 1833 and published more than a score of articles inspired by material that had previously appeared in the *Phalanstère*.[63]

The importance of these developments should not be overestimated. The *Phalanstère* never acquired anything like the influence or the readership of the Saint-Simonian *Globe,* or of subsequent Fourierist journals such as the *Phalange* and the *Démocratie Pacifique*. It did, however, lay the groundwork for the success of these journals and, more generally, for the development of the Fourierist movement that was to become an important part of the ideological landscape in France during the 1840s. And its most immediate, tangible result was to give "Fourierism" a life of its own, a life independent not only of Fourier himself but also of his disciples in Paris. This was most evident at Lyon where, during the mid-1830s, an important Fourierist movement developed, and where, between 1835 and 1838, the *chef d'atelier* Michel Derrion made the first significant attempt to create cooperative institutions based on Fourier's ideas. But the story of the Lyon Fourierists, like that of the other isolated groups of disciples who emerged in Europe and America during the fifteen-year period that began with the publication of the *Phalanstère,* takes us farther beyond Fourier's biography than we can now go.

23

The Creation of a Phalanx

DURING THE years 1832 and 1833 the energies of Fourier and his disciples were only partly absorbed by the task of publishing a journal. Their second preoccupation was the attempt to create a trial Phalanx in the commune of Condé-sur-Vesgre, not far from Paris. Since this was the one effort at organizing an actual community in which Fourier himself was directly involved, it deserves a chapter to itself.[1]

I

From the outset of his career as a thinker Fourier distinguished his doctrine from those of his enemies, the philosophers, on the ground that it alone was subject to experimental verification. All he needed was a square league of land and a wealthy benefactor who would create a model community according to his precise specifications. Within two months, Fourier believed, the success of such a community would prove to the world that the passions, which philosophers had traditionally regarded as enemies of concord, were indeed meant to be harmonized. This emphasis on the testing or "realization" of the theory appealed to Fourier's early disciples and notably to the large group of former Saint-Simonians who joined the ranks of the Fourierists during the first six or eight months of 1832. Many of them believed that the major weakness of the Saint-Simonian religion was precisely its abstraction, its lack of a concrete "plan" for the reorganization of society; and they shared, or came to share, Abel Transon's conviction that Fourier's theory of association provided the means by which the goals of the Saint-Simonian movement could best be realized. As the Polytechnicien Charles Didion put it in a letter to Transon: "It seems to me that to this original genius [Fourier] must belong the *Realization* of the general *Promises* made by Saint-Simonism."[2]

In many of his writings, most notably the *Nouveau monde industriel,* Fourier had sought to provide blueprints for the organization of a model community. But the creation of the *Phalanstère,* the express aim of which was the establishment of such a community, gave Fourier the opportunity to draw up yet another set of plans, this time in collaboration with his disciples. The result of their collaboration was a document that appeared in the first issue of the journal under the title "Statutes of the Founding Society."[3] This document, which was signed jointly by Fourier, Muiron, and Paul Vigoureux, specified that the trial Phalanx was to include "roughly eleven hundred men, women, and children, chosen at first from the lower class." In accordance with Fourier's belief that agricultural work was inherently more attractive than industrial work, the community was to be composed principally of farm workers: four-fifths of the members were to be *cultivateurs* and only one-fifth *manufacturiers.* A working capital of four million francs was to be raised through the sale of shares valued at one thousand francs each. On the actual operation of the Phalanx the statutes had little to say, except that the main responsibility for organizing the community would rest in the hands of three managers (*gérants*), whose work would be overseen by a committee of syndics to be elected from among the shareholders.* The statutes specified that profits were to be "distributed according to the societary system, in a manner proportional to the contribution of each

---

*The three *gérants* designated by the statutes were Paul Vigoureux, treasurer, Just Muiron, *gérant ordonnateur,* and Charles Fourier, *gérant directeur.* Fourier's functions as *gérant directeur* were to "preside over the organization of the whole mechanism of the Phalanx" and to "supervise the application of the societary mechanism." The committee of seven syndics was to be elected by a general assembly of shareholders. Two provisional syndics, however, were named in the statutes: Désiré-Adrien Gréa, who had been elected deputy from the Department of the Doubs in 1829, and Dr. Alexandre Baudet-Dulary, a young deputy from the Seine-et-Oise of whom more will be said later.

member in work, capital, and talent." Each member was also guaranteed the right "to choose freely whatever jobs correspond to his taste in farming and manufacturing work."⁴

Along with the "Statutes for the Founding Society," the first number of the *Phalanstère* also contained an article by Fourier entitled "Program for the Proposed Foundation."⁵ Apparently this article was supposed to elaborate on the information contained in the statutes. But like many of Fourier's subsequent articles in the *Phalanstère,* it was a rambling and diffuse piece in which he spent more time railing against the Owenites and Saint-Simonians than discussing his alleged subject matter. Fourier did, however, specify that the community he proposed to create would be a form of simple association appropriate to the transitional historical stage of Sociantism. He also rather laconically provided some information on how he expected the four million francs capital to be spent. Land for the Phalanx would cost "not more than 1,500,000 francs," he said. Construction of temporary buildings (and not the "sumptuous edifices" necessary for an experiment in full association) would cost another million francs. The purchase of livestock and the planting of fruit trees and the preparation of gardens would require 500,000 francs. The same sum would be spent on furnishing the living quarters and workshops. Finally, another 500,000 francs would be needed to buy the food and clothing to be advanced to members during the first year. This would not enable the initial Phalansterians to live on "bisque and caviar." But it would permit eleven hundred "proletarians" to enjoy cuisine far superior to anything they had previously known. And Fourier insisted that this was no trivial matter. "The trial Phalanx will have its bakery, its butcher's shop, its *charcuterie,* its candy store, its pastry shop, etc. It will sell the lower grades of the meat it produces to the neighboring peasants, and it will keep the good grades for the twelve hundred [*sic*] members. The excellence of the food and the gaiety of the work done in short sessions under mobile tents will be two powerful means of making the societary system beloved by everyone from the very first days of its establishment."⁶

This was, in essence, the "program" that Fourier offered to the readers of the *Phalanstère.* It was not, to say the least, a very precise or detailed program. But Fourier does not seem to have felt that details were necessary, since readers who wanted them could always consult his books. Nor did Fourier think of money as a problem. He was convinced that once work had started on the trial Phalanx, investors would be begging him to accept their money. "In reckoning on an estimate of four million," he wrote, "we ought to start work as soon as we have 500,000 francs. For the sight of the preparations, their strangeness, their contrast with present methods, will be the guarantee of a sudden vogue. In witnessing the arrangement of the gardens, the stables, and above all the covered passageways, people will realize that the human race is about to enter a new industrial world. . . . Then the enterprise will obtain all the credit it needs. Investors will come running; the value of the shares will rise."[7]

II

During the months of June and July 1832, as they were trying to get their journal established, Fourier and his disciples also faced the practical problems of raising money and finding a satisfactory piece of land on which to establish the trial Phalanx. Although the reports that appeared from time to time in the journal were consistently optimistic, these problems proved to be more difficult than they had anticipated. By the end of August they had received numerous pledges of financial support, but these were to become binding only upon the official establishment of the Founding Society. The value of the shares actually purchased was negligible. As for the problem of a site, Fourier had often specified that the trial Phalanx should be located within a day's journey of Paris to assure the essential "bénéfice des curieux." But property in the environs of Paris proved to be prohibitively expensive. So the disciples widened their search. They made inquiries about properties in Normandy, Touraine, the Vendée, Les Landes. All proved to be infertile or too costly. Fourier himself attempted to interest rich philanthropists in donating a site for the experiment. He did manage to elicit an offer of twenty thousand arpents of land from Laîsné de Villevêque. Unfortunately it was in Mexico.[8]

On July 19 the *Phalanstère* appealed to its readers to join in the search for land for the Phalanx. They were told that the ideal property would be twelve to fifteen hundred hectares in size. Ideally the land would be hilly and suitable for the cultivation of a wide variety of fruits and vegetables. Woods, fields, and waterways were essential but, as good Fourierists, the editors specified that the land needn't be suitable for the cultivation of grain. Although the nature of the existing buildings was unimportant, a "vast castle" could certainly be "turned to account." As for payment, landowners were advised that they would be amply reimbursed with shares in the enterprise.[9]

At the beginning of August 1832 would-be shareholders were called to Paris for a general assembly. To make the enterprise more appealing to investors, it was decided to constitute the Founding Society as a *société anonyme* (a joint-stock company with limited liability) rather than the then more customary *société en commandite par actions* (a partnership directed by a *gérant* with unlimited financial responsibility). Ministerial authorization was necessary, however; and until it was granted the disciples had to postpone the official formation of the society.[10]

Just Muiron had come to Paris for the general assembly, and one of Fourier's "written conversations" with him shows that at this point Fourier's hopes were still high.

> Our best chance for success is to work on readied land. We ought to finish the job in six weeks. We might begin in February, provided the land could be plowed and seeded in March. Our six weeks should date only from about the first of May. If the weather is good, we could begin about the twentieth or the twenty-fifth of April. We only need a few arpents of grain to vary things.
>
> Rambouillet sounds very good. I know there is a stream of water and the land is varied. . . .
>
> The tactic I shall follow henceforth will be to sound out societies like that of M. Laîsné de Villevêque.
>
> We had to wait long enough for the journal to acquire assurance and consistency. Two months. Now that the two months are past, I am going to widen the scope of my efforts. We are at the beginning *of the second act.*[11]

Beginning in late July Fourier devoted a number of his articles in the journal to general discussions of the trial Phalanx. He added nothing new to what he had already said many times over in his books. But he did revise downward—to 2,500,000 francs—his original estimate of the cost of the trial Phalanx.[12] And he also took his disciples to task for what he described as their excessive interest in "experiments with livestock, tools, crop rotation, breeding, etc." He reminded them that the point of the trial Phalanx was not to create a model farm but to liberate and utilize the repressed passions.[13]

From the middle of August until mid-November 1832 the *Phalan-stère* published no information, apart from Fourier's articles, concerning the activities of the Founding Society. Behind the scenes, however, things were happening. A deputy from Seine-et-Oise, Dr. Alexandre-François Baudet-Dulary, had become interested in the project.* A man of wealth and influence, Baudet-Dulary took Fourier's ideas far more seriously than any *candidat* who had yet emerged. He had also managed to communicate some of his enthusiasm to an acquaintance named Joseph-Antoine Devay. Devay was an agronomist who had received his training at the famous Institut Agricole run by Mathieu de Dombasle at Roville. He was a partisan of Dombasle's pragmatic and experimental methods, and he had been attempting to apply them without great success on a farm he had purchased two years earlier in the commune of Condé-sur-Vesgre, about thirty-five miles southwest of Paris on the outskirts of the forest of Rambouillet.[14]

At the time the Fourierists began to take an interest in it, Devay's farm was not a going enterprise. The soil was sandy and infertile, and very little of the land was under cultivation. A Paris manufacturer who had purchased the estate in 1792 had done considerable building. But since his time the property had changed hands four times. The barns and stables had fallen into decay, and game from the forest of Rambouillet had been allowed to ravage the woods and meadows. Devay was frank about all these things in a letter he addressed to the disciples at the end of August.[15] The land needed clearing, marling, and fertilization, he explained, and he advised the disciples "to undertake preliminary work before you attempt to establish anything according to the societary system." As for the fertility of the land, Devay was downright discouraging. "I don't pretend to say . . . that all the land is *currently* productive: I would even say that, despite appearances, it

*Alexandre-François Baudet-Dulary (1792–1878) belonged to a prosperous bourgeois family with large landholdings in the Seine-et-Oise. He received his medical degree at Paris in 1814. Although he appears to have abandoned the active practice of medicine before he joined the Fourierists, he retained a lifelong interest in physiology and popular hygiene—and in the then quasi-reputable science of phrenology. In 1831 he was elected deputy from the arrondissement of Etampes, and he resigned his seat in 1834 to devote all his energies to the attempt to establish a trial Phalanx. Although his enthusiasm for Fourier's ideas cost him a very large fortune, he remained until his death one of Fourier's most dedicated disciples. In addition to the standard reference works, see the text by Jules Prudhommeaux, reprinted in Henri Desroche, *La Société festive*, 220–235.

would be completely sterile after being worked purely and simply by a plow." It had an acidic quality, which would have to be eliminated by grubbing and burning.

In light of this gloomy assessment, one might well ask just what it was that prompted Fourier and his disciples to select Condé as the site for their crucial *essai*. An important consideration, no doubt, was that the land was near Paris. And it was cheap. After some persuasion by Baudet-Dulary, Devay agreed to accept shares in the Founding Society in lieu of cash payment for the estate. Baudet-Dulary, for his part, was willing to purchase enough adjoining land to make the property as a whole total five hundred hectares (about 750 acres). But what most effectively stilled all doubts was probably Baudet-Dulary's own enthusiasm and obvious good faith. All the disciples were impressed by his willingness to risk his fortune in the enterprise. As Jules Lechevalier wrote to Clarisse Vigoureux in September: "No doubt you admire, as do we all, the wonderful conduct of Baudet-Dulary. With two or three more like him and Devay, our prospects will be brilliant. In any case they are sure, for we are all resolved like stoics to be ready [by next spring]."[16] Thus by the end of September 1832, after Fourier, Muiron, Considerant, and others had visited Condé, the decision was made. A site had been found for the model community that was meant to vindicate Fourier's system in the eyes of the world.

The news was made public in an article that appeared in the *Phalanstère* on November 15. Its author was Baudet-Dulary, who described the property in terms considerably more seductive than those employed by Devay in his letter to the disciples.

> The region is picturesque; a small river, the Vesgre, winds across our property and turns a mill, which belongs to us. There is a sizable bank of chalk, which will be very easy to work, and there are a large number of meadows, which may be irrigated. These are the principal components of success on a property admirably suited to the growing of vegetables, which will be the basis of our enterprise. A quarry of potter's clay, the good qualities of which have long been known, will enable us to establish a factory of fine pottery. Fairly substantial buildings will provide lodging for an initial group of laborers. The preparations for planting have begun; the architect is on the spot, readying the materials for construction.

Baudet-Dulary added that since the term *Phalanstery* had been judged "bizarre" by some individuals, it had been decided to call the community simply a Societary Colony.[17]

In another article the following week Baudet-Dulary added further details. He and Devay proposed to establish a *société anonyme* with a capital of 1,200,000 francs. They themselves would be contributing the land, which was worth 280,000 francs. The rest of the capital would come from individual shareholders. Baudet-Dulary now conceded that half the land was still covered with briars and needed clearing. But he added that almost all of it was "capable of yielding a large crop once it had been marled and cultivated."

> We already have a considerable supply of livestock and tools, which will permit us to proceed quickly this winter with the clearing, marling, and other tasks. Thus it should be possible to arrange for the establishment of six hundred colonists in successive waves from March 21 to October 1, 1833. The buildings that are now standing can accommodate the first wave of workers; and new structures, built easily and economically out of wood and brick, will be ready during the month of May. Monsieur Colomb Gengembre, an architect known for major works (including the Mint of Nantes and the Porte Saint-Ouen) and a friend of the principal shareholders, will give all of his attention to the construction.[18]

The date for the official opening of the Societary Colony was set at March 21, 1833.

In both of Baudet-Dulary's articles there were intimations that the colony at Condé was going to represent a retreat from the initial specifications. Its size had been reduced to six hundred people, and the working capital to 1,200,000 francs. Furthermore the provisional *acte de société* published in the journal on November 22 specified that work in the colony would be organized "*insofar as possible* according to the method of Charles Fourier."[19] The meaning of these qualifications and reductions was spelled out clearly by Jules Lechevalier in another article when he distinguished between the work of "the theorists" and that of "the executors." "In our prospectus we asked for executors," wrote Lechevalier dramatically. "They have appeared." Now it was time for the theorists to efface themselves in order to make way for "those who are going to put into practice what they have found to be immediately realizable in the theory of Charles Fourier." According to Lechevalier, Baudet-Dulary and Devay were presenting the enterprise to the public "in the terms that they judge to be good and practicable."

> They have modified the original act according to the dictates of reality. They have changed several of the conditions of the experiment. They have replaced the name we had inscribed on the face of the edifice as the symbol of a new world by a term appropriate to the customs and usages of the men whom they are asking to enter into the contract of association. In making these changes, they have received the approbation of Fourier and his disciples. The theorists have played their part; they have been rigid, absolute, dogmatic. The executors have not failed to play their part. They are prudent, modest, flexible in the face of obstacles, and submissive to the *common sense* of humanity.

Lechevalier concluded his article by observing that in the negotiations over the execution of his ideas, Fourier himself had been "just as agreeable, just as accommodating . . . as he is firm and inflexible in theoretical calculations. 'I am the pilot,' he says, 'I will show you the solutions to be sought for, the pitfalls to be avoided. After listening to my advice, you will be free to act as you wish.' "[20]

Fourier's attitude toward the experiment of Condé actually seems to have been rather less than accommodating. Judging from the private correspondence of his disciples, it would appear that by November of 1832 there was already considerable tension between them and him over just what should be done at Condé. Thus Victor Considerant could write on November 23 that Baudet-Dulary and Devay were "masters of their fortune" and "if they want to modify Fourier's plans in any way that they think necessary to bring in shareholders, they have every right to do so and they *should* do so." And Considerant continued:

> Monsieur Fourier must not be an absolute master in selecting different types of industry and agriculture. That would, on the contrary, be a very bad thing because, as far as practical matters are concerned, he has ideas that are entirely false and even ridiculous. His manias could do us a great deal of harm. Ah, my God, don't we have an understanding of the Phalanstery? Don't we know that the tasks to be performed in the trial Phalanx must be as attractive as possible in themselves? And if Monsieur Fourier wrongly imagines that such and such a job is repugnant or attractive in itself when experience proves the

contrary, are we necessarily obliged to accept the erroneous ideas that have become lodged in his head?[21]

In November of 1832 Fourier was still far from having given up on Condé. But he had begun to adopt a rather detached attitude toward the colony. The following month, while Baudet-Dulary and Devay were attempting to raise money, Fourier coolly began to discuss in the journal the desirability of establishing *multiple* trial Phalanxes.[22] And there are hints in his correspondence of disagreements with the architect hired by Baudet-Dulary and Devay. "I have not been tempted to write you for some time," he wrote Muiron in January 1833, "because affairs haven't been going the way I wished."[23]

III

Throughout the winter of 1832–1833 Fourier remained in Paris along with most of his disciples. Their main preoccupation was still the publication of the *Phalanstère* and, more generally, what they had come to refer to as the work of "propagation"—the spread and popularization of Fourier's ideas by means of lectures and articles. Devay and Baudet-Dulary were in residence at Condé, however, and a number of the Paris disciples made regular visits to the site of the colony. In December 1832 Victor Considerant could report to readers of the journal that hired workers were clearing the land and readying it for the spring planting.

> For some time a small army of laborers belonging to three neighboring villages and divided into three companies, has taken up positions on the land of the colony. More than sixty men are scattered about and executing preparatory tasks. They are digging drainage ditches, cutting briars, and burning their roots. Meanwhile wagons are crisscrossing the fields and restoring to productivity soil that contemporary society ought to be ashamed of leaving sterile when it is cluttered with such a large number of starving people.[24]

By February two hundred workers were engaged at Condé, and the progress reports that appeared regularly in the *Phalanstère* continued to be optimistic. But then toward the end of March Joseph Devay felt obliged to publish a long article refuting various "allegations" concerning the infertility of the soil at Condé as well as "salon gossip" that members of the colony were "practicing free love with bacchantes."[25] In addition, Baudet-Dulary had to report on March 15 that because of difficulties in his own attempts to buy land adjacent to Devay's property, he had only managed to submit his formal request for government authorization of the *société anonyme* on March 1. There was no chance that authorization would be granted prior to March 21, the scheduled date of opening. "We are thus obliged to postpone the opening of the society until May 1," wrote Baudet-Dulary. "But this involuntary delay in preliminary formalities will cause no delay in the work of farming and construction," he added, urging his readers to take the trip out to Condé in the mild April weather to see things for themselves.[26]

Baudet-Dulary's decision to postpone the official opening of the colony was a blow to many of Fourier's followers and particularly to those provincial disciples who, having previously expressed their desire to participate in the experiment, were now awaiting the word to come to Condé. But these people would have been even more distressed if they had known what was really going on. For Baudet-Dulary and Devay were actually confronted by difficulties far more serious than those mentioned in print. The most pressing problem was a lack of capital. Baudet-Dulary and Devay were attempting to create a joint-stock company with a capital of 1,200,000 francs. They estimated their own contribution in land at 280,000 francs. There remained over 900,000 francs to be collected, and the value of the shares actually purchased between May 1, 1832, and March 1, 1833, reached a grand total of 10,750 francs.[27] In order to pay the workers who were clearing and cultivating the land at Condé, Baudet-Dulary had already drawn heavily on his personal funds.★

Finally at the end of May 1833, Baudet-Dulary conceded to the public that the Societary Colony was in serious trouble. As he described the situation to the readers of the *Phalanstère:* "The absence of a definitive mode of organization and, as a consequence, the absence of the aid promised by the shareholders, necessarily served to impede our initial labors and we have not been able to do everything we hoped." Baudet-

---

★In his efforts to raise money Baudet-Dulary received no help whatsoever from that other rich deputy with Fourierist sympathies, Désiré-Adrien Gréa. In July of 1832 Gréa had written Fourier to decline the position of syndic, which he had been assigned in the original Société de Fondation. In June of the following year Just Muiron reported that Gréa had refused to allow his name to be used in any way in fund-raising activities for Condé. See Gréa to Fourier, July 11, 1832, AN 10AS 25 (3), and Muiron to Clarisse Vigoureux, June 9, 1833, AN 10AS 40 (5).

Dulary went on to observe that another source of the trouble at Condé might have been "the lack of a single directing authority." For this reason, he announced, he and his associates had decided to give up their efforts to establish a *société anonyme*. Instead they were going to set up, for the time being at least, a *société en commandite* with a single responsible director. As the principal shareholder Baudet-Dulary himself had agreed to accept the responsibility. "I have accepted," he wrote, "because it is less a question now of realizing the magnificent promises of the theory than of yielding some result, however feeble it might be."[28]

Two weeks later, on June 14, the definitive text of the agreement constituting the "first Societary Colony" was published in the *Phalanstère*. Fourier's ideas were watered down even more than in the provisional *acte de société* published the previous November, and a note by Baudet-Dulary stressed the modest and pragmatic character of his approach. "I announce nothing absolute. I am not beginning with 600 colonists but with 150 workers, of whom 60 are now lodged and fed in the first buildings of the future colony." Baudet-Dulary also took upon himself full responsibility for the success or failure of the enterprise. Henceforth Fourier's role was to be that of an "indispensable counselor" but one without any formal responsibilities or powers.[29]

Fourier was anything but pleased with the new arrangements. It seemed to him that he was simply being denied a voice in the running of affairs at Condé, just as his disciples had earlier tried to deny him a voice in the running of the journal. Thus in early July he wrote sarcastically to Muiron about the "dictatorship" of Baudet-Dulary.[30] And in a note written at about the same time he carried on about the "incompetence" of his collaborator.

> For the past six months I have not dared to say a word in the journal about Condé. If [the journal] were in our hands, you would see how I would speak and how I would make the money come. But Dulary by weakness and incompetence is upsetting all our plans. You cannot count on him for anything. He falls into every trap. He only loves those who deceive him.[31]

But Baudet-Dulary was not the only target of Fourier's wrath. For some time previously his general dissatisfaction with the way things were going at Condé had been focused on the work of the architect, Colomb Gengembre.

The main problem seems to have been that Gengembre, who was a friend of both Baudet-Dulary and Devay, was a professional with exacting "civilized" standards. He found it hard to adapt his style and his plans to the aesthetic dictates and the limited financial resources of "amateurs." As early as March Fourier had already begun to fume about Gengembre in his letters to Muiron. The architect had wanted to spend twenty-five thousand francs on the purchase of lumber alone, and it had taken all of Fourier's powers to persuade him and Baudet-Dulary of the imprudence of spending "everything we have" on the purchase of a single kind of material. "This makes me worry," Fourier wrote, "about the kind of resistance I'm going to encounter when things are actually under way."[32]

By May of 1833 Fourier had become convinced that the architect was a man of dubious character as well as limited competence and excessively grandiose ideas. "We are getting a few shareholders now," he wrote Muiron.

> We could have ten times as many if the architect hadn't slowed everything up in an attempt to make us adopt, out of exhaustion, the plans that he kept urging on us, which he now admits are ridiculous. But he was tormented by pride. He's a quibbler who wants things round if you want them square, or square if you want them round. I have let it be known that we ought to fire him and take on a master mason, who would do a perfectly satisfactory job of constructing the rustic sort of buildings we want.[33]

By early summer Fourier was beginning to wonder if Gengembre was not in fact a saboteur bent on "aborting the whole project by wasting money in crazy constructions and baubles."[34] This seemed the more likely to Fourier in view of the architect's steadfast opposition to the construction of a "rue galerie," the architectural innovation that Fourier counted on to attract the attention of potential investors and shareholders.

Few of Fourier's disciples shared his suspicions concerning the motives of the architect.[35] But as the summer wore on, a number began to share Fourier's doubts about his competence and his judgment. These doubts can only have been intensified in July when (according to Fourier) Gengembre produced his ultimate extravagance: a pigsty with stone walls eighteen inches thick and no entrance! As Fourier described it to Muiron:

This man who kept saying, "We lack materials," when he was supposed to be building lodgings, has now managed to find enough materials to produce a hundred horrors. To speak only of the most recent ones, he has since the establishment of the new regime, or dictatorship, constructed the following *piggeries*.

1. A pigsty or stable for pigs with superb stone walls eighteen inches thick. The building for their human masters is only meant to have mud walls six inches thick. Thus the pigs will be three times better lodged than the gentlemen. Can't we spare these materials and put the pigs for the time being in a pen made of boards? That is the way the horses of the officers are kept at Besançon, and those horses are certainly more gentlemanly than these pigs.

The amusing thing about the pigsty is that he put up the walls without making a door, which means that the pigs are going to have to be hoisted in and out every day by means of pulleys.[36]

Fourier then went on to enumerate Gengembre's other "horrors," including the construction of no less than twelve handsome portable latrines. "There is no denying it," he concluded, "the colony has been ravaged."

During the hot summer months of 1833, while Fourier was fretting about the architect and about the "dictatorship" of Baudet-Dulary, a number of the disciples (including several of the most active collaborators on the journal) left Paris to go to Condé to do whatever they could to rescue the colony. Among them were Considerant, Transon, and Paul Vigoureux, and also such newer Fourierists as A. Maurize, Alphonse Morellet, a Captain Gérardin from Besançon, Adolph Brac de LaPerrière from Lyon, and the Spanish republican Joaquin Abreu. Some of these individuals like Brac de LaPerrière were well-to-do young gentlemen from the provinces; others were engineers with degrees from the Ecole Polytechnique; Abreu was a middle-aged former navy officer. But all of them joined in the manual work of clearing land and plowing and planting fruit trees that had been started in the spring by the day laborers hired by Baudet-Dulary. There was also much construction to be done. The architect Gengembre was finally forced to leave in late July. But work continued on the temporary lodgings for workers that he had started. The construction of a brickworks was undertaken on the banks of the Vesgre. And on a promontory overlooking the rest of the property, a beginning was even made on the construction of a wing of the future Phalanstery.

On July 19 Jules Lechevalier could write in the *Phalanstère* of the "great activity" displayed by "our most dedicated associates" at Condé.[37] But on the spot the situation looked much less encouraging than it did from Paris. For despite the hard work, there were few people who really seemed to know what they were doing at Condé; and as the summer wore on, there was increasing tension and even a threat of violence between the hired workers and the middle-class disciples.[38] At the very moment when Lechevalier's optimistic progress report was appearing in the journal, Victor Considerant, who described himself as "dropping with fatigue," wrote a letter to Charles Pellarin in Paris, lamenting the chaotic state of affairs at Condé and urging Pellarin not to bring any visitors to the colony.[39] And those who did make the visit to Condé were struck not only by the disorganization but also by the gloom and the absence of enthusiasm. Many years later in his *Mémoires épisodiques d'un vieux chansonnier saint-simonien,* Jules Vinçard could recall the "profound disappointment" he felt at "the bleak and chilling appearance" of Condé and of the people whom he encountered during a visit there in the summer of 1833. "The newly cleared land was bare and dark as if it had just been burned over. During the meal we shared everyone remained in deep silence. There was no talking, no laughing, no spontaneity among all these workers." At the end of the meal Vinçard entertained the group with his songs and managed to shake them out of their lethargy. But, he recalled, "during the course of my song, I noticed that Monsieur Baudet-Dulary . . . remained motionless with his elbows on the table and his head in his hands. When I had finished, he stood up and said with emotion: 'That's just what we lack here: warmth, expansiveness.' " "Well then," replied Vinçard, "you are going to struggle vainly against the old world."[40]

By the middle of August it had become apparent to the group at Condé that nothing significant could be accomplished during the remainder of the summer. A huge amount of money had been spent, apparently to little purpose. It is true that hundreds of trees had been planted and that despite the dryness of the summer, the vegetable garden was thriving. The mill had been repaired and enlarged; a brickworks had been established; and a complex of farm buildings had been created with "lodging for sixty people, common rooms, a blacksmith's and wheelwright's workshop, a carpenter's and cabinetmaker's shop, and immense stables."[41] But all of this was designed to serve a community that could not come into being without the expenditure of much more money than Baudet-Dulary and all of Fourier's other disciples possessed.

On August 16 a brief note appeared on the back page of the *Phalanstère* under Fourier's signature.

> The preparatory work at the colony of Condé-sur-Vesgre having undergone delays, the mechanism of attractive industry cannot be activated [at this time]. Since the summer season is already well advanced and since the inauguration cannot take place outside the months of planting, the inauguration is postponed until next spring. Meanwhile work will be continued and the beginnings will be so much the easier in May of 1834.[42]

Despite Fourier's effort to put a good face on things, there was a mood of frustration among his disciples. And now that the architect was gone, many of them tended to put the blame on Baudet-Dulary, whom some regarded as fatally indecisive and whom Considerant described as a man who "keeps making mistakes . . . not every day but every hour of the day."[43] Both Fourier himself and a number of the disciples began to look elsewhere for a *fondateur*. Thus Jules Lechevalier could write to Fourier at the end of August: "Transon sent me news about Condé this morning. Things are going badly, he says; and I have no trouble believing him. Nevertheless, I haven't totally lost hope. Perhaps we can still manage to win enough sympathy from the public to find other *fondateurs*."[44] As for Fourier himself, he was now convinced that there was nothing more to hope for from Baudet-Dulary's efforts at Condé. Thus he began to turn his attention elsewhere; and in a series of articles published in the *Phalanstère* between late June and early August he developed his ideas for a children's Phalanx, an experiment in association that might be organized cheaply and rapidly with as few as five hundred children under the age of twelve. This was to be the last in his long succession of efforts at "stripping down" and simplifying his formula for association.[45]

On September 22, 1833, the first general assembly of the shareholders of the Societary Colony was held at Condé. Fourier himself took the daylong trip from Paris to be in attendance. Just Muiron, Victor Considerant, and Abel Transon were there too. But out of a total of forty-eight shareholders, only thirteen managed to be present.

The main business of the meeting was the reading of a long and gloomy report by Baudet-Dulary. Tracing the various stages in the life of the colony, he noted that his own attempt to set up a *société en commandite* with a working capital of 1,200,000 francs was still far from realization. The total of the funds that had been gathered came to 378,000 francs, and of that sum by far the greater part was Baudet-Dulary's own contribution. "With such feeble resources," he wrote, "we have not been able to create a Phalanstery."

> What we can do next year, we don't yet know; that will depend on the help we can get during the winter. The public, especially in the provinces, is beginning to pay serious attention to the societary theory. A large number of generous individuals are interested in the enterprise at Condé, and we may hope that in the springtime we shall be able to build a portion of the great edifice.[46]

Although it was not recorded in the journal, Fourier seems to have followed Baudet-Dulary's report with a statement of his own.[47] Apparently it was largely a résumé of the misdeeds of the architect. But Fourier also seems to have had more to say about the proposal for a children's Phalanx, which he had advanced earlier in the summer and which had been welcomed enthusiastically by several of the disciples.[48]

This meeting at Condé was neither an end nor a beginning as far as the life of the Societary Colony was concerned. Within a few months the disciples had launched a new campaign to raise the funds necessary to establish a children's Phalanx the following year. This project, which would involve 250 children, was to cost a mere 250,000 francs.[49] But even this sum proved to be more than the disciples could raise. In 1836 the society formed by Baudet-Dulary was legally dissolved. The property at Condé-sur-Vesgre remained in his hands, but he took it upon himself to reimburse in full all the other shareholders. In the final reckoning his losses amounted to 487,000 francs.[50]

In later years the property at Condé was the scene of renewed attempts to realize Fourier's ideas in one form or another. But most of these were modest efforts; and by the end of the nineteenth century Condé had become hardly more than a country retreat for individuals sympathetic to what was left of the Fourierist movement. A country retreat is what it remains today for the grandchildren of the grandchildren of Fourier's disciples.

Even though the general assembly of September 1833 was not a terminal point in the life of the Societary Colony, it did mark an end to Fourier's association with the colony. He was never again to return to Condé, and he had nothing to do with subsequent efforts to breathe life into the Societary Colony. Henceforth his main concern was to dissociate himself and his doctrine from what came to be known as the "failure" of Condé.

> It has been spread about that I made a trial at Condé-sur-Vesgre, and that "it did not succeed." This is another one of the calumnies of our depraved society. I did not do anything at Condé. The architect who held sway there did not want to accept any part of my plan. . . . He began by constructing a great *provisional rhapsody* on muddy ground below water level. I could not approve of this ramshackle joke. I threw in the towel. I didn't have anything more to do with it.[51]

This statement in the *Fausse Industrie* was Fourier's own final judgment on the Societary Colony of Condé-sur-Vesgre.

24

Last Years

BY THE FALL of 1833 it was clear to most of Fourier's disciples that there was little to hope for from the two projects on which they had so enthusiastically embarked some eighteen months earlier. The effort to create a Phalanx at Condé was moribund, having been abandoned by Fourier himself as well as by most of his disciples. The journal was still being published, but only as a monthly; the original editors—Considerant, Lechevalier, Transon—had all ceased to regard it as an effective vehicle for the spread of Fourier's ideas. During a year and a half of close collaboration with Fourier these three, and most of the other Parisian disciples, had become convinced that the man was impossible to work with. They resented his dogmatism and intransigence—what Victor Considerant described as his "arid and exclusive nature"[1]—and they found him crude and inept as a popularizer of his own ideas.

The result was that in the last months of 1833 a number of the disciples began to strike off on their own. Without ceasing to consider themselves his followers and disciples, they began to create a Fourierist movement independent of Fourier himself. Leaving Fourier to do whatever he wanted with the journal, Considerant, Jules Lechevalier, and Adrien Berbrugger embarked on extensive speaking tours of the provinces. Between August and December of 1833 Lechevalier lectured to

large audiences at Rouen, Bordeaux, and Nantes; Considerant spoke at
Montargis, Orleans, and Besançon, and Berbrugger at Dijon and Lyon.
On these tours, which they sometimes described in Saint-Simonian
fashion as Phalansterian "missions," they downplayed Fourier's effort
to present his theory as a science and a profit-making scheme, a practical and experimentally verified theory of industrial organization that
would yield a profit to shrewd investors. Instead they tried to awaken
the generous and humanitarian impulses of the public. "We must . . .
make our appeal above all to the social sentiments," explained Considerant. "We must present the work at Condé as a tentative venture in
high philanthropy rather than a pure business speculation, and [we
must] interest men through their love for the public welfare . . . rather
than through their selfish interest."[2] Just a year later, in the fall of 1834,
Considerant published the first volume of his *Destinée sociale,* a lively
and lucid exposition of Fourier's doctrine that presented it in just this
light while ignoring or disguising its eccentricities. It proved to be so
much more accessible, and popular, than any of Fourier's books that
Hubert Bourgin could describe it as "the first exposition of Fourierism
that counts in the history of ideas."[3]

In the midst of all this activity on the part of his disciples Fourier
went his own way. He expected nothing to come from appeals to
generosity, and he took little interest in the effort to reach a wider
public. "All the small backers, the petty partisans, are useless and difficult to control," he wrote Muiron. "A great protector must be found
who will accomplish more all by himself than a hundred thousand
pygmies."[4] Fourier did, however, play an important role in the publication of the journal, and in December 1833 and January 1834 he also
gave a series of public lectures on his doctrine at the Société Universelle
de Civilisation. This was an athenaeum created by a group of noted
political liberals in 1829 and offering evening courses attended primarily
by "ladies and *gens du monde.*"* The disciples were apprehensive about

---

*In 1835 the Société Universelle de Civilisation was placed under surveillance by the
Paris prefect of police as a possible breeding ground of subversion similar to the outlawed
Société libre pour l'Education du Peuple. At that time its regular lecturers included Victor
Considerant, teaching a course entitled "Science Sociale," Fourier's doctor, Léon Simon
("Médecine Homéopathique"), and the ubiquitous system-maker, Hyacinthe Azaïs ("Ex-
plication Universelle"). See the police dossier on the society, AN F⁷ 6699 (dr. 29).

In reconstituting the society in 1836 its president, F. de Moncey, wrote Fourier asking
him "to accept the title of president of a special section of social science according to your
system. . . . I wish to side with you in this way and to give you and your disciples the

the lectures, fearing that Fourier might make a spectacle of himself. In fact, he came close to doing so. At one point he had to be restrained from devoting a whole lecture to rebutting a member of the audience, a Monsieur Desplanches, who had criticized his economic views. In another response to a question about freedom in the Phalanx he simply bewildered the audience with a detailed account of passionate maid service in Harmony. Even Muiron complained about his "eternal jeremiads" on the sufferings of inventors in France. But Muiron concluded that on the whole Fourier's performance was "passable."[5] Fourier himself was rather more satisfied. In a letter to Muiron he railed against the efforts of members of the audience to link his views on property to those of the Saint-Simonians, but he continued: "Despite the predominance of Saint-Simonism, most of the audience keeps coming back to see me. Yesterday's lecture convinced me of this. Already the two principal critics D . . . and L . . . have stopped finding fault with my ideas. Yesterday to intimidate them I made a systematic denunciation of political economy and proved that, out of the nine conditions it should meet, none has been satisfied."[6]

Between August 1833 and the end of February 1834 Fourier shared with Charles Pellarin responsibility for the publication of the *Phalanstère*. Pellarin left a beautiful portrait of Fourier at this time.

> The thing that first struck everyone who met Fourier, the most simple man in the world in his dress and manners, was his piercing glance. Above this eagle eye . . . rose a broad, high and remarkably beautiful forehead. The frontal parts of his skull, the seat of the intellectual faculties according to the phrenologists, were extraordinarily large compared to the rest of his head, which was rather narrow. His aquiline nose had been bent to the left as the result of a fall in his youth; but this did not harm the harmonious quality of the whole face. His thin lips, habitually pressed tight together and drooping at the corners, denoted perseverance, tenacity, and gave to Fourier's physiognomy a certain expression of gravity and bitterness. His blue eyes seemed to dart lightning in moments of animated

---

opportunity once again to win appreciation for the theories you have developed with so much talent in your writings and occasionally also at our rostrum. We are not always entirely in agreement, but we coincide on several points and that will be so much the better for humanity and civilization." De Moncey to Fourier, October 24, 1836, AN 10AS 25 (3).

conversation when, for example, he was doing justice to some sophistical attack on social truth or confounding a civilized quibbler. But at other times his eyes shone with a gentle, melancholy, and sad luster.[7]

During this period Fourier's main occupation was the writing of articles for the journal. Pellarin recalled that Fourier was usually at his desk by six or seven o'clock in the morning and that faithful to his Butterfly passion, he worked in short sessions, getting up every two hours or so to take a walk through the Sentier, where he could often be seen lost in his thoughts, talking to himself and occasionally stopping to jot down a note on the pad of paper that he always carried with him.[8]

During its last few months the journal consisted almost entirely of articles by Fourier himself; unfortunately, they were noteworthy more for their invective and for their picturesque titles than for their content. Most of them were either violent attacks on the "poltroons" and "snarling critics" of the Parisian intellectual establishment or appeals for money and patronage. Fourier did devote a series of articles to his proposal for the establishment of a children's Phalanx. But these were vague and insubstantial.[9] As usual Fourier continued to make changes until the last moment. "The journal was very late this time," he wrote Muiron on February 4, 1834, "because about January 20 I decided to change the whole subject [of the issue], and to include in it two articles that can be sent to Monsieur Thiers. One is to call attention to the monetary advantages; the other is to disabuse him about my cosmogony."[10]

At the end of March 1834, just a month after the publication of the last issue of the *Phalanstère*, the journal's office on the rue Joquelet was closed and Fourier had to move out of the apartment there, which he had occupied for the previous two years. His period of regular daily contact with the disciples was thus over. For the rest of his life Fourier was to live by himself in a small apartment at 9, rue Saint-Pierre-Montmartre (now rue Paul Lelong) in the same quarter of the Sentier that had been his home in Paris ever since 1822.

I

When Fourier moved out of the offices of the *Phalanstère* and into a private apartment in the spring of 1834, his disciples hoped his days as a journalist were over. For some time Considerant and Muiron had been urging him to cease writing popular expositions of his ideas and to get back to work on the big theoretical treatise of which the two-volume *Traité* of 1822 represented only a beginning. In September 1833 Considerant even managed to extract from Fourier a formal commitment to produce "a third volume" of the *Traité*. Considerant agreed to raise fifteen hundred francs for the purchase of the manuscript and also to pay all the costs of printing it. Fourier in turn promised to complete the work in seven months and to focus on a list of topics ranging from "the external relations of Phalanxes in High Harmony" to the "invariable theory of passional types and the rigorous demonstration that they are 810 in number . . . as it has been asserted without proof in previous volumes."[11] Eight months later, in a letter to his American disciple Albert Brisbane, Fourier was still speaking of this volume, which he now described as a "romantic" exposition of the doctrine as opposed to the "classic" presentation of the *Nouveau monde industriel*.[12] But it never appeared.

The fact of the matter is that even if he had tried, Fourier could probably no longer have written a third volume of his *Traité*. For more than ten years he had been simplifying and restating his basic ideas in the effort to find a protector. By the 1830s his creative powers were so diminished that he could do little more than repeat himself. His late manuscripts show a few halfhearted stabs at a third volume, but nothing sustained. Thus when Muiron and Considerant pressed Fourier to get down to work, he responded evasively, sometimes insisting on the need to begin the volume with a recapitulation of his earlier works "in the familiar mode."

> The Master seems to want to prove to me that a pamphlet by him is worth more than the volume we are asking for [complained Muiron]. It is always the same vicious circle, the same illusion from which he never seems to be able to escape and which makes him believe in his aptitude for spreading the doctrine. One must have great perseverance and extreme cleverness to make him understand that he should work for the small number of superior minds that rise to his level and not for the common horde who remain dumb before his great discoveries. This is what I have been telling him for almost fifteen years now.[13]

Fourier was not convinced. His fixed idea was to find a powerful protector, an individual who would do for him what had been done for Christopher Columbus by the confessor of Queen Isabella. And he believed, more firmly now than ever, that the way to reach such an individual was not through the fuller elaboration of his doctrine but rather through the presentation of his ideas in their simplest form with an emphasis on the rewards that would accrue to the lucky patron.

During the spring and summer of 1834, as he was settling into his new apartment, Fourier continued to draft appeals for support from prominent political figures. One of his principal targets was the minister of the interior, Adolphe Thiers. Fourier's manuscripts include at least five drafts of a letter to Thiers, urging that the government subsidize the founding of a trial Phalanx to be composed of three hundred children and forty adult regents. This proposal for a children's Phalanx, which had first been publicly advanced in his articles in the *Phalanstère,* would cost 600,000 francs. But it would win for the ministry the support of every deputy in the Chamber, including the legitimists and republicans; it would double the nation's economic output in a single year; and it would allow France to complete the conquest of Algeria without taking any further military actions. "Starting next year," Fourier wrote, "Algeria can become a superb kingdom for the king's second son; and if [France] wishes, the Bedouins, Moors, and Kabyles will turn into more docile and more active farmers than the gardeners of the Paris suburbs."[14]

In August of 1834 Fourier was at it again. This time the news that the Chamber of Deputies had formed a committee to consider the abolition of slavery prompted him to begin work on a pamphlet, to be published as a *Lettre aux Députés,* advising the members of the committee that he alone possessed the knowledge to bring about the emancipation of all slaves, everywhere, and without violence. Fourier originally intended his pamphlet to run to no more than seventy-two pages. But once he was embarked on it he couldn't stop. Eventually it turned into a very long and very strange book entitled *La Fausse Industrie morcelée, répugnante, mensongère, et l'antidote, l'industrie naturelle, combinée, attrayante, véridique, donnant quadruple produit.*

II

There may have been something to Fourier's claim that a cunning design lay behind the bizarre presentation of the *Théorie des quatre mouvements.* But this was not the case with *La Fausse industrie,* an even more bizarre work without end or beginning, a work that began on page 409 and required the use of so many different typefaces that Fourier's publishers were already complaining after three months that they were running out of type.[15] The book was actually a "mosaic" of articles, pamphlets, arguments, replies to particular critics, enticements to potential protectors, and "confirmations" of claims made elsewhere.

Fourier explained in the text itself that he had not originally intended to write a book, but that his pamphlet on the abolition of slavery had simply gotten out of hand. "I was working on the sixth chapter," he wrote, "when a journalist's insult determined me to reply harshly." So he included in his pamphlet a scheme for "the grafting of the press" in which he advised governments and police chiefs on how they might protect the rights of "obscure inventors" against "the despotism of the anarchical press." Shortly thereafter, having received "precise documents" on the economic policies of the Paraguayan dictator, José Gaspar Rodríguez Francia, Fourier decided to turn the brochure into a book and to change its character.

> Scarcely had I begun the second section [he wrote] than my plans were changed by the arrival of an unexpected piece of information. I received precise documents on the Paraguayan affair. It provides me with a FACTUAL PROOF . . . that Francia, although limited to a twentieth of the means that I possess . . . is realizing *in a very low degree* the mechanism of combined industry.[16]

The documents received by Fourier could not have been very precise. For the despotic little police state ruled by Dr. Francia actually bore no resemblance to the Phalanx.* But Fourier desperately wanted to believe

*Fourier's enthusiasm for the work of Dr. Francia (1766–1840) recalls that of many earlier French utopians for the "communistic" communities of Indians established by the Jesuits in Paraguay in the seventeenth and eighteenth centuries. Fourier did not share that enthusiasm, however. He wrote in *La Fausse industrie* that he had originally taken little interest in Francia because "I believed him to be the continuator of the Jesuits of Paraguay. He isn't that at all. He is a man who, without theory, has an instinct for the combined order." OC VIII, 431.

The source of Fourier's (mis)information about Francia appears to have been a Monsieur d'Epagny whom Fourier had met in 1830. In a letter to d'Epagny of April 1834 Fourier thanks him for "the details you were kind enough to give me last Monday evening on the social method of Francia." Fourier then formulates nine specific questions. (For example: "Are Francia's gatherings of fifteen hundred people jointly responsible for the care of the sick and the feeble and the small children of the poor?") It took d'Epagny six months to answer the letter (it is docketed "replied 15 October"). But the answers were apparently sufficient to convince Fourier that Francia's method was somewhat similar to his own. See Fourier to d'Epagny, April 24, 1834 (cancellation), Manuscript Department, Historical Society of Pennsylvania.

that his theory could be put into practice. He was quite ready to assume that the test had already been made, and even that it had been made ("in a very low degree") by someone else.

Having convinced himself that his theory was already "factually proven," Fourier no longer saw any need to persuade his readers of its subtlety and logical rigor. He could simply point to Paraguay and say, "Look, it works!" The important thing now more than ever was to stress the results of the theory—the quadruple product, the architectural splendors, the taming of the elements, the psychic gratifications, the "prodigious rewards" in store for the founder—and at the same time to dispel whatever misconceptions might exist in the minds of his readers. Thus Fourier repeatedly insisted that unlike the ideas of the Owenites and Saint-Simonians, his doctrine posed no threat to private property.[17] He carefully explained that "during the first two generations" of Harmony there would be "absolutely no change in amorous customs" and subsequent innovations would be "voted unanimously by fathers and husbands." He warned against various "ridiculous" interpretations and "insipid calumnies" concerning his cosmogony. And finally, he offered an extended analysis of the "abuse and spitefulness" of his detractors, whom he divided into three categories: the envious, the minotaurs, and the mongrels.[18]

For about a year Fourier worked on *La Fausse industrie*. He sent his manuscript off to the press chapter by chapter; and when each set of proofs returned, he made such extensive changes that the publisher complained that the cost of composition had been increased by two-thirds.[19] Finally, in September 1835 the printing and binding were done. As in the past, Fourier sent copies of his book to provincial disciples, to old friends like Amard and the younger Bousquet, to new acquaintances like Flora Tristan,* and to such potential founders as the duc de Broglie and Adolphe Thiers.[20] He might have spared himself the

---

*The great French feminist Flora Tristan (1803–1844) was still virtually unknown when she introduced herself to Fourier in August of 1835. Two months later she wrote him: "Every day I become more thoroughly penetrated with a sense of the sublimity of your doctrine." Although Flora Tristan was too independent ever to identify herself completely with any one ideology, she seems to have believed for a while that her "ardent desire to render [herself] useful" to the cause of the poor and the oppressed might best be realized in association with the Fourierists. Flora Tristan to Fourier, October 11, 1835, Bibliothèque de documentation internationale contemporaine B1040, cited in Jules-L. Puech, *La Vie et l'oeuvre de Flora Tristan* (Paris: Rivière, 1925), 70. See also Tristan to Fourier, April 22 [1836], AN 10AS 25 (3).

effort. For in addition to being an embarrassment to the disciples, *La Fausse industrie* had even less impact on public opinion than his previous works. The problem was that the work was simply unintelligible to anyone not already familiar with Fourier's ideas.

Fourier's reaction was to blame himself for not giving the work sufficient publicity. Thus in November he began work on a brochure the purpose of which would be to draw attention to *La Fausse industrie*. A month later this brochure had exceeded fifty pages and Muiron was complaining bitterly to Clarisse Vigoureux.

> It always crushes me to see him squandering his prospects and wasting his money as well as his time in printing such ill-conceived works of publicity. He tells me that his new factum will be seventy-two pages long and that he will circulate a thousand copies of it in Paris, etc., etc. I keep coming back to my idea that we should only give him money in exchange for manuscripts according to the terms of his promise of September 1833.[21]

Fourier spent another year working on this factum, which eventually became the second volume of *La Fausse industrie*. In it he appealed more crudely than ever before for aid from potential protectors. He announced that if Baron Rothschild would undertake to found the first Phalanx, he would be rewarded by the return of the Hebrews to Jerusalem and the establishment of "a Rothschild dynasty . . . on the throne of David and Solomon." To Daniel O'Connell he offered the deliverance of Ireland and the entire world "by the end of June 1837." Czar Nicholas I of Russia would gain ice-free ports north of the Arctic Circle. The pope would "rally to Christianity the majority of Mohammedans, Brahmans, Buddhists, and idolators."[22] This second volume appeared at the beginning of 1837. Like the first, it was hardly noticed; and *La Fausse industrie* remains, as Michel Butor has written, "a bottle in the sea, an enormous letter thrown out in search of its recipient, the possible candidate."[23]

III

For years prior to the publication of *La Fausse industrie* Fourier had been telling all who would listen that since France was "the paradise of sophists and the hell of inventors," it was likely that sponsorship for the establishment of the first trial Phalanx would come from outside France. The failure of the venture of Condé-sur-Vesgre only served to intensify Fourier's disgust with his own compatriots. But he wavered in his attitude toward other nations, sometimes (despite his habitual Anglophobia) looking to England for a protector and at other times asserting that since the West was rotten, the experiment would have to be made in a "sociable" Eastern nation such as Russia.[24] There was also a brief period in the mid-1830s when it seemed as if, regardless of Fourier's preferences, the honor of establishing the first Phalanx might fall on the Danubian principality of Walachia in present-day Romania.

During the last few years of his life Fourier was in fairly regular contact with a group of Romanian students, liberal aristocrats and young landowners from Walachia, who saw in his ideas a possible remedy for the poverty and backwardness of their homeland.[25] The most dedicated of these Romanian admirers was a young man named Teodor Diamant, a graduate of the French College of Saint-Sava at Bucharest, who had come to Paris apparently to study law and had met Fourier in 1832 after a brief flirtation with the Saint-Simonians.* During a stay at Paris that lasted until March 1834 Diamant contributed both money and time to the Fourierist cause: he purchased shares in *Le Phalanstère,* did some street-corner proselytizing among the Paris workers, and published at his own expense a short Fourierist brochure on "the means of ending the debate between the haves and the have-nots, without taking from the haves."[26] Diamant also introduced Fourier to a number of his compatriots. One of them, Ion Ghica, attended Fourier's lectures at the Société de Civilisation in the winter of 1833–1834 and was deeply touched by what he described as "the eloquence and poetry" of Fourier's language.

> The beauties, the pleasures, and the spiritual and emotional satisfactions offered by the Phalansterian community were described with great charm. . . . There was such power and such grace in his manner of speaking that it would have been impossible for the audience not to be captivated. I left these talks at once astonished and exalted, convinced I should say.

*On Teodor Diamant (or Mehtupciu-Diamant) see, in addition to the sources cited in note 25, Gromoslav Mladenatz, Introduction to Diamant's *Scrieri economice* (Bucharest, 1958). According to the Romanian sources Diamant had received training as an engineer and surveyor, but in Castelvera to Fourier, April 29, 1832, AN 10AS 25 (9), Diamant is identified as a law student and Saint-Simonian residing at 78, rue de la Harpe.

Ghica went on to note that he had been so moved by the poetic quality of Fourier's lectures that afterward, as he walked through the Champs-Elysées, he had the impression of being surrounded by "antilions gentler than lambs," of being "drawn across waters" by antidolphins and antiwhales, and "lifted up into the sky on the wings of antivultures."[27]

Teodor Diamant, who returned to Bucharest in May 1834, was more taken by Fourier's economic ideas than by his zoological poetry. But he was no less fervent in his commitment to the doctrine. According to the recollections of his cousin, Nicholas Cretulescu (whom he had also introduced to Fourier), Diamant had "no other aspiration on his return from Paris than the establishment of Phalansteries" and he preached Fourierism "with all the ardor of which he was capable." In June 1834 Diamant published an article on Fourier's system in a leading Bucharest journal, and he also attempted to interest the ministers and even the Russian governor, Count Paul Kiselev, in Fourier's ideas.[28] Diamant failed to convince the authorities. But he was more successful in arousing interest in the theory among liberal Walachian landowners. Thus in June 1834 he wrote a long letter to Fourier, urging him to come to Bucharest to supervise an *essai.*

> Is there any hope of making a trial next spring at Condé or elsewhere in France? If you don't think so, Monsieur, I beg you to let me know as soon as possible so that before the beginning of the winter we may send you the money you would need to come here to Bucharest, where I have had the good luck to obtain fairly good results in the twenty days since my arrival. Three cultivated sites, each one of which is good for a colony and on which there are already several buildings to house the first colonists, are offered by their proprietors who have become zealous partisans of the societary method and admire your genius. Several other boyars, doctors, professors, offer money. I would have established a share-holding company, but I think it wise to wait for the return of our worthy prince, so that he may be the first subscriber.

Diamant went on to say that he was in the process of drawing up plans and asked for specific advice concerning "the number and dimensions of the seristeries, rooms, dormitories, dining halls, kitchens, etc."[29]

Fourier was actually quite skeptical about Diamant's proposal. Not long after receiving this letter Fourier told Cretulescu that he feared

Diamant was getting carried away by his imagination, and that the theory demanded longer study than Diamant had yet given it.[30] Nevertheless, Fourier remained in touch with his Romanian disciple, and in 1835 the two exchanged letters concerning the possibility of establishing a children's Phalanx near Bucharest.[31] Meanwhile, however, one of the young noblemen to whom Diamant had preached Fourierism decided to organize a "Fourierist" community of his own consisting largely of freed serfs from his estate.

In March 1835 on the property of Manolake Emanuel Balaceanu in the Walachian village of Scaeni a purportedly Fourierist "Agricultural and Industrial Society" was officially established. It bore little resemblance to the Phalanx of Fourier's dreams. It had just over fifty members, most of them freed serfs, whose time seems to have been divided between farm work, crafts, and an educational curriculum, which included geography, arithmetic, drawing, music, French, Romanian, and catechism.[32] Nonetheless it is clear that Balaceanu thought of the community as an application of Fourier's ideas. He was, in Diamant's words, bent on securing for himself "the honor of becoming the founder of the first Phalanstery."* It is also clear that however watered-down this early experiment in practical Fourierism may have been, it was altogether too radical for most of the local boyars. Denouncing the community as a "fruit of the seditious French spirit," they brought pressure on the authorities to dissolve it. Apparently it was dissolved by force in December of 1836.[33]

Apart from the abortive trial Phalanx at Condé-sur-Vesgre, this "Agricultural and Industrial Society" established in a Walachian village was the only serious experiment in applied Fourierism undertaken during Fourier's lifetime. Fourier himself may have been unaware of its ultimate fate: the last news he had of it was apparently Diamant's letter of June 1836 denouncing Balaceanu as "a Jacobin" of "bad reputation" and "beset by debts." But in any case it is doubtful that Fourier ex-

---

*Diamant to Fourier, Bucharest, June 3/15, 1836, AN 10AS 25 (3). Diamant had apparently initially agreed to collaborate with Balaceanu: his name is listed on the contracts of association signed by members of the community as offering instruction in mathematics, "social economy," and French. But when Balaceanu proved unwilling to modify his plans according to Fourier's advice and to participate jointly in the preparation of a children's Phalanx near Bucharest, Diamant broke with him. Diamant's 1836 letter to Fourier is full of warnings against Balaceanu's "blind ambition" and general bad character.

pected much to come of it. As he wrote a year or two before his death, "Many people have, without meaning ill, a mania for correcting, mutilating, and dismembering inventions. They might attempt to found a bastard Phalanx or something else ambiguous, obtain little or no success in the equilibrium of the passions, and conclude that my theory is worthless. I disavow in advance all these mutilations. Their authors will fail, through philosophical prejudices, to accomplish things I could do if I were in charge."[34]

IV

Despite all the failures and disappointments of the 1830s, Fourier began to acquire a considerable amount of notoriety during the last years of his life. The publication of the *Phalanstère* and of Considerant's *Destinée sociale* widened the circle of Fourier's disciples, and by the mid-1830s small groups of Fourierists had begun to spring up all over Europe.[35] In Germany popularizations of Fourier's theory were published at Heidelberg, Augsburg, and Gotha. In Spain the republican navy officer Joaquin Abreu began in 1835 to publish articles on Fourier in the journals of Cadiz and Madrid.[36] In Italy there were signs of interest in Fourierism from Milan to Palermo, and in 1836 the young Giuseppe Mazzini's critical confrontation with Fourier's thought resulted in a substantial series of articles in the émigré press.[37] Even in the Russia of Nicholas I the future revolutionaries Alexander Herzen and Nicholas Ogarev eagerly followed the debates that Fourierists and Saint-Simonians carried on fifteen hundred miles away in the pages of the Paris journals. Much later Ogarev could still evoke nostalgically the heated atmosphere in which "we . . . disciples of a new world, disciples of Fourier and Saint-Simon . . . swore to dedicate our whole lives to the people and to their liberation."[38]

Fourier was not aware of the existence of his eclectic Russian "disciples." Nor (with the exception of the Romanians) does he seem to have had much knowledge of the other groups of foreign admirers. But he could not ignore the continued growth of interest in his ideas in France itself. During his last years he received letters from admirers all over France. Some sent poems in his honor. Others wrote to volunteer their services at Condé, or to ask questions about the doctrine. A few like Dr. Décheneaux, a professor of chemistry at the College of Sorèze, even made pilgrimages to the rue Saint-Pierre-Montmartre to meet face to face with the "Illustrious Revealer of the Harmonian World."[39]

But by the mid-1830s Fourier's theory had finally entered the public domain, and it was not merely the true believers who took an interest in it. The threat of violent class conflict that hung over the cities and industrialized regions of France and the consequent growth of concern with the "social question" had at last given his ideas about work and association and social harmony a relatively broad appeal. Thus in the last few years of Fourier's life sympathetic discussions of his ideas began to appear in large-circulation newspapers like Emile de Girardin's *La Presse* and in influential journals like the *Revue des deux mondes*.[40] Established writers such as George Sand and Sainte-Beuve took notice of Fourier, and a long article by Louis Reybaud in the *Revue des deux mondes* provided a tolerant if skeptical synopsis of Fourier's ideas, grouping him for the first time with Owen and Saint-Simon as a "modern socialist."[41]

For most of his contemporaries, however, Fourier was still an object of curiosity. And if Reybaud treated his ideas with a certain bemused detachment, other more hostile writers and journalists began to resurrect Fourier's early speculations on cosmogony to entertain their readers with accounts of antilions and planetary lovemaking. Thus in 1834 in his truculent preface to *Mademoiselle de Maupin* the young Théophile Gautier ridiculed the prophecies of the "madman" Fourier as the absurd culmination of the faith in progress and utility.[42] Word of Fourier's *archibras* and of his seas of pink lemonade had crossed the Channel by 1836, when Henry Bulwer could purport to "startle the grave and prudent people" of London with news of "a sage who asserts that the sea is, in its natural process, turning into lemonade; and who logically proves that the fate of humanity, in distant generations, will be to sustain an ornament behind, which it would be rather difficult to arrange with a pair of breeches."[43]

A few years later in his *Monographie de la presse parisienne* Balzac provided the formula, explaining how "the Wag, the second variety of minor journalist," could make ten francs a day embroidering on the *Théorie des quatre mouvements*.

The *Phalange* is founded to make known the doctrine of Fourier. The Wag sees ten articles in this philosophy, and he begins:

"Saint-Simon had proposed to make twenty paupers with the fortune of a rich man. But the *Quatre mouvements* by Fourier, a former proof corrector in his lifetime, expresses a very different social philosophy: you are going to work with your arms crossed, you won't have any corns on your feet, lawyers will get rich without taking a penny from their clients, legs of lamb will walk down the street already cooked, chickens will roast themselves on the spit. About the age of fifty you will grow a modest tail thirty-two feet long, which you will maneuver with elegance and grace. The moon will have babies, liver pâtés will grow in the fields, the clouds will rain champagne, the frost will be made out of Roman punch, and ten sou coins will be worth forty francs, etc., etc."[44]

Before 1840 it had not yet become the habit of cartoonists to represent Fourier and Victor Considerant with a tail or *archibras*. But already in Fourier's lifetime stories of his "extravagances" gained such currency that now and then children who encountered him walking in the garden of the Palais Royal would taunt: "Voilà le fou: riez!"[45]

Finally neither the taunts nor the sympathy appeared to make much difference to Fourier. At the end he retreated into an almost impenetrable shell. When he appeared in public he remained silent and impassive, keeping his true feelings to himself. And if he devoted much of *La Fausse industrie* to rebutting his detractors, he does not seem to have been greatly pleased by the more favorable reviews. He could not tolerate the condescending compliments of a George Sand; and when Louis Reybaud compared him to Prosper Enfantin and the abbé Châtel, both the inventors of new religions, Fourier commented dryly in his notebook that, like Jesus, he was being placed "between two thieves."[46] Then, less than a year before he died, when he learned that the Vatican had placed his works on the Index along with those of Saint-Simon and the abbé Lamennais, he responded with Olympian sarcasm. The Index, he wrote, was a "worn-out weapon," a "comic thunderbolt," and the Vatican was using it against an odd assortment of enemies. "One might say that Rome in its distress wants to stake everything on one card. It proscribes all at once the present poet of Christianity [Lamennais] and the manifest enemy of Catholicism [Saint-Simon]. It lumps me in that mess of incongruous elements. . . . The only thing that could be added to that crude gesture would be to proscribe the chorister of Christianity, Monsieur de Chateaubriand."[47]

V

Although Fourier never stopped arguing with his critics, he did in his last years become increasingly detached from the movement that had grown up around his name. He let it be known that he was not a "Fourierist," not the head of a party, and not responsible for the actions and words of his disciples. Thus in 1835, when Victor Considerant was attacked in two Catholic journals for a strongly anticlerical speech, Fourier took pains to separate himself from his disciple. "I am not responsible for things I have neither said nor written," he wrote the *Gazette de France*. "Many people are my disciples on one point and not on another." And he went on: "What is Fourierism? I don't know. My theory is the continuation of that of Newton on attraction. . . . I am a continuator and I have never accepted the term Fourierist."[48] Fourier made it plain that if his disciples wished to espouse his ideas in public, they did so at their own risk.

Fourier had always been a difficult man, and age did nothing to mellow him. The correspondence of his disciples for the mid-1830s is full of complaints about his dogmatism and his "arid and exclusive nature," and long after his death Considerant could still describe him as "at times extravagantly unjust toward those who did not think as he did."[49] To be sure, even in his last years there were moments when Fourier was, as Charles Pellarin put it, "delightful to see and to listen to."

> Were he asked, for example, about the analogy of such and such an animal, which represents one of our caprices and social follies? He would explain it in a manner at the same time most picturesque and most comical, imitating the bearing, the gait, the cry, and the habits of the animals of which he was speaking. . . . At these times one could see in Fourier something of La Fontaine and Molière.[50]

Others who knew Fourier well described him as delicate, uncomplaining, always eager to do whatever he could to relieve the pains of others, and "so impassive in the face of [his own] suffering that you would have thought him a stranger to his own personality."[51] At the same time, however, it is clear that Fourier became more and more irascible in his old age, more and more prone to explode in fits of anger against overattentive friends, against "Jacobins" masquerading as disciples, and even against the Paris wine merchants whose poisonous adulterations were, he felt (and perhaps rightly so), speeding him to his grave. Fourier also became increasingly secretive during his last years, and increasingly reluctant to engage in any serious discussion of his theory. He never lost the fear that his discovery might be stolen. And often, when people came to ask him questions, he brusquely turned them aside. As Albert Brisbane recalled later, "Any familiar conversation with him was out of the question. . . . 'There are the books,' he would say. 'Explanations can be found there.' "⁵²

There had never been much real intellectual interchange between Fourier and his disciples. The most he had ever done was to answer their questions and correct their errors. But in his last few years even this modest dialogue came virtually to an end, and Fourier's contacts with the disciples were limited largely to social occasions. They invited him to their homes for dinner and arranged meetings for him with prospective backers. Occasionally he consented to be taken by them to dine out or to visit the salons of their elegant friends. But his health, which had long been failing, made it difficult for him to enjoy fine cuisine, and the company of inquisitive strangers was often an ordeal for him.

> Although born with an affectionate disposition [wrote Pellarin], Fourier always lived a solitary life. During the last five or six years of his life, when his name began to be known, people started seeking him out just as any celebrity is sought out at Paris. Desiring to hear him speak about his theory, many people attempted to attract him to their homes by inviting him to dinner or for an evening. But jealous of his dignity as well as of his independence, Fourier accepted the invitations that were made to him only with extreme caution and only when he knew the people involved quite intimately. From the moment when he thought he perceived that they wished to exhibit him, to show him off as a spectacle to the curious, or when he saw that they were trying to steal from him the secret of some of his theoretical combinations, Fourier would entrench himself in an obstinate silence that nothing could break or else he would answer with evasions to all the questions they kept asking him.⁵³

On one such occasion Fourier and Considerant were invited to dine in Neuilly at the elegant home of Benjamin Appert, a philanthropist and prison reformer and an influential figure in Orleanist society. The company, which included the physiologist Dr. Broussais, was distinguished and the conversation lively. But Appert's attempts to draw Fourier out were unsuccessful. "I would have listened attentively to Fourier talk about his system," recalled Appert. "But he had little to say and he gave the impression of a man who was suffering inside himself."[54]

If Fourier revealed much of himself to anyone during his last years, it was most likely to several women whose company he particularly enjoyed. One of these was Clarisse Vigoureux, who had moved to Paris in 1832, establishing herself and her daughter Julie in a large apartment on the rue des Saints-Pères. Their household (where Julie's fiancé, Victor Considerant, was often present) was probably as much of a home as Fourier had at the end of his life, but he valued his independence and his privacy too much to accept Clarisse's standing invitation to move permanently into one of her rooms. Another of Fourier's closest friends during these years was Louise Courvoisier (*veuve* Lacombe), a widow from Besançon whom Fourier had met in 1832 and whose brother had served briefly as keeper of the seals under Charles X. She was devoted to Fourier, and she found in him a tenderness and a delicacy and a generosity that he generally kept hidden from the world at large. In the brief reminiscence of Fourier that she published after his death he emerges as an almost Christ-like figure, doing good turns to needy widows and overworked servant girls, and attempting in a variety of ways to alleviate the pains of civilization where he found them.[55]

For all Louise Courvoisier's admiration of Fourier, his image does not come very sharply into focus in her recollections. More revealing is the correspondence of Désirée Veret, a young dressmaker who met Fourier in 1832 at the age of twenty-two, having already passed through the Saint-Simonian movement and edited a journal initially called *La Femme libre,* which played a major role in what Evelyne Sullerot has described as "the feminist explosion of 1831–1832."[56] More than fifty years later Désirée Veret could still vividly recall her conversations with Fourier and the letters he wrote her after 1833 when she left for London to seek her fortune.

> Fourier was a consoler of sorrows for me as for others whom he cared for. My youth, my social enthusiasm, my lack of experience in life, inspired in him observations drawn from his theory as to the cause of my unhappiness. "You have too many

dominant passions," he wrote me. "They cannot develop in civilization, above all the alternating passion, which you have to a high degree."

"If I hadn't been an old man," he wrote, "whom you would disdain, I would have let you know my feelings, and if I had been rich, you would not have left. For I have missed you very much."[57]

Although Fourier's letters to Désirée Veret are lost, we do have four that she wrote to him while in England in 1833 and 1834. They are wonderfully rich and intimate letters dealing both with her amorous adventures in England and with her contacts with the Owenites and with Fourier's friend, Anna Doyle Wheeler.

> You hope, my good Monsieur Fourier, that love will come to distract me. The love of an Englishman! Do you really think so? They make love like they make machines. They only understand the physical side of things, or else a chimerical love affair that can only exist in the imagination. I have had lovers here, I can confide this to you, but they have only given me sensual pleasures. The English are cold, egotistical, even in their pleasures, in making love, in dining. Each thinks only of himself. . . .
>
> There is an Italian Saint-Simonian here named Fontana who is making the Owenite ladies turn their heads and is bringing frowns to the face of Mr. Owen, who is not happy to have his lovely converts taken from him. I have sent many ladies to his talks, and now they are all quasi Saint-Simonians. Is this for love of the doctrine or the speaker? I don't know. . . .
>
> My good Monsieur Fourier, if you were not a great genius, I wouldn't dare to write you these silly things. I let my pen wander, knowing that for you nothing is trivial and that in the middle of these complaints of a poor civilized girl, you will find a few germs that would have made a happy Harmonian.[58]

There is much about Fourier's inner life that will probably never be known. But it is interesting to note that age seems to have been no barrier to his affections—or to his ability to inspire affection. He once observed that one of the few times he ever thought of marriage he was twenty-five years old and the woman in question was eighty.[59] One thing these letters from Désirée Veret show is that at the age of sixty-two, when he appeared to the rest of the world as an embittered and cranky monomaniac, Fourier had the ability to win the confidence and affection of a woman forty years his junior.

VI

From the latter part of 1835 Fourier's health began to decline notice-ably. He suffered from chronic stomach disorders and frequently com-plained of cramps, nausea, and fever. As a result of sickness, and also growing indifference, he became almost entirely cut off from the activi-ties of his disciples. He was unable to assist Victor Considerant in the launching of a new journal, *La Phalange,* which began to appear on July 10, 1836.[60] And while he left no doubt that he approved of Consider-ant's assumption of leadership of the movement, he had little to say (at least in public) when a dissident group of provincial disciples, including Just Muiron, began to protest against Considerant's authoritarianism and his preoccupation with the journal rather than with new ventures in applied Fourierism.★

By the end of 1836 Fourier's condition had worsened, and he even had to give up his customary stroll to the Tuileries each morning to witness the changing of the royal guards. Still, he resisted all of the efforts of the disciples to provide him with better lodging than the damp and drafty apartment on the rue Saint-Pierre-Montmartre, and he adamantly refused their offers to look after him during his sicknesses. "Never, even when he was in the direst extremity," wrote Pellarin, "would [Fourier] consent to have someone stay with him in order to take care of him. He refused such offers with all the strength of his will,

★There are two good articles by Emile Poulat on the origins of the conflict within the Fourierist movement between various "dissident" provincial groups and the "orthodox" Parisian disciples. See Emile Poulat, "Sur deux textes manuscrits de Fourier," in Henri Desroche et al., *Etudes sur la tradition française de l'association ouvrière* (Paris, 1956), 5–19, and "Ecritures et tradition fouriéristes," *Revue internationale de philosophie,* XVI, 2 (1960), 221–233. The history of the conflict lies largely outside the scope of this biography. But it should be noted that matters first came to a head in the summer of 1836 when, just as the first issues of *La Phalange* were appearing in Paris, Just Muiron attempted to organize what amounted to a Fourierist corresponding society, the aim of which was to establish closer ties between the Fourierist circles and groups throughout the French provinces. In late August, Considerant criticized this proposal for a "Union Phalansterienne" in a 123-page "Mémoire confidentiel," and at about the same time Fourier himself drafted a letter to Muiron criticizing the "extreme sterility" of the proposal. See Fourier to Muiron, draft, August 26, 1836, AN 10AS 16 (42).

which, like his intelligence, remained in full vigor up to the last moment. 'I don't need to be looked after,' he would answer. 'I like being alone. I don't want to cause any trouble on my account.' "[61]

Fourier attributed his stomach problems principally to the bakers and wine merchants of Paris. In his view the latter were "public poisoners" and the bakers of the capital consistently adulterated their dough and then only half baked it. Fourier had a particular aversion to the soggy bread and foul wine served in most Paris restaurants, and when he dined out he usually made a point of taking his bread and wine with him. This was a habit that Heinrich Heine was to recall much later. "How often I used to see him," wrote Heine, "strolling under the arcades of the Palais Royal with both pockets of his old gray frock coat bulging so that out of one the neck of a bottle would protrude and out of the other a large loaf of bread."[62] Fourier had always been fond of good wines, and Pellarin writes that on occasion "he did not disdain to derive from them a slight degree of gaiety."[63] But at the end of his life, apparently he frequently drank to excess. "I am more sad than surprised," wrote Muiron to Clarisse Vigoureux in March 1836, "to learn from you that the health of Monsieur Fourier is precarious. The brother of [Amédée] Paget wrote the other day that he had just seen the Master completely drunk in the Luxemburg Gardens. So he just keeps on drinking too much, all the while protesting that he's being poisoned!"[64]

Throughout the winter of 1836–1837 Fourier was virtually confined to his apartment. "I am so weak," he wrote his disciple Charles Harel in January of 1837, "so tired out by my upset stomach and by the disgust I feel for food, that I won't be able to dine with anyone. . . . I will stay on my diet of abstinence and isolation." A few weeks after writing this letter Fourier had a serious accident. He was climbing the stairs late one night when he slipped and fell, fracturing his skull. The fracture healed after several months, but Fourier's face remained badly swollen.[65]

In the spring of 1837 with the return of warm weather Fourier's health and spirits improved, and there were times when he seemed to be his old self. His English disciple Hugh Doherty recalled one such instance.

About four months before he died, on asking him for an explanation of certain parts of his theory, as we were wont to do whenever we met with a difficult point, he was more than usually gay, and in order to give a clear idea of one of the words which he used, he declaimed, with appropriate action, several verses from Molière in which his meaning was happily expressed. Though we had been in the habit of conversing with him frequently, this was the first time we ever saw him laugh heartily.[66]

Only a few weeks after this, however, Fourier was described by a provincial disciple, Alphonse Tamisier, as hopelessly diminished in both mind and body.

The genius of Fourier is extinct forever [wrote Tamisier in July]. I am back from Paris, where I had the honor of seeing him and of shaking the hand of the liberator of humanity. Age and sickness have smothered the last flashes of that vast intelligence. Fourier could not even enjoy his triumph if it were announced to him now.[67]

The reports of other disciples suggest that Fourier's decline was neither so rapid nor so complete: Pellarin, Doherty, and Fourier's doctor all speak of him as retaining his mental alertness to the last. Nonetheless it is clear that by July 1837 Fourier was in much too weakened a condition to play a significant role in two events that might otherwise have been important to him. These were his meeting with Robert Owen and his attempt to mediate in the dispute between his disciples.

The meeting with Owen took place on July 17, 1837.[68] The occasion was a grand banquet in Owen's honor attended by over two hundred people and presided over by a liberal editor well known to Fourier, Marc-Antoine Jullien. Fourier's name was listed on the program as a subscriber—it is hard to imagine that this was his doing—and it appears that he and Owen were introduced to one another by their disciples. It is inconceivable that, under the circumstances, there could have been any significant exchange between the two. But still one can't help wondering what was going through Fourier's mind when he at last encountered the man whose "snares and charlatanry" he had denounced so vigorously just five years earlier.

Just two weeks after Fourier's encounter with Robert Owen a meeting was held in Fourier's presence between Victor Considerant and a number of the dissident disciples who were unhappy with Considerant's leadership of the Ecole Sociétaire.[69] What the dissidents wanted was the coordination of the Fourierist movement on a national level through the creation of a "Societary Institute," which would establish closer ties between Fourierist groups in different parts of France. Considerant objected that this proposal (like the similar proposal for a "Phalansterian Union" advanced in 1836 by Just Muiron) could only undermine his own efforts to raise money and publish a journal. Fourier himself seems to have asked for the meeting, and his original intention was apparently to mediate between Considerant and the dissidents.* But when the two parties met, on July 31, 1837, it was Considerant who did most of the talking. Fourier spoke briefly, declaring "that he wished to see unity maintained and that mutual concessions would have to be made."[70] But there were no concessions on either side, and the result of the meeting was simply to reaffirm the split within the ranks of the Fourierists.

Not long after this meeting, probably at Considerant's prodding and perhaps with his help, Fourier composed, or dictated, a declaration expressing his full support for "the direction given to our propaganda by my disciple and friend Victor Considerant."[71] This declaration, which may in fact have been written for the dying man by Considerant, was to be Fourier's ultimate statement on the movement that, in spite of his own disclaimers, now bore his name.

Beginning in late June 1837 Fourier was regularly visited by a doctor, one Léon Simon, a partisan of homeopathic medicine who was also one of many Fourierist refugees from the Saint-Simonian religion. Fourier was not exactly enthusiastic about Simon's visits: the doctor later wrote that he "endured rather than accepted" them. He was vague and reticent when questioned about his symptoms; he never consented to undergo a full physical examination; and "everything in his attitude and look announced his little confidence in the art of healing." In any case, it soon became evident that, as one disciple put it, Fourier's "whole frame was . . . hurrying on to dissolution." In addition to nausea, diarrhea, and various urinary problems, Fourier's digestive system was

---

*In a brochure issued by the dissidents in August 1837 Fourier is described as having initially been sympathetic to their proposals but then, after talking to Considerant, fearful of a schism. "M. Fourier told us that even though our proposal was good, it was necessary to see it from all sides, that the division of efforts might have a harmful effect on the movement, and that this was what we should try to avoid. 'I have talked with M. Considerant,' added M. Fourier, 'and I believe I should try to serve as an intermediary between you. Give me a summary of your proposal or let us set a day for you to explain things to Considerant in my presence.' " *Aux Phalanstériens.* La commission préparatoire de l'institut Sociétaire (Paris, August 1837), 23. AN 14AS 1–8, Institut Français d'Histoire Sociale.

simply breaking down. There were periods when he suffered from so strong a disgust for food that it was feared he might die of malnutrition. Dr. Simon tried various prescriptions and diets, but Fourier would not stick to them.[72]

Although he became increasingly weak and emaciated, Fourier continued until mid-September to try to lead a relatively normal life. But one day, in climbing his staircase, he suffered a stroke, which left him with a paralyzed right arm and pains in his right thigh. The pains gradually diminished, but the paralysis remained and his disgust for food only increased. By the end of September Fourier had virtually ceased to eat, and he refused free access to his apartment to anyone but a cleaning lady who looked in on him several times a day. On the morning of October 10, 1837, she found him dead at his bedside, dressed in his old frock coat.

EPILOGUE

Before burying Fourier, his disciples took what Pellarin described as "a religious care" in preserving all that could be preserved of their Master's mortal remains. A death mask was made, and in the course of his autopsy Dr. Simon recorded for posterity the exact dimensions of Fourier's brain. By his graveside in the Montmartre Cemetery Victor Considerant delivered a funeral oration that "summed up in a striking manner the whole life of Fourier" and contained a series of images that were to become standard in Fourierist hagiography: Fourier's early "Hannibalic oath" against commerce, his invention of the railroad train "while amusing himself at the age of nineteen," his great discovery of 1799, his long period of neglect and derision, and his final "crucifixion" by the society he had condemned. All of these images were invoked in the official biography of Fourier first published by Charles Pellarin in 1839; and the Christian religious imagery in particular assumed a prominent place in the brief accounts of Fourier's life subsequently written by other disciples. By the 1840s when Jean Czynski published a short popular biography, the apotheosis was complete. Fourier had become "the savior of humanity" and Besançon "the modern Bethlehem."[1]

Although Fourier had occasionally referred to himself as "the Messiah of Reason" and had more than once compared his own sufferings to those of Christ, there are obviously many respects in which both the man and the doctrine were ill suited to the sort of sanctification his disciples attempted to foist upon them. The man was scarcely a saint, and in his time he had treated with scorn and withering sarcasm the attempts of secular radicals like the Saint-Simonians to clothe their ideas in the language and symbolism of the Christian religion. More significantly, I believe, there was a fundamental, if unacknowledged, difference in temper or sensibility between Fourier and his disciples. Fourier was in some important respects a man of the eighteenth century. He was a hedonist in theory and the "inventor" of a "science" of human nature and society, who shared with Mandeville and Adam Smith and Helvétius and Jeremy Bentham the belief that, under the right conditions, the individual's pursuit of self-interest would necessarily lead to social harmony. In practice his disciples of the 1830s and 1840s did not really accept his view of human nature and human motivation. In their attempts to popularize the doctrine they made it clear that for them the way to realize the vision of the good society was to appeal to the individual's higher self, the capacity for self-abnegation and the love of humanity. Whereas Fourier's fundamental categories were "passion," "desire," and "interest," theirs were "dévouement," "sentiment humanitaire," and "démocratie pacifique." Thus in their propaganda they transformed his doctrine into a sort of democratic humanitarianism that he would surely have disavowed. And they found it easy to employ Christian rhetoric and imagery of the kind that he himself had dismissed in the Saint-Simonians as a "religious masquerade."[2]

If Fourier's French disciples rarely made their reservations about his doctrine explicit, there were a number of Americans of the same generation who were both more candid and more critical about what they regarded as the hedonism and immorality of Fourier's theory. Ralph Waldo Emerson, who expressed admiration for the "noble and generous" impulses of the creators of the Fourierist community at Brook Farm, could nevertheless describe Fourier as "one of those salacious old men" in whose imaginations it was always "the universal rutting season." Nathaniel Hawthorne was at once intrigued and appalled by Fourier's ideas. For Hollingsworth in Hawthorne's novel *The Blithedale Romance,* there was something diabolical about Fourier's insistence on making man's regeneration hinge on the free play of the base passions, "the portion of ourselves which we shudder at and which it is the whole aim of spiritual discipline to eradicate." Hawthorne's wife went further. For Sophia Peabody Hawthorne, Fourier was the author of a "monstrous system" the "abominable, immoral [and] irreligious" character of which could only be explained by the fact that he "wrote just after the Revolution" when "the people worshipped a naked woman as the Goddess of Reason."[3]

From the perspective of the late twentieth century Fourier's sexual radicalism seems less disturbing. And few of our contemporaries would share the horror of Hawthorne's Hollingsworth at Fourier's attempt to enlist the selfish passions as the instruments of man's regeneration. But still the limitations of Fourier's thought seem even more obvious now than they did in the 1840s. One could easily argue that although Fourier's theory is interesting as speculation and as a statement of ideals, it is simply not germane to the real world. One of Fourier's most fundamental premises, after all, was what most reasonable people would regard as a hopelessly unrealistic belief that the universe is intrinsically harmonious. Fourier also had what many would describe as a grotesquely exaggerated confidence in our ability as human beings to understand, and ultimately to alter, the world in which we live. He completely lacked a tragic sense. And he simply refused to admit that in a rightly ordered world there could be any disparity between a person's desires and his or her ability to gratify them. Indeed, one of the assumptions on which his whole system rested was a denial that a just God could have created any desires *not* meant to be satisfied.

In all these respects Fourier's thought rests on premises that today seem even less axiomatic than they seemed in the nineteenth century. But in making this point, one cannot help being struck by the closeness of the connection between Fourier's limitations as a thinker—his naiveté or simple-mindedness—and his deepest, most original insights. If Fourier lacked a tragic sense, it is not because he ignored pain and suffering but because he refused to accept their inevitability. He refused to accept pain as a necessary part of things. And, as I have tried to show, it was his conviction that most forms of human suffering were avoidable that gave his social criticism its remarkable urgency and compelling force. If Fourier denied there was any such thing as a natural aversion to work, this denial enabled him to take seriously the possibility of attractive work and to explore it with a care and imagination not to be found in the writing of any of his contemporaries. Fourier was, I have argued, almost unique among the early socialists in his concern with establishing work as a vital fulfillment of human personality. His design for utopia was, in one of its most fundamental senses, an attempt to specify the conditions in which work could become the pleasurable and gratifying experience that he believed it was always meant to be.

At the center of Fourier's whole utopian vision there was an affirmation of the power of human beings to shape their own universe. This affirmation was obviously central to his plans for the Phalanstery. But, I have suggested, it was also crucial to his cosmology. Fourier's theory was a celebration of man's power not only to change society but also to control the weather, to cleanse the seas, to alter the arrangement of the solar system. Here, it might be argued, Fourier's thought is at its most absurd. And here a long line of scoffers from Balzac's *blagueur* to modern historians of socialism have dispatched Fourier to their own satisfaction simply by evoking his more "absurd" prophecies such as the *archibras,* the Northern Crown, and the seas of lemonade. In the view of the more indulgent scoffers Fourier's thought is not devoid of interest, but the only way to make sense of it is to establish a clear distinction between Fourier's occasional insights as a critic and planner and the fundamental absurdity of his cosmology and metaphysics. I have suggested that if one's goal is to understand Fourier and not simply to appropriate his more "advanced" ideas for one's own purposes, this sort of critical distinction is not helpful. What it fails to recognize is that in Fourier's thought as in so many other things, there is a close connection between the sublime and the ridiculous. Fourier's criticism, his utopian plans, and his picture of the cosmos were all of a piece. The cosmology presented an image of ordered spontaneity that mirrored the sexual and spiritual life of the Phalanx. And elements of parody and social criticism were embedded within the descriptions of Phalansterian life. What lay behind all the aspects of Fourier's doctrine was his conviction that we are capable of creating a world consistent with our needs and expressive of our powers. Fourier's criticism, his cosmology, and his design for utopia were all rooted in the belief that the only limit to our possibilities is our desire.

Among Fourier's later disciples there were a few, like the bohemian prophet Jean Journet, whom Courbet painted in 1850 "setting out for the conquest of Universal Harmony," who were utopians as complete as Fourier himself and who shared his faith in the imminence of a total transformation of nature and society. But the majority of the later disciples were more cautious and practical individuals whose veneration of Fourier did not prevent them from seeking to accommodate his ideas to what they considered to be the constraints of reality. In their popularizations, the theory of passionate attraction was tamed, narrowed, sentimentalized, and ultimately transformed into a program for the organization of work. In the process, however, they gained for Fourier's doctrine a following that it had never had in his lifetime.

During the 1840s Fourierist groups and movements sprang up throughout Europe and America. The French disciples led by Victor

Considerant transformed Fourierism into a socialist movement for "peaceful democracy" that became an intellectual and even political force of some significance during the last years of the July Monarchy and the early phases of the Second Republic. In America, with the help of Albert Brisbane's salesmanship, Fourierist communities were established during the 1840s throughout the Northeast and as far west as Iowa. Even in czarist Russia, where there was no real possibility for the establishment of a "movement" or a viable community, Fourier's ideas cast their spell on the radical Westernizer Alexander Herzen and his circle; and the Fourierist study group formed at Saint Petersburg about 1845 by M. V. Butashevich-Petrashevsky attracted a remarkably talented group of young intellectuals, including Dostoevsky and the philosopher Danilevsky.

But the heyday of the Fourierist movements was short-lived. The exalted conversations of the Petrashevtsy were terminated in the spring of 1849 by the intervention of the Czarist police. And few of the American communities survived for more than two or three years. They were badly financed to start with; and experience showed that, like the Owenite and Icarian ventures, they lacked the cohesiveness of the sectarian religious communities established in America. Their members were modest people for the most part, many of them small tradesmen and artisans, unable to raise anything like the capital required by Fourier for a trial of his system. The Fourierist communities organized in Europe fared no better. There too the brief history of practical Fourierism was marred by schism and lack of capital, and most of the communal experiments were short-lived.

In France the Fourierist movement led by Considerant met its downfall, along with all of the other socialist sects, in 1848. After the June insurrection of that year, its program of "peaceful democracy" ceased to have any political meaning. Considerant and his followers were drawn into an alliance with the neo-Jacobin left, which Fourier himself had so detested. After his participation in the abortive uprising of June 13, 1849, Considerant was obliged to leave France. Subsequently he emigrated to the United States, where in the 1850s he led an unsuccessful attempt to establish a Fourierist community on arid land overlooking the west fork of the Trinity River in Texas. Just about all that remains of this last significant venture in practical Fourierism is a graveyard. The chalky bluffs on which the Phalanstery was supposed to rise have been dug out by a cement plant, and in the place of seristeries and street galleries stand the shopping centers and drive-in theaters and tract housing of a suburb of Dallas. What has survived is a vision of the good place that is alive in Fourier's writings and in the minds of those whom these writings retain the power to touch. This is what Dostoevsky described, in looking back on the youthful enthusiasm for Fourierism on the part of members of his own generation, as the dream of restoring the freedom of man "in a form of unheard-of majesty" and "on a new and adamantine foundation."[4]

ABBREVIATIONS

AN   Archives Nationales

ADD   Archives du Département du Doubs

AMB   Archives Municipales de Besançon

ADR   Archives du Département du Rhône

AML   Archives Municipales de Lyon

OC   *Oeuvres complètes de Charles Fourier.* 12 vols., Paris: Editions Anthropos, 1966–1968.

PM   *Publication des manuscrits de Charles Fourier.* 4 vols., Paris: Librairie Phalanstérienne, 1851–1858. (These four volumes are photographically reproduced in OC X–XI.)

NOTES

INTRODUCTION

1. Friedrich Engels, *Herr Eugen Dühring's Revolution in Science (Anti-Dühring)* (New York, 1939), 23–33, 281–325.

2. This is true even of the best Soviet writing on Fourier. See the massive, erudite, and sympathetic study by I. I. Zil'berfarb, *Sotsial'naia filosofiia Sharlia Fur'e i ee mesto v istorii sotsialisticheskoi mysli pervoi poloviny XIX veka* (The social philosophy of Charles Fourier and its place in the history of socialist thought in the first half of the nineteenth century) (Moscow, 1964). For an overview of Soviet Fourier scholarship see my review essay on Zil'berfarb's book in *Kritika: A Review of Current Soviet Books on Russian History*, II, 3 (Spring 1966), 44–58.

3. See for example Eric J. Hobsbawm, "Marx, Engels and Pre-Marxian Socialism," in E. J. Hobsbawm (ed.), *The History of Marxism*, 4 vols. (London, 1982), I, 1–28. It should be added, however, that the first major reinterpretation of utopian socialism since Engels comes from within the Marxist tradition. See the brilliant and strikingly original essay by Gareth Stedman Jones, "Utopian Socialism Reconsidered: Science and Religion in the Early Socialist Movement" (unpublished paper).

4. Hubert Bourgin, *Fourier. Contribution à l'étude du socialisme français* (Paris, 1905). Charles Gide, *Fourier, précurseur de la coopération* (Paris, 1924), and *Les Prophéties de Fourier,* in Gide's *La Coopération. Conférences de propagande* (Paris, 1900), 276–311. See also the first volume of Jean Gaumont's richly documented *Histoire générale de la coopération en France* (Paris, 1924).

5. See the special issue of *Topique. Revue freudienne,* 4–5 (October 1970), edited by Simone Debout and with contributions by Maurice Blanchot, Pierre Klossowski, Michel Butor, Dominique Desanti, and others. See also Jean-Paul Thomas, *Libération instinctuelle, libération politique. Contribution fouriériste à Marcuse* (Paris, 1980).

6. The second edition of Breton's *Ode à Fourier* (Paris, 1961) includes a long introduction by Jean Gaulmier with suggestive commentary on Fourier's influence on French literature from Baudelaire to the surrealists. See also Emile

Lehouck, "La Lecture surréaliste de Charles Fourier," *Australian Journal of French Studies,* XX, 1 (1983), 26–36.

7. See René Schérer's excellent anthology, *Charles Fourier ou la contestation globale* (Paris, 1970).

8. Michel Butor, *La Rose des vents. 32 Rhumbs pour Charles Fourier* (Paris, 1970). Roland Barthes, *Sade, Fourier, Loyola* (Paris, 1971), 7–16, 94–96. See also Simone Debout, *"Griffe au nez" ou donner "have ou art:" Ecriture inconnue de Charles Fourier* (Paris, 1974).

9. Two studies offering shrewd comment on the literary qualities of Fourier's work are Emile Lehouck, *Fourier aujourd'hui* (Paris, 1966), esp. 159–258, and Michael Spencer, *Charles Fourier* (Boston, 1981).

10. Simone Debout, *L'Utopie de Fourier: l'illusion réelle* (Paris, 1978), 22. For the works by Poulat, Hémardinquer, Riberette, and Lehouck see the Bibliography.

11. For Fourier's papers see Archives Nationales (hereafter: AN) 10AS 1–25. The papers of Victor Considerant and the Ecole Sociétaire are 10AS 26–42. A collection of printed materials originally part of the Archives de l'Ecole Sociétaire is now held at the Institut Français d'Histoire Sociale. There is a manuscript inventory of the Fourier papers by Edith Thomas. Emile Poulat's valuable *Les Cahiers manuscrits de Fourier. Etude historique et inventaire raisonné* (Paris, 1957) offers an inventory of the manuscript notebooks (10AS 1–11) and an account of the history of the manuscripts. Poulat's inventory does not include the correspondence or the large mass of loose papers collected in a *côte supplémentaire* (10AS 12–21).

12. In Fourier's code the five vowels are numbered 1 to 5; the first four consonants are numbered 6 to 9; and the other letters are represented by various symbols. When Fourier wrote in code, it was usually to indicate proper names.

13. For examples of the censorship of Fourier's manuscripts by the disciples see my article "L'Archibras de Fourier. Un manuscrit censuré," *La Brèche,* 7 (December 1964), 66–71, and Emile Lehouck, "Psychologie et morale dans l'oeuvre de Charles Fourier (1772–1837)," *Revue des sciences humaines,* Fasc. 107 (July-September 1962), 436–437. The text of the *Nouveau monde amoureux* was established by Simone Debout-Oleskiewicz and appeared as Volume VII of the twelve-volume *Oeuvres complètes de Charles Fourier* (Paris, 1966–1968) prepared under her direction. (Subsequent references to this edition will take the form OC I, II, etc.) Fourier's manuscripts were published principally in the Fourierist journal *La Phalange,* 10 vols. (1845–1849), and in four separate volumes entitled *Publication des manuscrits* and dated 1851, 1852, 1853–1856, and 1857–1858. These four volumes are reprinted in OC X and XI. About one-third of the manuscripts published in *La Phalange* are reprinted in OC XII.

14. OC X, PM (1851), 1–53.

15. Barthes, *Sade, Fourier, Loyola,* 95.

16. Spencer, *Fourier,* 9.

17. The fullest edition and that which is referred to here unless otherwise indicated is the second, Charles Pellarin, *Charles Fourier, sa vie et sa théorie*

(Paris, 1843). It includes large excerpts from Fourier's correspondence with Muiron not included in other editions.

18. Pellarin to Considerant, November 23, 1842, AN 10AS 41 (6).

19. Pellarin, *Fourier,* 5th ed. (Paris, 1871), i-xxxvi.

20. See especially Jean-Jacques Hémardinquer, "La 'Découverte du mouvement social': Notes critiques sur le jeune Fourier," *Le Mouvement social,* 48 (July-September 1964), 49–58; Pierre Riberette, "Charles Fourier à Lyon: ses relations sociales et politiques," *Actes du 99ᵉ Congrès national des sociétés savantes. Besançon, 1974. Section d'histoire moderne et contemporaine* (Paris, 1976), II, 267–289; Emile Lehouck, *Vie de Charles Fourier* (Paris, 1978), esp. 8–9, 91–92, 97–98, 167–174.

21. Riberette, "Fourier à Lyon," 271.

CHAPTER I

1. Claude Brélot, *Besançon révolutionnaire* (Paris, 1966), 37.

2. *Almanach historique de Besançon et de la Franche-Comté pour l'année bissextile 1772,* 94–95. On Besançon at the end of the Old Regime see also Claude Fohlen (ed.), *Histoire de Besançon,* 2 vols. (Paris, 1964–1965), II, 135–232.

3. "Note sur les prétentions des Bourguignons à frustrer Besançon de l'école d'artillerie et du chantier de construction," (1830), AN 10AS 19 (10).

4. "Délibérations municipales de la ville de Besançon, 26 nivôse an VII" (January 15, 1799), cited in Brélot, *Besançon révolutionnaire,* 40.

5. Fourier to François Devay, October 26, 1835, collection of Dr. E. G. Gobert, Aix-en-Provençe. I am grateful to Dr. Gobert for sending me copies of two letters of Fourier to his great-grandfather, François Devay. On the question of Fourier's ancestry see the "added chapter" to Pellarin, *Fourier* (5th ed.), 163–176; Pierre Renouard, *Saint Pierre Fourier et Charles Fourier. Contribution à l'étude des origines de la municipalité* (Paris, 1904), 6–9; and Auguste Castan, *Notes sur l'histoire municipale de Besançon* (Besançon, 1898), 509.

6. Pellarin, *Fourier* (2d ed.), 9, 167–168. Unless otherwise indicated, the second edition of Pellarin's biography will be cited henceforth.

7. Pellarin, *Fourier,* 10.

8. *Exposition des preuves qui doivent résulter de la procédure criminelle . . . contre Auguste-Ignace Renaud-Ducreux, accusé de banqueroute frauduleuse. . . .* (Besançon, 1787), 4ff., and *Mémoire pour le Sieur Jean-Claude Ventrillon, appellant, contre le Sieur François Muguet et autres, intimés* (Besançon, 1789), in ADD 4 B 520.

9. The machinations of François Muguet are untangled and viewed in a wide perspective in Alain Roquelet's very helpful doctoral thesis, *Les Forges comtoises en crise. Les structures sclérosées du commerce (1783–1787)* (Thèse du doctorat: Ecole Nationale des Chartes, 1977), 141–146, 157–158, 280–283, 309–312,

342–360, 424–426. I wish to thank François Lassus of the Institut d'Etudes Comtoises et Jurasiennes for calling my attention to this thesis and for sharing with me his considerable knowledge of the economic history of the region.

The evidence against Muguet is assembled in two thick dossiers at the Archives du Département du Doubs, ADD 4 519: "Pièces de la procédure intentée contre Muguet"; and ADD 4 B 520: "Pièces et comptes relatifs à la procédure contre Muguet (1786–1789)." Much of the material in these dossiers consists of printed tracts for and against Muguet.

10. Jules Michelet, *Histoire de la Révolution française,* 2 vols. (Paris: Bibliothèque de la Pléiade, 1952), I, 681.

11. Pellarin, *Fourier,* 11.

12. "Correspondance de la famille de Fourier," AN 10AS 25 (4). There is considerable information on the Muguet family in Georges Blondeau, "Portraits de Wyrsch peints par lui-même. Ses oeuvres en 1778 et 1779," *Mémoires de la Société d'émulation du Doubs,* X^e série, II (1932), 138–140. See also the fairly substantial obituary notices of Denis-Louis and Felix Muguet in *L'Impartial de Besançon,* I, 35 (November 15, 1829) and VI, 68 (January 8, 1835).

13. Pellarin, *Fourier,* 168.

14. The parish register of the Eglise Saint-Pierre at Besançon indicates that Antoinette-Marie-Françoise Fourrier died in 1784 at the age of seventeen. AMB GG 238, f° 16.

15. "Régistres Paroissiaux," AMB GG 226, f° 8. Fourier's earliest surviving letter is signed without the extra *r*. But he continued occasionally to sign himself Fourrier until he was past thirty. Fourier's papers include a false birth certificate (issued for reasons unknown, in December 1799), which records his date of birth as April 7, 1768, AN 10AS 25 (10). Fourier apparently had a younger brother, Frédéric-Hugues-Philippe Fourrier, who was born on April 1, 1773, and died on October 29, 1774. See AMB GG 227, f° 8v. and GG 228, f° 14v.

16. OC X, PM (1851), 274.

17. Georges Gazier, "Les Maisons natales de Fourier et de Proudhon," *Mémoires de la Société d'Emulation du Doubs,* VIIe série, VIII (1903–1904), 144–155.

18. "Fourier peint par une de ses soeurs," Pellarin, *Fourier,* 297–301. Pellarin also received some information from the brothers Jean-Jacques Ordinaire (1770–1843) and Désiré Ordinaire (1773–1847). A few other details concerning Fourier's childhood can be found in an unpublished twenty-five-page biographical sketch of Fourier by Constantin Pecqueur, Archief Pecqueur, Manuscripts I, International Institute for Social History, Amsterdam.

19. See the revealing letter written in the winter of 1788–1789 by Lubine Fourrier to her mother and reproduced in Pellarin, *Fourier,* 168–170.

20. Pecqueur, "Charles Fourier," p. 5, Archief Pecqueur, Manuscripts I, International Institute for Social History, Amsterdam.

21. Pellarin, *Fourier,* 300.

22. Pellarin, *Fourier,* 297–300.

23. Pellarin, *Fourier,* 16, 298.

24. Pellarin, *Fourier*, 298.

25. Pellarin, *Fourier*, 13, 297.

26. "Du groupe d'amitié," *La Phalange*, III (1846), 327.

27. OC V, 41–42.

28. Philippe Breton to Victor Considerant, November 7, 1837, AN 10AS 36 (10).

29. OC X, PM (1852), 78–79.

30. "Des Trois groupes d'ambition, d'amour et de famillisme," *La Phalange*, III (1846), 33.

31. "Des Trois groupes," *La Phalange*, III (1846), 33. The story is repeated in AN 10AS 9 (9), p. 15, and 10AS 4 (5), p. 85.

32. AN 10AS 4 (5), p. 85; "Des Trois groupes," *La Phalange*, III (1846), 33.

33. Pellarin, *Fourier*, 299.

34. Pellarin, *Fourier*, 297.

35. "Analyse du mécanisme de l'agiotage," *La Phalange*, VII (1848), 9. See also OC X, PM (1851), 274.

36. La Phalange, IIe série, I, 34 (October 1837), col. 1075.

37. OC X, PM (1851), 274, and see below, chapter 3, section i.

38. Pellarin, *Fourier*, 171–172; *Journal du Palais*, V, 178 (15 fructidor an XI), 515.

39. For the following see Bernard Lavillat, *L'Enseignement à Besançon au XVIIIe siècle (1674–1792)* (Paris, 1977), 25–55, and Lavillat's article "Les Etudiants à Besançon au XVIIIe siècle," *Mémoires de la Société d'émulation du Doubs*, Nouvelle série, 5 (1963), 3–18.

40. Lavillat, *L'Enseignement à Besançon*, 53–54.

41. See Louis Villat, "Le Premier Recteur de l'Académie de Besançon, Jean-Jacques Ordinaire (1770–1843)," *Bulletin trimestrial de l'Académie des sciences, belles-lettres et arts de Besançon* (1928), No. 3, 117–152; Comte Pajol, *Pajol, général en chef*, 3 vols. (Paris, 1874); Maurice Dayet, *Un Révolutionnaire franc-comtois: Pierre-Joseph Briot* (Paris, 1960). For a picture of student life at Besançon in Fourier's time see Arthur Chuquet (ed.), *Mémoires du General Griois 1792–1882*, 2 vols. (Paris, 1909), 11–12.

42. OC X, PM (1852), 144.

43. OC X, PM (1852), 252.

44. OC X, PM (1852), 252–253.

45. Neither Besançon's Bibliothèque Municipale nor Paris's Bibliothèque Nationale has *almanachs* for the years 1787 and 1788.

46. Pellarin, *Fourier*, 173–174.

47. Pellarin, *Fourier*, 301.

48. Pecqueur, "Charles Fourier," p. 5. Archief Pecqueur, Manuscripts I, International Institute for Social History, Amsterdam. See also OC X, PM (1852), 265.

49. Fourier to François Devay, Paris, October 26, 1835. Collection of Dr. E. G. Gobert, Aix-en-Provençe. See also Pellarin, *Fourier*, 21, 174–175.

50. See Jean Girardot, "Le Constituant Muguet de Nanthou (1760–1808)," *Bulletin de la Société d'agriculture, lettres, sciences et arts du département de la Haute-*

Saône (1938), 43–67, and, on Antide de Rubat (1751–1803), Emile Poulat, "Note sur un beau-frère de Fourier: le sous-prefet Rubat," *Le Bugey,* Fasc. 45 (1958), 60–66.

51. OC I, 2–3.
52. Pellarin, *Fourier,* 301.
53. AN 10AS 1 (5). This comment appears on an unpaged sheet following p. 36 of the fifth cahier of the *ancien côte* 9.
54. "De la Sérigermie composée ou binisexe," *La Phalange,* VIII (1848), 9–10.
55. Fourier to his mother, January 8, 1790, Pellarin, *Fourier,* 175.
56. OC II, *Sommaires,* 209.
57. Arthur Young, *Travels in France* (London, 1890), 113.
58. Fourier to his mother, January 8, 1790, Pellarin, *Fourier,* 176.
59. Fragment entitled "Pauvreté attribuée aux grandes propriétés faussement," probably dating from the years 1800–1803, AN 10AS 14 (3).

CHAPTER 2

1. AN 10AS 20 (11); OC II, *Sommaires,* 209.
2. OC I, 2–13; OC X, PM (1851), 1–24; "Lettre au Grand Juge," published by Jean-Jacques Hémardinquer in *Le Mouvement social,* 48 (July–September 1964), 59–69. Hémardinquer's article, "La 'Découverte du mouvement social': Notes critiques sur le jeune Fourier," *Le Mouvement social,* 48 (July-September 1964), 49–58, has been of great value to me in my own attempts to establish a critical perspective on the sources for this and the following chapter.
3. On Lyon at the end of the eighteenth century see Louis Trénard, *Lyon de l'Encyclopédie au préromantisme,* 2 vols. (Paris, 1958); Maurice Garden, *Lyon et les lyonnais au dix-huitième siècle* (Paris, 1975); Pierre Grosclaude, *La Vie intellectuelle à Lyon dans la deuxième moitié du dix-huitième siècle* (Paris, 1933). The most recent general history of Lyon is André Latreille (ed.), *Histoire de Lyon et du lyonnais* (Toulouse, 1975), but two older works still of value are A. Kleinclausz, *Histoire de Lyon,* 3 vols. (Lyon, 1939–1952), and Sébastien Charléty, *Histoire de Lyon depuis les origines jusqu'à nos jours* (Lyon, 1903).
4. On the Lyon silk industry, Justin Godart's *L'Ouvrier en soie. Monographie du tisseur lyonnais* (Lyon, 1888) is still unsurpassed. See also E. Pariset, *Histoire de la Fabrique lyonnaise* (Lyon, 1901), and Maurice Garden, *Lyon et les lyonnais au dix-huitième siecle,* 207–242.
5. For a vivid and richly documented evocation of the predicament of working-class women at Lyon in 1791 and 1792 see Richard Cobb's essay "A View on the Street: Seduction and Pregnancy in Revolutionary Lyon," in his *A Sense of Place* (London, 1975), 77–135.
6. On Lyon as a center of mystical speculation prior to the Revolution see especially Trénard, *Lyon, de l'Encyclopédie au préromantisme,* I, 76–79, 175–189, 294–304; Auguste Viatte, *Les Sources occultes du romantisme. Illuminisme—*

théosophie: 1770–1820, 2 vols. (Paris, 1969), I, 45–71, 139–152, 188–195, 270–292; René Le Forestier, *La Franc-Maçonnerie templière et occultiste aux XVIIIe et XIXe siècles* (Paris-Louvain, 1970), 275–378, 433–475, 679–706, 835–846; Alice Joly, *Un Mystique lyonnais et les secrets de la France-Maçonnerie* (Macon, 1938); Paul Vulliaud, *Les Rose-Croix lyonnais au dix-huitième siecle* (Paris, 1929).

7. Trénard, *Lyon, de l'Encyclopédie au préromantisme,* I, 234–249, 335–348; Jean Gaumont, *Histoire générale de la coopération en France,* 2 vols. (Paris, 1924), I, 17–99.

8. On L'Ange and the question of his influence on Fourier see, in addition to the works by Trénard and Gaumont cited above, François-Joseph L'Ange, *Oeuvres,* edited by Paul Leutrat (Paris, 1968); Bourgin, *Fourier,* 94–101; Jean Jaurès, *Histoire socialiste de la Révolution française,* 4 vols. (1901–1908), III, 328–347, IV, 165; Fernand Rude, "Genèse et fin d'un mythe historique: le pré-fouriérisme de L'Ange," in *Topique. Revue freudienne* 4–5 (October 1970), 175–189. Rude summarizes L'Ange's long-lost final work, *Remède à tout, ou Constitution invulnerable de la félicité publique* (Lyon, 1793), and argues that because there is little similarity between L'Ange's ideas and Fourier's finished system, "it will no longer be possible to count the works of L'Ange among the sources of Fourier." Rude's argument is less conclusive than he claims, since he ignores the possibility that L'Ange may have influenced Fourier's thinking as he worked on the schemes of "limited association" that preceded his principal discoveries. See below, chapter 3.

9. See the document from AN 10AS 25 (4) in which Madame Fourrier pays Bousquet nine hundred francs to cover her son's living costs.

10. Pellarin, *Fourier,* 179. François-Antoine Bousquet was born in 1736. Under Napoleon he became a member of the Conseil Municipal de Lyon and served as an administrator of the Hospices Civiles. See ADR 1Q 819, ADR 2L 91, and *Almanachs de Lyon.*

11. On Marseille at this time see Edouard Baratier (ed.), *Histoire de Marseille* (Toulouse, 1973); Felix-L. Tavernier, *La Vie quotidienne à Marseille de Louis XIV à Louis-Philippe* (Paris, 1973); A. Bouyala d'Arnaud, *Evocation du vieux Marseille* (Paris, 1959); Paul Masson, *Marseille depuis 1789. Etudes historiques* (Paris, 1921), esp. 1–347, "Le Commerce de Marseille de 1789 à 1814."

12. Jaurès, *Histoire socialiste de la Révolution française,* I, 55; AN 10AS 13 (36), p. 10; "Analyse du mécanisme d'agiotage," *La Phalange,* VII (1848), 126; OC VIII, 43.

13. There are two articles on Fourier and the French Revolution: Robert Bowles, "The Reaction of Charles Fourier to the French Revolution," *French Historical Studies,* I, 3 (1960), 348–356, and J. Zil'berfarb, "Charles Fourier et la Révolution française," *Annales historiques de la Révolution française,* No. 184 (April-June 1966), 53–75. Unfortunately both articles are merely compilations of the general comments on the Revolution in Fourier's published works, and neither tells us much about his specific experiences and positions or about the evolution of his attitudes during the course of the Revolution.

14. On May 26, 1793, Fourier was issued a passport "pour aller à Lyon et Marseille pour affaires de commerce." He was described as being five feet three

inches tall with chestnut hair and gray eyes. AMB "Régistres des passeports," I²
8, #1003.

15. This chapter in the history of Lyon, and of the French Revolution, is
vividly evoked in Edouard Herriot, *Lyon n'est plus,* 4 vols. (Paris, 1937–1940).

16. Pellarin, *Fourier,* 31.

17. Herriot, *Lyon n'est plus,* III, 27.

18. ADR 2L 91 "Surveillance des suspects après le siège de Lyon"; ADR
42L 135 "Dossiers particuliers": ADR 1Q 819 "Séquestres mainlevées Lyon
ville"; ADR 1Q 864 "Séquestres mainlevées Lyon campagne." The names of
both the elder Bousquet and his surviving son are included in a list of "Contre-
révolutionnaires, Agioteurs, Accapareurs" found among the papers of Couthon, AN T566 2.

19. This means little, since the archival records of the repression at Lyon are
notoriously incomplete, much of the material having been destroyed on the
orders of Joseph Fouché during his tenure as Napoleon's minister of police.
(Information kindly communicated by the director of the Archives du
Département du Rhône, Monsieur René Lacour.)

20. Pellarin, *Fourier,* 33–34.

21. OC V, 484.

22. The Jacobin journal *La Vedette* noted on November 5, 1793: "Subscriptions for the forced loan were opened the day before yesterday. Several citizens
hastened to pledge considerable sums. Muguet, who is never tardy when there
are sacrifices to be made, has deposited fifty thousand livres in the district
treasury." *La Vedette, ou Journal du département du Doubs,* IV (15 brumaire an II),
711.

23. Pellarin, *Fourier,* 34–35, 102.

24. *Moniteur* (August 23, 1793), XVII, 478.

25. Pellarin, *Fourier,* 36. Contrary to Pellarin, however, Brincour only became colonel of Fourier's regiment in September 1795. See Hémardinquer,
"Notes critiques," 50.

26. The following account of a soldier's life in the eighth regiment of light
cavalry is based largely on the following sources: Gay de Vernon, *Essai historique sur l'organisation de la cavalerie legère . . . suivi d'une notice historique sur le
huitième des chasseurs* (Paris, 1853), 173–178; Comte de Margon, *Historique du
huitième régiment de chasseurs de 1788 à 1888* (Verdun, 1889), 41–50; Henry Bourdeau, *Les Armées du Rhin au début du Directoire* (Paris, n.d.), 137–167, 203–245,
299–380; Edouard Desbrière and Maurice Sautai, *La Cavalerie pendant la
Révolution,* 2 vols. (Paris-Nancy, 1907–1908); Ramsay Weston Phipps, *The
Armies of the First French Republic,* 5 vols. (Oxford, 1929), II, 116–136, 197–257;
Marechal Gouvion Saint-Cyr, *Mémoires sur les campagnes des armées du Rhin et de
Rhin-et-Moselle,* 2 vols. (Paris, 1829), II, 133–155.

27. Gouvion Saint-Cyr, *Mémoires,* II, 153. The reference above to the diet of
the troops is also from Saint-Cyr's *Mémoires,* II, 150.

28. Bourdeau, *Les Armées du Rhin,* 96, 300.

29. Desbrière and Sautai, *La Cavalerie pendant la Révolution,* II, 101.

30. Military discharge dated 3 pluviôse an IV, AN 10AS 25 (10).

31. "De la Sérigermie composée ou binisexe," *La Phalange*, VIII (1848), 52.

32. OC X, PM (1851), 267.

33. Fourier to Luc Preisverch, draft, 5 floréal an IV (April 24, 1796), AN 10AS 16 (42). See also AN 10AS 20 (10): Fourier's account with F. Roux of Livorno, September 27, 1796.

34. Pellarin, *Fourier*, 31.

35. Pellarin, *Fourier*, 20, 171–172; *Journal du Palais*, V, 128 (15 fructidor an XI), 515; "Tableau des bénéfices qu'Antoine Pion a eu l'art de se créer dans la succession de Charles Fourrier, en s'associant avec sa veuve," AN 10AS 20 (10).

36. Fourier's letter is published in Jean-Jacques Hémardinquer, "Fourier stratège (1796) et fonctionnaire (1815)," *Cahiers d'histoire*, XI, 1 (1966), 97–105. Fourier actually received a courteous reply signed by Lazare Carnot. See figure 3 for the reply.

37. There is a reference to such a proposal in a much later essay on the same subject, 10AS 21 (5).

38. Pellarin, *Fourier*, 37. Pellarin's informant was probably Désiré Ordinaire.

39. Richard Cobb, *Reactions to the French Revolution* (London, 1972), 44.

40. "Certificat de non-rébellion" dated 19 frimaire an III (December 9, 1794), ADR I 819.

41. "Diligences de Lyon à Paris. Départ du 28 frimaire an V" (December 18, 1796), AN F^7 6239^A, plaq. 2, pièce 107.

42. On Marseille during the Directory see, in addition to the works cited above in note 11, G. Rambert, "Marseille en l'an VIII d'après un haut fonctionnaire de la police," *Mémoires de l'institut historique de Provence*, III (1926), 47–61, and Paul Gaffarel, "Le Gouvernement de General Willot à Marseille (mars 1796–mars 1797)," *Révolution française*, LXV (August 1913), 133–166. I have also made use of René Gérard, *Un Journal de province sous la Révolution. Le "Journal de Marseille" de Ferréol Beaugeard (1781–1797)* (Paris 1964), and of the file of Marseille's neo-Jacobin journal *L'Observateur du Midi de la République ou le Marseillais en vedette* (March 21, 1796–March 26, 1797) at the Bibliothèque Nationale.

43. Masson, *Marseille depuis 1789*, 196.

44. A vivid picture of the violence and lawlessness of the area around Marseille, and of the destitution of all those who had traditionally made their living from the port, may be found in the report of the Marseille police commissioner, Lecointe-Puyraveau, published in *Mémoires de l'institut historique de Provence*, III (1926), 47–61. The flavor of this period throughout the south of France is also powerfully evoked in Richard Cobb, *Reactions to the French Revolution*, 19–62, and in Gwynne Lewis and Colin Lucas (eds.), *Beyond the Terror: Essays in French Regional and Social History, 1794–1815* (Cambridge, England, 1983), esp. 152–231.

45. Quotation from *Journal de Marseille*, November 6, 1796, cited in René Gérard, *Un Journal de province*, 251.

46. Letter to Fourier dated 19 floréal an V (May 8, 1797), AN 10AS 25 (2). The Place de la Liberté, which had previously been named the Place de la Tour and the Place Necker, was one of the main squares in Marseille.

47. OC XII, 478.

48. Bill drawn up by Frederic Fournier, 22 frimaire an V (December 12, 1796): "M. Fourrier doit à Frédéric Fournier pour les articles suivantes: gantes de soye . . . bourses de soye . . . bas blancs de soye . . . 5,650 livres 14 sous." AN 10AS 20 (10).

49. OC I, 239.

50. Pellarin, *Fourier,* 38–39; OC I, 3.

51. OC VI, 400.

52. OC I, 3.

53. See the report on Fourier's proposal and the reply to "Citizen Fourrier," dated 1 thermidor an IV (July 19, 1796), in AN F^{12} 1253^A "Commerce et industrie: Foires et marchés," pièces 535–539.

54. See Delacroix to Fourier, 19 floréal an V (May 8, 1797), AN 10AS 25 (2), and Fourier's article "Invitation aux échos," *Journal de Lyon,* 7 nivôse an XII.

55. Memoir signed "Fourrier" to Citizen ? of the municipality of Bordeaux, 20 frimaire an V (December 10, 1796), AN 10AS 15 (18).

56. AN 10AS 15 (18).

57. This paragraph and the next are based primarily on Fourier's own account of "the indices and methods that led to the discovery," OC I, 2–12, and on a thirteen-page manuscript "Note sur le développement de la conception de Fourier," by Victor Considerant, AN 10AS 26 (8).

58. OC I, 7.

59. OC X, PM (1851), 21.

60. Abel Lefranc, "Le Collège de France pendant la Révolution et le Premier Empire," *Revue internationale de l'Enseignement,* XXII (1891), 513–543; Henri Gouhier, *La Jeunesse d'Auguste Comte et la formation du positivisme,* II (Paris, 1936), 170–171; Hémardinquer, "Notes critiques," 54–55.

61. AN 10AS 25 (9). Jean-Etienne Montucla, *Histoire des mathématiques,* 4 vols. (Paris, ans VII–X); René-Richard Castel, *Histoire naturelle des poissons. . . . Ouvrage classé par ordres, genres et espèces, d'après le système de Linné,* 10 vols. (Paris, an IX).

62. "Lettre au Grand Juge," 60.

63. Hémardinquer, "Notes critiques," 52–53. See also Pellarin, *Fourier,* 31: "In the disaster of Lyon the greater part of Fourier's fortune was lost; let us add at once that the remainder was swallowed up in the wreck of a boat out of Liverpool several years later."

CHAPTER 3

1. OC V, 230–231.

2. OC III, 391.

3. OC V, 230.

4. OC III, 282–283. See also OC XII, 657–659.

5. "Formation d'une Phalange d'attraction dans laquelle s'organisent les

sectes groupées," OC X, PM (1851), 80–174. For the completion of the calculus in 1806 see OC X, PM (1851), 46.

6. OC IX, F5; Victor Considerant, "Note sur le Développement de la conception de Fourier," AN 10AS 26 (8), p. 1.

7. OC II, *Sommaires,* 209.

8. OC X, PM (1851), 17. Fourier used the term *Guarantism* to refer to a transitional historical stage between civilization and Harmony. See below, chapter 16, section iii.

9. "Fourrier" to the Municipality of Bordeaux, 20 frimaire an V (December 10, 1796), AN 10AS 15 (18).

10. AN 10AS 15 (18). The *toise* was roughly six feet. For a discussion of similar contemporary proposals see Richard Etlin, "L'Air dans l'urbanisme des lumières," *Dix-huitième siècle,* 9 (1977), 123–134.

11. See especially "Plan d'une ville de 6ᵉ période," OC XII, 695–717, and OC IV, 300–308. Portions of each of these texts (which date from the early Restoration) are identical with Fourier's memoir of 1796 to the city of Bordeaux.

12. OC XII, 700. See also OC IV, 303.

13. OC X, PM (1851), 274.

14. OC X, PM (1851), 274. See also OC VIII, 358.

15. OC X, PM (1851), 249–252; OC XI, PM (1853–1856), 19–20.

16. "Concurrence réductive et fédération commerciale," OC XI, PM (1853–1856), 59–67. See also *La Phalange,* X (1849), 209–224.

17. OC XI, PM (1853–1856), 200–206; "Crimes du commerce," *La Phalange,* II (1845), 195–223.

18. On possible links between Fourier's ideas and the theory and practice of association in eighteenth-century France see the valuable and carefully documented studies by A. R. Ioannisian, "Istochniki proektov assotsiatsii Fur'e," *Istorik Marksist,* I (1939), 101–124, and *Genezis obshchestvennogo ideala Fur'e* (Moscow-Leningrad, 1939), 125–183. See also the general study by André Lichtenberger, *Le Socialisme au XVIIIᵉ siècle* (Paris, 1895), 325–344.

19. *Encyclopédie, ou Dictionnaire raisonné des sciences, des arts et des métiers,* X (Neufchâtel, 1765), 704–706, article "Moraves" by Faiguet de Villeneuve. This article was reprinted in the widely read *Encyclopédie méthodique,* Histoire III (Paris-Liège, 1788), 630–634. On associations at Lyon see Gaumont, *Histoire de la coopération,* II, 29–30, 52; Justin Godart, *Travailleurs et métiers lyonnais* (Lyon, 1909), 24; and I. I. Zil'berfarb, "Tvorcheskii put' Sharlia Fur'e," *Frantsuskii Ezhegodnik* (1959), 303. On the *Fruitières* see OC II, 37; OC VI, 7; Bourgin, *Fourier,* 46; Ioannisian, *Genezis,* 168–169.

20. OC I, 6–7.

21. AN 10AS 20 (11): "I undertook (*entrepris*) the calculus of association in April 1799, and I succeeded in finding the germ, the fundamental operation, and the organization of tasks and of the members into series of affiliated and contrasted groups."

22. OC I, 8.

23. OC I, 11.

24. OC I, 12.

25. For further discussion of this problem see chapter 11, section ii, and chapter 17, section i.

26. Bourgin, *Fourier*, 56–137. This study is flawed by Bourgin's neglect of Fourier's published manuscripts and by his failure to consider Fourier's scientific sources. For a telling critique of Bourgin see Lehouck, *Fourier aujourd'hui*, 168–172.

27. Bourgin, *Fourier*, 120–128, 135.

28. Bourgin, *Fourier*, 60–61.

29. "Des cinq passions sensuelles," *La Phalange*, IV (1846), 6–8; OC IV, 334.

30. AN 10AS 24 (2), #100. The article is by the abbé Nauton, "Essai sur la cause physique de la couleur des différens habitans de la terre," in the journal edited by the abbé Rozier and Mongez le jeune, *Observations sur la physique, sur l'histoire naturelle et sur les arts*, XVIII (September 1781), 165–184. This journal was subsequently named the *Journal de physique*.

31. See for example OC V, 47–49; OC VI, 175, 202–203, 461; OC VII, 33, 111, 223, 261–262; OC XII, 609.

32. For Fourier's knowledge of the Physiocrats and Bernardin de Saint-Pierre see below, chapter 10, section i, and chapter 17, sections iii and iv. On the abbé Raynal see for example OC I, 59–60, 254–255; OC X, PM (1851), 259, 293, 309. On Mably see *La Phalange*, VIII (1848), 151; OC XI, PM (1853–1856), 129; OC XII, 667. On Fénelon see OC II, *Sommaires*, 24–25, 116; OC V, 477–485.

33. "Des trois passions distributives," *La Phalange*, III (1846), 520–521.

34. Léon Cellier, *Fabre d'Olivet. Contribution à l'étude des aspects religieux du romantisme* (Paris, 1953), 12, 400. See also André Monglond, *Le Préromantisme français*, 2 vols. (Grenoble, 1930), II, 263–277. The following remarks also apply, with some qualifications, to the work of such minor mystics and visionaries as Hyacinthe Azaïs, François-Guillaume Coessin, and Fabre d'Olivet.

35. OC I, 2; Henri Saint-Simon, *Du Système industriel*, in *Oeuvres de Saint-Simon et d'Enfantin*, 47 vols. (Paris, 1865–1878), XXX, 182; Pierre-Simon Ballanche, *Du Sentiment considéré dans ses rapports avec la littérature et les arts* (Lyon, 1801), 56–57; Louis de Bonald, *Mélanges littéraires, politiques et philosophiques*, 2 vols. (Paris, 1858), II, 406.

36. Henri Saint-Simon, *Esquisse d'une nouvelle encyclopédie*, in *Oeuvres*, XV, 92.

37. *Le Producteur*, III (1826), 105.

38. Joseph de Maistre, *Considérations sur la France*, in *Oeuvres complètes*, 14 vols. (Lyon, 1884), I, 7.

CHAPTER 4

1. *Les Annales Lyonnaises*, June 30, 1814, cited in Georges Ribe, *L'Opinion publique et la vie politique à Lyon: 1815–1822* (Paris, 1957), 74.

2. Louis Reybaud, *Le Dernier des commis-voyageurs,* 2d ed. (Paris, 1856), 19–21. For a similar, if more hyperbolic, description of Lyon at this time see Lamartine, *Histoire des Girondins* (Paris, 1860), V, 273ff.

3. Mazade d'Avèze, *Lettres à ma fille sur mes promenades à Lyon* (Lyon, 1810), II, 177.

4. "Lettre au Grand Juge," *Le Mouvement social,* 48 (July-September 1964), 65.

5. AML, "Régistres des passeports," I^2 154 (11), #3860. Fourier's age is erroneously given on this passport as thirty-two instead of twenty-nine. For reasons unknown he similarly added three or four years to his age in other passports dating from the Directory and the Consulate.

6. OC X, PM (1851), 1–24.

7. OC X, PM (1851), 23.

8. "Analyse du mécanisme d'agiotage," *La Phalange,* VII (1848), 117.

9. Auguste Ducoin, "Particularités inconnues sur . . . Charles Fourier," *Le Correspondant,* XXVII (1851), 484. This article, which is the source of many of the details in this paragraph and the preceding, was based largely on the notes and reminiscences of Fourier's friend Jean-Baptiste Dumas. Pierre Riberette has discovered a paper on Fourier, read by Dumas to the Academy of Lyon in 1838, that was clearly Ducoin's principal source. See Riberette, "Fourier à Lyon," 268–272, citing Bibliothèque du Palais des Arts de Lyon, Ms. 293, fol. 57–67.

10. See "Stances à MM. D. et T., auteurs de deux épitres en petits vers pour et contre la fidélité," AN 10AS 23 (16), published anonymously by Fourier in the *Bulletin de Lyon,* 10 fructidor an XIII (August 23, 1805), and Henri Brun to Fourier, May 9, 1808, AN 10AS 25 (3bis). See also Riberette, "Fourier à Lyon," 274–275, and the full discussion of the "Vieux Coin" in Lehouck, *Vie de Fourier,* 109–115. Lehouck, who seeks to rectify Pellarin's picture of the young Fourier as a solitary and frustrated man, organizes one of his seven chapters around the image of Fourier as "le convive du Vieux Coin." The role of the "Vieux Coin" in Fourier's life at Lyon obviously needs to be clarified. But I do not believe that the evidence we have will bear the weight Lehouck seeks to put on it. Nor do I believe that our understanding of Fourier is deepened by substituting for the image of a solitary Fourier the image of Fourier as a "jovial bon vivant."

11. For the letters to Fourier of Paul François Henri Brun "de Pézénas" see AN 10AS 25 (2) and (3bis). See also Hémardinquer, "Notes critiques," *Le Mouvement social,* 48 (July-September 1964), 58. The tone of Brun's letters is familiar, and the man was obviously sympathetic to some of Fourier's ideas; but it seems to be stretching the point to describe him, as does Hémardinquer, as "the first disciple."

12. On Jean-Baptiste Gaucel see ADR 1M7 (1), "Personnel administratif," and 2F 328, "Correspondance Banque Guérin"; AML $I^2$97, $I^2$99, $I^2$111, "Régistres des passeports"; AN 10AS 25 (2) and 10AS 19 (4), correspondence with Fourier.

13. Clarisse Vigoureux to Fourier, June 20, 1834, AN 10AS 25 (3bis). On Louis Desarbres, who was born in 1770 and came from a prominent Ville-

franche family, see ADR 1M7 (1) as well as his letters to Fourier in AN 10AS 25 (3), 10AS 15 (33), and 10AS 21 (10). The evidence does not in my view support Lehouck's claims (*Vie de Fourier*, 24, 112, 143–145) concerning the intimacy of Fourier and Desarbres.

14. For an extensive discussion of Jean-Baptiste Dumas' relations with Fourier see Riberette, "Fourier à Lyon," 269–280. On Dumas' career as a journalist see Riberette's article "Pierre-Simon Ballanche et le *Bulletin de Lyon*," *Actes du 96ᵉ Congrès national des sociétés savantes. Toulouse, 1971. Section d'histoire moderne et contemporaine* (Paris, 1976), I, 481–512. Dumas the academician is maliciously described in the anonymous *Biographie contemporaine des gens de lettres de Lyon* (Lyon, 1826) as "poeticizing right and left, the cornerstone of the public meetings, always ready to read an insignificant tract of his own composition . . . has had the merit to compose an ode to Chateaubriand containing only one mistake in French."

15. For these poems see AN 10AS 23 (16).

16. Fourier to Georges de Rubat, August 1818, AN 10AS 20 (2), p. 1.

17. Ducoin, "Particularités inconnues," 486.

18. Letters to Fourier from Delphine Constant and Pauline Guyonnet, AN 10AS 25 (1). See also the discussion of the letters from Guyonnet in Lehouck, *Vie de Fourier*, 164–166. Lehouck notes that in 1808, when Fourier moved to 6, Place du Plâtre, he was still sharing an apartment with Pauline Guyonnet and, apparently, her sisters.

19. Fourier to Georges de Rubat, August 1818, AN 10AS 20 (2), p. 1. For Dumas' reference to Fourier's "amours faciles" see Riberette, "Fourier à Lyon," 277.

20. Madame Laporte to Fourier, two undated letters, AN 10AS 25 (2) and AN 10AS 25 (3bis).

21. OC VII, 389.

22. Lehouck, *Vie de Fourier*, 10, 157. See also Frank E. Manuel, *The Prophets of Paris* (Cambridge, Mass., 1962), 202, 247–248.

23. "Du Clavier puissanciel des caractères," *La Phalange*, VI (1847), 117. For Fourier's description of himself as an omnigyne see *La Phalange*, VI (1847), 110. See also OC VII, 98.

24. Even in Louis Trénard's compendious and valuable social history of Lyon intellectual life, *Lyon, de l'Encyclopédie au préromantisme*, 2 vols. (Paris, 1958), Fourier's name is only mentioned a few times—primarily with regard to his brief career as a journalist.

25. Dumas to Fourier, August 13, 1820, AN 10AS 25 (2).

26. OC I, 317.

27. OC I, 102.

28. OC X, PM (1851), 12.

29. "Lettre au Grand Juge," 65; OC X, PM (1851), 1.

30. Pellarin, *Fourier*, 39.

31. Letters to Fourier from the commissioner of the Nineteenth Military Division, Lyon, March 25 and June 13, 1811, and from the Ministry of War, Paris, August 9, 1820, and February 10, 1824, refusing his requests for 190

francs in vacation pay, AN 10AS 25 (2). J.-B. Dumas to Fourier, August 13, 1820, AN 10AS 25 (2). Eventually Fourier took his case to the readers of the *Traité de l'association domestique-agricole*. See OC II, *Argument*, xxxviii.

32. Hémardinquer, "Fourier stratège (1796) et fonctionnaire (1815)," *Cahiers d'histoire*, XI, 1 (1966), 97–100. This rectifies Pellarin, *Fourier* (5th ed.), 64, 163–176.

33. Bourgin, *Fourier*, 32; Ducoin, "Particularités inconnues," 485.

34. The following discussion of brokerage in Fourier's time is based primarily on A. Durand-Saint-Amand, *Manuel des courtiers de commerce* (Paris, 1845); A. Genevet, *La Compagnie des agents de change de Lyon* (Lyon, 1890); L. de Lanzac de Laborie, *Paris sous Napoléon,* Vol. VI; *Le Monde des affaires et du travail* (Paris, 1910); and ADR 14M, "Industrie et commerce. Agents de change et courtiers, 1808–1825." General studies that have helped provide perspective include Bertrand Gille, *La Banque et le crédit en France de 1815 à 1848* (Paris, 1959); Jean Bouvier, "Le Système de crédit et l'évolution des affaires de 1815 à 1848," *La Pensée,* 71 (January-February 1957), 35–46, and 72 (March-April 1957), 63–78; Louis Bergeron, *Banquiers, négociants et manufacturiers parisiens du Directoire à l'Empire* (Paris, 1978); and Fernand Braudel, *The Wheels of Commerce,* trans. by Siân Reynolds (New York, 1982), 97–114.

35. On the derivation of the term see Lanzac de Laborie, *Paris sous Napoléon,* VI, 278.

36. "Analyse du mécanisme d'agiotage," *La Phalange,* VII (1848), 198.

37. Drafts of Fourier's letter to Prefect Herbouville, January 30, 1808, AN 10AS 25 (9) and 10AS 16 (42); Herbouville to Fourier, February 18, 1808, AN 10AS 25 (2); Pellarin, *Fourier,* 39–41.

38. "Analyse du mécanisme d'agiotage," *La Phalange,* VII (1848), 215.

39. ADR 14M, "Industrie et commerce. Agents de change et courtiers."

40. Memorandum to the prefect of the Department of the Rhone, undated (but 1812), signed by the representatives of two dozen Lyon business houses, ADR 14M. Although this document is not signed by Fourier, the handwriting is clearly his. An early draft of the memorandum is also to be found among his manuscripts. See AN 10AS 17 (8).

41. "Analyse du mécanisme d'agiotage," *La Phalange,* VII (1848), 198.

42. "Sur le monopole exercé par les agents de change ou courtiers," AN 10AS 17 (8). See also 10AS 13 (36).

43. "Sur le monopole exercé par les agents de change ou courtiers," AN 10AS 17 (8).

44. "Analyse du mécanisme d'agiotage," *La Phalange,* VII (1848) and also AN 10AS 16 (13).

45. Honoré de Balzac, *L'Illustre Gaudissart, Gaudissart II* (Geneva: Skira, 1946); Louis Reybaud, *Le Dernier des Commis Voyageurs,* 2d ed. (Paris, 1856), esp. 9, 85–91, 150.

46. There is, to my knowledge, no monograph dealing in any detail, or with any degree of comprehensiveness, with the *commis voyageur* during the revolutionary and Napoleonic periods. In addition to the works of fiction cited above, the following account is based on B. Nogaro and W. Oualid, *L'Evolution du*

commerce, du crédit et des transportations depuis 150 ans (Paris, 1914), esp. 50, 64–66, 72–77; J. Labasse, *Le Commerce des soies à Lyon sous Napoléon et la crise de 1811* (Paris, 1956); A. Chabert, *Essai sur les mouvements des revenus et de l'activité économique en France de 1789 à 1820* (Paris, 1949), esp. 279–283, 305–306; H. A. O. Reichard, *Guide des voyageurs en France* (Weimar, 1810). See also the literature on trade fairs cited below.

47. Labasse, *Commerce des soies,* 27.

48. Cited in Nogaro and Oualid, *Evolution du commerce,* 73.

49. On the trade fairs see G. Zetter, *Evolution des foires et marchés à travers les siècles* (Paris, 1923); P. Léon, "Vie et mort d'un grand marché international. La Foire de Beaucaire (XVIIIᵉ–XIXᵉ siècle)," *Revue de géographie de Lyon,* 4 (1953), 309–328; Charles de Gourcy, *La Foire de Beaucaire, étude d'histoire économique* (Montpellier, 1911); L. Arque, "La Foire de Leipzig dans les temps passés," *La Science sociale,* XXV (May 1910), 17–88; and Braudel, *Wheels of Commerce,* 82–94.

50. Labasse, *Commerce des soies,* 55–56; E. Pariset, *Histoire de la fabrique lyonnaise* (Lyon, 1901), 291–292.

51. AN 10AS 6 (5).

52. AML I²111 and I²114; AN F⁷3559.

53. "Des cinq passions sensuelles," *La Phalange,* IV (1846), 37.

54. "Des cinq passions sensuelles," *La Phalange,* IV (1846), 39.

55. Pellarin, *Fourier,* 23.

56. OC II, 189, 209. The building in question is the Hotel de Thélusson in Paris, constructed by Ledoux between 1778 and 1781. See also OC XII, 705.

57. AN 10AS 9 for Basel, and AN 10AS 5 (8), p. 40, for the *Kellner.*

58. "Du Clavier puissanciel des caractères," *La Phalange,* VI (1847), 23.

59. AN 10AS 7 (1): "It is quite possible that foreign thinkers do not share the mania [for denigrating original ideas] that is common to those of France. What makes me think so are the contacts I have had with foreigners of the bourgeois class. Each time I have discussed [the theory of] attraction with Germans, with northerners, and even with Italians, who are supposed to be superficial, I have found in them a rectitude of judgment that is alien to the French."

60. See for example OC VII, 387: "If you discuss amorous manias with women who have had many lovers and men who have had many mistresses, you will learn from their accounts that their manias are infinitely varied." See also AN 10AS 7 (1), p. 19; 10AS 7 (2), p. 101; 10AS 7 (3), pp. 22, 35–36; 10AS 3 (4), p. 46.

61. OC VIII, 189.

CHAPTER 5

1. On journalism in Napoleonic France see André Cabanis, *La Presse sous le Consulat et l'Empire (1799–1814)* (Paris, 1975); Eugène Hatin, *Histoire politique et*

littéraire de la presse en France, 8 vols. (Paris, 1859–1861), VII, 377–604; Henri Welschinger, *La Censure sous le Premier Empire* (Paris, 1882); Robert B. Holtman, *Napoleonic Propaganda* (Baton Rouge, 1950).

2. On Lyon journalism during the Napoleonic period see Pierre Riberette, "Pierre-Simon Ballanche et le *Bulletin de Lyon,*" in *Actes du 96ᵉ Congrès des sociétés savantes (Toulouse, 1971). Section d'histoire moderne et contemporaine,* I (Paris, 1976), 481–512, and Aimé Vingtrinier, *Histoire des journaux de Lyon depuis leur origine jusqu'à nos jours* (Lyon, 1852), 86–117. See also Sébastien Charléty, "La Vie politique à Lyon sous Napoléon," *Revue d'histoire de Lyon,* IV (1905), esp. 375–378, and Louis Trénard, *Lyon, de l'Encyclopédie au préromantisme,* II, 522–527.

3. The letter, signed by both Martainville and "Fourrier," was written in the former's hand. It was published in full in Vingtrinier, *Histoire des journaux de Lyon,* 88.

4. Verninac to Fouché, 24 thermidor an VIII, AN F⁷ 3452, "Police des Journaux," pièce 44.

5. There is a sizable dossier concerning the proposed journal in AN F⁷ 3452, pièces 40–56. Some of the material in this dossier suggests that Fourier and Martainville were in fact acting as "fronts" for the royalist printers Tournachon and Molin, who had previously been granted, and then denied, authorization to publish a journal of their own. See Verninac to Fouché, 19 thermidor an VIII, AN F⁷ 3452, pièce 46. After the authorization given to Tournachon-Molin had been withdrawn, wrote Verninac, "on a cherché un expédient et c'a été de mettre la permission sur la tête d'un nommé Martainville et d'un autre mauvais sujet, tous les deux sans aveu, tous les deux plus immoraux et plus réacteur encore que Tournachon-Molin et qui sont evidemment à ses gages." For a detailed discussion of this episode see Riberette, "Fourier à Lyon," 280–284.

6. Martainville, who was born at Cadiz in 1777 and died of gout at Paris on the last of the *Trois Glorieuses,* still awaits his biographer. This account is based mainly on Henri Corbel, *Figures du passé: Martainville (1777–1830)* (Paris, 1911). See also Jules Janin, *Histoire de la littérature dramatique,* 2d ed. (Paris, 1854–1858), II, 74ff., and Hatin, *Histoire de la presse,* VIII, 492–494. On Martainville's theater see Paul Ginisty, *La Féerie* (Paris, 1910), 75–133.

7. Léon Thiessé, *M. Etienne, essai biographique et littéraire* (Paris, 1853), xxii.

8. Benjamin Constant, "Journaux intimes" (1804) in *Oeuvres* (Paris: Bibliothèque de la Pléiade, 1957), 423. See J-B. Dumas, *Notice historique sur la vie et les ouvrages de A-F. Delandine* (Lyon, 1820), and the article on Delandine by J-J. Hémardinquer in Roman d'Annat and R. Limousin Lamothe (eds.), *Dictionnaire de biographie française,* X (Paris, 1963), 682–683. On Jean-Baptiste Dumas' role in Lyon journalism see Pierre Riberette, "Ballanche et le *Bulletin de Lyon,*" cited above in note 2.

9. *Journal de Lyon et du Midi,* 5 and 19 nivôse, 3, 5 and 15 ventôse an X. The third article mentioned, "Conseils à un jeune homme par une femme," may well be by Fourier, who was later accused in another journal of just such a ruse as the title would imply. The author advises her (his?) "jeune homme" that he will please others by obeying his passions—whatever they may be—rather than by trying to be amiable.

10. *Journal de Lyon et du Midi,* 19 nivôse an X. Fourier uses the same example to make the same point in his 1803 manuscript "Petitesse de la Politique," OC X, PM (1851), 253.

11. According to the reminiscences of his sister, Fourier was a precocious versifier. Although none of his childhood efforts have survived, his papers include a number of poems dating from his early years at Lyon. Among them are a few love poems, several "Chansons Bachiques," a quite irreverent ode "Sur le Rétablissement du Temple de la Magdelaine à Genève," and a "Pastorale sur les jolies fêtes de l'Ile-Barbe à Lyon." The last, which is dated germinal an XI (April 1803), was apparently submitted to the *Bulletin.* AN 10AS 23 (16), "Pièces de vers."

12. "Satire envoyée a M. A. J. . . . sur son énigme, aux devins de laquelle il promet deux prix, l'un de saucissons et l'autre de marrons; et sur une réponse a cette énigme, sous la signature de Femme A. F. . . ." *Bulletin de Lyon,* 1 frimaire an XII. This poem was signed "Fourrier" as were all of his contributions to the *Bulletin.*

13. J. . . ne, "A M. Fourrier, auteur d'une satire des lyonnaises," *Bulletin de Lyon,* 11 frimaire an XII. Although these lines were signed "J. . . ne," Fourier recognized their author to be none other than Femme A.F.

14. "Harmonie universelle," *Bulletin de Lyon,* 11 frimaire an XII.

15. "Conversation sur l'homme du jour," signed "La belle Cordière, descendant de la belle Cordière qui faisait des vers et pour qui on en faisait du temps de François Ier." Although this poem appeared in the *Bulletin de Lyon* on 2 nivôse an XII, it was published as a broadside two weeks earlier. See P.-M. Gonon, *Bibliographie historique de la ville de Lyon pendant la Révolution française* (Lyon, 1844), 500 (#2736).

16. Vingtrinier, *Revue du lyonnais,* IV (1852), 108–109.

17. "Triumvirat continental et paix perpétuelle sous trente ans," *Bulletin de Lyon,* 25 frimaire an XII.

18. Drafts of such articles can be found among Fourier's 1803 manuscripts. See especially OC X, PM (1851), 224–235, where Fourier predicts the burning of Paris by Russian and "Tartar" invaders.

19. *La Phalange,* 2d series, II (1838), 1; Pellarin, *Fourier* (5th ed.), 55, 165. In Paul Janet, "La Philosophie de Charles Fourier," *Revue des deux mondes,* XXXV (October 1, 1879), 628–629, one finds Napoleon offering Fourier "a job in the Ministry of Finance"!

20. Adolphe Brac de LaPerrière to Fourier, December 15, 1834, AN 10AS 25 (3).

21. OC I, 316–317.

22. "Zacharie Delyror, habitué de Charenton," letter to the editors of the *Journal de Lyon. Nouvelles de la France et de l'étranger,* 30 frimaire an XII. This journal had been founded as a rival to the *Bulletin* just a few weeks earlier, and it survived for less than two months. Sébastien Charléty has attributed its "suppression" to the "intemperate verve" of Fourier's articles, *Revue d'Histoire de Lyon,* IV (1905), 376. It is more likely, however, that it died a

natural death—from a lack of subscribers. See Vingtrinier, *Revue du lyonnais,* IV (1852), 179–180.

23. "Lettre à Monsieur Delyror," *Journal de Lyon,* 5 nivôse an XII.

24. "Invitation aux échos," *Journal de Lyon,* 7 nivôse an XII.

25. During the Consulate the High Judge exercised functions that were later to be divided between the ministries of justice and the police. For the manuscript of Fourier's "Lettre au Grand Juge" see AN F^7 3455. It was dated 4 nivôse an XI (*sic* for XII). It was first published in 1874 and is here cited from the text established by Jean-Jacques Hémardinquer and published in *Le Mouvement social,* 48 (July–September 1964), 59–69.

26. "Lettre au Grand Juge," 60–61.

27. "Lettre au Grand Juge," 61.

28. AN F^7 3455 ("Police des Journaux").

29. "A l'auteur de l'inventaire des plaisirs de Lyon," *Bulletin de Lyon,* 20 nivôse an XII; "Acceptation des lettres de change," *Bulletin de Lyon,* 27 nivôse an XII.

30. Fourier cited in Pellarin, *Fourier,* 107: "I dined for four years at the same table with the editor of the Lyon journal to which I contributed articles in verse and prose."

31. "Sur les Quais de la Saône," AN 10AS 19 (2): "Sur l'incommodité de la reconstruction du pont de change," AN 10AS 13 (47); "Question de morale et de politique commerciale," AN 10AS 13 (31) and OC XI, PM (1853–1856), 32–37. In the last article Fourier denounces the Jews as an immoral band of "social lepers" and as a "parasitical sect that tends to usurp the commerce of states at the expense of the nationals."

32. Fourier's poem, "Stances à MM. D. et T., auteurs de deux épitres en petit vers, l'une contre la constance, l'autre contre l'inconstance," appeared in the *Bulletin de Lyon,* 10 fructidor an XIII (August 28, 1805). For Fourier's manuscript draft see AN 10AS 23 (16). See also the commentary in Lehouck, *Fourier aujourd'hui,* 110–111.

33. "A Monsieur H.T.", *Bulletin de Lyon,* February 21, 1807; "Les Plumes de Monsieur H.T.", *Bulletin de Lyon,* May 27, 1807. Both articles are signed "X." For Fourier's manuscript draft of the latter see AN 10AS 14 (33).

34. "Sur la décadence des grands théâtres de province," signed "X.", *Bulletin de Lyon,* December 20, 1806, and AN 10AS 13 (21) for the manuscript. After stigmatizing the Revolution for having produced a decline in taste and morals, Fourier concludes: "The establishment of schools of drama and opera must be envisaged today as a branch of national policy. Our triumphs are spreading our language throughout all the civilized regions; it is imperative to restore the luster of the theatrical art, which will contribute to ensuring the universality of that language."

35. OC I, 255–261n. Fourier's peculiar seven-page footnote in the *Quatre mouvements* on "the current distress of the theater" was simply a revised and expanded version of this article.

36. OC I, 98.

37. OC I, 27.

38. "Notice pour servir d'annonce à la Découverte du Calcul Géometrique des Destinées universelles et de l'Harmonie Sociale du Globe humain," AN 10AS 23 (16).

39. AN 10AS 23 (16).

40. OC I, 98, 160, 181, 307. OC X, PM (1851), 1.

41. AN 10AS 16 (2) and OC X, PM (1852), 54.

42. AN 10AS 13 (17) and 10AS 16 (8). The former, which is marked "Cahier Eleuthère," was published by Fourier's disciples in *La Phalange,* V (1847), 193–228, 289–321, 385–413. It has been reprinted in Charles Fourier, *L'Ordre subversif. Trois textes sur la Civilisation* (Paris, 1972), 45–190, and in OC XII, 587–682.

43. Among Fourier's papers at the Archives Nationales there are more than two dozen separate manuscripts that can be assigned on the basis of internal evidence to the period 1803–1806. (Such evidence includes allusions to "recent" newspaper articles and events, to the "First Consul," and to the sixteen-stage schema of historical periodization, which Fourier abandoned prior to the composition of the *Quatre mouvements.*) The fragmentary and sometimes bowdlerized form in which Fourier's disciples published these manuscripts obscures the fact that most of them are actually early drafts of his "manifesto against the three uncertain sciences."

44. There are two full drafts of "Petitesse de la Politique": AN 10AS 16 (3) and 10AS 14 (6). The former was published, together with excerpts from the latter, in OC X, PM (1851), 217–316.

45. OC I, 319. It was principally in the third part of the *Quatre mouvements,* which consisted of a series of "demonstrations" of the "methodical mindlessness" of the civilized philosophers, that Fourier made use of the material contained in the various drafts of the *Egarement.*

46. AN 10AS 16 (17). Fourier does not name the academicians with whom he conferred, but among his known friends Amard, Dumas, and Aimé Martin were all members of the Academy of Lyon.

CHAPTER 6

1. "Le Sphinx sans Oedipe, ou l'énigme des quatre mouvements," *La Phalange,* IX (1849), 197; AN 10AS 23 (10), p. 2.

2. Brunot-Labbe, bookseller, to Fourier, January 14, 1809, AN 10AS 25 (2).

3. OC I, 28.

4. OC I, 97n.

5. OC I, 31–32.

6. Fourier may well have had a specific audience in mind, an audience that included a number of individuals who had already "heard [his] accounts of the

pleasures of the Combined Order" and had "shuddered with impatience at [his] descriptions of these pleasures." OC I, 27.

7. OC I, 94.

8. The fullest statement of Fourier's explanation of "the riddle of the *Quatre mouvements*" is to be found in an 1816 manuscript entitled "Le Sphinx sans Oedipe, ou l'énigme des Quatre mouvements," AN 10AS 16 (21), published in *La Phalange,* IX (1849), 193–206. It was apparently meant to be published as an introduction to a projected second prospectus. AN 10AS 16 (1) and 10AS 23 (10) are drafts of the same with some variants. The riddle is discussed more briefly but in similar terms in a number of manuscripts dating from 1811 to 1818. See for instance OC XI, PM (1853–1856), 167–169, and AN 10AS 13 (32); 10AS 14 (49); 10AS 16 (12); 10AS 16 (17); 10AS 23 (6).

9. "Le Sphinx sans Oedipe," *La Phalange,* IX (1849), 194.

10. "Le Sphinx sans Oedipe," *La Phalange,* IX (1849), 205.

11. "Le Sphinx sans Oedipe," *La Phalange,* IX (1849), 197.

12. AN 10AS 23 (10), p. 1. See also *La Phalange,* IX (1849), 195: "This prospectus recommended itself by its very bizarreness, and if I demonstrate today that this bizarreness, which in truth is natural to me, was upon this occasion affected and exaggerated from the title onward, that it was a ruse to sound out the century and to entrap a few rascals, one must admit that the book was a good deal less bizarre than its critics."

13. Bill for 170 livres from Imprimerie et librairie de Tournachon-Molin, April 9, 1808, marked "Paid, April 26, 1808," AN 10AS 25 (2).

14. The copy of the *Quatre mouvements* in the archives of the Societary Colony, which still exists at Condé-sur-Vesgre (Seine-et-Oise), is inscribed by Fourier to Alexandre Emmanuel Louis de Bauffremont (1773–1833). An émigré who fought against the French revolutionary army, de Bauffremont was named duke and peer of France during the Restoration.

15. Braunberger and Co. to Fourier, May 5, 1808, AN 10AS 25 (2); François (last name illegible) to Fourier, May 10, 1808, AN 10AS 25 (2).

16. Manget and Cherbuliez to Fourier, May 14, 1808, AN 10AS 25 (2).

17. Madame de Staël to Fourier, cited in Bourgin, *Fourier,* 157. Fourier's initiative was less spectacular—and ultimately no more fruitful—than Henri Saint-Simon's earlier proposal of marriage to Madame de Staël. But he was touched by her courteous acknowledgment. In later years he was frequently to cite her as one of the "expectant" philosophers and as an ideal candidate for "the palm of foundress of universal unity." See for example OC VI, 14.

18. Schramm, Therstens and Co. to Fourier, July 15 and August 8, 1808, AN 10AS 25 (2); bill "for storage of a crate of books since 1808" to Fourier from Dufour *freres* and Co., November 5, 1812, AN 10AS 25 (2); J. B. Champon and Co. to Fourier, August 25, 1808, AN 10AS 25 (2).

19. See Brun to Fourier, September 5, 1808, AN 10AS 25 (2). For a specimen of the kind of review that Fourier submitted to the *Journal de l'Empire* see "Hypothèse d'une critique judicieuse sur le prospectus des destinées ou Théorie des quatre mouvements," *La Phalange,* V (1847), 490–492.

20. Henri Brun to Fourier, May 9, 1808, AN 10AS 25 (3bis).

21. Fourier does refer in his manuscripts to a review by a "journalist of Grenoble" who couldn't get beyond the introduction, *La Phalange*, IX (1849), 197. I have been unable to locate this review.

22. *Journal de l'Empire*, May 23, 1808; Lenormant to Fourier, June 1, 1808, AN 10AS 25 (2).

23. Henri Brun to Fourier, September 5, 1808, AN 10AS 25 (2).

24. Henri Brun to Fourier, September 5, 1808, AN 10AS 25 (2).

25. Brunot-Labbe to Fourier, January 14, 1809, AN 10AS 25 (2). Shortly thereafter (seven months after its actual publication) the *Quatre mouvements* was "announced" in two trade journals: *Journal typographique et bibliographique*, XI, 45 (November 14, 1808), p. 284; *Journal général de la littérature de France*, 9 (1808), p. 282.

26. Honoré de Balzac, *Monographie de la presse parisienne* (Paris: Pauvert, 1965), 168–169.

27. *Journal du commerce*, November 30, 1808.

28. L.V.P., "Variétés," *Gazette de France*, December 1, 4, 9, and 14, 1808.

29. *Gazette de France*, December 14, 1808. For excerpts from a third and particularly negative review, see OC I, 313. I have been unable to locate this review, which is erroneously attributed by Fourier's disciples to *Le Publiciste* of December 14, 1808.

30. Brunot-Labbe to Fourier, January 14, 1809, AN 10AS 25 (2).

31. "Le Sphinx sans Oedipe," *La Phalange*, IX (1849), 195.

32. The following section is based primarily on a series of manuscript fragments (most of them prologues to a "second prospectus" that Fourier never completed) written during the seven years that followed the publication of the *Quatre mouvements*. The bulk of the unpublished manuscripts utilized are to be found in 10AS 14 and 10AS 15. The relevant published manuscripts are the following: "Devoirs de la critique envers les inventeurs illettrés," OC X, PM (1851), 24–37; "Le Sphinx sans Oedipe," *La Phalange*, IX (1849), 193–206; "L'Entretien," *La Phalange*, IX (1849), 206–211; "Annonce d'une nouvelle publication," *La Phalange*, IX (1849), 211–216; "Du Monopole de génie qu'exerce la ville de Paris," *La Phalange*, IX (1849), 216–236; "La Nouvelle Isabelle," *La Phalange*, IX (1849), 237–240; and excerpts published in *La Phalange*, X (1849), 465–473. Some of this material has been given penetrating psychological interpretation by Frank Manuel in *Prophets of Paris*, 243–248.

33. AN 10AS 14 (49).

34. OC X, PM (1851), 24.

35. "L'Entretien," *La Phalange*, IX (1849), 206–211.

36. "La Nouvelle Isabelle," *La Phalange*, IX (1849), 237–240.

37. AN 10AS 16 (20).

38. "Du Monopole de génie," *La Phalange*, IX (1849), 222.

39. OC X, PM (1851), 28.

40. "Du Monopole de genie," *La Phalange*, IX (1849), 223.

41. OC XI, PM (1853–1856), 170.

42. *Journal de Lyon,* October 19, 1811, in OC X, PM (1851), 48.

43. "Réponse à l'article signé: Philoharmonicos," *Journal de Lyon,* October 31, 1811, in OC X, PM (1851), 48–51.

44. This letter, addressed in 1813 to "the Mayors and Principals of the Colleges of Aberdeen," is summarized in a manuscript dated January 23, 1815, AN 10AS 14 (49), p. 18.

45. The three manuscript fragments that constitute Fourier's unfinished draft of the "Discours sur les attributs de Dieu" are dispersed among his papers, AN 10AS 16 (7), 10AS 13 (2), 10AS 13 (3). They were published as a whole by the disciples in OC XI, PM (1853–1856), 115–195. In fact Fourier had much less to say in this rambling and chaotic essay about God than about commerce. As he advised the Scottish judges: "As long as the system of lying commerce exists and dominates in our societies, we insult God by seeking proofs of his justice and his goodness" (p. 144).

46. AN 10AS 14 (49), p. 21.

47. "De l'entrepôt fédérale ou de l'abolition du commerce," OC XI, PM (1853–1856), 68–114; "Concurrence réductive et fédération commerciale," OC XI, PM (1853–1856), 58–67.

48. OC X, PM (1851), 2–3.

49. "Testament de Marie Muguet, veuve Charles Fourrier, rentière," January 14, 1809, AN 10AS 25 (6).

50. "Note pour Madame la Supérieure du Monastère de Notre Dame," AN 10AS 25 (2).

51. "Testament de Marie Muguet, veuve Fourrier," AN 10AS 25 (6). See also the dossier "Concernant la succession de Madame Fourrier," 10AS 25 (5).

52. On the occupation of Lyon (March 21 to June 9, 1814) see Henry-Auguste Brölemann, *Souvenirs et portraits* (Lyon, 1882), 123–145, and Charles Guillemain, "Lyon et les occupations étrangères de 1814 à 1815," in *Albums du crocodile* (Lyon, 1945).

53. OC XI, PM (1857–1858), 348–349.

54. Bill dated July 11, 1814, AN 10AS 25 (2).

55. AML I² 124, "Passeports étrangers": Passport issued September 6, 1814, to "Charles Fourrier, voyageur. Destination Naples."

56. This letter, discovered by Pierre Riberette in the Archives du Ministère des Affaires Etrangères (Mémoires et documents, Vol. 675, pièce 29), is reprinted in Riberette, "Fourier à Lyon," 286.

57. E. Welvert, *Napoléon et la police sous la première Restauration d'après les rapports du comte Beugnot à Louis XVIII* (Paris, n.d.), 47 (report of July 8, 1814), cited in Riberette, "Fourier à Lyon," 286–287.

58. On Fourier's Bonapartism in 1814 see also the somewhat mysterious letter to Fourier from the aide-de-camp of Marshal Augereau, thanking him for the loan of maps, published by Jean-Jacques Hémardinquer in "Fourier stratège (1796) et fonctionnaire (1815)," *Cahiers d'histoire,* XI, I (1966), 105.

59. AN F¹ᵇII Rhone 4, published in Riberette, "Fourier à Lyon," 287.

60. For the (unsubstantiated) claim that Fourier was appointed head of the

Bureau of Statistics at the Prefecture of the Rhone during the Hundred Days by his namesake and distant cousin, the prefect Jean-Baptiste Fourier, see Pellarin, *Fourier* (5th ed.), 64, 165.

61. Hémardinquer, "Fourier stratège et fonctionnaire," 97–100, citing letter of Louis Desarbres to J. B. Planque, May 16, 1815.

62. For a fuller presentation and analysis of the evidence on which this account of Fourier's activities during the First Restoration and the Hundred Days is based see Riberette, "Fourier à Lyon," 284–288, and Lehouck, *Vie de Fourier,* 140–147.

63. OC X, PM (1851), 319, 321.

64. "Sur Napoléon Bonaparte," OC X, PM (1851), 317–334.

65. OC X, PM (1851), 319–320.

66. OC X, PM (1851), 223ff., 231ff.; OC I, 101; OC XI, PM (1853–1856), 118–215; OC III, 123, 229–230; OC V, 406–407: "The intention of establishing a universal monarchy was the wisest of Napoleon's ideas."

67. AN 10AS 13 (55), p. 1n; AN 10AS 16 (17), p. 4.

68. *La Phalange,* X (1849), 465–466. On the general clavier of creation see *La Phalange,* VI (1847), 6–12: "Du clavier puissanciel des caractères" ("Antimède").

69. OC I, 32.

70. "Réponse aux conjectures de l'astronome Herschell sur la Structure de l'univers," Belley, December 27, 1815, AN 10AS 23 (6), p. 9.

71. OC X, PM (1851), 3. See also "Découverte du Calcul de L'Association Simple en 1819," AN 10AS 20 (11).

72. Fourier to Georges de Rubat, draft [1818], AN 10AS 20 (2), p. 2: "I arrived here with a *plan* in thirty-two parts." See also OC X, PM (1851), 3: "I brought with me a ful'y elaborated *plan.*"

CHAPTER 7

1. All scholars working on this period of Fourier's life owe a great debt to the painstaking research of Emile Poulat. Particularly helpful for this chapter have been Poulat's articles "Le Séjour de Fourier en Bugey (1816–1821)," *Le Bugey,* Fasc. 43 (1956), 5–27; "Note sur un beau-frère de Fourier: le sous-préfet Rubat," *Le Bugey,* Fasc. 45 (1958), 60–66; and his *Les Cahiers manuscrits de Fourier: Etude historique et inventaire raisonné* (Paris, 1957), 66–82.

2. Shortly after his arrival in Bugey Fourier estimated that in the seventeen years since his discovery he had scarcely had time for "five years of real labor because of the occupations that absorbed me." AN 10AS 23 (6), "Réponse aux conjectures," Belley, December 1815, p. 7.

3. See, for example, AN 10AS 17 (6), p. 13; 10AS 9 (1), p. 3; 10AS 13 (3), p. 46D; and OC IV, 12 ("1819").

4. See, for example, OC XI, PM (1857–1858), 220–221; *La Phalange,* VIII

(1848), 46–47; OC X, PM (1852), 190; and 10AS 3 (4), p. 78, p. 192: "I went to live in the virtuous countryside, a sanctuary of innocence, and I learned from the most trustworthy people that not one pretty peasant girl was still a virgin at the age of ten."

5. On Fourier's family see Emile Poulat's articles "Note sur un beau-frère de Fourier" and "Le Séjour de Fourier en Bugey," pp. 6–8, as well as AN 10AS 25 (4), "Lettres de la famille de Fourier," and AN 10AS 40 (5), Just Muiron to Clarisse Vigoureux, October 24, 1837.

6. Clarisse Brun (née Rubat) to Fourier, August 30, 1832, AN 10AS 25 (4).

7. Note dated November 24, 1804, in which "Jeanne Marie Lambert, racomodeuse de dentelle à Lyon" promises "M. Charle Fourrié de réservoir sa niece aux pré de moy et luy enseignié à racomodé et blanchis la dantelle blonde tulle et crepe." AN 10AS 25 (4).

8. Fourier to Georges de Rubat, March 19, 1813, AN 10AS 25 (9).

9. Georges-Jean de Rubat was born in 1788. The only one of the children who had managed to leave Talissieu, he had studied at Paris and worked as a secretary at the Bureau of Seals before going into business. See Muiron to Clarisse Vigoureux, October 24, 1837, AN 10AS 40 (5). On his difficulties in providing for his mother see his letter to Fourier of May 4, 1816, AN 10AS 25 (4).

10. The following account of Fourier's escapades at Talissieu is based largely upon the drafts of four letters in which Fourier subsequently attempted to justify his own conduct in relation to his nieces. Since they clearly do not tell the whole story, the reader is advised that we have only Fourier's account to rely upon. Three of the letters are from AN 10AS 15 (31): Fourier to Mlle. Labatie, June 30, 1816; Fourier to the judge of Belley, February 1, 1817; Fourier to Mme. (?) of Lyon, August 8, 1817. The fourth and most important letter is from AN 10AS 20 (2). It is a résumé of the whole affair, an epistle of twelve folio pages and some ten thousand words, written in a microscopic and at times virtually illegible hand. Internal evidence suggests that it should be dated about August 1818. The story it tells is consistent with the information contained in the other letters. But it is far more complete—notably with regard to Fourier's difficulties with his treatise and his infatuation with Hortense. It is the source of most of the unfootnoted quotations.

11. Fourier to Georges de Rubat, August 1818, AN 10AS 20 (2), p. 1.

12. Fourier to Georges de Rubat, August 1818, AN 10AS 20 (2), p. 2. See also OC VIII, 236: "Several times women have provided me with new ideas and with precious solutions to problems that had tortured my mind."

13. Fourier to Georges de Rubat, August 1818, AN 10AS 20 (2), p. 2.

14. The *côte supplémentaire* of Fourier's papers at the AN (10AS 12 to 10AS 22) includes a large number of the "preliminary studies" that Fourier produced in great quantity at the outset of his stay at Talissieu. These were the *pré-, cis-, trans-,* and *post-liminaires,* which he planned to intersperse throughout his treatise in order to make the "dogmatic" portions more palatable. But it was impossible for Fourier to fit all the shorter writings that flowed from his pen

within the cadre of the treatise. Among the "occasional pieces" he produced during his first year in Bugey, many concerned problems of astronomy and cosmogony. The 1814 discoveries had renewed his interest in these matters; and he avidly followed the contemporary discussion of Sir William Herschel's discoveries, as well as the hot debate over the relationship between sunspots and climatic disturbances. Fourier hoped that by intervening in these controversies with a few decisive "revelations" of his own, he might generate interest in his theory, and a number of his writings seem to have been destined for publication. See below, note 22, and AN 10AS 23 (6), 10AS 23 (7), 10AS 13 (18), 10AS 16 (36), 10AS 16 (37): five drafts of an article entitled "Réponse aux conjectures de l'astronome Herschell sur la structure de l'univers" (the first of these is dated "Belley, December 27, 1815"). See also "Invitation à MM. les Astronomes de rechercher les deux planètes inconnues Protée et Sapho, les seuls qui restent à découvrir dans notre tourbillon," AN 10AS 13 (19), and "Horoscope des nombreux systèmes universels," Belley, June 20 and 25, 1816, AN 10AS 13 (12).

15. Fourier to Georges de Rubat, August 1818, AN 10AS 20 (2), p. 3.

16. Fourier to Georges de Rubat, August 1818, AN 10AS 20 (2), p. 3.

17. Fourier to Georges de Rubat, August 1818, AN 10AS 20 (2), p. 4.

18. Fourier to Madame (?) of Lyon, August 8, 1817, AN 10AS 15 (31).

19. Fourier to the judge of Belley, February 1, 1817, AN 10AS 15 (31).

20. Fourier to Mlle. Labatie, June 30, 1816, AN 10AS 15 (31).

21. The Lyon plot of January 19, 1816, and the Grenoble insurrection of May 4 are two of the more obscure chapters in the history of conspiratorial activity in France during the first years of the Bourbon Restoration. For differing interpretations of the Lyon affair—its political significance and possible links with the activities of a so-called Société de l'Indépendance Nationale—see Henry Dumolard, *Jean-Paul Didier et la Conspiration de Grenoble* (Grenoble, 1928), esp. 71–75, and Léonce Grasilier, *Simon Duplay (1774–1827) et son Mémoire sur les Sociétés Secrètes et les Conspirations sous la Restauration* (Nevers, 1913), 23–27. For a shrewd and penetrating overview of the whole problem of conspiratorial activity during the early Restoration see Alan Spitzer, *Old Hatreds and Young Hopes* (Cambridge, Mass., 1971).

22. "Sur les progrès de l'intempérie," *Journal politique et littéraire du département du Rhône,* I, 52 (July 11, 1816). The article was signed "C.F." and appeared under the rubric "Variétés." Two rather abusive replies signed "M." and "Chol." were published in the *Journal,* I, 54 and 56 (July 16 and 20, 1816). Thereupon Fourier penned an indignant "Réponse aux beaux esprits qui nient les maladies des astres," AN 10AS 13 (22). But the prefect Chabrol refused to allow its publication.

23. OC XI, PM (1857–1858), 307–309.

24. Fourier to Madame (?) of Lyon, August 8, 1817, AN 10AS 15 (31).

25. OC XI, PM (1857–1858), 221–222. See also the texts cited above, note 4.

26. Fourier to Muiron, August 21, 1816, Pellarin, *Fourier,* 247–249.

27. "Découverte du Calcul de l'Association Simple en 1819," AN 10AS 20

(11). See also Pellarin, *Fourier,* 193, 199; and Fourier to Georges de Rubat, August 1818, AN 10AS 20 (2), p. 7: "I made the mistake of working on an abridgment that reduced [the *Grand Traité*] to a quarter of its length. This idea was most prejudicial to my work. I lost eight or nine months at it. I got nothing done at Talissieu except for this useless draft. I saw my work ruined. That grieved me a great deal, but I no longer had the courage to pursue work on the *Grand Plan.*"

28. Fourier to the judge of Belley, February 1, 1817, AN 10AS 15 (31).

29. Fourier to the judge of Belley, February 1, 1817, AN 10AS 15 (31).

30. Fourier to Georges de Rubat, August 1818, AN 10AS 20 (2), p. 9.

31. Fourier to Georges de Rubat, August 1818, AN 10AS 20 (2), p. 12.

32. AN 10AS 12 (6), p. 20. This reference is in the code that the secretive Fourier often used to designate proper names in his manuscripts. On the models for the "Hierarchy of Cuckoldom" see also OC XI, 564.

33. Olympe Carrier (née Parrat-Brillat) to Fourier, January 16, 1834, AN 10AS 25 (4); C. Baroud (on behalf of his employer Bousquet) to Fourier, February 25, 1820, referring to "the amusing games like *Dos Condos* that you told us about on your last trip here and which charm your evenings at Belley." AN 10AS 25 (2).

34. AN 10AS 5 (9), p. 4. Concerning the system of passional accords, Fourier's complex rationale for the interaction of the human passions that was to take place within properly constituted groups and series, see OC IV, 352–380; OC V, 377–476; OC VI, 52–65, 270–334.

35. On the composition of the *Grand Traité* see Poulat, *Cahiers manuscrits,* 66–82.

36. OC I, 108n. Note that "false Agnes" was the phrase Fourier had applied to his "innocent" niece, Fanny.

CHAPTER 8

1. OC I, 8, 27, 98, 160, 181, 307; OC X, PM (1851), 1.

2. Dumas to Fourier, August 13, 1820, AN 10AS 25 (2); "A M. Fourrier, auteur d'une satire des lyonnaises," *Bulletin de Lyon,* 11 frimaire an XII; Henri Brun to Fourier, May 9, 1808, AN 10AS 25 (3bis); OC I, 204n; OC X, PM (1851), 48.

3. AN 10AS 14 (42), p. 17.

4. These comments apply to such early readers of the *Quatre mouvements* as Désiré-Adrien Gréa, Raymond de Raymond, Simon de Troyes, Roselli Mollet, Désiré Ordinaire, and Clarisse Vigoureux, as well as to Felix Bernard and Just Muiron.

5. I have been unable to determine the connection (if any) between Felix Bernard and Jean-Jacques Bernard (1791–1820), an influential figure in illuminist circles during the early Restoration.

6. Bernard to Fourier, September 28, 1818, AN 10AS 25 (2).

7. Bernard to Fourier, November 1818, AN 10AS 25 (2).

8. See Considerant to Gréa, October 10, 1833, AN 10AS 28 (7).

9. See the excellent discussion of the "renaissance of illuminism" in France during the early Restoration in Auguste Viatte, *Les Sources occultes du romantisme. Illuminisme-théosophie: 1770–1820*, 2 vols. (Paris, 1928), II, 243–276. See also Léon Cellier, *Fabre d'Olivet. Contribution à l'étude des aspects religieux du romantisme* (Paris, 1953), 315, 352.

10. The following account of Muiron's discovery of the *Quatre mouvements* is based on a "Petite notice" written by Muiron for Clarisse Vigoureux and dated March 25, 1845, AN 10AS 40 (6). See also the autobiographical portions of Virtomnius (Just Muiron), *Les Nouvelles transactions sociales, religieuses et scientifiques* (Paris, 1832), esp. 145–157.

11. Muiron, *Nouvelles transactions*, 149.

12. Although Muiron's name figures prominently in all the literature on the Fourierist movement, the only study of his life is Georges Gazier, "A propos du centenaire de la mort de Charles Fourier. Le Premier disciple: le bisontin Just Muiron (1787–1881)," *Académie des sciences, belles-lettres et arts de Besançon: procès-verbaux et mémoires* (1938), 1–14.

13. Muiron, *Nouvelles transactions*, 146–147.

14. Muiron, *Nouvelles transactions*, 148–149.

15. Muiron, *Nouvelles transactions*, 150.

16. Georges de Rubat to Fourier, May 4, 1816, AN 10AS 25 (4).

17. Fourier to Muiron, April 30, 1816, AN 10AS 25 (1).

18. Muiron, *Nouvelles transactions*, 150.

19. Muiron to Fourier, October 4, 1820, AN 10AS 25 (2). Fourier's answer to this query is, unfortunately, unknown.

20. Fourier to Muiron, February 20, 1818, Pellarin, *Fourier*, 194.

21. Fourier to Muiron, February 20, 1818, Pellarin, *Fourier*, 188.

22. Fourier to Muiron, February 20, 1818, Pellarin, *Fourier*, 194.

23. What particularly impressed Muiron was the "true" (and quite innocuous) sense that Fabre d'Olivet had managed to "restore" to the doctrine of Original Sin. A twelve-page sketch of his memoir, dated September 6, 1818, is inserted in one of Fourier's manuscript cahiers, AN 10AS 9 (1). See also Muiron, *Nouvelles transactions*, 1–88, and Muiron's letter to the baron de Villeneuve, mayor of Belley, September 8, 1818, announcing that he has lent the town library's copy of Fabre d'Olivet's *Langue hébraïque* to Fourier. Archives Communales de Belley, Serie R, 2ᵉ partie, #12. For general comment on the uses to which Fabre d'Olivet's biblical exegesis was put by Fourierists like Muiron, Considerant, and Ange Guépin, see Cellier, *Fabre d'Olivet*, 353–355.

24. Fourier to Muiron, February 29, 1820, Pellarin, *Fourier*, 256–257. Fourier states that he was informed of Muiron's proposal by a friend named Roselli Mollet. A lawyer from the Ain and the son of the *conventionnel* Jean-Luc-Anthelme Mollet, Roselli had been in personal contact with Fabre

d'Olivet and had apparently tried to interest him in Fourier's theory. See Fourier to Muiron, October 6, 1818, Pellarin, *Fourier,* 194–196.

25. Fourier to Muiron, February 16, 1817, Pellarin, *Fourier,* 253–254.

26. Fourier to Muiron, October 28, 1817, Pellarin, *Fourier,* 193.

27. Fourier to Muiron, December 24, 1818, Pellarin, *Fourier,* 193–194.

28. Fourier to Muiron, February 20, 1818, Pellarin, *Fourier,* 194.

29. Muiron, "Petite notice," AN 10AS 40 (6). This constitutes the major source for my discussion of Muiron's stay at Belley and his efforts to finance the publication of Fourier's treatise.

30. Pellarin, *Fourier* (5th ed.), 71; Pellarin, *Fourier* (2d ed.), 189.

31. Muiron, "Petite notice," AN 10AS 40 (6).

32. The manuscript of Fourier's unfinished *Grand Traité* is contained, along with other notes and manuscripts, in the sixty-four multicolored cahiers that constitute the *ancienne côte* 9 of Fourier's papers at the Archives Nationales (10AS 1 through 10AS 8). Substantial excerpts from these cahiers were published—in haphazard fashion—by Fourier's disciples during the 1840s. But only since the appearance of Emile Poulat's invaluable "reasoned inventory," *Les Cahiers manuscrits de Fourier* (Paris, 1957), has it become possible to establish the various stages in the composition of the treatise. The following account is based on Poulat and on a study of the manuscripts themselves and of the diverse outlines included among them. I have relied particularly on the most complete of these outlines, a "Plan du Traité de l'Attraction Passionnelle qui devait être publié en 1821," AN 10AS 23 (17) and 10AS 24 (1).

33. AN 10AS 5 (9), p. 4.

34. OC I, 108–109n; "Des Trois groupes," *La Phalange,* III (1846), 241.

35. "Plan du Traité," AN 10AS 23 (17) and 10AS 24 (1).

36. OC I, 62–72, 86–92, 117–130; OC X, PM (1851), 6–7.

37. OC X, PM (1851), 6.

38. AN 10AS 5 (9), p. 4: "During my first nineteen years of study . . . I believed that societary harmony required the complete development of the twelve passions. . . . Only in 1819 did I recognize the possibility of proceeding in a limited way through the exclusion of the minor accords that are contrary to [civilized] law."

39. For the following see AN 10AS 5 and 6 (cahiers 36, 37, 38 *ancienne côte* 9). These cahiers were published in *La Phalange,* IX (1849), 385–450; X, 5–62, 161–183, under the title "De la Sérisophie ou épreuve réduite."

40. Fourier to Muiron, April 3, 1819, Pellarin, *Fourier,* 196–197.

41. See AN 10AS 5 (8), published in *La Phalange,* VIII (1848), 5–76, as "De la Sérigermie composée ou binisexe."

42. Fourier to Muiron, May 11, 1819, Pellarin, *Fourier,* 197–198. See also AN 10AS 20 (11): "Découverte du Calcul de l'Association Simple en 1819."

43. Fourier to Muiron, May 11, 1819, Pellarin, *Fourier,* 198.

44. Fourier to Muiron, May 11, 1819, Pellarin, *Fourier,* 200.

45. Fourier to Muiron, August 21, 1816, Pellarin, *Fourier,* 247.

CHAPTER 9

1. "Le Sphinx sans Oedipe," *La Phalange,* IX (1849), 200. See also OC XI, PM (1853–1856), 339–342.

2. "Réponse à l'article signé Philoharmonicos," *Journal de Lyon,* October 31, 1811, OC X, PM (1851), 48–51; "Sur les progrès de l'intempérie," *Journal politique et littéraire du département du Rhône,* I, 52 (July 11, 1816).

3. This paragraph and the following are based on two drafts of a letter written by Fourier to baron de Villeneuve, mayor of Belley, and dated October 25, 1821, AN 10AS 20 (2) and 10AS 1 (5). Once again Fourier's purpose in chronicling a family quarrel was to defend his reputation against "calumnies" circulated by his own relatives.

4. The following is based on Emile Poulat, "Le Séjour de Fourier en Bugey (1816–1821)," *Le Bugey,* Fasc. 43 (1956), esp. 23–27, as well as the manuscript sources cited below.

5. Both documents are in AN 10AS 25 (2), which includes a printed invitation to the meeting of March 25, 1821.

6. The *Note remise à l'Académie de Belley* is from AN 10AS 14 (25) and has been published by Emile Poulat in *Le Bugey,* Fasc. 43 (1956), 28–42. Drafts of the *Mémoire à l'Académie de Belley* may be found in AN 10AS 1 (8), 10AS 7 (7), and 10AS 17 (3). The first of these is a notebook of 154 pages.

7. AN 10AS 1 (8), pp. 49–59.

8. On Joseph Bruand's career see the article by Charles Weiss in the Michaud *Biographie universelle ancienne et moderne,* LIX (Paris, 1835), 331–333. The only subsequent document concerning the academy in Fourier's papers is a printed invitation to its meeting of March 25, 1821.

9. OC V, 317.

10. Fourier to M. Palehoud, editor of the *Bibliothèque universelle,* January 11, 1820. Personal collection of Monsieur Edmond Bomsel, Paris.

11. Fourier to the editor of the *Censeur européen,* draft, June 18, 1820, AN 10AS 14 (32).

12. Muiron to Fourier, October 4, 1820, AN 10AS 25 (2).

13. Lubine Clerc to Fourier, February 26, 1818, AN 25 (4).

14. Pellarin, *Fourier,* 300–301.

15. See Pellarin, *Fourier,* 59, 86–87, 204–207, 224–240, and AN 10AS 19 (10), 10AS 20 (9), 10AS 23 (18).

16. Pellarin, *Fourier,* 59.

17. The following account of the quarrel over Fourier's annuity is based primarily on a large amount of material in AN 10AS 25 (5): "Succession de Mme. Fourrier"; 10AS 25 (6): "Rente viagère"; and 10AS 20 (10): "Compte remis par Ch. Fourier a ses Cohéritiers Solidaires," etc.

18. Fourier to Georges de Rubat, September 14, 1820, AN 10AS 25 (1).

19. Georges de Rubat to Fourier, October 27, 1820, AN 10AS 25 (4): "Vous vous livrez à mille suppositions désobligeants sur mon silence."

20. Fourier's demands are summarized in Philibert Parrat-Brillat to Fourier, January 22, 1821, AN 10AS 25 (4).

21. Copy of document from Bureau de la Conservation des Hypothèques de Besançon, January 20, 1821, AN 10AS 25 (6).

22. Document signed by Fourier and others, March 20, 1822, AN 10AS 25 (2).

23. Pellarin, *Fourier,* 60–61.

24. This paragraph is based on two drafts of Fourier's letter to baron de Villeneuve, mayor of Belley, October 25, 1821, AN 10AS 20 (2) and 10AS 1 (5).

25. OC III, 1–3, 60–84; Fourier to Muiron, February 10, 1821, Pellarin, *Fourier,* 190.

26. Fourier to Muiron, March 10, 1821, Pellarin, *Fourier,* 190.

27. OC III, 84–107.

28. Fourier to Muiron, March 7, 1821, Pellarin, *Fourier,* 191.

29. Fourier to Muiron, April 18, 1821, Pellarin, *Fourier,* 192–193.

30. OC X, PM (1852), 156.

31. OC V, xi, 380–382. OC IV, 287, 325.

32. OC III, 7; OC IV, 328; OC III, 396–397.

33. OC II, *Avant-propos,* 14.

34. OC IV, 98.

35. The preceding is based largely on a "Comte des impressions des ouvrages de Ch. Fourier" drawn up in Muiron's handwriting and marked: "Certified at Paris, August 2, 1832," AN 10AS 25 (9). A similar document, dated February 20, 1843, may be found in AN 10AS 40 (5). According to Muiron's reckoning, the total cost of printing and publishing Fourier's *Traité* (and the *Sommaires,* which appeared in 1823) came to 5,419 francs and 20 centimes. To make this sum meaningful it might be said that this was roughly three times the annual wage paid to Fourier when he was employed as a full-time clerk a few years later. Muiron's expenses (1,178 francs and a substantial interest payment on the loans received from others) were considerable and represented a great personal sacrifice for a man of some inherited wealth but very modest earned income. On Muiron's role in subsidizing the publication of Fourier's work see also his letters to Clarisse Vigoureux of December 12, 1835, and June 2, 1839, AN 10AS 40 (5). In the latter Muiron writes with some bitterness: "It is on me that fell the burden as well as the honor and the privilege of having *alone* seen to the publication in 1822 of this great work, notwithstanding the obstacle presented by the scantiness of my personal resources."

36. Delaunay to Fourier, August 23, 1822, AN 10AS 25 (2); Brunot-Labbe to Fourier, August 27, 1822, AN 10AS 25 (2).

37. Mongie *aîné* to Fourier, September 25, 1822, AN 10AS 25 (2). If Mongie had a weakness for unsalable books, he also had an eye for talent. Another work he published in 1822 was a *rossignol* entitled *De l'amour* by a little-known Grenoblois named Henri Beyle.

38. Amard to Fourier, December 7, 1821, AN 10AS 25 (2).

39. Jordan's statement is quoted in Muiron, "Petite notice," AN 10AS 40 (6). There is also a detailed statement of Fourier's efforts to conform to the censorship laws in the draft of his letter of November 18, 1822, to the minister of the interior, AN 10AS 16 (42).

CHAPTER 10

1. OC I, 3–5.
2. OC I, 2.
3. OC I, 191.
4. OC II, 78.
5. On Fourier's anti-Semitism see Edmund Silberner, "Charles Fourier on the Jewish Question," *Jewish Social Studies,* VIII, 4 (October 1946), 245–266.
6. *De l'anarchie industrielle et scientifique* (Paris, 1847), 4–5.
7. OC II, viii.
8. See for example OC I, 7; OC II, 25; OC III, 11–12.
9. On Fourier's analysis of "plethoric" crises of overproduction see below, chapter 19, section iii.
10. OC IX, 799.
11. OC IV, 173–179.
12. OC IV, 92.
13. *De l'anarchie industrielle,* 25.
14. OC I, 228.
15. OC I, 222.
16. "Crimes du commerce," *La Phalange,* II (1845), 5–32, 193–224; "Analyse du mécanisme d'agiotage," *La Phalange,* VII (1848), 5–32, 97–136, 193–244; OC I, 222–276; OC XI, PM (1853–1856), 5–251.
17. OC I, 229.
18. Honoré de Balzac, *Histoire de la grandeur et de la décadence de César Birotteau,* chapter XIV.
19. This sampling of types of bankruptcy is from OC I, 228–237: "Spoliation du corps social par la banqueroute."
20. OC I, 237.
21. OC I, 246. On the so-called "affaire des négociants réunis" see A. Chabert, *Essai sur les mouvements des revenus et de l'activité économique en France de 1789 à 1820* (Paris, 1949), 362–367; G. Ramon, *Histoire de la Banque de France* (Abbeville, 1929), 64–78; A. Duchêne, *Guerre et finances: Une crise du Trésor sous le Premier Empire* (Paris, 1940).
22. OC X, PM (1851), 266–267; *La Phalange,* V (1847), 317–320.
23. See for example OC I, 265–267: "Décadence de l'ordre civilisé par les maîtrises fixes qui conduisent en 4ᵉ phase."
24. OC I, 116–117.

25. OC I, 121–125.

26. OC I, 112.

27. OC IV, 69–76. See also OC I, 111–112.

28. OC I, 127–128, 114.

29. OC XI, PM (1853–1856), 252–272. See also the separate edition: Charles Fourier, *Hiérarchie du cocuage* (Paris, 1924), with an introduction on "Fourier et les cocus" by René Maublanc.

30. Some of Fourier's manuscript drafts of the "Hierarchy of Cuckoldom" include references in code to various acquaintances of Fourier's. See for example AN 10AS 12 (6): "Cocus: orgueilleux—Bohaire; rehaussé—Parrat."

31. OC VII, 235.

32. OC I, 130.

33. OC I, 150.

34. OC I, 147.

35. OC I, 147, 149. See also OC V, 186–190.

36. This point emerges clearly in the chapter on Fourier in Marguérite Thibert's still valuable *Le Féminisme dans le socialisme français de 1830 à 1850* (Paris, 1926), 99–121. See also Elizabeth C. Altman, "The Philosophical Bases of Feminism: The Feminist Doctrines of the Saint-Simonians and Charles Fourier," *Philosophical Forum,* VII, 3–4 (Spring-Summer 1974), 277–293, and Claire Goldberg Moses, *French Feminism in the Nineteenth Century* (Albany, 1984), 90–98.

37. OC I, 131.

38. OC I, 150, 131. See also OC XII, 608–610.

39. OC I, 132–133. Italicized in Fourier's text.

40. Karl Marx and Friedrich Engels, *The Holy Family* (Moscow, 1956), 259; Friedrich Engels, *Anti-Dühring,* 3d ed. (Moscow, 1962), 355; Flora Tristan, *L'Emancipation de la femme, ou le Testament de la paria* (Paris, 1845).

41. OC III, 121.

42. OC III, 110.

43. OC I, 192–193. Fourier's italics.

44. Fourier's critique of metaphysics is most fully elaborated in the first section of *L'Egarement de la Raison,* OC XII, 588–620.

45. OC XII, 591.

46. OC XII, 593.

47. OC XII, 611–612.

48. OC XII, 618–620; OC XI, PM (1853–1856), 295–296.

49. OC X, PM (1851), 216–217; OC XII, 623–624. For Fourier's critique of politics see especially OC XII, 621–652, and OC X, PM (1851), 217–239, 276–316.

50. OC X, PM (1851), 221; OC XII, 623. See also OC VII, 413.

51. "Analyse du mécanisme d'agiotage," *La Phalange,* VII (1848), 117–119. OC III, 184.

52. OC XII, 624; OC X, PM (1851), 222.

53. OC XII, 624; OC X, PM (1851), 222.

54. OC XII, 625.

55. OC XI, PM (1853–1856), 280. Fourier's most extensive critique of "the moralists" is to be found in *L'Egarement de la Raison,* OC XII, 653–671.

56. OC VI, 162.

57. OC III, 118.

58. OC XII, 656.

59. OC VIII, 409.

60. OC III, 41.

61. Engels, *Anti-Dühring,* 355.

62. "Des Transitions," *La Phalange,* VI (1847), 233–234.

63. OC IX, D7.

64. OC II, viii.

65. Edmund Wilson, *To the Finland Station* (Garden City, N.Y., 1953), 87. See also on this point the thoughtful remarks in Nicholas V. Riasanovsky, *The Teaching of Charles Fourier* (Berkeley, 1969), 177.

CHAPTER II

1. On the role of the passions in seventeenth- and eighteenth-century French thinking about ethics and psychology see Lester G. Crocker, *An Age of Crisis: Man and the World in Eighteenth-Century French Thought* (Baltimore, 1959), 218–255; Jean Ehrard, *L'Idée de la nature en France à l'aube des lumières* (Paris, 1970), 223–240; Robert Mauzi, *L'Idée du bonheur dans la littérature et la pensée françaises au XVIIIe siècle,* 3d ed. (Paris, 1967), 437–458.

2. Alès de Corbet, *De l'origine du mal,* 2 vols. (Paris, 1758), I, 60, cited in Crocker, *An Age of Crisis,* 229.

3. Mauzi, *L'Idée du bonheur,* 451; Crocker, *An Age of Crisis,* 231; Ehrard, *L'Idée de la nature,* 224.

4. Claude-Adrien Helvétius, *De l'Esprit,* Discours III, chap. 8.

5. Sade, *Histoire de Juliette* (Sceaux: Pauvert, 1954), IV, 180–181, and V, 177–178, cited in Crocker, *An Age of Crisis,* 234.

6. Ehrard, *L'Idée de la nature,* 233; Crocker, *An Age of Crisis,* 235.

7. Diderot's *Supplément au voyage de Bougainville* offers a particularly vivid evocation of such a society.

8. On the persistence of providentialist thinking through the eighteenth century see Jacob Viner, *The Role of Providence in the Social Order* (Princeton, 1976), esp. 19, and Georges Gusdorf, "Déclin de la providence?", *Studies on Voltaire and the Eighteenth Century,* CLIII (1976), 951–990.

9. OC I, 19.

10. OC III, 258–271.

11. OC III, 264.

12. On the strain of "moral Newtonianism" in eighteenth-century thought see Elie Halévy, *The Growth of Philosophical Radicalism* (Boston, 1960), 6, 13, 19,

29, and Georges Gusdorf, *Les Principes de la pensée au siècle des lumières* (Paris, 1971), 151–212.

13. David Hume, *A Treatise of Human Nature* (Oxford, 1955), 12–13.

14. OC VI, 47.

15. This section is an expanded version of Jonathan Beecher and Richard Bienvenu, *The Utopian Vision of Charles Fourier* (Boston, 1971), 37–39.

16. OC I, 79.

17. "Des cinq passions sensuelles," *La Phalange*, IV (1846), 25.

18. OC I, 77; OC VII, 440–443.

19. On the sensual passions see "Des cinq passions sensuelles," *La Phalange*, IV (1846), 5–51, 97–135, 193–224, 289–310, 385–412.

20. OC VI, 70.

21. OC IV, 408–409.

22. See Fourier's manuscript "Du Clavier puissanciel des caractères," *La Phalange*, V (1847), 5–47, 97–135.

23. See for example OC I, 88–90, 176.

24. "Du Clavier puissanciel des caractères," *La Phalange*, VI (1847), 23–24.

25. OC XI, PM (1857–1858), 320–321. For interesting commentary on this passage and on Fourier's concept of the Phalanx as the "integral man" see Riasanovsky, *Teaching of Fourier*, 186–189.

26. OC VI, 57.

27. OC VI, 55.

28. OC IV, 341.

29. OC VIII, 353.

30. See OC I, 294.

31. OC VI, 59.

32. "Des Trois groupes d'ambition, d'amour et de famillisme," *La Phalange*, III, (1846), 231.

33. OC IV, 345; "Des Trois groupes," *La Phalange*, III (1846), 26–27, 226–231.

34. OC IV, 347.

35. OC IV, 340.

36. OC VI, 52.

37. OC VI, 63; OC IV, 139–140.

38. OC XI, PM (1857–1858), 146.

39. OC III, 241.

40. OC VI, 403.

41. OC VII, 391. Fourier had probably read little of the Marquis de Sade, but this appreciation of the general character of de Sade's thought was uncommon for the time.

42. Lehouck, *Fourier aujourd'hui*, 34.

43. OC III, 323.

44. OC IV, 33.

45. "De la méthode mixte," *La Phalange*, VII (1848), 113–114.

46. OC X, PM (1851), 59.

CHAPTER 12

1. OC X, PM (1851), 95.
2. OC IV, 495.
3. On the appearance and architecture of the Phalanx see especially OC IV, 425–504; OC VI, 99–129; and OC X, PM (1851), 8–175.
4. See especially "Des Modifications à introduire dans l'architecture des villes," OC XII, 683–717.
5. OC IV, 460.
6. OC IV, 463–464, 468. See also OC VI, 272.
7. OC IV, 465.
8. Walter Benjamin, "Paris, Capital of the Nineteenth Century," in *Reflections,* trans. by Edmund Jephcott (New York, 1978), 148–149.
9. Johann Friedrich Geist, *Arcades: The History of a Building Type,* trans. by Jane O. Newman and John H. Smith (Cambridge, Mass., 1983), 457. This magnificently produced and illustrated book is a mine of information on the whole topic. See also Henri-Auguste-Ottocar Reichard, *Le Véritable Conducteur parisien* (Weimar, 1828), 114.
10. See for example OC XII, 707, and OC II, *Sommaires,* 209. Also see above, chapter 3, section i.
11. On Ledoux (1736–1806) and the other visionary architects see Mona Ozouf, "Architecture et urbanisme: L'Image de la ville chez Claude-Nicolas Ledoux," *Annales, Economies, Sociétés, Civilisations,* XXI, 6 (November-December 1966), 1273–1304; Bronislaw Baczko, *Lumières de l'utopie* (Paris, 1978), 325–360; Allan Braham, *The Architecture of the French Enlightenment* (Berkeley, 1980), 111–117, 159–209, 231–232; Emile Kaufmann, *Three Revolutionary Architects: Boullée, Ledoux, and Lequeu* (Philadelphia, 1952), and Kaufmann's *Architecture in the Age of Reason: Baroque and Post-Baroque in England, Italy, and France* (Cambridge, Mass., 1955); and the valuable exhibition catalogue prepared by J.-C. Lemagny, *Visionary Architects: Boullée, Ledoux, Lequeu* (Houston, 1968). See also Claude-Nicolas Ledoux, *L'Architecture considérée sous le rapport de l'art des moeurs et de la législation,* 2 vols. (Paris, 1804).
12. OC II, *Sommaires,* 189, 209; OC IX, 701; OC XII, 705; *La Phalange,* X (1849), 225. See also AN 10AS 20 (11), where Fourier gives a list of architectural models, which includes both the "Hotel Théllusson" and Ledoux's "Barrières."
13. OC XII, 705. On the Hotel de Thélusson see Braham, *Architecture of the French Enlightenment,* 186–189.
14. OC IX, 701.
15. Ledoux, *L'Architecture,* I, 181. See also I, 2 and 202, and II, 89 and 103.
16. Ledoux, *L'Architecture,* I, 18.
17. OC IV, 445, 516–518; OC V, 502–514.
18. "Lettre au Grand Juge," 62.
19. OC V, 5–6. For a full discussion of Fourier's views on education see the following chapter.
20. OC V, 445–446.

21. OC VII, 126.

22. On food in the Phalanx see Rolande Bonnain-Merdyck, "Fourier gastrosophe," in Henri Lefebvre et al., *Actualité de Fourier* (Paris, 1975), 145–180, as well as the brief but suggestive comments in Barthes, *Sade, Fourier, Loyola,* 83–86, 120–122, and Spencer, *Fourier,* 69–71.

23. Jean-Paul Aron, *Le Mangeur du XIXe siècle* (Paris, 1973), esp. 5–6, 13–25; Grimod de la Reynière, *Manuel des Amphitryons* (Paris, 1808), *Almanach des gourmands* (1803–1810); Joseph de Berchoux, *La Gastronomie, ou l'Homme des champs à table* (Paris, 1801); Anthelme Brillat-Savarin, *La Physiologie du gout* (Paris, 1825); Marie-Antonin Carême, *Le Maître d'hôtel français,* 2 vols. (Paris, 1822), and *L'Art de la cuisine française au XIXe siècle,* 2 vols. (Paris, 1833).

24. OC VI, 255; OC VIII, 283.

25. OC VII, 131; OC VI, 71–72; OC V, 110–112.

26. OC IV, 404.

27. OC I, 167; OC IV, 19; OC X, PM (1852), 159–161.

28. OC IV, 139; "De la médecine naturelle ou attrayante composée," *La Phalange,* VII (1848), 417–448.

29. *La Phalange,* VII (1848), 434.

30. OC XII, 482; Henri Desroche, *La Société festive* (Paris, 1975), 144.

31. OC VII, 142–143.

32. OC VI, 114.

33. OC VI, 113; OC IV, 447.

34. OC XI, PM (1857–1858), 170. See also OC III, 368–385; OC VI, 376–380.

35. See for example Fourier's "Ralliement d'ambition en direct ou ascendant par les souverainetés progressives et échelonnées" with its "Tableau des sceptres d'Harmonie," OC XI, PM (1857–1858), 170–190.

36. OC V, 21.

37. OC V, 32–33. On the role of peer group discipline in education see below, chapter 13, section ii.

38. OC X, PM (1851), 149–150. On "eclipsing" and work discipline see below, chapter 14, section iii.

39. OC V, 467.

40. OC XII, 481.

41. "Du Groupe d'amitié," *La Phalange,* III (1846), 353.

42. OC V, 429–431; OC VI, 248; OC X, PM (1851), 121–125.

43. OC I, 159.

44. OC V, 26.

45. OC X, PM (1851), 194.

46. *Le Phalanstère,* II, 38 (January 31, 1834), 410.

CHAPTER 13

1. Fourier's writings on education comprise more than six hundred pages in his collected works. See esp. OC V, 1–309; OC VI, 166–244; OC X, PM

(1852), 73–314. See also David Zeldin, *The Educational Ideas of Charles Fourier (1772–1837)* (London, 1969); Jean Dautry, "Fourier et les questions d'éducation," *Revue internationale de philosophie,* XVI, 60 (1962), 234–260; Hubert Bourgin, "La Pédagogie de Fourier," *Revue internationale de l'enseignement,* LV (1908), 130–143; Emile Lehouck, *Fourier aujourd'hui,* 78–103; Jean Goret, *La Pensée de Fourier* (Paris, 1974), 46–66, 111–138.

2. OC VI, 167.

3. OC V, 1–2.

4. Fourier had little liking for the "dogmatic follies" of Fénelon, which he dissected in a special "ultra-pause" in his *Traité* (OC V, 477–485). But his extensive critical comments on Rousseau's *Emile* show some appreciation of Rousseau's critique of contemporary educational practice. See, for example, OC V, 47–49, 292; OC VI, 175, 202–203; OC X, PM (1851), 111–112.

5. Rousseau, *Emile* (Paris: Garnier, 157), 22; Fourier, OC V, 31.

6. OC V, 201–205, 4–5.

7. OC V, 5.

8. OC VI, 175.

9. OC X, PM (1852), 109.

10. OC V, 50–53; OC VI, 170–175.

11. OC VI, 176.

12. OC VI, 181.

13. OC X, PM (1852), 117.

14. OC VI, 196; OC V, 121–122.

15. OC V, 72.

16. OC X, PM (1852), 141. See also OC V, 75.

17. OC X, PM (1852), 121. See also OC V, 111.

18. OC V, 112.

19. OC V, 6.

20. OC V, 77.

21. OC V, 83. For a more extensive discussion of the role of opera in Harmony see Nicole Beaurain, "Où la science-fiction se fait opéra" in Lefebvre et al., *Actualité de Fourier,* 207–238.

22. On the Little Hordes and the Little Bands see OC V, 138–166, and OC VI, 207–218. For a fuller discussion of the Little Hordes and the problem of repugnant work see below, chapter 14, section iii.

23. OC V, 149.

24. On the Vestals and Damsels in Harmony see OC V, 217–265; OC VI, 225–236; OC VII, 433–436.

25. OC V, 236; OC VI, 230.

26. OC V, 248; OC VI, 234.

27. OC VII, 434–435.

28. Victor Hennequin, *Les Amours au Phalanstère* (Paris, 1849), 3.

29. OC X, PM (1852), 190.

30. OC II, *Sommaires,* 22–23.

31. OC V, 448.

32. OC V, 23.

33. On the Fourierism of Jean Macé and the remarkable women who founded the *école maternelle* see Theodore Zeldin, *France, 1848–1945. Vol. II, Intellect, Taste, and Anxiety* (Oxford, 1977), 151–154, 186–189.

34. OC X, PM (1852), 190; OC V, 195.

35. Spencer, *Fourier*, 86.

36. Compare with Fourier the accounts given in Melford E. Spiro, *Kibbutz: Venture in Utopia* (New York, 1970), 110–139, and in *Children of the Kibbutz* (New York, 1965), and in Bruno Bettelheim, *The Children of the Dream* (New York, 1969).

37. See A. S. Neill, *Summerhill: A Radical Approach to Child Rearing* (New York, 1960).

38. On this point see the penetrating remarks of René Schérer, *Fourier ou la contestation globale*, 93.

CHAPTER 14

1. In my own efforts to confront the larger issues raised by this chapter I owe much to Richard Bienvenu. General studies of the history of work that have been helpful to me include P. D. Anthony, *The Ideology of Work* (London, 1977), Hannah Arendt, *The Human Condition* (Chicago, 1958), Parts III and IV, Alisdair Clayre, *Work and Play: Ideas and Experience of Work and Leisure* (London, 1974), José Artur Giannotti, *Les Origines du dialectique du travail* (Paris, 1971), David Meakin, *Man and Work: Literature and Culture in Industrial Society* (London, 1976), Pierre Naville, *De l'alienation à la jouissance. La Genèse de la sociologie du travail chez Marx et Engels,* 2d ed. (Paris, 1970), and especially William H. Sewell, Jr., *Work and Revolution in France: The Language of Labor from the Old Regime to 1848* (Cambridge, England, 1980).

2. *Le Dictionnaire de l'Académie Françoise,* 2 vols. (Paris, 1694), II, 511–512, cited in Sewell, *Work and Revolution,* 22; Jean de La Bruyère, *Les Caractères, ou les Moeurs de ce siècle,* ed. by Robert Garapon (Paris: Garnier, 1962), 339.

3. *Oeuvres de Saint-Simon et d'Enfantin,* XVIII (Paris, 1868), 128. This paragraph and the following are based largely on Beecher and Bienvenu, *The Utopian Vision of Charles Fourier,* 27–28.

4. OC VI, 94; OC VIII, 401.

5. OC IV, 515; OC VI, 75.

6. *De l'anarchie industrielle,* 21.

7. OC V, 546.

8. OC IV, 191–193.

9. OC III, 15–16.

10. OC VI, 52.

11. OC I, 294.

12. OC VI, 303–323.

13. OC VI, 67.

14. OC VI, 68.

15. Herbert Marcuse, *Eros and Civilization: A Philosophical Inquiry into Freud* (New York, 1962), 199.

16. OC X, PM (1851), 191–193.

17. OC X, PM (1852), 152. See the critique of Fourier in Paul Janet, "La Philosophie de Charles Fourier," *Revue des deux mondes,* XXXV (October 1, 1879), 643.

18. OC VI, 69.

19. AN 10AS 4 (5), p. 131.

20. AN 10AS 4 (5), p. 131.

21. Louis-Sébastien Mercier, *L'An 2440, rêve s'il en fut jamais* (London, 1773), 123–127.

22. OC V, 153.

23. OC V, 149.

24. *De l'anarchie industrielle,* 22.

25. OC VI, 151.

26. OC VI, 91–95.

27. OC VI, 209; OC VI, 151–153.

28. Robert R. Palmer and Joel Colton, *A History of the Modern World,* 2d ed. (New York, 1961), 435. See also David Meakin, *Man and Work,* 39: "Fourier's greatest limitation . . . lies in his failure to foresee and take account of the problems posed by industrialism."

29. Edward Mason, "Fourier and Anarchism," *Quarterly Journal of Economics,* XLII, 2 (February 1928), 261.

30. AN 10AS 2 (8), pp. 78–79. This passage was too raw for the taste of Fourier's disciples. They omitted it—without acknowledgment—from the published version of this manuscript. It should appear in "Du Parcours et de l'unitéisme," *La Phalange,* V (1847), 37.

31. OC I, 67. See also OC X, PM (1851), 237.

32. See, for example, *De l'anarchie industrielle,* 18–25.

33. For good summaries of a vast literature see Sewell, *Work and Revolution,* 143–161, and Roger Price, *The French Second Republic: A Social History* (London, 1972), 5–30, 56–82.

34. Sewell, *Work and Revolution,* 194–242; Louis Chevalier, *Classes laborieuses et classes dangereuses à Paris pendant la première moitié du XIXᵉ siècle* (Paris, 1958); Armand Cuvillier, "Les Antagonismes de classe dans la littérature sociale française de Saint-Simon à 1848," *International Review of Social History,* I (1956), 433–463; John M. Merriman (ed.), *Consciousness and Class Experience in Nineteenth-Century Europe* (New York, 1979).

35. Pierre-Joseph Proudhon, *Système des contradictions économiques ou philosophie de la misère* (Paris, 1923), II, 371.

36. Antonio Gramsci, *Selections from the Prison Notebooks* (New York, 1971), 297.

37. Karl Marx and Friedrich Engels, *The German Ideology,* in *Collected Works of Marx and Engels,* V (New York, 1976), 47.

38. Engels in *The New Moral World* (November 4, 1843), in *Collected Works of Marx and Engels,* III, 394–396; Engels, "A Fragment of Fourier's on Trade" from *Deutsches Bürgerbuch für 1846,* in *Collected Works of Marx and Engels,* IV, 613–644. On Fourier as Marx's source see Jerrold Siegel, *Marx's Fate: The Shape of a Life* (Princeton, 1978), 166.

39. A fuller discussion of Marx's and Fourier's views on work from a point of view somewhat similar to mine may be found in Janina Rosa Mailer, "Fourier et Marx," in Lefebvre et al., *Actualité de Fourier,* esp. 264–283. For a different perspective see Pierre Naville, *De l'aliénation à la jouissance,* esp. 65–75, 488–499.

40. Karl Marx, *The Grundrisse,* ed. and trans. by David McLellan (New York, 1971), 124.

41. Karl Marx, *Capital,* III (New York, 1967), 820.

CHAPTER 15

1. For the history of the manuscript and problems relating to the establishment of Fourier's text see OC VII, vii–xxviii, and Poulat, *Cahiers manuscrits,* 37–60, 66–82.

2. But see the remarkable introduction by Simone Debout-Oleskiewicz to her edition of the text, OC VII, vii–cxii, the critical analysis in Catherine Francblin, "Le Féminisme utopique de Charles Fourier," *Tel Quel,* 62 (Summer 1975), 44–69, and the shrewd observations in Spencer, *Fourier,* 91–95.

3. "Toward a Psychological History of Utopia," in Frank E. Manuel (ed.), *Utopias and Utopian Thought* (Boston, 1967), 72–79.

4. Tommaso Campanella, *The City of the Sun: A Poetical Dialogue,* trans. by Daniel J. Donno (Berkeley, 1981), 63.

5. Gabriel de Foigny, *A New Discovery of Terra Australia Incognita or the Southern World,* in Glenn Negly and J. Max Patrick (eds.), *The Quest for Utopia: An Anthology of Imaginary Societies* (New York, 1952), 403.

6. Louis-Sébastien Mercier, *L'An 2440* (London, 1773), 26.

7. Diderot, *Oeuvres philosophiques* (Paris: Garnier, 1956), 480.

8. Morelly, *Naufrage des îles flottantes,* in Frank E. Manuel and Fritzie P. Manuel (eds.), *French Utopias: An Anthology of Ideal Societies* (New York, 1966), 93–100.

9. Diderot, *Oeuvres philosophiques,* 470.

10. See Mark Poster's valuable study, *The Utopian Thought of Restif de la Bretonne* (New York, 1971), 33–50.

11. Poster, *Restif de la Bretonne,* 136, referring only to the connection between Fourier and Restif. Poster offers (132–138) a balanced overview of the whole question of the influence of Restif on Fourier. For suggestive rapprochements of Sade and Fourier see Simone Debout-Oleskiewicz in OC VII, lxxvii–lxxxix; Pierre Klossowski, "Sade et Fourier," *Topique. Revue freudienne,* 4–5

(October 1970), 79–98; and Barthes, *Sade, Fourier, Loyola*. For Frank E. Manuel and Fritzie P. Manuel, in *Utopian Thought in the Western World* (Cambridge, Mass., 1979), 546, Fourier was "doubtless" influenced by Sade. Debout-Oleskiewicz is rightly more cautious.

12. Sigmund Freud, *Civilization and Its Discontents*, trans. by James Strachey (New York, 1962), 50, 55.

13. OC VII, 47.

14. OC VII, 2.

15. "Le Sphinx sans Oedipe," *La Phalange*, IX (1849), 200.

16. OC VII, 253.

17. OC VII, 257.

18. OC VII, 386.

19. OC I, 133.

20. OC XII, 622.

21. OC I, 117–130.

22. On the sexual minimum see OC VII, 439–445.

23. For a fuller discussion of this point see the introduction to Beecher and Bienvenu, *The Utopian Vision of Charles Fourier*, 55–58.

24. OC VII, 37, 95.

25. OC VII, 50, 98.

26. The first half of this section is based largely on Beecher and Bienvenu, *The Utopian Vision of Charles Fourier*, 54, 61–63.

27. OC VII, 51.

28. OC VII, 432–435.

29. OC VII, 387.

30. OC VII, 209–220; OC XI, PM (1857–1858), 25–29.

31. OC VII, 260.

32. OC VII, 121–124, 264–272.

33. Choderlos de Laclos, *Les Liaisons dangereuses* (1782).

34. OC VII, 92.

35. OC VII, 327–328.

36. OC VII, 328. Fourier's source is identified by Alexandrian, *Les Libérateurs de l'amour* (Paris, 1977), 148, as Charles Masson, *Mémoires secrets sur la Russie* (1801).

37. OC VII, 328.

38. OC VII, 320, 329.

39. OC VII, 220.

40. OC VII, 32, 157.

41. Muiron to Fourier, October 4, 1820, AN 10AS 25 (2).

42. OC VII, 151–154, 160, 206, 309, 432–436.

43. Spencer, *Fourier*, 71.

44. OC VII, 47, 80, 120, 361.

45. OC VII, 80–81, 90–93, 118–126.

46. OC VII, 47, 168, 22.

47. Mikhail Bakhtin, *Rabelais and His World*, trans. by Helene Iswolsky (Cambridge, Mass., 1968).

48. OC VII, 375–376, 268.

49. OC VII, 268.

50. OC VII, 78.

51. AN 10AS 3 (7), p. 191.

52. "Des cinq passions sensuelles," *La Phalange,* IV (1846), 197.

53. James Mill to Francis Place, December 6, 1817, cited in Elie Halèvy, *The Growth of Philosophical Radicalism,* 451.

CHAPTER 16

1. Judith Shklar, "The Political Theory of Utopia," in Frank E. Manuel (ed.), *Utopias and Utopian Thought* (Boston, 1967), 104.

2. Frank E. Manuel, "Toward a Psychological History of Utopia," in *Utopias and Utopian Thought,* 79.

3. The main sources for Fourier's theory of historical development are OC I, 33–37, 52–57; OC III, 33–50; OC XII, 434–473; and "Des Lymbes obscures ou périodes d'enfer social et de labyrinthe passionel," *La Phalange,* IX (1849), 5–40, 97–110.

4. Manuel, *Prophets of Paris,* 211.

5. Henri Saint-Simon, *Catéchisme des industriels. Deuxième cahier,* in *Oeuvres,* VIII, 96; OC I, 16.

6. OC I, 89.

7. OC I, 89. Fourier's italics.

8. OC XII, 622. See above, chapter 15, section ii.

9. "Des Lymbes obscures," *La Phalange,* IX (1849), 12.

10. OC I, 52–56.

11. OC I, 56–58.

12. "Des Lymbes obscures," *La Phalange,* IX (1849), 27.

13. OC I, 62.

14. OC I, 36, 67–68.

15. OC VI, 441.

16. OC VI, 9.

17. OC VI, 386–387.

18. OC X, PM (1851), 52, 312; I, 89–90.

19. Friedrich Engels, *Herr Eugen Dühring's Revolution in Science (Anti-Dühring)* (New York, 1939), 284–285; Felix Armand, *Fourier: Textes choisis* (Paris, 1953), 24; Zil'berfarb, *Sotsial'naia filosofiia Sharlia Fur'e,* 94–106. For non-Marxist appreciations of Fourier's historical dialectics see Raymond Queneau, "Dialectique hégélienne et séries de Fourier," in his *Bords* (Paris, 1963), 37–51 (suggestive), and Maurice Lansac, *Les Conceptions méthodologiques et sociales de Charles Fourier. Leur influence* (Paris, 1926), 73–134 (superficial).

20. "Tableau du cours du mouvement social. Succession et relation de ses 4 phases et 32 périodes. Ordre des créations," OC I, insert. OC VI, 110–111.

21. Fourier's most extensive discussions of reforms appropriate to the inter-

mediate stages between Civilization and Harmony are OC IV, 276–313; OC VI, 427–442; OC XI, PM (1853–1856), 59–114, 213–234; OC XII, 683–717; and "Du Guarantisme," *La Phalange,* IX (1849), 289–336. Fourier's fullest descriptions of a small-scale Phalanx are "De la Sérigermie composée ou binisexe," *La Phalange,* VIII (1848), 5–76, and "De la Sérisophie ou épreuve réduite," OC XII, 217–365.

22. See OC III, 140–148; OC VI, 442–444; "Des Lymbes obscures," *La Phalange,* IX (1849), 5–38, 97–110; "Des diverses issues de la civilisation," *La Phalange,* X (1849), 184–256.

23. OC IV, 281, and Just Muiron, *Statuts pour un comptoir communal ou établissement rural et commercial* (Besançon, 1824). This is a separately published extract from Muiron's *Sur les vices de nos procédés industriels, aperçus démontrant l'urgence d'introduire le procédé sociétaire* (Paris, 1824).

24. For Fourier's influence on the cooperative movement, the principal source is Jean Gaumont's remarkable *Histoire générale de la coopération en France,* 2 vols. (Paris, 1924), I, 85–182: "Les sources de la coopération dans le socialisme sociétaire de Fourier." See also Charles Gide, *Fourier, précurseur de la coopération* (Paris, 1924); Celestin Bouglé, *Socialismes français,* 5th ed. (Paris, 1951), 111–138; Henri Desroche, *La Société festive,* 275–320.

25. "Plan d'une ville de 6ᵉ période," OC IV, 300–304; "Fourrier" to Citoyen (?) of Bordeaux, 20 frimaire an V, AN 10AS 15 (18). See also OC X, PM (1851), 17, and my discussion of these texts in chapter 3, section i.

26. OC X, PM (1851), 274; "Notice sur la découverte des lois intégrales du mouvement," Istituto Giangiacomo Feltrinelli (Milan), cited in Lehouck, *Vie de Fourier,* 81.

27. On Fourier's theory of "bicompound immortality" see especially OC III, 304–346.

28. OC III, 330.

CHAPTER 17

1. "Lettre au Grand Juge," 60. The following secondary sources have been particularly helpful to me in my own effort to gain an understanding of Fourier's "theory of the destinies": Emile Lehouck, *Fourier aujourd'hui,* esp. 131–229; Simone Debout-Oleskiewicz, "L'Analogie ou 'Le poème mathématique' de Charles Fourier," *Revue internationale de philosophie,* XVI, 60 (1962), 176–199; Michel Nathan, *Le Ciel des fouriéristes. Habitants des étoiles et réincarnations de l'âme* (Lyon, 1981); Helène Tuzet, *Le Cosmos et l'imagination* (Paris, 1965); and Auguste Viatte, *Les Sources occultes du romantisme,* 2 vols. (Paris, 1969).

2. "Le Sphinx sans Oedipe," *La Phalange,* IX (1849), 193–206; OC IX, 708.

3. Ange Guépin, *La Philosophie du socialisme* (Paris, 1850), cited in Maurice Dommanget, *Victor Considerant* (Paris, 1929), 17. Pellarin, *Fourier,* 81–82.

4. Lansac, *Conceptions méthodologiques,* 2; Zil'berfarb, *Sotsial'naia filosofiia Sharlia Fur'e,* 17, 71–84.

5. OC I, v–viii, "Préface des editeurs." For Fourier's corrections see OC I, 32, 38, 41, 46, 50, 51. An example of the kind of correction made by Fourier was to increase from eighteen to twenty-six his estimate of the number of separate "creations" that would occur during the course of the earth's history, OC I, 38. Far from constituting a disavowal of his speculations on cosmogony, such corrections merely indicate that Fourier never worked out his cosmogony to his full satisfaction.

6. See for example OC IV, 212.

7. Lehouck, *Fourier aujourd'hui,* 157.

8. OC XII, 606–607.

9. OC I, 30–31.

10. On the influence of Linnaeus and on the concept of the series in natural history see Henri Daudin, *De Linné à Jussieu. Méthodes de la classification et idée de série en botanique et en zoologie (1740–1790)* (Paris, 1926).

11. Nicolas Lemoyne to Lechevalier (1832), AN 10AS 39 (10).

12. OC I, 49.

13. OC I, 40.

14. OC IV, 257. See also OC XI, PM (1857–1858), 325.

15. For an analysis of the eighteenth-century debate on this question see Arthur O. Lovejoy, *The Great Chain of Being* (New York, 1960), 208–226.

16. OC VI, 449. See also OC XII, 52.

17. OC XII, 53.

18. OC XII, 63.

19. OC IV, 258–262; OC XII, 57. On Fourier's vendetta against the moon see "Les Ennemis de la lune" in Raymond Queneau, *Bords* (Paris, 1963), 53–57.

20. OC I, 41–52.

21. OC I, 45.

22. OC IV, 254–255.

23. OC I, 55; OC X, PM (1851), 44; OC XII, 64.

24. AN 10AS 6 (10), pp. 56–58. For the full text see Jonathan Beecher, "L'Archibras de Fourier: Un manuscrit censuré," *La Brèche. Action surréaliste,* 7 (1964), 66–71.

25. OC I, 31–32.

26. OC IV, 214.

27. OC VI, 461.

28. OC II, 145.

29. OC VI, 464.

30. OC XII, 201–202.

31. OC IV, 266.

32. OC XII, 93n.

33. OC VI, 460. See also OC VIII, 330.

34. OC XII, 203–206. See also OC I, 288–289.

35. OC IV, 462; OC XII, 93–95.

36. OC VI, 464. See also OC XII, 135–136.

37. Simone Debout, article on "illuminisme" in the glossary to her critical edition of the *Théorie des quatre mouvements* (Paris: Pauvert, 1967), 376–379; introduction to OC I, xi–xii. Gérard Schaeffer, "L'Ode à Charles Fourier et la tradition," in Marc Eigeldinger (ed.), *André Breton. Essais et témoignages* (Neuchâtel, 1950), 88.

38. Lansac, *Conceptions méthodologiques,* 8; Adrien Dax, "A propos d'un talisman de Charles Fourier," *La Brèche. Action surréaliste,* 4 (February 1963), 18–23.

39. OC XII, 405–406.

40. Poster, *Restif de la Bretonne,* 132–138. For Fourier and Saint-Martin see the articles by Debout cited above, note 37. For Fourier and Swedenborg see the caustic and, I believe, fundamentally sound remarks of Emile Lehouck, *Fourier aujourd'hui,* 209–214.

41. Alexandrian, *Le Socialisme romantique* (Paris, 1979), 129.

42. OC I, 184; OC IV, 199–200, 266, 350; OC VIII, 151; OC X, PM (1851), 208; OC XI (1857–1858), 19; OC XII, 205, 405–407. *La Phalange,* III (1846), 425; IV (1846), 111, 504; VI (1847), 219; IX (1849), 231; X (1849), 210.

43. OC VI, 14.

44. OC X, PM (1851), 22. See also Bourgin, *Fourier,* 63.

45. For a helpful overview of these traditions and a taxonomy of the various doctrines that view man as a microcosm of the universe see Rudolf Allers, "Microcosmus from Anaximandros to Paracelsus," *Traditio,* II (1944), 319–406.

46. Rudolf Wittkover, *Architectural Principles in the Age of Humanism* (London, 1952), esp. 90–99.

47. For Kepler see Arthur Koestler, *The Sleepwalkers: A History of Man's Changing Vision of the Universe* (Harmondsworth, England, 1977), 249–269, 393–404.

48. John Cotton, cited in Perry Miller, *The New England Mind: The Seventeenth Century* (Boston, 1961), 212.

49. See for example OC I, 289–290; OC IV, 180; OC XII, 411.

50. Simone Debout-Oleskiewicz, "Aperçus de l'influence de Kepler sur Fourier," *Revue internationale de philosophie,* XVI, 60 (1962), 195–199.

51. For helpful guides to the varied romantic reformulations of illuminist and analogical thinking see Viatte, *Sources occultes du romantisme,* II, and various articles by Frank Paul Bowman, notably "Illuminism, utopia, mythology," in D. G. Charlton (ed.), *The French Romantics,* 2 vols. (Cambridge, England, 1984), I, 76–112. See also Lehouck, *Fourier aujourd'hui,* 201–228.

52. Jean Pommier, *La Mystique de Baudelaire* (Geneva, 1967), 55–68; Paul Arnold, *Esotérisme de Baudelaire* (Paris, 1972); Spencer, *Fourier,* 150–153; and diverse articles by Peter Hambly, notably "The Structure of *Les Fleurs du mal:* Another Suggestion," *Australian Journal of French Studies,* VIII, 3 (1971), 269–296.

53. In addition to the works cited in note 1, above, see Roland Barthes, *Sade, Fourier, Loyola,* 81–124; Raymond Queneau, "Dialectique hégélienne et

séries de Fourier," in *Bords* (Paris, 1963), 37–51; and Emile Lehouck, "La Lecture surréaliste de Charles Fourier," *Australian Journal of French Studies,* XX, 1 (1983), 26–36.

54. Simone Debout, "Des Manies au cosmos, ou le dedans et le déhors sans frontière," *Australian Journal of French Studies,* XI, 3 (1974), 264; Lehouck, *Fourier aujourd'hui,* 133–157.

55. Spencer, *Fourier,* 99.

56. See the citations and evidence presented in the introduction to this chapter and in the discussion of "the riddle of the *Quatre mouvements,*" chapter 6, section i.

57. Felix Armand and René Maublanc, *Fourier,* 2 vols. (Paris, 1937), II, 114–115.

58. OC IV, 241, 257; OC XI, PM (1857–1858), 325; OC XII, 23.

59. OC VII, 487. On this theme in the work of Thomas Burton, Thomas Burnet, Henry More, and others see Marjorie Nicolson, *The Breaking of the Circle,* rev. ed. (New York, 1960), 188–190.

60. OC VII, 485–487.

61. Blaise Pascal, *Pensées,* ed. by Louis Lafuma, 3 vols. (Paris, 1951), I, 55 (*Pensée* 68).

62. OC XII, 5.

CHAPTER 18

1. Gaudillot to Fourier, November 9, 1822, AN 10AS 25 (2). The total printing of the *Traité* was one thousand copies.

2. Pellarin, *Fourier,* 262–263.

3. "Détérioration matérielle de la planète," *La Phalange,* VI (1847), 504.

4. Honoré de Balzac, *Illusions perdues* (Paris: Classiques Garnier, 1961), 272.

5. Most of the names are from a list in Fourier's hand, headed "Emplois d'exemplaires" and covering the period November–December 1822, AN 10AS 12 (6).

6. Fourier to Villèle, draft, January 31, 1823, AN 10AS 15 (1); Fourier to Muiron, February 1823, Charles Pellarin, *Lettre de Fourier au Grand Juge* (Paris, 1874), 38; Fourier to Count Grégoire, January 14, 1823, Bibliothèque de l'Arsenal, Fonds Enfantin, Imprimés 264, letter bound into Fourier's book.

7. Fourier to the minister of the interior, draft, November 18, 1822, AN 10AS 16 (42); Villèle to Fourier, February 21, 1823, AN 10AS 25 (2).

8. Fourier to Count Chaptal, draft, February 12, 1823, AN 10AS 16 (42). For a summary of Fourier's other appeals to learned societies see his undated draft of a letter to Count d'Argout, AN 10AS 20 (1).

9. "Notice explicative envoyée circulairement à MM. les Rédacteurs des journaux de Paris," 16 pp., AN 10AS 19 (11) and AN 10AS 17 (4). For the

complete list of journals contacted by Fourier see his "Emplois d'exemplaires," AN 10AS 12 (6).

10. *Annonce* of the *Traité de l'association domestique-agricole* by "Th. Fourier" (*sic*) in *Le Courrier français*, February 23, 1823.

11. *Le Miroir*, March 17 and 18, 1823.

12. This review is discussed by Fourier and attributed to "M. Pictet, de Genève," in OC II, *Sommaires*, 95–97. I have been unable to locate the source of either this review or the following.

13. OC II, *Sommaires*, 79–80.

14. *La Revue encyclopédique*, XVIII (May 1823), 380–381. Owing to Fourier's title this review appeared in a section devoted to works on agronomy.

15. OC II, *Sommaires*, 66.

16. Fourier's version of the conspiracy directed against him is most explicitly developed in "Le Dessous des cartes ou le comité directeur," OC II, *Sommaires*, 233–236.

17. OC II, *Sommaires*, 2, 20.

18. OC II, *Sommaires*, 22.

19. OC II, *Argument*, xxvii.

20. OC II, *Sommaires*, 78.

21. OC II, *Argument*, xxxvi.

22. AN 10AS 11 (6), p. 5.

23. AN 10AS 19 (3) includes eight copies of this statement, each written in Fourier's neatest and most careful hand.

24. Cited in Victor Considerant, *Au Texas* (Paris, 1854), 175–176.

25. Undated draft in AN 10AS 11 (6), pp. 55–56.

26. "Plan d'exercice d'opposition scientifique-industrielle dans un journal quotidien" and Fourier to M. de Maizières, director of *Le Drapeau blanc*, draft, October 14, 1823, AN 10AS 16 (42).

27. *Bulletin universal des sciences et de l'industrie*, Sixième section: *Bulletin des sciences géographiques; économie politique; voyages*, I (February 1824), 114–116. See also Férussac to Fourier, February 16, 1824, AN 10AS 25 (2).

28. Cited in Considerant, *Au Texas*, 176.

29. Fourier to Muiron, January 3 and February 1, 1824, Pellarin, *Fourier*, 206–208.

30. The literature on Robert Owen is voluminous. A good recent work is John F. C. Harrison, *Quest for the New Moral World: Robert Owen and the Owenites in Britain and America* (New York, 1969).

31. On the early diffusion of Owen's ideas in France see Jacques Gans, "Les relations entre socialistes de France et d'Angleterre au début du XIXe siècle," *Le Mouvement social*, 46 (January–March 1964), 105–118; and Henri Desroche (ed.), "Owenisme et utopies françaises," special issue of *Communautés. Archives internationales de sociologie de la coopération et du développement*, No. 30 (July–December 1971). A number of the sources for this section have been published in both of the above.

32. AN 10AS 14 (25), 10AS 1 (8), and OC XI, PM (1853), 222–223.

33. OC III, 8.

34. OC III, 3–8. See also AN 10AS 3 (8), pp. 124ff.

35. OC III, 33, 42.

36. Much of what Fourier knew about Owen seems to have come at second or even third hand. See his reference (OC III, 7) to a review signed "Huard" of a French translation of Henry Gray Macnab's *Examen impartial des nouvelles vues de M. Robert Owen* (1821). See also OC II, *Sommaires,* 30: "I have read in the *Revue encyclopédique* the maxims that Monsieur Owen circulates among his pupils."

37. Benjamin Disraeli, *Lord Beaconsfield: Correspondence with His Sister* (London, 1886), 15, cited in Sadleir, *Bulwer,* 140.

38. OC II, *Sommaires,* 30–31. The "societary-agricultural community" to which Fourier refers was doubtless the short-lived Owenite experiment at the country estate of Archibald James Hamilton at Motherwell in Lanarkshire.

39. Fourier to Owen, draft, April 2, 1824, AN 10AS 10 (8), pp. 75–81. This letter does not appear in either Gans or Desroche.

40. Skene to Fourier, June 28, 1824, AN 10AS 25 (2). The full text of this letter is published in Desroche (ed.), "Owenisme et utopies françaises," 142–144. On Philip Orkney Skene (1793–1837) see George J. Holyoake, *The History of Cooperation* (London, 1906), I, 221–222.

41. Pellarin, *Fourier,* 76.

42. Fourier to Skene, draft, September 14, 1824, AN 10AS 25 (2). This letter has been published in its entirety in Gans, "Relations entre socialistes," 106–109, and in Desroche (ed.), "Owenisme et utopies françaises," 144–146.

43. Fourier to Muiron, April 1, 1825, Pellarin, *Fourier,* 208.

44. Bourgin, *Fourier,* 108.

45. "Des Diverses issues de civilisation," *La Phalange,* X (1849), 231. This is from a draft of *Le Nouveau monde industriel* that includes extensive commentary on Owen and Owenism. See also *La Phalange,* X (1849), 191, 205, 230–245.

46. Fourier to Muiron, April 5, 1826, Pellarin, *Fourier,* 214.

47. Cited in Gans, "Relations entre socialistes," 110.

CHAPTER 19

1. Pellarin, *Fourier,* 82.

2. Pellarin, *Fourier,* 272–273.

3. This image was conjured up by François-Joseph Génisset in a report delivered to the Academy of Besançon in August 1825. Although nominally devoted to a work by Just Muiron, the report was in fact the first formal assessment of Fourier's doctrine by a group of his compatriots. See *Séances publiques de l'Académie des sciences, belles-lettres et arts de Besançon.* Séance du 24 août, 1825, 62–63.

4. Gabet to Fourier, October 2, 1824, AN 10AS 25 (2).

5. Pellarin, *Fourier*, 80.

6. Pellarin, *Fourier*, 83–84.

7. Fourier to Muiron, January 3 and February 1, 1824, Pellarin, *Fourier*, 206–207.

8. Fourier to M. Jaquet of Jaquet Bouchardier and Co., draft, February 17, 1824, AN 10AS 21 (10).

9. Gaucel to Fourier, February 12–13, 1824, AN 10AS 25 (2); Bousquet to Fourier, February 26, 1824, AN 10AS 25 (2). See also Saint Aubin to Fourier, May 26, 1824, AN 10AS 25 (9). Among Fourier's many correspondents, Gaucel and Bousquet were the only ones to use the familiar "tu."

10. "Analyse de mécanisme d'agiotage," *La Phalange*, VII (1848), 104.

11. See Bousquet to Fourier, April 22, 1824, AN 10AS 25 (2).

12. See receipts for the period May–August 1824 in AN 10AS 20 (10) and 10AS 20 (1).

13. Pellarin, *Fourier*, 80.

14. Gabet to Fourier, October 2, 1824, AN 10AS 25 (2).

15. Pellarin, *Fourier*, 73.

16. Fourier to Muiron, July 9, 1824, Pellarin, *Fourier*, 203.

17. See Gabet to Fourier, November 29, 1824, AN 10AS 25 (2).

18. *Mnémonique géographique, ou méthode pour apprendre en peu de leçons la géographie, la statistique et la politique* (Paris, 1824). This brochure was reprinted, presumably as a curiosity, in *Le Mercure de France au dix-neuvième siècle*, XXXI (1830), 400–412, 443–453. It also appears in OC X, PM (1852), 267–288.

19. Bourgin, *Fourier*, 166. See also Pierre Guiral, "Un Aspect peu connu de Fourier: Fourier géographe et climatologue," in *Livre jubilaire offert à Maurice Zimmermann* (Lyon, 1949), 373–379.

20. OC X, PM (1852), 268.

21. OC X, PM (1852), 288.

22. Fourier to Monsieur Brodart, November 25, 1824, draft, AN 10AS 16 (42). Half a dozen drafts of similar letters may be found in AN 10AS 16 (42), 10AS 20 (12), 10AS 15 (22), and 10AS 19 (4). See also manuscript "Plan d'instruction en 12 leçons," AN 10AS 15 (34).

23. OC X, PM (1852), 287.

24. Draft of a letter to an unnamed school director, AN 10AS 15 (22). See also AN 10AS 19 (4).

25. OC X, PM (1852), 284, 272, 273.

26. *La Pandore. Journal des spectacles, des lettres, des arts, des moeurs et des modes*, No. 488 (November 15, 1824). This journal was actually quite similar to *Le Miroir*, which had published a mocking but not totally unsympathetic review of the *Traité*. It was described by Stendhal as "the most impudently deceitful of our small journals." Stendhal, *Courrier anglais* (Paris: Le Divan, 1936), V, 85.

27. Fourier to the editor of *La Pandore*, draft, n.d., AN 10AS 17 (1).

28. Bousquet to Fourier, January 12, 1825, AN 10AS 25 (2); Muiron to Fourier, April 1, 1825, AN 10AS 40 (4); Fourier to Muiron, April 19, 1825, Pellarin, *Fourier*, 209; *Almanach du Commerce* (Paris: Bottin, 1825).

29. AN 10AS 16 (42) includes a number of drafts of business letters written by Fourier at this time, some with corrections in François Bousquet's hand.

30. Gabet to Fourier, August 17, 1825, AN 10AS 25 (2).

31. Fourier to Muiron, August 17, 1825, Pellarin, *Fourier,* 83.

32. Pellarin, *Fourier,* 81–85; Muiron to Fourier, August 8, 1829, AN 10AS 40 (4).

33. OC VI, 392–396. See also Fourier's manuscript comments on the crisis in AN 10AS 13 (3), esp. p. 46J.

34. On the economic crisis of 1826 see Arthur L. Dunham, *The Industrial Revolution in France* (New York, 1955), esp. 360–363, 376–377.

35. OC VI, 393.

36. Muiron to Clarisse Vigoureux, August 4, 1827, AN 10AS 40 (4).

37. Pellarin, *Fourier,* 87.

38. "Du Parcours et de l'unitéisme," *La Phalange,* V (1847), 31–32.

39. Fourier to his cousin Laure, August 24, 1827, draft, AN 10AS 15 (5); Reichard, *La Véritable Conducteur Parisien* (Paris, 1828).

40. Pellarin, *Fourier,* 142, 160–161.

41. Stendhal, *Mémoires d'un touriste* (Paris: Le Divan, 1929), III, 277.

42. Eugène-Emmanuel Amaury-Duval, *Souvenirs (1829–1830)* (Paris, 1885), 19. On the Nodier circle see especially Michel Salomon, *Charles Nodier et le groupe romantique* (Paris, 1908), 116–224.

CHAPTER 20

1. Not to be confused with Jean-Baptiste-André Godin (1817–1888), the stove manufacturer and founder of the Familistère de Guise. For Jean-Antoine Godin's letters and a long poem in honor of Fourier see AN 10AS 25 (2) and 10AS 38 (8).

2. On Gabriel Gabet (1763–1853) see the notice in Jean Maitron (ed.), *Dictionnaire biographique du mouvement ouvrier français: 1789–1864* (Paris, 1965), II, 221, and the note by Jules Puech in his edition of Flora Tristan, *La Tour de France. Journal inédit, 1843–1844* (Paris, 1973), 55n. For a very different picture of Gabet from the one that emerges from his correspondence with Fourier see the sarcastic comments in Flora Tristan's *Journal,* 52.

3. Gabet to Fourier, August 17, 1825, AN 10AS 25 (2).

4. Muiron, *Nouvelles transactions,* 153.

5. This report, which was delivered by François-Joseph Génisset, a professor of Latin at the University of Besançon, is reproduced in *Séances publiques de l'Académie des sciences, belles-lettres et arts de Besançon.* Séance du 24 août, 1825, 52–79. Although Génisset made some effort to be generous to Muiron—and to Fourier—he concluded by identifying himself with the "expectants."

6. Muiron, *Nouvelles transactions,* 160. Fourier also could write bitterly several years later about "the malicious citizens who defamed me at the Academy,

against the wishes of the reporter whose hand was forced." Fourier to Muiron, May 17, 1830, Pellarin, *Fourier*, 237.

7. Marguérite Thibert, *Le Féminisme dans le socialisme français* (Paris, 1926), 130–133. On Clarisse Vigoureux (1791–1869) see also Clarisse Coignet, *Victor Considerant, sa vie, son oeuvre* (Paris, 1895), 11–12.

8. See Considerant's thirteen-page letter to Paul Vigoureux, May 24, 1826, AN 10AS 28 (6).

9. Muiron to Clarisse Vigoureux, August 4, 1827, AN 10AS 40 (4).

10. Considerant to Clarisse Vigoureux, July 15, 1828, AN 10AS 28 (6).

11. The standard works on Victor Considerant (1808–1893) are still Hubert Bourgin, *Victor Considerant. Son oeuvre* (Lyon, 1909), and Maurice Dommanget, *Victor Considerant. Sa vie. Son oeuvre* (Paris, 1929).

12. See Pellarin, *Fourier*, 206–212.

13. Fourier to Muiron, June 28, 1826, Pellarin, *Fourier*, 211.

14. Fourier to Muiron, July 12, 1826, Pellarin, *Fourier*, 212.

15. OC VI, 1–46. A dozen of Fourier's drafts of the preface may be found in AN 10AS 9 and 10AS 10. One of these drafts was published separately by Fourier's disciples in 1847 under the title *De l'anarchie industrielle et scientifique*. On Fourier's difficulties with the preface see Poulat, *Cahiers manuscrits*, 63–66.

16. Muiron to Clarisse Vigoureux, August 4, 1827, AN 10AS 40 (4). In fact Gréa did no more than help secure a loan. In a statement dated August 2, 1832, Muiron described the publication costs of the *Nouveau monde industriel* as met by loans from Mlle. Bruand (2,400 francs) and himself (504 francs 85), AN 10AS 25 (9).

17. Fourier to Muiron, May 2, 1828, Pellarin, *Fourier*, 90.

18. Pellarin, *Fourier*, 91.

19. The main source for the information in this paragraph is the draft of a letter from Fourier to an unnamed priest written about July 1829, AN 10AS 9 (2), pp. 91–92. In this letter Fourier observes that his niece Lubine had been received without charge at the convent of Notre-Dame-du-Roule "because she is, as I am, a direct descendant of the Blessed Pierre Fourier of Lorraine," who founded the order that ran the convent. See also the letters of the priest to Fourier and the draft of a "Note" by Fourier to the mother superior of the convent of Notre-Dame-du-Roule, AN 10AS 25 (2).

20. Pellarin, *Fourier*, 242–243.

21. Pierre-Joseph Proudhon, *De la Création de l'ordre dans l'humanité* (Paris, 1927), 168.

22. Pierre-Joseph Proudhon, *Avertissement aux propriétaires ou lettre à M. Considerant* (Paris, 1841), 114.

23. Pierre-Joseph Proudhon, *Carnets*, I (Paris, 1960), 180. On the general problem of Fourier's influence on Proudhon see Fernand Rude, "Proudhon et Fourier," in Henri Lefebvre et al., *Actualité de Fourier*, 33–55, and Pierre Haubtmann, *Pierre-Joseph Proudhon. Sa vie et sa pensée (1809–1849)* (Paris, 1982), 82–86.

24. OC VI, iii, "Avertissement des éditeurs." The cuts are restored in Michel Butor's edition of *Le Nouveau monde industriel et sociétaire* (Paris, 1973).

25. Fourier to Considerant, October 23, 1831, AN 10AS 21 (13).

26. OC VI, 340. See also OC VI, 96–98 ("Chapitres omis").

27. OC VI, 473; "Confirmation tirée des Saints Evangiles," OC VI, 357–380.

28. Fourier to Férussac, March 1829, draft, AN 10AS 15 (69). The actual letter, dated March 21, 1829, is in the possession of Monsieur Edmond Bomsel of Paris. Fourier had concluded the *Nouveau monde industriel* by calling for the creation of such a Société de réforme industrielle.

29. AN 10AS 21 (12).

30. See for example the terse letter of acknowledgment to Fourier from N.-L. Lemercier and the kinder one from Paulin of *Le National*, AN 10AS 25 (2).

31. *Journal des débats*, May 2, 1829.

32. *L'Universel, journal de la littérature, des sciences et des arts* (June 22–23, August 6, 1829), I, 173–174, 218.

33. *La Revue française* (May 1829), 277–278.

34. AN 10AS 24 (1), pp. 39–59. See also AN 10AS 9 (9), pp. 29–35.

35. Muiron to Fourier, August 8, 1829, AN 10AS 40 (4).

36. *Livret d'annonce au Nouveau monde industriel* (Paris, 1830), 619.

37. *Le Mercure de France au dix-neuvième siècle*, XXVIII (1830), 51–62.

38. *Le Mercure de France au dix-neuvième siècle*, XXVIII (March 13, 1830), 477–490.

39. Fourier to the editor of the *Mercure*, draft, December 20, 1831, AN 10AS 16 (42).

40. *Le Mercure de France au dix-neuvième siècle*, XXX (July 10, 1830), 51–66. See Fourier's manuscript of this article, AN 10AS 13 (10).

41. On *L'Impartial* see Eugène Tavernier, "La Presse bisontine et la Révolution de Juillet," *Académie des sciences, belles-lettres et arts de Besançon. Procès-verbaux et mémoires. Annee 1908* (Besançon, 1909), 36–91. Muiron's official title was *gérant,* or managing editor.

42. Pellarin, *Fourier*, 102–103.

43. Pellarin, *Fourier*, 103.

44. Pellarin, *Fourier*, 106–107.

45. For a list of Fourier's articles in *L'Impartial* see the Bibliography.

46. Fourier to Muiron, September 13, 1829, Pellarin, *Fourier*, 104.

47. Fourier to Muiron, June 23, 1830, Pellarin, *Fourier*, 221–222.

48. A sampling of Fourier's voluminous letters on these topics is included in Pellarin, *Fourier*, 224–240.

49. *L'Impartial*, II, 26 (August 29, 1830).

50. "Note sur les prétentions des Bourguignons à frustrer Besançon de l'école d'artillerie et du chantier de construction," 10 pp., AN 10AS 19 (10).

51. *L'Impartial*, II, 7 (May 9, 1830).

52. Fourier to Muiron, May 17, 1830, Pellarin, *Fourier*, 237.

53. Xavier Marmier, "Charles Fourier," *La France littéraire*, II, 5 (1832), 336, 354–355.

54. See AN 10AS 15 (3) and 10AS 19 (13).

55. See drafts of Fourier's letter to Casimir Périer, June 1831, AN 10AS 16 (42) and Fourier's *mémoire* to the Committee on Agricultural Progress, January

1832, AN 10AS 21 (2), 10AS 19 (5), and 10AS 20 (6). For the acknowledgments of Jacques Laffitte, June 8, 1831, and Casimir Périer, June 15, 1831, see AN 10AS 25 (3).

56. Fourier to Dugas-Montbel, October 6, 1831, draft, AN 10AS 19 (4) and 10AS 21 (6). For Dugas-Montbel's perfunctory reply of November 14, 1831, see AN 10AS 25 (3).

57. See for example Polignac to Fourier, April 29, 1830, AN 10AS 25 (2), and Pellarin, *Fourier,* 109.

58. "Complément au Ministre des Travaux Publiques," AN 10AS 21 (1); Capelle to Fourier, June 19, 1830, AN 10AS 20 (5); Capelle to Fourier, July 24, 1830, AN 10AS 25 (2).

59. AN 10AS 19 (5).

60. Fourier to Muiron, August 23, 1830, Pellarin, *Fourier,* 223.

61. *Le Mercure de France au dix-neuvième siècle,* XXXI (January 1831), 335–336.

62. "Inconvenances de la salle Grenelle," AN 10AS 19 (3).

63. Fourier to Muiron, cited in Muiron to Gréa, February 20, 1831, AN 10AS 40 (5).

64. Muiron to Gréa, February 20, 1831, AN 10AS 40 (5).

CHAPTER 21

1. Pellarin, *Fourier* (5th ed.), 111.

2. On early socialism George Lichtheim, *The Origins of Socialism* (New York, 1969), is still of value. But see Gareth Stedman Jones, "Utopian Socialism Reconsidered: Science and Religion in the Early Socialist Movement," for an illuminating reassessment of the whole problem of "utopian socialism." On Saint-Simon in particular, Frank E. Manuel, *The New World of Henri Saint-Simon* (Cambridge, Mass., 1956), is excellent. In addition to the older and still valuable works by Maxime Leroy, Georges Weill, and Georges Gurvitch, see the special issue on Saint-Simon of the *Revue internationale de philosophie, 53–54* (1960).

3. Henri de Saint-Simon, *Le Nouveau christianisme et les écrits sur la religion,* ed. by Henri Desroche (Paris, 1969), 149.

4. On the "scientist hubris" of the Saint-Simonians see Friedrich A. Hayek, *The Counter-Revolution of Science* (Glencoe, Ill., 1952), Part II, esp. 105–116 and 143–155. Also G. Pinet, "L'Ecole Polytechnique et les Saint-Simoniens," *Revue de Paris,* I, 8 (May 15, 1894), 73–96.

5. The best general work on the Saint-Simonians remains Sébastien Charléty's venerable *Histoire du Saint-Simonisme* (Paris, 1931), but see also Frank Manuel's suggestive essay "The Children of Saint-Simon" in his *Prophets of Paris,* 149–193, and Henry-René d'Allemagne, *Les Saint-Simoniens, 1827–1837* (Paris, 1930).

6. See the superbly annotated edition prepared by Celestin Bouglé and Elie Halèvy (Paris, 1924).

7. The following discussion of Fourier's relations with the Saint-Simonians owes much to the valuable work by Henri Louvancour, *De Henri Saint-Simon à Charles Fourier. Etude sur le socialisme romantique français de 1830* (Chartres, 1913).

8. See Fourier's manuscript comments on a review in *Le Constitutionnel,* September 19, 1820, of Saint-Simon's brochure *Considérations sur les mesures à prendre pour terminer la Révolution,* AN 10AS 1 (1) and cited in Louvancour, *De Saint-Simon à Fourier,* 91–92.

9. Fourier to Muiron, May 22, 1829, Pellarin, *Fourier,* 215–216.

10. Fourier to Muiron, May 22, 1829, Pellarin, *Fourier,* 215.

11. Fourier to Enfantin, May 21, 1829, Bibliothèque Nationale, Papiers Saint-Simoniens (Don Alfred Pereire), Nouvelles Acquisitions Françaises 24614 (ff. 313–320). Henceforth this collection will be identified by the abbreviation BN NAF.

12. Enfantin to Fourier, May 22, 1829, AN 10AS 25 (3bis). Apparently more than a month passed before Enfantin actually sent this letter. There is a second letter from Enfantin to Fourier dated June 29, 1829 (AN 10AS 25 [3bis]), in which Enfantin explains that he was "prevented by numerous occupations" from finishing his first letter. Enfantin also makes the following observation: "I do not expect that this correspondence between us will yield fruit if the books we have exchanged fail to do so by themselves. It seems to me that we are both too accustomed to seeking out and to handling abstract ideas to make discussion valuable if the books do not themselves suffice."

13. Fourier to Enfantin, cited without date in Louvancour, *De Saint-Simon à Fourier,* 100–101. I have been unable to locate the original letter. The citations and summary above are taken from Louvancour.

14. Enfantin to Fourier, n.d., copy, Bibliothèque de l'Arsenal, Fonds Enfantin, Ms. 7668, #76, published in Pellarin, *Fourier* (5th ed.), 197–204.

15. Fourier to Muiron, cited in Louvancour, *De Saint-Simon à Fourier,* 103n.

16. Fourier to Muiron, June 5, 1829, Pellarin, *Fourier,* 216.

17. Fourier to Muiron, August 30, 1830, Pellarin, *Fourier,* 112.

18. *Le Mercure de France au dix-neuvième siècle,* XXXI (February 1831), 430: "On Saturday the second session of the preaching of Fourrierism [*sic*] was suddenly interrupted by the Saint-Simonian sabbath going on one floor below. Forty-seven, rue de Grenelle has become a real religious Babel."

19. Pellarin, *Fourier,* 112.

20. Fourier to Muiron, July 18, 1831, Pellarin, *Fourier,* 243.

21. *Le Globe,* June 27, 1831; Lambert, "Enseignement sur Fourier," Bibliothèque de l'Arsenal, Fonds Enfantin, Ms. 7803.

22. Muiron quoted in Pellarin, *Fourier,* 242–244; Abel Transon in *La Revue encyclopédique* (1832), 291n, cited in Louvancour, *De Saint-Simon à Fourier,* 126–127.

23. Fourier to Muiron, July 18, Pellarin, *Fourier,* 242.

24. *Le Globe,* VII, October 19, 1831.

25. *Le Globe,* VII, October 19, 1831.

26. See Abel Transon to Enfantin, January 1832, BN NAF 24611 (f. 278): "This letter was inserted with your knowledge and with the formal intention of crushing Fourier by ridicule."

27. Jules Lechevalier, *Cinq leçons sur l'art d'associer* (Paris, 1832), 133.

28. See Fourier's seven-page draft of a letter to the editors of *Le Globe,* October 2, 1831, AN 10AS 20 (11).

29. Fourier to Muiron, November 10, 1831, Pellarin, *Fourier,* 221.

30. On the "conversions" of Jules Lechevalier and Abel Transon to Fourierism and on their contributions to the development of a Fourierist movement, see Louvancour, *De Saint-Simon à Fourier,* 253–310; Charles Pellarin, *Notice sur Jules Lechevalier et Abel Transon* (Paris, 1877); and Jules Lechevalier, *Etudes sur la science sociale* (Paris, 1834), 18–23. Louvancour's study has been particularly helpful to me in the writing of this section.

31. Lechevalier, *Etudes sur la science sociale,* 21; *Le Globe,* July 25, 1831; Lechevalier to Fourier, January 16, 1832, AN 10AS 25 (3bis).

32. Considerant to Clarisse Vigoureux, November 13, 1831, AN 10AS 28 (7).

33. Considerant to Fourier, January 5, 1832, AN 10AS 25 (3bis).

34. *Religion Saint-Simonienne. Réunion générale de la Famille. Séance des 19 et 21 novembre, 1831* (Paris, 1832), cited in Manuel, *Prophets of Paris,* 149.

35. Jules Lechevalier, *Aux Saint-Simoniens. Lettre sur la division survenue dans l'association saint-simonienne* (December 20, 1831), 56.

36. Lechevalier to Fourier, January 16, 1832, AN 10AS 25 (3bis).

37. Fourier to Lechevalier, January 20, 1832, Houghton Library, Harvard University.

38. Transon to Enfantin (January 1832), BN NAF 24611 (ff. 278–279).

39. Gabet to Fourier, February 11, 1832, AN 10AS 25 (3); Devoluet to Olivier, February 21, 1832, Bibliothèque de l'Arsenal, Fonds Enfantin, Ms. 7609.

40. *Simple Ecrit d'Abel Transon aux Saint-Simoniens* (Paris, 1832), 2–3.

41. Louvancour, *De Saint-Simon à Fourier,* 301.

42. Lechevalier, *Etudes sur la science sociale,* 23.

43. Lechevalier to Fourier, January 28, 1832, AN 10AS 39 (9).

44. Lechevalier to Fourier, February 3, 1832, AN 10AS 39 (9).

45. Lechevalier, *Cinq leçons sur l'art d'associer,* 132–133.

46. The *Cinq leçons* were reprinted in 1834 in Lechevalier's *Etudes sur la science sociale,* 125–410.

47. Muiron to Clarisse Vigoureux, March 1 and 10, 1832, AN 10AS 40 (5); *L'Impartial,* III, 10 (March 11, 1832).

48. Pellarin, *Fourier,* 114; Eugénie Niboyet to Lechevalier, July 16, 1832, AN 10AS 41 (1); Imbert to Lechevalier, August 16, 1832, AN 10AS 39 (3).

49. Jullien to Lechevalier, June 18, 1832, AN 10AS 39 (3).

50. Pierre-Jean Béranger, *Chansons de P.-J. Béranger: 1815–1834,* Edition Elzévirienne (Paris, 1863), 560. Note to "Les Fous."

CHAPTER 22

1. Considerant to Clarisse Vigoureux, February 24, 1832, AN 10AS 28 (7); Muiron to Clarisse Vigoureux, March 1, 1832, AN 10AS 40 (5); Gabet to Fourier, February 11, 1832, AN 10AS 25 (3); Fourier to Muiron, February 17, 1832, cited in Muiron to Clarisse Vigoureux, March 10, 1832, AN 10AS 40 (5).

2. In addition to Transon's expositions of Fourier's thought in the *Revue encyclopédique,* see especially the long and sympathetic article on Fourier by the young Bisontine writer Xavier Marmier in *La France littéraire* (May 1832), II, 332–356.

3. On the appeal of Fourierism to dissident Saint-Simonians see Louvancour, *De Saint-Simon à Fourier,* 214–252.

4. OC VI, 485; Fourier to Muiron, October 26, 1831, Pellarin, *Fourier,* 221.

5. Letters of Amédée Pichot to Paul Lacroix, 1829–1830. Bibliothèque de l'Arsenal, Ms. 9623. Fonds Lacroix #2600.

6. Considerant to Fourier, January 5, 1832, AN 10AS 25 (3bis).

7. Muiron to Clarisse Vigoureux, March 27, 1832, AN 10AS 40 (5).

8. See list in Fourier's hand entitled "Actionnaires propag[ation]," AN 10AS 19 (2). The banker, who contributed three thousand francs, was a Monsieur de Birague, a representative of the English banking house of R. R. Hunter.

9. On September 7, 1832, beginning with the fifteenth number of the journal, its title was changed to *La Réforme industrielle ou le Phalanstère. Journal proposant la fondation d'une Phalange, réunion de 1100 personnes associées en travaux de culture, fabrique, et ménage.* To avoid confusion it will be referred to throughout this chapter as *Le Phalanstère.*

10. *Le Phalanstère,* undated prospectus.

11. *Le Phalanstère,* I, 1 (June 1, 1832), 2.

12. *Le Phalanstère,* I, 6 (July 5, 1832), 55.

13. Lemoyne to Pellarin, June 22, 1833, AN 10AS 39 (10); Bertin to Lechevalier, July 9, 1832, AN 10AS 36 (4); Pinet to the editor of *Le Phalanstère,* July 4, 1832, AN 10AS 38 (6); Lanet to Lechevalier, June 22, 1832, AN 10AS 39 (7).

14. Lemoyne to Transon, March 16, 1833, AN 10AS 39 (10).

15. Gerardin to Lechevalier, July 28, 1832, AN 10AS 38 (8); Lemoyne to Transon, July 16, 1832, AN 10AS 39 (10).

16. Anonymous letter signed J. . . to Fourier, July 24, 1833, AN 10AS 40 (5).

17. Lemoyne to Pellarin, April 1833, AN 10AS 39 (10).

18. See Fourier's comments on journalism in the letters reprinted in Pellarin, *Fourier,* 231–237.

19. *Le Phalanstère,* I, 4 (August 9, 1832), 89.

20. Fourier to Muiron, May 9, 1830, Pellarin, *Fourier,* 233.

21. Pellarin, *Fourier,* 121; Lemoyne to Transon, July 3, 1832, AN 10AS 39 (10).

22. Considerant to Gréa, October 10, 1833, AN 10AS 28 (7).

23. *Le Phalanstère,* I, 1 (June 1, 1832), 7.

24. *Le Phalanstère,* I, 8 (July 19, 1832), 69.

25. *Le Phalanstère,* I, 10 (August 2, 1832), 81.

26. These letters are *not* cited in Pellarin's biography. But there are echoes of them in Muiron's side of the correspondence with Fourier, which has been preserved. The above phrase is quoted in Muiron to Fourier, June 29, 1830, AN 10AS 40 (5). In a subsequent letter to Clarisse Vigoureux, Muiron identifies articles by Guillemon and Constantin Pecqueur as the particular objects of Fourier's wrath. Pecqueur's name is worth noting, since he was in fact one of the most gifted of Fourier's disciples and was subsequently to become a major socialist thinker in his own right.

27. *Le Phalanstère,* I, 15 (September 7, 1832), 132.

28. Quoted in Muiron to Clarisse Vigoureux, June 6, 1832, AN 10AS 40 (5).

29. Lechevalier to Clarisse Vigoureux, August 20, 1832, AN 10AS 39 (9).

30. Lechevalier to Clarisse Vigoureux, September 29, 1832, AN 10AS 39 (9).

31. See the "Compte de M. Lamorinière" drawn up by Fourier, July 31 [1832], AN 10AS 19 (2).

32. Honoré de Balzac, "Lettre sur Paris," October 9, 1830, in *Oeuvres Diverses* (Paris: Louis Conard, 1938), II, 74.

33. Considerant to Gréa, October 10, 1833, AN 10AS 28 (7).

34. Muiron to Clarisse Vigoureux, February 27, 1834, AN 10AS 40 (5).

35. Albert Brisbane, "Memoir of Charles Fourier," in *A Concise Exposition of the Doctrine of Association,* 6th ed. (New York, 1843), 78–79.

36. Pierre Joigneaux, *Souvenirs historiques* (Paris, n.d.), I, 22–24.

37. Fanny Schmalzigang to Lechevalier, July 25, 1832, AN 10AS 41 (13).

38. Fourier to Muiron, February 17, 1832, quoted in Muiron to Clarisse Vigoureux, March 10, 1832, AN 10AS 40 (5).

39. Fourier quoted in Muiron to Clarisse Vigoureux, April 15, 1832, AN 10AS 40 (5).

40. Considerant to Clarisse Vigoureux, November 23, 1832, AN 10AS 28 (7).

41. Clarisse Vigoureux to Fourier, December 3, 1832, AN 10AS 25 (3bis).

42. All the citations in this paragraph are from an unsigned nine-page memorandum in Abel Transon's hand on the aims and policies of the journal. AN 10AS 33 (10).

43. *Le Phalanstère,* I, 31 (December 27, 1832), 268. The editors went on to identify a number of questions of "la politique industrielle" that they proposed to treat in forthcoming issues. These included taxation, fiscal policy, the expropriation of private property, communal organization, public education, public health, and architecture.

44. *Le Phalanstère,* I, 31 (December 27, 1832), 267.

45. See *Le National* (January 12 and 27, 1833) and AN 10AS 25 (8): bill for the insertion of advertisements. Fourier's disciples spent close to eight hundred

francs on these advertisements. See accounts for the *Phalanstère* in AN 10AS 19 (2).

46. Transon to Fourier, undated note of five pages, AN 10AS 42 (4).

47. Transon to Fourier, undated note of five pages, AN 10AS 42 (4).

48. "Les Alliés dangereux," *Le Phalanstère*, II, 13 (March 29, 1833), 149; "Sur un éloge de la théocratie et de la main-morte," *Le Phalanstère*, II, 15 (April 12, 1833), 176–177; "Les Disciples aventureux," *Le Phalanstère*, II, 27 (July 5, 1833), 314.

49. *Le Phalanstère*, II, 15 (March 29, 1833), 148.

50. Bucellati to Fourier, July 10, 1833, AN 10AS 36 (12).

51. J. . . to Fourier, July 24, 1833, AN 10AS 40 (5).

52. Considerant to Clarisse Vigoureux, August 15, 1833, AN 10AS 28 (7).

53. See Baudet-Dulary to Fourier (?), August 6, 1833, AN 10AS 36 (3).

54. Lechevalier himself had already begun to publish in *Europe littéraire*. In 1834 he was to found a journal of his own, the *Revue du progrès social*. By the end of 1834 he had drifted away from Fourierism. On this phase of his career as an independent journalist see Herbert J. Hunt, *Le Socialisme et le romantisme en France* (Oxford, 1935), 116–130.

55. *Le Phalanstère*, II, 29 (July 19, 1833), 334.

56. *Le Phalanstère*, II, 33 (August 16, 1833), 372.

57. Considerant to Gréa, October 10, 1833, AN 10AS 28 (7).

58. *Le Phalanstère*, I, 11 (August 9, 1832), 97.

59. Charles Pellarin, *Souvenirs anecdotiques* (Paris, 1868), 152.

60. *Le Phalanstère*, I, 22 (October 25, 1832), 188.

61. Article from the *Vigilant de Seine-et-Oise*, cited in *Le Phalanstère*, I, 18 (September 27, 1832), 159.

62. This is a general impression based on a study of the correspondence received by the editors of the *Phalanstère* and on the information contained in several partial lists of the journal's subscribers, AN 10AS 19 (1). See also Bourgin, *Fourier*, 453.

63. The influence of Fourierist (and Saint-Simonian) ideas among the *canuts* at Lyon is touched upon in the standard works on the history of the Lyon silk industry in the first half of the nineteenth century (notably Rude and Bezucha). Although the subject has not yet been explored in any depth, further information may be found in two works: Maximilien Buffenoir, "Le Fouriérisme à Lyon (1832–1848)," *Revue d'histoire de Lyon*, XII, 6 (November–December 1913), 444–445; and especially Jean Gaumont's suggestive *Le Commerce Véridique et Social (1835–1838) et son fondateur Michel Derrion* (Amiens, 1935).

CHAPTER 23

1. This chapter is based largely on the "Bulletins sur la Colonie sociétaire," which appeared in the *Phalanstère* in 1832 and 1833 and on the following dossiers in the Archives de l'Ecole Sociétaire: AN 10AS 19 (1) and (2); 10AS 25

(11); and 10AS 31 (1). See also AN F^{12} 6809. The published literature on the Fourierist experiment at Condé is scant, but see Jules Prudhommeaux, Manuscript on the Colonie sociétaire (1913), published in Henri Desroche, *La Société festive*, 220–235; Gabriel Vauthier, "Un essai de Phalanstère à Condé-sur-Vesgre," *La Révolution de 1848*, XXI (February 1925), 327–344, and XXII (April 1925), 417–432; and Jules Duval, "Le Ménage sociétaire de Condé-sur-Vesgre," *Annuaire de l'Association pour 1868*, 141–158. I wish to thank the members of the modern Colonie sociétaire de Condé-sur-Vesgre, and especially Madame Jules Castier and Marie-Hélène Castier, for their kindness and warm hospitality during the weekend I spent with them in April 1964.

2. Didion to Transon, July 2, 1832, AN 10AS 37 (9). See also Thomas to Transon, July 28, 1832, AN 10AS 42 (1).

3. "Statuts de la Société de Fondation," *Le Phalanstère*, I, 1 (June 1, 1832), 2.

4. *Le Phalanstère*, I, 1 (June 1, 1832), 14 (articles 37 and 33).

5. "Programme de la Fondation Proposée," *Le Phalanstère*, I, 1 (June 1, 1832), 7–12.

6. *Le Phalanstère*, I, 1 (June 1, 1832), 10.

7. *Le Phalanstère*, I, 1 (June 1, 1832), 10.

8. Laîsné de Villevêque to Fourier, August 11, 1832, AN 10AS 25 (3).

9. *Le Phalanstère*, I, 8 (July 19, 1832), 72.

10. *Le Phalanstère*, I, 11 (August 9, 1832), 92.

11. Notes in Fourier's hand, AN 10AS 19 (15).

12. *Le Phalanstère*, I, 9 (July 26, 1832), 73–75.

13. *Le Phalanstère*, I, 10 (August 2, 1832), 81.

14. On Joseph Devay see Guy Frambourg, *Un Philanthrope et démocrate nantais: le docteur Guépin, 1805–1873* (Nantes, 1964), 14–15, 71–73.

15. Devay to Lechevalier (?), August 22, 1833, AN 10AS 19 (1).

16. Lechevalier to Clarisse Vigoureux, September 29 [1832], AN 10AS 39 (9).

17. *Le Phalanstère*, I, 25 (November 15, 1832), 208.

18. *Le Phalanstère*, I, 26 (November 22, 1832), 220.

19. "Fondation de la Colonie sociétaire. Projet d'acte de société," Article 3, *Le Phalanstère*, I, 26 (November 22, 1832), 218. Italics mine.

20. *Le Phalanstère*, I, 26 (November 22, 1832), 217.

21. Considerant to Clarisse Vigoureux, November 23, 1832, AN 10AS 28 (7).

22. *Le Phalanstère*, I, 29 (December 13, 1832), 245, and II, 1 (January 4, 1833), 3.

23. Fourier to Muiron, January 1833, Pellarin, *Fourier*, 244.

24. *Le Phalanstère*, I, 30 (December 20, 1832), 254.

25. *Le Phalanstère*, II, 12 (March 22, 1833), 143–144.

26. *Le Phalanstère*, II, 11 (March 15, 1833), 132.

27. Accounts for the Société de Fondation, AN 10AS 19 (2).

28. *Le Phalanstère*, II, 22 (May 31, 1833), 264.

29. "Acte de Société de la Colonie sociétaire de Condé-sur-Vesgre," *Le Phalanstère*, II, 24 (June 14, 1833), 277–280.

30. Fourier to Muiron, July 10, 1833, Pellarin, *Fourier,* 245.

31. Undated note by Fourier, probably a draft for a letter to Muiron, AN 10AS 31 (1).

32. Fourier to Muiron, March 9, 1833, Pellarin, *Fourier,* 244–245.

33. Fourier to Muiron, May 2, 1833, Pellarin, *Fourier,* 245.

34. Manuscript fragment from statement delivered by Fourier to shareholders of the Colonie sociétaire, September 22, 1833, AN 10AS 19 (1).

35. Pellarin, *Fourier,* 246. But see the letter from the disciple Maurize to Fourier, June 19, 1833, AN 10AS 40 (1): "The incompetence of this man is simply unimaginable. As for me, I would go so far as to believe that his mind is unhinged. As to his dedication, it is pure make-believe by which Monsieur Dulary has been fooled, because you don't dedicate yourself to something about which you don't understand a word."

36. Fourier to Muiron, July 10, 1833, Pellarin, *Fourier,* 245.

37. *Le Phalanstère,* II, 29 (July 19, 1833), 333.

38. Fugère to Considerant, May 27, 1836, AN 10AS 38 (7).

39. Considerant to Pellarin, July 18, 1833, AN 10AS 28 (7).

40. Vinçard *ainé, Mémoires épisodiques d'un vieux chansonnier saint-simonien* (Paris, 1878), 158–160.

41. Baudet-Dulary, Report to the General Assembly of the Colonie sociétaire de Condé-sur-Vesgre, September 22, 1833, *Le Phalanstère,* II, 36 (November 16, 1833), 396.

42. *Le Phalanstère,* II, 33 (August 16, 1833), 372.

43. Considerant to Clarisse Vigoureux, August 15, 1833, AN 10AS 28 (7).

44. Lechevalier to Fourier, August 30, 1833, AN 10AS 39 (9).

45. See "La Théorie familière ou l'Ecole d'éclosion des instincts, appliqués à tous genres de travaux et d'études. Plan d'essai sur 500 enfans de 5 à 12 ans," *Le Phalanstère,* II, 26 (June 28, 1833), 301–306, and similar articles in *Le Phalanstère,* II, 29 (July 19, 1833), 334–338; II, 30 (July 26, 1833), 346–348; II, 31 (August 2, 1833), 349–352.

46. *Le Phalanstère,* II, 36 (November 16, 1833), 396.

47. A portion of what appears to be the draft of Fourier's statement to the shareholders has survived in AN 10AS 19 (1).

48. See Considerant to Fourier, August 17, 1833, and August 31, 1833, AN 10AS 28 (7) and *Le Phalanstère,* II, 36 (December 16, 1833), 396.

49. *Le Phalanstère,* II, 36 (December 16, 1833), 396.

50. Baudet-Dulary to shareholders in the Colonie sociétaire, April 15, 1836, AN 10AS 31 (1).

51. OC IX, 725.

CHAPTER 24

1. Considerant to Gréa, October 10, 1833, AN 10AS 28 (7).

2. Considerant to Gréa, October 10, 1833, AN 10AS 28 (7).

3. Bourgin, *Victor Considerant*, 8.

4. Pellarin, *Fourier*, 127.

5. On these lectures see Muiron to Clarisse Vigoureux, January 31, 1834, AN 10AS 40 (5); Monternault to Fourier, two undated letters, AN 10AS 25 (3); Philippe Breton to Considerant, November 7, 1837, AN 10AS 36 (10).

6. Fourier to Muiron, January 4, 1834, Pellarin, *Fourier*, 118.

7. Pellarin, *Fourier*, 119.

8. Pellarin, *Fourier*, 141–145.

9. "La théorie familière, ou l'école d'éclosion des instincts, appliqués à tous genres de travaux et d'études. Plan d'essai sur 500 enfants de 5 à 12 ans," *Le Phalanstère*, II, 26 (June 28, 1833); "Détails sur l'épreuve minime, en travaux à courtes seances, appliquée à 160 enfants de 3 à 12 ans," *Le Phalanstère*, II, 30 and 31 (July 26 and August 2, 1833).

10. Pellarin, *Fourier*, 127.

11. "Plan du 3ᵉ volume," AN 10AS 20 (4); Considerant to Gréa, October 10, 1833, AN 10AS 28 (7).

12. Fourier to Albert Brisbane, May 22, 1834, Houghton Library, Harvard University.

13. Muiron to Clarisse Vigoureux, October 25, 1834, AN 10AS 40 (5).

14. Fourier to the minister of the interior, draft [May 1834], AN 10AS 13 (9). For other drafts of this letter see AN 10AS 16 (24) and 10AS 16 (25).

15. Davies J. Robertson to Fourier, November 9, 1834, AN 10AS 25 (9).

16. OC VIII, 430.

17. OC VIII, 420, 169, 290, 267–268.

18. OC VIII, 281, 162–166, 439–445, 247–304.

19. Davies J. Robertson to Fourier, November 9, 1834, AN 10AS 25 (9).

20. List of "emplois non payables," AN 10AS 12 (7).

21. Muiron to Clarisse Vigoureux, December 27, 1835, AN 10AS 40 (5).

22. OC IX, 659–660, 785, 781, 506.

23. Michel Butor, "Preface" to *Le Nouveau monde industriel* (Paris, 1973), 20–21.

24. OC II, 5; Ion Ghica, *Opere*, I, 239, cited in Zil'berfarb, *Sotsial'naia filosofiia*, 311.

25. The following remarks on early Romanian Fourierism are based primarily on Gromoslav Mladenatz, "L'Influence de Charles Fourier sur les économistes roumains," *Archives internationales de la sociologie de la coopération et du développement*, 21 (January–June 1967), 15–46; Zil'berfarb, *Sotsial'naia filosofiia*, 309–315; and the letters of Teodor Diamant to Fourier in AN 10AS 25 (3).

26. Teodor Diamant, *Aux amis de la Liberté, de la Justice et de l'Ordre. Sur un moyen de faire cesser le débat entre ceux qui ont et ceux qui n'ont pas, sans prendre à ceux qui ont* (Paris, April 25, 1834).

27. Ion Ghica, *Scrisori catre V. Alecsandri* (Bucharest, 1887), 325, in Mladenatz, "L'Influence de Charles Fourier," 18.

28. Nicholas Cretulescu, "Amintiri istorice," *Ateneul romin*, 8 (1894), 590, cited in Mladenatz, "L'Influence de Charles Fourier," 25. Diamant's article appeared in *Curierul rominesc* (The Romanian courier), June 7, 1834.

29. Teodor Diamant to Fourier, Bucharest, June 24, 1834 (old style), AN 10AS 25 (3).

30. Cretulescu, "Amintiri istorice," 590–591, cited in Mladenatz, "L'Influence de Charles Fourier," 29.

31. Diamant to Fourier, Bucharest, June 3/15, 1836, AN 10AS 25 (3), refers to a letter from Fourier of October 24, 1835: "I have read the advice you give me to make the experiment on three hundred boys and girls from three to thirteen years old. . . . I will follow your advice to the letter, Monsieur, because I too believe that it is the most economical approach. We can take the majority of children as boarders if this polytechnical school is organized near Bucharest."

32. Mladenatz, "L'Influence de Charles Fourier," 28. There were also to be thirty-six "agronomes associés étrangers" not all of whom lived on the premises. The most readily accessible account of this experiment in French, that contained in Henri Desroche, *La Société festive*, 200–202, errs both in attributing to it a membership of four hundred families and in making Diamant its ("meticulous and overworked") accountant.

33. There is some conflict in the sources concerning the manner in which the community was disbanded. Some accounts suggest that it was actually put to siege by the local militia. See Mladenatz, "L'Influence de Charles Fourier," 29, and Zil'berfarb, *Sotsial'naia filosofiia*, 313–314.

34. AN 10AS 20 (3).

35. Much the best guide to Fourierism as an international movement is the comprehensive survey in Zil'berfarb, *Sotsial'naia filosofiia*, 252–382. The brief remarks on international Fourierism that follow refer only to the period preceding Fourier's death.

36. For German and Spanish Fourierism see Zil'berfarb, *Sotsial'naia filosofiia*, 257–270, 295–296. A résumé of the remarkable career of Joaquin Abreu (1782–1851) may be found in the *Almanach phalanstérien pour 1852* (Paris, 1852), 175–176.

37. Giuseppe Mazzini, "De quelques doctrines sociales. Ecole fouriériste," *La Jeune Suisse* (April 30, May 18 and 25, June 8, 1836). On Italian Fourierism see Zil'berfarb, *Sotsial'naia filosofiia*, 272–295; Carlo Francovich, *Idee sociali e organizzazione operaia nella prima meta dell' 800 (1815–1847)* (Milan-Rome, 1959), 83–87, 111–114; and Franco Della Peruta, "Note e documenti per la storia delle idei sociali in Italia 1830–1849," *Annali, Istituto Giangiacomo Feltrinelli*, III (1960), 547–560.

38. N. P. Ogarev, *Izbrannie proizvedeniia*, II (Moscow, 1956), 252. On early Russian Fourierism see Zil'berfarb, *Sotsial'naia filosofiia*, 330–341, and O. V. Orlik, *Peredovaia Rossiia i revoliutsionnaia Frantsiia* (Moscow, 1973), 171–203.

39. Décheneaux to Fourier, Sorèze, June 16, 1836, AN 10AS 19 (2).

40. Constantin Pecqueur, "Analyse du système d'association de M. Charles Fourier," *La Presse*, I, 32 and 33 (August 6 and 7, 1836); Louis Reybaud, "Fourier," *Revue des deux mondes*, 4ᵉ série XII (November 15, 1837), 455–487, reprinted in Reybaud's *Etudes sur les réformateurs contemporains ou socialistes modernes. Saint-Simon, Charles Fourier, Robert Owen*, 2d ed. (Paris, 1841), 139–204.

41. George Sand, "Lettres d'un voyageur," *Revue des deux mondes*, 4ᵉ série, VIII (November 15, 1836), 429–432; Sainte-Beuve, "Chronique littéraire," *Revue des deux mondes*, 2ᵉ série, I (February 15, 1833), 432–433, reprinted in Sainte-Beuve, *Oeuvres* (Paris: Pléiade, 1949), I, 499–501.

42. Théophile Gautier, *La Préface de Mademoiselle de Maupin*, Edition critique par Georges Matoré (Paris: Droz, 1946), 36–38.

43. H. L. Bulwer, *The Monarchy of the Middle Classes, or France, Social, Literary, Political*, second series (Paris, 1836), 97.

44. Honoré de Balzac, *Monographie de la presse parisienne* (Paris: Pauvert, 1965), 168–169.

45. Wladimir Gagneur, letter in *L'Impartial*, VIII, 58 (July 20, 1836).

46. For Fourier's notes on George Sand see AN 10AS 12 (7) and OC IX, 830–839. His response to Louis Reybaud is headed "Cabinet de lecture, 29 decembre 1833: Louis Reybaud" and must therefore refer to an earlier article than the one by Reybaud cited above. See AN 10AS 12 (4).

47. Notes scrawled on the back of a funeral notice dated January 1, 1837, AN 10AS 24 (1).

48. Fourier to the editor of the *Gazette de France*, drafts dated December, 1835, AN 10AS 19 (3) and 10AS 20 (7). In this letter, which was never published, Fourier was responding to articles in the *Gazette de France*, December 18 and 19, 1835, and *L'Univers religieux*, December 12 and 24, 1835.

49. Considerant to Gréa, October 10, 1833, AN 10AS 28 (7), and Considerant, *Le Socialisme devant le vieux monde* (Paris, 1849), 123.

50. Pellarin, *Fourier*, 120–121.

51. Louise Courvoisier cited in Pellarin, *Fourier*, 267.

52. Redelia Brisbane (ed.), *Albert Brisbane: A Mental Biography* (Boston, 1893), 186.

53. Pellarin, *Fourier*, 119–120.

54. Benjamin Appert, *Dix ans à la cour du roi Louis Philippe* (Paris, 1846), III, 12. See also II, 313, and III, 108. In his time Benjamin Appert was well known as a prison reformer, and it is in that role that he makes his way into the opening pages of Stendhal's *Le Rouge et le noir*.

55. Louise Courvoisier, letter to the editor of *La Phalange*, published July 1, 1838, and reprinted in Pellarin, *Fourier*, 264–268.

56. Evelyn Sullerot, *Histoire de la presse féminine en France, des origines à 1848* (Paris, 1966), 143–163. On the crucial role of this journal in the birth of an autonomous women's movement in France see also Claire Moses, "Saint-Simonian Men / Saint-Simonian Women: The Transformation of Feminist Thought in 1830s France," *Journal of Modern History*, 54 (June 1982), 240–267.

57. Désirée Veret, veuve Gay, to Considerant, October 9, 1890, AN 10AS 42 (8).

58. Désirée Veret to Fourier, August 14, 1833, AN 10AS 42 (8). This letter is more fully cited in Lehouck, *Vie de Fourier*, 224–226.

59. AN 10AS 3 (4), p. 46.

60. Fourier did contribute five articles to *La Phalange*, but several were actually manuscripts dating from a much earlier period.

61. Pellarin, *Fourier,* 163.

62. Heinrich Heine, *Lutezia,* Paris letter of June 15, 1843, in *Werke* (Frankfurt am Main: Insel Verlag, 1968), III, 560.

63. Pellarin, *Fourier,* 159.

64. Muiron to Clarisse Vigoureux, March 15, 1836, AN 10AS 40 (5).

65. Fourier to Charles Harel, January 29, 1837, reproduced in Harel, *Ménage sociétaire* (Paris, 1839), facing p. vii. Hugh Doherty, *False Association and Its Remedy . . . to Which Is Prefixed a Memoir of Fourier* (London, 1841), 18.

66. Doherty, *False Association,* 15.

67. Tamisier, letter of July 12, 1837, published in *Correspondance harmonienne,* August 15, 1837.

68. For this paragraph see Jacques Gans, "Robert Owen à Paris en 1837," *Le Mouvement social,* 41 (October–December 1962), 35–45. The encounter of Fourier and Owen is also mentioned in Désirée Veret to Considerant, October 9, 1890, AN 10AS 42 (8).

69. The best account of this episode is to be found in Poulat, "Sur deux textes manuscrits de Fourier," in Henri Desroche et al., *Etudes sur la tradition française de l'association ouvrière* (Paris, 1956), 5–19.

70. *Aux Phalanstériens,* 27 ("Comte rendu du 31 juillet").

71. AN 10AS 22 (1), published in full in Poulat, "Sur deux textes manuscrits de Fourier," in Desroche et al., *Etudes sur la tradition française de l'association ouvrière,* 14–15. The manuscript of this declaration does not seem to be in Fourier's handwriting. Nor is it signed and dated. Although some of the language is clearly Fourier's and the content is perfectly consistent with positions taken by Fourier elsewhere, it is not implausible to suppose that at least a part of this statement may have been dictated *to* Fourier by Considerant.

72. Dr. Léon Simon, "Rapport sur la maladie de M. Fourier," in Pellarin, *Fourier,* 285–291; Doherty, *False Association,* 18.

EPILOGUE

1. Pellarin, *Fourier,* 164, 277–280. *La Phalange,* 2d series, I, 34 (October 1837), cols. 1075–1078. Jean Czynski, *Notice biographique sur Charles Fourier,* 2d ed. (Paris, 1841).

2. On the difference in sensibility between Fourier and the disciples see especially the twenty-page letter of Considerant to Gréa, October 10, 1833, AN 10AS 28 (7).

3. Ralph Waldo Emerson, *Journals* (March–June 1845), in Joel Porte (ed.), *Emerson in His Journals* (Cambridge, Mass., 1982), 337; Nathaniel Hawthorne, *The Blithedale Romance* (New York, Norton, 1978), 50; Julian Hawthorne, *Nathaniel Hawthorne and His Wife: A Biography,* 2 vols. (Boston, 1884), I, 268–269.

4. F. M. Dostoevsky, *The Diary of a Writer,* trans. by Boris Brasol, 2 vols. (New York, 1949), I, 7.

BIBLIOGRAPHY

This Bibliography is limited to works by and about Charles Fourier. The listing of works by Fourier is as complete as I have been able to make it. The listing of secondary sources is highly selective and emphasizes recent and scholarly works that I have found valuable. The Bibliography does not include general works on French history or the history of ideas. Works on local history that have been useful to me have been cited at appropriate points in the notes. Works dealing primarily with the Fourierist movement are not listed here unless they bear directly on topics or issues considered in this book. Good general bibliographies on the Fourierist movement may be found in Giuseppe Del Bo, *Charles Fourier e la Scuola Societaria (1801–1922). Saggio Bibliografico* (Milan, 1957), and in I. I. Zil'berfarb, *Sotsial'naia filosofiia Sharlia Fur'e* (Moscow, 1964), 460–532. Del Bo's study is thorough in its descriptions and summarizes the contents of most of the Fourierist periodicals. But it is limited to the holdings of the Feltrinelli Institute of Milan and does not include works published after 1922. Zil'berfarb's listing runs to several thousand works in a dozen languages. The titles of non-Russian works are given in Roman characters.

PRIMARY SOURCES

Manuscripts

Archives de l'Ecole Sociétaire (Archives Nationales 10AS)

This is the essential manuscript source for the study of both Fourier and the Fourierist movement. It is divided into two sections. The "fonds Considerant" (10AS 26 to 10AS 42) includes the papers of Victor Considerant as well as a collection of several thousand letters exchanged by the disciples from the 1820s until the end of the nineteenth century. The principal section (10AS 1 to 10AS 25) consists of manuscripts and personal papers left by Fourier at the time of his death. It includes 98 manuscript cahiers of roughly one hundred closely written pages each, 331 separate pieces or folders, twenty notebooks, and several hundred letters addressed to Fourier. (There are very few letters written by Fourier himself. His important correspondence with Just Muiron originally belonged to this collection, but it was lost or stolen during the nineteenth century.)

Fragmentary and sometimes bowdlerized excerpts from Fourier's manuscripts were published by his disciples during the 1840s and 1850s. But the sheer bulk—and confusion—of the collection discouraged scholars from making much use of it until the completion of an initial inventory by Edith Thomas in 1949 and the subsequent publication of Emile Poulat's admirable *Les Cahiers manuscrits de Fourier. Etude historique et inventaire raisonné* (Paris, 1957). Although devoted only to the 98 cahiers (10AS 1 to 10AS 11), this work constitutes an indispensable *instrument de travail*.

Fourier Papers

10AS 1 to 10AS 8: sixty-four multicolored cahiers dating primarily from 1817 to 1822 and including drafts of Fourier's unpublished *Grand Traité* and of the "partial treatise" that did appear in 1822 under the title *Traité de l'association domestique-agricole*. See Poulat, *Cahiers manuscrits*, 93–181.

10AS 8 to 10AS 11: thirty-four cahiers dating from 1824 to 1830 and mainly consisting of drafts of the *Nouveau monde industriel*. See Poulat, *Cahiers manuscrits*, 183–222.

10AS 12 to 10AS 21: 311 pieces and folders (*ancienne côte supplémentaire*) including: (1) a number of Fourier's earliest manuscripts; (2) numerous drafts of letters by Fourier; (3) draft introductions to the *Grand Traité* and fragments from a shorter treatise on which Fourier worked in 1816; (4) numerous manuscripts dating from the years 1830–1837 (especially 10AS 19 to 10AS 21); corrected proofs of *La Fausse industrie*.

10AS 22: twenty personal notebooks.

10AS 23 and 10AS 24: twenty folders of miscellaneous papers, verse, and reading notes.

10AS 25: letters addressed to Fourier and personal documents.

"Fonds Considerant"

10AS 26 to 10AS 27: manuscripts of Considerant.

10AS 28: letters of Considerant.

10AS 29 to 10AS 33: letters and documents concerning the Fourierist movement.

10AS 34 to 10AS 35: photographs.

10AS 36 to 10AS 42: correspondence of the disciples, classified alphabetically.

[Bibliography]

Other Manuscript Holdings

Institutions and Public Archives

Archives du Département du Rhône (Lyon). Petition to the prefect of the Rhone on the brokerage monopoly, February 1812 (14 M: "Industrie et commerce: Agents de change et courtiers, 1808–1825").

Archives du Ministère des Affaires Etrangères (Paris). Letter to General Bertrand, June 14, 1814 (Mémoires et documents, Vol. 675, pièce 29).

Archives Nationales (Paris). Dossier on journal to be edited by Fourier and Martainville, 1800 (F^7 3452); "Lettre au Grand Juge" and police dossier, 1803 (F^7 3455); response to Fourier's memoir to the Ministry of the Interior on the organization of the Beaucaire Fair (F^{12} 1253); dossier on the trial Phalanstery of Condé-sur-Vesgre, 1833 (F^{12} 6809). The Fichier Charavay (carton 20) includes extracts from half a dozen letters by Fourier.

Bibliothèque de l'Arsenal (Paris). Much of the material in the Enfantin and d'Eichthal papers is of interest to the student of Fourierism. See especially copies of correspondence exchanged by Fourier and Enfantin (Ms. 7643 and Ms. 7668) and letters of Fourier to Madame Dupouy, 1831 (Ms. 15032, copy) and to Count Grégoire, 1823 (bound in F.E. Impr. 264).

Bibliothèque Nationale (Paris). In addition to a collection of letters addressed to Fourier's disciple Jaenger of Colmar (N.A.F. 22050), one letter from Fourier to Enfantin, May 21, 1829, accompanied by a long "Note sur l'invention des séries passionnées" (N.A.F. 24614).

Boston Public Library (Boston, Mass.). Letter of Fourier to the booksellers Treuttel and Wurtz, March 16, 1824 (Ch. N 6.36).

British Library (London). Fourier proof sheet with autograph corrections (Add. Mss. 33,230 f. 28).

Ecole Normale Supérieure (Paris). The very rich Archives Victor Considerant include some Fourier manuscript material and letters to Fourier from Considerant.

Feltrinelli Institute (Milan). Two manuscripts: "Notice sur la découverte des lois intégrales du mouvement," 64 pp.; "Préambule à la Fausse industrie," 4 pp.

Historical Society of Pennsylvania (Philadelphia). Letter of Fourier to Monsieur d'Epagny, April 24, 1834, on Francia's community in Paraguay.

Houghton Library, Harvard University (Cambridge, Mass.). Letters of Fourier to Jules Lechevalier, January 20, 1832, and to Albert Brisbane, May 22, 1834.

Institute of Marxism-Leninism (Moscow). Letter of Fourier to the editor of the *Courrier français*, July 6, 1820. Three draft articles, 1822–1833 (Fond. 471, Op. I, d. 7).

International Institute for Social History (Amsterdam). Letter of Fourier to Gabet on the Saint-Simonian schism, February 15, 1832.

Private Collections

Archives of the Colonie sociétaire de Condé-sur-Vesgre (Seine-et-Oise). Some Fourier memorabilia along with much material concerning the history of the
Fourierist communities at Condé.
Collection of Edmond Bomsel (Paris). Letters of Fourier to Baudet-Dulary, Ba-
ronne Vassal-Roger, and Madame Dupouy, 1832–1834. Memoir to the
baron de Férussac, 20 pp., March 21, 1829. Letter to the editor of the
Bibliothèque universelle, January 11, 1820, with three-page article entitled "In-
dication des cinq planètes inconnues."
Collection of E. G. Gobert (Aix-en-Provençe). Two letters of Fourier to Joseph
Devay, October 16, 1833, and October 26, 1835.

Fourier's Published Writings

Works Published during Fourier's Lifetime

Newspaper Articles

Journal de Lyon et du département du Rhône. Prospectus, 23 thermidor an VIII
(August 11, 1800), signed Martainville and "Fourrier." This journal was
never published.
Journal de Lyon et du Midi (1801–1802):
"Au Rédacteur du Journal de Lyon" (19 nivôse an X), 74–76. Signed
"Four. . ."
Anonymous articles possibly by Fourier:
"Théorie de l'égoisme" (5 nivôse an X), 21–23.
"De la Gaieté" (19 nivôse an X), 78–79.
"Conseils à un jeune homme par une femme" (3 and 5 ventôse an X), 254–
256, 262–263.
"Observations sur les faillites, addressés a la Commission chargée d'examiner
le projet de code du commerce (15 ventôse an X), 303–304.
Bulletin de Lyon. Articles signed "Fourrier" (1803–1804):
"Satire envoyée à M. A.J. . . , sur son Enigme, aux devins de laquelle il
promet deux prix, l'un de saucissons et l'autre de marrons; et sur une
réponse à cette Enigme, sous la signature de femme A.F. . ." (1 frimaire
an XII).
"Réplique à Clothilde D." (8 frimaire an XII).
"Ode à Madame A.F., reconnue" (11 frimaire an XII).
"Harmonie universelle" (11 frimaire an XII).
"Clôture des débats sur la satire F. Stances aux Lyonnaises sur la médiocrité
des champions qui ont pris leur défense" (15 frimaire an XII).
"Le ballon de Zambeccari qui fait 300 lieues d'un seul trait" (25 frimaire an
XII).

"Triumvirat continental, et paix perpétuelle sous trente ans" (25 frimaire an XII).

"A l'auteur de l'inventaire des plaisirs de Lyon" (20 nivôse an XII).

"Acceptation des lettres de change" (27 nivôse an XII).

Journal de Lyon. Nouvelles de la France et de l'étranger. Articles signed "Fourier" (1803):

"Sur les empires qui ont des vapeurs comme les jolies femmes" (2 nivôse an XII).

"A Monsieur Delyror" (5 nivôse an XII).

"Invitation aux échos" (7 nivôse an XII).

Bulletin de Lyon. Articles signed "X." (1805–1807):

"Stances à MM. D. et T., auteurs de deux épîtres en petit vers, l'une contre la constance, l'autre contre l'inconstance," (10 fructidor an XIII).

"Sur la décadence des grands théâtres de province" (December 20, 1806).

"A Monsieur H.T." (February 21, 1807).

"Les Plumes de Monsieur H.T." (May 27, 1807).

Journal de Lyon et du département du Rhône (1811):

"Réponse à l'article signé Philoharmonicos" (October 31, 1811).

Journal politique et littéraire du département du Rhône (1816):

"Sur les progrès de l'intempérie," I, 52 (July 11, 1816). Signed "C.F."

Journal des débats (1829):

Paid annonce of *Le Nouveau monde industriel* (May 2, 1829). Unsigned but undoubtedly written by Fourier.

L'Impartial, Feuille Politique, Commerciale et Littéraire de la Franche-Comté. This was a journal of the *juste-milieu* founded in 1829 by Fourier's disciple Just Muiron as a commercial venture and not primarily as an organ of Fourierist propaganda. The articles that Fourier published in it were unsigned. But the following anonymous articles (1829–1831) can be attributed to him on the basis of manuscripts and receipts included among his papers at the Archives Nationales:

"Guerre d'Orient," I, 22 (August 15, 1829).

"Politique extérieure," I, 27 (September 20, 1829).

"Théorie de la population," I, 43 (January 10, 1830).

"Urgence de rectifier la division territoriale de la France," I, 51 (March 7, 1830).

"Inconstance des saisons," II, 4 (April 18, 1830).

"Les Messageries. Cercle vicieux de la concurrence actuelle," II, 5 (April 25, 1830).

Letter "Au Rédacteur" on the destruction of the grove of Chamars, II, 7, (May 9, 1830).

Letter "Au Rédacteur" on the "intrigues" of the Dijonnais, II, 26 (August 29, 1830).

Untitled article on the conquest of Algeria, II, 29 (September 19, 1830).

"Civilisation," III, 18 (June 2, 1831).

"Du gouvernement à bon marché," III, 34 (July 24, 1831).

Mercure de France au dix-neuvième siècle (1830):
  "Dénouement des utopies anciennes et modernes," XXX, 51–66 (July 10, 1830). Signed "Ch. Ph."
  "Mnémonique géographique," XXXI, 400–412, 443–454 (November 13 and 27, 1830). Originally published as a brochure in 1824.
Le Globe. Journal de la religion saint-simonienne (1831):
  "Lettre au rédacteurs" (October 19, 1831).
La Réforme industrielle ou le Phalanstère (1832–1834). For a complete listing of the eighty-three articles that Fourier published in this, the first journal of the Ecole Sociétaire, see Bourgin, *Fourier*, 15–18.
La Phalange. Journal de la science sociale, 2ᵉ serie (1836–1837):
  "Remède aux divers esclavages," I, 161–169 (August 20, 1836).
  "La Chute de l'homme, ou le double mécanisme des passions," I, 317–323 (October 10, 1836).
  "Société primitive, dite Eden. Ses phases d'enfance, ses progrès, son déclin, sa caducité et sa chute," I, 417–421 (November 10, 1836).
  "Analyse de la chute de l'homme. Carrières et phases du pêché originel," I, 672–681 (February 1, 1837).
  "Introduction à la théorie des quatre mouvements" (written in 1818), I, 707–715 (February 10, 1837).

Books and Brochures

Sur les charlataneries commerciales. Lyon, 1807. The text of this sixteen-page pamphlet is known through its republication in *La Phalange,* 3d series, II (April 11, 1841), cols. 732–736 from "a copy that is probably unique."
Théorie des quatre mouvements et des destinées générales. Prospectus et annonce de la découverte. Leipzig [Lyon], 1808. (Anonymous).
Traité de l'association domestique-agricole. 2 vols. Paris and London: Bossange and Mongie, 1822.
Sommaires et annonce du Traité de l'association domestique-agricole. Paris and London: Bossange and Mongie, 1823.
Mnémonique géographique, ou méthode pour apprendre en peu de leçons la géographie, la statistique et la politique. Paris: Impr. Carpentier-Méricourt, 1824. (Anonymous).
Le Nouveau monde industriel et sociétaire, ou invention du procédé d'industrie attrayante et naturelle distribuée en séries passionnées. Paris: Bossange and Mongie, 1829.
Le Nouveau monde industriel, ou invention du procédé d'industrie attrayante et combinée, distribuée en séries passionnées. Livret d'annonce. Paris: Bossange, 1830.
Pièges et charlatanisme des deux sectes Saint-Simon et Owen, qui promettent l'association et le progrès. Moyens d'organiser en deux mois le Progrès réel, la Vraie Association, ou combinaison des travaux agricoles et domestiques, donnant quadruple produit, et élevant à 25 milliards le revenu de la France, borné aujourd'hui à 6 milliards un tiers. Paris: Bossange, 1831.

La Fausse industrie morcelée, répugnante, mensongère, et l'antidote, l'industrie naturelle, combinée, attrayante, véridique, donnant quadruple produit. Mosaïque des faux progrès, des ridicules et cercles vicieux de civilisation. Parallèle des deux mondes industriels, l'ordre morcelé et l'ordre combiné. 2 vols. Paris: Bossange, 1835–1836.

Plan du Traité de l'Attraction Passionnelle, qui devait être publié en 1821. Paris: Impr. Duverger [1836].

Post-scriptum to the *Lettre confidentielle des membres de la réunion du 31 juillet, en réponse à une brochure intitulée: "Aux Phalanstériens, la Commission préparatoire de l'Institut Sociétaire."* Paris: Impr. De Decourchant, 1837.

Posthumous Publication of Fourier's Manuscripts

Manuscrits de Fourier published in *La Phalange. Revue de la Science Sociale.* 10 vols. Paris, 1845–1849. This was the major theoretical organ of the Fourierist movement during its greatest days. Most of the thirty-one manuscripts that were published in the *Phalange* were fragments from Fourier's *Grand Traité* and they date from the years 1817–1819. A number of these manuscripts were also published separately as brochures. For a detailed listing see Bourgin, *Fourier,* 20–21.

De l'anarchie industrielle et scientifique. Paris: Librairie Phalanstérienne, 1847. The work published under this title by Fourier's disciples was the draft of a preface to the *Nouveau monde industriel.* It was probably written in 1827.

Fragments on "les ralliements passionnels" published in *La Démocratie pacifique,* June 7 and 8, 1848.

Publication des manuscrits de Charles Fourier. 4 vols. *Années 1851, 1852, 1853–1856, 1857–1858.* Paris: Librairie Phalanstérienne, 1851–1858. Most of the manuscripts published in these volumes were drawn from the *côte supplémentaire* of Fourier's papers, and they date primarily from the Napoleonic period.

Fragments published in *Le Bulletin de mouvement sociétaire en Europe et en Amérique.* Brussels, 1857–1860. Twenty-seven fragments of diverse dates. See Bourgin, *Fourier,* 22–23, for a complete listing.

Lettre de Fourier au Grand Juge (4 nivôse an XII). Paris: Dentu, 1874. Presented by Charles Pellarin. This text has also been published by Felix Rocquain, *Revue de France,* X (April 30, 1874), 152–164, and by Jean-Jacques Hémardinquer, *Le Mouvement social,* 48 (July–September 1964), 59–64.

Hiérarchie du cocuage. Edition définitive colligée sur le manuscrit originel par René Maublanc. Paris: Ed. du Siècle, 1924.

"Sur deux textes manuscrits de Fourier." Presented by Emile Poulat in Henri Desroche et al., *Etudes sur la tradition française de l'association ouvrière.* Paris: Eds. de Minuit, 1956, 9–19.

"Un inédit de Fourier: Note remise a l'Académie de Belley. Sur une des entraves à surmonter," in Emile Poulat, "Le Séjour de Fourier en Bugey (1816–1821)," *Le Bugey,* Fasc. 43 (1956), 31–45.

"Des sympathies puissancielles." A few unpublished texts presented by Simone Debout-Oleskiewicz in the catalogue of the *Exposition internationale du Surréalisme, 1959–1960*. Paris: Galérie Daniel Cordier, 1960, 27–31.

"Textes inédits de Charles Fourier," presented by Simone Debout-Oleskiewicz, *Revue internationale de philosophie*, 60, 2 (1962), 147–175. Texts dealing with the theory of universal analogy.

"Un Divertissement linguistique de Fourier," presented by Emile Lehouck, *La Brèche. Action surréaliste*, 4 (1963), 24–25.

"L'Archibras de Fourier: Un manuscrit censuré," presented by Jonathan Beecher, *La Brèche. Action surréaliste*, 7 (1964), 66–71.

"De l'orgie de musée ou omnigamie mixte en ordre composé et harmonique," text from *Le Nouveau monde amoureux* presented by Simone Debout-Oleskiewicz in the catalogue of the *Exposition internationale du Surréalisme, 1965*. Paris: Galérie de l'Oeil, 1965.

Memoir addressed to Reubell (3 messidor an IV) concerning troop movements, presented by Jean-Jacques Hémardinquer, "Fourier stratège (1796) et fonctionnaire (1815)," *Cahiers d'histoire*, XI, 1 (1966), 97–105.

Le Nouveau monde amoureux, extracts presented by Simone Debout-Oleskiewicz in her new edition of the *Théorie des quatre mouvements et des destinées générales*. Paris: Pauvert, 1967, 245–311.

Le Nouveau monde amoureux. Manuscrit inédit, texte intégral, edited and presented by Simone Debout-Oleskiewicz. Paris: Editions Anthropos, 1967. This constitutes Volume VII of the Anthropos edition of the *Oeuvres complètes*.

L'Ordre subversif. Trois textes sur la Civilisation, ed. by René Scherer and Jean Goret, Paris: Aubier Montaigne, 1972. Includes *L'Egarement de la Raison*, correcting errors and omissions made by disciples in publishing this text in *La Phalange* in 1847.

Collected Works

Oeuvres complètes de Charles Fourier. 6 vols. Paris: Bureaux de la Phalange and Librairie Sociétaire, 1841–1845.

Oeuvres complètes de Charles Fourier. 12 vols. Paris: Editions Anthropos, 1966–1968. This is the most recent and fullest edition of Fourier's works, though it is still far from complete. It is cited throughout this biography. Since every volume but one of this edition is a photographic reproduction of earlier editions, a full reference to each volume is given here.

OC I: *Théorie des quatre mouvements et des destinées générales*. 3d ed. Paris, 1846.

OC II–V: *Théorie de l'unité universelle*. 4 vols. 2d ed. Paris, 1841–1843. This work was originally published under the title *Traité de l'association domestique-agricole*.

OC VI: *Le Nouveau monde industriel et sociétaire*. 3d ed. Paris, 1848.

OC VII: *Le Nouveau monde amoureux.* Paris, 1967. This volume, edited and with an introduction by Simone Debout-Oleskiewicz, consists almost entirely of previously unpublished material.

OC VIII–IX: *La Fausse industrie morcelée, répugnante, mensongère.* . . . 2 vols. Paris, 1835–1836.

OC X: *Publication des manuscrits de Charles Fourier. Année 1851. Année 1852.* 2 vols. Paris, 1851–1852. This volume of the Anthropos edition has two paginations, which are referred to as PM (1851) and PM (1852).

OC XI: *Publication des manuscrits de Charles Fourier. Années 1853–1856. Années 1857–1858.* 2 vols. Paris, 1853–1858. This volume of the Anthropos edition also has two paginations. They are referred to as PM (1853–1856) and PM (1857–1858).

OC XII: *Manuscrits publiés par la Phalange.* This volume includes ten substantial manuscript texts originally published in *La Phalange* between 1845 and 1849.

SECONDARY WORKS

Fourier's Biography

Although numerous biographical sketches of Fourier were published by his disciples in the 1840s, they all derive from a single source: the "official" biography of Charles Pellarin. They are therefore not included in this listing.

Manuscripts

Considerant, Victor. "Note sur le Développement de la conception de Fourier." 13 pp. AN 10AS 26 (8).

Dumas, Jean-Baptiste. Paper read to the Academy of Lyon in 1838 on Fourier's years at Lyon and on his works. Bibliothèque du Palais des Arts de Lyon, Ms. 293, fol. 57–67. This paper (discovered by Riberette) was the principal source for the article by Ducoin cited below.

Pecqueur, Constantin. "Charles Fourier," unpublished twenty-five-page biographical sketch dating from 1833–1837. Archief Pecqueur, Manuscripts I, International Institute for Social History (Amsterdam).

Published Works

Considerant, Victor. Article "Fourrier" in William Duckett (ed.), *Dictionnaire de la conversation et de la lecture,* XXVIII (1836), 73–76.

Ducoin, Auguste. "Particularités inconnues sur quelques personnages des

XVIIIe et XIXe siècles: Charles Fourier," *Le Correspondant,* XXVII (January 25 and February 10, 1851), 480–490, 541–550.

Gazier, Georges. "Les Maisons natales de Fourier et de Proudhon," *Mémoires de la Société d'Emulation du Doubs,* VIIe series, VIII (1903–1904), 144–155.

Hémardinquer, Jean-Jacques. "La 'Découverte du mouvement social': Notes critiques sur le jeune Fourier," *Le Mouvement social,* 48 (July–September 1964), 49–70.

Hémardinquer, Jean-Jacques. "Fourier stratège (1796) et fonctionnaire (1815)," *Cahiers d'histoire,* XI, 1 (1966), 97–105.

Lehouck, Emile. *Vie de Charles Fourier.* Paris: Denoël-Gonthier, 1978.

[Pellarin, Charles]. Obituary notice on Fourier in *Annuaire statistique et historique du département du Doubs pour l'année 1838,* XXVI, 128–150. Contains some extracts not published elsewhere from Fourier's correspondence with Muiron.

Pellarin, Charles. *Notice biographique sur Charles Fourier, suivi d'une exposition de la théorie sociétaire.* Paris: Bureaux de la Phalange, 1839.

Pellarin, Charles. *Charles Fourier, sa vie et sa théorie.* 2d ed. Paris: Librairie de l'Ecole Sociétaire, 1843. 3d ed. rev. 1844; 4th ed. rev. 1849. The second edition, which is cited here unless otherwise specified, is the most complete and the most useful for scholarly purposes. Its voluminous supplementary material includes long excerpts from the correspondence with Muiron.

Pellarin, Charles. *Charles Fourier, sa vie et sa théorie.* 5th ed. Paris: Dentu, 1871. Although much shorter than the second edition, the fifth contains some new material, notably "Chapitres ajoutés en 1871," 163–192.

Poulat, Emile. "Le Séjour de Fourier en Bugey (1816–1821)," *Le Bugey,* Fasc. 43 (1956), 5–42.

Poulat, Emile. "Note sur un beau-frère de Fourier: le sous-préfet Rubat," *Le Bugey,* Fasc. 45 (1958), 60–66.

Renouard, Pierre. *Saint Pierre Fourier et Charles Fourier. Contribution à l'étude des origines de la mutualité. (Thèse).* Paris: A. Rousseau, 1904.

Riberette, Pierre. "Charles Fourier à Lyon: ses relations sociales et politiques." *Actes du 99e Congrès national des sociétés savantes. Besançon, 1974. Section d'histoire moderne et contemporaine* (Paris, 1976), II, 267–289.

Trénard, Louis. *Lyon, de l'Encyclopédie au préromantisme.* 2 vols. Paris: Presses Universitaires de France, 1958. Trénard's discussion of Fourier (II, 613–618) is brief. But this is the essential general study of the social and intellectual history of Lyon during Fourier's years there.

Fourier's Doctrine

This is a highly selective bibliography emphasizing recent and scholarly works. But mention might be made at the outset of a few nineteenth-century expositions and evaluations of Fourier's doctrine that can still be read with profit. In the vast body of literature produced by Fourier's disciples three works stand out. Jules Lechevalier, *Etudes sur la science sociale. Année 1832. Théorie de Charles Fourier* (Paris, 1834), was the work of a talented refugee from the Saint-Simonian religion. Victor Considerant, *Destinée sociale,* 3 vols. (Paris, 1834–1844), was the most substantial and lucid popularization of the doctrine by any of the disciples. More widely read, however, was Hippolyte Renaud, *Solidarité. Vue synthétique sur la doctrine de Charles Fourier* (Paris, 1842), which was later to inspire Zola's "Fourierist" novel, *Le Travail.* In all of these works the disciples practiced what Ange Guépin termed a "salutary weeding-out" of the "extravagant" elements of the doctrine; and in explicitly propagandistic writings such as Considerant's *Exposition abrégé du système phalanstérien de Fourier* (Paris, 1845) the theory of passionate attraction was reduced to a scheme for the organization of labor.

Significant evaluations of the doctrine by contemporary nonbelievers may be found in Louis Reybaud, *Etudes sur les réformateurs contemporains ou socialistes modernes. Saint-Simon, Charles Fourier, Robert Owen,* 2 vols. (Paris, 1840), and Lorenz von Stein, *Geschichte der socialen Bewegung in Frankreich,* 3 vols. (Leipzig, 1851). Reybaud's study was condescending and ironic but not devoid of sympathy. In the wake of June 1848, however, he was to ridicule the Phalansterians in his *Jérome Paturot à la recherche de la meilleure des républiques,* 4 vols. (Paris, 1849). Fourier's ideas were widely disseminated during the 1840s; and barely five years after his death Marx and Engels had already begun to discover the "vein of true poetry" in his writings. Their early works, notably *The German Ideology* and *The Holy Family,* bear traces of his influence. But the most substantial Marxist appreciation of Fourier, and still one of the shrewdest assessments of his gifts as a social satirist, is contained in Engels's *Anti-Dühring.* Significant later efforts on the part of militant socialists to specify Fourier's place in their ideological heritage are to be found in Benoît Malon, *Histoire du socialisme,* 5 vols. (Paris, 1882–1883), and August Bebel, *Charles Fourier. Sein Leben und seine Theorien* (Stuttgart, 1890). By 1890, with Paul Leroy-Beaulieu's lectures at the Collège de France and the publication of Charles Gide's first essays, the debate over Fourier's socialism had become an academic matter; and it was long to dominate scholarly discussion of his thought.

Alexandrian. *Les Libérateurs de l'amour.* Paris: Seuil, 1977. "Charles Fourier et la polygamie," 126–159.

Alexandrian. *Le Socialisme romantique.* Paris: Seuil, 1979, 77–137.

Altman, Elizabeth C. "The Philosophical Bases of Feminism: The Feminist Doctrines of the Saint-Simonians and Charles Fourier," *Philosophical Forum,* VII, 3–4 (Spring-Summer 1974), 277–293.

Armand, Felix, and Maublanc, René (eds.). *Fourier. Textes choisis.* 2 vols. Paris: Editions Sociales Internationales, 1937.

Barthes, Roland. *Sade, Fourier, Loyola.* Paris: Seuil, 1971.

Beecher, Jonathan, and Bienvenu, Richard (eds.). *The Utopian Vision of Charles Fourier: Selected Texts on Work, Love, and Passionate Attraction.* Boston: Beacon Press, 1971. "Introduction," 1–75.

Bénichou, Paul. *Le Temps des prophètes.* Paris: Gallimard, 1977. Section on Fourier, 241–247.

Bouglé, Celestin. *Socialismes français.* 5th ed. Paris: Colin, 1951. "Bilan du fouriérisme," 111–138.

Bourgin, Hubert. *Fourier. Contribution à l'étude du socialisme français. (Thèse).* Paris: Société Nouvelle de Librairie et d'Edition, 1905.

Bowman, Frank Paul. "Fouriérismes et christianisme: du Post-curseur à l'Omniarque Amphimondain," *Romantisme,* 11 (1976), 28–42.

Breton, André. *Ode à Fourier.* 2d ed. Introduction and notes by Jean Gaulmier. Paris: Klinckseick, 1961.

Crastre, Victor. "Fourier," *Critique,* V, 39 (August 1949), 754–761.

Dautry, Jean. "La notion du travail chez Saint-Simon et Fourier," *Journal de psychologie normale et pathologique,* LII, 1 (January–March 1955), 59–76.

Dautry, Jean. "Fourier et les questions d'éducation," *Revue internationale de philosophie,* XVI, 60 (1962), 234–260.

Debout-Oleskiewicz, Simone. "L'Analogie ou 'Le poème mathématique' de Charles Fourier," *Revue internationale de philosophie,* XVI, 60 (1962), 176–199.

Debout-Oleskiewicz, Simone. "Introduction" to *Oeuvres complètes de Charles Fourier.* I. Paris: Anthropos, 1966, i–xxvii.

Debout-Oleskiewicz, Simone. "Préface" to *Le Nouveau monde amoureux. Oeuvres complètes de Charles Fourier.* VII. Paris: Anthropos, 1967, vii–cxii.

Debout, Simone. "La Théorie des quatre mouvements, ou le dessein d'un 'grand oeuvre,' " in *Théorie des quatre mouvements et des destinées générales.* Nouvelle edition. Paris: Pauvert, 1967, 19–68.

Debout, Simone. *"Griffe au nez" ou donner "have ou art." Ecriture inconnue de Charles Fourier.* Paris: Anthropos, 1974.

Debout, Simone. "Des manies au cosmos, ou le dedans et le déhors sans frontière," *Australian Journal of French Studies,* XI, 3 (1974), 263–287.

Debout, Simone. *L'Utopie de Charles Fourier: l'illusion réelle.* Paris: Payot, 1978.

Desroche, Henri. "Fouriérisme ambigu. Socialisme ou religion?" *Revue internationale de philosophie,* XVI, 60 (1962), 200–220.

Desroche, Henri. *Les Dieux rêvés. Théisme et athéisme en utopie.* Paris: Desclee de Brouwer, 1972, 87–145.

Desroche, Henri. *La Société festive. Du fouriérisme ecrit au fouriérismes pratiqués.* Paris: Seuil, 1975.

Francblin, Catherine. "Le Féminisme utopique de Charles Fourier," *Tel Quel,* 62 (Summer 1975), 44–69.

Friedberg, Morris. *L'Influence de Charles Fourier sur le mouvement social contemporain (Thèse).* Paris: Giard, 1926.

Gans, Jacques. "Les relations entre socialistes de France et d'Angleterre au début du XIXe siècle," *Le Mouvement social,* 46 (January–March 1964), 105–118.

Gaumont, Jean. *Histoire générale de la coopération en France.* 2 vols. Paris: Fédération nationale des coopératives de consommation, 1924.

Gide, Charles. *Les Prophéties de Fourier.* Nîmes: Veuve Laporte, 1894.

Gide, Charles. *Fourier, précurseur de la coopération*. Paris: Association pour l'Enseignement de la Coopération, 1924.

Gide, Charles. "Introduction" to Charles Fourier, *Pages choisies*. Paris: Sirey, 1932, xii–lxv.

Goret, Jean. *La Pensée de Fourier*. Paris: Presses Universitaires de France, 1974.

Ioannisian, Abgar R. *Genezis obshchestvennogo ideala Fur'e*. (The genesis of Fourier's social ideal.) Moscow-Leningrad: Izdatel'stvo Akademii Nauk SSSR, 1939.

Ioannisian, Abgar R. "Istochniki proektov assotsiatsii Fur'e" (The sources of Fourier's projects of association), *Istorik Marksist,* 1 (1939), 101–124.

Ioannisian, Abgar R. *Sharl' Fur'e.* (Charles Fourier.) 2d ed. Moscow: Izdatel'stvo Akademii Nauk SSSR, 1958.

Janet, Paul. "La philosophie de Charles Fourier," *Revue des deux mondes,* XXXV (October 1, 1879), 619–645.

Lansac, Maurice. *Les Conceptions méthodologiques et sociales de Charles Fourier. Leur influence. (Thèse)*. Paris: Vrin, 1926.

Larizza, Mirella. "I Presupposti Teoretici dell'Anarchismo di Charles Fourier," in *Anarchici e Anarchia nel mondo contemporaneo*. Turin: Fondazione Luigi Einaudi, 1971, 320–344.

Lefebvre, Henri, et al. *Actualité de Fourier. Colloque d'Arc et Senans*. Paris: Anthropos, 1975.

Lehouck, Emile. "Psychologie et morale dans l'oeuvre de Charles Fourier (1772–1837)," *Revue des sciences humaines,* Fasc. 107 (July–September 1962), 423–437.

Lehouck, Emile. *Fourier aujourd'hui*. Paris: Denoel, 1966.

Lehouck, Emile. "La Lecture surréaliste de Charles Fourier," *Australian Journal of French Studies,* XX, 1 (1983), 26–36.

Leroy, Maxime. *Histoire des idées sociales en France*. 3 vols. Paris: Gallimard, 1947–1954. "Charles Fourier ou la mathématique des passions," II, 246–292.

Lichtheim, George. *The Origins of Socialism*. New York: Praeger, 1969. Section on Fourier, 31–38.

Louvancour, Henri. *De Henri Saint-Simon à Charles Fourier. Etude sur le socialisme romantique français de 1830 (Thèse)*. Chartres: Durand, 1913.

Majler, Janina. *Doktryna etyczna Karola Fouriera*. (The ethical doctrine of Charles Fourier.) Warsaw, 1965.

Majler, Janina. "Fourier et Marx," in Henri Lefebvre, et al., *Actualité de Fourier*. Paris: Anthropos, 1975, 239–290.

Manuel, Frank E. *The Prophets of Paris*. Cambridge, Mass.: Harvard University Press, 1962. "Charles Fourier: The Burgeoning of Instinct," 195–248.

Manuel, Frank E., and Manuel, Fritzie P. *Utopian Thought in the Western World*. Cambridge, Mass.: Harvard University Press, 1979.

Mason, Edward. "Fourier and Anarchism," *Quarterly Journal of Economics,* XLII, 2 (February 1928), 228–262.

Mladenatz, Gromoslav. "L'Influence de Charles Fourier sur les économistes roumains," *Archives internationales de la sociologie de la coopération et du développement,* 21 (January–June 1967), 15–46.

Moneti, Maria. *La Meccanica delle passioni: Studio su Fourier e il socialismo critico-utopistico.* Florence, 1979.

Nathan, Michel. *Le Ciel des fouriéristes. Habitants des étoiles et réincarnations de l'âme.* Lyon: Presses Universitaires de Lyon, 1981.

Poulat, Emile. *Les Cahiers manuscrits de Fourier. Etude historique et inventaire raisonné.* Paris: Editions de Minuit, 1957.

Poulat, Emile. "Ecritures et tradition fouriéristes," *Revue internationale de philosophie,* XVI, 60 (1962), 221–233.

Queneau, Raymond. *Bords.* Paris: Hermann, 1963. Two essays on Fourier: "Dialectique hégélienne et séries de Fourier," 37–51, and "Les Ennemis de la lune," 53–57.

Renouvier, Charles. "La Philosophie de Charles Fourier," *La Critique philosophique, scientifique, littéraire,* XXII and XXIV (1883), Nos. 14, 16, 21, 28, 29.

Riasanovsky, Nicholas V. "L'emploi des citations bibliques dans l'oeuvre de Charles Fourier," *Archives de Sociologie des Religions,* No. 20 (1965), 31–43.

Riasanovsky, Nicholas V. *The Teaching of Charles Fourier.* Berkeley and Los Angeles: University of California Press, 1969.

Saitta, Armando. "Charles Fourier e l'Armonia," *Belfagor,* II, 3 (1947), 272–292.

Schaeffer, Gérard. "L'Ode à Charles Fourier et la tradition," in Marc Eigeldinger (ed.), *André Breton. Essais et témoignages.* Neuchâtel: La Baconnière, 1950, 83–109.

Schérer, René. *Charles Fourier ou la contestation globale.* Paris: Seghers, 1970.

Seillière, Ernest. *Le Mal romantique.* Paris: Plon Nourrit, 1908.

Silberling, E. *Dictionnaire de sociologie phalanstérienne. Guide des oeuvres complètes de Charles Fourier.* Paris: Rivière, 1911.

Silberner, E. "Charles Fourier on the Jewish Question," *Jewish Social Studies,* VIII, 4 (October 1946), 245–266.

Spencer, Michael. *Charles Fourier.* Boston: Twayne, 1981.

Spencer, Michael. "A(na)logie de Fourier," *Romantisme,* 34 (1981), 31–46.

Stedman Jones, Gareth. "From Cagliostro to Fourier: Some Non-Enlightenment Sources of Socialism," unpublished paper.

Stedman Jones, Gareth. "Utopian Socialism Reconsidered: Science and Religion in the Early Socialist Movement," unpublished paper.

Thibert, Marguérite. *Le Féminisme dans le socialisme français de 1830 à 1850.* (*Thèse*). Paris: Rivière, 1926. On Fourierist feminism, 99–146.

Thomas, Jean-Paul. *Libération instinctuelle, libération politique. Contribution fouriériste à Marcuse.* Paris: Le Sycomore, 1980.

Tuzet, Helène. "Deux types de cosmogonie vitaliste. II: Charles Fourier, Victor Hennequin," *Revue des sciences humaines,* Fasc. 101 (January–March 1961), 37–54.

Vergez, André. "L'Intuition fondamentale de Charles Fourier, philosophe franc-comtois, ou les très riches heures du Phalanstère," *Mémoires de la Société d'Emulation du Doubs,* Nouvelle Série, 8 (1966), 17–39.

Vergez, André (ed.). *Fourier*. Paris: Presses Universitaires de France, 1969. "Introduction," 5–57.

Viatte, Auguste. *Les Sources occultes du romantisme. Illuminisme—théosophie: 1770–1820.* 2 vols. Paris: Honoré Champion, 1928. Section on Fourier, II, 263–268.

Volgin, Viacheslav Petrovich. "Sistema Fur'e" (Fourier's System), *Pod Znamenem Marksizma,* No. 7–8 (July-August 1929), 102–126.

Volgin, Viacheslav Petrovich. "Sotsiologicheskie vzgliady Fur'e" (The sociological views of Fourier), *Arkhiv Marksa i Engel'sa,* IV (1929), 92–122.

Zeldin, David. *The Educational Ideas of Charles Fourier (1772–1837).* London: Cass, 1969.

Zil'berfarb, Ioganson Izaakovich. "Tvorcheskii put' Sharlia Fur'e" (The creative path of Charles Fourier), *Frantsuskii Ezhegodnik* (1959), 295–334.

Zil'berfarb, Ioganson Izaakovich. "Les études sur Fourier et le fouriérisme, vues par un historien," *Revue internationale de philosophie,* XVI, 60 (1962), 261–279.

Zil'berfarb, Ioganson Izaakovich. *Sotsial'naia filosofiia Sharlia Fur'e i ee mesto v istorii sotsialisticheskoi mysli pervoi poloviny XIX veka.* (The social philosophy of Charles Fourier and its place in the history of socialist thought in the first half of the nineteenth century.) Moscow: Izdatel'stvo "Nauka," 1964.

Zil'berfarb, Ioganson Izaakovich. "Charles Fourier et la Révolution française," *Annales historiques de la Révolution française,* No. 184 (April-June 1966), 53–75.

Zil'berfarb, Ioganson Izaakovich. "L'Imagination et la réalité dans l'oeuvre de Fourier," *Le Mouvement social,* No. 60 (July-September 1967), 5–21.

Special issues of the following journals have been devoted in whole or in part to Fourier:

Australian Journal of French Studies, XI, 3 (1974).

Autogestion et socialisme, 20–21 (September-December 1972).

Esprit, XLII, 4 (April 1974).

Revue des études coopératives, LI, 170 (October-December 1972).

Revue internationale de philosophie, 60, 3 (1962).

Topique. Revue freudienne, 4–5 (October 1970).

INDEX

years in Bugey (1816–1821), 140–57, 165–85; early relations with Just Muiron, 161–70; publicizing his ideas, 355–64, 372–75, 377, 391–92, 395–400, 405–8, 432–39, 448–53, 473–80; Paris years (1822–1837), 355–495; contacts with Robert Owen, 364–71, 493; contributions to the Besançon *Impartial,* 400–404; contacts with the Saint-Simonians, 409–30; collaboration on *Le Phalanstère,* 431–53; the Societary Colony of Condé-sur-Vesgre, 454–71; Romanian disciples, 480–84; notoriety, 484–86; sickness and death, 491–95

—problems of interpretation: sanity, 2, 3, 12, 107, 110, 126; influence, 2–4, 74, 216–17, 239, 271–73, 292–96, 328–29, 453, 484–85, 500–502; place in utopian tradition, 2, 216–19, 241, 246–47, 298–302, 318–19, 411, 485, 505n.3; literary strategies, 4, 8–10, 116–22, 127, 311–15, 349–51; as "maligned inventor," 7–8, 127–30, 361, 478, 480; use of parody, 9, 217–18, 269, 284, 308, 313–15, 317; sources, 68–70, 96–97, 222–23, 275, 301–2, 334–35, 345–48

—thought: formation of theory, 36, 52–56, 57–67; impact of French Revolution, 71–74; critique of civilization, 195–219; theory of human nature, 220–40; ideal community, 241–58; Phalansterian architecture, 242–46; social relations within Phalanx, 246–50; gastronomy, 250–53; discipline and punishment, 253–56; education in Phalanx, 259–73; work and self-realization, 274–96; love and sexual relations, 297–317; theory of history, 318–29; theory of metempsychosis, 329–31; cosmology and cosmogony, 332–41, 345–52; theory of universal analogy, 341–52

—works: *Nouveau monde amoureux* (1817–1818), 7, 84, 156, 238–39, 268–69, 298, 302–17; *Grand Traité* (1816–1820), 7, 139, 145, 152, 156, 168–75, 533n.32; *Egarement de la*

Raison (1806), 113–14, 210–16; *Théorie des quatre mouvements* (1808), 114, 116–30, 140, 161, 163–65, 176, 297, 326, 334, 350; *Traité de l'association domestique-agricole* (1822), 189–92, 355–64, 365, 366, 535n.35; *Nouveau monde industriel* (1829), 225, 312, 374–75, 382–83, 391–400, 415, 455; *Mnémonique géographique* (1824), 378–80; *Pièges et charlatanisme des deux sectes Saint-Simon et Owen* (1831), 419–20, 422; *La Fausse Industrie* (1835–1836), 471, 477–80

Fourier, Jean-Baptiste (mathematician), 135, 528n.60

Fourier, Pierre (Catholic reformer), 16, 17, 556n.19

Fourierist movement, 387–90, 422, 429–30, 432, 441, 446, 452–53, 484–85, 491; growth after Fourier's death, 2, 453, 500–502; outside France, 484, 501–2; Fourier not a "Fourierist," 487. See also Disciples of Fourier

Fournier, Frédéric (cloth merchant), 52, 77, 134

Fourrier, Antoinette (sister of Charles), 18, 508n.14

Fourrier, Charles (father of Charles), 17, 18, 19, 20, 24–25, 27, 31, 41n, 94

Fourrier, Frédéric-Hugues-Philippe (brother of Charles), 508n.15

Fourrier, Marie (née Muguet; mother of Charles), 17, 18, 19, 21, 33, 34, 39, 40; and Charles' inheritance, 27, 28, 49; and Charles' career, 30, 31, 35; death of, 133, 182

Francblin, Catherine, 545n.2

Francia, José Gaspar Rodríguez, 478–79

Fraudulent bankruptcy, 17, 26n, 91, 101, 201

Freedom. See Liberty/liberation

Freemasonry: at Lyon, 38–39, 80, 85, 130n, 346; at Besançon, 161, 372

French literature, Fourier's knowledge of, 29

French Revolution, 6, 16, 32, 33, 36–58, 71–74, 88, 275, 402, 411; Fourier's reaction to, 32, 52, 54, 57, 58, 71–74, 231–32, 511n.13; Fourier's life during, 36–52; ideals of, criticized by

cursor of Marx, 2, 411; career, 53, 364–65; Fourier compared to, 136, 289, 398, 411, 485; diffusion of his ideas in France, 365, 366, 552n.31, 553n.36; criticized by Fourier, 365–71, 395, 396, 434; Fourier's overtures to, 367–70; Fourier's meeting with, 493, 569n.68

Owenites, 366–71, 456, 479, 490, 501

Paget, Amédée, 448, 449, 492
Pajol, Pierre-Claude, 29, 509n.41
Palais Royal, 195, 376, 385, 486, 492; Fourier's first visit to, 33–34, 59; galleries of, 245
Palmer, Robert R., 289
Panckoucke, Charles-Joseph, 69
Paris: Fourier's first visit to, 33–34, 36, 59, 245, 251; trips to, during 1790s, 53, 54n, 55, 65–66; literary monopoly of, 114–15, 127, 190, 196, 374, 386, 392, 475; arcades of, 245; Fourier's life in, after 1822, 355–495 *passim*
Paris Commune, 11
Parody, Fourier's use of, 9, 217–18, 269, 284, 308, 313–15, 317
Parrat-Brillat, Agathe (niece of Fourier), 155, 178
Parrat-Brillat, Olympe (niece of Fourier), 155
Parrat-Brillat, Philibert (brother-in-law of Fourier), 141–42, 178, 183, 251, 537n.30
Parrat-Brillat, Sophie (sister of Fourier), 18, 133, 141–42, 155, 178, 183
Pascal, Blaise, 317, 351
Pasqually, Martinès de, 161n
Passional accords, system of, 156, 171, 531n.34
Passionate attraction, 4, 55, 66, 105, 108, 117n, 171, 223–25; defined, 225
Passionate series, 117n, 169, 236–37, 336; defined, 236, 278; and social integration, 249–50; and work, 278–79
Passions, 220–40; in French thought, 221–23; and the divine plan, 223–25; Fourier's taxonomy of, 226–29; and Fourier's classification of personality types, 229; Fourier's theory of, criticized, 229–31; and group activity,

231–37; repression of, 237–39; and work, 278–82, 295
Patriarchate, 320, 323–324
Paulin (editor of *Le National*), 557n.30
Peasants. *See* Agriculture; Rural France
Pecqueur, Constantin, 508n.18, 562n.26
Pellarin, Charles: as Fourier's biographer, 10–11, 21, 165, 355, 497; on Fourier's family, 19, 24, 142; on Fourier's early years, 43, 49, 87, 514n.63; on Fourier's cosmogony, 333; on Fourier's character and personality, 374, 487, 488, 491–92; becomes a Fourierist, 428; Fourierist journalism of, 437, 448, 450, 452; on Fourier as a writer, 438; and other disciples of Fourier, 442, 444, 468; criticized by Fourier, 448–49; portrait of Fourier, 474–75; on Fourier's work habits, 475; on Fourier's health, 493
Pericles, 337
Périer, Casimir, 397, 406, 558n.55
Pestalozzi, Johann Heinrich, 260, 261
Phalanstère, Le (later *La Réforme industrielle*), 292, 432–53, 455–65, 468–69, 474–75
Phalanstery, 243–44
Phalanx, 4, 67n, 70, 117n, 172, 237, 241–58; architecture of, 243–46; classes in, 247; remuneration of members, 247–48; social relations in, 247–50; education in, 249, 259–73; cuisine and gastronomy in, 250–53; authority in, 253–55, 282; children in, 255, 259–73; discipline in, 255–56; entertainments in, 257; work in, 274, 277–96; love in, 302–17; and analogy, 327, 348
Philosophers/*philosophes*: and French Revolution, 54, 72; Fourier's knowledge of, 69–70; "philosophical cabale," 86, 121, 127–28, 130, 196; Fourier's critique of, 86–87, 95–96, 113, 119, 195, 209–16, 220, 232; "expectant philosophers," 209
Phrenology/phrenologists, 103, 448
Physics, 67n, 69
Physiocrats, 64, 70, 203
Pichegru, General Charles, 46

Designer: Sandy Drooker
Compositor: Huron Valley Graphics
Text: Linotron 202 Bembo
Display: Bembo and Caslon Openface
Printer: Braun-Brumfield, Inc.
Binder: Braun-Brumfield, Inc.